RELIGIOUS WOMEN IN EARLY CAROLINGIAN FRANCIA

FORDHAM SERIES IN MEDIEVAL STUDIES

Mary C. Erler and Franklin T. Harkins, series editors

RELIGIOUS WOMEN IN EARLY CAROLINGIAN FRANCIA

A Study of Manuscript Transmission and Monastic Culture

FELICE LIFSHITZ

FORDHAM UNIVERSITY PRESS

New York   2014

Fordham University Press has no responsibility
for the persistence or accuracy of URLs for
external or third-party Internet websites referred
to in this publication and does not guarantee that
any content on such websites is, or will remain,
accurate or appropriate.

Fordham University Press also publishes its
books in a variety of electronic formats. Some
content that appears in print may not be available
in electronic books.

Library of Congress Cataloging-in-Publication
Data is available from the publisher.

Printed in the United States of America

16 15 14   5 4 3 2 1

First edition

To Qianguo

From Felice

You Became Quinn

You Made me Mommy

With Love

Hineni!

CONTENTS

List of Maps and Color Plates / *xi*

List of Abbreviations / *xiii*

Preface: Medieval Feminism / *xvii*

Acknowledgments / *xxi*

PART ONE. INTRODUCTIONS: PEOPLE, PLACES, THINGS

1 Syneisactism and Reform: Gender Relations in the Anglo-Saxon Cultural Province in Francia / *3*

2 The Anglo-Saxon Cultural Province in Francia / *16*

3 The Gun(t)za and Abirhilt Manuscripts: Women and Their Books in the Anglo-Saxon Cultural Province in Francia / *29*

PART TWO. TEXTUAL ANALYSIS

4 "I Am Crucified in Christ" (Galatians 2:20): The Kitzingen Crucifixion Miniature and Visions of the Apostle Paul / *65*

5 "We Interpret Spiritual Truths to People Possessed of the Spirit" (1 Corinthians 2:13): Studying the Bible with the Fathers of the Church / *87*

6 "The Sensual Man Does Not Perceive Those Things That Are of the Spirit of God" (1 Corinthians 2:14): History and Theology in the Stories of the Saints / *112*

7 "An Eternal Weight of Glory" (2 Corinthians 4:17): Discipline and Devotion in Monastic Life / *148*

PART THREE. CONCLUSIONS

8 "Concerning Virgins, I Have No Commandment of the Lord" (1 Corinthians 7:25): Consecrated Women and Altar Service in the Anglo-Saxon Cultural Province in Francia / *185*

9 "Through a Glass Darkly" (1 Corinthians 13:12): Textual Transmission and Historical Representation as Feminist Strategies in Early Medieval Europe / *193*

Notes / *207*

Bibliography: Manuscripts and Printed Materials / *283*

Index / *337*

Color plates follow page 192

MAPS AND COLOR PLATES

MAPS

The Carolingian Rhineland / *xxiii*

Mainland Franconia / *xxiii*

COLOR PLATES (following page 192)

1. Basel, Öffentliche Universitätsbibliothek F III 15a folio 17r: Kitzingen Library Catalogue and related materials

2. Basel, Öffentliche Universitätsbibliothek F III 15a folio 17v: Kitzingen Library Catalogue and related materials

3. Basel, Öffentliche Universitätsbibliothek F III 15a folio 18r: Kitzingen Library Catalogue and related materials

4. Würzburg, Universitätsbibliothek M.p.th.f. 69 folio 7r: Kitzingen Crucifixion Miniature (also on cover)

5. Würzburg, Universitätsbibliothek M.p.th.q. 28b folio 43v: Kitzingen Isidore Lamb of God

6. Würzburg, Universitätsbibliothek M.p.th.q. 28b folio 60v: Kitzingen Isidore Eagle Illuminations

7. Würzburg, Universitätsbibliothek M.p.th.q. 28b folio 42v: Kitzingen Homiliary Call to Penance

8. Wolfgang-Bonhage-Museum Korbach inventory number Go 4/11: Cross Pin from Goddelsheim grave 23

9. Munich, Bayerische Staatsbibliothek Clm 14345 folio 7v: Paul preaching, Altmünster(?) Pauline Epistles

10. Volto Santo: Lucca, Cattedrale di San Martino

ABBREVIATIONS

AASS	Acta Sanctorum
AB	Analecta Bollandiana
BAV	Bibliotheca Apostolica Vaticana
BHL	Société des Bollandistes, *Bibliotheca Hagiographica Latina antiquae et mediae aetatis* plus Supplements (Subsidia Hagiographica 6, 12, 70; Brussels: Société des Bollandistes, 1898–1901, 1911, and 1986)
BLB	Badische Landesbibliothek
BM	Bibliothèque Municipale
BN	Bibliothèque Nationale de France
BR	Bibliothèque Royale de Belgique
BSB	Bayerische Staatsbibliothek
CCCM	Corpus Christianorum, Continuatio Medievalis
CCSL	Corpus Christianorum, Series Latina
CLA	Elias Avery Lowe, *Codices Latini Antiquiores. A Palaeographical Guide to Latin MSS. prior to the 9th Century,* 11 vols. plus Supplement (Oxford, 1934–71)
CPMA	Johannes Machielsen, *Clavis Patristica pseudepigraphicorum Medii Aevi* I-II: *Opera Homiletica* (CCSL CPMA I-II; Brepols: Turnhout, 1990)
CSEL	Corpus Scriptorum Ecclesiasticorum Latinorum
DACL	Cabrol, Fernand, and Henri Leclerc, with Henri Marrou, eds., *Dictionnaire d'archéologie chrétienne et de liturgie,* 15 vols. (Paris: Letouzey et Ané, 1907–53)
DEO	*De ecclesiasticis officiis*
EME	*Early Medieval Europe*
HAB	Herzog August Bibliothek
HE	Historia Ecclesiastica
Lipsius, *DAA*	Richard Adalbert Lipsius, *Die Apokryphen Apostelgeschichten und Apostellegenden. Ein Beitrag zur altchristlichen Literaturgeschichte,* 2 vols. plus Supplement (Braunschweig, 1883–90).

LSK	Bernhard Bischoff and Josef Hofmann, *Libri sancti Kyliani. Die Würzburger Schreibschule und die Dombibliotheck im VIII u. IX Jahrhundert* (Würzburg, 1952)
LTK	Lexikon für Theologie und Kirche
MGH	Monumenta Germaniae Historica
MGH AA	Auctores Antiquissimi
MGH Capit	Capitularia regum Francorum
MGH SRG	Scriptores rerum Germanicarum in usum scholarum separatim editi
MGH SRM	Scriptores rerum Merovingicarum
MGH SS	Scriptores
MS	Manuscript
ÖNB	Österreichische Nationalbibliothek
ÖUB	Öffentliche Universitätsbibliothek
PG	*Patrologia Graeca*, ed. J.-P. Migne (Paris, 1857–1866)
PL	*Patrologia Latina*, cursus completus, ed. J.-P. Migne (Paris, 1844–55)
PLS	*Patrologia Latina*, cursus completus ed. J.-P. Migne (Paris, 1958–), supplementum
RB	*Revue bénédictine*
SB	Stiftsbibliothek
SB-PK	Staatsbibliothek zu Berlin–Preußischer Kulturbesitz
SC	Sources Chrétiennes
Settimane	*Settimane di Studio del Centro Italiano di Studi sull'alto Medioevo*
SFG	Eugen Ewig, *Spätantikes und Fränkisches Gallien. Gesammelte Schriften (1952–73)*, ed. Hartmut Atsma, 2 vols. (Munich, 1979)
Tangl	*Die Briefe des heiligen Bonifatius und Lullus*, ed. Michael Tangl (MGH: Epistolae Selectae, vol. 1, Berlin, 1916; 2nd ed.; Berlin, 1955)
TSMAO	Typologie des Sources du Moyen Âge Occidentale
UB	Universitätsbibliothek
Vienna 751	Vienna, Österreichische Nationalbibliothek MS 751
Vienna 2223	Vienna, Österreichische Nationalbibliothek MS 2223

VKB 1966 · Friedrich Oswald, Leo Schaefer, and Hans Rudolf Sennhauser, *Vorromanische Kirchenbauten. Katalog der Denkmäler bis zum Ausgang der Ottonen* (Munich: Prestel Verlag, 1966)

VKB 1991 · Werner Jacobsen, Leo Schäfer, and Hans Rudolf Sennhauser with Matthias Exner, Jozef Mertens, and Henk Stöpker, *Vorromanische Kirchenbauten. Katalog der Denkmäler bis zum Ausgang der Ottonen. Nachtragsband* (Munich: Prestel Verlag, 1991).

WDGB · *Würzburger Diözesangeschichtsblätter*

PREFACE: MEDIEVAL FEMINISM

The best-known emplotment of the rise of feminist consciousness, history, thought, activism, and the like considers such phenomena to be characteristically modern (as well as Euro-American). For instance, Miriam Schneir's 1972 reader, *Feminism: The Essential Historical Writings*, the classic introduction to the field for over four decades, places the origins of "old feminism" (represented by the likes of Abigail Adams and Mary Wollstonecraft) "in the eighteenth-century democratic revolutions of the propertied middle class."[1] Accordingly, the collection begins with those authors, who have come to represent the beginnings of feminism for most students. Yet Schneir also mentioned the works of Christine de Pizan (1364–c. 1430), Moderata Fonte (1555–92), and François Poulain de la Barre (1647–1725) in her introductory remarks, albeit without including selections from their writings among those considered as "essential."[2] Clearly, specialists in the history of feminist thought have long considered "medieval" figures such as Christine de Pizan to be part of the story.

Furthermore, already in the 1970s, feminist scholarly activists were pushing the genealogy of Euro-American feminism back beyond Christine. In 1975, Eleanor McLaughlin labeled the twelfth-century philosopher Peter Abelard's work on the dignity of women as an example of "feminism," but guardedly so, retaining quotation marks around the F-word.[3] There was probably no need for such hesitancy. Indeed, had not Herbert Grundmann already in 1935 spoken of a religious women's movement, or *Frauenbewegung* (the same term used to describe modern feminist movements) as characteristic of the European Later Middle Ages, when beguines and female mystics played a central role in the cultural life of Christendom?[4] McLaughlin was far less hesitant in another 1975 article, in which she advanced the thesis "that Christian tradition under certain conditions and at certain times was radically supportive of women"; she illustrated her thesis with "glimpses of a feminist heritage in the Christian tradition," taken from the *Life* of Christina of Markyate and the *Revelations of Divine Love* of Julian of Norwich.[5] A slightly abbreviated version of this essay was included in another classic, and still used, feminist reader of the 1970s, Carol Christ and Judith Plaskow's 1979 *Womanspirit Rising*.

Thus, from its beginnings as a field of academic inquiry in the 1970s, feminism has been recognized by specialists as more than a modern revolutionary movement. Since that time, much work has been done to incorporate the centuries of Abelard, the beguines, Christina, Fonte, and Poulain into the scholarly narrative of the history of feminist thought.[6] The Middle Ages even boasts subtypes of feminism, such as "matristic feminism" and "marian feminism," as well as a genuine superstar figure, Abbess Hildegard of Bingen and her "theology of the feminine."[7] If there is reluctance to push the origins of European feminism back beyond Christine de Pizan—as reflected in the periodization used by the "Six Waves" research project on the history of feminism in Europe (which begins in 1400), in the introduction that accompanies all the books in the series "The Other Voice in Early Modern Europe" (which celebrates Christine as the harbinger of a completely new era after a "three thousand year history of the derogation of women"), and in other commonly encountered periodization schemes (such as "The Misogynist Tradition, 500 BCE–1500 CE")—it is at least now axiomatic that "from the fifteenth century onward 'pro-woman' arguments took an increasingly central place in European literature."[8] Meanwhile, medievalists who do see feminism in their eras can number some very big names among their supporters. For instance, the doyenne of women's history, Gerda Lerner, in 1993 confidently described the creation of feminist consciousness in Europe as beginning at least as early as the seventh century, and one of the gray eminences in the field of the history of Christianity, Rosemary Radford Ruether, also began arguing in the 1990s that feminism has very old roots in that religion.[9]

None of this was known to me when, in 1997, I embarked on the project that became *Religious Women in Early Carolingian Francia*. I was attracted by a group of eighth-century manuscripts in the University Library of Würzburg that had been associated with the Anglo-Saxon cultural province in Francia— the world of (just to name two famous individuals) Bishop Boniface of Mainz and his "beloved," Abbess Leoba of Tauberbischofsheim. They and their fellow (so-called) "Anglo-Saxon missionaries to the continent" are among the best known and most studied personalities of the entire European Middle Ages. Yet, despite oceans of scholarship and intense interest, no one had tried to delve into the details of their intellectual and cultural lives by studying the manuscripts that appear to have been produced in their scriptoria and used in their communities. This was all the more surprising in that the Würzburg manuscripts included a subgroup of books associated with women's houses. Given the rarity of sources allowing direct access to women's experiences before the modern era, it was actually shocking that no one had examined these in particular.

As I studied the women's manuscripts, I found many things, some novel, some unsurprising. Among them was something that looked to me like "feminism," although I never dared to call it that, for I did not imagine that there was any warrant for asserting the existence of a feminist consciousness in the eighth century. Instead, I used a variety of substitute terms to convey this aspect of the thought-world evidenced in the manuscripts, such as *profeminist, protofeminist, prefeminist, quasi-feminist, prowoman, profemale, antimisogynist, antisexist, gender-egalitarian, universalizing, nonandrocentric*, and even for a time the uniformly ridiculed *heterosocial*. Some of my early medievalist colleagues have been equally reticent to take the plunge, as evidenced by this randomly selected remark on the powerful maternal imagery of the Anglo-Saxon poet

Cynewulf: "we need not identify Cynewulf as an early proto-feminist."[10] The double remove from "feminism" startles by its timidity; Cynewulf was not a feminist, he was not a protofeminist, he was not even an early protofeminist.

But I wrote the version of the book that was actually submitted to a publisher between summer 2011 and summer 2012 in radically altered circumstances: not in a Department of History, teaching the early Middle Ages, but in a Program in Women's Studies, teaching "The History of Feminist Thought." This exposed me to the works just cited and much more besides. Of paramount importance was Lerner's approach in *The Creation of Feminist Consciousness*, which involved defining "feminist consciousness" broadly enough to show that "women's resistance to patriarchal ideas" and "feminist oppositional thought" had a very long history indeed, even if this meant including women who "would not have defined themselves as feminist in their own time."[11] Lerner was particularly interested in the women's and mixed-sex communities that flourished during the seventh and eighth centuries and even mentioned Leoba and Boniface by name; she knew that the women of Chelles and Laon and Nivelles and other houses were educated and active, but she was unable to provide any details for the content of the "feminist consciousness" that presumably must have accompanied their educational and intellectual efforts, for no specialized studies existed to help her peer into the inner workings of the communities.[12] *Religious Women in Early Carolingian Francia* provides those details, alongside many other glimpses into the intellectual and monastic culture of the Anglo-Saxon cultural province in Francia. I describe various aspects of that world, but have chosen to give particular prominence to features that manifest the presence of a feminist consciousness.

I use the term *feminist* unapologetically. However, I also use it in a very limited and conservative sense, that is, as defined by Gerda Lerner: a resistance to patriarchal ideas, particularly as they concern women. Eighth-century Christian nuns would never have subscribed to the more radical definitions of feminism that are central to contemporary feminist theory, for which "feminism" involves a resistance to any and all kinds of hierarchy, domination, inequality, or oppression on the basis of race, religion, creed, sexual orientation, gender identity, physical or mental ability, or relationship to the means of production. Aristocratic exploitation of agricultural laborers (to take but one issue) surely did not bother them. But the denigration of their capacities and dignity as women absolutely did. I believe I have shown that what Ruether said of Hildegard and Mechthild and Hadwijch and others can (with slight modifications, as indicated by the ellipses) also be said of the women of the monasteries of Karlburg and Kitzingen: "they reshaped the gender symbolism of [Christian] spiritualities in a way that clearly made them agents of their own lives . . . as well as . . . pastoral teachers for their communities, who valued them and carefully preserved their teachings for us to read today. This is surely some part of feminism."[13]

ACKNOWLEDGMENTS

This book has been very long in the making. My research was funded by the DAAD (the German Academic Exchange Service), twice by the Alexander von Humboldt Stiftung, and twice by Florida International University. I researched and wrote early drafts of the book while resident at the Abteilung Landesgeschichte of the University of Freiburg, the Historisches Seminar at the University of Frankfurt (twice), the Forschungsstelle Mittelalter of the Österreichische Akademie der Wissenschaften in Vienna (twice), the Institute for Advanced Study in Princeton, the Wissenschaftskolleg in Berlin, and Florida International University. I could never have completed the project without the warm welcome and gracious cooperation of librarians at those institutions and elsewhere, from manuscript conservators to interlibrary loan specialists. I presented my work in progress for audiences at all those institutions, sometimes on multiple occasions, as well as (also sometimes on multiple occasions) at the Central European University in Budapest, the International Medieval Congress in Leeds, the Arbeitskreis für Hagiographische Fragen (in Stuttgart and Weingarten), the International Congress on Medieval Studies in Kalamazoo, the University of Vienna, Princeton University, Johns Hopkins University, the Mid-America Medieval Academy, the University of South Florida, the American Historical Association, the University of Bielefeld, the University of North Carolina at Chapel Hill, New York University, the University of Texas at Austin, the Nuns' Literacies in Medieval Europe Conference at the University of Missouri at Kansas City, the University of Alberta, and the University of British Columbia.

My debts are immense. I am grateful to Thomas Zotz, Gundula Grebner, Beatrice Lafarge, Johannes Fried, Peter Scholz, Felicitas Schmieder, Olaf Schneider, Angelika Pabel,Walter Pohl, Tina Lutter, Helmut Reimitz, Maximilian Diesenberger, Henrietta Leyser, Caroline Walker Bynum, Giles Constable, Vance Smith, Colum Hourihane and the staff of the Index of Christian Art, Katrinette Bodarwé, Conrad Leyser, Kate Cooper, Hedwig Röckelein, Celia Chazelle, Charles Bowlus, Barbara Bowlus, Martin Eggers, Rob Meens, Melanie Holcolmb, Helene Scheck, Lisa Bitel, Walter Goffart, Jane Rosenthal, Virginia Brown, Mildred Budny, Martha Newman, Diane Ahl, Kathleen Davis, Jo Ann McNamara, Larry Nees, Madeline Caviness, Paula Gerson, Margo Fassler, Virginia Blanton, Maryanne Erler, Hagith Sivan, Julian Hendrix, Gabrielle Spiegel, David Nirenberg, Kirsten Wood, Lara Kriegel, Elizabeth Cooper, Aurora Morcillo, James D'Emilio, Anna Latowsky, Luca Giuliani, Horst Bredekamp, Frank Rexroth, Christian Kroetzel, Dipesh Chakrabarty, Hsueh-mann Shen, Angela Albanese, Rick Russom, David Ganz, Michael Allen, Michele C. Ferrari, Fiona Griffiths, Kathryn Smith, Alison Frazier, Anna

Taylor, Richard Unger, Gordon Blennemann, and Dieter Bauer. I remain painfully aware that I must have forgotten to include many names, and I beg the pardon of anyone who feels slighted.

Those debts that are the freshest loom the largest. I thank my chair and deans at the University of Alberta (Lise Gotell of the Department of Women's and Gender Studies, Lesley Cormack of the Faculty of Arts, and Marc Arnal of the Faculté St.-Jean) for the research appointment in winter term 2012 that enabled me finally to produce a draft of the book good enough to submit to a publisher. I thank the editors at, and readers for, Fordham University Press, for what has been a smooth and seamless publication process. I thank Igor Jakab of the Digital Imaging Lab in the Department of Geography at the University of Alberta for his indispensable help in making the two maps. I thank Andrew Gow, Director of the Religious Studies Program at the University of Alberta, to which I am jointly appointed, for providing me with a research assistant to produce a draft of the index for this book (along with various other duties), and I thank that RA, Nicholas Majaesic, for his excellent work. I also thank Robert Swanson for his (indispensible) professional indexing help.

My husband, Joseph F. Patrouch, and our daughter, Quinn Bellamy Patrouch Lifshitz, have been with me every step of the way as I wrote this book. It has been an adventure, and a challenge. QBPL—this book is for you!

The Carolingian Rhineland

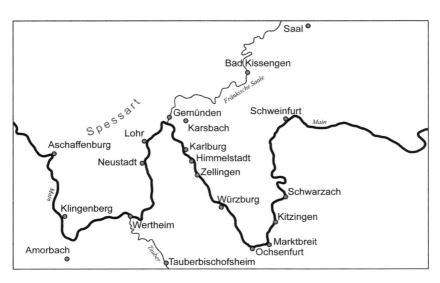

Mainland Franconia

PART ONE

INTRODUCTIONS:

PEOPLE, PLACES, THINGS

CHAPTER ONE

SYNEISACTISM AND REFORM: GENDER RELATIONS IN THE ANGLO-SAXON CULTURAL PROVINCE IN FRANCIA

PROLOGUE: REGIONAL HISTORY AND THE HISTORY OF IDEAS

This book is a study of manuscripts produced during the eighth century in the Anglo-Saxon cultural province in Francia, and it argues that the Christian culture of that region was thoroughly gender-egalitarian and in many ways feminist. Before moving on to description (chapter 3)[1] and analysis (chapters 4 through 7) of the manuscripts, I introduce the individuals and issues at stake in the area (chapter 1) and the region itself (chapter 2).

My approach is unusual. A 1999 study of "regional history and religious history" using "a new methodology which locates the development of the Church in the context of what will be termed the north Italian human environment" never addressed ideas, as opposed to institutions and events, and utilized no manuscript evidence.[2] In the definitive regional history of the area covered by this study, neither ideas nor manuscripts made an appearance.[3] Even in the midst of pleading for a regional approach to religious and ecclesiastical history ("*Landeskirchengeschichte*"), another specialist on the area covered by this study made no reference to manuscripts, although he held a position at the University of Würzburg, where the manuscripts I discuss are located.[4] To my knowledge, the only regional study of a premodern place to have treated manuscript evidence as an integral part of the source base is Patrick Sims-Williams's "coherent picture" of the kingdoms of the Hwicce and the Magonsætan during the seventh and eighth centuries.[5] Like Sims-Williams, I examine ideas within a regional context, on the basis of a corpus of relevant local manuscripts.

A treasure trove of eighth-century manuscript material survives to illuminate the "distinct area of Anglo-Saxon influence and Anglo-Saxon script [that] was established in Germany by the activities of Boniface and his pupils, as well as by the monks and nuns who followed them."[6] Yet, these manuscripts have barely been noticed by early medieval historians. Indeed, the vast majority of historical, literary, theological, and art historical scholarship has failed even to register the connection between women and the Würzburg manuscripts, let alone actively explore the intellectual worlds of the women who produced and used the codices. Instead of using the manuscripts examined here, scholars have repeatedly mined a single source: a famous collection of letters. This particular source has led scholars to highlight the prominence of women, as intellectual intimates, in the personal lives of Boniface and Lul; their collaboration, as spiritual equals, in all aspects of the professional lives (pastoral care, mission, education, liturgy) of those successive Mainz prelates; and the high quality of their own minds, based on the literary prowess displayed in the letters.[7] I, too, begin with that letter collection, before moving on to the manuscripts.

SYNEISACTISM AND MARRIAGE: FRAMEWORKS FOR GENDER RELATIONS IN THE ANGLO-SAXON CULTURAL PROVINCE IN FRANCIA

Soon before 786, an unidentified individual collected dozens of letters written over the course of the previous century by Archbishop Lul of Mainz (d. 786), his predecessor Boniface (d. 754/755), and many of their colleagues, relatives, and friends on both sides of the English Channel.[8] Of the sixty-nine letters in this collection, twenty-five (eight of the first twenty, and eighteen of the first thirty-eight) were to, from, or between female members of the group.[9] Some of the women were named, such as Abbess Eadburga (of Minster-in-Thanet or Wimbourne), heartily thanked by Boniface for sending him books, and elsewhere asked by Lul to support his weakness with her strength.[10] Others were anonymous, such as the *ancilla Dei* to whom Boniface turned for solace after run-ins with "pagans, false Christians, fornicating clerics and pseudo-priests."[11] Because letters constituted "proof that disembodied friendships between members of the opposite sex subsist on ideas,"[12] the compiler of the letter collection made an important ideological point about gender and intellectuality. She or he also produced a monument to syneisactism, a (always slightly controversial) form of religious life that encouraged sexually chaste contact between men and women.[13]

Syneisactic practices existed everywhere from Egypt to Ireland, and from paleo-Christian times through the Reformation.[14] Syneisactic forms ranged from sustained friendships or even spiritual marriages between professed women and men, through the convention of attaching small, informal women's communities to a major men's community, to the formal institution of the full-fledged double monastery. The apostle Paul referred approvingly to the practice (1 Corinthians 7:36–38) and may have engaged in it himself, for he once asked, "have we not power to lead about a sister as a wife?" (1 Corinthians 9:5). From a very early date, there was a thriving settlement of monks and virgins at Seleucia, all governed by a deaconess, around the tomb of Paul's most famous female companion, St. Thecla.[15] Furthermore, cenobitic (community-based) monasticism was frequently a "domestic ascetic movement" instigated by a female member of the family, involving "the commitment of the entire family to pursuing a life of Christian piety."[16] Such mixed-sex communities were created by orthodox-minded women throughout the Mediterranean world.[17] Most important, however, the seventh and eighth centuries in England and parts of Western Europe, including the Anglo-Saxon cultural province in Francia, represented a high point of syneisactism.[18]

For instance, Leoba may have ruled both the women's house at Tauber-bischofsheim and the men's house at Fulda as a double community.[19] As Boniface's "beloved," her corpse was brought to Fulda (in 782) from her property at Schornsheim near Mainz (where she had died) so that she might be buried next to Boniface.[20] The burial of male and female corpses in a single grave was not uncommon among Anglo-Saxon ecclesiastics,[21] and Boniface had requested that the two be buried in a single grave, but the monks of Fulda (founded in 744 by Boniface's student, Sturm) instead buried Leoba in an adjacent spot.[22]

Syneisactic monastic practices bled easily into that other key framework for gender relations, namely, marriage. Several members of the monastic circles around Boniface, such as Bugga's mother, Eangyth; Abbess Adela of Pfalzel; and Bilhildis of Altmünster in Mainz, came to monastic life after extensive heterosexual experience.[23] Lul's aunt Cynehild crossed the Channel to take up the monastic life alongside her unnamed husband and their children Baldhard and Berhtgyt; the latter worked for decades in Thuringia as a *magistra* (teacher) and regularly exchanged books with her cousin Lul.[24] Theoretically, married women and men could make vows of chastity only with the permission of their spouses, but churchmen in the region offered discontented wives (not husbands) the opportunity to purge the sin of illicitly abandoning a husband through penance.[25] This made it possible even for less prominent women to turn to religion after a life of marriage and procreation, such as the unidentified *Gottgeweihte* (consecrated to God) Bertrada (or Berta), mother of Heribert, who donated property to Echternach in 721.[26] Furthermore, some women in the monastic circles of the Anglo-Saxon cultural province in Francia later married.[27] Whether she had been a formally professed and consecrated nun, or a widow or virgin who had converted by changing her vestments while living in her own home, a woman could subsequently (re)marry and remain a full member of the local Christian community, as long as she and her new husband did penance.[28]

Detailed information on the institution of matrimony during the early Middle Ages is hard to come by; nevertheless, evidence relevant to the Anglo-Saxon cultural province in Francia implies that married women were understood to be full autonomous human beings who could make choices and even mistakes. For instance, ecclesiastics provided penitential remedies for Christian husbands who wished to remain married to adulterous wives[29] or to separate from a pagan or infidel wife who refused to abandon her own religious convictions;[30] likewise, abandoned husbands were required to take back penitent wives who decided to return home.[31] Meanwhile, eighth-century ecclesiastics gave women permission to leave a husband who had (through theft or fornication) made himself a *servum* ("slave").[32]

The level of independence for married women indicated in these examples was tied to their control of property. Women in Francia inherited and possessed property as fully entitled individuals. Both married women and married men sometimes disposed of their property independently, but more commonly both spouses held and disposed of property together, so that women participated in the disposition of their husbands' personal inherited properties, and vice versa. In the eighth century east of the Middle Rhine, women (consecrated and lay, married or single) not only enjoyed legal autonomy alongside financial and property rights but also chose to exercise their freedom in large numbers by generously and visibly supporting monastic institutions, through public acts in public fora.[33]

No constitutive nuptial rites existed during the early Middle Ages.[34] However, many manuscripts (albeit none from our region) contained an *accio nuptialis* giving prayers and offerings to help a woman and her husband produce posterity. The *accio* urged brides to be loving, wise, and fruitful, but never obedient, and the couple took communion only to affirm their togetherness and facilitate their fecundity.[35] The spirit (if not the text) of this *accio* clearly penetrated the Anglo-Saxon cultural province, where a local scribe replaced Isidore of Seville's visions of the sacrament of marriage as a divinely ordained institution intended to assure the subordination of women to men with a discussion of fertility entirely in keeping with the *accio nuptialis*.[36] This is consistent with the way the family was conceptualized in the region, as witnessed by local extracts from the "Family Relations" section of Isidore's *Etymologies* (Book 9, chapters 5–7):[37] a multipolar network in which male and female members participated in equivalent ways, rather than a male-dominated and male-defined lineage such as appeared in other copies of the *Etymologies*.[38]

Rather than being a mechanism for the subordination of women, marriage could provide the framework for spiritual attainments, as it did in works celebrating virgins penned by Abbot Aldhelm of Malmesbury (c. 639–c. 710), a member of the letter-exchange circle whose letters to women showed true emotional warmth.[39] Aldhelm celebrated the chaste marriages of Chrysanthus and Daria and of Julian and Basilissa, brilliant rhetors who together studied canonical writings and exegetical commentaries and converted multitudes to Christianity.[40] These treatises were undoubtedly available in the Anglo-Saxon cultural province in Francia from the mid eighth century onward;[41] there they were taken as a literary model by Boniface, Lul (who studied at Malmesbury), Leoba, and Berhtgyt.[42]

The Anglo-Saxon cultural province in Francia was a place where people expected the active and self-directed participation of women in all aspects of culture, including the political realm. In the opening years of the eighth century, when newcomers from Wessex, Northumbria, and Kent were settling into Merovingian-ruled Francia, the wives of the Carolingian mayors of the palace (who dominated the Merovingian kings) were so politically significant that forgers included them to make falsified documents seem authentic. The widow of one mayor, namely, Plectrude (d. 717), even seized power herself.[43] Queens who actively participated in politics after the Carolingian royal coup included Bertrada (751–783), Hildegard (771–783) and Fastrada (783–794).[44] Fastrada, who based her court in her home territory at Frankfurt and was always accompanied by her daughters, was the key figure in the politics of the Main Valley until her death in 794 at the Council of Frankfurt, sited there so that she could participate.[45]

Leoba also possessed political clout, serving as one of Charlemagne's (768–814) royal counselors and as Queen Hildegard's spiritual director, which led her to attend the Worms Reichstag of 781.[46] But politics were a sideline. Boniface called Leoba from England during the 740s "to instruct the [female] servants of God in the monasteries of Germany in divine scriptures."[47] The letter collection showed Leoba as a prominent teacher, sought out by women eager for higher education.[48] The present study explores the intellectual culture of Leoba, her colleagues, and her students through analysis of the eighth-century manuscripts from the region associated with women's religious communities. Those books reflected the gender-egalitarian, even feminist, values of the Anglo-Saxon cultural province in Francia, values that accompanied and supported syneisactism. The existence of this feminist tradition has been invisible under medieval Christian culture's misleading reputation for misogyny.[49]

The women's manuscripts included a number of male-authored texts conventionally ignored by feminist scholars, who have tended to examine only those male-authored texts whose explicit topic was women.[50] Yet the latter constituted a preferred locus for the articulation of antiwoman ideas, whereas positive ideas about women were embedded in many sorts of writings. The evidentiary base for my study is neither a series of texts by women, nor a series of texts about women, but rather a series of texts dealing with a variety of subjects, all contained in manuscripts that were produced and utilized by women. When viewed through the lens of gender, these manuscripts help us grasp the feminist strategies of eighth-century religious women, as they negotiated the changing political waters of early Carolingian Francia.

THE CAROLINGIAN REFORM MOVEMENT IN THE ANGLO-SAXON CULTURAL PROVINCE

While some of the women's manuscripts from the Anglo-Saxon cultural province were produced as early as the 740s, others dated from the final decades of the eighth century, when a new generation came to power and rejected the traditions of Boniface and Leoba.[51] Most of the books in this study were therefore intended to defend women's central place in the intellectual and religious life of Francia, in the face either of a full-blown movement for "correction" and "renewal" or of that movement's preparatory rumblings.

Reform legislation of the end of the eighth century attacked as "abuses" the various priestly and episcopal activities commonly pursued by consecrated women.[52] For instance, the *Admonitio generalis* (789) prohibited abbesses from making blessings on men's heads with their hands and the sign of the cross and from veiling virgins with a sacerdotal blessing.[53] Already in 755, King Pippin had issued (at Verneuil) a capitulary aimed at restricting the movements of abbesses and limiting their political importance, specifically by prohibiting abbesses from being pluralistic or from leaving their monasteries except in specific circumstances (such as a royal summons) and by requiring that *monachae* ("nuns") conduct their business through representatives rather than travel to royal palaces in person.[54] At the moment of formulation in western Francia, Pippin's capitulary was irrelevant to the abbesses and nuns of the Anglo-Saxon cultural province; in fact, it became irrelevant in western Francia, for the chapter in question was omitted from all west Frankish copies of the capitulary.[55] However, it became relevant when it was included in a spate of east Frankish manuscripts of the turn of the eighth century, including Vatican City, BAV, MS Palatinus latinus 577, either from the men's monastery of St. Alban's in Mainz or from Fulda.[56] Furthermore, the best extant copy of the *Admonitio generalis* appeared in a Fulda manuscript of c. 800, while the archbishop of Mainz responsible for the Anglo-Saxon cultural province from 787 to 813 (Riculf) was a disciple of a key architect of the reform program (Alcuin). Clearly, enforcement of reform ideals was attempted in the region.[57]

A closer look at Alcuin and Riculf reveals how attitudes toward women among some leading male ecclesiastics were fraught with contradictions and ambiguities by the end of the eighth century. Amid the reform program, these men had to negotiate the multiple dissonances between their lived experience of learned and/or powerful women, on the one hand, and gender-hierarchical ideologies on the other. Alcuin crafted key planks of the reform program during the 790s while enmeshed in a number of close relationships with consecrated intellectual women who were his good friends, respected intellectual equals, and affectionately regarded colleagues.[58] The very man who sought to restrict women's activities in the sacred sphere has been described as able "to transcend traditional views of gender and to promote instead an egalitarian basis for understanding what it is to be human."[59]

As for Riculf, he was appointed by Queen Fastrada (possibly a relative), who raised him from her own *comitatus* when her husband, Charlemagne, was absent from Francia.[60] Riculf could not, therefore, have seen influential women as per se a scourge. He was not, however, a particular friend of religious women. One of Riculf's major projects (between 796 and 805) was the creation of a men's monastery at St. Alban's in Mainz, theretofore a mere burial church (of c. 430) in an ancient cemetery (where Fastrada was buried in 794), and its development into a major educational and spiritual center.[61] Riculf's strong support for this male community, which competed for resources with older women's communities in the area, was part of the process whereby women's houses such as Leoba's Tauberbischofsheim lost much of their importance as schools. More telling is the likelihood that St. Alban's produced, under his direction, the Vatican manuscript containing the capitulary of Verneuil, with its draconian restrictions on the autonomy and activities of consecrated women.

Of particular interest is the fate of the letter collection described at the beginning of this chapter during the reign of Riculf at Mainz. No "pure" copies of the original collection have survived. We know of it only because it was copied, and simultaneously supplemented, by someone working in the Mainz archives early in the ninth century.[62] This scribe copied the older collection, including its uniform and regularized salutations and orthography, through folio 39v, then (beginning with a new numbering system) almost doubled the total size of the collection (to a total of seventy-seven folios) by copying (with no uniformization) from the Mainz archives dozens of additional letters,[63] only one of which had a female sender or addressee.[64] At the same time, another scribe was mining the Mainz archives, compiling a separate collection of letters by Boniface, Lul, and related figures.[65] Six of the women's letters from the original collection that had been included in the other ninth-century version were omitted from this one,[66] which also added dozens of letters from male ecclesiastics, swelling the (completely homogenized) new collection to 128 folios.[67] Whether or not it was a conscious goal of the compilers of these ninth-century Mainz collections to dilute the evidence for a thriving syneisactic network among Anglo-Saxons active on the continent during the eighth century, they certainly diminished the relative visibility of women among the collaborators of Boniface and Lul.[68]

Nevertheless, these Mainz scribes transmitted evidence of women's eighth-century activities.[69] The two ninth-century Mainz scribes, Alcuin, and Riculf are all paradigmatic for our region, where there was a certain hesitancy to endorse the reform program in full. I ascribe this hesitancy both to the deeply rooted nature of syneisactic values in the area and to the success of Leoba and her students—along with their male allies—in defending regional traditions. Manuscript evidence from the Main Valley often displayed some level of feminist push-back against reformist ideals. Examination of some canon law collections from the region will illustrate the situation, for the reform program was expressed and transmitted above all through the creation of such collections.[70]

Canon law collections brought together legislation that could date from early Christian times through the moment of compilation and derive from anywhere there had ever been a Christian population. The majority of the materials assembled in Carolingian-era legal collections originated far from the Main Valley, often in contexts marked by a strong degree of gender hierarchy. Incorporation into a canon law collection transformed what might have been a curious relic of a different age into a diktat for the present. Ancient eastern Mediterranean conciliar pronouncements were a powerful weapon in the hands of those who wished to diminish the political power, intellectual influence, and sacramental standing of women in eighth-century Francia.

Copies of a variety of canon law collections were produced in the Anglo-Saxon cultural province during the eighth and early ninth centuries.[71] In the following pages, I discuss those that offer the most salient evidence for the dynamics of reform in the area: a local copy of a widespread collection (the so-called *Collectio Vetus Gallica*), a unique local collection (the so-called *Collectio Wirceburgensis*), and a local copy of a central reform text (the so-called *Institutio sanctimonialium*). Where relevant, I also draw on the commonly cited printed editions of reform legislation.

The *Collectio Vetus Gallica* was a systematic collection of canon laws, made or at least initiated at Lyons by bishop Etherius (c. 586–602), although possibly not completed before 627. A substantial excerpt from the collection was included in Würzburg, UB M.p.th.q. 31 folios 42–51, of the late eighth or early ninth century, a codex marked by clear connections to Bonifatian circles.[72] Whoever selected the extracts from the *Vetus Gallica* in this particular collection rejected one key provision: she or he edited chapter 28 to omit canon 4, according to which a woman, no matter how *docta* ("learned") and *sancta* ("holy"), should not teach men.[73] This decision, one of many similar interventions in the textual transmission process that I document in this book, means little in isolation; seen together, however, they reveal a consistent pattern of scribal activity: to select for copying texts that supported the full participation of women alongside men in intellectual and cultural life, to edit texts to bring them in line with that orientation, or both. Such scribal intervention was a fact of life under the old regime of information technology; the well-known malleability of texts (including biblical ones) went hand in hand with a conscious scribal impetus to modify them.[74] In some cases, the syneisactic, gender-egalitarian, and feminist leanings in the codices were reflections of shared values taken for granted by the Anglo-Saxon immigrants to Francia and their continental collaborators; more often, however (including in the case of Würzburg, UB M.p.th.q. 31), they represented positions staked out in the midst of debates over gender roles precipitated by the Carolingian reform program.

More evidence of the approach to reform legislation in the region can be found in the *Collectio Wirceburgensis*, a chronologically ordered collection of ancient conciliar canons uniquely witnessed in Würzburg, UB M.p.th.f. 146. This manuscript was produced during the first third of the ninth century by a male scribe who described himself as being "in communion with" the women's community "*ad lapidum fluminis*," that is, Karlburg.[75] The codex reproduced an early sixth-century collection that itself incorporated fifth-century Italian and African collections.[76] In this collection, the syneisactic community of Karlburg attempted to transmit from Christian antiquity—and thereby depict as relevant to current discussions—ecclesiastical legislation that supported their own orientation, for all of the canons relevant to gender represented the ancient church as a community in which women were thoroughly involved.[77]

The *Collectio Wirceburgensis* contained numerous references to women in clerical positions, either in their own right or because of their (generally marital) relationship with male clerics. For instance, the very first set of canons (the "Canons of the Apostles") included four separate items concerning the kinds of women bishops, priests, and deacons could licitly marry and under what circumstances, and also forbidding clerics from leaving their wives under the pretense of religion.[78] The very apostles themselves were thus pressed into service to testify to the dignity expected from the wife of a bishop or a priest or a deacon (she could not be a prostitute or slave or engage in public spectacles). Readers also learned that the Council of Chalcedon required a woman to wait until her fortieth year, and to prove herself worthy, to be ordained as a *diaconissa*; further, a deaconess who married after engaging in her *ministerium* would be anathematized, along with her husband.[79] The Council of Carthage set the minimum age for the ordination of deacons as thirty-five years and for the consecration of virgins at twenty-five years, implying that a certain gravitas pertained to the (female) *virgo*.[80] Finally, the Council of Laodicea Canon 11 stated that it would not be permitted to establish in a church the women whom the Greeks called "*praesbyterae*" and whom the Latins called "*viduae seniores, univirae, et matriculariae*," even if they had been ordained (*tamquam ordinatas*).[81] Although this canon was negative, it added to the overall impression that historical Christian practice included official roles for women and even female ordination. Otherwise, the *Collectio Wirceburgensis* included no provisions restricting the autonomy or activities of consecrated women.[82]

A high point of the Carolingian reform movement was reached in 813, when reform councils were held at Reims, Mainz, Tours, Arles, and Chalons. Each gathering issued different decisions, all reassessed when the bishops subsequently reassembled at Aachen.[83] The dignitaries gathered at St. Alban's in Mainz issued restrictive legislation, but it weighed as heavily on monks as on nuns.[84] Meanwhile, their provision that priests should enter women's houses only to perform mass and then leave immediately (canon 26) would have had the inevitable effect of leaving many responsibilities, such as hearing confessions, in the hands of abbesses or other members of the women's communities.[85] Furthermore, both men's and women's communities were supposed to be assured of good buildings and sufficient resources (canon 20).[86] It was only in their attempt to require abbesses (but not abbots) to secure permission from their diocesan bishop to travel (canon 13) that the Mainz legislators participated in some antifemale aspects of the reform movement.[87] Yet this provision was never enforced, for the bishops subsequently adopted a unified "Concordia," according to which the canons of the Chalons council would govern abbesses and nuns. According to the concordance, abbesses would not need episcopal permission to travel when an imperial order was involved or when the bishop was too far away for them to easily get permission.[88] Furthermore, according to Canon 62 of the Council of Chalons, abbesses were envisioned to travel with a retinue of *sanctimoniales,* who could also travel on their own (either with the permission of their abbess or because they had some need to do so) and conduct business in a central room in the monastic complex (although it was preferable to delegate business matters to male or female servants).[89]

The next critical stage in the reform movement was reached in 816 and 817, when a series of councils at Aachen articulated a new vision for the empire of Louis the Pious (814–840), largely under the influence of his adviser, Benedict of Aniane. One aspect of this program was the requirement that all religious communities organize themselves either according to the Benedictine Rule or according to a form of life whose details were set forth in two new rules, one for canons (the *Institutio canonicorum*) and one for canonesses (the *Institutio sanctimonialium*). As it happened, the new rule for women was received only in select places, despite the fact that Louis considered his legislation concerning female religious to be one of the most important planks in his entire program. One place he and Benedict did see success was in the Anglo-Saxon cultural province, for the important women's house of Schwarzach was intimately connected with the reformers at the time.[90] One of the few surviving copies—indeed, the oldest surviving one—of the *Institutio sanctimonialium* was made around 820, at Würzburg, for one of the women's houses in the diocese.[91] It, too, followed the pattern of modifying potentially antiwoman texts.

The *Institutio sanctimonialium,* as formulated at Aachen, prescribed strict enclosure for canonesses, discouraged abbesses from traveling, prohibited abbesses from plural office holding, and insisted that women who professed do so for a lifetime. Realistically speaking, such prescriptions were ideological pronouncements that were impossible to implement; indeed, the legislating family itself (the Carolingians) never implemented the prescriptions where their own family institutions (such as Argenteuil, Chelles, or St. Salvator in Brescia) were concerned.[92] The *Institutio sanctimonialium* imposed many obligations on the women of canonial communities (such as to provide hospitality and to care for the poor and the sick) that required them to remain connected with the outside world, as did their individual responsibilities to visit and administer their personal properties; furthermore, many ninth-century Carolingian princesses were pluralistic abbesses of several houses and held these positions after betrothals or even after marriages.[93] More striking, however, is the evidence that Würzburg scribes did not rely on the impact of "reality" to soften strict reform legislation, but intervened directly in the text, indeed, precisely at the two points where the *Institutio sanctimonialium* threatened to become outright misogynistic.

The opening section of the *Institutio sanctimonialium,* as legislated at Aachen, consisted of a series of patristic texts, most of which had nothing but praise and inoffensive advice for religious women, including Jerome's letters to his female friends Eustochium and Demetriades; Caesarius of Arles's "Gaudete et exultate" letter enjoining nuns to read, pray, and work rather than simply be proud of their virginity; and an "exhortatio ad sponsam Christi" glorifying brides of Christ as the most sacred and consecrated form of humanity.[94] However, two of the texts in this prefatory section were problematic, and one deeply so: Jerome's letter to Furia, discouraging women from going out in public at all, and Cyprian's *De habitu virginum*, a notoriously misogynistic diatribe arguing that virgins should never be seen at all lest they attract men's eyes and arouse the latters' libidos. It cannot be a coincidence that two folios, containing the final portion of Jerome's letter and the entire Cyprian text, have been cut out of the codex[95] because the chapter of the rule that these patristic opinions undergirded has also been manipulated. Chapter 16 recommended against girls who were being educated in the community leaving the cloister lest they be seen by people in the city and their modesty be thereby damaged, or lest they be exposed to foods that they should not eat. However, this section of the chapter was omitted from its proper place in connection with girls in the school and located instead in a section dealing with sick or infirm nuns who wished to confess to a priest and who were thus encouraged to wait until a priest could come to them, rather than to go looking for one in the town; this transformed a sexist recommendation into a sensible one.[96]

Carolingian-era reformers were unable to enforce many aspects of their programs.[97] The legal materials discussed in the preceding paragraphs allow us to glimpse how implementation of reform ideals concerning gender roles was thwarted at the local level by those who controlled the processes of textual transmission and reproduction. Nevertheless, the reform movement was not toothless, and relations between professed men and women in the Anglo-Saxon cultural province in Francia were very different by the 830s from what they had been a century earlier.

The full participation of religious women in the intellectual life of the Anglo-Saxon cultural province in Francia during the eighth century had been based on the existence of a sufficient number of monastic houses to support their vocations. The seventh and much of the eighth century had seen the foundation, by a variety of aristocratic families, of numerous monastic institutions intended for and governed by female members of those families. These institutions formed part of the regional power base of each family and, as such, were attacked by the Carolingian dynasty as part of their efforts to eliminate potentially disloyal forces. The men's house of Fulda was key to the Carolingian strategy. Taken over by King Pippin in 765, it was subsequently used by Pippin and, above all, by Charlemagne to indirectly subject smaller communities to the ruling family through a series of hostile takeovers.[98] From the 780s through the 830s, Fulda gained control of the resources (in land and personnel) of a number of formerly independent women's houses, most of which were located at crucial river crossings and road intersections. The strength and wealth of the regional aristocracy were thereby diminished, and those of the ruling family increased.[99]

The treatment of the smaller communities by Fulda was at first benign, as the monks attempted to guarantee a devout lifestyle to the inhabitants,[100] but the smaller houses were all eventually closed down.[101] Furthermore, an imperial capitulary, given in 803/804 at Salz on the Frankish Saale, forbade girls to enter a religious community temporarily and solely to acquire an education, forbade women's communities to offer such training, and forbade boys to receive any part of their education in women's religious communities; this legislation must have crippled many of the houses, increasing their vulnerability and the temptation of Fulda to shut them down as useless drains on resources.[102]

The changed situation of the ninth century, in which religious women were much less visible and much less important in the region than they had been earlier, is evident from the conflicted nature of the memory of Leoba, as she appeared in her biography by Rudolf of Fulda (d. 865). The text was composed around 836 on the basis of a lost older narrative, along with information garnered from Leoba's disciples.[103] Rudolf's Leoba was the very epitome of a Christian teacher, knowledgeable in all aspects of Christian literate culture, including scientific methods of biblical study. She was also a great missionary, called to the life by prophetic designation; trained for that life through the study of "the Holy Fathers," canonical decrees, and "the laws of the entire ecclesiastical order"; and finally confirmed in that life by Archbishop Boniface, who even left to her his cowl (and with it, perhaps some of his official authority). Rudolf showed Leoba performing the sacramental rite of the washing of the feet. Rudolf also narrated the many trips Leoba made to meet with Boniface, other bishops, or Kings Pippin and Charlemagne. He even recounted how Leoba traveled frequently with other *sanctimoniales* to Fulda, where she ate and slept with the monks, and how at the end of her life she forsook her monastery at Tauberbischofsheim and took up residence, with a small group of *sanctimoniales*, on her villa near Mainz, a gift from Charlemagne.[104] Yet, in contradiction of the contents of his own narrative but as a faithful echo of the Carolingian reform ideology, Rudolf simultaneously asserted that Anglo-Saxons in Germany all lived under a strict rule according to which men and women never visited one another, priests entered women's houses only to perform a mass, consecrated women were strictly cloistered, and even the abbess, as the only woman who could leave the confines of the community, did so only for very important reasons![105]

By Rudolf's day, the heritage of Anglo-Saxon syneisactic monasticism at Fulda had clearly become a controversial matter. Rudolf found it necessary to walk a very fine line between refashioning Leoba to suit his own interests and faithfully reflecting those aspects of her life that went back to the reports of contemporaries.[106] And he had to deal with an abbot, Raban Maur, who was alone among Carolingian ecclesiastics in espousing strongly misogynist views, including that woman was flesh (*caro*) and man spirit (*animus*), hierarchically understood; that only man, not woman, was made in the image of God; that woman was characterized by a *levitas mentis* ("lightness of mind"), requiring that a husband have authority over his wife and a father over his unmarried daughters; and that woman was particularly lustful.[107] In 782, the Fulda monks had denied Boniface's wish to be buried in a single grave with Leoba; in 836, they further separated the two saints, translating Leoba's relics into the crypt of a newly constructed church on a hill outside of town.[108] Although still treated with respect (she was surrounded by relics of the Savior, the twelve apostles, and a number of early Christian martyrs), Leoba was banished from the center, from Boniface, and from public view.[109] It was the end of an era.

"[D]espite changes in legislation and politics . . . religious women in [Saxony, Thuringia, and Hesse] continued the tradition of instruction and moral exemplarity first established by the women of Boniface's circle."[110] However, it appears that developments of the period around 800 put the brakes on women's involvement in the world of texts in the Main and Tauber valleys. The present study explores the contribution that women made to eighth-century Christian culture, often in the face of oppositional "reformist" currents, before the disappearance of the world of Boniface, Lul, and Leoba. Eighth-century Frankish culture was organized around the reception and transmission of the heritage of late ancient Mediterranean Christian communities, as contained in the writings of the Church Fathers and in other anonymous texts, such as martyr passions. Leoba and her students participated—as scribes and readers—in this foundational European cultural moment. The analytical chapters of this book reveal some details of their efforts, including their feminist concern with images of, and roles assigned to, women. Manuscript-based studies of other areas might well confirm Janet Nelson's intuition that egalitarian institutions and ideas were completely normal, at every social level and in every sphere, during much of the early Middle Ages, as they seem to have been in the Anglo-Saxon cultural province in Francia during the early Carolingian period.[111]

CHAPTER TWO

THE ANGLO-SAXON CULTURAL PROVINCE IN FRANCIA

MONASTERIES AND CHURCHES IN THE MAIN RIVER VALLEY BEFORE C. 740

During the late Merovingian and early Carolingian periods, Anglo-Saxon immigrants were active in many different parts of Francia and its neighboring territories. The present study, however, focuses only on their activities in the Middle Main and Tauber valleys, that is, in the portions of Franconia (*Franken*) defined by those two rivers, known as *Mainfranken* and *Tauberfranken*.[1] An agriculturally fertile territory, Franconia was, beginning in 496/497, integrated into Francia through subjection to families loyal to the royal dynasty of Merovingian Franks.[2] The region was even linguistically "frankicized," for the dialect spoken along the rivers Main, Tauber, Saale, and Neckar was closely related to the dialects of the Rhine and Moselle valleys;[3] for the elites, civilization in both the written and oral registers was bilingual, Latin and Germanic.[4]

By the eighth century, Franconia was among the richest and most economically developed areas of Francia,[5] which as a whole was more awash with aristocratic wealth than anywhere else in the former Roman world.[6] The area was heavily monetized and was plugged into multiple trade networks, both regional and long distance.[7] Mainz was both a key market (where grains and Franconian wines were exchanged for imported finished goods such as textiles and metalwork) and a key production center (for instance, of metalwork).[8] The substantial coterie of potential patrons must have been the main thing that attracted so many Anglo-Saxon intellectuals to the area, for Frankish aristocracies could support a much larger learned religious class than could the impoverished elites of post-Roman Britain.[9] And those Frankish elites were Christian, a *sine qua non* for potential patrons. In some places, such as Saxony and Frisia, Boniface and company did act as missionaries, but not in Franconia, where extensive Christianization activities had already been carried out from Trier, Mainz, Worms, and Speyer, as well as by the monasteries of Echternach and Weissenburg.[10] Thus, the vocabulary of baptism, ecclesiastical organization, and monasticism was derived, during the seventh century, from West Frankish.[11]

When the Anglo-Saxons began arriving in large numbers during the late Merovingian period, the distinguishing characteristics of Franconia were the openness of its terrain to the Middle Rhine and its multiple connections to the territories around Trier and Metz.[12] Even at this late stage, all the families ruling in the area, including the Hedeni based at Würzburg, came from West Francia.[13] But the Christian communities of Merovingian Franconia were also linked directly to the source of their Latin brand of Christianity: Rome. All over the Rhine-Main area, including at Würzburg itself, archeologists have found sixth-, seventh-, and eighth-century bronze keys, pilgrim souvenirs brought from St. Peter's in Rome.[14] Roman capital inscription practices were so rooted in the area that there is a "rhinefrankish writing type" based on the plethora of seventh- and eighth-century finds from Mainz.[15]

Thus, neither Mediterranean culture in general nor Christianity in particular was a new arrival in the Franconian portion of the Anglo-Saxon cultural province in Francia. The only evidence for "paganism" in eighth-century Franconia was a 742 letter of Boniface to Pope Zacharias, complaining that Frankish pilgrims to Rome were returning from the holy city corrupted, with "pagan" objects and practices![16] Most important, when, in the 740s, a new bishopric was created in the middle Main Valley, at Würzburg, it was possible to endow the see with twenty-seven Franconian churches (and one monastery), all of which dated at least to the seventh century, and most of whose dedications (e.g., to Martin of Tours and Remigius of Reims) bespoke early foundation specifically under the influence of west Frankish centers.[17]

Many of these seventh-century wooden churches (later rebuilt in stone) have been excavated, as have other contemporary wooden proprietary churches (*Eigenkirchen*) that were not given to the new bishop, such as at Kleinlangheim.[18] These excavations have revealed that the seventh-century wooden churches of the area were sometimes quite large and elaborate structures.[19] Significantly, the majority of the churches in the 740s endowment were located to the east and/or north of Würzburg, an indication of how far the Christian religion had already spread.[20] Meanwhile, the row grave field at Zeuzleben near Schweinfurt appears to have been the site of several monumental *ad sanctos* burials already during the sixth century.[21] Leoba and company joined a Christian society when they settled in the Main River valley.

In the following pages, I survey the institutional Christian world into which Boniface, Leoba, and their companions came when they first arrived in Franconia at the beginning of the 740s. However, there must have been even more of a preexistent ecclesiastical infrastructure than can be described here. Many small churches for the lay population, as well as small aristocratic *Eigenklöster* (private or family monasteries), are known only through offhand and fortuitously surviving references or chance archeological discoveries;[22] others must have escaped both medieval documentation and modern detection. Several women named as abbesses in contemporary documents ruled communities that have never been identified.[23] There were also professionally religious women living in private households.[24] However, such institutions, or individual households, are unlikely to have been significant intellectual centers, still less sources of book production. My concern here is, above all, the intellectual and educational centers of the region during the eighth century. As this chapter will show, those were predominantly women's communities, both before and after the arrival of the Anglo-Saxons.

As an old and important city, by 700 Mainz and its environs included a cathedral complex and numerous secular churches whose dedications spoke to relations with Christian communities throughout the Latin West and the Greek East.[25] The metropolis also boasted a women's monastery, namely, St. Mary inside the walls (Altmünster), which survived in its original spot inside the northwest corner of the city walls from the 690s into the seventeenth century.[26] Altmünster clearly had some connection with the bishops of Mainz and with local nobles, for it sat on land acquired by Bilihilt (Bilhildis) of Würzburg (wife of Hedan II) from her uncle Rigobert (Rigibert), bishop of Mainz (d. 720), and the only extant charter concerning its property was witnessed in 734 by (among other people) Rigobert's successor bishop, Gerold of Mainz.[27] Altmünster also ran a *Volkskirche* (or "people's church," the term for the sanctuary utilized by the lay populace as distinct from the religious community before the birth of the institutional parish) dedicated to St. Paul and had full ownership of the area of the town in which it was located, as well as of extensive properties throughout Mainz.[28] No men's community existed at Mainz before the very end of the eighth century, when Archbishop Riculf installed monks at St. Alban's. There were male clerics attached to the cathedral, but the oldest products of their scriptorium dated to the ninth century.[29]

The remainder of the lower Main Valley evidenced, by circa 700, significant institutional Christian development in terms of the presence of secular churches but did not include any monastic communities beyond a tiny, ephemeral men's community dedicated to St. Martin, about which nothing is known.[30] Neither the Spessart to the north nor the northern reaches of the Odenwald to the south was able to support anything more than tiny chapels.[31] Even at the spot where two ancient, well-traveled transport routes through the Spessart crossed one another, no permanent community grew up.[32] The river valley was very sparsely populated along this stretch, and the (seventh-century?) church of St. Michael at Lohr may have single-handedly served the population of the area. In contrast, farther up river, monastic life flourished.

The vibrancy of monastic life in the Middle Main was doubtless a result of its lush *Weinberge* (wine-producing hills), which guaranteed vitamins, pleasure, and income to religious communities, who sold their wines through the market at Mainz.[33] After the transitional town of Klingenberg, a documented site of both wine production and stone quarrying during the eighth century, gently rolling sun-drenched hills and a fertile littoral densely packed with orchards and farms (including for large-scale wheat production around Ochsenfurt and Schweinfurt) stretched for miles, all the way through to Schwarzach.[34] Three women's monasteries (Karlburg, Zellingen, and Ochsenfurt) were already in place here by the foundation of the see of Würzburg in 741.

Karlburg was probably founded, between 630 and 640, by Gertrude of Nivelles (626–653), using her own properties.[35] An enormously wealthy and important house, Karlburg possessed extensive properties, including a seventh-century fortress (further developed in the eighth century) that was key to Frankish domination of the fertile Middle Main region. Karlburg was the center of clearing and settlement for the surrounding territories, which it developed and ruled both as a secular mark and as a parish (centered on the church of St. Gertrude in Karsbach).[36] The women of Karlburg, like those of Altmünster and (as we shall see) Kitzingen, ran people's churches, which made them spiritual leaders for the region. Karlburg not only ruled an extremely fertile stretch of the Main River valley but also was located on one of the few direct east-west routes through the area, a road running through Frankfurt to the Rhine.[37]

The Karlburg complex was composed of a women's monastery (possibly dedicated to St. Martin of Tours), a monastic church (dedicated to Mary), a fortress (castellum or Burg), a villa or Hof engaged in export-oriented mass production of medium-quality goods alongside agriculture and viticulture, and a settlement populated by dependent personnel, all of which belonged to the Hausgut of the Pippinids (ancestors of the Carolingians).[38] It was a major elite settlement and gathering spot, possibly even a court or residence, where specialized metalworkers lived on a permanent basis, and where an extremely high percentage of the ceramics in daily use were high-quality imports.[39] Local workshops turned out high-quality and stylistically prized goods (including reliquaries and book covers), but much of the material culture of Karlburg was determined by its position in a network of trade, embassies, and gift exchange.[40] There is some debate over whether Karlburg was, in the seventh and eighth centuries, a center of production of objects made in a style associated with the Trier area or a center of consumption and distribution of products from the Trier area; either way, Karlburg was tightly connected with the Trier area, marked by the syneisactic scriptorial cultures of the monastic trio of Echternach (a men's house), Oeren, and Pfalzel (women's houses).[41]

Archeological finds, including the tools necessary for book production, attest to the presence of a scriptorium and a school at Karlburg.[42] The archeological profile of the house (writing tools, high-quality metal objects including spindle whorls and loom weights, religious artifacts, and signs of intermixing between members of the village and the monastic community) matched that of seventh- and eighth-century double monasteries in England,[43] although Karlburg was not a double house. Some male clerics lived in the complex, such as Reginmaar the deacon, early in the ninth century (see chapter 3), but they were not organized as a monastic community. Finally, it bears stating explicitly that all the bustling urban and courtly life of Karlburg unfolded not merely in the neighborhood of, but in connection with, the monastery.[44] As part of the process of endowing the new episcopal see at Würzburg during the 740s, Karlburg became an episcopal Eigenkloster, but was closed by the bishops before the end of the ninth century.[45]

The other two Middle Main Valley pre-Bonifatian women's monasteries (Zellingen and Ochsenfurt) were less significant than was Karlburg. Cellinga (Zellingen), located nine kilometers from Karlburg in the direction of Würzburg, is known primarily through archeological excavations, which have revealed a material culture similar (although on a smaller scale) to that of Karlburg, in the sense that the objects found were of very high quality, were the sorts of things associated with intellectual and social elites, and were acquired through networks of long-distance trade and elite gift exchange.[46] Although it never became a major center on the order of Karlburg, Cellinga did maintain its independence from both Fulda and Würzburg at least through the middle of the ninth century, when a servant of the abbess was healed by relics that had overnighted at the community (along with the monks engaged in the translation) in the course of transfer to Fulda.[47] The event was also a sign of the continued integration of religious women into the ecclesiastical life (if not the intellectual life) of the region. Farther up the Main River, beyond Würzburg, was Ochsenfurt, the smallest and least wealthy of the three but still a house of some significance due to its command of an important river ford and its status as the gateway city on the roads to Rome (via Augsburg and Innsbruck), into Bavaria (via Nuremberg), and to the Eastern Roman Empire and Black Sea regions via the Danube River; as the oldest settlement near the point where the Main flowed closest to the Danube (now at Marktbreit), eighth-century Ochsenfurt stood at one end of a 130-kilometer road linking the Main River valley to the most important ideas and most valuable goods on offer.[48]

Farther to the north, along the Saale River, indigenous Frankish aristocratic families had also founded women's (and possibly men's) houses; however, none of these is known to have had any intellectual aspirations, and all were gobbled up by nearby Fulda before the end of the eighth century.[49] The Frankish nobility was, in general, extremely supportive of all forms of religious life for women,[50] but the Main Valley was especially blessed in this regard. This preexistent orientation of the region may well explain why Boniface invited so many religious women into the area.

BONIFACE AND FRIENDS IN THE VALLEY OF THE MAIN

In the course of the decades after 741, Boniface, Carloman, Carloman's brother (and later king) Pippin (who deposed the last Merovingian king), and Pippin's son Carloman founded and endowed a bishopric in Würzburg and set on the episcopal throne (until 754/755) Boniface's fellow countryman Burkhard. Boniface's own status was both irregular and extraordinary. In the course of multiple trips to Rome, Boniface had been named bishop (722), archbishop (732), and papal legate (737), in each case without any fixed seat. He became bishop of Mainz only in 746 or 747, after deposing his enemy, Bishop Gewilib (745), son and successor of Gerold, who had died in battle in 737 supporting Charles Martel.[51] Following his father's example, Gewilib had killed his father's killer and returned trium-phant to Mainz with Charles Martel.[52] Boniface's failure to influence the choice of the new appointee in a direction more amenable to his vision of proper clerical behavior presumably caused him to agitate in Rome for the status of legate and to begin to assemble a team through whom he could penetrate the Main Valley, off-limits because of his poor relations with the "fornicating" bishops of Mainz.[53]

On his 737 trip to Rome, Boniface brought both Lul and Burkhard into his entourage, to which he subsequently added (in 740) Willibald, who would write his first biography.[54] By that date, he had also attracted the English nuns Thekla and Leoba to his team.[55] The group stood poised to move at the first opportu-nity. In 741, literally as Charles Martel (ally of the fornicating warrior-bishop Gewilib) lay on his deathbed, Boniface created for Burkhard the new bishopric of Würzburg and founded a new women's monastery in the Main River valley, at Kitzingen, for Thekla, to which he soon added a house for women in the Tauber Valley (Tauberbischofsheim) for Leoba, a bishopric for Willibald (at Eichstätt), and a house for men at the extreme northern reaches of the new diocese of Würzburg (Fulda).

I suspect that the endowment of Würzburg was made possible by the expro-priation of Martel's son by his second marriage (to Swanahild), namely, Grifo, who was immediately deposed from his position of rulership in Thuringia by Boniface's allies, Carloman and Pippin, sons from Martel's first marriage (to Chrotrud).[56] Churches such as St. Peter at Groß-Umstadt in the Odenwald, associated with a royal *Hof*, and the monastery of Karlburg, which ended up in the endowment for Würzburg, are exactly the sorts of properties the de-posed Grifo would have received from Charles Martel to enable him to rule in the area.[57] In addition to those properties, which had long been in Martel's family, Charles must have endowed Grifo with properties acquired from the former Würzburg ruling family of the Hedeni when he took personal control of the Thuringian duchy during the early 720s.[58] These properties also went to the new bishop. The basic procedure was repeated in 743, when Carloman and Pippin attacked their sister Hiltrud and her husband, Duke Odilo of Bavaria (whom she had married against their wishes in 741 or 742), and seized proper-ties in the Nordgau to create the bishopric of Eichstätt for Willibald.[59] Over the next two years, they gave substantial properties to Sturm and Boniface for the foundation and endowment of Fulda,[60] properties that may also have derived from the attacks on Odilo and Grifo. In 747, upon the retirement of Carloman, Pippin seized the Austrasian inheritance of his nephew Drogo. It is surely no coincidence that a second wave of endowments by Pippin for Würzburg took place in 747, drawing on property gained from Drogo's denied inheritance.[61]

Kitzingen quickly became the most significant women's monastery of the region, surviving until its secularization in 1544. Its significance derived in the first instance from its position as a replacement Pippinid (Carolingian) *Eigenkloster* for Karlburg that, in the course of the complex property transfers of the 740s, had been given by Carloman and Pippin to Würzburg.[62] The population in and around Kitzingen was extremely sparse before the implantation of the monastery, which had to pioneer the settlement and organization of the area, as well as its integration into local structures of lordship, which came to center on and radiate out from Kitzingen just as they had from Karlburg.[63] The *cella* at Ochsenfurt was also subjected to Kitzingen, giving the latter house a plethora of political and commercial advantages. The abbesses of Kitzingen also founded the people's church of the area and weathered (into the fifteenth century) periodic attacks by the bishops of Würzburg over the female monastery's control of the parish.[64] They may also have gained control of the *Volkskirche* at Ochsenfurt, although not until the ninth century.[65]

The abbesses of Kitzingen enjoyed *Reichsunmittelbarkeit*, that is, immediate, direct subjection and access to the imperial court.[66] The first abbess of Kitzingen, Hadeloga, was the daughter of Charles Martel and his second wife, Swanahild, and thus the half-sister of the ruthless fraternal pair Carloman and Pippin; unlike her less fortunate brother Grifo, Hadeloga securely retained her place in the political landscape of Franconia despite the machinations of her half-siblings.[67] The significance of Kitzingen also derived from its status as the institution with the most learned teacher in the entire region, namely, Thekla (d. after 747), one of the dedicatees of Aldhelm of Malmesbury's *Prosa de virginitate*.[68] Thekla, learned, experienced, and already advanced in age, became the *magistra* (teacher) responsible both for Kitzingen and nearby Ochsenfurt.

And then, of course, there was Leoba, who came to the continent to govern a new Bonifatian foundation at Tauberbischofsheim, where she established a major school.[69] Walburga (Walpurga), the younger sister of Bishop Willibald of Eichstätt, came from Wessex to study either at Kitzingen or Tauberbischofsheim, before succeeding her brother as the head of the community of Heidenheim, into which she integrated women.[70] The house attracted continental noble girls as well, such as the Thuringian Willeswind.[71] The valley of the Tauber had not previously been outfitted with women's monasteries, despite being fully incorporated into (Christian) Francia from the seventh century.[72] Yet the Tauber Valley was a natural for female monastic development because of its character as a stable wine-producing area, much like the Middle Main.

Despite its proximity to Würzburg, which could be reached via an easy and direct overland route, Tauberbischofsheim pertained to Boniface's diocese of Mainz, yet another sign of his close relationship with Leoba.[73] Leoba's connections to Mainz remained strong even after Boniface's death, for she founded a women's monastery at Schornsheim on the old Roman road south of Mainz, adding yet another female community to the Main Valley.[74] In contrast, Lul of Mainz established a men's monastic house, as his personal retreat and eventual burial church, far to the north at Hersfeld.[75] Even in his retreat, Lul could not leave women behind, for during his lifetime (and for a time afterward), there was also a women's Marian community, Frauenberg bei Hersfeld, right next to the men's house. The women's house, subject to Mainz not Hersfeld, was evidently Lul's answer to Boniface's Tauberbischofsheim.[76]

For all their glory, neither Kitzingen nor Tauberbischofsheim could compete with the other new foundation of the Bonifatian team, namely, the men's house of Fulda.[77] The monastery was founded in 744, in connection with a royal residence, and very soon began its march to major wealth (primarily based on endowments of *Weingut* in the Rhineland) and power, beginning with a papal exemption from the authority of the bishop of Würzburg (751), a grant of immunity from royal power (774), and a grant (from the royal fisc) of the entire Hammelburger Mark (777).[78] The bishops of Würzburg unsuccessfully fought both the exemption and Fulda's control of tithes on properties within the borders of their diocese.[79]

The appearance of the newcomers east of the Middle Rhine did not put a stop to monastic development programs on the part of indigenous aristocratic families. For instance, a certain Count Throand founded a church and a (probably men's) Marian monastery at Holzkirchen in response to letter of Pope Zacharias (748), calling upon the count and other lay nobles to undertake such projects. Holzkirchen attracted many donations from a broad spectrum of nobles under King Pippin (751–768) but was (in 775) seized by Charlemagne and given to Fulda, which by 800 had turned the institution into a Main Valley school for boys.[80] Likewise, Count Macco (Matto), who had earlier founded a women's house at Einfirst (in the 730s), established—probably during the 750s— another women's monastery at Wenkheim. Like Holzkirchen, it was very rich in property, relics, and unfree subjects by the time Matto's children donated it to Fulda (792).[81] But for many decades, Wenkheim had an independent existence, as when (in 762/763) a married couple (Hahbert and Hruadlaug) gave properties both to Fulda and to Wenkheim (under Abbess Hruadlaug).[82] Farther up the Saale from Wenkheim, Abbess Emhilt founded and governed a Marian women's house at Milz, to which she donated (in 783 or 784) her library and her relic collection; it is unclear what became of the books and the relics when, a few years later, the property of the house was given to Fulda and the nuns relocated to Tauberbischofsheim.[83]

Sometime late in the eighth century, Charlemagne founded a tiny retreat for monastic men in a royal *Hof* at Neustadt am Main.[84] Neustadt commanded a ford on the Main River and a key spot on north-south roads, both crucial features for an institution about which the earliest thing known for certain is that it was held successively (810–829) by three men who also served simultaneously as abbots of Amorbach in the Odenwald and as bishops of the new Saxon bishopric of Verden. Neustadt was of great strategic importance as an instrument of Carolingian policy in Saxony, but neither it nor Amorbach served as an intellectual or educational center.[85] Meanwhile, the Main River valley witnessed the rise of still another important women's house with a strong educational orientation: Schwarzach, within easy walking distance of Kitzingen, at the extreme edge of the fertile Middle Main. One author has suggested that the house was essentially a school for noblewomen run by lay abbesses,[86] but I would not discount its possible spiritual as well as intellectual significance. Like Einfirst and Wenkheim, the original aristocratic *Eigenkloster* at Schwarzach was founded and governed by members of the house of Count Macco (Matto), most importantly by Abbess Juliana, sister of Count Megingaud.[87] Schwarzach rose to glory as a royal monastery when Fastrada (d. 794), who was related to the Mattonen and was one of Schwarzach's major donors, became queen through her marriage to Charlemagne (783).[88] The royal couple in person laid the ground stone for a new abbey church in 793.[89] Under the patronage of Fastrada (one of the greatest landowners in the region), Schwarzach not only became fabulously rich but also acquired increasing political significance, to the extent that it appeared (in the same category as Fulda and Hersfeld) on an 819 list of Carolingian royal monasteries that owed services (monetary, military, and/or intercessory) to the Frankish Empire. Rule of the house was eventually assumed by Fastrada's daughter with Charlemagne, Theodrada, formerly abbess of Argenteuil near Paris.[90]

This book is a study of eighth-century manuscripts from the Main River valley. The Main Valley institutions most likely to have been able to produce books during that period were women's religious communities. During the 740s, when book production in the area began (the most important result of the arrival of the Anglo-Saxons),[91] Karlburg was the institution most capable of hosting a full-fledged scriptorium; by the 780s, Kitzingen had eclipsed Karlburg in terms of personnel and other resources. Surviving manuscripts from the region, which date approximately from the late 740s through the early 790s, and which are described in detail in chapter 3, were all written in "German-insular" script by a series of interrelated hands. The scenario that best explains the nature of the surviving manuscript evidence is that the women of the former (Karlburg) and the replacement (Kitzingen) Carolingian proprietary houses cooperated over the course of decades, with the bulk of the work taking place at Karlburg during mid-century (resulting in the Gun[t]za-group manuscripts) and shifting to Kitzingen over the course of time (resulting in the Abirhilt-group books). Near the end of the eighth century, all the books were concentrated at Kitzingen, as Karlburg was becoming ever weaker (and would soon be closed by the bishops of Würzburg). These two groups of codices, named for Gun(t)za and Abirhilt, are described in detail in chapter 3.

However, it is not possible to move immediately to a survey of those codices, for it is necessary first to address one additional aspect of the historiography of the region: a series of distorting myths surrounding the foundation of the bishopric of Würzburg contained in the biographies of Boniface and Burkhard that, taken together, have led some scholars to believe that the eighth-century manuscripts of the area were produced in a men's monastery in the diocesan seat, rather than in any of the women's houses described here.

THE FOUNDATION OF WÜRZBURG: MYTHIC NARRATIVES OF EXPULSION AND REMOVAL

The initial endowment of the see of Würzburg involved some unsavory politics and collusion in the expropriation of two potential Pippinid rulers (Grifo and Drogo). It was in the interests of both Würzburg bishops and Carolingian kings to obscure the course of events. A campaign to blacken Grifo's name[92] was accordingly supplemented with the creation of the legend of a pagan dynasty forced out of Würzburg by God and the righteous populace as a way to explain why lands and other resources were "available" to be transferred to the new bishopric. The first biography of Boniface was commissioned by Lul of Mainz and Megingoz of Würzburg (d. 783, Burkhard's successor and a former monk of one of Boniface's foundations, installed by Boniface in 754) from another beneficiary of the expropriations of the 740s, namely, bishop Willibald of Eichstätt (741–788).[93] This text was the first salvo in the process of casting confusion over the genuine history of the Anglo-Saxon cultural province in Francia.[94] Palmer has pinpointed the greatest point of divergence between the plot of Willibald's biography of Boniface (on the one hand) and the concerns of Boniface's own letters (on the other): "The arch-villains from Boniface's letters—notably Virgil of Salzburg and Gewilib of Mainz—are passed over by Willibald in favor of secular leaders like Hedan of Thuringia, about whom Boniface himself left no surviving comment."[95]

The focus on Hedan of Thuringia, presented in the narrative as a tyrannical duke based in Würzburg and as the perpetrator of a long list of crimes (rather than as the pious donor to Christian churches that he historically was), was intended to divert attention from the true stories of Grifo of Thuringia and Drogo of Austrasia.[96] Even egregious villainy, however, will fade from memory without a victim to commemorate. That victim would be Kilian, martyred evangelist of the Würzburg area and future patron saint of the diocese.[97] This next stage in the development of the legend was owed to Megingoz's successor, Charlemagne's ally Berowelf, whose orchestration of a cult to Kilian further obscured the process by which the see had been founded. The birth of Kilian (that is, his first appearance in the record) coincided with a major change in the position of the bishop of Würzburg: the 779 *Würzburger Markbeschreibung* defined a contiguous territory around the diocesan seat that was to be under the control of the bishop and labeled the territory as the property of Saint Kilian.[98] Based on his improved resources, Berowelf began construction of a worthy cathedral; meanwhile, Kilian was included in the personal calendar of Queen Hildegard and King Charlemagne (in the Godescalc Gospel Lectionary) produced at the Carolingian courts of Verona and Aachen in the years following 781, a way for the royal couple to honor the importance of Würzburg.[99]

The details of Kilian's life and death were fleshed out at Würzburg in the course of the 780s.[100] Some ideas for the character of the saint congealed in 783, in connection with the funeral of the retired Bishop Megingoz in a tiny cruciform oratory, centered upon a well in the heart of Würzburg.[101] Both the well and Megingoz's sarcophagus are still in their original location (now the crypt of the church of Neumünster), to which Bishop Adalbero moved the saint's relics in 1057 because he believed the well to be the site of Kilian's martyrdom, as described in his passion narratives. The person most likely to have invented the association between Kilian and the well (along with the remainder of the story of the saint) is the man who performed the funeral for Megingoz: Bishop Berowelf, who would—a scant five years later, in 788—consecrate his new cathedral, in the presence of Charlemagne, by installing relics of Kilian. The saint's ability to divert attention from unscrupulous Carolingian (Pippinid) expropriations of their relatives' property became keenly relevant again in that year when Charlemagne seized the property of his cousin Duke Tassilo of Bavaria. This event transpired at Ingelheim, a town whose lordship was split between the king and the bishops of Würzburg.[102] The alliance of Charles and Berowelf was absolutely cemented in that year, which also saw the composition of a full-fledged passion narrative (the *passio minor*) of Kilian.[103]

This story of Kilian and his two companions, martyred Irish missionaries, continued the silence of the *vita Bonifatii* about the real issues in the region and instead inflated to monumental proportions the ersatz villains of the biography of Boniface: the local Würzburg dynasty of the Hedeni. The *passio* culminated with the populace accepting Christianity and killing or expelling their former ruling family: Duchess Geilana was killed through possession by an evil spirit, Duke Gozbert was killed by his servants, their son Hetan was driven out of realm, and every member of the line was hunted down and executed.[104] This elaborate story of the freeing of the region from evil pagan rulers neatly explained why the area was available to be granted to the new bishops of Würzburg; it became a core feature of local and regional identity, as the memory of Kilian and his companions was intensively cultivated over subsequent centuries.[105] Currently, however, even books meant for popular consumption have begun rejecting the Kilian myth.[106] In contrast, little has been done to debunk an outgrowth of the Kilian story: the tale of Immina of Würzburg. Despite the clear assertion of the *passio minor Kiliani* that all the Hedeni were hunted down and killed and that the populace converted to Christianity in the wake of Kilian's martyrdom, the author of a twelfth-century *vita* of Bishop Burkhard posited the survival of a daughter of that family, named Immina, who (with her community of nuns) practiced Christianity amid a pagan population.

Immina has functioned to obscure the important roles played by women's monasteries in and around the diocesan seat during the eighth century. One way to approach this issue is to begin with the seventh-century (or older) church in Würzburg that was part of the original endowment of the see. This "basilica infra praedictum castrum [uuirziburgensis] in honore sanctae mariae constructa" served as the bishop's church until Berowulf's grand edifice was constructed during the 780s.[107] There is a long-standing controversy concerning whether the Merovingian-era church was located in the commercial town on the Main's right bank or in the aristocratic fortress on its left bank. The weight of the evidence speaks overwhelmingly for the right bank, where the cathedral has always stood.[108] The sole "source" that advocates for a left-bank location is the twelfth-century *vita* of Burkhard noted earlier, which identifies the Marian church of Würzburg as having been, before the erection of the bishopric, the chapel of Immina's female religious community.[109]

According to the *vita Burkhardi*, Immina and her nuns had been waiting for decades for the arrival of a man who could found a legitimate Christian church in the town, something they did not feel worthy to do. Moreover, Immina and her companions longed to leave the world behind and devote themselves entirely to contemplation but were stuck in Würzburg. Burkhard saved them by trading Karlburg to Immina (in usufruct) in exchange for her left-bank Würzburg properties, including the Marian church.[110] Having cleansed the diocesan seat of consecrated women, Burkhard watched passively from across the river as monks established themselves in a left-bank monastery dedicated to Mary and the apostle Andrew.[111] This text has been attributed both to Ekkehard of Aura, writing before 1126,[112] and to Engilhard, monk of St. Stephen's in Würzburg, writing between 1145 and 1150.[113] It was intended to support the autonomy of the men's monastery of St. Burkhard in Würzburg, which claimed descent from the house of Mary and Andrew, for the story of the introduction of the male community was told so that Bishop Burkhard had no hands-on involvement. It fit perfectly into the context of battles between bishops and local monastic communities typical of eleventh- and twelfth-century Latin Europe.[114] There is, however, no reason to accept it as a reliable depiction of the eighth century.

In fact, the majority of scholars reject the information in the *vita Burkhardi*, except for the Immina episode,[115] which has been interpreted as evidence that the 740s witnessed a peaceful transfer of secular power over the Würzburg area from a dying, feminized dynasty to the new bishop.[116] I, along with Alfred Wendehorst, reject the Immina episode as well.[117] The purging of religious women from his diocesan seat is the last thing we should expect from the historical Burkhard, especially at a time (the early 740s) when he (along with Lul and Denehard) looked to Abbess Cyneburg of Inkberrow as his spiritual mentor, legal protector, and secular lord (*domina* and *hlaford*).[118] Burkhard began his career in England when the archbishop of Canterbury, Theodore (d. 690), could call double monasteries "the custom in this region"[119] and then spent approximately his first twenty years on the continent in Echternach, a syneisactic monastic community comprising not only the men's house at Echternach but also the two local women's houses, Oeren in Trier and Pfalzel by Trier.[120] Burkhard came to Würzburg knowing that the female religious in Oeren and Pfalzel had produced manuscripts for the bishopric of Trier,[121] and the first book that he commissioned for his cathedral library was a copy of Augustine's *De Trinitate*, ordered from the nuns of the Parisian-basin house of Chelles.[122] As the first bishop of a newly founded see in desperate need of books, Burkhard would have embraced a female monastery in Würzburg (had there been one).

Unfortunately, the twelfth-century legend of the replacement of Immina's women's monastery with a community of monks, in combination with a fleeting reference by Ekkehard (or Engilhard) to Burkhard as having written books, has led some scholars to attribute the eighth-century German-insular manuscripts of the Main Valley region to a scriptorium established by Burkhard in a men's monastery of St. Andrew in Würzburg (or to refugee monks from St. Andrew's working in Neustadt),[123] rather than to the securely attested women's communities described in this chapter. They have not been dissuaded by the fact that there is no independent evidence of the existence of a men's monastery at Würzburg before the late tenth century, at which point a left-bank house was already dedicated to Burkhard.[124]

Bernhard Bischoff placed the beginning of book production in Würzburg under Bishop Wolfgar (810–832), with output revving up considerably under Bishops Hunbert (832–842) and Gozbald (842–855).[125] Meanwhile, he connected the eighth-century manuscripts of the region with female religious communities and suggested that women in England (such as Bugga, who promised around 720 to send *passiones martyrum* to Boniface) or on the continent produced the books in use in the newly founded diocese.[126] Nowhere did Bischoff suggest that the see of Würzburg possessed a functioning (male-staffed) scriptorium during the eighth century or even early in the ninth century, either at the cathedral itself or in a (left-bank) men's monastery. In fact, he explicitly rejected the possibility that Reginmaar, the early ninth-century scribe who described himself as "in communion with" the women's community "ad lapidum fluminis," was a Würzburg cathedral cleric, on the grounds that Reginmaar's high-quality work could not have been produced in Würzburg early in the ninth century, in the absence of any preparatory steps in the development of a scriptorium.[127] The attribution of the eighth-century manuscripts of the area east of the middle Rhine to women's houses is not only plausible but also virtually the only logical possibility open to us, given the nature of the intellectual infrastructure of the region at the time. Some men's houses did exist, but they were smaller, less wealthy, and less stable than the most important women's houses at Karlburg and Kitzingen.

CHAPTER THREE

THE GUN(T)ZA AND ABIRHILT MANUSCRIPTS: WOMEN AND THEIR BOOKS IN THE ANGLO-SAXON CULTURAL PROVINCE IN FRANCIA

PROLOGUE: TEXTUAL TRANSMISSION AS A FEMINIST STRATEGY

This prologue considers the evidence for book ownership by women's communities in the Main Valley before the establishment of scriptoria during the 740s. It should be noted that no comparably early evidence concerning book ownership can be brought forward for men in the region.

Altmünster in Mainz owned one of the oldest books present in the area, an Italian uncial codex of the fifth century containing the only extant copy of works by Priscillian (bishop of Avila 381–385) and his circle.[1] The volume was at some point in the possession of Bilhildis, retired duchess of Würzburg and benefactress of the house.[2] Priscillian and his leading associates (both male and female) were executed, by imperial order, in 385, on charges of practicing black magic, holding secret nocturnal reunions, praying nude, and sexual libertinage.[3] Priscillianist men and women lived together in ascetic communities without being either married or related by family ties.[4] They believed in the equal capacity of men and women to be vehicles of the Spirit[5] and sometimes used neuter, rather than masculine, pronouns to refer to the Father, the Son, and the Holy Spirit.[6] One or more of the anonymous tractates may have been penned by Euchrotia and/or Procula, two women prominent in the movement,[7] perhaps drawing on the writings of Agape, one of Priscillian's main teachers (according to Sulpicius Severus).[8] One tractate in Bilhildis's collection seems to have been written by a woman named Amantia for a man named Amantius.[9]

This codex, containing writings by male and female members of a syneisactic spiritual group, was owned by an aristocratic woman and then by a women's monastic community. It was quite an extraordinary possession, for works of "heretics" had almost no chance of escaping annihilation.[10] Its very existence suggests that the transmission of favorable texts was a core feminist strategy during late antiquity and the early Middle Ages. We probably owe the preservation of the Priscillianist tractates to a women's (or syneisactic) network centered on the Italian peninsula, where the codex was produced in the fifth century and still remained at the beginning of the eighth century, when notations in eighth-century north Italian cursive minuscule were added to it.[11]

Yet another hint of the existence of a female, or a syneisactic, transmission stream of books from the Mediterranean world to the Main River valley is that both the Priscillianist syneisactic group and the women of the syneisactic Anglo-Saxon cultural province shared an interest in the Apocryphal Acts of the Apostles. The Apocryphal Acts of the Apostles were popular in the ancient Mediterranean[12] and were sometimes used for the creation of orthodox liturgical texts.[13] Nevertheless, the narratives were considered dangerous by many Christians. Priscillian and his companions incorporated apocryphal narratives concerning the apostles into their liturgy in the face of vocal opposition,[14] which they sought to neutralize by means of the third apologetic tractate in Bildhildis's codex (a sustained defense of the spiritual value of apocryphal texts).[15] Likewise, the women of Karlburg produced the oldest extant copy of the collected Apocryphal Acts of the Apostles (Würzburg, UB M.p.th.f. 78, the Karlburg Passionary), at a time when opposition to such materials may already have been on the rise (culminating in the command of the *Admonitio Generalis* of 789 that all such texts be burned).[16] It is possible that the passion narrative of Thomas, one of the individual texts in the Karlburg collection that appears to have arrived there from the Italian peninsula, made its way to the Main Valley in the company of the rare Priscillianist codex.

The only other old book (also a fifth-century Italian uncial codex) that was demonstrably present in the Anglo-Saxon cultural province in Francia before the middle of the eighth century was also in the possession of women. It contained the oldest extant copy of Jerome's (d. 419/420) *Commentary on Ecclesiastes* (c. 389).[17] Around 700, the book was owned by Abbess Cuthswith (Cuthsuuitha) of Inkberrow near Worcester (c. 693–709), who inscribed her *ex libris* in the manuscript.[18] Her royal successor, Cyneburg, was the *domina, hlaford,* and possibly teacher of Burkhard, Denehard, and Lul.[19]

Jerome's commentary on Ecclesiastes, dedicated to the Roman matron Paula and her daughter Eustochium, was originally written for the scholar's female friends and followers, during a stretch of years (386–393) when he wrote nine treatises for this mother–daughter pair.[20] Jerome recommended Ecclesiastes as especially well suited for female readers[21] and reminisced in the preface about the pleasures of reading the biblical book with his disciple Blasilla.[22] As a classical textual commentary on the most "intellectual" book of the Old Testament, Jerome's commentary proved that late ancient and early medieval religious women were able to handle challenging texts.[23] Given that the text was originally written (and considered particularly suitable) for women, and that the manuscript was owned around 700 by a woman, it is likely that the codex was gifted by Cyneburg to Kitzingen, rather than to any of her Anglo-Saxon male contacts.[24] Indeed, the women of Kitzingen were demonstrably interested both in the text (centonized in the Kitzengen homiliary) and in Paula, its dedicatee.[25]

More evidence of women's involvement with literate culture in the region from before the middle of the eighth century is provided by one of the books in Boniface's personal traveling library, the very book with which, according to tradition, the martyr tried vainly to protect himself.[26] Known as the Ragyndrudis codex, because it was commissioned for Boniface by a Frankish patroness, Ragyndrudis,[27] it contained anti-Arian texts alongside a copy of Isidore's *Synonyms*. Ragyndrudis was a nun mentioned in a 755 letter of Lul as having donated gold and silver to the church of Mainz; she was the daughter of Athuolf, probably the father of Boniface's companion Hathuolf (listed on folio 2v of the manuscript as having acquired the book, presumably then passing it on to the saint). Although scholars have localized both the production of the codex and Ragyndrudis herself to Mainz,[28] none has specified a producing institution. One possibility might be Altmünster. Wherever it was produced, in having been commissioned by a woman, the Ragyndrudis codex hints at the existence of gendered networks of textual transmission, in that its principal content (Isidore of Seville's *Synonyms*) was a particular favorite of the women of the Anglo-Saxon cultural province.

Medieval book production was not a matter of random chance. It required much time and immense resources, both financial and material. The entire process involved a series of deliberate choices concerning the specific texts to be acquired and copied, as well as substantial effort to identify potential sources of exemplars for copying. The process was governed by the values of the producing institution and conditioned by that institution's connections with other libraries and scriptoria. When the women's communities of the Anglo-Saxon cultural province in Francia began producing books around the middle of the eighth century, they didn't prefer the *Synonyms* to other works by Isidore, or the Apocryphal Acts of the Apostles to narratives concerning other saints, simply because of chance or necessity; they deliberately selected those texts, alongside certain others, on the basis of recommendations from like-minded colleagues. One of the key values governing book production in the Anglo-Saxon cultural province was a commitment to gender egalitarianism that was pointed enough to be considered feminist. Furthermore, the ability of the women of Karlburg and Kitzingen to carry out a program of book production governed by such values depended on the existence of a broader feminist network for textual and manuscript transmission.

THE GUN(T)ZA AND ABIRHILT MANUSCRIPTS

In the middle of the twentieth century, Bernhard Bishoff identified two clusters of manuscripts as the oldest surviving products of scriptorial activity in the Main Valley. He associated one cluster with the woman's name Gun(t)za and dated this group to the second third of the eighth century: Würzburg Universitätsbibliothek manuscripts M.p.th.f. 13, M.p.th.f. 17, M.p.th.f. 78, and M.p.th.q.

28a.[29] He associated the other group with the woman's name Abirhilt and dated this group to the final third of the eighth century: Würzburg Universitätsbibliothek manuscripts M.p.th.f. 45, M.p.th.f. 69, and M.p.th.q. 28b.[30]

All these manuscripts show continental students trying to work in insular traditions, while introducing some continental motifs; the result was a mixed insular-continental style with a uniquely local stamp.[31] The dominant script at both houses was a German-insular minuscule, also with a local stamp. This is exactly what we would expect to find in books produced at an established Frankish monastery such as Karlburg under the influence of teachers newly arrived from England.[32] The mixing of styles makes sense for the later Abirhilt (Kitzingen) codices as well, for insular immigrants continued to influence the Anglo-Saxon cultural province until practically the end of the century, and the first wave of women trained in the 740s and 750s to produce books would have tutored their students in insular techniques. At the same time, the majority of the members of the community would have come from continental backgrounds.

In the decades since Bischoff's identification of the Gun(t)za and Abirhilt groups, the existence of the two sets of books (with attributions either to Kitzingen or to Karlburg) has gradually become better known, and many other examples of books produced by religious women have been uncovered.[33] This has been part of a general trend toward recognizing that women played a major, constant, public, recognized, and respected role in the production of literary culture throughout the Middle Ages.[34] Yet there have also been pockets of resistance to the very idea that women (aside from a handful of famous exceptions) could or did write during antiquity and the Middle Ages.[35] Neither Gun(t)za nor Abirhilt appeared in the purportedly comprehensive guide to all named medieval scribes compiled by the Benedictine monks of Bouveret, although they knew and used Bischoff's study, listed many males as scribes on the sole basis of having written their names, not full colophons, and even listed Burkhard of Würzburg as a scribe based on the (unreliable) claim of his twelfth-century biography that he wrote books.[36]

The present study should put all such doubts to rest. The Gun(t)za and Abirhilt manuscripts were, indeed, women's books, for they appeared on the library catalogue of Kitzingen in Basel, Öffentliche Universitätsbibiliothek F III 15a folios 17v–18r (Plates 1 and 2).[37] The booklist in the Basel manuscript has been almost entirely erased. However, a handful of titles can be deciphered as "certamina apostolorum omnium" (Würzburg, UB M.p.th.f. 78, a collection of apocryphal passions of the apostles), the "sententialis liber" (Würzburg, UB M.p.th.f. 13, a collection of "sententiae" known as the *Liber Scintillarum*), "sancta Eugenia" (Würzburg, UB M.p.th.q. 28a, the passion narrative of Eugenia combined with Isidore's *Synonyma*), "sanctae ceciliae passio" (Würzburg, UB M.p.th.q. 28b part 1, a collection of passion narratives beginning with that of St. Cecilia), "synonyma sancti isidori" (Würzburg, UB M.p.th.q. 28b part 3,

Isidore's *Synonyma*), "gregorius in evangelio" (Würzburg, UB M.p.th.f. 45, Gregory I's homilies on the Gospels), "epistolae apostolorum" (Würzburg, UB M.p.th.f. 69, the letters of Paul), "sermones sancti Augustini" (Würzburg, UB M.p.th.f. 17, Augustine's commentary on the gradual Psalms), and "omilia" (Würzburg, UB M.p.th q. 28b part 2, a collection of homilies).[38] Furthermore, Jerome's Commentary on Ecclesiastes (Würzburg UB M.p.th.q. 2), a collection of wisdom teachings believed by Jerome and others to have been written by Solomon, likely also appeared on the list, as the illegible entry immediately after "libri salamonis tres et sapientia."[39]

The list has heretofore been identified as the library catalogue of Fulda, where the manuscript was produced (in the eighth century), bound (in the ninth century), and given a shelfmark (in the fifteenth century).[40] Nevertheless, this identification is mistaken. The erasure of the booklist from a codex in Fulda's library in and of itself demonstrates that the catalogue did not refer to Fulda, but to another collection whose contents once seemed important to record, then became irrelevant.

Every early library catalogue, booklist, or lending list was arranged in a vertical column (or columns) to facilitate the organization and management of the collection, and many included notations concerning the location of specific books. In contrast, the catalogue in the Basel manuscript was written in full lines, rendering it unsuitable for the actual management of a collection. It was therefore a *copy* of a library catalogue but was not itself a library catalogue.[41] Furthermore, the community whose books were listed in the catalogue possessed none of the particular texts or manuscripts that were certainly present at Fulda by c. 800: the Benedictine Rule, a *vita* of Boniface, letters of Boniface, and the three *codices Bonifatiani* believed to have belonged to Boniface.[42] Indeed, the Basel catalogue included only one liturgical manuscript, dramatically fewer than on other extant book lists;[43] this made little sense for the priest-heavy community of Fulda but was consistent with the needs of a women's house. Finally, there was virtually no overlap between the contents of the Basel catalogue and the contents of the five separate booklists attesting to the over-stuffed shelves of the Fulda library in the middle of the ninth century.[44] Scholars have expressed both astonishment and puzzlement at these lacunae, but have nevertheless—with two exceptions—ignored their own misgivings.[45]

The title of the list was absolutely not "Isti sunt nostri libri" ("These are our books") as has been suggested.[46] There was no room for "nostri" ("our") even as the abbreviation "nri." The first letter was not an *I*,[47] for there was more to that initial than a vertical stroke; both a small hook and a short line come out from the right side of the vertical stroke, matching the initial *K*s and *F*s in the codex (as in "Kalends" and "Februarius"). Finally, the second and fifth letters were not *s* (as in "Isti sunt"), for they included the curved forms of the minuscule *s*, which was never used by any scribe anywhere in this codex; instead, those scribes exclusively used the insular long *s* (similar to *f* but without the crossbar). Curved forms would, however, appear in a *g*, as Degering recognized when he suggested (in turn) the readings "Argentei libri" and then "Aptio digni libri."[48] Therefore, the best reading of the remaining ink marks, including the letters *K* and *g*, was some form of the place name Kitzingen (written, in the earliest sources, as "Kizinga").[49] It makes perfect sense that a Fulda monk eventually erased a list titled "Kitzingen Books" (Kizinga Libri).

The Kitzingen booklist, along with a handful of other texts, was written into some blank spaces between the main text in the Basel codex (an extract from the late seventh- or early eighth-century English long recension of Isidore of Seville's *De natura rerum* on fols. 1v–17r) and its supplementary astronomical tables (fols. 18v–23v).[50] Analysis of these three pages' worth of additions, in the context of the intertwined histories of Fulda and Kitzingen, has led me to conclude that a traveling Fulda monk copied the additions into his community's copy of the *De natura rerum*, which he was reading while visiting Kitzingen.

Isidore's *De natura rerum* was extremely popular between 650 and 800.[51] The English long recension, first witnessed in Basel ÖUB F.III.15f (an English codex of c. 750) was in the Anglo-Saxon cultural province in Francia before the end of the eighth century, where it served as the exemplar for the Fulda copy in Basel ÖUB F III 15a[52] that accompanied a Fulda monk to Kitzingen. There, the first addition to fill up the blank space was the rubric "Titulus sepulchri Paulae" (fol. 17r; Plate 3). The monk was planning to acquire, but never did, the section of Jerome's Letter to Eustochium on the death of her mother, Paula, in which Jerome quoted the epitaph he had composed for Paula's tomb in Bethlehem.[53] The Fulda monk's interest in an epitaph suitable for the tomb of a holy woman of noble birth who had left her native land to settle in foreign territory was surely a result of the presence of Leoba's tomb at Fulda.

Next the Fulda monk wrote in the famous "Basler Rezepte" (Basel recipes; fols. 17r–17v) three pharmacotherapeutic texts, the first in Latin and the next two in Old High German. He wrote one of the latter in a dialect (east Frankish with Bavarian traits, current only on the Franconian-Bavarian border) completely different from those in vernacular texts from Fulda, leading some scholars to question the connection of the recipes to Fulda.[54] The only two monastic houses on the linguistic borderline were Tauberbischofsheim and Kitzingen,[55] and the location of Kitzingen in the commercially thriving Rhine-Main thoroughfare would have brought every ingredient necessary for the remedies to medical specialists there. One fermented drink required thirteen different drugs and two bottles of wine to treat an unspecified problem variously identified as simple fever, epilepsy, or typhoid fever accompanied by hallucinations, whereas the concoction of salt, soap, and oyster shells "widar cancur" (either against boils or against cancerous growths) called for rubbing an external tumor with caustic ingredients until it bled and then dressing the wound with egg whites and honey.[56]

It is simple to pinpoint the circumstances under which a Fulda monk would have copied down pharmacotherapeutic texts while visiting Kitzingen, where Abbot Sturm of Fulda had been, over a one-month period probably in 748, nursed or doctored back to health after being taken ill on a journey.[57] Early medieval religious women regularly engaged in medical practice. For instance, the seventh-century *Regula Cuiusdam ad Virgines* mandated an exterior area used for caring for sick people, as well as entertaining guests and visitors.[58] The special medical expertise of the Kitzingen women was praised in Sturm's biography, written (during the 810s) by Eigil of Fulda at the request of Angildruth, abbess (or nun) of Kitzingen and dedicatee of the narrative.[59] Eigil must have visited Kitzingen shortly before 800, where he became acquainted with various aspects of the nuns' medical prowess and recorded some of what he learned (along with a copy of the nuns' library catalogue) in the blank pages of Isidore's *De natura rerum*, which he then brought back to Fulda.[60] This scenario accounts perfectly for the linguistic features of the First Basel Recipe as reconstructed by specialists, who have suggested that the person who dictated the remedy was east Frankish (as many of the nuns of Kitzingen would have been) and the person who wrote it down was Bavarian (which Eigil was).[61]

It is inconceivable that the final addition to the blank leaves in the Basel codex was made by Fulda monks for Fulda monks. The "Basler Blutsegen" (folios 17v–18r) was a charmlike prayer against excessive and painful menstruation.[62] There was a large category of blood-stanching charms and recipes, many of which incorporated references to biblical figures such as Longinus, Judas, and the Jordan River, and most of which were for types of flux other than menstrual blood (such as wounds or nosebleeds).[63] The Basel hemostatic charm was unusual in its concern with menstruation and in its invocation of a female figure.

The speaker of the Basel blood charm began by calling three times on "Beronice" and quoting Psalm 50:16, which began "libera me de sanguinibus . . ." ("liberate me from blood"). Veronica (or Berenice) appeared, by the eighth century, in many Latin legends as a contemporary of Christ who owned (or commissioned) a miracle-working painting of Christ's face (made from direct observation). She was identified as the woman in the Gospels cured of excessive bleeding by touching the hem of Jesus' garment.[64] The Basel *Blutsegen* continued, in Latin, for many more lines.[65] Most sections of the *Blutsegen* were paralleled in another codex (and only there), namely, the Royal Prayerbook, a late eighth- or early ninth-century Mercian prayer book containing four separate charms to staunch bleeding: three from the period around 800 and one from the twelfth century.[66] In the older royal charms, as in the Basel text, the key figure was Beronice, the woman cured of bleeding by Christ.[67] The two sets of charmlike prayers represented parallel developments from a single tradition, neither having been copied from the other.[68] That tradition, probably an originally oriental one dating to the sixth century, was a female one, for the Royal Prayerbook was owned by a female physician in a nunnery.[69] This transfer of gynecological texts most likely transpired through female networks of textual transmission.

Around 800, Fulda monks had a genuine interest in the library collections of women's houses such as Kitzingen, for they were becoming increasingly responsible for the governance of religious women in small communities all across Franconia. When the opportunity presented itself, as it apparently did very early in the ninth century, to acquire a record of books of interest to a female community, the Fulda monk (and future abbot) Eigil made a copy of the Kitzingen library catalogue. It is not surprising that he also acquired the *Blutsegen*.

At the beginning of the ninth century, as evidenced by the copy of their library catalogue in the Fulda *De natura rerum*, the women of Kitzingen possessed both the Gun(t)za and Abirhilt manuscript groups (having absorbed the former from Karlburg) and a number of other codices. While the titles of some of their other holdings were clear (such as the *Sentences* of Isidore of Seville), I did not attempt to discover the particular copies of those works that were in the Kitzingen library. Nevertheless, the Basel booklist has furnished invaluable additional information for this study. For instance, Kitzingen also had a copy of the (Pseudo-Isidoran) "Liber de ordine creaturarum" (in the catalogue as "Liber de creaturarum sancti esidori"), a seventh-century visionary text that provided inspiration for the crucifixion miniature analyzed in chapter 4. I thus draw on the booklist when titles from the catalogue help fill out the picture of the intellectual life of the women of the Anglo-Saxon cultural province in Francia.

The chart on the following page shows the Gun(t)za and Abirhilt manuscripts, in the order in which they are described in the remainder of this chapter (which nonspecialists may wish to skip) and discussed in part II.

The Kitzingen Paul (Würzburg, Universitätsbibliothek, M.p.th.f. 69)

The subject of chapter 4 is an Abirhilt (Kitzingen) group copy of the Pauline Epistles, produced during the second half of the eighth century.[70] The translation of Paul's (Greek) Epistles in this codex followed (in most cases) the text as found in eighth-century English copies of the Epistles and was therefore based on an English exemplar.[71] The codex also contained a series of prologues and chapter headings keyed to each letter, essential for locating the readings from the Epistles used on different feast days.[72] The prologues and headings also functioned as an apparatus for the understanding of scripture and exercised some influence on the crucifixion miniature that was created as a frontispiece for the text.[73] Chapter 4 is devoted entirely to elucidating this full-page miniature (Plate 4 and cover).

Kitzingen Catalogue (Basel, ÖUB F III 15a fols. 17v–18r)	Gun(t)za/Abirhilt Manuscript
epistolae apostolorum	Letters of Paul (Würzburg, UB M.p.th.f. 69, the Kitzingen Paul)
sermones sancti Augustini	Augustine's Commentary on the Psalms (Würzburg, UB M.p.th.f. 17, the Karlburg Augustine)
gregorius in evangelio	Gregory I, Homilies on the Gospels (Würzburg, UB M.p.th.f. 45, the Kitzingen Gregory)
certamina apostolorum omnium	Passions of the Apostles (Würzburg, UB M.p.th.f. 78, the Karlburg Passionary)
sanctae ceciliae passio	Passion of Cecilia (Würzburg, UB M.p.th.q. 28b part 1, the *Deus per Angelum libellus*)
synonyma sancti isidori	Isidore of Seville, *Synonyma* (Würzburg, UB M.p.th.q. 28b part 3, the Kitzingen Isidore)
sancta Eugenia	Passion of Eugenia + Isidore of Seville's *Synonyma* (Würzburg, UB M.p.th.q. 28a, the Karlburg Isidore)
sententialis liber	"Liber Scintillarum" Florilegium (Würzburg, UB M.p.th.f. 13, the Karlburg Florilegium)
omilia	Homilies (Würzburg, UB M.p.th q. 28b part 2, the Kitzingen Homiliary)

With the exception of textile production, Carolingian-era women are much better known as patrons (matrons) or collectors of art than as producers of art.[74] Despite widespread acknowledgment that the codex was produced (or at least owned) by women,[75] previous scholars have all tacitly assumed that the artist of the miniature was a man. Mine is the first treatment of the crucifixion image to recognize that the artist would have been a woman. She may also have drawn the simple Annunciation on folio 1r: a large male figure with "big hair," flowing robes, and either a flowing cape or very ethereal wings (the angel Gabriel), depicted as if in motion across the page, moving from left to right, while gesturing across his body with his raised right hand toward a (veiled or haloed) seated female figure (the Virgin Mary). Someone (later?) also drew two heads on the bottom part of the page.

The Kitzingen Paul was clearly not the only book of the Bible owned at Karlburg or Kitzingen, for several biblical books were listed on the Kitzingen library catalogue of c. 800, including a Gospel of Luke.[76] I believe that the canon tables currently bound with the Burkhard Gospels (Würzburg UB M.p.th.f. 68, a sixth-century Italian uncial manuscript that Burkhard brought to Würzburg either from England or from Echternach)[77] were originally made, in Karlburg, for that Luke codex. The canon tables (on a distinct quire, folios 1–9) were painted around the middle of the eighth century,[78] using decorative elements typical of eighth-century pin finds from Karlburg and of the bone and wood pendants worn by women in the region around 700 (e.g., the cross marks within a circle on fol. 2v and the almandine/leaf petals within the circles on fols. 3r and 3v).[79]

The canon tables have been ascribed to various production locales (Wearmouth-Jarrow, England, Italy, Langres or a similar continental center, a West Frankish scriptorium under Luxeuil influence, and the Bonifatian circle at Mainz) and are universally assumed to have been made for the Burkhard Gospels.[80] However, the manuscript was completely rebound in the eleventh century, when it was graced with a superb cover complete with ivory panels and silverwork.[81] The brightly colored canon tables were added (and mutilated) only at that time, when they were dramatically cut down to match the size of the Gospel book. For instance, the bird on the outer right side margin of folio 2v was cut off mid-body, even before the tail. Only folio 3v (a page with very simple décor) escaped serious damage from the cutting.

A ninth- or tenth-century hand on folio 1r, at the beginning of the canon tables, indicated that they were at that point placed before an "evangelium secundum Lucam," but the Burkhard Gospels started with Matthew. Furthermore, the Gospels were massively marked up during the eighth, ninth and tenth centuries with ink and dry point glosses, but no one ever made a single mark on the canon tables. Clearly, the latter were not part of the codex until the eleventh century, when it was transformed into a contact relic for St. Burkhard, after which point no additional entries were made on the Gospel texts. The canon tables must, therefore, have been removed from a different older manuscript available in Würzburg during the eleventh century, very possibly the now-lost Karlburg-Kitzingen Gospel of Luke.

Augustine's Commentary on the Gradual Psalms (Psalms 119–130)
(Würzburg, UB, M.p.th.f. 17)
Augustine (354–430) was bishop of Hippo in North Africa. His longest single work, which took him approximately thirty years (c. 392–c. 422), to write, was his commentary on the Psalms.[82] This Karlburg copy of Augustine's *Commentary on the Psalms* is discussed in chapter 5, along with the other patristic manuscript in my study, Gregory the Great's *Homilies on the Gospels*. Homilies and commentaries were related forms of interpretation of scripture; indeed, both

texts were examples of "homiletic commentary," for—like fully one third of extant biblical commentaries—both were originally preached by their episcopal authors as a sermon series and then revised and polished for publication.[83]

Due to its great length, Augustine's Psalm commentary circulated in fragments. This Gun(t)za (Karlburg) group manuscript contained his exposition of Psalms 119 through 130, most of the section devoted to the "gradual Psalms" (119–133), or "Songs of Ascents," originally preached in December 406 and the following months (or over the same period a year later).[84] Augustine's scriptorium at Hippo issued booklets containing only this section of the text.[85] The Karlburg copy, in its current state, runs through the beginning of the explication of Psalm 130, which ends (incomplete) on folio 45v. The original manuscript would certainly have continued through the end of this comment and also included a protective, but now lost, extra leaf; the current final folio—dirty and beat-up—served as the back cover for many centuries. The question, however, is whether the Karlburg copy originally included Augustine's comments on Psalms 131 and 132/133 (a bipartite single text).[86]

All of the homiletic comments, through 133, were certainly contained in the exemplar used at Karlburg, for that very (lost) codex, itself dating from the sixth century or earlier and a direct descendant of one of the original Hippo booklets, also served as the exemplar for a complete copy made by a male scribe, Gundheri, somewhere in the Anglo-Saxon cultural province early in the ninth century (Würzburg, UB M.p.th.f. 64).[87] That lost ancient manuscript was also used for the copy of Augustine's exposition of Psalm 119 included in the small sermon collection that is now Würzburg UB M.p.th.f. 43, containing four of Augustine's Psalm comments and two of Gregory's homilies on Ezekiel.[88] Given that this latter collection was made in England around the middle of the eighth century, the lost ancient codex must have traveled from there to Karlburg very early in the history of the new continental scriptorium; it was very likely accompanied by the small sermon collection itself, probably the volume described as "Gregory on Ezekiel" in the Basel library catalogue, which then likely served as the model for a similar sermon collection produced at Kitzingen later in the century (Würzburg, UB M.p.th q. 28b part 2, the Kitzingen Homiliary).[89]

Thus, the Karlburg scribe had available to her, and could have copied, the entire "gradual Psalms" section of Augustine's vast commentary; at the same time, she had available to her a model of an alternative approach, namely, to select only certain portions of a text for copying (as the compiler of the short sermon collection in Würzburg UB M.p.th.f. 43 did). Nothing implies that the Karlburg Augustine ever contained the comments on Psalms 131–133. Indeed, the current state of the codex is best explained if it is missing only two leaves, namely, the other halves of the two singletons folios 40 and 41; the replacement of two lost leaves (folios 46 and 47) would result in a standard eight-leaf quire, as throughout the majority of the codex. Those two leaves would have been sufficient to complete the comment on Psalm 130, leaving a blank final verso.

I discuss the Karlburg Augustine on the premise that the female scribe deliberately omitted the closing sections. The comments on Psalms 131 and 132/133 largely reiterated, for the umpteenth time, points hammered home in the preceding sermons or introduced material of acute relevance to early fifth-century Africa that would have been baffling to eighth-century readers, such as long discussions of Circumcellions and Donatists.[90] Most important, however, these comments utilized women as figures of weakness or subordination, expressing some virulently misogynistic ideas (the only ones in the Gradual comments). The comment on Psalm 133 presented Eve in all her fetid glory as the dangerous temptress of Adam and of all men after him and then moved to a similar image of another holy man (Job, a new Adam) fending off another evil woman (his wife, a new Eve) trying to turn him away from God.[91] There was no motivation for the women of Karlburg to permit their copy of a spiritual classic to culminate in such offensive imagery, so they omitted it. The nuns of Chelles took a different approach to Augustine's misogynistic outburst: they surgically excised only the offending lines from the two copies of the text produced in their scriptorium.[92]

The manuscript contained one vernacular dry point (or scratched) gloss in Old East Frankish: the word *laitent* on the lemma "lator legis," that is, legislator (fol. 42v).[93] Vernacular dry point (that is, without ink) glosses, comments scratched into books as quick "notes to self," first emerged as a reading practice in the Anglo-Saxon cultural province on the continent, at a time when parchment was still in short supply; readers took notes using wax tablets and scratching pens and were sometimes moved to write directly in the books they were reading.[94] In addition to the single word on the Psalm commentary, there was a single word on the Kitzingen Gregory and five words on the Karlburg florilegium. The other women's manuscripts were unglossed in the vernacular. This contrasted sharply with the manuscripts of the area that were used by men, such as the Würzburg cathedral copy of Isidore's *Synonyms* (Würzburg UB M.p.th.f. 79), which contained dozens of vernacular glosses.[95] In contrast to their male counterparts, women only rarely felt moved to comment in their books in the vernacular language (as opposed to in Latin) and did so only on patristic manuscripts (Augustine on the Psalms, Gregory on the Gospels, and the florilegium of patristic extracts), precisely the type of text most often glossed in this way.[96]

Gregory the Great's Homilies on the Gospels 21–36, 39,
and 40 (Würzburg UB M.p.th.f. 45)
Gregory I was bishop of Rome from 590 to 603. In the very first years of his pontificate (590–593), he preached a series of forty sermons on the Gospel readings used in the liturgy of the Roman church.[97] The recorded version of these

sermons represented a straightforward discussion of central biblical texts, "filled with clear directives and comforting miracles,"[98] and written in a lively, conversational tone. The seventh and eighth centuries witnessed a steady stream of visitors from beyond the Alps seeking copies of Gregory's works in Rome,[99] and the homilies in particular became wildly popular. They were singled out for praise in his biography, written at the very beginning of the eighth century by a nun or monk of Whitby, indicating also that they were of particular importance in the Anglo-Saxon syneisactic tradition.[100] Many copies were made in the Anglo-Saxon cultural province in Francia,[101] all participating in a remarkably stable textual transmission.[102]

Gregory's Gospel homilies were transmitted in two separate books, each containing twenty sermons. Half of the sermons (homilies 1–20) were composed by Gregory and then, on account of his ill health, read out to the people by deputies but revised for publication by Gregory as Book I. Popular discontent pressured Gregory to deliver homilies 21–40 himself and have his words recorded by stenographers, enabling their authorized publication as Book II.[103] Confusion in the Kitzingen scriptorium led to the unintended omission of homilies 37 and 38.[104] Homilies 39 and 40 were copied by Abirhilt, who signed folio 71v; because her section of the text contained fewer corrections than did parts written by other scribes, and the corrections may even be in her hand, she probably played a leading role in the scriptorium.

Passions of the Apostles (Würzburg Üniversitätsbibliothek M.p.th.f. 78)
This Gun(t)za Group/Karlburg codex, containing nothing but passions of the apostles, is the oldest surviving example of such a homogeneous collection.[105] Such manuscripts are often said to transmit a collection originally produced in the late sixth or early seventh century by Pseudo-Abdias, a notion derived from the fact that some versions of the *passio* of Simon and Jude included an epilogue describing "the preceding work" as the Latin version of a Greek translation of a Hebrew text by Abdias, bishop of Babylon. Based on collections in which the *passio* of Simon and Jude appeared in last place, a sixteenth-century scholar (Wolfgang Lazius) attributed all of the apostolic passions (i.e., a new understanding of "the preceding work") to Pseudo-Abdias.[106] But the manuscripts varied considerably on this point (as on all points); for instance, the Karlburg passionary placed the *passio* of Simon and Jude, including the Abdias appendix, in next to last place and clearly attributed only that text to the putative bishop of Babylon. While individual narratives "of diverse background and character" eventually did coalesce into "a more or less coherent series of texts describing the acts and martyrdom of the twelve apostles" frequently titled *Virtutes Apostolorum*, that "collection" was always a protean organism whose form shifted from codex to codex.[107] I therefore treat the Karlburg passionary as a unique collection.

In addition to the homogeneous Karlburg passionary, a handful of heterogeneous collections, including but not limited to apostolic materials, were produced during the eighth century. Most important among these was Montpellier, Bibliothèque Interuniversitaire, Faculté de Médecine, H.55, containing the same passion narratives as the Würzburg manuscript and in the same order, accompanied by three additional apostolic passions and other narratives, including the earliest Latin versions of several Marian texts.[108] Given the prominence of women (Mary, female saints and martyrs, female associates of the apostles) in this manuscript, it may also have been made in a women's community.

The similarity between the Karlburg passionary and the Montpellier collection raises the possibility that the Würzburg codex originally contained three more apostolic passions, for it is now mutilated at both ends.[109] Its run of seven texts from John the Evangelist through Philip matched the Montpellier collection, but the latter opened with *passiones* of Peter, Andrew, and James the Lesser. However, it would be foolish to extrapolate from the Montpellier collection to a hypothetical pretruncation Karlburg passionary, for a comparison of the *passiones* of Thomas and Bartholomew in the two codices shows that neither was copied directly from the other.

The Karlburg and Montpellier collections were independent creations; both, however, likely drew on a women's (feminist) textual transmission network for their (related) versions of the *passio* of Thomas, presumably the same network hypothesized also as the source of the (Iberian) Priscillianist tractates discussed at the beginning of this chapter. The first Greek apostolic acts were owed to female authors and/or women's oral traditions and were aimed at the liberation of women;[110] the reworked Latin versions of those narratives were equally feminist. We can pinpoint the most likely specific conduit to the Latin West for some of these Greek texts, including the *passio* of Thomas: Egeria, a wealthy Iberian who spent three years on pilgrimage in the east near the end of the fourth century, acquired texts concerning the apostles Thecla and Thomas when she visited their shrines.[111]

To understand the process whereby the Karlburg passionary was assembled, we must attend to the uneven quality of the texts written by scribe 1 (folios 1–33), who was able to read some of her exemplars better than others and who was sometimes copying from an undivided uncial exemplar, sometimes from a minuscule one.[112] The passionary was therefore a new collection compiled from multiple exemplars. Because scribe 1 had to deal with disparate exemplars, she made grammatical errors and even reversed the order of brief passages when copying some of the passion narratives (John, James, Thomas),[113] yet she produced completely accurate versions of other texts (Bartholomew and Matthew). Her copy of the passion narrative of Thomas featured a peculiar double opening that resulted in a particular sentence being copied twice, first at the beginning of the text (folio 6r) and then at the end (folio 13v); she made a number of copying errors the first time that she avoided on the second go-round, having become familiar with the script in her exemplar.[114] Scribe 3, responsible for the passion narrative of Philip, was also able to produce error-free text.[115]

In the following pages, I discuss the disparate origins of the different *passiones* and how they arrived at Karlburg, where, in a creative historiographical act, they were forged into an apostolic passionary.

Folios 1v–3r: The Passion of John the Evangelist

The Karlburg compiler began with John's *transitus* (since technically he never died but was assumed into heaven), a Latin version of a Greek text written by Melitus of Laodikeia at or near Ephesus during the latter part of the fifth century on the basis of a lost older text.[116] A Latin version of Melitus's narrative was available in Gaul by the end of the sixth century, which suggests that the text reached the Main Valley through West Francia; to judge by the many errors in the Karlburg passionary, the West Frankish exemplar was written in a script that was unfamiliar at the new insular scriptorium.

There was another copy of Melitus's *transitus* in the "Veri Amoris" *libellus* (Würzburg, UB M.p.th.q. 26) listed in the Basel catalogue as part of the Kitzingen collection, which is discussed in detail later.[117] Both copies seem to have been made from the same exemplar. The "Veri amoris" copy lacked the prologue and most of the introduction, beginning only with the very last line of the introduction (folio 43r),[118] probably reflecting the state of its exemplar. I conclude that, before it was damaged, the Karlburg copy also began at that point.

Folios 3r–6r: The Passion of James, Brother of John the Evangelist

The earliest narrative devoted to James was a "catholic" Latin *passio* (BHL 4057), perhaps composed as early as the second half of the fourth century in Gaul or Spain,[119] perhaps composed as late as the early sixth century in the area between Narbonne, Lyons, and Marseilles.[120] Legends connecting James with Spain, ascribed to heterodox groups such as fifth-century Priscillianists or eighth-century Spanish Adoptionists, had no impact on the catholic *passio*, the tradition embraced at Karlburg.[121]

I compared the Karlburg copy with three different published versions of the catholic *passio*: the one published by Mombritius in Milan before 1480;[122] the one originally published in Paris in 1571, whose variant readings vis-à-vis the Mombritius version were listed by the monks of Solemnes, who reprinted Mombritius in 1910;[123] and the version published in 1898 by a canon of the cathedral of Santiago from a late twelfth- or early thirteenth-century passionary (the *Pasionario Tudense*) preserved at the cathedral of Tui, in the province of Pontevedra.[124] The Karlburg copy was closest to the sixteenth-century Parisian edition, but there is no way to tell which manuscript the editor used. At most, I can very tentatively suggest that the Karlburg passionary was closer to a "French" transmission of the *passio* than to an "Italian" or "Spanish" one and perhaps traveled to the Main Valley from West Francia along with the *transitus* of John, brother of James.

Folios 6r–15v: The Passion of Thomas

Next, the Karlburg compiler produced the oldest extant copy of Thomas's Latin *passio*, adapted from a pre-fourth-century Greek version of Thomas's acts and available in a critical edition by Klaus Zelzer.[125] Zelzer dated the composition of the text to the 370s on the grounds of its concern with the same debates (confrontations with Arian Christians and with devotees of the Sun God) that obsessed Ambrose at Milan during those years.[126] However, the theological statements Zelzer attributed to the fourth century were likely not older than 400.[127] Because the manuscript transmission of the *passio* was particularly widespread and particularly high quality on the Italian peninsula from an early date,[128] the narrative was likely produced on the Italian peninsula early in the fifth century, probably based on a copy of the Greek acts imported to the west by Egeria, in time to be known to Augustine and when concerns over Arianism had hardly vanished.[129] The text came to the Anglo-Saxon cultural province in Francia in an unfamiliar script, perhaps directly from the Italian peninsula, perhaps via Frankish Gaul, for the version of the text in the Karlburg passionary was most closely related to those in West Frankish manuscripts produced at Fleury, Moissac, and somewhere in northeastern Gaul.[130]

The copy of the text in the large Montpellier collection discussed earlier also belonged broadly to the "French" transmission of the text but not to the Fleury-Moissac strand.[131] The relationship of the Karlburg and Montpellier texts was that of grandchildren in two different lines of descent from a single grandparent. They shared a very similar (and otherwise unattested) opening sentence to the effect that Thomas was preaching chastity and the worship of Christ in India, which outraged the king, who had Thomas brought before him with bound hands.[132] The Montpellier version then jumped to the saint's martyrdom in (Zelzer's) Chapter 51, the opening sentence having provided a (highly condensed) summary of the action up until that point. In contrast, in the Karlburg manuscript, the summary sentence introduced (with a large decorated initial) the full narrative, which then leaped backward in time to the standard opening sentence (and another decorated initial) to find Thomas in Caesarea, with his entire Indian adventure still in his future. If read straight through, the (literary) effect was analogous to that of the cinematic flashback technique.

But readers at Karlburg (and eventually Kitzingen) could select an alternative to working all the way through the narrative in flashback mode; that is, they could choose to read only the abbreviated version of Thomas's story, focusing on his martyrdom, by skipping ahead seven folios to the point when the saint was led before the king; this passage was easy to spot because the key phrase (describing how the king commanded Thomas to be brought before him with bound hands) was placed in the bottom margin of the page, with a sign to where it belonged in the flow of the text (folio 13v). The presence of two decorated initials within lines of one another at the head of the narrative (on folio 6r) was the scribe's way of proposing two alternative texts. This "two-for-one" scheme was unique to the Karlburg passionary but was not the brainchild of the Karlburg scribe; instead, it already characterized the (lost) exemplar used at the house, for the Montpellier codex also descended, albeit indirectly, from a "flashback" copy of the *passio*. I draw this conclusion from the way the name of the king appeared in the different copies of the text.

In witnesses to the full narrative, including the Karlburg manuscript, the name of the king of India was Misdeus until the trial and martyrdom scene (i.e., the substance of the abbreviation). Then, in all of the "French" manuscripts of the *passio*, confusion set in, and the king was called sometimes "Migdeus," sometimes "Migdonius." The only exception was Montpellier 55, which gave the king's name throughout as Migdonius. I hypothesize that the Montpellier scribe corrected the name "Misdeus" in the opening sentence of the exemplar because she or he could see that the king's name in the immediately following martyrdom portion of the narrative was Migdonius and wanted to homogenize the text. In contrast, the scribe of the exemplar used by the Montpellier scribe made the choice to copy only the abbreviation after having seen the flashback text as well and accepted Misdeus as the king's name in the opening summary sentence; this scribe then utilized the alternative name after turning many pages to find the passion portion of the narrative. The Karlburg scribe, who copied (but did not invent) the full flashback version, accepted the name Misdeus in the summary opening sentence because it matched most of the narrative, unaware of what awaited in the trial and martyrdom scene.

We now move to a different portion of the passionary, in which grammatically correct versions of the texts were copied from (a) familiar exemplar(s).

Folios 15v–20v: The Passion of Bartholomew
From the late fourth through the late sixth century, the cult of Bartholomew flourished in Armenia, where a Nestorian Christian community composed a (lost) Greek *passio* of the saint, which was translated into Latin between 450 and 480.[133] The Latin text (BHL 1002), which was very poorly edited by Bonnet, came west along with relics of the saint in the wake of various sixth-century military disruptions.[134] By the time the Latin text was utilized for the Karlburg passionary, it had undergone a major modification: the original version of the narrative had set the action in Armenia, but at some stage the text was modified so that the action of the *passio* of Bartholomew as it was known throughout the Latin west was set in India.[135]

Bonnet believed that Bartholomew's Latin *passio* (whose manuscript witnesses he divided into families Γ and Δ) represented a straightforward translation of the lost Nestorian original but that his Greek *passio* (dated to sometime between 450 and 550) represented a substantial reworking of the Nestorian original. Nevertheless, he used the Greek "reworking" to establish his edition of the Latin "translation," sometimes by drawing on the Greek text as a determinative criterion for deciding among variant readings in the Latin witnesses, sometimes by permitting the Greek text to override all the readings of the Latin manuscripts. Furthermore, he did not take into account the Karlburg copy of the text, probably the best available witness. Thus, in Bonnet's edition, Bartholomew was made to teach that the Holy Spirit emanated from the Father alone (in eastern fashion, probably in keeping with the original text), whereas the entire Γ family, most of the Δ family, and the Karlburg copy omitted this controversial phrase, in keeping with the Latin belief in the dual procession of the Spirit.[136]

In some cases, the Karlburg passionary's unique readings were surely the correct ones, such as to have the king honor with gold and jewels the attendants ("*camillos*") of the priests who assisted Bartholomew at an exorcism, rather than to have the king honor with gold and jewels the camels ("*camelos*") of those priests.[137] In other cases, the superior readings of the Karlburg copy were matched by other witnesses, such as when the Karlburg passionary and most representatives of the Δ family used the masculine "sanctus" to modify the masculine "filius Dei," rather than the neuter "sanctum" chosen by Bonnet (edition p. 136, line 3). The Karlburg copy—which sometimes agreed with one or the other of Bonnet's families as a whole, sometimes agreed with one or more manuscripts within a family, and occasionally offered a unique reading—possibly hearkened back, with only a single intermediary, to the lost copy that stood at the head of both families of transmission in the Latin west.

Bartholomew's Latin cult spread from its earliest western center of gravity in southern Italy, a region that profoundly affected the early Anglo-Saxon sanctoral.[138] Veneration of Bartholomew, and presumably the text of his Latin *passio*, must have come to England directly from that area. Guthlac, who received his education at the monastery of Repton under abbess Ælfthryth, subsequently set himself up in a hermitage where he was tormented by anxiety and depression until he was joined by St. Bartholomew as a spiritual mentor. Guthlac died in approximately 715, and his attachment to Bartholomew was a central theme of his biography by Felix, written between 721 and 749.[139] Whether or not Guthlac acquired his devotion to Bartholomew from his former abbess, which would indicate involvement on the part of the women of Repton in the development and transmission of the passion narrative, the intense Guthlac–Bartholomew connection demonstrates the existence of strong feelings for Bartholomew in Anglo-Saxon circles just when immigrants from England were transforming the culture of Karlburg. The exemplar used at Karlburg for the passionary probably came from England and was therefore clear and readable to the women working in the new insular scriptorium, who were able to produce an excellent copy of the text.

Folios 20v–28v: The Passion of Matthew

The Karlburg passionary's copy of this text (BHL 5690) was not used for, but differed only slightly from, its most recent (1958) edition, made by Atenolfi primarily on the basis of Vatican City, BAV, MS lat. 5771, a late ninth-century manuscript from Bobbio.[140] Where the texts did differ, however, the (older) Karlburg copy was superior.[141] Atenolfi dated and localized the composition of the text to a monastic center under Frankish influence, possibly but not necessarily in Italy, during the Carolingian period.[142] I suggest that the Carolingian monastic community that produced the narrative was a women's community with connections to the ruling family, possibly even Karlburg itself. This would explain the one feature of the *passio* of Matthew that Atenolfi did not consider: the central importance of the queen and the princess, the latter along with her house of virgins located just by (or possibly in) the royal palace.

There are several reasons to peg Karlburg as the place of composition of the *passio*. First, the Karlburg scriptorium produced the oldest extant copy of the narrative. Second, the Karlburg scriptorium considered the narrative to be particularly significant, marking it (on fol. 20v) with the first elaborate decorated initial in the codex, a letter Q by scribe 2.[143] Scribe 2 went on (fol. 29r) to produce another elaborate decorated initial for the next text, the *passio* of Simon and Jude.[144] Third, the Karlburg scriptorium produced a stellar copy of the *passio* in terms of grammar, spelling, word separation, and sentence divisions (via slightly larger initials marking the beginning of each sentence), such as would characterize a copy made from an exemplar in completely familiar script using the scribe's own habitual conventions. Scribe 1 did make a few errors, but they were painstakingly corrected by scribe 2, who intervened more in this text than in the others and who very likely was its original author, for her "corrections" were effectively improvements to an initially misformulated foreign language composition.[145]

The final passage of the *passio* of Matthew linked the activities of this apostle with those of Simon and Jude. It described how the rival magi Zaroes and Arfexar, bested by Matthew in the Ethiopian narrative just ended, fled to Persia, where they were definitively defeated by Simon and Jude (fol. 28v), whose exploits were contained in the next *passio*. The Karlburg author of the *passio* of Matthew thus created a tight connection between "her" apostle and Simon and Jude; why she wished to do so will become clear momentarily, when we see what that apostolic pair meant in the Anglo-Saxon cultural province in Francia.

Folios 29r–35r: The Passion of Simon and Jude by Pseudo-Abdias

The *passio* of Simon and Jude in the Karlburg passionary included an epilogue in which the author claimed to be Abdias, a recent convert of the apostles whom they had ordained as bishop of Babylon (fol. 35r).[146] Pseudo-Abdias's *passio* of Simon and Jude has been dated to the late sixth or early seventh century.[147] This early dating is problematic. The tradition of venerating Simon and Jude together and as companion missionaries in Persia was Latin; eastern Christian churches cherished multiple traditions concerning the two apostles but venerated them as separate individuals whose deeds were unrelated to those described by Pseudo-Abdias.[148] Many medieval Latin texts were consonant with eastern rather than Pseudo-Abdian traditions,[149] whereas none of the oldest evidence for veneration of Simon and Jude in the Latin west drew on or even seemed to know the information in the *passio* of Pseudo-Abdias.[150] The earliest certain benchmark was Bede (d. 735), who singled out a "suspect" *passio* of the apostolic pair for censure.[151]

Els Rose, who uncovered only twelfth-century and later dedications to the apostolic pair, recognized that any progress in understanding the history of their cult would depend on charting additional dedications.[152] Yet, we already know more than she realized. Lul of Mainz placed his personal retreat and burial church at Hersfeld under their patronage.[153] Perhaps at the urging of Lul, the apostolic pair played a major role in Charlemagne's policies almost from the very beginning of the latter's reign, particularly in connection with the Saxon wars.[154] I suggest that the brand-new Latin story of Simon and Jude as a pair, which suddenly appeared on the continent as a supplement to existing eastern traditions of two separate apostolates, originated in England, where Bede knew it, and whence Lul brought it south. Lul surely had personal connections with the Englishwomen who established the scriptorium at Karlburg, who may even have known the author of the *passio*. This would explain why scribe 2 honored Simon and Jude with a moderately elaborate decorated initial (fol. 29r) and why the Karlburg author of the *passio* of Matthew wanted to link "her" apostle to them.

I compared the text in the Karlburg passionary with that published by Mombritius.[155] The two texts lined up reasonably well at the beginning, but the final few folios (34r–35r) contained a fuller and more detailed text (and one probably closer to the original) than that printed by Mombritius.

Folios 35r–35v: The Passion of Philip

Sitting at the culmination of the passionary, the *passio* of Philip opened with the most elaborate decorated initial in the codex, a large *P* complete with rosettes, interlace, and animal heads.[156] It was the creation of scribe 3, whose only contribution to the codex was this final text. Given the elaborate initial, the text of the *passio* in the Karlburg manuscript must have originally been complete. The entire remainder of the *passio* of Philip would have fit on the recto side of a single sheet of parchment, and the passionary must have contained this additional leaf (whose verso side was likely blank) that has since gone missing due to wear and tear.

Philip's Latin *passio*, whose original composition has never been dated or localized, was used by Bede.[157] Given that the copy of the text in the Karlburg passionary was an excellent and grammatical one and was written by a scribe who used a distinctively insular "nail type" script, it seems quite likely that the exemplar for the *passio* came to Karlburg from England. It contained roughly the same text published by Mombritius.[158]

The "Deus per angelum" Libellus (Würzburg, Universitätsbibliothek M.p.th.q. 28b Codex 1)

The current codex is composed of three originally separate smaller *libelli* (or booklets), corresponding to folios 1–25, 26–42, and 43–64, all produced in the same Abirhilt-group (Kitzingen) scriptorium during the final third of the eighth century and bound together in the Würzburg Cathedral Library during the fifteenth century.[159] I call the first *libellus*, an extremely sophisticated work by the Kitzingen Anonyma, "Deus per angelum" after its opening words and provide a breakdown of its contents here.[160]

Folios 2r–5r: Preface/Opening (Marian) Frame

Text I: Abbreviated Christmas Homily [of Pseudo-Fulgentius?] (folios 2r–3r)   The Kitzingen Anonyma began "Deus per angelum" with an original, abbreviated version of a homily[161] that enjoyed wide diffusion due to its inclusion in the much-copied sermonary that Alan of the Marian house of Farfa (d. 770) began compiling during the abbacy of his predecessor, Abbot Fulcoald (744–757).[162] Alan's collection, based on a Roman sermonary of perhaps the sixth century, spread extremely rapidly; five copies were made in Bavaria alone before the middle of the ninth century.[163] The homily, one of Alan's additions to the Roman collection, also circulated independently, including in other booklets.[164] The sermon was normally attributed either to Augustine or to Fulgentius (attributions rejected by modern scholars).[165] The number of sermons pseudonymously attributed to Augustine far exceeded those ascribed to any other single figure, so no individual attribution was particularly significant.[166] The attribution to Fulgentius, on the other hand, was. A particular individual, active either in North Africa or Italy, deliberately composed works in the style of Fulgentius, bishop of Ruspe in North Africa (c. 467–532).[167] Several of this person's sermons appeared alongside a complete version of the homily abbreviated at Kitzingen for "Deus per angelum" (folios 10v–13r) in the late eighth- or early ninth-century north Italian codex Vienna ÖNB MS 1616, a copy of a sermon collection originally compiled c. 650–750, at whose core was a sixth-century African homiliary.[168] Perhaps this homily really was a product of pseudo-Fulgentius.

Text II: Interpolated Description of Mary by Isidore of Seville (folios 3r–3v)
The Kitzingen Anonyma followed the homily with the chapter concerning Mary from Isidore of Seville's (c. 560–636) work *De ortu et obitu patrum*.[169] The version in the "Deus per angelum" *libellus* included an interpolated passage concerning the Annunciation, copied from the sermon of Bartholomew to

king Polymius in the Karlburg passionary, including the formulation (shared by these two women's manuscripts, against the readings of all other exemplars) to have Gabriel say to Mary "concepisti" ("you have conceived") rather than "concipies" ("you will conceive").[170]

Text III: Extract from Cassiodorus's Revision of Pelagius's Commentary on Paul (folios 3v–5r) The interpolated Isidoran extract was followed by Pelagius's commentary on Paul's Letter to the Romans 12:9–17, as revised by Cassiodorus.[171] Pelagius's commentary on the Pauline epistles was written between 405 or 406 and 410 for lay Christian aristocrats in the city of Rome for whom Pelagius served as teacher and spiritual advisor.[172] Pelagius, who championed human free will in opposition to Augustine's doctrine of original sin, was condemned by Emperor Honorius in 419; he and his followers were persecuted throughout the 420s. Nevertheless, his commentary remained popular. Cassiodorus encountered the text near the end of the sixth century, recognized it as "heretical," and devised a strategy to counter its influence: he put into circulation an expurgated revision, replacing some of Pelagius's words with Augustine's interpretations.[173]

Folios 5r–16r: Female Martyrial Center
Text I: The Abbreviated Passion of Cecilia of Rome (folios 5r–9r) The *passio* of Cecilia was originally composed during the sixth century (or perhaps at the very end of the fifth century), perhaps by an African refugee (from the Vandals) in Rome, and became extremely widespread.[174] The Kitzingen Anonyma created an original abbreviated version, from which a few extracts have been published.[175]

Text II: The Abbreviated Passion of Juliana of Nicomedia (folios 9r–12r) According to Geith, the *passio* of Juliana was composed in Byzantine south Italy (perhaps in Cumae or Naples, the centers of the saint's cult) during the middle decades of the sixth century.[176] He hypothesized a single sixth-century southern Italian archetype, from which all extant manuscripts descended, and dated that original *passio* to before the Lombard invasion of 568 on the grounds that the report of the translation of Juliana's relics to Cumae (which did not appear in the oldest copies of the legend) referred to that invasion. Because this argument was founded on the untenable assumption that the Lombard invasion caused a complete rupture in the literary culture of the Italian peninsula,[177] it is perfectly possible that the original text dated from the Lombard period.[178] The Kitzingen Anonyma created an original abbreviated (and unpublished) version of the *passio*, the sole member of Geith's Group IV of Family 1.[179]

Text III: The Abbreviated Passion of Agnes of Rome (folios 12r–14r) The lively veneration of Agnes in Rome already in the fourth century generated images of her (on numerous gold glass bowls and in the cemetery of Commodilla) as a very young female "orans," or full frontal figure praying with outstretched palms, wearing the dress of a Vestal Virgin and a stole.[180] The oldest and very popular *passio* of Agnes (BHL 156) may have been composed as early as the first quarter of the fifth century, although it more likely dated from the opening decades of the sixth century.[181] The Kitzingen Anonyma created an (unpublished) abbreviated version (BHL 157) for "Deus per angelum."

Text IV: "On the Death of Agatha of Catania" ("De Obitu sanctae Agathae"; folios 14r–16r) Although one devotee of Agatha argued that her *passio* was an eye-witness account of her martyrdom during the mid–third century,[182] the original version of her *passio* was probably composed during the second half of the fifth century in Sicily, where her cult was centered.[183] However, the surviving version of the narrative (BHL 133) was a mid–sixth-century reworking by an African refugee, perhaps Ferrandus, biographer of Fulgentius of Ruspe.[184] The original abbreviated version in the Kitzingen *libellus* (BHL 134) was published with multiple serious errors.[185] It was probably copied (with the exception of the final few lines) by a student for, unlike the remainder of the texts in the *libellus*, "On the Death of Agatha" was dramatically error-laden.[186]

Folios 16r–25v: Epilogue/Closing (Dominical) Frame
Text I: "Lectio sancti Evangelii secundum Matheum incipit, id est praedicatio Capitolii" (Commentary on Matthew 26:1–30; folios 16r–20r) There was a rich tradition of writing commentaries on Matthew during the early Middle Ages. Many examples have only recently come to light.[187] At least three Carolingian-era commentaries on Matthew (one by Wigbod, a member of the court of Charlemagne, the second possibly by Charles's key advisor Alcuin, and the third a revision of an eighth-century commentary traditionally attributed to a certain Frigulus) were discovered in 2002 and 2003 alone.[188] As Michael Gorman wrote in 2005, "it is difficult to evaluate any early medieval commentary on Matthew . . . many discoveries are still to be made . . . little detailed research has been devoted to how biblical commentaries in the early medieval period were transmitted. . . . Epitomes (or abbreviated versions) were much more popular than we might have supposed, and so were interpolated versions."[189] Even a cursory dip into manuscript catalogues reveals multiple unstudied texts to which the heretofore unknown Kitzingen commentary could be related.[190]

There was, however, one relatively well-known text from which the Kitzingen Anonyma could have extracted her brief commentary: the *Opus Imperfectum in Matthaeum*, written between 425 and 430 by Annianus of Celeda, a deacon based somewhere in the Latin west who avidly supported the Pelagian cause.[191] The "Deus per angelum" *libellus* was also Pelagian in its sympathies (Chapter Six). Whatever transmission stream brought the revised Pelagian commentary on Romans discussed above to Kitzingen could also have brought

Annianus's Pelagian commentary on Matthew. Several of the eleven eighth- and ninth-century manuscripts of the *Opus Imperfectum* had connections with the Anglo-Saxon cultural province in Francia, so the text could have been available there.[192] The mysterious reference to a "praedicatio Capitolii" in the title of the text in the Kitzingen *libellus* conceivably referred to something in the exemplar connecting the *Opus Imperfectum* with the Capitolium in Constantinople, an auditorium where Annianus attended lectures.[193]

It is nevertheless impossible to make a certain determination concerning the relationship of the two commentaries. The *Opus Imperfectum* survived only through the end of the comment on Matthew 25, while the Kitzingen text commented on Matthew 26:1–30. Both used the format of classical textual commentary, citing a portion of the Gospel text, then commenting, then citing another portion, and so on (as opposed to quoting the biblical text in its entirety and then interpreting it). However, the "Deus per angelum" commentary was drastically abbreviated in terms of how much commentary followed upon each phrase of scripture when compared with those portions of the *Opus Imperfectum* that survive; nevertheless, this difference cannot decisively eliminate Annianus's comment from consideration, for the Kitzingen Anonyma abbreviated most of her sources. In the end, the fact that so many authors felt free to produce original commentaries on the Gospel of Matthew during the early Middle Ages indicates that the Kitzingen Anonyma would have felt similarly authorized to create precisely the text she required for her *libellus*. Thus, it is likely that the commentary on Matthew 26 was an original composition.

Text II: Description of the Holy Sepulchre (folios 20r–21r) The Kitzingen Anonyma followed the commentary with a description of the sepulchre of Christ and a list of the hours at which various events in sacred history transpired. The description clearly pertained to the grand edifice built by Constantine between 325/6 and 335, known as the Anastasis (from the Greek word for "resurrection"): a rotunda containing the Edicule (or "little house") and accessed through a triportico.[194] Scholarship on the tomb of Christ has been extensive; the fact that the "Deus per angelum" text matched no previously known verbal description or visual depiction of the tomb from the fourth through the eighth century[195] indicates that it was an original composition.

Significantly, no two early descriptions or depictions matched exactly.[196] The Edicule was sometimes hexagonal, sometimes square, sometimes octagonal; it was sometimes surmounted by a dome, sometimes by a conical roof, sometimes by a rotunda, sometimes by an octagonal roof; some depictions crowned the entire edifice with a cross, and some did not.[197] Written descriptions and artistic depictions were not intended to convey precise details about the tomb; rather, they were memorial records of individual features that particularly struck different observers over time.[198]

The feature that most struck the author of the description in "Deus per angelum" was the five columns surrounding the tomb.[199] Columns were not mentioned in any known verbal descriptions of the tomb before the late ninth century, when their number was given as nine or eleven.[200] The fact that the Kitzingen Anonyma mentioned columns suggests that she was drawing on pilgrim vial(s), just as the Kitzingen theologian-artist drew inspiration from these sources for her crucifixion miniature.[201] Several pilgrim vials depicted the encounter of the women with the angel at the tomb, shown as the Constantinian structure; these frontal views clearly invited interest in the columns.[202] These mass-produced, mid– and late–sixth-century hammered-metal containers, worn as pendant necklaces, have mostly been destroyed because of the fragility of their closures.[203] But they were certainly known in the women's communities of the Anglo-Saxon cultural province in Francia, for some were used as models, possibly at Karlburg, for the famous Pettstadt pyxis, and three silver ampullae were inventoried at Milz in 799.[204]

Still, none of the depictions on surviving vials suggested that the number of columns around the tomb was five, and the "real" number seems to have been nine: five built into the rotunda housing the tomb, four at the corners of the square porch in front of the Edicule. Yet someone familiar with a three-dimensional model of the Edicule, such as the fifth-century one now in the Musée archeologique of Narbonne, might well have hit upon the number five for the tomb columns.[205] Knowledge of such a model would also lead someone to describe the Edicule as both round and square, the geometric configuration ascribed to the tomb by the Kitzingen Anonyma.[206] Indeed, this same conclusion would be drawn by someone who had seen monument itself. If the compiler of the *libellus* did not have personal experience of Jerusalem, she may have learned about the site from an associate, perhaps a member of the community of Latin nuns attached to the church of the Holy Sepulchre.[207]

Text III: *Lectio evangelii secundum Matheum Incipit* (Homily on Matthew 28:1–20; folios 21r–24r) The reading from Matthew 28, a standard lesson for the Easter Vigil mass, was followed by a sermon keyed to that feast, which incorporated portions of a relatively widespread letter of pseudo-Jerome (fols. 23r–23v) concerning the Easter vigil.[208] The Kitzingen Anonyma incorporated no other verbatim quotations from earlier works into this original sermon, but she did draw some inspiration from Gregory's Gospel Homily 25, a text contained in another Abirhilt-group codex that also inspired the Kitzingen crucifixion miniaturist: she described how, through the crucifixion, God caught the Devil (the sea monster Leviathan) like a fish by fooling him with the bait of Jesus' apparent humanity, then piercing him with the hook of Jesus' divinity (fols. 22v–23r).[209] The homily also discussed the woman who found the lost drachma (subject of Gregory's Gospel Homily 34).[210] It is written clearly and well, additional evidence that it was a Kitzingen creation rather than a text copied from an arcane exemplar.

Text IV: A Sermon on the Second Coming (fols. 24r–24v)   Although lacking a rubric, this sermon was clearly a separate text, beginning with a decorated initial after Text III wound up with "Finit Deo gratias." Like Bede's discussion of the Last Judgment in *De temporum ratione*, the work cited Revelations 21:1, Revelations 20:11, and Isaiah 30:26.[211] Beyond this minor debt to Bede, the work was original.

Text V: Praedicatio incipit pascuae minoris. Lectio sancti evangelii secundum Johannem (Commentary on John 10:1–15; folios 24v–25v)   Like Text I in the closing frame, this piece took a classical textual commentary approach to a biblical passage, in this case Jesus' "I am a good pastor" speech, warning against future dangers such as bad pastors, bad rulers, and heretics. The most unusual feature of this brief, original commentary was its enumeration of five (rather than the more traditional seven) key vices: *ira* (wrath), *invidia* (envy), *fornicatio* (fornication), *blasfemia* (blasphemy), and *superbia* (pride).

The Kitzingen Anonyma clearly constructed her *libellus* from multiple sources (in addition to penning original texts). One of these must have been a lost collection of martyr passions closely related to Paris BN 10861, produced at Christ Church, Canterbury, or by an Anglo-Saxon working on the continent or in another English house related to Christ Church, such as the women's houses of Minster-in-Thanet or Winchcombe, during the 810s or 820s.[212] This codex contained copies of the full passion narratives of Cecilia (BHL 1495), Agnes (BHL 156), Agatha (BHL 134), and Juliana (BHL 4522), along with a number of other saints, and undoubtedly shared a close common ancestor with the codex used for the Kitzingen *libellus*.[213] It is also possible that Vienna ÖNB 1616, discussed above in connection with the abbreviated Christmas homily at the start of the opening frame, was itself the source of that pseudo-Fulgentian text; produced in the late eighth century at a Carolingian royal residence in Monza, it could have spent time at the Carolingian *Eigenkloster* of Kitzingen before eventually making its way to Salzburg, given that it contained tenth-century pen trials calling on "christe martyr sancte chiliane" (fols. 100v and 110r), that is, Kilian of Würzburg. None of the oldest copies of Isidore's *De ortu et obitu patrum* was particularly related to the copy used by the Kitzingen Anonyma.[214] The state of scholarship on the remaining texts is insufficiently advanced to support speculation concerning possible sources.

The Synonyms of Isidore of Seville (Würzburg Universitätsbibliothek M.p.th.q. 28a and Würzburg Universitätsbibliothek M.p.th.q. 28b Codex 3)
Both the older Gun(t)za group of manuscripts and the younger Abirhilt group of manuscripts included a copy of the *Synonyms* of Isidore of Seville.[215] The

bishop of Seville polished this text between 604 and 617, apparently on the basis of two different working copies. The result was that the text circulated in two slightly different recensions.[216]

The Karlburg copy (Würzburg UB M.p.th.q. 28a) preserved the rare Λ recension, titled *Sinonima*, which included a prologue ("Prologue 1") added in the British Isles.[217] This recension was best represented by St. Petersburg, Rossijskaja Nacionalnaja Biblioteka, Lat. Q.v.I.15, an early eighth-century English codex in which the young Boniface himself may have written a creed; other witnesses of this recension included Würzburg UB M.p.th. f. 79 (likewise from early eighth-century England) and Würzburg UB M.p.th. f.33 (copied from Würzburg UB M.p.th. f. 79 in the Würzburg cathedral between 832 and 842).[218] The Karlburg Isidore and the St. Petersburg codex were copied from the same exemplar; this (lost) common exemplar was made on the Ur-exemplar of the entire Λ recension, as was Würzburg UB M.p.th. f. 79.[219] The common exemplar of the St. Petersburg and Karlburg Isidores must have traveled to the Anglo-Saxon cultural province in Francia with the Anglo-Saxon immigrants who established the scriptorium (the first in the region) at Karlburg.[220] In contrast, Würzburg UB M.p.th. f. 79 did not move from England to the Würzburg cathedral until after the creation of that institution's library catalogue around 800. The fact that the *Synonyms* was not on the cathedral catalogue and that Würzburg UB M.p.th. f. 79 (rather than Würzburg UB M.p.th.q. 28a) was utilized to make a new copy of the text there is further evidence that the Gun(t)za group codices were not produced by males associated with the cathedral.[221]

The Kitzingen copy of Isidore's *Synonyms* (Würzburg UB M.p.th.q. 28b Codex 3) preserved the common Φ recension (which included Isidore's own Prologue 2 and was entitled "Liber Soliloquiorum"). This recension was best represented by Fulda Dommuseum Bonifatianus 2 (the Ragyndrudis codex, produced at Mainz for Boniface shortly before the middle of the eighth century) and Paris, BN 14086.[222] The Paris codex and another now-lost manuscript were made directly on the Ur-exemplar for the Φ recension; the latter codex then served as the common exemplar both for the Kitzingen copy and for the Ragyndrudis codex. Thus, the very manuscript used for Boniface's personal copy of the *Synonyms* found its way to Kitzingen, eloquent testimony to the intellectual culture of the syneisactic world of Boniface and Leoba.

In addition to belonging to two different recensions, the Karlburg and Kitzingen Isidores differed in other ways. For instance, the Kitzingen copy was skillfully illuminated, whereas the Karlburg copy was minimally decorated.[223] Furthermore, the Kitzingen copy was both complete and free-standing, whereas the Karlburg copy was both deliberately edited (through the excision of Book II chapter 27 to Book II chapter 81)[224] and combined with *passiones* of the martyrs Eugenia and Potitus.[225] Finally, the Kitzingen Isidore was produced by a single scribe, whereas two scribes combined to create Würzburg UB M.p.th.q. 28a (one using a "more stately" script, the other a "more cursive" one).[226] They alternated in copying the *Synonyms* (fols. 1–36); then one copied most of the *passio Eugeniae* (fols. 37–63) while the other copied most of the *passio Potiti* (fols. 63–70).[227] One of them may have written her name, for on the otherwise blank last folio (71v) are the remains of a word that, under blue light, might be a name ending in "-hilt."

The story of Eugenia derived from a corpus of at least seven legends of female transvestite saints produced in Egypt between the mid–fifth and the early sixth century.[228] The only other eighth-century copy of the version of the *passio Eugeniae* found in the Karlburg Isidore, whose original date of composition is uncertain, was made by monks of Corbie, who regularly collaborated on scriptorial projects with a nearby community of nuns.[229] Insofar as Corbie also owned the St. Petersburg *Synonyms* manuscript (the Karlburg Isidore's closest relative) and produced a copy of the *passio Potiti* during the mid–eighth century,[230] it is possible the texts in the Karlburg Isidore had a deep history of interconnection in syneisactic circles.

The Karlburg Isidore also included a formula for "a mass which should be sung daily to the public, a mass for all Christian people" added in the ninth century to the protective leaves at the end of the codex (fols. 70v–71r).[231]

The later (Kitzingen) copy of Isidore's *Synonyms* (Würzburg, UB M.p.th.q. 28b Codex 3; i.e., fols. 43r–64v) was more straightforward.[232] The text currently runs only through Book II chapter 18 (column 849B line 9 in PL 83) but was originally complete. The peculiarity of the codex is that it was illuminated, probably by the scribe herself, who displayed artistic creativity in laying out the text as a block and adjusting her Anglo-Saxon minuscule hand in the uncial direction, in imitation of Würzburg UB M.p.th.q.2, an ancient Jerome codex (discussed at the beginning of this chapter) that had already served as a model for uncial scripts in England.[233] Furthermore, she added orange rubrics and colored in almost all the sentence initials (usually alternating yellow with red-orange), rendering the text not only pleasing to the eye but also extremely easy to read. She also used color (orange and yellow) for the names of the characters "homo" and "ratio," thus underlining the dramatic nature of the text as a dialogue between a human being and reason (particularly visible on fols. 50v–51r, 53v, 54r, and 55v). And she began the entire work with a charming decorated "In" using yellow, orange, and brown, making use of the bird-head ornamentation that appeared so frequently in the Kitzingen Paul (fol. 43r). Finally, she added two important illuminations, a Lamb of God at the beginning of Book I (fol. 43v)[234] and a set of birds at the beginning of Book II (fols. 60v–61r; Plates 5 and 6).

The Karlburg Florilegium *(Würzburg, Universitätsbibliothek M.p.th. f. 13)*

This oldest witness of the florilegium known as the "Liber Scintillarum," one of the most popular works of the entire Middle Ages, was entitled in the *explicit* (fol. 57v) "Liber Sententiarum de diversis voluminibus coaptatum" ("Book of Sentences Drawn Together from Various Volumes") and bore no authorial attribution.[235] The twentieth-century editor and translator of the text, Henri Rochais, invented an author and the conventional title for the work.[236] In thirty-two (mostly Milanese) manuscripts from the eleventh century or later, a certain Defensor was named in a prologue as the *concinnator* ("one who chained together") the extracts, and his *nutritor* (patron) was named as Ursinus; in four of those manuscripts, Defensor was localized to Ligugé near Poitiers. Those Italian prologues had already been called to the attention of scholars by Jean Mabillon (1632–1707),[237] but centuries passed before Rochais (a monk of Ligugé) accepted them as sufficient evidence to identify the original author as Defensor, a monk of Ligugé circa 700, when the name Ursinus was attested around Poitiers.

Rochais's attribution needs to be rethought.[238] The prologues identifying Defensor as the *concinnator* are too late to be taken seriously. Indeed, Rochais himself rejected the later manuscripts as useless for establishing the text or even the stemma, precisely on the grounds that florilegia are prone to radical transformation over the course of transmission.[239] Furthermore, the compiler made very heavy use of Isidore's *Synonyms*, a text at the time virtually confined to Anglo-Saxon circles and very unlikely to have been known at Ligugé.[240]

The collection was not diffused from Ligugé. The (lost) archetype had two direct descendants and one indirect descendant, from which all extant manuscripts in turn descended, in three interrelated traditions. The Karlburg manuscript, the oldest extant copy, was made around the middle of the eighth century directly on the compiler's original and then served as the examplar for another eighth-century copy (Munich BSB Clm 4582) made in Benediktbeuern or Kochel.[241] The second branch of transmission began with a copy made, also on the compiler's original, during the late eighth or early ninth century in Alemannia, possibly in the monastery of St. Gallen.[242] The third branch began with a copy made in the Salzburg area around 816/817 from one or more lost earlier copies made from the archetype.[243] The oldest west Frankish copy, produced in the middle of the ninth century at St. Martin of Tours, fused the Salzburg and Alemannic traditions[244] and must have been introduced there from the east (rather than directly from nearby Ligugé), possibly by Alcuin, who created the Tours scriptorium and clearly knew the florilegium.[245]

Finally, the character of the florilegium did not match the strictly ascetic character of Ligugé. The compilation certainly originated in clerical circles that emphasized interior spiritual orientation over overt signs of corporeal self-control like sexual purity and other types of abstinence from material pleasures, such as the group of noncelibate, nonascetic clergy in the Trier area, all closely allied, around 700, with the circles around Willibrord of Echternach, Irmina of Oeren, and the early Carolingians, whose *Eigenkloster* Karlburg then was. This social group included a family that, in the late seventh and early eighth century, monopolized the see of Trier by passing the episcopal office not only from uncle to nephew but also from father to son.[246] This family also included a Gun(t)za, the name of one of the scribes of the codex who twice wrote her name in it: Gun(t)za of Trier, sister of one early eighth-century bishop of Trier, mother and grandmother of his successors, and in later life a widowed aristocratic matron who could have retired to Karlburg and brought with her—or later acquired—a copy of the florilegium.[247] Multiple points of connection between the regions of Trier and Würzburg might have led Gun(t)za to look to the Main Valley as a retirement site. For instance, Willibrord was active in and around Würzburg in the 700s and 710s, when the ducal couple of Würzburg twice donated properties to him and to Echternach, and the archeological finds at Karlburg point to ties with the Moselle region around Trier.[248]

Although the codex is missing the first quire, containing the chapters on Charity, Patience, Love of God and Neighbor, and Humility, they were part of the original manuscript, which served as an exemplar for other complete copies. The Karlburg scribes decorated the manuscript throughout with a series of charming, lighthearted, and colorful (mostly orange and yellow) initials and rubricated it in a very light orange fading into yellow. Readers also scratched many Latin glosses into the book that have never been deciphered, although five East Frankish scratched glosses have been.[249] Based on the sheer volume of glosses, it is clear that the codex was heavily used at Karlburg.

The Kitzingen Homiliary (Würzburg, Universitätsbibliothek M.p.th.q. 28b Codex 2)

The middle portion of the artificial collection that is now Würzburg, UB M.p.th.q. 28b was an Abirhilt group homiliary produced by a single scribe.[250] This scribe also wrote "explicit deo gratias. Gaude maria virgo" ("the end, thank God! Rejoice, virgin Mary!") on the last page of the Kitzingen Gregory (Würzburg UB M.p.th.f. 45 fol. 72v), although she did not otherwise work on that codex (the one copied in part and containing the colophon of Abirhilt on fol. 71v).

The sermons in the homiliary, which had no authorial attributions in the manuscript itself, have long been identified as widespread works and have all been published before. No part of the codex represented a composition original to Kitzingen, but the combination of the texts into a single homiliary almost certainly was the work of the women's scriptorium. The component parts were:

> Folios 26r–28v: "De Mysterio Trinitatis et Incarnationis," frequently attributed to Augustine, possibly by Vigilius of Thapsus.[251]
> Folios 28v–33r: Caesarius of Arles, "Epistola de Humilitate."[252]
> Folios 33r–36v: "Sermo in Natale Domini," or "Doctrina cuiusdam sancti viri," a seventh-century Septimanian or Iberian text containing Arian Christological statements and frequently attributed to Caesarius.[253] It was a model for the scarapsus of Pirmin.[254]
> Folios 36v–38v: "Sermo de resurrectione Domini," an abbreviated version of a sermon frequently attributed to Augustine.[255]
> Folios 38v–42v: A possibly unique cento or chain of extracts from the first three-quarters of Jerome's Commentary on Ecclesiastes.[256] The cento

was not made using the fifth-century copy of the text available at Kitzingen (Würzburg, UB M.p.th.q.2) and was therefore probably not originally produced there.[257] Additional copies of this cento could lurk among the twenty-six anonymous, unedited comments on Ecclesiastes in medieval manuscripts.[258]

The centonization process radically transformed the character of Jerome's original, which had quoted and elucidated every word of the biblical text; in contrast, the cento loosely addressed the single phrase "Vanity of vanities, vanity of vanities, all is vanity" ("Vanitas vanitatum, vanitas vanitatum, omnia vanitas est") from Ecclesiastes 1:2, rarely including subsequent biblical lemmata. The extracts conveyed Jerome's general message of contempt for the transitory things of this material world, but they did so without a cogent flow of ideas. For instance, without the citation of a biblical passage concerning wisdom and stupidity, it was unclear why the text commented on wisdom and stupidity, but those comments nevertheless constituted useful nuggets of insight, such as: "The more one pursues wisdom, the more one realizes that s/he is subject to vices and far from the virtues s/he sought."[259] Another example of the tenuous relationship of the cento to Jerome's commentary concerned Ecclesiastes 3:2, the lyrical favorite "a time to be born and a time to die, a time to plant and a time to uproot." Jerome connected birthing and planting with fear (*timor*) through Isaiah 26:18, then quoted 1 John 4:18 on how perfect love banished fear ("Perfecta quippe dilectio foras mittit timorem"),[260] whereas the extractor simply quoted 1 John, which hardly conveyed the texture of Jerome's comment, or much about Ecclesiastes. This series of disconnected quotations from Jerome's work (plus a few original sentences) was effectively a florilegium on *contemptus mundi*.

Although the text was probably not original to Kitzingen, its deliberate graphic culmination was. The scribe placed the final lines of the text (a call to do penance while time remained) within the diagram of a military camp (Plate 7). The text could have fit along the top of the page, had the scribe wished to divorce the words from the image; instead, she called attention to the relationship between the two. She wrote the lines, with multiple abbreviations, precisely so as to form an inverted cone down the center of the page, plunging into the heart of the diagram, written in the same hand as the text. Given the absence of signs of erasure on the diagram where the text penetrated the graphic, the diagram did not predate the text but constituted an integral part of the Kitzingen homiliary.

APPENDIX: THE "AD LAPIDUM FLUMINIS" MANUSCRIPTS

Besides the Gun(t)za and Abirhilt codices, Bischoff identified a third group of women's manuscripts, written around 800 in a combination of Carolingian minuscule and German-insular hands, one of whose scribes, Reginmaar the deacon, described himself as living in communion with a congregation of women "ad lapidum fluminis."[261] His colophon, at the end of a copy of homilies by Caesarius of Arles, included a request for prayers from these women, articulated in language nearly identical to that used by Lul, Denehard, and Burkhard to Abbess Cyneburg.[262] The denizens of this community, a women's house to which male secular clerics were attached, were continuing the syneisactic traditions of the Anglo-Saxon cultural province in Francia. Karlburg, Kitzingen, Ochsenfurt, and Tauberbischofsheim, all situated on rivers where there were stony crossings, have been suggested as candidates for the house in question; nevertheless, the "ad lapidum fluminis" manuscripts were made in an established scriptorium, leaving only Karlburg and Kitzingen in question. I follow most commentators in locating the production of the manuscripts at Karlburg.[263] The decoration on the initial *G* on folio 7r of Vienna ÖNB 2223 looked exactly like one of the Karlburg crosses (*X*-shaped, with four circles around the outside), and the initials on folios 45v and 46r of that same codex were especially reminiscent of the Karlburg jewelry-style initials in Würzburg UB M.p.th.f. 13.[264]

Although the books were made at Karlburg, they were neither used there nor transferred with the rest of the library to Kitzingen; accordingly, they did not appear on the Basel booklist. The codices were almost certainly made for the Würzburg cathedral clerics, who were just beginning to produce books for themselves, albeit at a much lower level of quality and using very different hands.[265] The Karlsruhe Caesarius was demonstrably in the cathedral library by the tenth century at the latest.[266] Two of the "Ad lapidum fluminis" manuscripts furnish crucial evidence concerning values in the diocese: the *Collectio Wirceburgensis*[267] and, above all, the Vienna Penitentials (Vienna ÖNB 2223).[268] The latter manuscript may have been made in the eighth century, for the German-insular hand of the main scribe (who wrote all but the final text, a later addition) was consistent with eighth-century scripts.[269] It is still in its Würzburg cathedral binding, which is falling apart as a result of heavy use. Small, light, and eminently portable, it was certainly used in the care of souls.[270] Its contents follow here.

> Folios 1–17: the seventh-century Penitential of Archbishop Theodore of Canterbury in the *Discipulus Umbrensium* version, including Books I and II but without the preface.[271]
>
> Folios 17–22: a fragment of the eighth-century penitential of Pseudo-Bede, composed in an Anglo-Saxon center in the Rhine-Main area.[272]
>
> Folio 22r: the preface to the penitential of Cummean.[273]
>
> Folios 22v–41r: the *Capitula Iudiciorum* penitential, composed during the second half of the eighth century in northern France or (more likely) southern Germany.[274]
>
> Folios 41–44: an epilogue added to the *Capitula Iudiciorum* during the second half of the eighth century, somewhere between the Alps and the

Main Valley, comprising extracts from Gregory the Great's *Libellus responsionum*; it also appeared in St. Gallen Stiftsbibliothek 150 part 4 (c. 800).[275]

Folios 44–45: an extract from Gregory the Great's *Libellus responsionum*.

Folios 45–54: Gregory the Great, *Libellus responsionum*.[276]

Folios 54–55: a text on the importance of penance, "*Tres autem syllabae sunt.*"[277]

Folios 55–56: selections on kinship relations from Isidore's *Etymologies*.[278]

Folios 56–76: Pseudo-Fulgentius, "Letter to Peter on the Faith," chapters 47–87,[279] and Fulgentius, "Letter 8 to Donatus."[280]

Folios 76–77: Gregory of Elvira's "Fides catholica," a creed statement with particular emphasis on the Trinity.[281]

Folios 77r–77v: Latin translation of Gregory the Thaumaturge's "Fides catholica."[282]

Folios 77v–87r: the penitential of pseudo-Egbert, written in an Anglo-Saxon center in the Rhine-Main area in the late eighth or early ninth century (a later addition by a second scribe).[283]

PART TWO

TEXTUAL ANALYSIS

CHAPTER FOUR

"I AM CRUCIFIED IN CHRIST"

(GALATIANS 2:20): THE KITZINGEN

CRUCIFIXION MINIATURE AND VISIONS

OF THE APOSTLE PAUL

AN IMAGE AND ITS THEOLOGIAN-ARTIST

This chapter analyzes the full-page Crucifixion miniature (Plate 4) that was created as a frontispiece for the Kitzingen Pauline Epistles.[1] The image is both famous (according to one specialist, the most famous of all the insular and insular-inspired manuscripts of the early Middle Ages)[2] and little understood. It is commonly treated as a copy of a lost model and explained through the prism of ethnic (or national) artistic traditions. One recent treatment, for instance, described how the artist combined "oriental," "insular" and, "continental" elements by depicting Christ and his companions in an "Egyptian" bark of the dead, while utilizing "Frankish" ornamental motifs (rosettes and interlace in the arcade) and an "Irish" color scheme (orange, yellow, and black); another appealed to its "bright colors" as a sign that the miniature might have been copied from an Irish model.[3] This view of the image persists despite Spilling's 1982 demonstration that the grounds for positing an Irish model are slim at best; for instance, the Kitzingen image placed Stephaton (represented by his sponge, a triangle at the tip of Christ's beard) on the left of Jesus and Longinus (represented by his lance, whose tip is aimed at Christ's belly) on the right, following Anglo-Saxon and continental practice, whereas Irish crucifixion images reversed the sides.[4] As for the color scheme: it reproduced the palette of the Spessart in the autumn; no Irish experience was required for a visual artist to think in these pigmented terms.

The paradigm according to which early medieval art was primarily an expression of racially based aesthetic preferences is now being vigorously questioned. For instance, ideas about which artistic elements (such as bright color) "must" derive from Irish tradition have been shown to be especially suspect and linked to modern racist stereotypes about the (feminine) "nature" of the Irish people.[5] Furthermore, the paradigm according to which early medieval art was essentially imitative is also under attack[6] and is particularly unhelpful for understanding eighth-century crucifixion imagery. Depictions of the crucifixion were just becoming common only when the Kitzingen artist was at work, virtually requiring her to construct her own iconographic program.[7] She was part of a broader trend, during the reign of Charles the Great, to massively increase the number and significance of pictures in books, so much so that we can truly speak of the development of a (theologically stamped) visual culture.[8]

The Pauline miniaturist certainly found inspiration in preexisting images, possibly including the famous Holy Land pilgrim souvenir vials available all over Europe by the eighth century, including at the Franconian women's houses of Karlburg and Milz.[9] For instance, the motifs of Christ crucified between the two thieves and of the cross under a decorated arch appeared both in the crucifixion image and on a number of the extant vials.[10] Furthermore, the scenes along the bottom rims of the reverse sides of some of the vials created a boat-like effect, as Mary and the apostles stood on a line, rather than directly on the semicircular edge of the ampulla.[11] Some version of the fourth-century bronze lamp in the shape of a ship, with a cross for a mast and Peter (or Paul) as its rudderman, found near St. Stefano Rotundo in Rome, might also have made its way north and inspired our artist.[12] Far more important, however, were a series of textual sources, discussed at length in this chapter.

The intensive study that Éamonn Ó Carragáin has devoted to decoding the theology, and discerning the devotional uses, of eighth-century objects such as the Ruthwell Cross (whose anonymous creator could have been a woman) and the Book of Kells (a Gospel book) is a model for what can be done with the Kitzingen Paul.[13] The Pauline miniature provides the first opportunity to glimpse the mentality pervading all the codices analyzed in this study, in which "liturgical practice, private devotion and theological reflection [functioned] as complementary activities within the monastic life."[14] Objects such as high crosses and illuminated books were manipulated, shown, and touched during the liturgy and were always understood in light of that liturgy, for it remained in memory during moments of private devotion or theological reflection. Later in the chapter, we shall see how the crucifixion image may have functioned both liturgically and devotionally; however, the ability of the image to function in such spheres derived from its theological content, to which I turn first.

The Kitzingen miniaturist, like so many of her contemporaries and near-contemporaries, was not first and foremost an artist, but rather a theologian who used visual images to convey Christian doctrine.[15] Her compositional strategies were typical of eighth-century theologian-artists. For instance, the simultaneous presence of the lance (with which Longinus pierced the side of the already-dead Jesus) and the vinegared sponge (with which Stephaton gave a final "drink" to the still-alive Jesus) conveyed the paradoxical ambiguity of Christ as both dead and alive.[16] Also like her contemporaries, the Kitzingen artist used numerical symbolism to make theological points.[17] For instance, she drew twelve fields on each side of the arch around the cross, leading to a single field at the keystone position above Christ's head. Yet this structural symmetry was accompanied by ornamental asymmetry, such as the eight-petal asterisk on the right side of the arch corresponding to a four-petal asterisk on the left side. The potential for all creation to stand in the identical relation to Christ was expressed through the equivalence between the two sides of the arch, but the divergent fates of the saved (symbolized by the Repentent Thief Dysmas, toward whom anthropomorphic birds/angels rose) versus the damned (symbolized by the Unrepetent Thief Gestas, at whom crows pulled and pecked) was expressed through the divergent ornamental detailing.

My discussion of the image differs from previous ones in several ways. First, I analyze the Kitzingen crucifixion miniature in relation to the text it was intended to introduce, namely, the letters of St. Paul. Second, I do not identify the key figures in the image (the large central figure in the boat and the figure on the central cross) solely—or even primarily—as Jesus. Third, I treat the theologian-artist as a woman. Fourth, I subject the image to a gendered analysis.[18]

Significantly, gendered difference was not overtly thematized in the miniature, which focused instead on the key sacramental moment of Christianity: Christ's voluntary, redeeming, and triumphant death on the cross. The sparsity of overt evidence for female book production in Anglo-Saxon England has been tied to the theory that "women simply did not feel the need to draw attention to their gender when labouring this way in the service of their God."[19] After all, Paul himself had helpfully asserted that there was no male or female in Christ Jesus (Galatians 3:27–28). Therefore, in creating a suitable frontispiece to introduce the message of Pauline Christianity, a message identical for men and for women, the Kitzingen theologian-artist emphasized the (gender-egalitarian) universal over the gender-differentiated. But the significance of the image in terms of gender did not stop with its fundamentally universalizing orientation. The Kitzingen theologian-artist expressed—amid the controversies of the Carolingian reform movement—views designed to counter attacks on the central role that professed women had been playing in the churches of the Anglo-Saxon cultural province in Francia. She filled the image with covert messages relevant to gender roles, messages that could be clarified during discussions between the artist and those who mattered most: other members of her community, her male and female colleagues associated with other ecclesiastical institutions and the powerful lay aristocrats (including the royal family) with whom the Kitzingen community was regularly in contact.

ILLUSTRATING THE PAULINE EPISTLES

Fifth- and sixth-century artisans occasionally marked the outside front covers of books of scripture with crosses (e.g., jeweled inset crosses, hammered metal crosses), either in doorways or under arches; during the seventh and especially the eighth century, artists transferred the motif to frontispiece and explicit pages inside their books.[20] The nuns of Chelles particularly developed a repertoire of such introductory pictures, frequently stationing a cross under an arch as the frontispiece to a text.[21] A key function of such miniatures was to adumbrate the essential themes of the texts for which they served as entryways. Because the motif signaled "the entranceway to heaven that Christ's salutary death provided," it was logical to apply it to a crucifixion scene.[22]

The appropriateness of a crucifixion to illustrate the letters of Paul, who wrote repeatedly about the crucified Lord, has been noticed but has not formed the basis of an analysis of the Kitzingen image.[23] Instead, the most commonly invoked textual referent has been Augustine's *Commentary on the Psalms*, particularly Psalm 103:25–28, which evoked a "great sea" teeming with creeping things, creatures little and great, and a sea dragon.[24] According to Augustine's comment, the sea was the temptation-filled world, filled with satanic traps and enemies of the church. When a Christian ship (understood to be the church) sailed in such dangerous waters, its Christian passengers were urged to stand vigilantly "in ligno" (translatable both as "by the [wooden] cross" and "in the [wooden] boat"), so that Christ could calm the sea for them.[25] Individual scholars have rung minor changes on this theme and have seen in the miniature (alongside Augustine on Psalm 103) allusions to the ending of the *Dream of the Rood* (when the souls of the blessed were borne to eternal bliss on a cross functioning as a ship) or to Cassiodorus's commentary on Psalm 106 (the church as a ship piloted by Christ and rowed by the apostles).[26] But all in all: "The identification of the image as Christ calming the seas is undisputed."[27]

Yet, this common interpretation of the image as an illustration of Augustine's Psalm commentary is not fully satisfactory; even an adherent of this view writes that "the seemingly bizarre conflation of the cross and the boat . . . has caused some consternation."[28] Artists juxtaposed images of the human (incarnate, bearded) Christ with the (beardless, androgynous) divine Logos, the theophanic Christ of the Second Coming from at least the seventh century.[29] Yet, there was no logic to, nor precedent for, stacking the (human) Christ on a cross above the (theophanic) Christ in a boat (indeed, there was neither logic nor precedent nor parallel for locating the theophanic Christ of the Second Coming in a boat at all). Furthermore, it was the followers of Christ who were urged to stand vigilantly in the boat and/or by the cross, not Christ himself, whose proper place was either on the cross or in the kingdom of heaven, but not at the base of the cross. Finally, the most serious problem with the standard interpretation is that there is no reason that an artist would illustrate the Pauline epistles with an image drawn from an unrelated text such as Augustine's commentary on Psalm 103.

We will never understand the Kitzingen crucifixion as a specific image if we approach it primarily in connection with well-worn naval themes such as Jesus as a ship's pilot and the cross as a ship.[30] "Sea imagery abounds in patristic and homiletic writing of the early Middle Ages. It appears in such abundance, in fact, that it is perhaps tantamount to insisting on a truism to refer to specific examples."[31] Even the most basic image of a ship held deep significance in Christian symbolic systems, as is clear from the (third- or fourth-century) ship graffito in the foundations underneath the Constantinian Church of the Holy Sepulchre in Jerusalem.[32] The miniaturist undoubtedly had many maritime referents in the back of her mind as she constructed the overall composition, and educated viewers (beginning with the eighth-century nuns of Kitzingen) undoubtedly found the scene reminiscent of many widespread literary motifs and of many oft-repeated patristic biblical interpretations.[33] A densely packed Carolingian-era crucifixion miniature could easily suggest to its viewers many levels of meaning.[34] My interpretation does not exclude previous readings, for the miniature was surely both drawn and viewed within an intricate matrix of cultural referents. However, I advance an additional interpretation of the miniature as relevant to the text it illustrates.

Copies of the Pauline epistles were rarely illuminated, but those that were repeated a small number of themes: portraits of Paul, portraits of the addressees of his letters, scenes of Paul with the addressees of his letters, the moment of Paul's conversion, or scenes of Paul preaching the gospel.[35] In the scenes of Paul preaching either to individuals or to crowds, one of the most common ways to illustrate his letters, Paul was drawn larger than those to whom his words were addressed, and one of his hands was always raised in a gesture of speech.[36] The oversized figure in the boat, standing at the foot of the cross, looking up at the cross, and gesturing toward the cross, in an *Eingangsbild* (introductory picture) for the Pauline epistles, must be Paul preaching the cross.[37] One reason that this possibility has escaped previous commentators on the miniature is the widely held belief that Christ alone can be cross-nimbed in Christian iconography,[38] a myth shattered by more than eighty examples of the attribute on figures other than Christ (including angels, Anna, apostles, Daniel, David, evangelists, John the Baptist, various personifications and unidentified saints, and the Virgin Mary) in the Index of Christian Art database at Princeton University.[39]

The Kitzingen miniature was an author portrait, telling the reader about the author of the text to come. The theologian-artist showed Paul explicating one of his key themes, redemption through the death of Christ on the cross, in connection with which he wrote: "Jews ask for signs and Greeks search for wisdom, but we preach Christ crucified" (1 Corinthians 1:22–23).[40] Author portraits were standard features of illustrated biblical manuscripts.[41] This particular author portrait was constructed out of a variety of biblical and extrabiblical traditions concerning the person of Paul, set forth in the following pages.

VISIONS OF PAUL/SPURS TO PENANCE

As narrated in Acts 9:1–20, Paul began life as a Jew named Saul who persecuted followers of Jesus. One day he was struck blind. While physically blind, Saul had a vision of a man named Ananias curing his blindness, which indeed came to pass when Ananias was instructed by Jesus, also in a vision, to go to Saul.

Having regained his corporeal vision and repented of his former life, Saul/Paul began to preach Christ. Vision, in both its corporeal and ideational manifestations, was thus the central concern at the crucial moment in the life of Paul who, as shown in the Kitzingen miniature's boat, was not only preaching Christ crucified but also having a visionary experience of the crucified Christ. Accordingly, the artist created two stylistically divergent zones to represent two ontologically and perceptually divergent planes: the world of the vision (the top register) and the world of the person having the vision (the bottom register). In one zone, she depicted a bold crucifix-cum-arch almost popping off the page; in the other zone, she sketched an almost shadowy boat scene retreating into the distance under the advancing cross.[42] She also equipped the visionary Paul with two different eyes, one blacker than the other, with which to apprehend the different scenes.

The Kitzingen theologian-artist utilized several strategies to create the eye-catching crucifix-cum-arch, such as perching two expertly executed birds atop the main cross's arms. Birds were the preferred zoomorphic theme among eighth-century artists.[43] Similar birds recurred in the illuminated initial *P*s scattered throughout the epistle codex.[44] For the surface of the arch, as well as in the decorated initials throughout, she drew on a stock of ornamental motifs commonly found in eighth-century Frankish manuscripts (simple twists, rosettes, asterisks, saltire crosses over circles) while also utilizing the new motif of interlace bands, which almost rivaled bird heads in fashionability during the second half of the eighth century.[45] The Kitzingen artist-theologian also exerted herself to render, through irregular cross-hatchings and circles, the worked surfaces of three metal crosses. Both patterns were typical of seventh- and eighth-century metal objects from the region, but the objects that most closely resembled the metal crosses envisioned by the Kitzingen artist were found in women's graves, including a bronze cross-shaped pin of c. 800 from a woman's burial (Plate 8).[46] This contemporary object helps us see that the cross-hatching on the interior surfaces of Jesus' cross was set back from a border of unworked flat metal, represented in the drawing by the solid bright orange outline.

The effort lavished on the crucifixion-cum-arch was crucial to conveying the impression that the upper portion of the image belonged to a perceptual field distinct from that of the lower portion, whose inhabitants were depicted through extremely spare line drawings, with no trace of the modeling techniques long traditional in the Mediterranean world. In the absence of formal training in how to realistically depict the human form, sixth-, seventh-, and eighth-century artists east of the Middle Rhine frequently copied figures from Roman coins to render Jesus or Mary or copied the Roman "Victoria" symbol to render an angel.[47] Yet the human figures in the Würzburg manuscript were in no way reminiscent of Mediterranean artifacts. The artist-theologian simply drew the lower zone of the miniature with a few simple strokes, using her lack of specialized training to good artistic effect.

The Kitzingen theologian-artist took inspiration for her overall composition from many sources. For instance, Isidore of Seville's sketch of Paul's life in his *De ortu et obitu patrum* (utilized by the Kitzingen anonyma for *Deus per angelum*, analyzed in chapter 6) described the saint's conversion to Christianity through a divine cure of his blindness and his career as a traveling preacher who, among other things, experienced elevation to the Third Heaven in a vision.[48] It was not uncommon for artists to take inspiration from Isidore's biographical sketch of Paul when illustrating the latter's letters.[49] Isidore also described Paul's shipwreck, based on Acts 27:14–44. Paul was well known to have frequently traveled by sea,[50] during which voyages he certainly preached "Christ crucified."

The visionary register also included the two thieves, who conveyed the message that humans could either believe in the saving cross of Jesus and be saved or deny it and be damned.[51] Here the theologian-artist literally rendered Romans 6:3, in which Paul asserted that believers were baptized by Christ's crucifixion. On the right arm of the main cross, she placed red and black dots; one red drop, a fleck of blood, dripped from the cross arm toward the repentant thief, whose own cross was flecked with red drops of blood. In contrast, the left arm of the main cross was marked only by flecks of black not-blood, which neither baptized nor saved the unrepentant thief. The theology of redemption and perdition was also expressed through avian morphemes. The two eagles perched atop the cross symbolized resurrection; one eagle alluded to the resurrection of Christ himself, the other to the resurrection promised to his followers.[52] The artist also drew from Prudentius's *Dittochaeon* (or *Tituli Historiarum*) another avian theme: anthropomorphic doves rising toward the Repentent Thief and crows pulling at the Unrepentent Thief.

Prudentius's *Dittochaeon*, composed around 400, comprised captions for forty-eight biblical scenes.[53] The Spanish poet's caption for an ideal depiction of the conversion of Paul fit the Kitzingen image perfectly:

> The Chosen Vessel: here one who was formerly a ravening wolf is clothed in a soft fleece. He who was Saul loses his sight and becomes Paul. Then he receives his vision again and is made an apostle and a teacher of the nations, having power with his lips to change crows into doves.[54]

In the crucifixion miniature, crows (black birds) and doves (white birds) symbolized the effects of taking to heart—or not—the words emanating from Paul's lips: crows dragged to damnation those who did not heed Paul's teaching, whereas those who shared Paul's vision were transformed into white doves/angels and rose up to meet the Good Thief.[55]

The artist may have known the metaphor through a direct acquaintance with Prudentius, whose *Tituli Historiarum* may be what was listed as *cronih* ("chronicle") on the Kitzingen library catalogue.[56] If so, this would have added a deeply gendered charge to the image, for the first line of that collection of quatrains read: "Eve was then a white dove, but afterwards black";[57] whatever could turn birds from black to white would also reverse the "blackening" of Eve. She may also have known the image of transforming black crows into white doves as a general metaphor by which to evoke an evangelization effort, as Alcuin used it.[58] Most likely, however, she drew the image from the works of a member of the Anglo-Saxon syneisactic network, Aldhelm of Malmesbury, whose description of Paul in his verse treatise on virginity (dedicated to an unidentified Abbess Maxima) repeated all the elements of Prudentius's Pauline *titulus*.[59] There were two entries that could refer to Aldhelm's *De virginitate* on the Basel booklist.[60]

Eventually, it would become standard to pair crucifixions with depictions of the Last Judgment as a way to call sinners to faith and repentance, but the juxtaposition of visual references to these two pillars of Christian theology in early medieval art appeared only in the miniature under discussion here.[61] This aspect of the composition was one of the great inventions of the Kitzingen theologian-artist, who thus set before the eyes of her companions in the monastic community the specter of divine judgment as a way to reinforce their own vocations.[62] The call to repentance and penance on the last folio of the Kitzingen Homiliary (Plate 7) likewise tapped into the nuns' concern with penance, "the main theme of the eighth century."[63] The theme was also in evidence in the Karlburg penitential collection's original statement of the importance of penance; that codex also highlighted (through decoration and the use of a secret "Greek" script) the tenet from Fulgentius's *De Fide ad Petrum* that Jesus would return to resurrect the blessed as angels, while the devil and his companions would be thrown into hell (Rule 25).[64]

The miniature was probably used by the Kitzingen community in various contexts. For instance, it may have been held aloft to accompany the readings from the epistles that were a necessary part of virtually every Christian feast, although it had stronger connections to some than to others. As a frontispiece to the codex, the miniature was placed right before Romans 1:1–6, the opening epistle of the liturgical year, read on Christmas Eve.[65] Of course, the image of Christ on the cross was especially suited for Easter weekend, and perhaps the miniature was used in the rite of veneration of the cross that became common on Good Friday in the course of the eighth and ninth centuries, a rite that included physical contact with all types of crosses.[66] The artist placed a small cross in the water at the bottom of the picture, where the image has been rubbed away, possibly through repeated touching. And outside of such special liturgical moments, the image was likely contemplated, either alone or in the presence of others, as a spur to repentance, during confession, and in the final days or hours of life.[67]

In addition to this extraordinary example of visionary art, the Kitzingen community was well outfitted with visionary literature, at least three examples of which were inventoried on the Basel booklist, including two seventh-century texts, namely, the *Vision of St. Fursey* and a Pseudo-Isidorian "Liber de ordine creaturarum."[68] The latter text focused above all on the Good Thief, a special case of Jesus' promise, and must have been one of the sources of inspiration for the Kitzingen theologian-artist for, although there were other relatively early examples of crucifixions showing the thieves, none except the Kitzingen Paul showed the judgment on them.[69] Whether visual or literary, however, these early medieval visionary materials should not be conflated with late medieval "mystical" texts and images. Those later devotional texts and images were records of, and spurs to, passionate somatic and emotional visionary experiences; in contrast, early medieval visionary art and literature were pragmatic spurs to good behavior or at least to repentance for bad.

The third visionary text on the Basel catalogue deserves special attention: the "apocalypsis apostoli sancti pauli," which appeared immediately after the entry for the Pauline epistles and referred to the penance-inducing text commonly known as the *Visio Pauli* (*Vision of St. Paul*). This popular narrative was known in the circle of Boniface and Leoba, for it was mentioned by Aldhelm of Malmesbury and referenced in two of the epistles in the syneisactic group's letter collection.[70] It circulated in many versions,[71] yet we can know with relative certainty which version was used at Kitzingen. The "Latin transitional version" was written in the eighth century, somewhere between northern France, the Upper Rhine, St. Gall, and Fulda.[72] The best copy of the original eighth-century text, Vatican City, BAV Palatinus Latinus 220 (an early ninth-century manuscript from the Middle or Upper Rhine that was in Lorsch by the tenth century), took over wholesale from its eighth-century exemplar a series of characteristically insular (sometimes characteristically Anglo-Saxon) abbreviations, linguistic or orthographical peculiarities, and verbal formulae.[73] This version of the *Vision of St. Paul* was almost certainly created in the Anglo-Saxon cultural province itself.

The "insular" characteristics and connections of the eighth-century Latin transitional *Visio Pauli* led one critic to conclude that the redactor was "an Irish monk or nun, probably on the Continent . . . it is also likely that the redaction was made for a house of nuns."[74] Irrespective of the ethnic background of the insular immigrant to Francia who authored the Latin transitional *Vision of St. Paul*, the text surely derived from and was intended for a female environment, for it was also feminist in orientation. I will turn to the issue of feminism after demonstrating that the text was in fact a source of inspiration for the image.

The Kitzingen miniature was no mechanical rendering of the *visio Pauli*. For instance, instead of attempting to render the text's description of heaven above (the Son of God sitting at the right hand of the Father, a great city, and an altar, where the Son of Man stood radiant as the sun in shining white clothes),[75] the theologian-artist had Paul fix his hopeful eyes on Christ crucified, a substitution that accorded not only with the importance of the crucifixion in Paul's letters but also with another detail of Paul's conversion as narrated in Acts (discussed later). Nevertheless, many details of the Latin transitional version of the *Vision of St. Paul* did match the Kitzingen crucifixion miniature. All known older versions of the apocalypse of Paul had described seriatim the apostle's visions of heaven and hell, but the eighth-century adaptation moved back and forth between Paul's vision of the saved in heaven and his vision of the damned in hell.[76] The simultaneity of this literary treatment was paralleled in the miniature, for the visionary in the boat could see both the salvific cross above and the waters of hell beneath. The notion that hell was watery, extremely rare in the Christian tradition, was reflected in the Kitzingen miniature, as was the location of Paul's visionary experience on a boat, a theme unique to the "Latin transitional version" of the narrative.[77] Several of the simultaneous heaven–hell versions added the detail of beasts swimming in the middle of the water, like fish in the sea, also represented in the miniature.[78]

The underwater portion of the crucifixion image, particularly the eel-like sea beast and the cross, had significant theological import. The cross floating deep under the surface of the water was the theologian-artist's rendering of the teaching of another text in the Abirhilt group of codices, one on which the Kitzingen Anonyma also drew for her *"Deus per Angelum" libellus*, namely, Gregory the Great's Gospel Homily 25.[79] Reading the cross in light of Gregory's homily, as the women of Kitzingen would have done, reinforced the penitential message of the image. His Easter season sermon explicated John 20:11–18, explaining the theology of redemption by the cross through Job 40:19–21, where Leviathan was caught on a fishhook. According to Gregory, the sea monster Leviathan (represented by the large sea creature in the miniature) was the devil, whom God caught by throwing in Jesus (represented by the cross in the miniature) as bait. Leviathan was fooled and took the bait, thinking Jesus was human, but then "was pierced by the sharp hook of his divinity."[80] Gregory continued: "he did not deprive the sinner of hope, for he pierced Leviathan's jaw . . . and also gave a remedy to those who do sin, so that they might not despair. . . . He has set before us, as though in a sign which urges us to repentence, those whom he brought back to life when they repented. . . . I consider the thief crucified with Jesus. . . . I see nothing other in these figures than examples of repentence."[81] Another optimistic detail drew on Gregory's Gospel homily 24, where he explained that the shore represented "the enduring state of eternal rest."[82] Some fish lay on the bank, symbolizing the "good" human souls that had already reached safety.[83]

Identifying the version of the *Vision of St. Paul* that inspired the Kitzingen miniaturist, a text potentially even composed at Kitzingen itself, provides crucial insight into the self-conception of this particular group of religious women. First, Paul saw a single virgin, paired with a single aged bishop; both had been damned as a result of identical sins: a deficit of mercy and compassion and goodness, insufficient prayers and vigils and fasts.[84] Next, Paul saw five wise and five foolish virgins.[85] The former sat, with crowns on their heads, on shining thrones next to glittering palm trees as bright as the sun, surrounded by golden halos, while from their mouths came praise of God like flames of fire; they wore garments as white as snow, and they glowed like sun and gold; they all had books in their hands, and their voices praised God like the voices of many waters; they had done the will of God in life: spoken the truth, shown kindness and mercy, been constant in prayer and vigils, spoken no harsh words, thought no evil, and shown no avarice. Paul summed up his vision of the wise virgins: "I saw the five reading the books in their hands, and I heard their voices."[86] Meanwhile, the foolish virgins, damned for the very faults earlier imputed to the bishop and the single virgin, faced a horrific punishment: "the Lord did not hear their voices."[87]

Overall, the view of religious women attributed to Paul in the Latin transitional version of the *Visio Pauli* assumed that they were of a dignity equal to that of bishops, that they were literate, and that their active vocal participation in sacred contexts was pleasing to himself and to God. This eighth-century feminist text appealed to the authority of the apostle Paul to authorize women's vocal participation in the liturgy, a structured, formal way to praise God. It reflected the confident self-conception that was current among the women of the Anglo-Saxon cultural province in Francia during the eighth century, as well as a view of Paul consistent with modern feminist biblical scholarship, which has argued that Paul did not teach that women should be silent in churches.[88] We can conclude, from the combined evidence of the miniature itself and the fact that it must have been inspired by a Latin transitional version of the *Vision of St. Paul* also in the Kitzingen library, that the community explicated the image to itself (presumably in a variety of didactic, liturgical, and penitential contexts) in ways that supported the full human dignity and personhood of religious women.

WHEN CLOTHES MAKE THE CHRIST-FIGURE: VIRGINS PUT ON CHRIST LIKE A GARMENT

Paul preached redemption through faith in Jesus' death on the cross. This aspect of Paul's message was clarified for the Kitzingen readers of his letters by the chapter headings in the manuscript, written on the back of the frontispiece (that is, on the back of the miniature). For instance, one of the first chapter headings for Paul's Letter to the Romans read: "On the justification of a human being through faith without works."[89] Such *argumenta* were consulted by artists for inspiration concerning how to illustrate biblical texts,[90] and the Kitzingen theologian-artist was no exception. The final chapter heading introducing Paul's Letter to the Galatians read: "On the apostle bearing in his own body the crucifixion wounds of our lord Jesus Christ."[91] Galatians was the letter in which Paul wrote of himself, "I am crucified in Christ" (Galatians 2:20) and described "the cross of our Lord Jesus Christ, through which the world has been crucified to me, and I to the world" (Galatians 6:14). Isidore of Seville, in a text known and used at Kitzingen, asserted that "in imitation of Christ [Paul] underwent many sufferings and grave torments of his body."[92] The most efficient way to convey Paul's imitation of and identification with Christ was to put him on the cross. The Kitzingen miniature showed Paul visualizing himself as the crucified one.

Medieval Christian theology was deeply typological, in the sense that many important figures were both themselves and others at the same time. For instance, the biblical King David was also a type of Christ. Furthermore, it was a relatively popular strategy among eighth- and ninth-century theologian-artists to intermingle the conventional iconographies of separate individuals and create typological equivalencies to express these associations and identifications in visual terms. This technique was used particularly in author portraits for biblical manuscripts, including portraits of Moses (believed to have written the Pentateuch), of David (believed to have written the Psalms), and of the evangelist Mark. The ninth-century illuminator of the Moutier-Grandval Bible used the standard Pauline physical type (of which more anon) for his image of Moses receiving the law, rather than any of the standard ways to depict Moses, to link the two figures as the key prophets of the old and new laws;[93] this illuminator also drew on a version of the apocalypse of St. Paul.[94] The late eighth-century illuminator of the Corbie Psalter placed Christ, ancestor and prefiguration of David, on the king's royal throne to recall that the Psalms were regarded as the personal prayers of Jesus; the details for this portrait were drawn by the Corbie theologian-artist from Augustine's commentary on the Psalms.[95] Finally, the author portrait of Mark in the eighth-century Echternach Gospels rendered the Lion of Mark as Jesus by having the beast be partially confined by the frame and partially breaking through it, symbolizing Christ's dual nature.[96]

The Kitzingen theologian-artist worked squarely in this tradition when she utilized the "unmistakable" hallmarks of the apostle Paul, as witnessed in numerous depictions dating from the fourth through the ninth century, for the figure on the cross: dark hair, a droopy mustache, a pointed beard, a receding hairline to the point of baldness or half-baldness, and either a widow's peak or a single isolated tuft of hair in the middle of a high forehead.[97] This standard pictorial type appeared, for instance, in the depictions of Paul preaching that illustrated the Pauline epistles in Munich, BSB Clm 14345, a mid-ninth-century manuscript probably from the Mainz area, possibly from Altmünster (Plate 9).[98] Meanwhile, the figure in the boat beneath the cross was depicted as the young, beardless, flowing-haired type of the eschatological Christ.[99] Thus, while Christ was on the cross and Paul was in the boat, the artist depicted Paul as Christ and Christ as Paul. She also slipped the sound of the Roman *p* into the inscription atop the main cross by spelling the name of the crucified one as "IHS XΠS," substituting the Greek pi for the Greek rho in the abbreviated form of "Christus" (when correct spelling demanded a Greek P [rho], vocalized as an *r*) as a clue to the presence of Paul on the cross. She repeated the pun in the initial *P* for "Paulus," rendered by the capital Greek pi (Π) in the incipit for Paul's First Letter to the Thessalonians.[100]

By placing Paul on the cross at the moment after his conversion, when he regained his vision and began to preach Christ crucified, the Kitzingen theologian-artist also rendered another detail of Paul's story as described in Acts. In that biblical narrative, Jesus told Ananias (in the latter's vision) what he, Jesus, had in store for Paul. First, Paul would be the "Chosen Vessel" (*Vas Electionis*) to bring Christ to the multitudes; the decision to place the preaching Paul in a vessel neatly rendered this metaphor, quoted also by Prudentius and Aldhelm. Second, Paul would receive a vision from Christ, to "show him how much he must suffer for my name's sake."[101] The reader of Acts was specifically instructed to envision Paul as a traveling vessel, preaching Christ, while envisioning himself suffering as Christ—exactly what was shown in the Kitzingen miniature. Furthermore, as Christ's chosen messenger, Paul effectively became Christ in the eyes of his audience, who saw the haloed figure in the boat.

I now come to the final aspect of the appearance of the crucified figure. Paul "was" Jesus only in part as a result of his placement on the cross. In contrast to the overwhelming majority of early crucifixion images, in which Christ wore a loincloth (*subligaculum*),[102] the figure on the cross in the Kitzingen miniature was fully clothed in a tunic (the *colobium*) whose fabric folds were (I suggest) inspired by familiarity with how garments appeared on carved wooden monumental crucifixions such as the Udenheim crucifix, or the Volto Santo of Lucca (Plate 10).[103] A study of the rare tradition of clothed crucifixions found that every image of Jesus wearing a tunic showed him open-eyed, stiff-armed, and placid, even after images of the suffering Christ became common; the author concluded that the tunic was the key to the imagery of Christ's victory over death.[104] The Kitzingen theologian-artist showed Paul as the physical body on the cross but made him the triumphant Jesus through the garment that he wore, an allusion to Galatians 3:27–28: "For all of you who were baptized into Christ have clothed yourselves with Christ; there is neither Jew nor Greek, slave nor free, male nor female, for you are all one in Christ Jesus." This locus classicus for egalitarian interpretations of Paul, and for defenses of leading roles for women in Christian contexts, insisted that any person who put on the tunic, who took Christ as a garment, became one with Christ.

Paul urged his audience, with no distinction of gender, to strive for the kind of identification with Christ crucified that he had achieved: "For if we have become united with him in the likeness of his death, we will also be part of his resurrection; knowing this, that our old man was crucified with him, that the body of sin might be done away with. . . . If we suffer with him . . . we may be also glorified with him" (Romans 6:5–6 and 8:17). According to Paul, the pious "bear about in their body the dying of Jesus" and have "crucified the flesh with its affections and desires" (2 Corinthians 4:10 and Galatians 5:24). Most pointedly, he added: "I urge you then be imitators of me" (1 Corinthians 4:16). But a universal goal was not a universal accomplishment. As Ambrosius Autpertus observed, writing at St. Vincent in Benevento between 758 and 767, "the members of the elect participate in Christ's crucifixion through the physical suffering they endure from their own renunciation of worldly pleasures."[105] Some Christians were more Christlike than others.

Paul exhorted his entire audience "to offer [their] bodies as a living sacrifice, holy and pleasing to God" (Romans 12:1), but his words had, by the eighth century, become narrowly associated with female virgins as a result of Origen's interpretation of Romans 12 in his *Homilies on Numbers*. A copy of that biblical commentary, to which I shall return, was available at Kitzingen, but the women of that house would also have been familiar with—and more impressed by— the use of the Pauline citation in the rite for the consecration of virgins in the Gallican liturgy.[106] This rite paralleled virginity to Christ's sacrifice on the cross as an act of voluntary self-immolation bringing benefits to the entire church.[107] Selections from Romans 12 also occupied an important spot in the powerfully feminist "Deus per Angelum" *libellus* created at Kitzingen.[108]

The consecration of virgins was a rite that foregrounded female sacred authority, for it was performed in our period by abbesses (prompting attempts in 789 and 829 to reserve the liturgical prerogative to bishops).[109] Furthermore, this same rite—which encouraged female religious to recognize themselves in Christ's sacrifice on the cross—underlined the importance of the garments worn by consecrated women. This must have infused the notion of "putting on Christ like a garment" as a means to create a world without gendered hierarchies (as Paul promised in Galatians) with particular significance. Garments played a larger role in liturgical consecrations of women than in those of men, and there were scattered cases in which the totality of the rite pertained to the garment.[110] One of these, the Sacramentary of Gellone, was produced during the 790s in a syneisactic scriptorium (that of David and Madalberta) with a habit of making egalitarian gender statements through illuminated initials.[111]

The Gellone rite consecrated only the virgin's vestments, which became the visible sign of the humility of her heart, of her contempt for the world, of her status as closed to sexual activity, and of her salvation.[112] There was no reference in the rite to silence, obedience, meekness, claustration, or anything comparable. The consecrated virgin in her blessed vestments obtained "chaste liberty" (*casta libertas*), a recurrent theme in virtually every extant example of the rite;[113] indeed, the version in the Vatican Gelasian Sacramentary, written by the women of Chelles, placed particular emphasis on the personal liberty and charisma of the virgin.[114] Furthermore, the theological rationale for liturgically blessing the habits of female virgins was identical to that for blessing the vestments of (male) priests; both were paralleled with the vestments of Aaron the priest, blessed in Deuteronomy 29:4–9 and Leviticus 8:12, and both were, therefore, sacerdotal.[115] An example of the powerful clothing worn by consecrated virgins appeared in the Gellone initial depicting the sainted virgin Agatha: a vibrant full-length tunic boasting vertical strips of patterned fabric, plus a veil, a belt, and sleeves, all in contrasting patterns.[116] The forceful vibrancy of the vestment in the image testified to a consciousness of the power of the virgin's garment.

The consecrated women of Kitzingen would have had all these associations concerning the vestments of a virgin in their minds when viewing the tunic of the crucifixion miniature, a garment powerful enough to clothe Paul in/as Christ. They certainly recognized that there was something special about their own garments, for the only difference between the sinful *virgo* and the sinful bishop in the Latin transitional version of the *Vision of St. Paul* was that the former had put on the "vestments of salvation" (*vestimenta salutis*) and nevertheless fallen short in her behavior.[117] The decision of the miniaturist to place the physical body of Paul on the cross and then to clothe him with the tunic that had come to represent Christ's salvific triumph called attention to the transformatory power of vestments and inevitably evoked the key egalitarian Pauline citation: "For all of you who were baptized into Christ have clothed yourselves with Christ; There is neither Jew nor Greek, slave nor free, male nor female, for you are all one in Christ Jesus" (Galatians 3:27–28).

More evidence that the creator and viewers of the miniature would have known the interpretation of Romans 12:1 according to which virgins were the most perfect imitators of Christ crucified (and therefore visualized themselves in the crucifixion image) can be found in Origen's *Homilies on Numbers*, the original source of this liturgical imagery. The Greek homilies of Origen (c. 185–254) on the Book of Numbers survived only in the Latin translation produced, around 410, by Rufinus of Aquileia (c. 345–410).[118] A copy of the commentary was produced in the Anglo-Saxon cultural province during the second half of the eighth century and was certainly available at Kitzingen; one scholar even claimed that codex (Würzburg, UB M.p.th.f. 27) for the Abirhilt group because of the similarity of its initials to those in the Pauline Epistle codex and other Kitzingen manuscripts.[119] Regardless of where it was produced, the Origen manuscript was housed in the same library as the Kitzingen Paul, the Kitzingen Isidore (Würzburg UB M.p.th.q. 28b Codex 3), and the ancient copy of Jerome's *Commentary on Ecclesiastes* that served as a model for some of the Abirhilt-group manuscripts, for all four of these codices contained an identical pen trial in their margins.[120]

Origen was supported by wealthy matrons for much of his career; he had many female disciples, including students at his school in Alexandria; and he owed the propagation of much of his writing to female-staffed scriptoria, both during his lifetime and after his death.[121] It is therefore not surprising to discover a feminist tenor in his work. The key homily in the Numbers commentary was the twenty-fourth, concerning sacrifices and vows. It was Origen's creative linkage of these two themes that elevated vows of consecrated virginity to a Christlike level of sacrifice, forging the association that would be exploited in the liturgy for the consecration of a female virgin. Origen also exploited the Pauline distinction between the inner and the outer man to identify the "image of God" (the *imago Dei*) of the Book of Genesis with the interior, incorruptible, invisible, immortal, and noncorporeal *homo*, where bodily and gendered difference did not apply.[122] Origen also declared that the possession of eminent virtue (a feature of the inner man) granted a woman autonomy and liberated her from authority, including that of a husband.[123]

The most salient passages from Origen's homily for our purposes were those that glorified voluntary self-immolation in imitation of Christ and ascribed this intensity of *imitatio Christi* preeminently to the apostle Paul and to consecrated virgins who became (like Christ) both priests and victims in the sacrificial process:

> Paul offered himself as a burnt offering. . . . Listen to his words elsewhere: "For I am now being sacrificed." . . . Now a vow is when we offer something of ourselves to God. . . . In fact, the one who is called a Nazarene has made a vow of his own self to God. . . . For to offer up a son or a daughter or cattle or land, all this is outside ourselves. But to offer oneself to God, and to please him not with someone else's effort, but with one's own, this is more perfect and more excellent than all vows. For whoever does this is an "imitator of Christ" . . . has offered to God its very self, that is, its own soul. The one who lives in chastity, vows his body to God in accordance with him who said: "Now the virgin thinks about how she may be holy in body and spirit." For even the word "holy" [*sancta*] has this in view; for they are called saints who have vowed themselves to God. . . . If you are vowed to God, you must imitate the calf. . . . [124]

The apostle Paul hung visibly on the cross in the Kitzingen miniature, but the consecrated virginal audience of the image knew that they belonged there, too.

A NEW PAUL: BONIFACE AND COMPANY IN THE VALLEY OF THE MAIN

At its most superficial level, the Kitzingen crucifixion image may have lacked gendered significance, but the keys to unlock its feminist implications (the Latin transitional version of the *Visio Pauli*, the consecration rite for virgins, and Origen's twenty-fourth homily on the Book of Numbers) were passed on through discussion and teaching in the community or simply gained through experience (for instance, of consecration). The perspective gained from discussion, study, and experience would have influenced the way community members comported themselves and how they argued for their "place" in Francia with those who were not part of the community.

This same dynamic obtained in connection with Paul's companions in the boat, all of whom have been identified as men by previous commentators on the image. In fact, there were both men and women in the boat, as well there should be in the frontispiece to a copy of the letters of Paul created for a women's monastic community. The identity and significance of these figures would also have been explained by the image's creator and the community's teachers in the course of the utilization of the book, including at key points in the liturgical year.[125] As a crucifixion miniature, the image would have been most particularly used during the Easter season, and attention to the Easter liturgy provides the key to identifying the occupants of the boat, whose number has proven baffling to previous commentators.

The reading for the Friday after Easter in the Roman tradition (the practice followed in the Würzburg area during the eighth century) was 1 Peter 3:18–22, which explained that the waters of the flood prefigured the waters of baptism, with the following difference: only eight people, including Noah, listened to God's message at the time of the flood and entered the ark, which brought them to safety, whereas now many accept God's message and reach salvation through baptism into Jesus' resurrection.[126] The passengers in the boat alluded to the eight souls who survived the flood: Noah, his wife, his three sons, and his three daughters-in-law. The large figure in the center of the vessel would, for this layer of the miniature's multiple meanings, be the Risen Christ, Paul having been reduced to the ancillary role of oarsman. Whether or not the theologian-artist intended such detailed correspondences, every member of the Kitzingen community would have been familiar with the passage concerning Noah and his family that was read every year during Easter week, and they would have understood the image of the boat and its passengers in that context. Given the deeply entrenched liturgical linkage between Easter and the flood, they would automatically have understood the individuals in the boat to be both male and female, for the continuation of the human race after the recession of the waters depended on the ability of the inhabitants of the ark to reproduce.

The association with Noah's ark was an important aspect of the theological dimension of the crucifixion image, but even without it, people in the Anglo-Saxon cultural province in Francia would have imagined the passengers of any boat to include both men and women. This assumption would have been particularly strong in a place such as Kitzingen (and its dependency, nearby Ochsenfurt), where crucial ferry crossings, for which the women's houses were responsible, were located.[127] Indeed, the theologian-artist clearly had her own riverine environment in mind, for her boat was a standard river barge such as plied the Main and Rhine rivers.[128] Finally, the fact that the audience of the image was primarily women actually provided an additional rationale for the theologian-artist's decision to include the image of a boat trip as part of the composition. Everything connected with the act of pilgrimage (including metaphorical understandings of it) was almost an obsessive theme in the writings of the women of the Bonifatian syneisactic circle, whereas men never thematized the issue at all.[129] Even outside of discussions of travel and pilgrimage, women from this group expressed themselves through naval metaphors.[130] It is no wonder that a female artist, working for a female audience, constructed an image that brought together the central Christian icon of the crucifixion with a depiction of a boat trip (a combination that "has caused some consternation").[131]

When we approach the image with a full understanding of its context rather than with a set of androcentric assumptions, it becomes virtually impossible to see only males in the boat. Some bearded and bald figures were clearly male, but others (such as the third and fourth figures on the right of the central figure) not only were beardless but also had quite a bit of hair (unless we read the lines around their heads as stripes on fabric head coverings rather than as strands of hair). Furthermore, attention to all the typological reminiscences reverberating through the image leads to the following realization: just as the central figure was both Jesus and Paul, their companions were both Noah's family and Paul's followers. The most famous of Paul's followers was Thecla, his companion in mission, who was always depicted as young, almost always with an uncovered head, and frequently even naked (or nearly so).[132] The beardless figure immediately to Paul's left possessed youthful feminine features and (to judge by the single line running from the crown of her head to below her shoulders on the right side of her back) long, uncovered hair. Even if this figure was not meant to be Thecla, any relatively youthful-looking figure could be her, including ones clearly drawn as male, for the popular Thecla of legend traveled disguised as a man.[133]

Paul and Thecla were no distant exotic figures in the Anglo-Saxon cultural province in Francia; on the contrary, their modern analogues were prominent in the regional devotional landscape. Boniface of Mainz, latter-day Paul to the two Theklas of Kitzingen, consistently utilized Pauline reminiscences in his letters to his female disciples so as to style himself as heir to the apostle.[134] Of the 150 total biblical citations in Boniface's surviving letters, sixty were to the Pauline epistles alone, a staggering proportion of the whole.[135] Boniface's Pauline self-fashioning was accepted and further developed by his first biographer, Willibald of Eichstätt, who used the conceit that Boniface was a second Paul as a leitmotif of his *vita* of the saint and ended each chapter of the *vita* with a quotation from the Pauline epistles. Significantly, Willibald first introduced the theme when Boniface began to make a name for himself as a teacher of both men and women, describing how the saint's male Bible students "flocked to hear him," whereas his female Bible students ("unable continually to come to his lectures") took their classes in their own monasteries, where they "applied themselves with diligence to the study of the sacred texts."[136] Immediately thereafter, Willibald explicitly paralleled Paul with Boniface, who "followed both the example and the teaching of the Apostle of the Gentiles."[137] The fashioning of Boniface as Paul was so insistent that the chapter on the saint's ascetic practices ended: "With the Apostle of the Gentiles he could say: 'I pommel my body and subdue it . . .'" (1 Corinthians 9:27), and Boniface's return to England from an unsuccessful preaching trip to Frisia was cast as a fulfillment of "that passage in the writings of the Apostle of the Gentiles, where it says: 'For I have decided to spend the winter there'" (Titus 3:12).[138]

When, therefore, women in the Anglo-Saxon cultural province pictured Paul, they also pictured Boniface, "their" Paul, and themselves, Boniface's helpers. The women who supported Boniface surely saw in themselves not only Paul's special companion, Thecla, but also the dozens of women mentioned and/or addressed by Paul in his letters as leaders of Christian communities. Their consciousness could accurately be described as feminist, for "the cult of Saint Thecla remained closely linked with communities of women among whom Thecla's example was a source of empowerment."[139] Veneration of Thecla was strong in the Anglo-Saxon cultural province, for there were at least two important women named Thekla at Kitzingen (where the Pauline crucifixion miniature was produced) during the eighth century, and one of Leoba's disciples still bore the name in 836, when she conveyed memories of her *magistra* to Rudolf of Fulda.[140]

The Greek *Acts of Paul and Thecla* were not included in the canon of the New Testament, but—had things developed differently—they might have been, for they were considered canonical by many Christians as late as 500 and perhaps into the next century.[141] But these acts were controversial, for they depicted Thecla as a self-baptizing missionary.[142] Tertullian wrote a treatise aimed specifically against the claim that women could baptize and teach that was so clearly articulated in the Thecla stories, stories to which women in his Carthaginian circle explicitly appealed to claim those powers for themselves.[143] Later Latin Fathers such as Ambrose, Jerome, and Augustine took a subtler approach to the challenges posed by Thecla and transformed her into a paragon of virginity, suppressing her personality as the missionary companion of Paul.[144] But Thecla's fans carried on: Tertullian's treatise was transmitted only in a single thirteenth-century manuscript from Troyes, whereas a Latin version of Thecla's passion narrative was widely available from the fourth century onward. Even more important, there were areas in northern Italy and southern France where the *Acts of Paul and Thecla* were treated as canonical. Thecla also appeared in the *Martyrology of Pseudo-Jerome* with no fewer than five separate festivals.[145] And westerners visited her pilgrimage centers in the east, bringing back with them souvenirs such as gold glass, pilgrim ampullae, and oil lamps on which her exploits were depicted; examples of such souvenirs dating from the fourth through the seventh century have been found in and around the Anglo-Saxon cultural province in Francia.[146]

Not that it was necessary to travel to the east to venerate Thecla, for there was a basilica in her honor in Milan from the fifth century and, more important, a church of Thecla right next to S. Paolo fuori le mure in Rome; visitors to Rome (among whom members of the Anglo-Saxon syneisactic circles were prominent during the eighth century) could conveniently worship at the neighboring shrines of Paul and his companion Thecla.[147] The proximity of their Roman shrines also reflected the knowledge that Thecla might have been Paul's *agapeta*, to whom he referred when he wrote: "Have we not power to lead about a sister as a wife, as do other apostles, and the brethren of the Lord, and Cephas?"[148] Careful readers of Paul would never have imagined that he traveled with an all-male posse, yet another reason to recognize the gendered diversity of Paul's companions in the crucifixion miniature's boat.

Feminist scholars have demonstrated how men's greater access to positions of authority and greater control over writing and textual transmission distorted certain aspects of early Christian history and constructed a canonical New Testament that was far more gender-hierarchical than necessary.[149] No ancient books celebrating women's apostolic activity (such as the *Acts of Paul and Thecla*), containing women's words (such as collections of oracles of female prophets), or transmitting women's teachings (such as the *Gospel of Mary*) were included in the canon; instead, such texts were labeled as apocrypha or as heretical. One of the greatest casualties of the centuries of masculinist editorial interventions in the developing Christian tradition was Thecla's companion, Paul. The apostle was saddled with a reputation as a misogynist that conveniently exculpated Christians by attributing to Paul "the Jew" the antifeminist tendencies in Christian tradition.[150] As I have already noted, contemporary biblical critics have explained the antiwoman views that Paul seemed to espouse (such as the idea that women should be silent in churches) either as the misleading result of distorting punctuation introduced by editor-scribes or as outright malicious interpolations.[151]

Even without the techniques of contemporary feminist biblical criticism, women in the early Middle Ages who admired Thecla found it natural to admire Paul and managed to overlook his bizarre and inconsistent outburst on the subject of women's spiritual authority. Paul, companion of Thecla and correspondent of many female Christian leaders, was a figure of great importance to religious women in Francia, and not only because of his association with Boniface.[152] Eighth-century women east of the Middle Rhine had a very positive vision of Paul, reflected both in the crucifixion miniature and in the Latin transitional version of the visionary text associated with his name. In their own way, they practiced feminist theological hermeneutics as a way to deal with a Bible that had already been constructed as patriarchal and with a Paul who was being used against their aspirations. The women of Kitzingen produced a copy of the letters of Paul and intervened in the text by means of an elaborate frontispiece whose meanings could be coordinated with what may also have been a product of their scriptorium, namely, a new version of the *Vision of St. Paul*. Their Paul, the Paul of the visionary text and of the visionary *Eingangsbild*, authorized their lifestyle, encouraging them to run schools for boys and girls, to operate *Volkskirchen*, and to work together with men in their scriptoria. The Pauline crucifixion image, produced when the Carolingian reform was calling the syneisactism of the Anglo-Saxon cultural province into question, was a defensive attempt to shape understandings of Paul's authoritative message along gender-egalitarian lines.

CONCLUSION: GENDER, ART, AND SPIRITUALITY

Jeffrey Hamburger has brought attention to inexpert devotional pictures (including crucifixion scenes) created by Dominican nuns in Germany between the thirteenth and sixteenth centuries and explained the need for those images as a function of the nuns' inability to engage in rationalist spirituality because of their low educational level; instead, "corporeal images proved uniquely suited to the somatic character of female spirituality."[153] However, the vast gulf that separated the world of the Kitzingen theologian-artist from that of Hamburger's Dominican nuns raises grave questions about the notion of "female spirituality."

The Kitzingen crucifixion miniature was an exegetical work by a female theologian-artist. It was, ultimately, a biblical commentary, because it elucidated the central themes of Paul's teachings with the goal of furthering understanding of the text of his letters. There was a very broad spectrum of ways to interact with scripture, but all came down to the same thing: they were all ways to comment on and interpret it. Illustrating a biblical text, providing it with explanatory and supplementary pictures, was a way to practice scriptural exegesis.[154] The aristocratic women of the Anglo-Saxon cultural province in Francia produced sophisticated theological art, nourished by their study of the Bible but also by their study of other Christian texts, including the patristic commentaries I discuss in the next chapter. The women and men of these syneisactic circles shared a common set of textual referents, which informed their art and their devotional lives. For instance, when Boniface wrote to thank Abbess Eadburga for sending books to Germany, he constructed his letter out of allusions to the Pauline epistles (the subject of this chapter) and the Psalms, plus citations from the writings of Gregory the Great (the Psalms and Gregory being the subject of the next chapter).[155]

The women of Kitzingen did not labor under educational liabilities that rendered them incapable of "male spirituality" and thus doomed them to a "somatic" brand of spirituality dependent on pictures rather than words. The Kitzingen crucifixion miniature did not substitute for verbal understanding; it supplemented verbal understanding by conveying—graphically and efficiently—ideas that would have required (and in this chapter did require!) dozens of pages to set forth in words. The nuns of Kitzingen did not possess a crucifixion miniature because of their deficiencies as women, which required recourse to visuality, but because of the lucky chance that provided their community with a particular rare bird: a talented theologian-artist who could take the traditions of her community and translate them into a powerful image.

CHAPTER FIVE

"WE INTERPRET SPIRITUAL TRUTHS TO PEOPLE POSSESSED OF THE SPIRIT" (1 CORINTHIANS 2:13): STUDYING THE BIBLE WITH THE FATHERS OF THE CHURCH

WOMEN AND PATRISTIC BIBLICAL COMMENTARY

It is clear from the sophisticated work of the Kitzingen theologian-artist, whose full-page miniature functioned as a visual commentary on the Pauline epistles, that the women of the Anglo-Saxon cultural province in Francia devoted time and effort to biblical study. But the significance of the Christian Bible was far from self-evident, for "the prophets spoke in riddles, concealing their real meaning within figurative expressions like the wrappings of mysterious parcels."[1] The superficial story of a given passage could seem quite clear, but Gregory the Great, for one, insisted on the necessity to delve deeper into the hidden mystery of the text.[2] Accordingly, the libraries at Karlburg and Kitzingen contained at least two helpful patristic texts: a Gun(t)za group copy of Augustine's commentary on the gradual Psalms and an Abirhilt group copy of a portion of Gregory's commentary on the Gospels. The former text provides the Pauline title for the present chapter: "We interpret spiritual truths to people possessed of the spirit" (1 Corinthians 2:13).[3]

The two commentaries analyzed in this chapter figured among the most popular patristic works during the medieval period, in part because clerics were always obligated to preach on the Psalms and the Gospels.[4] More than four hundred integral witnesses of Gregory's homily set have survived, in addition to innumerable fragments and individual sermons copied into other collections.[5] Augustine's sermons on the Psalms constituted his most widely read work, far outpacing the rest of his oeuvre, throughout the entire Middle Ages.[6] Therefore, the two texts analyzed in this chapter evidence ideas that were widespread across Latin Europe. Nevertheless, I focus on what the texts reveal about the intellectual and spiritual lives of women in the Anglo-Saxon cultural province during the eighth century.

The two texts related to different aspects of monastic life. The impact of Gregory's Gospel homilies was most felt during the Easter season, for homilies twenty-one through twenty-six explicated the biblical portions for Eastertide feasts, whereas the impact of Augustine's Psalm commentary was pervasive, for the Psalms were the centerpiece of all monastic liturgy.[7] Considered to be the prayers that Jesus spoke through his ancestor, King David, all 150 canonical Psalms were recited in a standard weeklong cycle by the sixth century.[8] Communities gathered to psalmodize either six (every four hours) or eight (every three hours) times a day. The latter rhythm, known as the *laus perennis* (perennial praise), was used at the women's houses of Laon, Remiremont, Notre Dame de Soissons, and Fécamp.[9] The gradual Psalms were sung before matins.[10] Because only the fuller schedule (nocturns, matins, prime, secunda, terce, sexts, nones, and vespers) included matins, the fact that Karlburg produced a commentary on the gradual Psalms indicates that they likely held to the more demanding version of the liturgy of the hours.

The women of Karlburg and Kitzingen were not alone in embracing patristic writings. Fourteen percent of the named scribes in the *CLA* (a survey of Latin manuscripts older than 800) were female; all copied exclusively patristic texts.[11] Clearly, religious women found something to value in the writings of the Fathers of the Church, yet the best known scholarship on patristic views of women has painted these men as misogynists.[12] One scholar summed up the situation thus: "the paradigm of patristic thought on women was that women were not holy; they were creatures of error, of superstition, of carnal disposition—the Devil's gateway. This being so, anyone holy enough to be an exemplar of the faith could not be a woman."[13] This assertion paints with far too broad a brush. In the patristic works copied at Karlburg and Kitzingen, many women served as exemplars of the faith.

This chapter looks by turns at Augustine's holy women and at Gregory's holy women. Both Augustine and Gregory treated biblical characters and other saints as embodiments of particular virtues, normally with the additional sense that they could be role models for others. This approach was congenial to scribes during the Carolingian period, when sermons "taught a sort of 'behavioral' Christianity to their audience" by treating saints as "manifestations of the holy."[14] For all the differences between them, in these exegetical works aimed at broad popular audiences (as opposed to their treatises aimed at scholars), the two bishops were largely either indifferent to or outright positive about female embodiments of Christian virtue. And that is why the scribes of Karlburg and Kitzingen contributed to the enormous popularity of these particular patristic texts during the Middle Ages by transmitting them to future generations. Patristic misogyny, such as it was, could not propagate itself without the active collaboration of scribes.

During the first centuries of the transmission of Mediterranean Christianity to other parts of Europe (and for quite a long time thereafter), any given library contained only a fraction of the writings of any individual patristic theologian, and no community could boast a complete set of all patristic works. The very notion that certain texts by certain theologians might constitute a repository of authoritative pronouncements on matters Christian was itself only beginning to be formulated during the Carolingian period.[15] The "authority of the Fathers" was a creation of the period studied here, not a precondition of it. Scribes of the eighth and ninth centuries were engaged in the project of deciding which books to copy and which to disregard, all the while dissimulating the traces of their own intervention by presenting themselves as merely transmitting the writings of the "Fathers."[16] And different scriptoria reproduced and thus transmitted different texts.

I argue here that one factor conditioning scribal decisions was the relative degree of misogyny as opposed to gender egalitarianism present in the works available for reproduction and transmission. Few if any of the Fathers of the Church produced uniformly misogynist works, in part because devout women were part of the process by which the Fathers formulated Christian doctrine in the first place, providing a check on the extent to which patristic pronouncements could be antiwoman.[17] Even Augustine ("the man whom feminists love to hate")[18]—who avoided women as much as possible after his conversion from the world to Christianity—carried on letter exchanges with women in which he "took the women and the issues and questions contained in their letters seriously . . . [thinking] them capable not only of deep and prayerful spiritual lives but also of sound practical judgment."[19] Some of Augustine's letters to women were long and complex enough to count as theological treatises, as were many of the letters Jerome addressed to female correspondents.[20] Indeed, Jerome was specifically memorialized as a teacher of both men and women in an illumination in the First Bible of Charles the Bald (the Vivian Bible).[21] Having championed women's right to read scripture by dedicating twelve of his surviving twenty-three biblical commentaries to women, Jerome deserved this reputation.[22] His meditations usually followed the traditional format of classical textual commentary on Greek and Latin literature, involving dramatic atomization of the base text into a series of lemmata, as well as long excurses on the possible significance of individual words or phrases or on the complexities of grammar and syntax.[23] Such fragmented commentaries were reference works for scholars who pored over texts in search of deeper understanding.[24] It was shocking to act as if women needed such books.

A key result of the respect that many patristic theologians had for women's intellects, combined with the active participation of intellectual women in the Christian theological conversation, was that the "paradigm of patristic thought" concerning women was actually quite variegated, even within the corpus of an individual author. Although fallout from the garden of Eden story is often believed to have been monolithically disastrous for women, exegesis concerning Eve from patristic times through the ninth century was neither uniform nor consistently negative.[25] This permitted feminist scribes and librarians to prefer positive patristic discussions of holy women to negative patristic diatribes concerning "woman" or Eve. Thus, the early Christian "inferiority thesis" concerning women made particularly little headway in the Anglo-Saxon cultural province in Francia,[26] where feminist values guided many scribal decisions.

Intervention in chains of textual transmission was a crucial feminist strategy during the manuscript era. It may well have been widely practiced. Tertullian's infamous description of women as the "devil's gateway" (referenced by another scholar as if it were pervasive) is attested by one ninth-century parchment (Paris, BN lat. 1622) plus five fifteenth-century paper copies of a single lost exemplar; indeed, the total number of manuscripts containing any portion of Tertullian's work is eleven, eight of which are early modern humanist books.[27] Meanwhile, leading theologians continued to act, in the tradition of Jerome, as if religious women were suitable consumers of theological treatises. For instance, Bede wrote an allegorical exposition of the Canticle of Habacuc for a women's community so that the sisters could better understand the text they sang at Lauds every ferial Friday.[28] The status of women as readers of works of theology was sometimes highlighted in eighth-century Francia, where a copy of Isidore's *De fide catholica contra Judaeos* (dedicated to his sister Florentina) was introduced by a full-page miniature showing the bishop and his sister and where the text was translated into Old High German, publicizing even more widely the interest that women appropriately took in theology.[29]

Religious women needed biblical commentaries.[30] When they chose which ones to acquire, they selected those that aligned with their feminist consciousness.

AUGUSTINE'S WOMEN: "IT IS GOD WHO WORKS IN YOU" (PHILIPPIANS 2:12)[31]

Augustine's career was marked by controversy, and the winter of 406–407, when he preached his sermons on the gradual Psalms, was no exception. The homilies were often polemical, aimed at "the unpersuaded, the indifferent and the downright disobedient."[32] Augustine countered challenges from the malcontents (for instance those conventionally labeled Donatists) by harping on the unity of the church, conceptualized as a single mystical body of Christ, whose head was Jesus, whose members were all Christians, and whose common, singular, unified emotions were expressed in the Psalms.[33] Another danger also loomed: the possibility that Christians might return to traditional pagan values in the hope of stemming the tide of troubles washing over the Roman Empire. To discourage this line of reasoning, Augustine formulated an apologetic doctrine that severed the commonsense connection between worldly benefits and divine favor or between earthly disasters and divine displeasure. Instead, he insisted in his comments on the gradual Psalms that ephemeral earthly successes and failures were meaningless to Christian pilgrims, who were merely passing through on their way to abiding heavenly bliss. True *peregrini* (pilgrims) sought only to ascend to God and lost all attachment to material things.[34]

These two themes (Christian unity and Christian indifference to material conditions) dominated Augustine's sermons on the gradual Psalms. Both were politically and pastorally expedient, given the challenges of his episcopate in early fifth-century Roman Africa. Moreover, both translated perfectly into the monastic worlds of eighth-century Francia, where Augustine's Psalm commentary served as a devotional text. The theme of unity was helpful to anyone attempting to negotiate the potentially turbulent emotions of a close-knit monastic family that ate, slept, worked, and prayed as a group and whose members would have recognized themselves immediately in the image of the mystical body of Christ singing as one individual. The discourse of unity must also have been useful to religious superiors who had to motivate self-willed community members into obedience.[35] Meanwhile, the radically antimaterialist teachings of the homilies strengthened the resolve of the wealthy, aristocratic nuns who had renounced riches and comforts to enter places such as Karlburg. For instance, it must have been a genuine consolation to, and corroboration of the lifestyle choice of, childless nuns to realize that children were not much of a blessing after all, for the command "increase and multiply" (Genesis 1:22) had been spoken to lowly beasts as well as to humans.[36]

The shift in audience and context for Augustine's Psalm commentary between its origin as a series of late Roman sermons "to the people" and its Carolingian adaptation as a devotional text for elite, professed monastics also transformed the text from a monument to social hierarchy into a spiritual classic.[37] It was one thing to tell "the people" of Hippo that worldly happiness was spurious, temporal goods useless, poverty transient, misery meaningless, and oppression tolerable, and to assert that "When at Christ's command you serve a human being, it is not he whom you are serving but Christ. . . . Paul does not try to turn slaves into free men and women, but bad slaves into good slaves."[38] It was quite another for such sentiments to be pondered by aristocrats who had voluntarily chosen a life of devotion and renunciation to seek spiritual riches. Augustine's insistent evocation of unity, prohibiting "unrest" and enjoining obedience to rulers, would also be experienced quite differently when preached to peasants in Africa and when read by Frankish nuns in a royal *Eigenkloster*.[39]

But one aspect of Augustine's message of unity in renunciation remained stable: he did not differentiate between the duties and capacities of men and those of women. On the level of its dominating themes, Augustine's exposition of the gradual Psalms avoided gendered differentiation, particularly along potentially hierarchical lines. In the vast majority of cases, his supporting subthemes were equally egalitarian in terms of gender. Although he addressed his audience with the masculine "brothers," linguistic analysis has shown that he was also referring to women.[40] The universal bipartite message of communal unity and material renunciation that permeated his sermons on the gradual

Psalms certainly applied equally to male and female monastics, a feature that helped ensure the widespread popularity of the text in monastic circles.

Augustine did occasionally utilize gendered imagery in his commentary on the gradual Psalms but in a fluid way that did not consistently map onto stable male–female binaries. One such instance, from a part of the text contained in the Karlburg codex, was completely evenhanded in its approach to men and women. Augustine began his exposition of Psalm 122 with the "Head + Members" metaphor for the unity of Christians with each other and with Christ.[41] This metaphor could easily have been exploited to support hierarchical statements, for instance, by associating males with the (ruling) head and females with the (ruled) members. But Augustine made not the slightest move in the direction of mapping head and members onto men and women. Instead, his interpretation was thoroughly anchored in the larger scheme of his goals for the "Songs of Ascents," namely, to underline that the only way Christians could ascend was to "lift their eyes to him who dwells in heaven," the risen Christ, who descended in order to lift humans up with him.[42] When Augustine finally injected gender into his Head + Members metaphor, he placed males and females in both categories, some exalted to the point of identification with God but most as sinful, submissive humans receiving a merited flogging:

> We are servants (*servi* [masculine]), and we are a maid (*ancilla* [feminine]); God is both our master (*dominus*) and our mistress (*domina*). . . . There is nothing strange in our being servants, with God as our master. . . . there is nothing really incongruous about our being a maid, because we are the Church. And indeed there is not even anything strange about Christ being our mistress, because he is the power and the wisdom of God. . . . When you hear the name of Christ, lift your eyes to the hands of your master; but when you hear him called the power and the wisdom of God, lift your eyes to the hands of your mistress, because you are both a servant, being his people, and also a maid, being the Church.[43]

Elsewhere in the text, Augustine did locate femaleness only on the human side of the God–human divide, in such a way as to both underline the dependency of humans and construct female figures as particularly dependent. He wrote, in his commentary on Psalm 131: ". . . the whole Church is one single widow, whether in men or in women, in those who are married, in the young or the old, or in virgins: the whole Church is one single widow, left alone in this world, insofar as she is conscious of her desolation and acknowledges her widowed state . . . let your place be among the members of the widow; look for help in God alone."[44] In the next sermon, only the laity (rather than the entire church) was gendered female, as those whose "business is in the world, a world continually revolving like a millstone."[45] Yet these final expositions were omitted from the Karlburg copy, an example of the sorts of targeted editorial excisions that could supplement larger feminist decisions about which texts to reproduce at all.

I approach the question of Augustine and women now from the angle of his views on saints, for the individual, named women—as opposed to the symbolic women—who appeared in his commentary were almost exclusively saints. The bishop of Hippo's homiletic treatment of male and female saints was entirely evenhanded, and here, too, his message was universal for all Christians. The women of the Anglo-Saxon cultural province in Francia (like the women of Chelles) must have seen the text in this light and therefore considered it worthy to transmit to future generations.

Like the other aspects of Augustine's thought described here, his ideas about saints grew out of the pastoral challenges he faced, in this instance the fact that the gulf between the ascetic elite and the rank and file had halted the Christianization process, for average people felt the challenges of a Christian lifestyle were insurmountable.[46] To make Christian achievement appear doable for all, Augustine taught that success in such endeavors was a result of the actions of Christ in the struggling human, rather than of any special abilities on the part of the human being in question, for "there was no effort, no matter how humble, that did not depend as absolutely on the free gift of God's grace as did the most spectacular manifestation of charisma."[47] To quote Augustine's comment on Psalm 129: "Nowhere is there a pure heart that can depend on its own righteousness. . . . let the hearts of all of us rely rather on the mercy of God."[48] The utter dependency of humanity on God was just one of the many ideas that Augustine derived from Paul, who wrote in Philippians 2:12 (or 2:13), "it is God who works in you."[49]

Augustine applied his theology of grace and human dependency equally to males and females and likewise to male and female saints.[50] Augustine has not, however, always been seen in this light; indeed, he has been accused of deep-seated misogyny.[51] In the particular sphere of the bishop's treatment of female saints, the tendency has been to see his "celebrations" of their fortitude as left-handed compliments. For instance, a selection of readings intended to introduce students to saint veneration practices included one of Augustine's sermons for the feast of Sts. Perpetua and Felicitas, martyred in nearby Carthage in 203.[52] The editor contrasted Augustine's comments on Perpetua with the saint's first-person descriptions of the martyrdom of her companions and of her own preparations to enter the arena, all of which featured robust images of heroic women. Unsurprisingly, given his theology, Augustine emphasized the power of God manifest in Perpetua's actions, rather than dwelling on her personal heroism. Yet the editor failed to mention the broader explanatory context of Augustine's anthropology in her elucidation of the selected reading and instead ascribed the sermon's deflation of Perpetua entirely to Augustine's desire to counter any uppity tendencies among women. Yet, when Augustine explained that Christians celebrated the women who were martyred at Carthage in 203 "because the weakness of women more marvelously did vanquish the ancient Enemy," he merely referenced the universally accepted notion that women were physically weaker than men and therefore less likely to be able to undertake gladiator-like combat in a Roman arena without some additional inspiration.[53] This was not tantamount to domesticating Perpetua and was likely not perceived as a negative comment by his audience.

Some interpreters might insist that the "weakness of women" trope in Augustine's homily for the feast of Perpetua did constitute a limiting swipe at the virtue of female saints and, by extension, a hierarchically gendered perspective on saintly heroism.[54] If so, then it is all the more significant that the treatment of female saints in Augustine's commentary on the *Song of Ascents*—namely, that portion of his oeuvre that was transmitted by the women of Karlburg—did not participate in the discourse of gendered weakness. When he celebrated the heroics of a female martyr in those homiletic commentaries, as he did in his sermon on Psalm 120, preached on the feast of St. Crispina,[55] he underlined how God helped her withstand her torments by enabling her to overcome the enfeebling effects of a pampered, upper-class lifestyle, more than any disabilities associated with biological sex:

> The persecutors. . . . unleashed their savagery against a rich woman, delicately nurtured, but she was strong, because the Lord was for her a better defense than the hand of her right hand, and he was guarding her. . . . she was extremely famous, of noble stock, and very wealthy. . . . Had the persecutor power to do anything, even against so delicate a woman? She was of the weaker sex, perhaps enfeebled by riches and quite frail in body in consequence of the life to which she had been accustomed. But what did all this signify, compared with the bridegroom whose left hand was beneath her head, whose right hand was embracing her?[56]

In the commentary just quoted, Augustine illustrated humanity's utter dependence on God through the example of a woman; elsewhere, he illustrated this same fundamental point through the example of male martyrs such as Vincent.[57] Even Paul owed everything to God. Indeed, God's decision to elect Paul, an undeserving persecutor, was—according to Augustine's comment on Psalm 130—motivated by the desire "to demonstrate that the gifts were from him, not derived from any human source."[58] Augustine's deflation of Paul was accompanied by similar points concerning the rest of the apostles and, in another sermon, concerning Stephen.[59] That Augustine's theology of grace over merit was both central to his teachings and void of gendered implications was clear to the women of Karlburg, whose copy of the homilies on the *Song of Ascents* pegged the comment on Psalm 123 as the centerpiece of the codex, through the elaborately decorated word "Bene" with which it opened.[60] This sermon contained the most emphatic, general statements of the theme in the entire collection, such as: "It is quite plain that you yourself are not the victor—only he is, who dwells in you . . . unless he who first of all conquered on your behalf is in you now, you will be overcome" and "you must never think you can achieve this by your own strength."[61]

Exceptionally, the theme of divine dependency did not appear in Augustine's explanation of Psalm 127, where he praised St. Felix of Nola as one who "had the strength to spurn the world. . . . [who] turned away from present joys. . . . [who] won the prize of eternal life . . . because he set his heart on these [eternal] things."[62] Clearly, it was tempting to attribute successes to human agency. Augustine's comment on Psalm 137, not part of the *Song of Ascents*, credited Crispina with similar resolve, speaking of the saint as if she personally deserved credit for her heroic choices, yet, at the last minute, the bishop of Hippo caught himself and tacked on the Pauline citation: " 'By grace you have been saved, through faith, and this is not your own doing but the grace of God' " (Ephesians 2:8).[63]

Consciously and deliberately, Augustine committed himself to "the somber view on human nature which he came to see in St. Paul's teachings."[64] His influence has long been "associated with the sad abandonment of a classical view of the human capacity for self-improvement."[65] But the triumph of Augustinianism should not be exaggerated.[66] The cult of the saints created an involuntary, almost magnetic, attraction to Pelagian ideas concerning human free will; most authors regularly succumbed to the lure of Pelagius's optimistic faith in human ability in narrating the deeds of their favorite holy men and women, whereas Augustine's steely resolve permitted only rare lapses in this regard. Pelagian ideas remained current in the Anglo-Saxon cultural province in Francia, for instance, in the many passion narratives copied at Karlburg and Kitzingen and discussed in chapter 6. The women of this region were well provided with images of powerful heroines and heroes, despite the strict demands of Augustinian orthodoxy as preached in the expositions of the Psalms. But whether they were being somberly Augustinian or tantalizingly Pelagian, the women of Karlburg and Kitzingen judged both male and female saints by a single gender-neutral standard.

"Augustine's Women" in the gradual Psalms also included a handful of biblical figures, such as when he addressed the fall, arguably the biblical episode that has been, historically speaking, most vulnerable to misogynistic interpretations. Yet, Augustine's musings on the tragedy in the garden of Eden steered clear of any antiwoman tendencies; this may not hold true across his vast oeuvre, but it was a feature of his homilies on the gradual Psalms that helps explain the willingness of the women of Karlburg to propagate the text.

Far from blaming Eve for the fall, Augustine's first two discussions of the Genesis story did not mention her at all. His comment on Psalm 121 explicated the philosophical basis of the theory of original sin, namely, a Neoplatonic reading of the naming of God as "I AM WHO AM" (Exodus 3:13): only God was absolute Being and thus the only possible source of lasting joy for humans.[67] The first falling away from Being occurred when the proud angel decided to trust in himself instead, leading to his own expulsion from paradise; then, out of envy, he dragged "homo" (a grammatically masculine noun meaning "mankind" or "humanity") down with him.[68] Augustine's second treatment of the fall concentrated on correcting the potential misapprehension of human blamelessness that might have emerged from the homily on Psalm 121. In his exposition of Psalm 122, Augustine insisted that (ever since the fall) humans were "rightly scourged" and "merited a beating."[69] This time, Augustine gave sinful humanity a name: "Adam," glossed as the *genus humanum*" (human race).[70]

Anyone attending Augustine's sermon series or reading through the written expositions would have encountered a woman, Crispina, as an exemplar of Christian heroism on the ascending path to God (albeit with God's help) and would have found the name associated with the male half of the primordial couple, namely, Adam, highlighted as the source of sin and scourges, before that reader or listener encountered a single word about Eve, hardly what one would expect from a stereotypically "misogynistic" patristic text. When he did finally discuss Eve, it was only in a positive manner, as the type of the church, created from the first Adam's side as he slept, just as the church would be created from the second Adam's side as he hung dead on the cross; furthermore, Eve, like the church, was fruitful and produced offspring.[71] Moreover, Augustine's first and fullest treatment of Eve (in his comment on Psalm 126) was permeated by an (uncharacteristically joyful) optimism concerning the ease with which a human soul could ascend to God through the simple measure of humbling itself as Jesus humbled himself.[72] The appearance of fecund Eve, mother of all humanity and type of Mother Church, in this context was uplifting. The implications of this good news were recognized in the Anglo-Saxon cultural province, where both local copies of the text exclaimed (uniquely) "amen allelulia!" at the end of the homily.[73]

Augustine's fourth discussion of the fall in the commentary on the *Song of Ascents* reverted to the practice of mentioning only Adam, and not Eve, and also introduced another female biblical figure, the woman with the alabaster jar who anointed Jesus soon before the crucifixion. There were four different versions of this story, one in each of the four canonical Gospels; Augustine took his details from the version of the event in the Gospel according to Luke, in which a sinful woman visited Jesus in the house of a Pharisee and there washed his feet with her tears, dried them with her hair, and anointed them with ointment, all to the approval of Jesus but to the chagrin of his Pharisee host (Luke 7:36–50).[74]

The story of the woman with the alabaster jar has been called "the most startling gender inversion in the gospels" for its depiction of a woman performing a priestly act on a male body.[75] It could easily be activated for feminist purposes, as it was in the Kitzingen "Deus per angelum" *libellus*, discussed in chapter 6, and even in Gregory's homilies on the Gospels discussed later in this chapter. Augustine did not exploit the story for feminist purposes; indeed, among the key battles of his lifetime, we may number invalidating women's Christian ministries and delegitimizing the many wealthy matrons who supported Pelagian and Donatist ideas.[76] But he did not fight those battles in his commentary on the gradual Psalms. Instead, Augustine utilized the story to criticize Jews for being like the Pharisee, who thought Jesus should have pushed the sinful (and therefore unclean) woman away from himself, for the Pharisee could understand purity only in a carnal sense and failed to see the inner purity of the woman's heart.[77] Just as Eve was a type of the church, the woman with the alabaster jar symbolized the potential for all of sinful humanity to find redemption in the wake of the fall. Once again, however, that fall was described without any reference to Eve; it was Adam who fell, "and Adam is all of us."[78]

The extent to which Adam truly was "all of us" goes to the heart of "the woman question" in Augustine.[79] Augustine articulated his views on the *imago Dei* (image of God) most fully in *On the Trinity*, the first book deliberately acquired for the Würzburg cathedral library by Bishop Burkhard, from the women's monastery at Chelles.[80] In this work, the bishop of Hippo accorded women full *imago Dei* status, as the image of the Trinitarian God, in that "part" of humans where there is no sex ("ubi sexus nullus est"), namely, the mind; there, in the tripartite, interior human soul (consisting of memory, intelligence, and will) both male and female *homines* reflected the Trinity.[81] Insofar as the spiritual realm was what mattered to Augustine, women were made in the image of God in every way that counted.[82] However, some scholars have emphasized that, for Augustine, woman in her bodily, sexual, and social nature was still a lesser creature and have insisted that his grudging recognition of women's spiritual status had no impact on their subordination in the temporal world.[83] This may well have been true in fifth-century Hippo.

However, women were not thoroughly subordinated in the Anglo-Saxon cultural province in Francia, the specific context in which Augustine's works (*On the Trinity* and his comments on the *Song of Ascents*) were read and understood. Furthermore, none of the other writings of Augustine that were necessary to activate (through intertextuality) the potentially subordinationist implications of his anthropology of the *imago* (such as *City of God* and *On the Literal Meaning of Genesis*) was available in the region to affect how *On the Trinity* was interpreted. In the absence of such promptings, there is no reason to believe that the women of Karlburg read the veil in the negative way required to make it a symbol of female concupiscence.[84] Quite the opposite, in fact, for (as we saw in the previous chapter) the garments worn by consecrated women in mid-eighth-century Francia were more likely to be understood as priestly than as punitive.[85] Therefore, when Augustine mentioned, in his homily on Psalm 129, that the *imago Dei* had been stamped upon "homo," readers at Karlburg must have understood him as did his most recent English translator, who rendered the passage in accordance with the spiritually egalitarian anthropology set out in *On the Trinity*:

> Our soul groans until it reaches him, until the image of God stamped upon
> human beings is released by God himself. In these deep places God's image,
> imprinted upon men and women at their creation, is so roughly tossed

about and worn away by the onslaughts of the waves that, unless it is rescued by God and renewed and restored by him, it remains sunk in the depths forever, because though men and women were able to effect their own downfall, they cannot bring about their own resurrection.[86]

Nothing suggests that the women of the Anglo-Saxon cultural province in Francia would ever have considered themselves not covered by the term *homo* or that they would have imposed a misogynistic perspective on a nongendered statement.

Even the classic piece of evidence for doubting inclusive understandings of "homo,"namely, the famous debate at the Council of Mâcon (585) concerning whether the category "homo" included women, did not support such a move.[87] Usually treated as a scandalous sign that sexist Christian ecclesiastics did not view women as humans fully in the image of God, the episode has been reconceptualized as a legal discussion designed to prevent women from exploiting a technical loophole by claiming that they were not covered by the term "homo."[88] More important, the resolution at Mâcon was that "homo" (human being) did cover both "vires" (men) and "mulieres" (women). The women of Karlburg surely thought, with Augustine, that Adam was "all of us."[89]

Augustine wrote many misogynistic things, leading one eminent specialist on gender and Christianity to believe that Augustine's women did not share fully in the image of God, in part because there could be nothing feminine in Augustine's God: "it is inconceivable to think of God as in any way feminine. God is wholly masculine-spiritual."[90] But Augustine also wrote many nonmisogynist things, nor did he express misogynist ideas in all of his works; some of his writings could even be used to support a feminist view of God and of humanity. The chastising God of Augustine's commentary on Psalm 122, who was both *dominus* and *domina* (discussed earlier), was one of many maternal and feminine images that the bishop of Hippo—in keeping with his Neoplatonic view of God as immaterial, "which virtually mandate[d] gender instability"—used for God and for Christ.[91] Augustine's homily series on the *Song of Ascents* was far more positive than negative in terms of women and gender; where it was not positive, as in the final sermon (on Psalm 133), it was edited, both at Karlburg and at Chelles.[92] Neatly pruned, Augustine's comment on the gradual Psalms was a text that female intellectuals were happy to transmit. They were part of the movement that made this particular work of Augustine his most popular in medieval Europe and thus part of the movement that created a monastic landscape in which women could thrive as intellectual and spiritual human beings.

GREGORY'S WOMEN: "DOERS OF THE LAW WHO WILL BE JUSTIFIED" (ROMANS 2:13)[93]

The other patristic text that was certainly transmitted by women in the Anglo-Saxon cultural province was the second set of Gregory the Great's homilies on the Gospels. By Gregory's pontificate, most of the readings (pericopes) used in the Roman liturgy were established by tradition.[94] Gregory therefore commented on the gospel texts that were read on predetermined days according to the custom of his church.[95] Most of the pericopes used by Gregory appeared in the celebrated *Comes romanus wirziburgensis* (Würzburg, UB M.p.th.f. 62), a guide to the biblical readings for the liturgy of the mass as they stood in Rome during the seventh century. This particular codex was produced before the middle of the eighth century in England, where it was believed still to reflect current practice, and was passed on to the Würzburg cathedral, thus (unwittingly) introducing a liturgical practice already outmoded in Rome.[96] Gregory's Gospel homilies were accorded extraordinary respect by Carolingian ecclesiastics but must have been particularly enthusiastically embraced in the Würzburg area, where they were keyed to the very readings in use locally.[97]

Female figures played prominent roles in many of the Roman Gospel pericopes, so Gregory's sermons provide rich material for a gendered analysis of his exegetical techniques. He did not work systematically through literal, moral/tropological, typological, and anagogical meanings, but found "a whole spectrum of spiritual or 'mystical' meanings symbolized by the literal details of the story."[98] Yet even the most "literal" exegesis reaccentuated scripture to serve the exegete's own agenda.[99] Moreover, Gregory, having once embarked on the exegetical journey toward spiritual or moral significance, pursued his interpretations with "an unlimited freedom from textual restraint."[100] His search for spiritual significance was so wide-ranging that his thought reflected the "intrinsic pluri-semantic potential" of scripture itself.[101] This imaginative, unconstrained approach to biblical exegesis was also opportunistic: Gregory seized on every chance to fight his various ongoing battles, none of which—significantly—were with women, either as individuals or as a group. Like Boniface, Gregory had (and was known to have had) many close female friends and associates, particularly during his time in Constantinople.[102] It should not be surprising to discover that Gregory took some solidly feminist positions, rendering his work congenial to female intellectuals and scribes.

A chasm lay between the theological fundamentals of Augustine and those of Gregory, and it was precisely because of the way he departed from his eminent predecessor that the bishop of Rome could articulate overtly feminist stances, something that was almost logically impossible (not to mention personally difficult) for Augustine. The bishop of Hippo systematically deflated the biblical figures and postbiblical saints about whom he preached, whether male or female, attributing their successes to God's grace. In contrast, Gregory built up his holy heroes and heroines, praising their works, their ascetic practices, in short, their human efforts.[103] He exhorted his audience to "live in a way that we may deserve to come to the eternal feast in heaven" for "faith without works is dead" (James 2:26) and urged his listeners to embrace ascetic deprivations in imitation of Christ, on the grounds that it was "not enough to receive the sacraments of our Redeemer . . . we need to combine this communion with good works."[104] Gregory did not completely reject the "orthodox" understanding of human dependency upon divine grace; for instance, his long sermon for the Sunday of Pentecost (on John 14:23–31) celebrated the ways that the Holy Spirit fortified human beings.[105] But the fine calibrations of theological caution rarely made an appearance in the Gospel homilies, where the pope who believed that "[s]ometimes saints achieve wonders on their own merit and by their own will" took center stage.[106] This perspective opened the door for the celebration of exemplary holy women (and holy men).

Unlike Augustine, Gregory consistently praised his human role models without recourse to modifying comments concerning their receipt of support from God. Even Paul was pressed into service as a preacher of works such as hospitality, for instance, in Homily 23 (on Luke 24:13–35), where Gregory quoted Romans 2:13, "It is not the hearers of the Law who are righteous in the sight of God, but the doers of the Law who will be justified."[107] The ranks of Gregory's exemplary "doers of the Law" included women, holy figures of the past who functioned as models for present behavior.[108] However, Gregory invoked female exemplars only in limited circumstances. There was a pattern to his decisions concerning when to develop, and when to ignore, the feminist opportunities inherent in the established Roman pericopes: the feasts that drew the largest crowds were exploited for his own institutional benefit, whereas those that attracted fewer worshippers were subject to a wide spectrum of arguments, including feminist ones.[109]

For instance, Homily 23, concerning the meeting of the disciples with the risen Christ on the road to Emmaus, was delivered on the Tuesday after Easter, a weekday when people were on their way to work, leaving time for only a few hurried words from the pope encouraging the small group of mass attendees to engage in charitable works.[110] This excellent sentiment was of little direct benefit to the papacy. The original impact of Gregory's quick sermon for the Tuesday after Easter was presumably modest, compared with the impact of Homily 21, on Mark 16:1–7, the Easter Sunday reading, delivered in 591 before the largest audience any sermonizer could expect to address within the regular annual liturgical cycle.[111]

The Easter Sunday Gospel pericope described how Mary Magdalen, Mary the mother of James, and Salome came to Christ's tomb to anoint his body, learned of his resurrection from an angel, and then were instructed by the angel to inform Peter and the other disciples of the event. Gregory's exegesis effectively disappeared the three women: "For in our creator's resurrection we discover his servants, the angels, to be our fellow-citizens."[112] In this summary formulation of what happened at the tomb, "we," God, and the angels were present; the holy women who actually met the angel according to the historical level of the pericope were obliterated. Having disappeared the women, Gregory instead underlined the angel's individual naming of Peter—according to the historical level of the pericope—as a prefiguration of the authoritative role of Peter (whose successors the bishops of Rome claimed to be) in the Church.[113] Gregory was not single-minded in the aggrandizement of his see; he also made appropriate theological points concerning the crucifixion and the resurrection, and he offered standard bromides such as "Let us cross over from vices to virtues."[114] But his invocation of biblical genealogical exemplarity on the highest of all Christian holidays was for his own institutional benefit, ignoring the women who could have been foregrounded. Gregory similarly disappeared Mary Magdalen from his homily on John 20:1–9 for the Saturday after Easter. The pericope described how Mary, having found Christ's tomb empty, subsequently brought Peter and John to the spot. Gregory's sermon, which could have lingered on Mary as the first to discover the resurrection, instead developed the theme of the race to the tomb between Peter and John as a device to criticize Jews. In Gregory's imaginative interpretation, John represented the Synagogue, which "came first to the tomb, but did not go in. . . . the Synagogue knew the meaning of sacred Scripture, and yet held back from entering into faith."[115]

The majority of both local Romans and visiting pilgrims could hear only a portion of Gregory's sermon series, depending on their life circumstances.[116] Knowing this, Gregory turned important preaching days to the advantage of the male clerical elite. Thus, the anti-Synagogue thrust of his homily for the Saturday after Easter gave way, in the culminating paragraphs, to a discussion of the special status of those clerics who managed to tame the flow of their own sexual desire and therefore deserved to preach sexual uprightness to others.[117] On Ascension Day, Gregory praised the slow belief of the male disciple Thomas (over the more ready faith of Mary Magdalen) as an example of the process leading to a certain and perfect faith.[118] On the Thursday after Easter, Gregory used Christ's appearance before the (male) disciples by the Sea of Tiberias to press the Petrine claims (amid an otherwise ungendered exhortation to embrace virtues and shun vices).[119] But the high point in Gregory's battling for clerical position came in Homily 26 for the octave of Easter, where his discussion of doubting Thomas (John 20:19–31) suddenly mutated into a pointed assertion of the authority of the bishop (for instance, "whether the bishop condemns justly or unjustly, let the flock still respect and fear his judgment").[120]

However, centuries after Gregory delivered his sermons to a live audience in Rome, their status had been transformed to that of a literary text. Fine calibrations of delivery date became irrelevant to their reception. The performative difference between the inflation of Peter on a well-attended day and the inflation of a female figure on a poorly attended day lost its edge in an eighth-century scriptorium or library; both texts carried equal weight for readers who encountered the text as a series of written homilies, all of which were equally and always available. The sermons in which Gregory did not disappear the women correspondingly gained in importance over time.

The most beloved sermon in Würzburg, UB M.p.th.f. 45, measured by the response it elicited from female readers, was Homily 25 (on folios 13r–18r), a sermon on the "Noli me tangere" pericope (John 20:11–18) in which Mary Magdalen encountered the risen Christ.[121] The pericope was assigned to the Friday after Easter, a day of mid-level importance in the liturgical year, likely to attract a fair number of average Christians but not the huge crowds of Easter Sunday.[122] (Not incidentally, the epistle reading for this day was one of the major sources of inspiration for the Kitzingen crucifixion miniature.)[123] Whereas on Easter Sunday, Gregory had disappeared the women at Christ's tomb, on the fifth day after Easter, he centered his exegesis precisely around the Magdalen, arousing the enthusiasm of the women who produced and utilized the manuscript: they marked his fulsome praise of Mary with an Andrew cross (fol. 13v) and a large, thick marginal cross (fol. 14v); they overlaid the text with glosses (Latin and vernacular, marginal and interlinear, dry point and wet ink, both red and black); and they highlighted (far beyond any other sermon in the codex) the portion of the homily in which the Magdalen was trumpeted as the ideal exemplar for all humans by coloring every single sentence initial with an eye-catching hue (fols. 17r–17v).[124] The pièce de résistance, however, was the late eighth- or early ninth-century red ink line drawing that appeared in the margin by the section of the homily in which Gregory discussed Mary's Christ-given role as announcer of the resurrection to the apostles: a woman's head, in profile, with an open mouth, certainly speaking, and possibly preaching (folio 16r).[125] Here a reader memorialized a familiar sight in the Anglo-Saxon cultural province.[126]

Mary Magdalen stood front and center among the female "doers of the law" who would be justified in Gregory's eyes. But she also stimulated some feminist argumentation on the part of the respected pope. The "Noli me tangere" episode, in which Christ commanded Mary Magdalen not to touch him, could be exploited by misogynists to support the theory of the ritual impurity of women. Gregory explicitly argued against such an interpretation:

> But her Master said to her, "Do not touch me." Now this was not because the Lord, after his resurrection, in any way rejected the touch of women. This can be seen when scripture says, concerning the two women who came together to his tomb, "They approached and grasped his feet." No, the real reason why he was not to be touched is given when the text continues, "For I have not yet ascended to my Father."[127]

Gregory went on to explain that only those people who had accepted the Nicene Christology, according to which the Son was the full equal of the Father (that is, had risen to his level), would be able to reach God. He skillfully turned a passage that could have been used to disadvantage women into a critique of Arian (or adoptionist) Christology, while advancing his own position on the topic of ritual purity, a stance he would articulate most forcefully in his *Responsiones* to Augustine of Canterbury (601).[128]

Gregory's correspondence with Augustine of Canterbury, whom he had sent to England to convert the population to Roman Christianity, was extremely well known and respected in the Anglo-Saxon cultural province; in fact, Boniface had specifically sought—and presumably acquired—a copy of the *Responsiones*.[129] Gregory's interpretation of the "Noli me tangere" Gospel reading would have been understood in the mutually reinforcing context of his arguments in the *Responsiones*, in which he argued for a spiritual interpretation of biblical purity regulations. Some people in the Latin west (including the British Isles) were receptive to ancient Hebraic ideas of pollution through sex, menstruation, and childbirth, as measured by the number of penitentials that treated menstruating or recently delivered women as "dangers" to ritual purity.[130] Gregory the Great specifically argued against this perspective in his *Responsiones*, insisting (for instance) that a menstruating woman should not be forbidden to take communion or enter a church.[131] It could not possibly be licit, he asserted, to prohibit menstruating women from entering a church and receiving communion, when Jesus himself had touched a woman suffering from a flux of blood (referring to the Gospel story at the core of the Basel "blood charm" accompanying the Kitzingen library catalogue).[132] He went on to counter a whole range of prohibitions born of pollution anxiety, inviting men who had had sex with their wives or nocturnal emissions to take communion, make confession, and celebrate the mass; inviting pregnant women to be baptized; and inviting new mothers to attend church. Gregory also bluntly insisted that to oppose such practices was "extremely stupid."[133]

Later scribes who shared Gregory's views on purity hit on the strategy of including a copy of his respected *Responsiones* in penitential collections and in compilations of canon law to mitigate or even invalidate the strictures of other texts in the collections, texts that were frequently either anonymous or attributed to far less prominent people than the beloved pope.[134] For instance, the Gregorian text traveled regularly with the anonymous canon law collection known as the *Vetus Gallica*.[135] This pattern of transmission of the *Libellus Responsionum* tempered strict ritual purity stances and created room for a diversity of practices based on personal, local, or regional preference.[136] The penitential collection compiled at Karlburg enthusiastically utilized Gregory's authoritative *Responsiones* as a counterweight to texts that participated in the misogynistic discourse of female ritual impurity, such as the prohibition in the *Discipulus Umbrensium* version of the Penitential of Theodore against lay or consecrated women entering a church and/or taking communion when menstruating[137] and the requirement in the same penitential that all new mothers undergo a three-month period of postpartum purgation.[138]

The scribes of at least twelve of the twenty-five known medieval manuscripts containing the *Discipulus Umbrensium* version of Theodore's penitential chose to offset it by including complete copies of Gregory's *libellus*.[139] The emphatic Karlburg scribe of the Vienna collection included two copies of the latter text (first in the form of the epilogue to the *Capitula Iudiciorum* penitential and then as an integral whole), all prefaced by titles and a table of contents, enabling her to repeat four separate times, within a span of fourteen folios, Gregory's key arguments against the ritual impurity of women.[140] She also designed the folios featuring the pope's writings so as to render them immediately visible to anyone leafing through the book: she introduced the opinions of "blessed pope Gregory" in the *Capitula Iudiciorum* appendix (Vienna, ÖNB 2223, folios 41r–41v) with multiple rubricated titles (in one case running to five lines), a table of contents, and an elaborate, colorful decorated initial (by far the main initial in the entire codex). Rubricated titles and multicolored decorated initials recurred throughout the set of antipollution-anxiety selections, lending added visibility to Gregory's jabs at proponents of ritual purity, such as when he labeled their views "extremely stupid" (a characterization our scribe was able to include a second time by quoting the relevant sentence from the *libellus* in her epilogue to the *Capitula Iudiciorum*).[141] The titles to her second iteration of Gregory's views on ritual purity called him "holy" or "saint" ("sanctus") Gregory (Vienna ÖNB 2223, fol. 44r), further authorizing his views.

Judging by the large number of marginal crosses and other marks of reading on the Gregory folios in the Karlburg penitential codex, plus their particularly dirty and beat-up condition, the scribe's strategy to call attention to the pope's humanitarian approach worked. She was aided by the fact that veneration of Gregory reached its historical apogee in Anglo-Saxon circles during the eighth century, when his status was comparable to that of Augustine and Jerome.[142] She took advantage of his reputation to justify an interpolation into the *Capitula Iudiciorum*, tempering that penitential's antimenses view ("neither consecrated women nor laywomen should enter a church or take communion during the time of menstruation, but should they presume to do so, let them do three weeks penance") by immediately adding: "But the blessed Roman pope Gregory conceded what is here prohibited to both kinds of women."[143] The scribe also placed a cross in the margin to call particular attention to Gregory's assertion, in the *Responsiones* proper, that menstruation was perfectly natural and that therefore menstruating women should be permitted to enter a church and take communion, but a later commentator, using a different (black) ink, eventually insisted "this is not valid."[144]

It was within this broader context of debate over women and pollution that Gregory's Homily 25 on Mary Magdalen was received and transmitted at Kitzingen. Yet, the particular issue of ritual purity was not an isolated case, for Gregory's writings were utilized during the Carolingian period to justify a whole range of egalitarian ideas.[145] For instance, his exegesis of Mary Magdalen in the "Noli me tangere" pericope (John 20:11–18), in which Mary brought news of the resurrection to the male disciples, contained typological elements that could be developed into a full-fledged argument concerning the reversal of the curse of Eve:

The sin of humankind was taken away in the same kind of circumstances from which it came. For, in Paradise, a woman brought death to a man; here, however, out of a tomb, a woman announces life to many men. She repeated to them the words of the one who gave her life, whereas, before, the woman had repeated the words of the death-dealing serpent. It is as if the Lord were saying to mankind, not through words but through physical circumstances, "From the same hand which previously brought you the drink of death, take now the drink of life."[146]

This theme would indeed be developed—fully, explicitly, and powerfully—in the Kitzingen *libellus*, "Deus per Angelum," analyzed in the next chapter, and would have a significant afterlife in regional thought.[147] Gregory's orientation here was consistent with his comment in the *Responsiones* that the punishment of pain in childbirth visited upon Eve was irrelevant to contemporary women.[148]

Unlike Augustine, Gregory conceptualized the achievements of women (and men) as resulting from human virtues. In Gospel Homily 25, the female Mary Magdalen became the ultimate symbol of virtue; "since she alone remained in order to continue searching, she alone then saw [Jesus]. For perseverance is the virtue underlying every good act."[149] Gregory underlined the active, voluntary achievement of the Magdalen, just as Augustine had emphasized the need for humans to rely on divine grace. Mary was the subject of the verbs of action that led her to her special position; she "was abandoning her own depraved ways" until "she found such a position of grace in his eyes, that she was the one who proclaimed his resurrection—even to the apostles."[150] Inspired by Mary, subsequent humans could likewise become the subjects of verbs of action, for "almighty God everywhere places before our eyes those whom we ought to imitate."[151] In keeping with his exaltation of a female human, Gregory ended the sermon with the feminine divine: "Return, dearest children, to the bosom of your true mother, eternal wisdom. Suckle at the generous breasts of God's mercy."[152]

Mary Magdalen was not the only female doer of the Law who would be justified in Gregory's preaching, which frequently emphasized the necessity for tearful self-sacrifice (in imitation of Christ) and purgative penitence.[153] Homily 34 (on Luke 15:1–10, concerning the "just penitent") featured a woman who was happier about finding the single coin she had lost than about the nine others she had always had with her, for "there is more joy in heaven over converted sinners than over the righteous who have stood firm" because "those who remember that they have done something forbidden . . . exercise themselves in extraordinary virtues."[154] To be safe, Gregory recommended an attitude of tearful penitence to the righteous as well, but the star of the homily was the woman who recovered her lost coin; she was also incorporated into the complex imagery of the "Deus per Angelum" *libellus* made at Kitzingen around the same time as this copy of Gregory's homilies, as was another one of the pope's female figures, the woman with the alabaster jar.[155]

The woman with the alabaster jar, whom we have already encountered in Augustine's sermon on Psalm 125, was identified by Gregory with Mary

Magdalen.[156] Her anointing of Jesus was described by all four evangelists, but only Luke's version of the story was read liturgically. Both Augustine and Gregory (in Gospel Homily 33) commented on the pericope Luke 7:36–50, the latter on an average weekday.[157] Yet the obscure circumstances of original delivery became meaningless once the homilies began to circulate as written texts. Like Homily 25 on the exemplarity of Mary Magdalen, Homily 33—another key text for feminist biblical interpretation—was decorated in the Kitzingen copy of Gregory's sermons to render the beginning and end of each sentence immediately visible to any reader.[158] And in Homily 33 (as in Homily 25), Gregory presented Mary as an active doer: she offered, she wept, she used, she found, "she converted the number of her faults into the number of virtues, so that she could serve God," she "completely burned away the rust of sin," and so forth.[159] "She came . . . she poured . . . she stood . . . she wet . . . she wiped . . . she did not cease . . . she represented us."[160] Mary stood and wept and wiped and kissed, and so should every member of Gregory's audience: "Dearly beloved, bring back to your mind's eye, bring before you the repentant sinful woman as an example for you to imitate."[161]

As we saw in connection with the crucifixion miniature in the Kitzingen Paul (the subject of chapter 4), confessional penance was a part of the devotional life of the women of that community. I argue in chapter 7 that Isidore of Seville's *Synonyms* functioned as a script for penitent community members who wished to engage in devotional monastic confession. In this context, we can understand the importance of Homilies 25 and 33, and of Mary Magdalen, in the Kitzingen copy of Gregory's Gospel commentaries: her exemplarity supported a central facet of monastic life at Kitzingen. For the women of Kitzingen, Gregory's Magdalen (in the Abirhilt group codex Würzburg, UB M.p.th.f. 45) embodied the main message of the crucifixion miniature (in the Abirhilt group codex Würzburg, UB M.p.th.f. 69) and effectively performed the penitential script of Isidore's *Synonyms* (in the Abirhilt group codex Würzburg, UB M.p.th.q. 28b). When the women of Kitzingen were not examining scripture with their minds, they were confessing their sins to God with the mouths and palates of their hearts, images used by both Augustine and Gregory.[162]

But there was more to Gregory's women than penitence. Previous scholarship has (mis)represented patristic gender ideology as identifying holy women exclusively as "fools for Christ" and "incarnations of simplicity and emotion" while reserving for males a rational, intellectual approach to religiosity.[163] As we saw earlier, on the major feast of Ascension Day, Gregory did highlight Doubting Thomas as the key exemplar of reasoned faith. But in his Gospel homilies as a whole, copied and read as a text independent of particular feasts, he exemplified this virtue more frequently through female figures. This motif was apparently noticed by the pope's fans, for all three of his earliest (eighth- and ninth-century) biographies included versions of an anecdote concerning a "doubting matron," that is, a woman who doubted the Real Presence until convinced of transubstantiation by a miracle that occurred when Gregory celebrated the mass and Christ's physical body appeared on the altar.[164] The initial articulation of this theme was owed to the anonymous nun or monk of the Northumbrian double monastery of Whitby who composed Gregory's earliest *vita* (c. 704–714); it was then picked up by Paul the Deacon (c. 750) and by John the Deacon (c. 875).[165]

Like the "doubting matron" in his biographies, female doers of the law who would be justified frequently symbolized "reason," "mind," and "spirit" in Gregory's Gospel Homilies. For instance, in Homily 32 (on Luke 9:23–27), for the feast of the male martyrs Processus and Martinianus, when there was absolutely no textual impetus from the pericope to mention women at all, Gregory introduced one: a certain very religious matron presented as a role model for his audience. The martyrs had appeared to that woman in the guise of pilgrims, demonstrating to her in a tangible way the reality of the life to come; as a result of the certain knowledge thus acquired, the matron redoubled her prayer activities. The point of the episode, according to Gregory, was that God "wanted us to know rather than to believe in the life to come."[166] Here, Gregory used a female protagonist to trumpet the (at least occasional) superiority of an intellectualized, proofs-oriented spirituality over "simple faith."

As a final example of Gregory's women, let us take the trio of Romans the pope celebrated in his last sermon, Gospel Homily 40 on Luke 16:19–31. Like most of his woman-centered discussions, it was probably originally preached on a run-of-the-mill weekday,[167] but as part of the Kitzingen codex, it could be read and contemplated at any time. The Lucan pericope concerned the rich man Abraham and the poor wounded Lazarus, but instead of developing themes related to these biblical men, Gregory focused on contemporary holy women who lived together near the Roman church of the Virgin Mary: Redempta, Romula, and a third woman whose name he didn't know. Gregory's sermon series thus culminated with an image of the eternal city hallowed by consecrated women. For Gregory, the exemplarity of Romula was that, despite suffering from paralysis, she produced a miracle through her prayers. "The damage to her body became for her a means to increase in virtue. The less strength she had for anything else, the stronger grew her attachment to the practice of prayer."[168]

Based on Gregory's *Pastoral Care* and the many letters he wrote to prominent women, Walter Wilkins painted Gregory as a pastor who sought to empower women: "[i]n a variety of places, Gregory subverts misogynistic attitudes and affirms the status of women. He does so not only by identifying with women's experience and empowering them . . . but also by affirming their competence."[169] In contrast, Carole Straw argued for a unified system structuring all of Gregory's works, a system that placed a hierarchical view of gender at the core of a fundamental set of binary oppositions, as illustrated in her "Synopsis of Oppositions in Gregory's World View" reproduced here:[170]

Nothingness	Virtue
Devil	Spirit
Sin	**Male**
Flesh	Strong
Female	Birds
Weak	Essential
Snakes	Heart
Newts	Mind
Superfluities	Wheat
Hair	Citadel
Excrement	Church
Chaff	Courtroom
Wild	Internal
Sea	Contemplative
Field	Dry
Ass	Firm
Wet	Human
Slippery	Stability
Animal	Joy
Mutability	Activity
Asleep	Warm
Dark	High
Night	Dry
Low	Light
Cold	Awake
Torpor	God
Sorrow	True Being

In keeping with this vision of Gregory as a devotee of binary oppositions, Straw declared categorically: "[b]y God's dispensation, a hierarchical order subordinate[d] barbarians to Romans, slaves to free men, women to men, and so on," yet went on to quote (with no recognition of the inconsistency) a letter of Gregory to the barbarian Queen Brunhilda of the Burgundians concerning her dominion over the subjects (many of Roman extraction) bound to her in servitude.[171] Wilkins used that same letter to show how Gregory "recognized the rational mind of woman and its ability to control the irrational flesh" and "plac[ed] within [Brunhilda's] sphere of responsibility the faith and ethics of her people, as well as the reform of the church bureaucracy."[172]

In fact, Gregory did not subscribe to an immutable binary system that mapped "flesh" onto the "female" and "mind" onto the "male"; for instance, in his treatment of the woman with the alabaster jar (Mary Magdalen) and her reluctant Pharisaic host in Homily 33, the male Pharisee symbolized the (Jewish) attachment to material goods and corporeal needs, while the female penitent symbolized the interior spiritual desires of converted gentiles who had come to know Christ. From the Pharisee, Jesus received physical food from an earthly table, "but he received internal nourishment with the woman. . . . because the Lord is fed by hearts which are not burnt by their physical desires. . . . The repentant woman gave the Lord more nourishment interiorly than the Pharisee did exteriorly."[173] Alcuin Blamires argued that Gregory used women to symbolize steadfast spirit and men to symbolize weak flesh in his *Moralia in Job*.[174] Finally, and most dramatically, no immutable binary system could coexist with the core pragmatic statement at the heart of Gregory's pastoral handbook, *Pastoral Care*: his argument that different people need to be motivated and exhorted in different ways, appropriate to their own situations.

Gregory's *Pastoral Care* was available at Kitzingen by the time the library catalogue was drawn up.[175] Although we possess the copy of the text produced during the eighth century by the women of the Bavarian house of Kochel,[176] it is impossible to identify the particular copy of the work owned by the Kitzingen community. However, a late ninth-century copy from the Würzburg cathedral scriptorium may speak to the way Gregory was understood in the Anglo-Saxon cultural province in Francia. It included a graphic, two-column vertical chart of the qualities and characteristics a pastor had to keep in mind, a chart on which maleness and femaleness utterly failed to line up in the lockstep hierarchy proposed by Straw.[177] At the top of the two columns stood the first set of variables: "Aliter namque ammonendi sunt viri, Aliter feminae" ("For men are to be admonished in one way, women in another"). But the other groups lined up in the "men" and "women" columns explicitly contradicted the placements on Straw's chart:

Men	Women
Iuvenes (Young)	Senes (Old)
Inopes (Poor)	Locupletes (Rich)
Laeti (Joyful)	Tristes (Sad)
Subditi (Subjects)	Praelati (Prelates)
Servi (Slaves)	Domini (Lords)
Benivoli (Benevolent)	Invidi (Envious)
Simplices (Simple)	Inpuri (Impure)

The crucial flaw in Straw's approach was her desire to find a homogeneous set of Gregorian teachings, a project doomed to failure when applied to a figure famous for the heterogeneity of his corpus, who avowed his willingness to change his mind.[178] Sometimes Gregory did associate a woman with flesh and a man with spirit, for instance, in his description of Eve as the flesh who felt pleasure and Adam as the spirit who consented near the end of his *Responsiones*.[179] But scattered comments did not a systematic ideology make, rendering equally difficult to sustain Blamires's contention that the transmission of the works of Gregory always constituted a contribution to a gender-egalitarian ideology. Many key features of the "case for women" as it crystallized by the twelfth century were traceable to Gregory, namely, how women had remained loyal to Jesus even when men deserted him (a fact many male biblical commentators tried to obfuscate, but Gregory frequently drove home) and the idea that anyone with talent or vocation, male or female, who could effectively control the flow of their own speech, should evangelize and preach (an asexual ruler model).[180] Nevertheless, dozens of authors over many centuries used Gregory the Great's writings on (for instance) sacred images to support virtually every position along the spectrum of iconoclastic and iconodule views, each insisting they were simply relying on Gregory.[181] His writings on women were likewise subject to interpretation. Building a feminist case involved a long, complex chain of preferential transmissions of the prelate's most evidently feminist works, combined with constant negotiation concerning their interpretation in the face of adherents of misogynist viewpoints.

CONCLUSION: THE COMPLEXITY OF PATRISTIC GENDER IDEOLOGIES

The simplistic stereotype of "patristic misogyny" is useless for grasping the nuances of ideas about women and gender in medieval Europe. A brief discussion of some patristic exegesis on the biblical figure of Job should suffice, as a final point, to reveal the nearly unfathomable complexities of the topic. Both Augustine and Gregory utilized Job to represent both negative and positive ways of thinking about women. We saw earlier in this chapter how Augustine (in a passage excised from the Karlburg copy of his Psalm commentary) utilized the Job story in a classically misogynistic way, letting Job remain male and his evil wife remain female.[182] Yet in the immediately preceding homiletic commentary, on Psalm 132, Augustine had identified his text's woman at the mill with Job to explain how both would ultimately be saved.[183] The same bifurcated treatment appeared in Gregory I's *Moralia*. There, Job was sometimes the good man beset by an unnamed wife who tempted Job "to moral weakness, weeping despair and suicide."[184] But Job's own suffering, which turned him into a Christ figure, also engendered him as feminine: Gregory's Job was "both an invincible, well-armed warrior and a sword-pierced sufferer."[185] As Ann Astell concluded concerning gender and biblical exegesis:

> *Woman* means opposite things, because "weakness" points to what is both the lowest and the highest; to the carnal sensuality of Eve, on the one hand, and the self-sacrifice of Christ, on the other. . . . the meeting of opposites in gender symbolism assumes a special force in the paradoxical language of Scripture, scriptural exegesis, and biblical imitation. United by a copulative

verb or the *id est* of an exegete, folly is wisdom; weakness, strength; death, life; the last, first; the servant, the master; and a female Job, greater than Job.[186]

The heterogeneity of the patristic corpus enabled feminist scribes to influence the developing Christian tradition by preferentially transmitting some works by certain authors, such as Gregory's *Homilies on the Gospels*, and avoiding (for instance) all the writings of Tertullian. The homiletic biblical commentaries of Augustine and Gregory that were copied by the women of Karlburg and Kitzingen were well suited to reinforce the main values of the Anglo-Saxon cultural province in Francia, including a leaning toward syneisactism and gender egalitarianism. It is regrettable that these female scribes did not do more with patristic-era theological writings; for instance, Augustine was involved in voluminous correspondences with various women, but only his side of the conversation was collected, preserved, and transmitted.[187] Perhaps they did their best, and the fault lies mainly with scholars of subsequent eras, early modern and modern. For instance, a long letter exchange between two late fourth-century Iberian women on various theological and practical topics was included in a ninth-century collection (St. Gallen, SB 190) that also preserved the unique surviving copies of similar letters by men such as Faustus of Riez and Desiderius of Cahors. The men's letters have all been carefully and repeatedly published, and thoroughly studied. Meanwhile, the letters of the women have been published (or even noticed) only once, in a little-known article whose entire "analysis" consisted of the point that a male secretary must have been involved.[188]

While the field of biblical commentary, in whatever form (epistolary, homiletic, etc.), lacks conspicuous female-authored survivals from the patristic era, there was another arena in which feminist authors and scribes made spectacular, often quite well-preserved, contributions: the production of (generally anonymous) narratives concerning saints. That supple sphere of developing Christian tradition offered almost unlimited possibilities for creativity. In many of these postbiblical and postpatristic texts, including the *passiones*, *vitae*, and snippets of homilies that fill the next chapter, active heroic women stood front and center.

CHAPTER SIX

"THE SENSUAL MAN DOES NOT PERCEIVE THOSE THINGS THAT ARE OF THE SPIRIT OF GOD" (1 CORINTHIANS 2:14): HISTORY AND THEOLOGY IN THE STORIES OF THE SAINTS

PASSIONS OF THE SAINTS IN THE ANGLO-SAXON CULTURAL PROVINCE IN FRANCIA

This chapter uses the "whole book" approach to analyze, holistically, the contents of the Karlburg apostle passionary (Würzburg, UB M.p.th.f. 78) and the Kitzingen *libellus* that I have named *"Deus per angelum"* for its opening words (Würzburg, UB M.p.th.q. 28b Codex 1).[1] Both books functioned historiographically, recounting (through a combination of texts) a particular stage in the spread of Christianity.[2] Furthermore, both constructed female figures as central to the conversion process, whether as main protagonists (as in the Kitzingen *libellus*) or as crucial supporters (as in the Karlburg passionary). The Karlburg passionary focused on a very early phase of Christianization, primarily in eastern lands, and the efforts of various apostles; the *"Deus per angelum" libellus* focused on a slightly later stage on the Italian peninsula and the efforts of various female martyrs (Cecilia, Juliana, Agnes, and Agatha).

Such stories were understood to describe real historical events, whose literal truth could often be "verified" by a visit to the grave of the saint in question. The city of Rome alone boasted dozens of such tombs, and one did not have to make the journey in person to know about the shrines, which were noted on the many pilgrim itineraries in circulation north of the Alps.[3] Closer to home, the historicity of Christian struggles with pagan Rome was demonstrated at the Mainz arena, where a chapel was used for Christian rites from the fourth to the eighth centuries. The arena was less than eighteen kilometers from Leoba's community at Schornsheim, which may have been the home base of the nursemaid of Christ ("ancella Christi") Rotsvintda named on the disk-shaped cover of a walrus ivory pyx inscribed with the beginning of the "Our Father" prayer, one of many ivory carvings found in the arena.[4]

Beyond the historicity of their surfaces, the narratives also possessed theological import for, like scripture itself, accounts of subsequent chapters of sacred history held multiple levels of meaning. The biblical Jesus was constructed in narrative form: things were narrated about Jesus, and it was narrated about Jesus, that he narrated.[5] For those with eyes to see and ears to hear, those narratives were more than stories. As the *passio* of Cecilia warned, quoting Paul, "The sensual man (*animalis homo*) does not perceive those things that are of the Spirit of God" (1 Corinthians 2:14).[6] "Animal" people did not see beyond the surface drama in a passion narrative to its theological import, but such limitations did not apply to the consecrated women of the Anglo-Saxon cultural province in Francia who, like the martyr Juliana, had "a rational soul and prudent council."[7]

There was often a substantial theological component to narratives of saints, just as there was to sermons concerning saints.[8] Take Heffernan's "theology of behavior": a hall-of-mirrors world of Christian exemplarity, where Christ, the saints, and the average Christian were interlocked in a complex communal nexus of action and imitation.[9] Passion narratives and lives of saints frequently reflected or contained theological ideas,[10] but they could also be contributions to theology in and of themselves, as in the case of Hugeburc of Heidenheim's *Vita Willibaldi et Wynnebaldi*, described by Palmer as an exegetical tool.[11] Marie Ann Mayeski has emphatically lobbied in favor of reading narratives concerning saints as theology, citing the assertion in Rudolf of Fulda's biography of Raban Maur that lives of the saints "are extensions of the revelatory narratives of Scripture and they contain genuine doctrine that must be both believed in faith and understood by theological reflection and mimetic action."[12]

The theological dimension was particularly strong in the two codices examined here. Their component parts were, for the most part, texts originally produced in circumstances of heated theological debate, perhaps even as contributions to those debates.[13] Although recent scholarship has associated the first Greek apostolic acts with female authors and/or women's oral traditions,[14] a previous stage of scholarship viewed the Greek apocryphal passions of the apostles as articulations of the doctrines of "heretical" communities such as Marcionites, Gnostics, and Manichaeans and viewed the surviving Latin versions of those texts in the Karlburg passionary as "catholic" antiheretical reworkings.[15] Though scholars have moved away from this perspective (while recognizing still that the Latin texts contained heterodox ideas),[16] what matters is that the theological content of the passion narratives was weighty enough to have given rise to such interpretations in the first place.

The women's *passiones* in the Kitzingen *libellus* belonged to a group of texts (sometimes described as "martyr romances": the "missing link" between the ancient novel and the medieval romance), penned by anonymous authors on the Italian peninsula during the fifth and sixth centuries.[17] Throughout the entire period when they were composed, the Italian peninsula was the object of fierce competition among claimants who differed on the fundamentals of Christian doctrine: "Catholic" western Roman emperors, "Catholic" eastern

Roman (Byzantine) emperors, "Arian" Ostrogoths, and "Arian" Lombards.[18] Many of the texts in the Kitzingen *libellus*, such as the selection from Cassiodorus's expurgated version of a commentary by the free-will "heretic" Pelagius, were clearly generated amid these circumstances of intense theological competition.[19] But the martyr narratives must also have been penned in part as contributions to doctrinal disputes; certainly, the author of the sixth-century pseudo-Gelasian decree, which prohibited reading *passiones* in churches to guard against heretical theological content, believed that they were.[20]

Scholars have suggested some specific theological contexts to account for the emphases of the texts. For instance, Dufourcq argued that a sixth-century resurgence of hyperascetic neo-Manichaeanism was responsible for many features of the martyr romances as a group.[21] Meanwhile, the *passio Agathae* (BHL 133) has been ascribed to Augustinian circles of African bishops exiled to Sardinia by the Vandal king Trasamondus (504–524), and the *passio Ceciliae* (BHL 1495) has likewise been attributed to an African refugee, who had fled the (Arian) Vandal kingdom for catholic Rome.[22] At the same time, the *passio Ceciliae* (like the *passio* of Agnes) has been dated to the reign of the "Arian" king of the Goths and the Romans, Theoderic the Great (493–526), whose palatine basilica in Ravenna (now S. Apollinare Nuovo) boasted a mosaic procession of martyrs including Cecilia, Agnes, and Agatha.[23] My own sense is that the influence of Pelagius was particularly marked; he was extremely popular among wealthy fifth-century matrons at Rome and elsewhere,[24] and this demographic must have been central in the development of the cults of the female martyrs commemorated in the Kitzingen *libellus*.

Indeed, the *passiones* of Cecilia, Juliana, Agnes, and Agatha all could have been written by women. There is certainly no evidence that they were written by men. Considering the criteria advanced by Janet Nelson for identifying female authorship of anonymous texts and the unrelieved prominence of women in the early history of Juliana's cult, it seems likely that at least the *passio Julianae* (BHL 4522), created somewhere in Campania (perhaps in Cumae or Naples, the centers of the saint's cult) during the tumultuous struggles of the sixth century, was written by a woman.[25] The Italian peninsula did not lack potential female authors.[26] Of the approximately 260 mentions of religious persons (cenobitic or individual) between the years 350 and 612/613, 87 were to individual women or women's communities; there were also a handful of chaste couples. Women outright dominated the statistics in the early period. By 500, there were large, documented women's monastic communities in Verona, Bologna, Turin, Rome, and Sicily, and inscriptional evidence from cemeteries suggests that in the sixth century there were women's communities attached to the Roman churches of St. Agnes, St. Cecilia in Trastevere, and St. Paul Outside the Walls (adjacent to the church of Thecla)—the last three institutions clearly being excellent candidates for authorship of some of the texts.

Late ancient martyr *passiones* advanced competing agendas. For instance, the oldest acts of Peter and the oldest acts of Paul contained overlapping episodes, yet the former was ideologically accommodating to political authorities and unfriendly toward the idea of women as leaders in Christian communities, whereas the latter was hostile toward political authorities and supportive of autonomous female leadership.[27] Insofar as all of the narratives described the progress of Christianization against enemies of that faith, they even offered models of disbelief.[28] Texts marked by the conditions of late antique controversies were then received in the eighth century by readers enmeshed in their own theological debates over icons, adoptionism, and the *filioque* clause.[29] A scholar who was baffled that he could not find evidence of those controversies in the Würzburg-area churches failed because he didn't consider looking for it in copies of passions of the saints.[30] When, for instance, in the Karlburg passionary, the apostle Thomas explicated to the assembled crowds of India the fundamentals of the Trinitarian faith, he took a stand on the question of the procession of the Holy Spirit: from the Father only, in Thomas's view, not from the Father and from the Son (*filioque*).[31] The interest of the author in doctrinal disputes over the Trinity could date the composition of the original *passio* to a number of moments, ranging from the fourth through the sixth century; its popularity in the eighth century was in part due to the continued relevance of Trinitarian disputes.

Eighth-century readers and scribes thus picked their way through a variegated theological inheritance. For example, the anonymous author of the *libellus* "*Deus per angelum*" worked from a manuscript that appears to have had virtually the same content as the current Paris, BN 10861.[32] From it, she selected texts connected with Cecilia, Juliana, Agnes, and Agatha, but she rejected passion narratives of other female saints in the same codex, such as Afra of Augsburg. The short *passio* of Afra (BHL 107b), the oldest narrative concerning a saint ever composed (c. 640) in what is now Germany, was developed during the eighth century (also in south Germany) into an elaborate narrative of the prostitute-saint's conversion and passion (BHL 108–9).[33] The eighth-century version, which appeared in the Paris manuscript, included two long debates on the theology of merit and grace; in both cases, the "bad guys" advanced the position that salvation for the egregiously sinful person was a lost cause, while the "good guys" (including Afra) advanced the position that forgiveness of sin was always possible through God's compassion (*pietas*). Clearly, theological arguments were being made in and through narratives of the saints in areas culturally and politically not far removed from the Main River valley during the period covered by this study. It is, however, quite striking that this text failed to resonate with the Kitzingen Anonyma; the *passio*'s insistent theology of grace simply did not fit well with the Anonyma's own (Pelagian) theology of merit, articulated throughout the *libellus*.

Beyond rejecting some texts and embracing others, eighth-century author-scribes such as the Kitzingen Anonyma altered and recombined the texts they selected for transmission to bring out new dimensions and, thus, did their own theological work. The scribe-authors of Karlburg and Kitzingen shaped the contents of the two collections into new wholes in support of their own gendered programs. For those goals, the martyrs were not enough. Theologically speaking, the most important figure in terms of the creation of a feminist sacred history was Mary, mother of Jesus. There was, by the eighth century, a highly developed tradition in both Greek and Latin Christianities of female orchestration of the cult of Mary as a way to justify women's real-world claims to power and influence. These female impresarios all realized "that how the Virgin was defined theologically would influence the extent and social meaning of her spiritual power."[34] The theological definitions of the Virgin in the two women's books analyzed in this chapter were about as woman-friendly as it was possible to get. As the only figure to appear in both codices, Mary's literary status matched her real-world status in a region where the majority of the women's monasteries, including Karlburg, were dedicated to her, at a time when the region's culture was being reshaped by immigrants from Anglo-Saxon England, where Mary was venerated in particularly elevated terms.[35]

THE KARLBURG APOSTOLIC PASSIONARY (WÜRZBURG UB M.P.TH.F. 78): SYNEISACTISM AND MARIAN DEVOTION

The apostles were missionaries, and their collected passionary could hardly avoid telling the story of the spread of Christianity, a story that held both historical and theological significance. The so-called Abdias appendix to the *passio* of Simon and Jude reflected consciously on its status as historical narrative, asserting that the very documentation of missionary efforts made a contribution to the progress of the faith (fol. 35r). Yet, from the very first destruction of a pagan temple by an apostle, namely, the destruction of a temple of Diana by John the Evangelist, the theological import of the events was broadcast, for the narrative self-interpreted to parallel worship of material idols to worship of the world instead of hidden spiritual reality (fol. 1r). Once John bested Diana's priest in a public display of power by calmly surviving a poisonous draft and resurrecting two poisoned corpses, all and sundry rejected the idols and embraced Christ (fols. 1v–2v), a development that any attentive reader was in a position to understand as symbolic for the rejection of materialism and the commitment to abstinence.

In connection with John the Evangelist, abstinence was primarily understood in sexual terms. John was the "virgin chosen by the Lord and beloved beyond all others,"[36] that is, the paradigmatic male virginal body to whom Jesus commended his mother, the paradigmatic female virginal body, "ut virginem virgo servaret." Knowledge of the evangelist's lack of fleshly corruption was ubiquitous in medieval Europe, propagated by the preface to his Gospel that was part and parcel of biblical manuscripts, including those available in the Anglo-Saxon cultural province in Francia.[37] We do not have a surviving Gospel book from Karlburg, but we know that John's virginal purity was recognized there, for he proclaimed to Jesus in his *passio*, "you have guarded my body from all pollution."[38]

In later medieval monasteries, paired male and female communities venerated John and Mary as a committed virginal couple whose companionship reflected the organization of the houses.[39] The presence of John's *passio* at the head of the Karlburg apostle collection shows that the function of his cult as a prop to syneisactism was already incipient in the eighth century, at least in the Anglo-Saxon cultural province; however, his female companion was not yet the Mother of God. Instead, the key dramatic episode in the *passio* of John the Evangelist concerned the saint's relationship with his beloved female follower Drusiana, who met an untimely death during John's exile to Patmos.[40] After his return, John immediately raised her from the dead so that she might see him again. Drusiana's relationship with John in the Karlburg passionary was special and affective, more so than in other versions of John's acts (including the late sixth-century Frankish *virtutes*) in which the resurrection of Drusiana by John was driven by the desires of Drusiana's husband and partner in chaste marriage, namely, Callimachus.[41]

The Karlburg *passio* thus imagined John the Evangelist, the most beloved disciple, a perfect man free from all fleshly corruption, to have been involved in a close emotional relationship with a woman, to the point that he raised her from the dead so that she could look upon him. The exemplary story of John and Drusiana authorized syneisactic practices by associating them with a man of extraordinary status. Alone among the apostles in the Karlburg passionary, John the Evangelist did not experience martyrdom or even death. Instead, his story—like that of the Virgin Mary—ended with his assumption: at the age of ninety-seven, John vanished in a great light, leaving nothing but manna behind (fol. 2v). This *transitus* (or μετάστασις) was generally understood to have been a special reward for John's extraordinary purity,[42] which was apparently not compromised by his special bond with Drusiana. Furthermore, his *passio* also functioned to elevate the self-esteem of the consecrated virgins of Karlburg, independent of syneisactic relationships, for the narrative was labeled a *passio* even though its protagonist suffered no martyrdom. Apparently, perfect virginity was the equivalent of martyrdom in the eyes of the Karlburg scribe.

John's incipient position as a poster boy for syneisactism was even clearer in the "Veri amoris" *libellus* available (albeit not necessarily produced) at Kitzingen; there his *transitus* was used to introduce stories of saints that were overwhelmingly syneisactic in their teaching.[43] But the theme resurfaced throughout the Karlburg passionary, for instance, in the final narrative: the *passio* of Philip. This apostle's twenty-year career preaching the gospel in Scythia was illustrated by a single dramatic episode at a temple of Mars, where he persuaded the assembled crowd to knock down their idol, commanded the dragon (formerly) inhabiting the idol to retreat, and miraculously undid all the physical harm the dragon had wrought. After baptizing thousands, explaining some fundamentals of Christian doctrine (second coming, virgin birth, resurrection, ascension, and Pentecost), and establishing a formal church complete with clergy, Philip returned to Hieropolis in Asia Minor, where, at the age of eighty-seven, he was crucified by infidels and buried. But the most important thing about Philip, in terms of the way the historical process of Christianization was imagined at Karlburg, was his companions, namely, his daughters the "sacratissima virgines" (most holy virgins), through whom the Lord gained a multitude of virgins. That "most holy virgins" were a *sine qua non* of missionary activity must have been taken for granted in the Anglo-Saxon cultural province in the middle decades of the eighth century when the passionary was compiled at Karlburg. Their passionary was organized to culminate with the closing image of those virgins, buried to the left and right of the apostle Philip. In the context of this cultural imaginary concerning the very apostles, we can easily see why Boniface wished to have Leoba buried by his side.[44]

The texts between the syneisactic bookends of the Karlburg passionary were all longer and more complex than the *passiones* of John and Philip. The three narratives at the heart of the codex (the *passiones* of Thomas, Bartholomew, and Matthew) went beyond the basic syneisactism of heterosocial companionship imputed to John and Philip into seriously feminist historiographical and theological territory, either through the espousal of radically Marian doctrinal positions or through the description of women playing crucial, active roles in the spread of Christianity. These three texts, which occupy the bulk of my analysis here, may all have been composed (as well as copied) by women. Bracketing the feminist core of the codex was another pair of narratives (the *passiones* of James the Greater and of Simon and Jude), arranged parenthetically inside the syneisactic frame; these two texts were fundamentally uninterested in female characters or the concerns of women. That any part of the Karlburg passionary omitted heroines set it apart from the "Deus per angelum" *libellus* analyzed in the next section of this chapter, for that later compilation was outright polemical in its aggressive assertion of the centrality of women to the spread of Christian religion. The Kitzingen *libellus* was created to argue in favor of a place for women in ecclesiastical and public life, at a time when such approaches to Christian leadership were under attack. In contrast, the compiler of the Karlburg passionary did not seem to have had to worry yet about such developments and could thus vary her sacred history to inform intellectually engaged Christians concerning a variety of historical and theological topics.

The main "informational" thrust of the second text in the collection, the *passio* of James the Greater, Brother of John, was how to use the Bible to dispute against Jews. The women of Karlburg may actually have harbored the ambition to convert the Jewish merchants serving the Carolingian court, whom they (as inhabitants of a royal *Eigenkloster* in a royal residence on the major Main River thoroughfare) would certainly have encountered.[45] Isidore of Seville had dedicated his major anti-Judaic tract to his sister, and that treatise was translated into one of the regional vernaculars before the end of the eighth century;[46] perhaps the women of Karlburg thought that anti-Jewish polemic was a particularly suitable topic for them to study.

The *passio* of James the Greater traced the apostle's successful preaching campaigns in the synagogues of Judaea and Samaria against the Jews, who, the text several times reminded the reader, crucified Christ.[47] Through a combination of miraculous signs and eloquent sermons, James proved that Christ fulfilled Old Testament prophecies and was therefore the messiah.[48] The heaviest concentration of theological content appeared in James's trial scene. In response to the claim by the Pharisees that the person crucified between the two thieves was simply a man (fol. 4r), James produced a very long and very erudite sermon larded with biblical allusions, decipherable only by someone well versed in the writings of the Old Testament prophets (fols. 4v–5v). This speech could have held the interest only of someone who could follow the references and who actually needed to know which passages in the Hebrew Bible were thought to foretell Jesus (and why). It is therefore a significant index of the interest in theology at the women's monastery of Karlburg that the word separation and grammar in their copy of James the Greater's long speech were particularly accurate; what is more, the scribe caught and corrected her own (very few) errors.

The main theological curiosity of the passion narrative of Simon and Jude, the closing bracket around the feminist core of the Karlburg passionary, lay in the radically dualist positions espoused by the adversaries of the apostles, whether magi expelled from Ethiopia by Matthew or local Persian pagan priests. These enemies of Christ's apostles taught that the God of the Old Testament, all of his prophets (including Moses), and indeed all created flesh were evil; accordingly, Jesus himself had no bodily or material reality: "he was a figment, not a true man born from the virgin" (fol. 29r).[49] Simon and Jude eschewed theological arguments in favor of more action-oriented responses to this challenge. For one thing, they modeled the love of one's enemy by repeatedly interceding with both God and earthly rulers to save the pagan pontiffs (for instance fols. 30v–31r) and even healing those priests to provide a chance for them to convert (e.g., fol. 33v). When given the choice by an angel, the apostles embraced voluntary martyrdom, preferring to die themselves than to punish their enemies. God had fewer scruples and incinerated the pagan priests with a thunderbolt. But the powerful apostles also bested their adversaries in agonistic competitions at least as often as they forgave them. And they placed their powers in the service of the Persian king, particularly by providing sterling advice concerning battle strategies. In the end, filled with gratitude, the Persian king Xerxes translated their bodies into a glorious octagonal tomb shrine built specially for them in the royal city. It is clear why these saints, celebrated by Lul at Mainz and at Hersfeld and by the women of Karlburg, came to play such a central role in Frankish military campaigns against the Saxons.[50]

The heart of the Karlburg passionary was a row of narratives set in exotic climes: India, the stomping grounds of Thomas and Bartholomew, and Ethiopia (by which was meant the region south of Egypt, namely, Abyssinia),[51] mission field of Matthew. The editor of the *passio* of Matthew saw that text as nothing more than a pious romance, an exotic and entertaining story of faraway lands, full of superstition and magic.[52] But George Boas found greater significance in these "exotic" apostolic acts: in his view, they were evidence that late ancient and early medieval people invariably despised "primitive," "inferior" "Others" living under "superseded" dispensations because, in the narratives, the latter always martyred their would-be evangelists.[53] I see more subtlety here: the apostles may have ended up martyred by the intransigent leaders of rival religious systems but not before they provoked mass conversions on the part of good people who embraced Christian teachings. In some cases, even the rival priests changed their tunes.

In fact, the process of evangelization proceeded smoothly and against little serious resistance throughout the Karlburg apostolic passionary, which never dwelt on any negative characteristics of the converts. Instead, the successes that the apostles racked up with the enthusiastic masses (including, ultimately, the Jewish ones persuaded by James) overshadowed the evil of a few leaders, and "proved" the universal appeal of Christianity.[54] Bartholomew in particular had an easy time of it: he converted all of India through very little more than a long Marianist sermon but sadly was decapitated during an extremely brief pagan reaction. This literature, as apostolic historiography, was thoroughly upbeat, in contrast to other historiographic *corpora* such as early eleventh-century Norman depictions of the initial evangelization of the borders of that region, which celebrated the missionary saint as a "warlike savior" of a "savage territory" through a thoroughly violent process[55] (demonstrating that "othering" discourses can be applied even to close neighbors). Far from fostering in its users a sense of distance from and superiority over Others, the Karlburg passionary more likely helped the women of the house imagine the similarities among themselves, the Indians, and the Ethiopians.

In the middle decades of the eighth century, as Anglo-Saxon newcomers were transforming the culture of the Main Valley, for instance, through the introduction of scriptoria, there must have been a keen interest in tales of cultural transformation. The apostle passions were classics of the genre, in part because the "primitive" peoples of the *passiones* were not "othered," they were "selved."[56] The alterity of the eager new Christians of India and Ethiopia must have been psychologically productive for the insular immigrants, looking for a way to approach the inhabitants of foreign territories, and local Franks would also have found in the Karlburg passionary a string of models for sympathetic and successful cross-cultural collaboration between outsiders and natives, a process that necessarily involved the possibility of self-mutation. The passion narrative of Thomas, the opening exotic tale, began with an Indian king who already possessed everything he could ever want, yet who reached out to Roman Caesarea with the explicit goal of borrowing from Others, learning their ways, and changing his own landscape through the importation of foreign things. Jesus himself negotiated with the king's emissary the engagement of his slave Thomas to design and build a Roman-style palace in India (fols. 6r–6v).[57]

That the portrait of exotic cultures in the Karlburg passionary was far more selfing than othering is important for another reason: once the composite narrative moved out of Palestine and Judaea, women exploded on the scene as crucial to the process of Christianization. The setting of these apostolic narratives was a way to articulate the historic role of individual women and sometimes of women's monastic communities (in the case of the *passio* of Matthew) in the Christian conversion process.

The first of the women central to the exotic apostle passions was the Hebrew musician who performed at the wedding of the king's daughter, a lavish affair that Thomas attended soon after his arrival in India. The *cantatrix* immediately understood the reason for Thomas's refusal to fully participate in the festivities and spontaneously began to preach—with Thomas's encouragement—to the assembled company on the one God, maker of heaven and earth (fol. 7r).[58] When Thomas became involved in an altercation with the wine steward, who had taken offense at the apostle's refusal to imbibe, the Hebrew *cantatrix* again spoke out, this time to explain Thomas's mystifying behavior and to hail him as a prophet of God (fol. 7r).[59] Her obviously valued intervention resulted in the king having Thomas bless the bride and groom. Here the "apocryphal" *passio* of Thomas, a female-transmitted and perhaps female-authored text, countered the male-authored narrative of the "canonical" *Acts of the Apostles*, in which the servant girl who announced to a skeptical public that Paul was teaching the true word of God was immediately exorcised by the apostle, on the grounds that such perspicacity and public bravery on the part of a girl could be due only to demonic possession (Acts 16:16–18). The intense discomfort felt by some men around the turn of the first century over female preaching and participation in the evangelization process was manifest in the biblical "cure" episode, while the *passio* of Thomas shows that other authors were committed to providing models of female contributions on the mission field. Nothing "factual" required that a female character play any role in jump-starting Thomas's mission in India. Only a deliberate authorial decision could have given Thomas a spiritually insightful female accomplice from the very beginning of his ministry and permitted him to embrace their partnership.

The next stage of the passion narrative created a syneisactic partnership between the princess and her new husband, as they converted to Christianity and embarked upon a chaste marriage that paralleled the syneisactic partnership between the apostle and the *cantatrix* (fol. 7v).[60] The rebirth of India as a Christian nation thus began with the chaste marriage of a spousal couple whose equality was underlined in their voluntary, bilateral, simultaneous embrace of the new lifestyle (fol. 8r).[61] Two angels descended to help, one for each of the new converts, and Thomas baptized and purified them together, the entire process serving as a symbol for gender equality in the syneisactic tradition. This parity stood in stark contrast to the asymmetrical chaste marriage of Cecilia in the Kitzingen *libellus* discussed later in this chapter, with its insistence on the primacy of the bride at every step, a contrast that reflected the changing circumstances of early Carolingian Francia: the compilers of the Karlburg passionary celebrated syneisactism when the influence of Anglo-Saxon newcomers was at its height in the Main Valley, whereas the Kitzingen Anonyma fought polemically against a rising hostility to women's leadership roles in matters ecclesiastical.

As Thomas's adventures in India continued, the concerns of women became ever more central to the very definition of Christianity. Thomas consistently taught rejection of the things of this world in ways strongly reminiscent of the main values of Augustine's *Comments on the Psalms,* another book produced at Karlburg. This message was conveyed, for instance, by the lavish palace that Thomas built for his royal employer, Gundoforus: it was in heaven, for Thomas spent all the funds intended for construction of the palace doing charitable works. The fortuitous (albeit temporary) death of the king's brother Gad enabled him to verify the existence of the celestial palace and commission a second such palace for himself (fols. 8r–9v).[62] But the main drama of the narrative resulted from the way two aristocratic women, spotlighted as the most significant of the apostle's new converts, understood the saint's teachings: as a call to refuse sexual relations with their husbands. Thomas converted many people to Christianity and performed several mass baptisms, but the text provided insight into the emotions of only these two women, Migdonia and Treptia, whose thoughts and words were frequently quoted. Furthermore, unlike other versions of Thomas's story (the Latin *miracula* and various eastern narratives) in which the apostle's earthly end was brought on by confrontations over political authority or royally supported religions, in the Latin *passio* Thomas was arrested, tried, and executed entirely because of his role in precipitating the defiant chastity of Migdonia and Treptia (fols. 13v–14r).[63] Thus, the values of aristocratic women became the defining values of Indian Christianity.

One double entendre used to describe the women's concerns may particularly point to female authorship. The apostolic sermon that changed the course of Migdonia's life (fols. 11r–11v), bringing her to Christianity and separating her from her husband, Caritius, advocated chastity (*castitas*) as one among many virtues.[64] Migdonia, however, elevated chastity to the key position and determined never again to *contingere* (touch) her husband's *thorum* (fols. 11v–12r).[65] Caritius's attempt to lure his wife back to his *thorum* (bed) through the intermediary of his sister, Queen Treptia, backfired; Treptia was persuaded by Migdonia to renounce sexual relations with her husband, King Misdeus, and to convert to Christianity (fols. 12r–12v).[66] *Thorum* (more commonly rendered as "*torum*") was a sharply polysemous term that vividly expressed the viewpoint of women like Migdonia and Treptia: it meant "bed" or "couch," but it also meant "swelling" or "protuberance."[67] The phrase thus alluded to the sexual act in two ways.

The exotic portion of the passion collection, with its focus on what Christianity meant to women, continued with Bartholomew's Indian mission. After having paralyzed the demon/idol/false god Astaruth, the apostle exorcised a demon from a "lunatic" princess but refused compensation for his services; impressed, the king and queen converted to Christianity, providing the apostle with an opportunity to preach a long, overwhelmingly Marian, sermon explicating the fundamentals of the new religion as a faith in which the Virgin was the key player and in which the incarnate savior (never named as Jesus or Christ) was more often the Son of the Virgin (*filius virginis*) than the Son of God (*filius dei*).[68] The sermon, which occupied almost the entire length of the *passio*, began on the central leaf of the codex.[69]

Bartholomew underlined the absolute inextricability of the incarnation from the virgin birth four times in four opening sentences and then moved into an account of the annunciation; this account was subsequently quoted by the author of the Kitzingen "Deus per angelum" *libellus* (discussed later in this chapter) as part of her broader retelling of the story of Christianity as a history of women's actions, including those of Mary. Bartholomew's Marian theology, as later reiterated by the Kitzingen Anonyma, made the annunciation/incarnation dependent on Mary's never-before-seen vow of virginity. It was not simply that she had not yet known a man and therefore possessed a virginal body suitable to give flesh to the savior; it was that she, alone among all humans being since the beginning of time, had deliberately, purposefully, autonomously, spontaneously decided that she would remain a virgin: "id est hoc constitui," she insisted, "that is, I decided it" (fol. 17r).

Mary's self-affirming clarification appeared in several extant copies of the *passio* of Bartholomew in addition to the one in the Karlburg passionary, as well as in the extract from the *passio* in the "Deus per angelum" *libellus* (Würzburg UB M.p.th.f. 28b fol. 3v), but was banished to the apparatus as a variant not "properly" part of the text in Bonnet's edition.[70] It is impossible to say whether the phrase was part of the original narrative but was removed in some strands of transmission or was inserted as an interpolation into only some strands of transmission; either way, it was part of the transmission known in the Anglo-Saxon cultural province in Francia, and its inclusion changed the entire complexion of the annunciation and incarnation. Scholars have argued that the most feminist way available to view Mary's role in the incarnation was as the first to believe and as willing to participate in an event that was in no way of her own making.[71] In contrast to that view of Mary as reactive, the theology of the *passio* of Bartholomew, both in the Karlburg passionary and in the Kitzingen *libellus*, treated Mary as proactive. Salvation history could never have been set in motion had Mary not made her unique decision.

Furthermore, according to Bartholomew, Mary transmitted her unique self-control to her son. It was precisely the perseverance of the "filius virginis sanctae" (son of the holy virgin) that canceled the problems created by the "filius terrae virginis" (son of the virgin earth), namely, Adam (fol. 18r)—a formulation that recast all of sacred history in terms of Virgin Mothers. *Terra* (earth) was a virgin willy-nilly, because no human blood had yet been shed on her, and no human corpse buried in her, at the time of his birth (fol. 17v).[72] In consequence, Adam had little special resolve and succumbed immediately to temptation when the devil came and tempted him to eat (Eve being noticeably absent from this version of the fall). In contrast, Mary was a virgin because she had decided to be one, the first human ever to imagine such a course of action. Therefore, when the devil tried to tempt Mary's son with food in the desert, the resolute son of the resolute virgin resisted those diabolic wiles. The typological equivalency here was not the typical patristic, originally Pauline, androcentric one (first Adam in paradise/second Adam in the desert),[73] but rather how "the one who conquered the son of a virgin was conquered by the son of a virgin" (fol. 17v).[74] This rousing conclusion was highlighted by the only marginal notation in the entire codex (℞).

Bartholomew's exegesis of the temptation of Jesus was unlike anything in the (orthodox) patristic theological tradition.[75] Latin patristic exegesis was unanimous in interpreting the typological parallel-cum-contrast of Adam versus Christ as a sign of the latter's divinity, of his paternal inheritance as the Son of God, which enabled him to withstand the devil.[76] In contrast, Bartholomew's radically feminist Marian exegesis attributed the Son's ability to withstand diabolic temptation to his perfect resolute human flesh, a maternal inheritance. This view was similar to the teachings of Paul of Samosata, a strong advocate of syneisactism whose ideas were condemned at the Council of Nicaea. The condemnation of the Paulianist position that "the Son of God took his beginning from his mother Mary" was noted in a marginal gloss on the early ninth-century Würzburg canon collection, a sign that his ideas were known in the Anglo-Saxon cultural province in Francia.[77] But Bartholomew's feminist Marianism was not Paulianist. In the Karlburg passionary, in Bonnet's Γ family of manuscripts, and in the Montpellier copy (here jumping its family grouping), after describing the incarnation and the virgin birth, Bartholomew noted that the human, fleshly incarnation did not mark the beginning of the son of God, "whose beginning is before the worlds, from the Father for whom there was never a beginning and who gave a beginning to all" (fol. 17r).[78]

The Mariology of the *passio* of Bartholomew was instead consistent with Nestorianism. Nestorius, bishop of Constantinople from 428 to 431, who was condemned at the Council of Ephesus (431), confessed two separate hypostases in Jesus, one for each of his natures, human and divine. Although Jesus was a unified figure when seen from the outside, internally speaking the two natures could not merge into a hypostatic union, for the transcendent Logos could not unify itself with mutable human flesh, nor could there be any restrictions on Jesus' complete humanity.[79] The *passio* of Bartholomew represented a maximally Marianist (and feminist) teasing out of the implications of this Christology, which furnished the basis on which to attribute the incarnate Jesus' triumphs to his maternal inheritance. Nestorius was long considered by scholars to have been insufficiently respectful of Mary, seeing her as the mother "only" of Jesus' human flesh, as if this minimized her significance.[80] Yet, it has recently become clear that Nestorius used the *Theotokos* ("Mother of God") title and also accepted Mary as the mother of God.[81] Since Nestorius's ideas about Mary were the primary cause of his downfall,[82] we should perhaps reevaluate whether at Ephesus those ideas might have been deemed excessively Marianist rather than insufficiently so.

The passion narrative of Matthew that followed Bartholomew's, itself probably the work of a Karlburg nun,[83] shared the older *passio*'s recognition of the importance of Mary in salvation history but was more conventional in its approach. Matthew's lengthiest sermon explained humanity's fall and redemption so as to put female figures in the center of the story while at the same time avoiding both misogynistic vitriol against Eve and Bartholomew-like adulation of Mary. According to Matthew, the fall was precipitated by a fallen angel, whose jealousy of humanity's paradisiacal condition caused it to enter the body of a serpent and speak to Adam's wife, persuading her to eat the forbidden fruit; the fall was reversed by a Savior born when a virgin filled with purity and faith was impregnated through her ear by the words of a different angel (fols. 23v–24r). The author of the *passio* of Matthew borrowed the idea of the envious fallen angel disguised as a serpent from the *passio* of Simon and Jude (fol. 32v), which her narrative was designed to complement.[84] At the same time as she borrowed from the older narrative, she also set herself theologically apart from it, in formulations that were more pro-Marian and less anti-Judaic than those of her source; for instance, statements such as "everyone knows that the Jews crucified Jesus" in the *passio* of Simon and Jude were replaced by descriptions of Jesus, such as "he who was born from the holy spirit and from the virgin Mary, whom Judas betrayed to the Pharisees, and they killed him."[85]

The feminism of the Matthew passion lay less in its theology and more in its emplotment. Like its source of inspiration, namely, the *passio* of Simon and Jude, the *passio* of Matthew pitted its protagonists against the magician pair, Zarues and Arfexar, whom Simon and Jude bested in a series of agonistic competitions.

In the case of the *passio* of Matthew, however, it was not the apostle himself but his most important female convert and disciple, Ephigenia, who achieved the greatest successes as an athlete of Christ.

At the beginning of Matthew's antimagi mission to Ethiopia, his only important ally was the baptized (by the apostle Philip) eunuch Candacis. King Aeglyppus, in contrast, remained completely duped by the evil magi, playing the role assigned in the "Deus per Angelum" *libellus* to a whole series of foolish, unseeing males. When the king's son Eufronus died, Candacis seized the opportunity to sing Matthew's praises to Queen Eufenosa, who (perspicacious female that she was) immediately sent for the apostle and commanded that the magi be imprisoned (fol. 24v). The queen's authority was evidently such that she could easily impose her will, indeed, luckily for Prince Eufronus (whose family adhered to maternal naming patterns), who was resuscitated by Matthew, whom the queen then publicly proclaimed as an apostle of the true God. Only a long sermon by the apostle clarified for the rather dense king that Matthew was an apostle of God, not God himself. Once that was settled, the royal family was baptized (including Princess Ephigenia, who became a virgin of Christ), the Ethiopian people were converted, churches were built, and priests ordained. After twenty-three happy years, the most religious (*religiosissima*) queen and the most Christian (*Christianissimus*) king passed away, and the drama began. Ephigenia was at the heart of it, for the *passio* of Matthew—like that of Thomas—put the concerns of aristocratic women front and center.

The new king Hyrtacus, whose relationship to the deceased rulers was never defined, wished to marry Ephigenia. Ephigenia, of course, refused, for she had received the veil from the hand of Matthew and was already not only dedicated to Christ ("Christo dedicatam") but also the head of a large community of virgins ("praeposita virginum amplius quentucentarum"; fol. 25r). Hyrtacus offered Matthew half the kingdom if he could persuade Ephigenia to change her mind (an alliance with her being evidently quite valuable), so the apostle slyly agreed to preach a sermon (fols. 25v–27r) on marriage to all the people, including the virgins of the princess's community, who were obviously not cloistered. The king was lured into a (false) sense of security when Matthew launched into a staunchly promarriage speech, explaining that God had blessed marriages, despite the fact that there were often problems (such as spouses who did not like each other), because of the need for procreation; therefore, a man took a woman and a woman took a man, creating a sexual bond exclusive to the two of them. Matthew then detailed additional goods of marriage, but eventually explained that Ephigenia was already married to the heavenly king; not only would it be impossible for her to find a better spouse but also it would be wrong for her to change spouses. The apostle ended the sermon by assuring the assembled crowds that they did not have to fear earthly kings, only the heavenly one.

Matthew's clear approval of her wishes led Ephigenia to declare her willingness to brave the earthly king's threats. But it bears underlining that at no point was Ephigenia constructed as a virgin-martyr whose corporeal purity was threatened. She was princess, a woman of royal stock, who decided to dedicate herself to Christ, without any explicit reference to a desire for bodily purity. Having made the commitment to Christ, she stuck to her decision, in part because there would have been major institutional implications had she renounced her position at the head of a community. The king wanted her at his side as queen, but she considered a royally governed monastery to be more beneficial in the long run. Therefore, she begged Matthew to protectively bless, through the imposition of his hands, all the virgins "consecrated to the Lord through your word" ("per verbum tuum Domino consecratas"), a phrase marked in the manuscript by an interlinear cross (fol. 27r), a sign that this scene struck a chord with the consecrated women of Karlburg. He indeed blessed them, and in explicitly egalitarian terms, addressing the Christian God as one"who spurns no age and rejects no sex, who considers no condition unworthy of your grace, but who [is] the equal creator and redeemer for all" (fol. 27r).[86] Throughout this drama of self-assertion by a noncloistered virgin in a public setting, the Karlburg manuscript correctly utilized (where appropriate) the nominative form for Ephigenia, as the subject of the verbs of action, whereas the published edition of the text, based on a Bobbio manuscript, incoherently cast her name into the accusative, literally objectifying the princess.[87]

Yet Ephigenia was so far from being a vulnerable, threatened damsel in distress in the Karlburg *passio* that Hyrtacus took his frustration out on Matthew, whom he had assassinated, but left the "most sacred virgin of Christ" ("sacratissima virgo Christi") unscathed. The princess immediately swung into action, using her gold, silver, and gems to build a basilica in honor of the slain apostle over his tomb and making massive donations to the poor, for—as she announced—"It behooves me to do battle with Hyrtacus" (fol. 28r).[88] Ephigenia's subsequent defeat of Hyrtacus—permitting her brother Pehor to succeed him on the royal throne—ensured the conversion of Ethiopia to Christianity, as a result of which everyone in the Catholic-filled provinces of the country blessed the royal virgin forever after. That the narrative constructed Ephigenia, rather than Matthew, as the apostle of the Ethiopians was noticed even by Els Rose, whose studies of the apocryphal acts never utilized gender as a category of analysis; the prominence of Ephigenia in the emplotment of the *passio* was simply impossible to miss.[89]

Significantly, the culmination of the battle between Ephigenia and Hyrtacus highlighted what the author of the *passio* considered the proper (or at least logical) location for a community of virgins founded and governed by a woman of royal stock: adjacent to the royal palace. Hyrtacus was definitively defeated when the ring of fire that he had set around Ephigenia's *praetorium* (a term for a palace that connoted some governmental functions) instead turned around and consumed his *palatium* (fol. 28r). Like Karlburg itself, Ephigenia's community— very likely the invention of a Karlburg nun—was closely associated with the ruling family and conceptualized as having a share in royal administration. Similarly situated women's houses were joined to the residences of eighth-century ruling families in Salzburg (the Nonnberg), Regensburg (Niedermünster), and Alsace (Hohenbourg).[90] The heroic, even pugilistic expectations that eighth-century aristocrats had for the aristocratic abbesses of such communities were reflected in a contemporary collection of epitaphs of abbesses, all of which labeled the departed woman an *"athleta Christi"* (athlete of Christ).[91]

In sum, at Karlburg the story of Christian beginnings was envisioned and told with a spotlight on a series of famous male apostles but with a plethora of crucial and at times indispensable supporting roles for a variety of women. This is exactly how the Anglo-Saxon immigrants were going about their work in Francia at the time the passionary was compiled. Their own approach was reflected in how they imagined their predecessors to have behaved. Once constructed, this vision of how the apostles comported themselves (namely, as collaborators with women) became the model for subsequent public collaboration in the syneisactic tradition.

THE KITZINGEN "DEUS PER ANGELUM"(WÜRZBURG, UB M.P.TH.Q. 28B FOL. 25): A WOMAN'S THEOLOGY OF WOMANHOOD

The accent of the Kitzingen *libellus* was less historiographical, and more theological, than that of the Karlburg passionary. Indeed, the Kitzingen abbreviator of the *passio Agathae* specifically cut the original author's announcement that she or he would recite the "historia" of the saint.[92] The texts in the Karlburg codex reliably provided specific names and places and boasted plots that were not only easy to follow but also neatly wrapped up with contextualized denouements. For instance, the passion of Thomas was resolved with a neat translation of his body from India to Edessa in Syria, his recognized resting place, and included the useful note that this was the town where King Abgar got the famous letter from heaven, written by the hand of Jesus.[93] Authors who inserted such specifics (whether "accurate" or "invented") desired to convey the impression that they were recounting "what actually happened"; in contrast, authors who omitted specifics blurred the focus on the level of emplotment and direct the reader's attention elsewhere.[94] Thus, the Kitzingen Anonyma omitted details from her abridgments of the passion narratives of Juliana and Agnes that were undoubtedly in her copies of the full texts, information such as the name of the woman who took Juliana's body from Nicomedia onto the ship bound for Rome, the name of the town where Juliana's body washed ashore after the shipwreck, and the names of the prefect and his son who were responsible for Agnes's troubles (fols. 11v–12r). A historical dimension remained in the Kitzingen *libellus*, but the author of "Deus per angelum" clearly intended to teach more than history.

Modern readers understand the tales in the Kitzingen *libellus* (abbreviated versions of passion narratives of Cecilia, Juliana, Agnes, and Agatha) to be set during the ascendancy of the *augusti* (emperors) over the ancient Roman Empire. However, the texts themselves did not thematize any concrete political context or historical setting. Indeed, the passion narrative of Agatha (fols. 14r–14v) set the death of the saint in the reigns of both the emperor Decius (d. 251) and the emperor Diocletian (d. 303).[95] This sort of "flirting with fictionality" was also practiced by some twelfth-century Latin authors, who deliberately inserted erroneous chronological or geographical references in order to play with truth claims.[96] Likewise, the Kitzingen abbreviator disguised the specific number of bystanders who were burned by the recalcitrant pot in Juliana's martyrdom scene. The relevant sentence was one of the simplest and most straightforward in the entire codex; even someone with a merely elementary knowledge of Latin would have understood that only a number could make sense at the particular spot, yet the scribe copied a nonnumber (indeed, nonword) "bexu."[97] The abbreviator's insertion here of a nonsensical detail opened a space of uncertainty, even unreality. Similarly, the anonymous author of the ninth-century Old French Sequence of St. Eulalia deliberately made "errors" with some of the most basic linguistic forms in order to draw attention to the issue of language itself.[98]

Another authorial technique to steer readers away from surface plotlines, the avoidance of narrative continuity, was also utilized by the Kitzingen Anonyma. For instance, in the abbreviated passion narrative of Cecilia, a mysterious character Almachius out of nowhere began searching for Cecilia to force her to sacrifice; readers of the full *passio* knew him to be the prefect under whose authority Cecilia's husband and brother-in-law had just been executed.[99] Furthermore, readers of the abbreviated passion were given no hint as to the audience of Cecilia's first missionary sermon; readers of the full *passio* knew that the listeners were guards sent by Almachius to arrest the saint.[100] In the Kitzingen Anonyma's abbreviated passion narrative of Agatha, the proconsul Quintianus called the saint to trial literally in the third line of the text, for no apparent reason; she arrived, only to announce that she has been healed of blows that the reader never knew were inflicted upon her (fol. 14v). Readers were thus discouraged from reading the *libellus* primarily for its plot.

It was, above all, through their near indifference to deeds that the *passiones* in this manuscript most clearly announced their transcendent purposes. This set them apart from most medieval saints' biographies, which had a "propensity . . . to emphasize dramatized action over complex argument" and an interest in "the primacy of the dramatic deed."[101] Yet, the Kitzingen Anonyma eliminated the most dramatic and entertaining scene in the entire Juliana narrative, in which the saint dragged a demon through the streets and threw him into a full sewer.[102] In the *passiones*, complex arguments flourished, particularly in the form of direct discourse, while action was kept to a minimum.

The Kitzingen texts familiarized readers with the saints primarily via oratorical displays, through which the interior worlds of the protagonists were made manifest, perhaps an example of how "in Germanic tradition, women normally use[d] speech rather than action to achieve their purposes, but they resort[ed] to action when speech fail[ed]."[103]

The female martyrs in the *libellus* "Deus per angelum" were all eloquent, powerful, and independent. The implications of their passion narratives for women and womanhood were unambiguously positive, including as inspirational models for the women who read and heard their stories. Oratory can evoke powerful feelings of identification in a listener. At least one future medievalist found herself, as a girl in twentieth-century France, watching the annual performance of the *Martyrdom of Saint Reine* in Alise-Ste-Reine, and "wishing with all my heart that it could be me up there on the stage, fighting those battles and speaking those lines."[104] Female martyrs constituted important sources of inspiration for Hrotsvitha of Gandersheim, Hildegard of Bingen, Joan of Arc, and other medieval women who identified with the martyrs' autonomy and defiance.[105] In the Kitzingen *libellus*, they became part of a celebratory theological statement concerning women and womanhood. The author of the *libellus* selected texts (that is, the full *passiones*) that already contained substantial material for thinking through a theologically charged female figure, but she also made completely new abbreviated versions of the preexisting narratives. She then combined them with a dizzying collection of revised extracts from additional texts, as well as with some original material, and forged everything into a single whole, in which she articulated a feminist, gender-egalitarian, liberationist theology of womanhood.

The heart of the *libellus* was the row of passion narratives (of Cecilia, Juliana, Agnes, and Agatha). Yet the narratives gained much of their meaning through interaction with the remainder of the *libellus*. They were framed by a series of prefatory texts concerning Mary and by a series of epilogual texts concerning Jesus. The Marian texts functioned as a preface for all four passion narratives, replacing the prefaces proper to the four individual *passiones*. The Marian prefatory texts overtly proclaimed the end of woman's subjection to man and thus primed the reader to discover both proof and illustration of woman's liberation in the passion narratives that followed. The closing portion of the frame functioned as a fifth *passio*, explicating the passion of Christ and effectively yoking the women martyrs to their prototype, Christ, as the Kitzingen Anonyma echoed Christ in her women, and vice versa.

This collection of materials was intended to work together as a whole theological tractate, in contrast to superficially similar contemporary manuscripts such as Vienna ÖNB 1556.[106] In the latter collection of sermons and martyr *passiones*, each passion narrative and each sermon was a discrete unit, while the codex was a collection of units equaling no more than the sum of its parts. A table of contents (folios 1v–2v) helped the preacher find a needed sermon or *passio*, each of which was clearly labeled according to the liturgical or homiletic occasion for which it was intended (such as the ordination of a bishop). In contrast, "Deus per angelum" liberated its component parts from any particular temporal or situational connection, permitting them to stand instead as eternally relevant theological statements. For instance, the opening text, an abbreviated version of a homily by Pseudo-Fulgentius, was normally presented in manuscripts as a sermon for the feast of the Nativity.[107] The Kitzingen Anonyma omitted both the usual title, through which the suggested utilization of the text was limited to Christmas Day, and the usual opening line, through which Christmas Day was colored as a Dominical (that is, connected with Jesus) holiday, rather than as a Marian one.[108] As a result, she harnessed the full power of the imagery in the sermon for her theology of womanhood.

The fact that the Kitzingen *libellus* provided no authorial attributions for any of its frame texts also contributed to the theological weighting of the codex. Instead of appealing to the authority of named authors, the compiler of the *libellus* presented her material as, effectively, a divine revelation of fact above and beyond human opinion, comparable to the fact reported in the simple past indicative in the opening sentence of the *libellus*: "Deus per angelum ad Mariam protulit verbum" (fol. 2r).[109] This sentence constituted a powerful and straightforward declaration, achieved by the Kitzingen Anonyma by trimming the second line of her source text (the pseudo-Fulgentian sermon) in addition to omitting title and author.[110] It was a bold decision to produce an entire *libellus* lacking in authorizing titles, given that the conventions of Latin-literate culture generally encouraged scribes to attribute texts to known author(ities), even in the absence of evidence. It is possible that the compiler of the *libellus* avoided all authorial attributions to avoid admitting through differential treatment that some texts were pseudonymous, of uncertain origin, of unorthodox background, or her own original compositions. Or perhaps the systematic omission of signs of authorship constituted something of a protest against developing traditions of canonical, authoritative, patristic textuality.[111] Whatever the explanation for the absence of authorial attributions in the *libellus*, it is clear that learned Christian women in the eighth century were able to find egalitarian texts and thereby circumvent the patriarchal traditions found in the writings of many a Church Father.

A case in point is the opening text in the *libellus*, a work of Pseudo-Fulgentius that trumpeted the liberation of all women from all the disabilities of Eve. Beginning with Philo of Alexandria, who may have been reacting against real-world gains made by women in Roman imperial social life, male theologians developed the notion that women were divinely subjected to men as a punishment for Eve's sin, itself presented as the origin of evil in the world.[112] Although some Fathers of the Church acknowledged the liberation of some special women from some disabilities of Eve as a result of the special virtues of Mary, no (orthodox) Father maintained that Mary had dissolved all the negative consequences of Eve's sin.[113] Like many theologians of his era, Fulgentius (bishop of Ruspe, c. 462–527)[114] enjoyed the elegance of the Eve–Mary parallel but never ascribed any liberating consequences for earthly women to Mary's achievements.[115] However, Pseudo-Fulgentius, whoever she or he was, was not Fulgentius. Both this pseudonymous author and those who transmitted his or her works injected into Christian theological discussion ideas that would have been vigorously repudiated by Fulgentius himself, whose letters to women emphasized subordination, humility, and self-abnegation, along with the idea that women were in no way responsible for their own virtues or good deeds.[116]

Codices containing the authentic works of known patristic authors had a better chance of survival over the long haul than did codices containing pseudonymous and anonymous attempts to redirect the emerging gender-hierarchical version of the Christian tradition. Nevertheless, the manuscripts from the Anglo-Saxon cultural province in Francia contained at least two examples of the work of Pseudo-Fulgentius. The Vienna penitential contained a pseudo-Fulgentian discussion of the fall, highlighting the equal guilt of the first "homines" (human beings), Adam and his wife, in the original sin, along with the disappearance of bodily gender in the resurrection of the flesh.[117] And the pseudo-Fulgentian sermon dramatically opened the "Deus per angelum" *libellus* with this rousing call to women everywhere: "Put down the curse of prevarication and assume the blessing of restoration, throw off the sorrows that Eve acquired through the serpent, and assume the honors that Mary received through the angel."[118]

Pseudo-Fulgentius's Mary was a new Eve ("nova Eva") through whom the curse ("maledictio") placed on Eve had ceased to be valid; the "bona Mariae" had, to the benefit of all women of succeeding generations, excluded all the "mala Evae" such as sorrow ("dolor"), sadness ("tristitia"), servitude ("servitus"), and placement under the domination of a husband (fols. 11v–12r). Under this new dispensation, women did not have to embrace virginity to escape the controlling power of men.[119] The text continued: "Thus does the virgin Mary receive in our lord Jesus Christ women at all stages of life, so that she, the new Eve, might support all women who flee to her and thus restore every type of woman who comes to her."[120] This opening text claimed real-world consequences for contemporary women as a result of the actions of the heroines of sacred history, directing readers to interpret the stories of powerful women that filled the subsequent pages of the *libellus* as models for the real world.

This pseudo-Fulgentian sermon became widespread during the eighth century through inclusion during the 770s in the homiliary of Alan of Farfa, a collection whose own popularity was curtailed when (as part of the reform program) Charlemagne commissioned Paul the Deacon to construct an alternative sermon collection containing no such apocryphal texts.[121] But the women of the Anglo-Saxon cultural province in Francia worked to circumvent this developing antifeminist tradition by continuing to transmit anonymous texts. Were the popularity of the Pseudo-Fulgentian sermon, with its explicit directive to read biblical women as exemplars for their contemporary descendants, better known, Carol Farr might have recognized the liberationist program of the female images on the monumental eighth-century Ruthwell Cross in Dumfriesshire, Scotland, that Meyer Shapiro had already pegged as both reflections of and prototypes for prominent female monastics, such as Hild of Whitby; unfortunately, Farr hesitated to follow this lead, on the following grounds: "One may search carefully, long, and fruitlessly for a patristic or early medieval exegesis of Mary Magdalen or Martha and Mary that says anything about their meanings as specifically female figures. . . . Nearly all interpretations allegorize them as seemingly gender-neutral types of the church or monastic ideals."[122] She therefore felt compelled, reluctantly and indeed unnecessarily, to deny that the prominent scene of the woman (generally understood to be the Magdalen) anointing Jesus' feet was intended to justify sacerdotal functions for women.[123]

Having made the fundamental point that, because of Mary, the postlapsarian gender hierarchy had been superseded, the author of "Deus per angelum" moved on to focus on some key moments in the life of Mary, above all the Annunciation, the scene invoked in the opening line of the *libellus*, when "God through an angel" (namely, Gabriel) spoke to Mary. The second text in the opening frame placed the driving force of the Annunciation in the mind and heart of Mary. After a list of some of Mary's titles and attributes, and the point that she "agnoscit" (recognized) the greeting from the angel and the mystery of conception (material drawn from Isidore of Seville's *De ortu et obitu patrum*), the Kitzingen Anonyma expanded, by means of a passage borrowed from the *passio* of Bartholomew in the Karlburg passionary, upon the drama as described in the Gospel of Luke.[124] In the Gospel account, Mary expressed shock that she was to bear a child on the grounds that she had not yet known a man, but she never expressed the intention never to know a man at all. According to the Anonyma's development of the Lucan text, as borrowed from Bartholomew's theology, Mary had already made a vow to God to preserve her virginity, the very first person since *homo* was created (since "homo factus est") to make such a vow. A few earlier authors had mentioned Mary's "vow of virginity," but the text in "Deus per angelum" went beyond them.[125] By drawing on material in the apocryphal acts of the apostle Bartholomew, the Kitzingen Anonyma constructed the Annunciation (and, by extension, the Incarnation) as preconditioned by and predicated on Mary's virginal resolution.

The order of events at the Annunciation/Incarnation according to the *libellus* was as follows. First, Mary did what no human being had ever done, when she said, "Domine, offero tibi virginitatem meam" ("Lord, I offer my virginity to you"), an act that rendered her (like Christ) a perfect priest and victim. The revolutionary uniqueness of Mary's resolve was emphasized by the Kitzingen Anonyma, who wrote: "she decided that she would remain a virgin, especially for the love of God, although she had been incited to this by no other human being, either through verbal teaching or through an example for imitation."[126] Mary's voluntary embrace of such a never-before seen or imagined sacrifice of self for the love of God immediately textually preceded and thus logically and historically precipitated the sudden appearance of Gabriel and the conversation between the angel and the virgin as reported in the Gospel of Luke, in which the angel announced that Mary had conceived a child. The human gift, never seen since "homo factus est," stimulated the divine gift, when God was made man (or "homo factus est"). The interpretive emphasis in the *libellus* was displaced from the simple fact of Mary having not yet known a man onto the autonomous decision of Mary not to know a man.

The *libellus* then returned to the Isidoran test and to the question of Mary's status as a martyr who "corporalis necis passione . . . ab hac vita migrasse" ("migrated from this life by the suffering of a bodily death"). There was, of course, no way to know for sure about this, for "her death is nowhere described in writing at all."[127] The basis of the tradition of Mary's passion was the prophecy of Simeon (Luke 2:35) that a sword would pierce her soul. Isidore had glossed the prophecy with the point that we do not know for certain if Simeon even meant a material sword, but the Kitzingen Anonyma integrated the text into her *libellus* by changing the "material" sword, in a unique variant, to a "martyrial" sword. Thus, within the context of the *libellus*, Mary's physical death, if it indeed transpired, would also have to be seen as a passion, linking her with Cecilia, Juliana, Agnes, Agatha, and Christ. The Kitzingen Anonyma here took a feminist stand on one of the flashpoint topics of Mariological (and therefore gendered) controversy among patristic authors, many of whom were eager to deny the possibility of Mary's coredemptive suffering at the moment of the crucifixion. Origen, for instance, interpreted the sword of Simeon's prophesy as the doubt Mary experienced at the crucifixion. Ambrose admitted that Mary had remained faithful to Christ at the crucifixion and felt emotional pain as well, but he explicitly denied that her suffering had any meaning or effect, for Jesus needed no help to save the world. For Bede, Mary's maternal sorrow at the sight of her son's suffering was nothing more than a symbol for the suffering of "the church."[128]

Isidore of Seville had closed his chapter on the mother of Jesus by noting that the location of her sepulchre was known (albeit without actually naming that location).[129] The Kitzingen Anonyma's modification of her source text here, leaving Mary's end shrouded in mystery, participated in an eighth-century trend to elevate the status of Mary by refusing to treat the end of her life as comparable to that of a normal human being. During the eighth century, the feast of Mary's Dormition, centered on her empty tomb in the church in the Valley of Josaphat, drew pilgrims from all over the Christian world, including (in 724/726) at least one member of the syneisactic Bonifatian circle, namely, Willibald.[130] Willibald was made bishop of Eichstätt by Boniface in 741, and he founded a double monastery at Heidenheim in 752. Writing some time during the 760s, 770s, or 780s, the nun Hugeburc of Heidenheim (also an immigrant from England) described Willibald's visit to the Holy Land church that was dedicated to Mary, "not because her body rests there, but in memory of her."[131] Accordingly, the Kitzingen Anonyma changed the final phrase of the final sentence of Isidore's text to read "her sepulchre has not been found" (folio 3v).[132] This deliberately mystifying ending ran counter to the effect of Isidore's original, which had slammed the brakes on any speculation concerning Mary as either immortal or risen from the dead along the lines of Christ himself. In assessing the impact of this information within the overall schema of the *libellus*, it is useful to keep in mind that readers of "Deus per angelum" were eventually led, in the closing portion of the frame, to another empty tomb, that of Christ. One aspect of the bookended opening and closing frames was therefore a Mary–Christ parallelism.

The third text in the opening frame of the *libellus* was an extract from Pelagius's commentary on Paul's Letter to the Romans 12:9–17, as revised by Cassiodorus. Pelagius opposed Augustine's developing doctrine of the congenital consequences of original sin, according to which humans could not avoid sinning; he championed, instead, a doctrine of Christian freedom, according to which humans possessed the capacity to choose between good and evil. His message was most clearly articulated in his 413 letter to the nun Demetrias: "since perfection is possible for man, it is obligatory."[133] After a number of trials, Pelagius was, in 418, both condemned by imperial rescript and excommunicated by the bishop of Rome.[134] Proponents of orthodoxy did their best to destroy Pelagius's writings, but they remained popular nonetheless, both in the British Isles and on the continent, well into the ninth century.[135] For instance, a copy of Pelagius's commentary on Paul's Letter to the Philippians, written in Northumbria during the first half of the eighth century, was present in one of the Anglo-Saxon monastic foundations in Germany during the ninth century.[136]

Of course, the Kitzingen Anonyma did not work from Pelagius's original commentary on Romans, but rather from Cassiodorus's revision of it. Cassiodorus actually made very few changes to this particular section (12:9–17), which therefore still conveyed numerous Pelagian ideas.[137] Furthermore, the way the selection was incorporated into the *libellus* accentuated its Pelagian leanings. The theme of Romans 12 was the call for all Christians to imitate or embody Christ.[138] As the final portion of a preface to four martyr passion narratives, followed by an account of Christ's own passion, this notion of the exemplarity of Christ helped the Kitzingen Anonyma set up her female saints as Christ figures taking full advantage of their liberation from the consequences of the sin of Eve.

Just as she began her extract from the Pseudo-Fulgentian homily in midtext, in order to open the *libellus* with the words "Deus per angelum," the Kitzingen Anonyma began her extract from the commentary on Romans partway through verse 9 of the Pauline text ("Cursing evil, adhering to the good") in order to foreground the theme of human choice.[139] The unaltered, optimistic, and exceedingly demanding Pelagian interpretation of this choice followed: "there must be total purity in a Christian, just as God is pure light."[140] For Pelagius, and for the Kitzingen Anonyma, "total purity" could be demanded of people because perfection was possible. In their evident control over their bodies and themselves, the female saints in her *libellus* illustrated and demonstrated womankind's ability to voluntarily avoid sin. Mary had, by her own autonomous and voluntary embrace of virginity, created a situation in which all women were free to exercise their unstained wills to "curse evil" and "adhere to the good," including through sharing in the passion of Christ. Any reader could see Cecilia, Juliana, Agnes, and Agatha do so.

As we saw in connection with Augustine's Psalm commentary (chapter 5), even the bishop of Hippo at times found it difficult to resist sounding like an ally of Pelagius. Although the latter's ideas were hereticated, "Pelagianism would remain endemic."[141] Pelagius's views could not be banished from the Christian tradition as long as scribes and authors, such as the women of Kitzingen, found his ideas to be congenial. The "Deus per angelum" *libellus* reveals one instance of just how "endemic" Pelagius's optimistic, confident view of human abilities remained. The Pelagianism of the Anglo-Saxon cultural province in Francia also supported syneisactic practices there; against any warning that concupiscence was inevitable amid the temptations of socializing with members of the opposite sex, Leoba and her followers could answer, flatly, that it was not, for "total purity" was a real option.

After the passion narratives of the four women martyrs (to which I turn later), the closing portion of the frame took the reader through another set of key moments in sacred history, moving from Christ's passion and resurrection all the way through to the Second Coming. To create her closing Christological frame, the Kitzingen Anonyma drew only on the Gospels of Matthew and of John, sometimes considered the more authoritative Gospels because (presumably) they were written by eyewitnesses, and left aside the Gospels of Mark and of Luke.[142] However, John and Matthew shared another trait that would have been relevant in the Anglo-Saxon cultural province in Francia and could account for their preferential usage here; both of their *passiones* were included in the Karlburg passionary, where they were characterized as staunch supporters of (respectively) syneisactism and of female monasticism.

The back frame opened with an original commentary on Matthew 26:1–30: the deliberations of the chief priests concerning how to dispose of Jesus, the anointing of Jesus by the woman with the alabaster jar, Judas's agreement with the priests to betray Jesus, the preparations of Jesus and the disciples for the passover feast and crucifixion, and the gathering of Jesus and the disciples on the Mount of Olives. It was certainly no accident that the Kitzingen Anonyma included here the woman with the alabaster jar, a recurrent figure in all four

Gospels, whom she would have understood to be Mary Magdalen (whose cult was already thriving in eighth-century England, substantially earlier than elsewhere).[143] Our author's exegesis of the woman who anointed Jesus took a unique path, consonant with the themes of the *libellus* as a whole. For her, the woman was neither Augustine's symbol of the possibility of redemption through grace nor Gregory's penitent sinner; instead, she was the clairvoyant who alone understood what was happening when the men around her were blind. The commentary explained: "In her spirit this woman foresaw that she would not be able to anoint the body of the Lord in his sepulchre, blocked by an extremely heavy rock" (fol. 17v).[144] This biblical woman shared her clear-sightedness with all the female martyrs at the heart of the *libellus*, as well as with the female characters in the Karlburg *passio* of Matthew. After the commentary explained the significance of the unction, Jesus declared that wherever the gospel was preached, what this woman did would also be narrated, "in memory of her" (Matthew 26:13). The women of Karlburg and Kitzingen, who repeatedly spotlighted the woman with the alabaster jar, worked to make this prediction come true.

The commentary on Matthew was followed by a description of the sepulchre of Christ and a list of the precise hours at which various events in sacred history transpired, above all those connected with the crucifixion (such as the hour at which Jesus was led before Pilate, the hour at which he cried out on the cross, the hour at which the good thief confessed, the hour at which the holy women came to the sepulchre, and the hour at which Nicodemus and Joseph buried Jesus). This original composition, created specifically for the "Deus per angelum" *libellus*, was a transitional text, intended to help the reader visualize the tomb of Christ in the next section of the work. It sewed together the most vital Gospel passages in terms of potential female claims to sacerdotal powers: the woman with the alabaster jar of Matthew 26, who anointed Jesus before the crucifixion, and the women with their unguents of Matthew 28, who came to anoint Jesus' body in his tomb. The third piece of the closing frame was a commentary on the latter text, Matthew 28:1–20, describing the women at the tomb, the risen Christ's appearance to them and then to the eleven disciples, and the charge to preach to and baptize the nations.

Most of this original commentary contained commonplaces concerning the meaning of Easter as (for instance) a time of transition from earth to heaven, from the devil to Christ, from the shadows of sin and ignorance to the light of truth and faith, and from hell to paradise or as a recapitulation of the passage of the Israelites through the Red Sea (fol. 22r). But no commentary on the biblical lemma Matthew 28:1–20 could fail to be significant from the perspective of gender. One study of the passage, by a Catholic male cleric, concluded that "Matthew presents the women headed by Mary Magdalene as true discipleship models" because of how both Jesus and the angel at the tomb deputized women to spread the word of the resurrection.[145] It is possible to go even further than this analyst, who drew his conclusions based solely on two explicit charges to female figures, ignoring a third—implicit—charge. Jesus told the women to go to the male disciples in Galilee, and the angel told the women they would see Jesus in Galilee. Therefore, when Jesus appeared to the disciples in Galilee and charged them with a global mission, the women may have been present at that key moment as well. Given that readers of "Deus per angelum" would already have encountered female saints (Cecilia, Juliana, Agatha, and Agnes) who did engage in missionary preaching, they were primed to understand Jesus' plan for spreading the gospel as an inclusive charge to male and female followers.

But the gendered significance of this third portion of the closing frame did not end with the implications of the biblical lemma, for the Kitzingen Anonyma's commentary also contributed to the overall feminist project. For instance, she drew a string of contrasts between the first and the second Adam that made Adam the subject of all the verbs of action leading to the fall; a fleeting reference to an unnamed woman (the first Adam fell by her persuasion) was countered by a reference to another woman who made things right (the second Adam stood up by birth from a virgin; fol. 22v). The renewal of humanity (*homo*) on Easter was then symbolized by a female figure: the woman who found the lost drachma in which the "imago Dei expremitur" (fol. 23r), celebrated by Gregory in his gospel homilies.[146] Finally, the restriction of ultimate salvation to a few special individuals (conveyed through a choice quotation from a letter of Pseudo-Jerome) was also symbolized by a female figure: the prostitute Rahab, whose house alone remained standing when the walls of Jericho came tumbling down (fol. 23v).[147] The Kitzingen Anonyma here chose Rahab to underline yet again how women were able to recognize truth when all around them (including men) were blindly misguided. The tiny remnant of the truth church was also symbolized by those who were with Noah in the ark (fol. 23v), a gender-mixed image that we encountered in connection with the Kitzingen crucifixion miniature (chapter 4).

Had the *libellus* ended at this point, it would have presented a perfectly polished encapsulation of a female-dominated version of sacred history, moving from the annunciation through the crucifixion. This "movement," theologically speaking, "went" nowhere, for the annunciation and the crucifixion were so intimately connected that the feast of the Annunciation, a new invention of the seventh century, was set on March 25, the traditional date (rather than the generally celebrated movable one) for the crucifixion.[148] A plethora of seventh- and eighth-century liturgical and poetical materials emphasized the interconnectedness between annunciation and passion as part of a larger understanding of the unity of Christ's life.[149] But the *libellus*, ultimately a treatise designed to intervene in contemporary debates, continued with a dramatic bipartite coda reminding readers that Christ would return (on the anniversary of the day when manna fell from heaven, when Jesus was baptized in the

Jordan, when he turned water to wine, and of the Pentecost) to judge heaven and earth and that—in the interim—they would often have to suffer (according to Christ's own warnings) under bad pastors and bad rulers (fols. 24r–25v).[150] This culmination of the *libellus* transformed it instantly into a critique of contemporary policy, as the Kitzingen Anonyma closed with the point that those who ruled in the world, in secular or ecclesiastical positions, did not always act correctly. Anyone who had read the *libellus* could clearly see how misguided were the recommendations of those Carolingian reformers who were attempting to limit the ecclesiastical activities of women. The *libellus* protested the reform movement by demonstrating that women, theologically and historically, deserved to play active roles in a Christian society.

LIBERATED WOMEN: HOW FOUR EARLY CHRISTIAN MARTYRS BUILT THE VISIBLE CHURCH

The passion narratives of the four female martyrs at the core of the *libellus* were intended to be read in light of their theological framing. Texts that, in other codicological contexts, might appear as mere romantic stories here were pitched in the same key as the letters of Paul and the Gospel of Matthew. There was an overarching thread running through the four passion narratives, namely, the progressive realization, externalization, and materialization of the Christian faith. The *libellus* began in the isolated and hidden interiors of Cecilia's heart and culminated with Agatha's miraculous ability to control the volcanic forces of nature. As faith materialized in external reality, the composite woman that was Cecilia-Juliana-Agnes-Agatha moved from control over only her own interior self to control over nature. Thus was fulfilled the promise of Christianity, through Mary, to women.

The central section of "Deus per angelum" began with the double entendre that Cecilia, an isolated Christian who dared not show her true self to the world, always carried the gospel of Christ hidden in her breast, implying both that she carried a gospel book under her clothing and that the knowledge of its contents was inscribed upon her heart.[151] Cecilia's dilemma was touchingly illustrated at her wedding, as she wore a hair shirt beneath her bridal finery. As instruments played for the wedding guests to hear in material reality, inside her own heart Cecilia sang audibly to God and the angels. Her control over her interior world was not matched by control over her social circumstances until she and her (non-Christian) husband, Valerian, approached the marriage bed. Suddenly, an object in material reality—namely, the bed—was described as hidden and secret ("she was to undertake, along with Valerian her betrothed, the silent secrets of the marriage bed"),[152] and Cecilia—speaking for the first time—was (a)loud. She revealed to Valerian that she had an angel as her lover, who would punish him if he tried to have sex with her, but whom he would never be able to see unless he became purified and adopted her religion. Christianity itself became a matter of being able to see that which was otherwise hidden, the things of the spirit beyond the sensual world.[153]

As the text began to grope toward a vision of Christianity as an external material reality, Valerian agreed to seek out an old man who knew how to purify him. Although Cecilia's instructions for how to find this man were reminiscent of plans for rendezvous with undercover agents in espionage novels, Valerian did manage to make contact with a certain Urban, who established conditions under which the mysterious old man could materialize out of thin air. This old man, probably St. Paul, successfully "purified" Valerian by having him read a passage from Ephesians.[154] "Purification" was therefore a function of engagement with (Pauline, sacred) text, something very much in keeping with the intellectual orientation of the professionally religious women of the Anglo-Saxon cultural province in Francia. The figure of Cecilia was defined entirely by the fact that she carried the Word, the gospel, always in her breast, and the Kitzingen abbreviator edited the text precisely to open the core of the *libellus* with that particular description of a woman.

When Cecilia began to make an impact on the exterior world by converting Valerian and then his brother Tiburtius, the circle of identifiable Christians spread beyond Cecilia herself, but the secret community connected with Urban did not come out of the shadows. It was only when Cecilia herself began preaching in public that a Christian society fully materialized. Her preaching resulted in more than 400 new converts, who were baptized in her house. The exterior of that building was the setting for the second half of the *passio* (Cecilia's trial), in keeping with the progress of the text toward externalization; the first half of the passion narrative, which began in her breast, had taken place largely inside Cecilia's house. Furthermore, the Anonyma edited the trial dialogue between Cecilia and the prefect Almachius to retain only statements relevant to the theme of appearance and reality, such as the passage in which Cecilia ridiculed her idol-worshiping interrogator for having apparently lost his eyes, since anyone with healthy eyes could see that the gods to which he sacrificed were just stone.[155] Cecilia's taunting of Almachius precipitated her martyrdom, but before her execution, she experienced the successful culmination of her efforts to shape the world around her: the saint's interior perceptions now corresponded to the external reality upon which "all" concurred. Only one stubborn yet powerful man could not see what was really there.

After being beheaded, Cecilia remained for three days with her followers. During this Christlike period, Cecilia taught the new Christians, donated property to them as a group, and transformed her own house into a church. The text thus moved from a single woman with the gospel hidden in her breast to an established Christian community with a church building and an endowment. The woman herself was the source and the driving force of the visible church community and the instrument of its establishment, thus reflecting "the historically significant donation of resources and status to the early church by Roman matrons."[156] Yet, the overtly theological frame that introduced the narrative in the Kitzingen *libellus* and the omission of all specific references to the city of Rome (such as the naming of Urban as its bishop) rendered the *passio Ceciliae* in this case more than a history of how Cecilia established a particular church (the *titulus Ceciliae*) in a particular city (Rome).[157] The narrative became a demonstration that Woman was essential to the creation of the visible Church.

What Cecilia founded, Juliana defended and cultivated. The clandestine Christian community of Cecilia's day gave way, in the passion narrative of Juliana, to an organized church. Yet, that church and its members were threatened by secular persecutors, including the man (Eliseus) who wanted to marry Juliana. Juliana demanded that Eliseus convert to Christianity to marry her and even convinced him of the truth of her faith, but his cowardice prevented him from publicly embracing Christianity for fear of reprisals from the emperor. And so the brave young woman ended up in prison, where she confronted and bound a demon, Jofer, from whom she wrung a confession: a catalogue of the demonic misdeeds behind every manifestation of evil in the world, beginning with the transgression of Adam and Eve.[158]

The Pelagian theology of the *libellus* thus continued. Against the Augustinian notion of original sin, according to which the transgression in paradise wrought a congenital alteration in human nature, vitiating human will and increasing human propensity to sin, the Anonyma taught that evil deeds from the primordial to the recent had a different cause: the promptings of demons, which humans could and sometimes did successfully resist. Jofer may have personally tricked generations of male patsies (including Cain, Nebuchadnezzar, Herod, Judas, and Nero), but the *libellus* put on parade a series of untrickable women with the gift of discernment. From Mary's recognition of the angel and his message, through Cecilia's ability to see angels hidden from those around her, to Juliana's recognition that the "angel" who approached her in prison was a demon in disguise, the daughters of Eve all put their "rational souls" and "willing minds" to work.[159]

The passion narratives of Agnes and Agatha provided additional impressive evidence of the exteriorized Christlike power of woman and of that power's connection with the spread of the Christian faith in the post-Marian, post-Incarnation world. The Anonyma introduced Agnes, a thirteen-year-old girl with an immeasurably old mind, as she was coming home from school.[160] She then showed us Agnes resisting the entreaties of the parents of a youth who had fallen in love with the girl to marry their son, despite their offer of many things and their promise of many more. Here the Anonyma substituted a large quantity of items for the original narrative's focus on specifically beautiful items and omitted both the full text's detailed descriptions of the gorgeous things on offer and Agnes's dreamy conceptualization of Christ as a lover who showered her with jewelry; these editorial changes broke the stereotypical connection between frivolous women and luxury goods that had been built into the full *passio* and was common in antiwoman literature. But Agnes's troubles were not over: a judge demanded that she sacrifice to a pagan deity, the goddess Vesta, or suffer the consequences. Again, Agnes stood firm, and she was punished by imprisonment in a brothel; there, protected by an angel, she transformed her surroundings into a sacred place of prayer, a powerful externalization of her faith. Cecilia was able to transform her private house into a church, but Agnes showed that Christianity could penetrate everywhere, even the most sullied of places, through the efforts of woman.

Greater deeds were yet to come, including Agnes's resurrection of her would-be husband, who met an untimely death in the brothel by attempting to touch the saint. The young girl thus performed the highest order of miracle, comparable to Jesus' resurrection of Lazarus (a parallel event included in the closing portion of the frame), and to great effect, for it persuaded huge crowds of people to convert to Christianity. The event transpired precisely at the midpoint of the *libellus*[161] and was set up by the saint's announcement that "because it is time that the power of my Lord Jesus Christ be made manifest, let us all go outside so that I may offer myself to God in my accustomed prayer."[162] The parallelism with Christ was strengthened as the Anonyma had Agnes offer herself (a sacrificial act) rather than her prayer, the infinitely more common formulation utilized in the full *passio*. The theme of Agnes as the sacrificed one continued after her death in her parents' vision of her with a lamb (*agnus*), a symbol of sacrifice. And as a sign of the increasing Christianization of the physical landscape, the text then lingered over Agnes's tomb, the focal point of veneration of a miracle-working woman.

The final text in the assemblage, "De obitu Agathae" (fol. 14r), was the most radically trimmed of all the narratives, compared with its source *passio*. "On the death of Agatha" provided the end-of-life and postmortem themes that had been largely absent from the previous three texts but were necessary to complete the parallels between Christ and his female imitators. It preserved the very end of the saint's trial before the proconsul Quintianus, as she declared the perspicacity of her interrogator inferior to her own and insulted him for being "without sense or intelligence" ("sine sensu et sine intellectu," folio 14v). Quintianus was unable to avenge himself on Agatha because his plans to torture her were foiled by an earthquake that crushed two of his advisors and precipitated a popular uprising, forcing him to flee. The earthquake recalled the geological and climatic events that accompanied Christ's paradigmatic passion on the cross. It was only the first of a series of authorial devices designed to model Agatha's death on that of Jesus.[163] By far the most significant of the parallels was the fact that Agatha's actual death appeared as the conscious and voluntary result of her own decision, an aspect of Christ's heroism that was frequently emphasized by Carolingian-era theologians.[164] Standing in prison and yet paradoxically remaining visible to many ("coram multis"), she told God she was ready to be taken and gave up the ghost "with an enormous cry" ("ingenti voce"). Woman had come very far since she first appeared in the person of Cecilia, who began the female journey hidden, silent, and subject to the control of her family. Agatha ended the journey visible, audible, and in control of her own body to the point of control over her physical death. The liberation of woman was the fulfillment of Christianity, and vice versa.[165]

The theme of liberation was literally monumentalized when a mysterious youth and his entourage placed a marble tablet over Agatha's tomb; the tablet bore the words: "mentem sanctam spontaneam deo et e liberationis" (fol. 15v). In virtually all copies of any version of the *passio Agathae*, her memorial inscription read "mentem sanctam, spontaneum honorem deo, et patriae liberationem,"[166] or "A holy mind, willing honor to God, and the liberation of the fatherland." The codex that is our best guide to the full *passio* utilized by the Kitzingen Anonyma, namely, Paris BN lat. 10861, gendered "spontaneam" as feminine and had it modify "mind" rather than "honor" but generally stuck to the common phrasing.[167] The text of the *De obitu Agathae* in "Deus per angelum" was extraordinarily error-ridden, so it is perhaps justifiable to treat the unattached letter *e* as an error and suggest the translation: "A holy willing mind, and for the God of liberation." This would represent an eighth-century version of liberation theology built on the ideas in the opening frame of the *libellus*: the (Pelagian) notion of the willing mind, which can make the right choices, and liberation.[168]

Agatha's tomb, springboard into the closing frame centered on Christ's passion and tomb, represented the monumentalized realization of woman in physical space and coincided with the full realization of Christianity in the world, for it became the focal point of a faith uniting local Christians, pagans, and Jews. At the start, the gospel was hidden in the breast of Cecilia (or, to return to the opening frame, in the womb of Mary); at the finish, Christian devotion had invaded every breast. Furthermore, "On the Death of Agatha" included postmortem miracles, a crucial dimension in projecting the significance of the woman Cecilia-Juliana-Agnes-Agatha into the infinite future. In the final episode in the saintly core of "Deus per angelum," the deadly molten lava flow belched forth from Mount Etna toward the city of Catania was halted, and the city saved, when the citizens betook themselves to Agatha's tomb. Agatha's power over the lava flow from Mount Etna also represented the culmination of the trajectory of the materialization, exteriorization, and realization of the Christian faith as a force in the world, from its humble beginnings in Cecilia's breast (or in Mary's imaginative will). Within the parameters of "Deus per angelum," Christianity was a faith brought to humans by women.

This composite holy woman Cecilia-Juliana-Agnes-Agatha cannot be forced into the category of the "virgin martyr," a figure who "is always beautiful, always of good family, her chastity always somehow threatened. She undergoes a series of tortures and confrontations, and inevitably dies."[169] With the exception that all died and were presumably virgins (albeit never described as such), the martyrs in "Deus per angelum" did not fit this description. In fact, the only figures described as "beautiful" in the entire *libellus* were the mysterious youth and his all-male entourage who came to place a marble inscription on Agatha's tomb (fol. 15r).[170] Instead, Cecilia, Juliana, Agnes, and Agatha all occupied themselves with preaching against pagan deities and never wasted a precious moment when facing their judges and the gathered crowds on the subject of sexuality. All were commanded to sacrifice to non-Christian deities, and all refused. They were treated as persons who counted in the public forum, expected to demonstrate their allegiance to the political structure in which they lived, not as sexual beings concerned with chastity. Not even in Agnes's narrative was sexual peril thematized, even though she was being held in a brothel rather than a prison (as were Juliana and Agatha). Indeed the *libellus*'s unusual spelling of the word for brothel ("lupinar," rather than "lupanar") desexualized Agnes's perils by alluding to a different nonsexual danger, namely, wolves.

The Kitzingen Anonyma's female martyrs ran counter to expectations that have characterized the entire spectrum of scholarship on women saints. The priest D'Arrigo, for instance, claimed that Agatha was not "actually" martyred as part of an imperial persecution of Christians, but as a result of the vendetta that Quintianus was waging against her because she had spurned his sexual advances; in fact, he wrote, "fascination with the beauty of Agatha was the true cause of her martyrdom."[171] Cross, a traditional male literary scholar, insisted that the defense-of-virginity theme really was present—in an "allusive" rather than "explicit" manner—in the Latin *passio Julianae*, despite its complete absence from that narrative.[172] Sorgo, a feminist literary theorist, found tales of female martyrs to be so thoroughly sexualized that she saw in them the roots of modern pornography.[173] Finally, squarely in the mainstream of feminist historical scholarship, Schulenburg and Consolino (respectively) argued that women won recognition as martyrs solely through defense of their virginal purity against lecherous men and that the only significant model of sanctity available to women in the fifth- and sixth-century martyr passions was devotion to virginity and chastity.[174] A few aspects of the full *passiones* of Cecilia, Juliana, Agnes, and Agatha had pointed to the classic "virgin-martyr" as described, but the Kitzingen Anonyma thoroughly purged her abbreviations of every component element of the iconic virgin-martyr connection, such as the potentially eroticized torture of Agatha's breast. Rather than all four representing a homogeneous ideal of femininity as bodily purity, the martyrs Agnes, Juliana, Cecilia, and Agatha instead embodied four distinct moments in the life-span (the "*cursus naturae*" of the pseudo-Fulgentian sermon) of Everywoman: the girl, the adult single woman, the wife, and the deceased woman.[175] The *libellus* therefore supports attempts to dissolve monolithic preconceptions concerning depictions of female martyrs.[176]

The Holy Everywoman of "Deus per angelum" was not markedly virginal. Juliana, for instance, appeared perfectly willing to enter into a full, normal marriage—she simply refused to do so with a man who persecuted her coreligionists. Already in the full *passio Julianae*, virginity (mentioned neither in her negotiations with her suitor nor in connection with her death) had appeared only once, as a source of the physical strength that enabled the saint to bind a demon;[177] even this offhand reference was cut from the abbreviation. Similarly, a subtly gentle—and absolutely noncausal—link between virginity and martyrdom in the full *passio Ceciliae* (an angel brought crowns covered with red roses and white lilies to Cecilia and Valerian to foreshadow how both would undergo bloody passions and be virginally pure)[178] was replaced in "Deus per angelum" by a simple angelic statement commending the virginity of the chaste couple ("commendavit virginitatem amborum," folio 7r). The Kitzingen Anonyma's theology of womanhood never gave virginity the pride of place (or connection to martyrdom) that modern scholars have sometimes assigned to the virginal state in their assessments of the nature of female sanctity.[179] Indeed, one of the sections cut from the opening pseudo-Fulgentian Marian sermon by the author of the *libellus* was the assertion that Mary's virginity was not violated by Jesus' birth (that is, that she continued to have corporeal integrity even after parturition).[180] The women of Kitzingen certainly valued virginity but not to the exclusion of all else; the Anonyma constructed a theology of womanhood that emphasized women's wills, actions, and words over their corporeal characteristics.

Another element of the iconic virgin-martyr figure as she is generally conceptualized was the endurance of horrific tortures.[181] Yet the Kitzingen Anonyma displayed a complete aversion to textualized violence. This reticence was in part an unremarkable function of cultural sensibilities shared with most Europeans of her era. The luxuriantly detailed and gruesome depictions of violence that characterized both the art and the literature of the later Middle Ages were far removed from eighth-century approaches.[182] European manuscript painters began creating graphic depictions of the violent torture of saints and martyrs (and mostly male ones, to judge by surviving evidence) only in the tenth and eleventh centuries; for inspiration, those artists drew on Mediterranean models dating from before 600.[183] But eighth-century artists rejected this aesthetic of violence, just as the Kitzingen Anonyma purged the pre-600 Mediterranean martyr *passiones* of their violent elements when she condensed them for her *libellus*. For instance, the full passion narrative of Juliana had included vicious torture episodes, in which the saint's body was broken and violated to the extent that marrow oozed out of her bones.[184] The author of "Deus per angelum" cut this scene entirely, along with a plethora of additional individual words and brief phrases, all with the goal of diminishing the level of vulgar bloodthirstiness in the text.[185]

Graphic depictions of bodily harm, whether textual or visual, are not necessarily ways to negatively abjectify/objectify the tortured person. Within a

Christian context, even gruesome images could be positive, rather than sadistic, when consumed in connection with images of Jesus' broken, bleeding body. Torture-induced wounds could then be authenticating signs of Christlike holiness, as were certain late medieval depictions of the torture of Agatha's breast.[186] However, in a cultural context in which Jesus was not seen visibly to suffer (and the Anglo-Saxon cultural province in Francia was such a context, as witnessed by the Kitzingen crucifixion miniature), it was far less possible to understand the position of "victim of violence" as ennobling. Just as the actual crucifixion of Jesus was skipped in the closing frame of "Deus per angelum," which jumped from the gathering on the Mount of Olives to the empty tomb, so did it prove impossible for the enemies of the saints to visit any violence upon the Christian heroines in the martyrial core of the *libellus*. For instance, Agnes's enemies tried to expose her naked body, but miraculous interventions frustrated their efforts, and the very pot of boiling lead itself refused to cooperate in the plans to torture Juliana (whereas this same pot had proven entirely pliable in the full narrative).[187] Most important, the reader was never explicitly shown the moment of execution of either Juliana or Agatha, and Agnes's decapitation by sword was over in the narrative blink of an eye.

Only Cecilia's extraordinary death was judged worthy of significant narrative attention because the half-decapitated saint—who miraculously lived for three days after a botched attempt to execute her—devoted her last days on earth to consecrating her house as a church, thus authorizing women to perform priestly acts. The famous episode of Cecilia's house–church consecration was later cited as justification for claims that the laity could perform minor sacraments and may have been similarly exploited already in the eighth century.[188] Combined with other examples of clerical behavior in the *libellus*, such as Juliana's extraction of a confession from the demon, Agnes's resurrection of the besotted youth while clad in an angelically produced and miraculously delivered *stola* (a clerical vestment worn by male priests during sacramental performances), and the frequent sermonizing of all the martyrs, the house consecration asserted a strong precedent for the sacerdotal role of women.[189]

The composite holy woman Cecilia-Juliana-Agnes-Agatha thus escaped virtually every stereotypical position known to scholarship on female sanctity: she was not particularly virginal or beautiful, nor did she suffer physically or emotionally. She never had to overcome the special frailty of her weaker sex to reach heights of holiness.[190] However, like many prominent male saints, she was vocal, performed miracles, and had sacerdotal aspirations, characteristics that explain why Juliana could be called "companion of the apostles, consort of the martyrs, partner of the patriarchs, companion of the angels."[191] And like the women of the Bonifatian movement, she enjoyed close spiritual camaraderie with men, on egalitarian terms. The chaste marriage of Cecilia and Valerian (structurally a ménage à trois with an angel, the lover of them both) could take place only after the purification of the bridegroom, a process effected by having Valerian read a markedly egalitarian Pauline passage: "One God, one faith, one baptism, one God and father of all, who is above all things and in us all" (Ephesians 4:5–6).[192] Cecilia had already been featured in Aldhelm's prose treatise on virginity, where she stood alongside Mary and Joseph as a linchpin of a group of chastely married men and women.[193] Flanked in "Deus per angelum" by Mary and Jesus, she was a worthy combatant in the battle against those Carolingian reformers who wished to limit the public and ecclesiastical roles of women.

Misogynistic moments in European history precipitated the creation of feminist works, both literary and artistic, designed to critique male domination.[194] "Deus per angelum" was one such work: a deeply intellectual feminist theological tractate necessitated by late eighth-century attacks on the position of religious women.

CHAPTER SEVEN

"AN ETERNAL WEIGHT OF GLORY" (2 CORINTHIANS 4:17): DISCIPLINE AND DEVOTION IN MONASTIC LIFE

AN ETERNAL WEIGHT OF GLORY

The Anglo-Saxon immigrants to Francia, along with their continental collaborators, advocated regulated lifestyles, that is, the organization of monastic life to the extent possible according to a *regula* (rule).[1] Their orientation was effectively Benedictine, in that they considered the Rule of St. Benedict to be a superlative source of guidance for the monastic lifestyle. Nevertheless, their communities did not formally or strictly follow the Benedictine (or any other) rule, particularly not as we know it (or them) today.[2] In this regard, Karlburg, Kitzingen, and the other Main Valley institutions were typical of early medieval women's communities, only a handful of which were organized in accordance with a rule.[3] In fact, they were typical of early medieval monastic communities in general, for the very notion of a "rule" was still a highly ambiguous concept before the ninth century.[4] Recent scholarship has emphasized the "remarkable range of experiences and practices" and the "state of vibrant chaos" that characterized monasticisms (deliberately pluralized) from the fourth into the ninth century, before the primacy of the prescriptive rule.[5]

Houses for noblewomen had rich endowments that were legally in the control of the community (and particularly the abbess), which in turn guaranteed a large degree of discretion concerning organizational forms.[6] Abbesses could decide to use a rule (as Adela at Pfalzel apparently decided to use the Rule of St. Benedict) but were not obligated to do so; they could just as easily decide themselves to be the rule.[7] Yet, lack of a formal rule was not tantamount to lawlessness, nor were abbesses devoid of textual(ized) support in their duty to guide their flocks. We should certainly not conclude from the relative rarity of formal written rules that women's houses were essentially "domestic" institutions serving the social needs of an aristocratic family but indifferent to the spiritual and intellectual needs of the inhabitants.[8] Instead, we must look to different sorts of manuscripts, not just copies of rules, to find the texts that served as blueprints for lives of monastic discipline and devotion.

A text could function as a monastic rule without conforming to the standard format of a monastic rule. This was the case in Ireland, where collections of sayings on the monastic life, penitentials, and other types of texts served as rule-equivalents.[9] Not the rule by Caesarius of Arles but rather other writings by and attributed to him (namely, sermons and letters) circulated widely as part of a relatively stable collection of texts aimed at dedicated women who, by the eighth century, "had more need of ideological works which left them free to find their own practical paths to holiness, than of rules which governed the *minutiae* of their existence."[10] Biographies of saints also functioned as "normative texts."[11] In this chapter, I treat a number of texts that appear to have functioned effectively as guidelines for a life of monastic devotion at Karlburg and Kitzingen for the women who produced and owned them: Isidore of Seville's *Synonyms* (in one case combined with a pair of narratives concerning saints), the florilegium known as the *Liber Scintillarum*, and a handful of sermons, including by Caesarius.[12]

These texts formed a coherent group. Isidore's *Synonyms* drew forty-three times on Jerome's *Commentary on Ecclesiastes*, a centonization of which appeared in the sermon collection; the *Liber Scintillarum*, in turn, drew heavily on Isidore's *Synonyms*.[13] And all the texts drew heavily on the letters of Paul. Certainly Carolingian-era scribes saw the texts as related. A substantial percentage of the surviving eighth-century copies of the *Synonyms* were codicologically combined, *ab initio*, with florilegia and devotional sermons. For instance, the Anglo-Saxon Peregrinus, working at Freising under Arbeo (764–784), combined the *Synonyms* (in the Λ recension used at Karlburg) with the *Liber Scintillarum*, a unique "Freising florilegium," and a few sermons by authors such as Caesarius.[14] Another scribe, active during the first third of the ninth century in what is now eastern France, also paired the *Synonyms* with the *Liber Scintillarum*.[15] A third scribe, active in early ninth-century southern Bavaria, combined extracts from the Λ transmission of Isidore's *Synonyms* with another unique florilegium, alongside several popular sermons.[16] Finally, at least eight manuscripts from the ninth century and later combined the *Synonyms* with a corpus of monastic rules; one of these (Lambach, Stiftsbibliothek 31) appears to have been produced at the Main Valley women's house of Schwarzach around the middle of the ninth century.[17]

I begin with Isidore's spiritual classic, the *Synonyms*, which found in Paul a justification for the disciplined monastic lifestyle, namely, that present suffering and tribulation would be rewarded with "an eternal weight of glory."[18]

THE SYNONYMS OF ISIDORE OF SEVILLE: SPIRITUAL CONSOLATION FOR THE ANGUISHED SOUL

Many works of Isidore of Seville (c. 560–636) were widely diffused throughout Latin Europe within a century of his death. His *Synonyms*, however, did not spread as quickly or as early outside Spain as did the bishop of Seville's other writings. Yet the text was a precociously popular source of devotional and penitential motifs, as well as a model of style in, the Anglo-Saxon homeland of Thekla and Leoba already in the time of Aldhelm.[19] Despite some debate concerning whether the young Boniface personally wrote in an early eighth-century English copy of the *Synonyms* (St. Petersburg, Rossijskaja Nacionalnaja Biblioteka, Lat. Q.v.I.15),[20] there is agreement that the text was of paramount importance in the Anglo-Saxon cultural zone on the continent and that the Anglo-Saxon newcomers were central in its early transmission and promotion.[21]

Fifteen of the thirty-eight extant extra-Spanish manuscripts of the *Synonyms* from the ninth century or earlier are in the Anglo-Saxon tradition.[22] Of the twelve that date from the eighth century (or possibly the very beginning of the ninth), eight were closely connected with the Anglo-Saxon immigrants to the region under study here, and one was more loosely associated with their network of friends and collaborators.[23] Those eight included (in addition to the St. Petersburg manuscript mentioned previously) Boniface's own personal copy (Fulda, Dommuseum, Bonifatianus 2). Whether or not the future prelate had already encountered the *Synonyms* as a youth in England, he prized the text enough in adulthood to bring it with him on his missionary journeys.[24] Other (fragmentary or complete) eighth-century copies demonstrate the interest of the Bonifatian circle in the text, including one from an unidentified Anglo-Saxon center on the continent that was at Fulda early in the ninth century,[25] one recently discovered fragment of the Φ recension,[26] a few leaves from another unspecified Anglo-Saxon center in the Rhine–Main region,[27] and an Anglo-Saxon copy that was at the cathedral of Würzburg by the end of the century (Würzburg, UB M.p.th.f. 79).[28] Most important, both the Gun(t)za[29] and Abirhilt[30] groups included copies of the text.

The *Synonyms* possessed a certain "polymorphous utility," enabling it eventually to become popular throughout Europe and across the entire spectrum of literate consumers of Christian texts.[31] Yet in each case, and for each group, certain specific characteristics of the text accounted for its appeal, particularly during the eighth century when few readers had yet grasped the potential of the work. We need to ask why Isidore's *Synonyms* held such an extraordinary status among the women of the Main Valley communities in order to understand what the text can tell us about their devotional and disciplinary lives.

Isidore wrote the *Synonyms* in a context in which double monasteries represented the outright standard approach to monastic organization.[32] Isidore himself was supportive of the syneisactic nature of Iberian monasteries. For instance, he recommended that monks and nuns engage in economies of exchange, with the women making clothes for the men in return for types of support that men could more easily provide.[33] He also presided at a church council (Seville II, held in 619) at which the gathered prelates (in canon 11) gave monks the responsibility for the spiritual and material well-being of nuns. This legislation departed from previous organizational models, which had subjected nuns to bishops rather than to monks, and signaled the end to centuries of episcopal endorsement of sex segregation in monastic contexts.[34] In Isidore's view, insofar as the internal working of their monastic communities was concerned, the lives of religious women were identical to those of religious men.[35]

Isidore of Seville thus knew that a substantial portion of his potential readership consisted of heterosocial religious communities. Not all his works were aimed at a monastic audience in need of devotional texts, but the *Synonyms* certainly was. Medieval bibliographical notices always discussed the text as a work of spiritual consolation.[36] Long misunderstood as part of a triptych of schoolbooks (along with Isidore's *Differences* and *Etymologies*) for training rhetors, whose specific purpose was to develop verbal agility by studying a tract in which every point was repeated between two and twelve times, in different words, the *Synonyms* has since been recognized as a moral or spiritual tract.[37] Isidore did organize his thinking and writing along the grammatical lines of generic schoolbook forms, but the content of his writings was always deeply spiritual. Put simply, Isidore of Seville developed a unique way of doing theology through grammar, putting the techniques of ancient rhetoric in the service of Christian morality.[38] Other works in the synonymic style consisted of repeated propositions that never added up to any larger point, whereas Isidore's *Synonyms* was a carefully crafted masterpiece with an internal progression and a coherent argument.[39]

The coherent structure of the *Synonyms* was absolutely straightforward. At the beginning of the text, *Homo* (Human Being) expressed a heartfelt plaint:

> My soul is in anguish, my spirit burns, my heart beats wildly, spiritual anguish overwhelms me. Anguish of the soul possesses me, anguish of the soul afflicts me. I am surrounded by evils, closed in by shadows, encircled by enemies, besieged by miseries, buried by unhappiness, oppressed by anguish. I do not find any refuge from such great evil. . . . [40]

Homo continued in this vein for several more lines. *Homo* then engaged in a dialogue with *Ratio,* who led *Homo* through an intensively emotional experience, at the end of which *Homo* repented of sins and decided to persevere, prompting *Ratio* to launch into a monologue whose contents amounted to a full-fledged moral manual. *Ratio* offered practical strategies for living a virtuous life at a point when the power of *Homo*'s emotional journey had prepared the soil of the reader's soul to absorb *Ratio*'s teachings. The synonymic repetitions, conducive to the (emotionally and intellectually challenging) processes of rumination and introspection, functioned perfectly in the spiritual text. What is more, the accumulation of words and phrases reinforced the deliberately hyperbolic content and consequently the expressivity of the text.[41] Finally, on a very mundane level, the frequent repetitions rendered the text easier to understand, even for someone with weak Latin knowledge, by maximizing the chance that a reader would be familiar with at least one of the formulations used to convey a given idea; this must have been extremely important in an area such as the Main River valley, where no one was a native speaker of Latin.[42]

The *Synonyms* of Isidore of Seville was thus a devotional and disciplinary treatise whose immediate "natural" audience was monastic communities, written when said monastic communities were predominantly syneisactic. Surely Isidore, as an effective spiritual teacher, intentionally shaped the treatise to render it of maximum utility and acceptability to associated groups of consecrated men and women. This context of original composition rendered the *Synonyms* immensely popular in syneisactic Anglo-Saxon circles on the continent during the eighth century, for the text was, from the moment it left the author's pen, emphatically universalizing. Both female and male readers could equally and easily identify with the universal human predicament of *Homo*. Texts intended to support men's monastic lifestyles were regularly repurposed to serve women's communities, and vice versa.[43] Isidore's *Synonyms*, however, required no alterations to be suitable for both male and female readers and was therefore particularly appealing to women and men committed to a syneisactic lifestyle.

Here is how Prologue 1 (probably added in the Anglo-Saxon cultural zone), which appeared in both the Gun(t)za and Abirhilt copies of the treatise, advertised the text:

> Isidore of holy memory, archbishop from Spain, introduces the character of *Homo* crying bitterly amid the hardships of the present world . . . whom Reason meets in a marvelous encounter, and consoles with gentle management. . . . Any reader who strives to proceed with an eager mind will without doubt learn in what manner to avoid vices, how to lament sins already committed, and how to be renewed through the laments of repentance . . . so as not to perish with desires for the things of this world, but rather to live with Christ, rewarded with eternal prizes.[44]

The announced intention of the *Synonyms* was to grapple with a universal situation: the tribulations of *Homo* in this world, tribulations keenly felt by all, including the author.[45] The prologue also guaranteed consolation for *Homo*'s experience of tribulation and foreshadowed how the answer would lie in penance, a practice equally open to women and men. Although the grammatically male *Homo* may not seem to be an unproblematically universal persona, no other term was available that could have better invited all readers to identify with the protagonist. For instance, Augustine's discussion of the "image of God" in his *On the Trinity* (the first book ordered for the newly founded Würzburg cathedral library by Bishop Burkhard) made it perfectly clear that a woman was a human being (*homo*).[46] Still, some highly gender-sensitive scribes, including the Kitzingen one, also intervened in the text of Prologue 1 to avoid an unnecessarily emphatic masculinization of the text's protagonist.[47]

Isidore's universalizing *Synonyms* was thus already designed to appeal to the women of the Anglo-Saxon cultural zone in Francia. Nevertheless, scribes at both Karlburg and Kitzingen found ways to increase the appeal of the text by shaping their copies to maximize its personalized relevance to local readers and to intensify their experience of the text. The Gun(t)za group (Karlburg) copy of the text (Würzburg UB M.p.th.q. 28a) personalized it by embodying the teachings of *Ratio* in two exemplary Christ-figure people, namely, St. Eugenia and St. Potitus, whose biographies were appended to the *Synonyms*. Even here, through having two passion narratives, the device of synonymic repetition of a single point in more than one way was maintained; that the martyrs were a woman and a man, rather than two men or two women, also underlined the applicability of the text across gender lines. I analyze these martyr passions and their relation to the text of the *Synonyms* later in this chapter. Here, I turn first to the strategies adopted by the Abirhilt group scriptorium in Würzburg UB M.p.th. q. 28b (the Kitzingen copy): to personalize and dramatize the meaning of the *Synonyms* through illustration with images and by structuring the text as a dramatic dialogue between *Homo* and *Ratio*.

ISIDORE AT KITZINGEN: ILLUSTRATION THROUGH ANIMAL IMAGERY IN WÜRZBURG UB M.P.TH.Q. 28B

The illustrations in the Kitzingen copy of Isidore's *Synonyms* were essential to the message of the text as understood by its scribe-illuminator. I have not come across any other examples of illuminated copies of Isidore's *Synonyms*; thus, the very decision by the Kitzingen artist to illustrate the text was significant and creative and must have been based on a strong desire to express something of her own understanding of the meaning of the text. The artist, certainly the same woman who drew the crucifixion miniature in the Pauline epistles, given the rarity of such talents at the time, also heralded the coming illustrations through a unique textual variant in her copy of the second (originally Isidoran) prologue. After a compressed statement guaranteeing the universal utility of the text, the second prologue introduced *Homo* and *Ratio*: "Duorum autem personae hic inducuntur, deflentis hominis, et admonentis rationis."[48] However, instead of "inducuntur" (that is, "brought forward" as in "introduced"), the scribe-illuminator wrote "indicantur" (fol. 43v), that is, "brought forward" as in "revealed," with a strong connotation of visibility. Thus, the scribe-artist explicitly announced her intention to reveal the characters by means of an illustration.

The illustration that followed immediately after the sentence just quoted was a haloed backward-looking four-footed animal in the shape of the letter *h* combined with the letters "omo" to create the word *homo* (Plate 5). *Homo* was evidently no mere word, but rather the protagonist of the text ("human being"), about to enter into dialogue with *Ratio*. Yet the text, with its plural "indicantur," had announced that both *Homo* and *Ratio* were revealed, and indeed they were, for in Christian art historical terms, a backward-looking four-footed animal with a cruciform halo was the Lamb of God (*agnus dei*), namely, Jesus, "the Lamb of God who takes away the sin of the world" (John 1:29).

The Lamb of God motif, attested on the Italian peninsula from the fifth century,[49] was scratched (before 700) as a graffito on one of the columns of the abbey church of St. Symphorien in Autun.[50] It became popular in eighth-century Northumbria, where it was utilized for the Codex Amiatinus (from Wearmouth-Jarrow) and for both the Ruthwell and Aycliffe crosses.[51] Further-more, at least four pins with the motif of a backward-looking four-footed ani-mal dating from around 700 have been found in Main Valley sites such as Kleinlangheim, located twelve kilometers from Kitzingen and five kilometers from Schwarzach. Although these lacked explicitly Christian iconography,[52] they could have furnished some inspiration to our artist. Yet the absolute closest analogue to the Kitzingen Lamb of God—indeed, its only truly close likeness—appeared in an eighth-century manuscript from another (Carolin-gian) royal women's monastery: the Laon Orosius, one of the Laon School az-manuscripts.

Laon, BM 137, a copy of Orosius's *Histories* produced around 750 or 760 at Sainte-Marie-Saint-Jean of Laon, boasted a full-page "Veneration of the Lamb" illumination on its title page (fol. 1v).[53] While the Lamb of God with the crossed nimbus in the central medallion was most closely related to the lamb of the Kitzingen *Synonyms*, the numerous backward-looking four-footers in the frame of the Laon Orosius also bore many marked similarities to the Isidoran figure. The only az-manuscript scribe known by name was Dulcia, who cer-tainly made Laon BM 423 and who may also have made Paris BN lat. 12168; she was not, however, the scribe of the Orosius, whose work was particularly close to Chelles products, above all to the Vatican Gelasian Sacramentary.[54] Although all the Laon az-manuscripts featured marked overlaps with books from the women's scriptorium at Chelles, the Chelles manuscript that was most closely related to the Laon az-group was Oxford, Bodleian, Laud misc 126, the copy of Augustine's *On the Trinity* made for the Würzburg cathedral.[55] The Kitzingen artist responsible for both the Isidoran Lamb of God and the Pauline crucifix-ion miniature may well have been trained by the very woman responsible for the Laon Orosius, for the latter image also had much in common with the frontispiece to the Kitzingen Paul, such as the important Chelles-school motif of the cross under an arcade and the device of hanging figures from the cros-sarms. Insofar as the abbesses of both Kitzingen and Sainte-Marie-Saint-Jean of Laon were Pippinid-Carolingian princesses throughout the eighth century, exchanges and connections between the two houses would have been easily established.

Like the crucifixion miniature, the illustrated *homo* in Isidore's *Synonyms* comprised a series of deeply entangled, overlapping identities. This artistic technique created unbounded complexity while simultaneously focusing the reader's eyes on a single, simple image. The word *homo* was also *Homo* the

Word: Jesus, who was regularly described not only as the *agnus Dei* but also with the phrase "Ecce Homo" (Behold, [the] Man). The four-footed animal/ *homo* was not simply suffering Everyman but also Jesus, and therefore the image did reveal both *Homo* and *Ratio*, for the *Ratio* of Isidore's *Synonyms* was not human reason but rather the Wisdom of God.[56] *Ratio* could be none other than Christ, for the final words of the text contained *Homo*'s profession of love for *Ratio* above all else.[57] The four-footer glowed with powerful, warm orange and yellow light, bright enough to illuminate the darkness and help the most pitiful lost soul find a way forward.

The opening illustration in Würzburg UB M.p.th.q. 28b was thus a succinct statement of the dual nature of Christ, as two persons, human and divine, both *Homo* and *Ratio*. By logical extension, it was also a succinct statement of the potential of human beings to accede to that duality themselves, to be like Christ in both his human and his divine aspects. The image depicted both the suffering human being, the anguished soul who cried out as the text opened, and the suffering Jesus, Lamb of God. It was particularly appropriate as an illustration for a gender-universalizing text in that it embodied Christ in an animal while avoiding any characteristics associated with biological sex, such as antlers or external genitalia. The image thus underlined the universal applicability of the model of suffering at the core of *Ratio*'s message.

Homo, the eighth-century equivalent of a deer caught in headlights, was trapped, hunted, surrounded, terrified, seeing no escape from or positive side to its suffering. This opening image of the four-footer looking back in fear over its own shoulder continued to function through the second chapter, deepening the emotional resonance of the text, for it was still visible to a reader whose focal point had shifted to folio 44r, where she could read:

> Wherever I flee, my misfortunes pursue me; wherever I turn, the shadow of my misfortunes accompanies me. Like the very shadow of my body, so am I unable to run away from my misfortunes. . . . although I have never done evil to anyone, I have never falsely accused anyone, I have never stood against anyone, I have never brought trouble to anyone . . . I have lived among my fellow humans without quarrel. . . .[58]

A reader of the Kitzingen *Synonyms* benefited from a powerful, visualized sense of the horrific feeling that, wherever she went, the shadows of her misfortunes followed inescapably like the shadow of her own body. Yet, as she continued to turn the pages, gradually, through dialogue with *Ratio*, she absorbed the consolatory implications of the fact that Human Being could also be Jesus, the voluntary sacrificial lamb whose suffering redeemed the world.

Illustration was not the only strategy utilized by the scribe-artist of the Kitzingen Isidore to heighten the emotional impact of the text and encourage the reader's identification with it; the text, like most representatives of the Φ recension, was also laid out as a dialogue between *Homo* and *Ratio*.[59] Human

Being spoke the opening lines, written right in front of the creature's back-turned mouth:

My soul is in anguish, my spirit burns, my heart beats wildly, spiritual anguish overwhelms me. Anguish of the soul possesses me, anguish of the soul afflicts me. I am surrounded by evils, closed in by shadows, encircled by enemies, besieged by miseries, buried by unhappiness, oppressed by anguish. I do not find any refuge from such great evil. . . . [60]

Ratio spoke for the first time on folio 47r, its words introduced by an orange "*ratio*"; the two *dramatis personae* then alternated in their dialogue for the remainder of Book I.[61] The situation was almost theatrical, and it is worth considering the possibility that the dialogue was at times performed.[62]

The illuminations and dialogue format in the Kitzingen copy of Isidore's *Synonyms* heightened the emotional impact of a text that was already saturated with feelings of pain and anxiety. In all copies of the text, the lamentable *mala* of Human Being were recounted in chilling detail: *Homo* was alone, friendless, spurned by all, and reduced to beggary through corrupt judgments, unjust persecution, unjustified hatred, tattling lies, false testimony, and unwarranted accusations.[63] Such feelings of isolation could have catastrophic consequences if not properly handled within the close quarters of a monastic community, where feelings of exclusion could push the inevitable strains of the common life to the breaking point. It is an indication of the visceral impact of Isidore's text that the scribe-artist of the Kitzingen manuscript at one point threw the text into the first person (when all other copies reported *Homo*'s thoughts as a rhetorical question to an interlocutor), exclaiming, "Whom can I believe? In whom can I have faith?"[64] She also highlighted one particularly intense articulation of the situation ("everyone is raging against me, everyone is intent upon my destruction, everyone is preparing their hands to kill me") by surrounding almost all the initial letters with clusters of red dots, a technique known as *Umpunkt* (fol. 45v).[65] The bloodied sentence strategically linked the textual sentiment with the (illuminated) Lamb of God, against whom all had once raised their hands in unjust judgment. Without complaint, and despite his innocence, he had accepted his suffering; therefore, Christians should likewise embrace their suffering. Isidore's message of human identification with the sufferings of Christ was underlined in the Kitzingen copy of the *Synonyms* through a series of visual cues, whereas it was conveyed in the Karlburg copy through the pairing of the treatise with martyr passions (as I discuss later).

The consolatory musings of *Ratio* soon clarified the logic of the Christian embrace of suffering in imitation of Christ: suffering comes from God, effects purgation from sin, and is therefore the route to eternal life. At both Karlburg and Kitzingen, the chapters containing these explanations (I.24–28) were given special prominence,[66] perhaps in part because the teachings of Christ/Ratio were articulated above all (in *Synonyms* I.27) through quotations from the beloved and authoritative apostle Paul: "For I reckon that the sufferings of this time are not worthy to be compared with the glory to come, that shall be revealed in us" (Romans 8:18) and "For this slight momentary affliction is preparing for us an eternal weight of glory beyond all comparison" (2 Corinthians 4:17).[67] The Kitzingen scribe here edited a key quote from Jerome's commentary on Ecclesiastes by replacing the relatively cryptic reading "Ad probationem sunt ista omnia quae sustines" ("all that you undergo is to test you") with the very explicit "purgationem" ("all that you undergo is to purify you").[68]

Through dialogue with *Ratio*, *Homo* recognized that human beings were far from being unjustly persecuted innocents; instead, their sinfulness justified both the suffering human condition in life and the eternal fires of hell. Isidore evoked this reality through a hunting metaphor ("you are pierced by your own arrows, you are wounded by your own darts") that cohered beautifully with the Kitzingen image of Human Being as a four-footed, potentially hunted beast.[69] Here the Karlburg scribe, who was not working with animal imagery, made the warning more direct by substituting "deliciis" ("pleasures") for "telis." But the most telling variant in this section was the Kitzingen scribe's unique substitution of "eternal judgment" for "eternal fire" as the thing of which *Homo* must be mindful.[70] This heightened sensitivity to the theme of judgment at Kitzingen was likewise manifested in their graphic and iconographically groundbreaking crucifixion miniature, an illumination that permitted the women to fulfill *Ratio*'s recommendation to have an image of the future judgment always before their eyes.[71]

But there was also a ray of hope in *Ratio*'s message of deserved eternal punishment: "through repentance, all sins are wiped away."[72] Isidore's *Synonyms*, like the crucifixion miniature, spurred its audience to penance. The effect on *Homo* was profound and immediate. *Homo* cried out: "I confess my error, I acknowledge my guilt . . . attend to the voice of this prayerful one, hear the voice of this crying out sinner. . . . I have sinned, God, have mercy on me."[73] The effects of *Homo*'s confession were likewise instantaneous, as *Ratio* announced: "God suspends your sins."[74]

But this was not the end of *Homo*'s spiritual odyssey, for the repentant *Homo* of the end of Book I, who accepted suffering as justified, had seemingly landed not far from the unrepentant *Homo* of the beginning of Book I, who railed against suffering as unjustified; either way, *Homo* was suffering![75] Nevertheless, we must not lose sight of the gulf between the mental state of unrepentant *Homo* and that of repentant *Homo*, for the latter, unlike the former, had both hope and a plan for the future and was fortified by *Ratio*'s assurance that "Whoever perseveres all the way to the end, this one will be saved" (Matthew 10:22).[76] Indeed, the scribe-artist called attention to *Homo*'s new mental state through the insertion of an illumination (Plate 6) between the "hic salvus erit" ("this one will be saved") and the "explicit liber I/incipit liber II" ("here ends book I/here begins book II").[77] Three birds were pictured, or rather, the same bird was pictured three times as it recapitulated *Homo*'s emotional cycle.

The artist drew the first and largest bird to look hunted, startled, scared, anxious, and angry, and looking over its shoulder like the four-footer in the first illumination, to recall the *Homo* of Book I's beginning. She placed a second, smaller bird somewhat higher on the page, turned its body 180 degrees, and raised its head and eyes to look upward. Using perspective, the artist showed that the second bird was farther away and had started its ascent. Her third and smallest bird, in full flight, its eyes locked onto its heavenly goal, soared upward toward salvation. *Homo* was no longer the Lamb of God (symbol of Christ's passion and crucifixion) but had been replaced by an aquiline creature soaring at full throttle: the eagle, symbol of Christ's resurrection.[78] Thus, Christ modeled for Human Being a trajectory that led from suffering to eternal life. Human Being was now filled with hope for the future and stood ready to receive the guidelines for a sinless lifestyle that *Ratio* would set forth in Book II.

KNOW THYSELF: PENITENTIAL CONFESSION AS THE CENTERPIECE OF THE MONASTIC LIFE

In the opening chapters of Book II of his *Synonyms*, Isidore of Seville turned to the famous "scito te ipsum" (know thyself) motif.[79] The core of the "know thyself" idea was that sin began in the mind (thoughts, feelings, desires) long before it manifested itself in actions. Therefore, the key to avoiding the commission of sins was to recognize any nascent leanings toward something that might eventually result in sinful behavior. *Ratio* thus recommended a practice of constant self-examination,[80] accompanied by a constant stream of plaintive confessions of sinful proclivity. Isidore helpfully provided a script for the practice of devotional confession by filling *Homo*'s mouth with repeated expressions of feelings of sinfulness and remorse, the performance of which could create in the speaker the desired emotional experience.[81] Some particularly moving lines from the *Synonyms* were even incorporated into the "Succurre mihi" prayer in the ninth-century Book of Cerne, the central prayer in a collection "designed to guide the reader through a penitential, meditative religious process or experience."[82]

The monastic practice of penitential confession, as it emerged from Isidore's *Synonyms*, was individual, private, and autonomous, independent of any institutional practice of penance in subordination to a superior. It revolved around the unmediated interaction between God and tearful, contrite *Homo*.[83] The midwife of *Homo*'s epiphany, *Ratio*, was no mere priest but rather the Wisdom of God, and *Homo*'s penitential journey in Book I of the *Synonyms* was filled with heartfelt prostrations directly before God; only once did *Homo* vary the routine by calling on the *chorus sanctorum* to beg for forgiveness on *Homo*'s behalf.[84] The practice of daily self-examination was another aspect of the universalizing tendency of the *Synonyms*, as it eschewed hierarchies in connection with penance (in contrast to the penitential of Pseudo-Bede, which recommended different forms of penance to different people, depending on their status as rich or poor, free or slave, and learned or ignorant).[85]

Muschiol's discussion of the monastic practice of devotional confession in Merovingian-era nunneries revealed a sacramental and liturgical system for guiding or disciplining nuns by an abbess, through the imposition of penitential tariffs (most commonly a prescribed number of days of fasting through abstinence from meat and wine) and other disciplinary measures, such as excommunication.[86] As one example of this, Diem's intensive study of the *Regula cuiusdam ad virgines* (a mid-seventh-century rule from the ambit of Luxeuil, perhaps written by Jonas of Bobbio) uncovered an elaborate, formal structure of near-permanent confession to a superior, complete with strict provisions for exclusion from the community for the sinful and the penitent.[87] However, Isidore's *Synonyms* supported a very different approach to devotional confession at Karlburg and Kitzingen.

There was room for variety in the penitential landscape of early Carolingian Francia, which witnessed an explosive growth in the production of new penitentials.[88] Some of them may have been used in formal, hierarchical settings such as episcopal courts,[89] but others may (at least sometimes) have been used in informal, relatively unhierarchical ways, pointing to the existence of a view of penance that was more individual and emotional than institutional and disciplinary. Some penitentials were essentially didactic works, florilegia for moral guidance rather than manuals for externally imposed discipline.[90] I do not reject the possibility that abbesses in the communities covered by this study confessed and disciplined their flocks; I do, however, suggest that disciplinary penance was not as important as devotional approaches that were supported by Isidore's *Synonyms*, which provided a script for the individual expression of feelings of sin and remorse.

The Penitential of Pseudo-Bede explained that the standard tariff of fasting could be replaced by giving alms, genuflecting in prayer, standing in the form of a cross, or singing Psalms.[91] Insofar as the *Synonyms* was effectively a new type of penitential psalm,[92] it would have served perfectly those alternative penitential devotions that Carolingian aristocrats came to favor. Alcuin created a program of private devotion for lay nobles that was built around the daily recitation of the seven penitential psalms plus a long litany, introduced by a "pure confession of sins" that twice quoted the *Synonyms* (I.57 and I.65) to provide language in which the penitent could appropriately address God.[93] It is unsurprising that the increasing popularity enjoyed by the *Synonyms* from the mid-ninth century onward extended beyond monastery walls to lay aristocrats such as Dhuoda, Eberhard of Friuli, and Eccard of Mâcon.[94]

This approach to devotional confession had deep monastic roots, particularly in the tradition of informal penance described by John Cassian, whose

Conferences (420s) listed almsgiving, shedding of tears, and avowal of one's faults as the techniques of repentance by which expiation of sin was achieved, rendering absolution by a priest unnecessary.[95] In 813, when the students of Boniface and Leoba still exercised some influence in Francia, the Council of Chalons recognized as valid and efficacious confession to God alone; later this came to seem inadequate to Carolingian authorities, giving rise to the demand that a priest be involved in the process.[96] The warm embrace of Isidore's *Synonyms* during the eighth century was surely keyed to the importance of informal penitential approaches to God because it provided a perfect script for such expressions of regret, something not every penitent heart could confect on its own. This informal approach to penance helped Christians to develop "the self-discipline without which recidivism is predictable."[97]

The key to avoiding sinful recidivism was, as noted earlier, the continuous self-examination inherent in the motto "scito te ipsum." There has been very little work done on the constellation of ideas and practices associated with the ancient oracular dictum "know thyself" in connection with the eighth and ninth centuries; indeed, the received view holds that the sentiment had little relevance to the Carolingian era beyond the idiosyncratic concerns of Paschasius Radbertus and Hincmar of Reims. Yet, the teachings of the *Synonyms* that were being actively propagated by the women of the Anglo-Saxon cultural zone in Francia during the eighth century were remarkably consistent with the "scito te ipsum" motif as it appeared in the writings of those ninth-century (and later) authors: self-knowledge required "meditation on the wretchedness of the human condition" and "was understood as being gained by mimesis of exemplars, and as being realized in the enactment of personae."[98] An example of such enactment was the technique of singing the Psalms in the persona of David.[99] The women of Karlburg and Kitzingen also possessed such personae, *Homo* and *Ratio*, whose dialogue could be recited to help them achieve empathy for the wretched condition of *Homo* and to learn to imitate the reasoned response of *Ratio*.

THE DEVIL IN THE DETAILS: THE GUIDELINES OF BOOK II

Neither of the Main Valley area women's copies of Isidore's *Synonyms* currently contains the complete text of Book II. The Kitzingen copy was originally complete but has lost its final quire, and now it breaks off in the middle of a sentence (at the end of the previously penultimate quire on fol. 64v) halfway through II.18.[100] In contrast, the Karlburg copy never included more than its current contents, that is, II.1–26 and II. 82 to the end of Book II.[101] The excised chapters were remarkably banal, even deserving of the negative evaluations ("immature," "rudimentary," "juvenile," and the like) to which the *Synonyms* has often been subjected.[102] Furthermore, they lacked monastic focus and were far more appropriate to those living fully in the world.[103] Finally, in the missing chapters, the emotional impact of the devotional treatise dissipated, and *Homo*'s *cri de coeur* was lost from view. From the monastic perspective, the abbreviated version of the *Synonyms* in the Karlburg codex formed a coherent whole.

The excision of so much of the text rendered that which remained all the more important. The centerpiece of what remained in the Karlburg copy, still present as well in the now mutilated but originally complete Kitzingen copy, was a program for avoiding fornication (the worst sin of all, in Isidore's view) by vanquishing libido (*Synonyms* II.10–II.18).[104] *Ratio*'s pragmatic program for maintaining *castitas* included remembering the perpetual fires of hell, spending the nocturnal hours to the extent possible in prayer and vigils, being abstemious in one's intake of food and wine, disciplining one's gaze to avoid seeing potential objects of desire, and working. *Ratio*'s recommendations concerning food and drink emphasized moderation rather than asceticism, an orientation consistent with the Karlburg florilegium discussed later in this chapter. Having dispensed with the particular theme of libido, *Ratio* added more details to the program for a disciplined, but not particularly ascetic, monastic lifestyle: engage frequently in reading and meditating on scripture, cultivate humility, and demonstrate compunction through frequent tears, sighs, and laments.[105] The majority of the remainder of *Ratio*'s Book II discourse was excised from the Karlburg copy, which retained only the chilling reminder that nothing could preclude a lapse into sinfulness (requiring recourse to God's mercy),[106] alongside some fundamental tenets of the monastic orientation, such as "therefore, renounce everything because of God."[107] The text reached full closure when *Homo*, the character with whom the reader was supposed to identify, explicitly accepted *Ratio*'s rule for living ("vivendi regula)."[108] This coercive form of textuality pushed the reader to follow in *Homo*'s footsteps and accept the *Synonyms* as her rule equivalent.

Nothing in the text of the *Synonyms* gendered the message of *Ratio* or limited its universal applicability. The universalizing slant of Isidore's *Synonyms* accounted in large part for its surge in popularity in monastic circles in eighth-century Francia, when gender egalitarianism and syneisactism were dominant values in the lives of the potential audience for the text. *Ratio* was a veritable font of good advice for a monastic life of discipline and devotion, advice aimed equally at men and women, including an emphatic command to keep silent and speak only when spoken to.[109] That such advice appeared in popular texts aimed at mixed-gender audiences deserves to be better known, as does the fact that the women of Karlburg considered the injunction to silence as not particularly relevant to them and thus omitted this section of the treatise.[110]

Only one line in the entire text explicitly thematized sexual difference, namely, when *Ratio* recommended discretion in vision, as part of the project to tame libido, because "the mind is captured through the eyes."[111] *Homo* was therefore counseled to avoid looking at women. A heteronormative reading of this sentence would deny its relevance to the female subject, but such a limited reading would be unwarranted, as is clear from the fact that the dramatic centerpiece of the *passio Eugeniae* (which followed the *Synonyms* in the Karlburg codex) was a proposal of marriage made to the saint by another woman, who was attracted by the sight of her. In fact, women living in a female monastic community had more need to avert their desiring gazes from the sight of women than did men living in a male community. I therefore turn to the Karlburg copy of the *Synonyms*, which illustrated *Ratio*'s message through the stories of two saintly humans, rather than through animal imagery.

ISIDORE AT KARLBURG: ILLUSTRATION THROUGH SAINTLY EXEMPLARITY IN WÜRZBURG UB M.P.TH.Q. 28A

In the Karlburg copy of the *Synonyms*, two saints (Eugenia and Potitus) embodied and illustrated the behaviors recommended by Isidore. The two martyrs, alternatives to the strategies of the Kitzingen scribe-artist (animal illuminations, dialogue labels), sometimes intensified the demands of the monastic life to a level of asceticism far surpassing *Ratio*'s moderate proposals. For instance, Isidore recommended humility, but Potitus performed vile abjection.[112] More often, however, Isidore's teachings on humility were perfectly calibrated to the behaviors of the exemplary saints, such as when Eugenia treated her high abbatial office as a *ministerium* that permitted her to serve others or when Eugenia and Potitus refused to accept riches, exactly as recommended by Isidore in chapters included in the Karlburg copy.[113]

The Karlburg scribe was not the only one to pair Isidore's devotional classic with biographies of saints and martyrs, but (as far as we can tell, based on the ages of extant manuscripts) she was the first to do so.[114] The *Synonyms* welcomed illustration through saintly exemplarity, for Isidore discussed the dynamics at work in both positive and negative behavioral modeling. The chapter in which the dynamic of exemplarity was most thoroughly explored was longer in the Λ (Karlburg) recension of the text than in the Φ recension;[115] furthermore, the Karlburg copy displayed a particular sensitivity to the importance of saints, substituting "sanctorum" for "iustorum" in *Homo*'s plea for intercession.[116]

The two saints selected to illustrate and embody the teachings of *Ratio* for the women of Karlburg were chosen for the way their personalities resonated with the figure of Christ through shared feast days: Christmas (Eugenia's feast, chosen by Christ as the day to welcome her into heaven)[117] and the octaves of Epiphany (Potitus's feast). Discussion and celebration of Eugenia helped call attention to how God became man, and discussion and celebration of Potitus helped call attention to how that man was recognized as God. Eugenia and Potitus worked together to recall and underline the dual nature of Christ and the salvific exemplarity of the God-Man, a message that was conveyed in the Kitzingen copy through the illuminations of *homo* and the eagle. Eugenia and Potitus were Christ-types suffering false accusations and torture, enacting an *imitatio Christi* exemplarity that helped bridge the gap between the God-Man and humans.[118] In their double reference to the sacrificed Christ and the necessity to imitate him, they conveyed the theology of Hebrews 13:12–13: the blood of the martyr is "always and above all that of Christ."[119]

Although scholars sometimes gender the Christian culture of suffering as a cult of female victimhood, in the martyr passions appended to the Karlburg copy of Isidore's *Synonyms*, both male and female martyrs experienced suffering.[120] In fact, the male martyr suffered far more than did the female one. Potitus's short life was virtually an unbroken *passio*, interrupted only by brief thaumaturgical episodes benefiting women, such as when he cured (of leprosy and diabolic possession, respectively) and converted to Christianity a wealthy senatorial matron and the daughter of the emperor.[121] Even the multicolored and extra-large-lettered rubric that announced his story in the Karlburg manuscript underlined the motif of suffering: "In the name of Christ, here begins the passion narrative of saint Potitus, who suffered under the emperor Antoninus and the governor Gelasius."[122] Accordingly, Potitus was almost constantly subjected to horrible physical torture, from the opening scene when his idol-worshiping father, Hylus, imprisoned him without food or drink, to his final hurrah when Roman executioners boiled him in oil and cut out his tongue before decapitating him.[123] When not being subjected to harsh corporeal tortures by others, Potitus voluntarily lived as an impoverished solitary, occasionally appearing in public to beg.[124]

Potitus not only suffered, he embraced his suffering, and thus embodied *Ratio*'s advice to welcome suffering as beneficial. For instance, the boy saint repeatedly declared during his extended imperial torture session how much he desired the tortures, which he characterized as a "great consolation," and even demanded to be on the receiving end of more.[125] That the fortitude of Potitus was intended to function as an example to the readers of the text cannot be doubted, for the theme of exemplarity was prominent in the narrative. The saint invoked his own exemplars: Daniel in the lion's den, David in battle with Goliath, Joseph in an Egyptian prison, Peter in Roman chains.[126] Those heroes had nowhere to turn but God and found their prayers answered. Isidore's *homo* faced the same horror and emerged filled with the knowledge that God was always nigh. Potitus's various rescues, from prisons and demons, by clouds and by angels, dramatized what transpired between *Homo* and *Ratio* and pointed readers back to trust in God at challenging moments. The saint's antisocial preference for solitude, which commentators have found curious,[127] enabled him to function as a model for the direct recourse to God that was cultivated through the penitential lamentations of *Homo* in the *Synonyms*.

While the extremely short life of the little-known Potitus consisted almost entirely of wretched suffering, the popular and well-known Eugenia (a Roman martyr buried in one of the Latin way cemeteries) was able fully to embody, through a long life connected with multiple monastic communities, many aspects of the recommended lifestyle sketched by Isidore.[128] Yet, despite Eugenia's greater importance, the brilliance of the Karlburg Isidore resided in the doubling of Eugenia and Potitus as embodiments of the teachings of *Ratio*. As noted, both of their feast days (Christmas and the Octaves of Epiphany) overlapped dominical feasts, making them types of Christ. But there was another aspect to the logic of their selection as exemplars: Eugenia and Potitus, an adult female monastic and a young boy, together represented the key demographics at Karlburg, namely, the female religious community and the boys attending the monastic school.[129] Potitus was a mere twelve years old at the time of his death (fol. 70v), and his extreme youth was repeatedly emphasized in the course of the narrative.[130] The adult woman and the adolescent boy both met their ends in a Roman arena, a venue that was hardly unfamiliar in the Anglo-Saxon cultural zone, for one of the largest Roman arenas north of the Alps sat just outside of Mainz.[131] Perhaps the eighth-century ivory pyx deposited there by Rotsvintda was brought by a nun of Karlburg on a field trip with her students, on an outing designed to reinforce the exemplary relevance and emotional impact of the martyrs.

HOMOEROTICISM AND TRANSVESTISM IN THE PASSIO EUGENIAE

Eugenia (according to her passion narrative) moved with her family (father Philip, mother Claudia, and two brothers) from Rome to Alexandria so her father could take up a post in the imperial provincial government;[132] after the death of her father, she moved with her mother back to Rome, where she was martyred and honored with a tomb cult. Like all the female martyrs in the "Deus per angelum" *libellus*, she contributed to the spread of Christianity; like many of them, she possessed a key characteristic congenial to intellectual women: she was highly educated, excelling because of her mental prowess in the study of Latin, Greek, and philosophical works by Plato, Aristotle, Socrates, and Epicurus.[133] At fifteen, she refused to consent to a marriage on the grounds that the proposed bridegroom did not have suitable "mores." Her conversion soon thereafter to Christianity resulted from reading the works of Paul and hearing the Ninety-Fifth Psalm chanted in the bishop's suburban villa; thus inspired by texts of great importance to the women of Karlburg and Kitzingen, she threw herself into a life centered on the study of scripture.[134] But there was more to Eugenia than this.

Her story contained two central dramas, one set in Alexandria and one set in Rome. The centerpiece of the Alexandrian portion was the story of how the noble widow Melantia was attracted to Eugenia, who, disguised as a man named Eugenius, was serving as abbot of a men's monastery. Melantia found the abbot elegant and tried—unsuccessfully—to persuade him to marry her, particularly by emphasizing how much wealth she was able to offer. Enraged at having been spurned, Melantia falsely accused Eugenia/Eugenius of sexual assault. The accusation led to a formal trial before the prefect (the saint's father, Philip), at which Eugenia dramatically disrobed to demonstrate that she was a woman, thereby "proving" the accusation to be false.[135] The centerpiece of the Roman portion was the story of the noble virgin Bassilla, whom Eugenia converted both to Christianity and to chastity, leading Bassilla to embrace execution by imperial order rather than marry her fiancé. This put Eugenia in the position of having to explicate, for Roman officials and the Roman public, Christian teachings on chastity. Multiple attempts to execute her for refusing to sacrifice to the goddess Diana finally succeeded on December 25.[136]

There were many points of resonance between Eugenia's story and Isidore's *Synonyms*. Just as Isidore's *Ratio* turned out to be Christ, so the Christ-figure Eugenia turned out to be *Ratio*, who not only offered emotional comfort but also drove out demons and restored sight to the blind.[137] From the moment she entered the monastery whose abbot she would become, Eugenia was a *Doppelgängerin* for *Ratio*: she had such "animi tranquillitas" that she appeared to be one of the angels, she was emotionally helpful to all (consoling the sad, mitigating the wrath of the angry, etc.), and she was able to remove all *dolor* (twice referenced in *Homo*'s opening cry of anguish in *Synonyms* I.1) from any sufferer.[138] She reacted to the experience of being unjustly persecuted, something that desperately tormented *Homo* (e.g., *Synonyms* I.13–16), with exemplary equanimity; indeed, Eugenia's comportment was explicitly described as "imitabilis . . . viris," that is, to be imitated by the men in her community.[139] Eugenia's greatest virtue, however, was that Christ had made her "a victor over all pollution of sexual desire."[140] She exemplified throughout the narrative the enviable state of being liberated from libido, the goal of *Ratio*'s multistep program as sketched out in Book II of the *Synonyms*.[141] After all, "fornication is greater than all other sins" ("omnibus peccatis fornicatio maior est"), "it is better to die than to fornicate" ("melius est enim mori quam fornicari"), and "sexual desire plunges a human being into hell" ("libido vero in infernum hominen mergit").[142]

For a monastic community, fornication and libido truly did represent crucial potential problems. The internal harmony of a monastic community could be completely wrecked through the emotions attendant upon such activities. Furthermore, rumors of sexual impropriety could damage the reputation of a community and cause lay support for the life of monastic devotion to dry up. Eugenia's problems with Melantia, like the false pregnancy accusation in Rudolf of Fulda's *vita Leobae*, clearly demonstrated the existence of anxiety over such matters among the monastic women of the Anglo-Saxon cultural province in Francia.[143] However, the Eugenia text (unlike the Leoba one) did not thematize heterosexual fornication, let alone false accusations of pregnancy. The only time libido reared its ugly head in the *passio Eugeniae* was in the homoerotic confrontation between Eugenia and Melantia.

Contextual evidence prods us to take seriously the homoerotic strand of the Eugenia narrative in connection with the danger of fornication that was so central to the *Synonyms*. The penitentials in the Vienna collection produced at Karlburg prescribed penances for a range of both male and female same-sex activities and fantasies.[144] A codex such as the *Synonyms-cum-passiones*, which functioned as a partial rule-equivalent for the women of Karlburg, was a logical tool for managing the danger of lesbian fornication in the community, a problem that may have been exacerbated by some nuns adopting male clothing.[145] The *Collectio Wirceburgensis*, a canon law collection also from Karlburg, displayed extreme interest in the canons of the fourth-century Council of Gangra, said to have been called to respond to a wave of female transvestites; this section of the manuscript opened with a special decorated initial to mark it as particularly important and was heavily glossed both in Latin and in the vernacular.[146]

The women of Karlburg, upon reading or hearing the story, may have seen themselves in Eugenia/Eugenius, in Melantia, or in both, but however they imagined themselves in relation to the narrative, the fact remains that the sexual drama in the *passio Eugeniae* took place between two women and thus necessarily addressed anxieties over the possibility that women might be attracted to one another. The story of Eugenia was originally generated, in the fifth or sixth century, as part of a movement of women who practiced transvestism and looked to transvestite saints (most famously Thecla) for empowerment; for instance, in the Syriac and Armenian versions of Eugenia's story, the saint was converted to Christ through reading "the story of the discipleship of Thecla the holy virgin, and of Paul the Apostle" and then further confirmed in her faith by studying the "book of Thecla."[147] Yet, such tales of disguised female monks have been seen primarily as evidence for the (often misogynist) subjectivities of men, including as creations of gender-segregated male monks secretly longing for female company.[148] Clearly, the fact that the narratives were transmitted through women's communities such as Karlburg and Essen demonstrates that they did not exclusively express male fantasies.[149] Schulenburg, at least, insisted that figures such as Eugenia were meant to be relevant to women but never explained how.[150] Meanwhile, other scholars have offered little more than cryptic allusions to the homoerotic charge in such stories.[151]

Ratio's advice to discipline one's gaze and avoid looking at women (*Synonyms* II.16) was hardly irrelevant to female readers of the text. When combined with the text of the *passio Eugeniae*, the Karlburg *Synonyms* codex offered a multipronged approach to discouraging lesbian sexuality. The author of the passion narrative of Eugenia, and the scribes who transmitted that text, taught that lesbian fornication was impossible, for what "proved" that "Eugenius" could not possibly have attempted to seduce Melantia was that "Eugenius" was really a woman. What was reinforced, above all, was a behavioral convention of female sexual passivity that logically precluded the possibility that any woman might act as a sexual aggressor. Within the diegesis of the narrative, all immediately accepted that a female could never have thrown herself at another person with sexual intentions. By defining women as "naturally" incapable of initiating a sexual encounter, the narrative recapitulated the key tropes of the late ancient and early Christian response to female homoeroticism as "monstrous," "worthy of death," and (above all) "contrary to nature"; because this position was associated with the apostle Paul (Romans 1:26), it must have been seen as authoritative at Karlburg.[152]

Previous discussions of Eugenia have uniformly ignored her homoerotic encounter in favor of a focus on her status as one of dozens of female transvestite saints venerated in both east and west during the Middle Ages.[153] Hotchkiss argued that (fictional) cross-dressers ultimately acceded to male hegemony because they left man as the measure of all things, denying femaleness in favor of a more desirable maleness; furthermore, because "femaleness and its attendant sinfulness cannot remain hidden," the disguise was always dissolved and the female body relocated in its inferior cultural place.[154] Scheck concluded that the narratives functioned, above all, to put women firmly in a subordinate place by "re-dressing" them properly as women and thus redressing their error in believing they could escape the limitations of their gender.[155] In a slightly more positive reading, Stofferahn suggested that women included these stories in their books to express their wish to live public, stimulating, scholarly, male lives, as if no woman's life could include such pursuits.[156] Finally, Roy wrote the following about the speech Eugenia gave just before she revealed herself as a woman: "Eugenia herself becomes the mouthpiece of the clearest expression in the *Passio* of the idea of male superiority and female inferiority."[157] However, none of these readings can be sustained for the Karlburg Isidore.

For instance, the speech to which Roy referred was not part of the Karlburg codex. In this manuscript, Eugenia began (as elsewhere) by quoting Paul, "the teacher of all Christians" ("magister omnium christianorum"), on how there was, in Christ, no distinction of male and female ("disceptio masculi et femine"), thus citing the crucial biblical proof text for egalitarian gender ideologies, namely, Galatians 3:28.[158] The copies of the text Roy analyzed then had Eugenia launch into a series of statements that indeed "indicate[d] an acceptance of the notion of male superiority and female inferiority" (e.g., "nolui esse femina" or "I did not want to be a woman"), effectively contradicting the core sense of the opening Pauline citation.[159] In these copies of the passion narrative, Eugenia did imply that, through her disguise, she had transcended her female sex and ascended to a better state of manliness.[160] However, this part of Eugenia's speech (if it ever existed in this form at all) was thoroughly erased from the Karlburg copy and replaced by the story of the women at the tomb in the Gospel of Matthew version, another key citation supporting the claims of women to equal positions with men in Christian institutions.[161] Karlburg's Eugenia scarcely endorsed the notion of women's inferiority, as she reminded those gathered in court that there was no distinction of male and female and that Jesus' faithful female disciples were the first witnesses of the resurrection. When, as her next move, she revealed herself to be a woman, the weight of the message of the codex fell firmly on the inconceivability of lesbian fornication, as everyone agreed that Eugenia could never have made a sexual advance upon Melantia.

For those who had read her story attentively, Eugenia's citation of Galatians at her trial made perfect sense. The saint's moment of conversion to Christianity had taken place after reading a work by the apostle, based on which she announced to her male slaves Protus and Hyacinthus that a "usurped power" ("usurpata potestas") had set her over them as a *domina* but they would henceforth be equal as brother and sister.[162] Every reader would have recognized the allusion to Paul's announcement, in Galatians 3:28, of the dissolution of status distinctions such as slave and free in the body of Christ. When Bishop Helenus later accepted the trio into the monastic community, he did so in full knowledge that all three were dissembling concerning their status, Eugenia by pretending to be a man and Protus and Hyacinthus by pretending to be free, indeed noble, Roman citizens.[163] The anonymous author of the *passio* thus endorsed the egalitarian nature of the monastic *familia*, where secular status distinctions vanished so thoroughly that Eugenia could rightfully exercise authority over the men in the house; after all, as she was assured by reading Matthew 20:25–27, Christian rulership was not like power among the gentiles.[164] Eugenia's citation of the egalitarian Galatians manifesto at her trial was the logical outcome of a life devoted to dissolving secular status distinctions.

The Galatians citation also provides a clue for understanding Eugenia's transvestism as something other than a desire to reject her womanhood: like Paul in the Kitzingen crucifixion miniature, Eugenia had clothed herself with Christ.[165] But we do not have to rely entirely on interpretations of the saint's biblical allusions, for Eugenia explained her adoption of male dress as a pragmatic decision designed to permit her to maintain a connection with Protus and Hyacinthus.[166] Remaining together was predicated upon Eugenia's adoption of a masculine disguise, given that she had decided that both she and her slaves would join the all-male monastic community attached to the bishopric of Alexandria; thus, she decided to tonsure her hair and adopt manly dress ("virili habitu").[167] The saint reiterated her desire not to be separated from Protus and Hyacinthus when, as spokesperson for the trio, she requested baptism from Bishop Helenus.[168] If we take the character Eugenia at her word, the driving force behind her transvestism was the depth of her feelings for her male companions, with whom she shared an unbreakable intellectual bond based on years of shared study of Plato and Aristotle; they continued this relationship in the "schola Christi" ("school of Christ"), making steady progress together in divine erudition.[169] From this perspective, the erasure of the speech about not wanting to be a woman improved the text by rendering it internally consistent and preserved the nature of the trio as symbols for the syneisactic circle around Boniface.

Furthermore, Eugenia was never "re-dressed" as a woman. One could only conclude that Eugenia dressed in women's clothing or joined a women's community by reading into the information that the saint buried her father next to the "monasterium Christi virginum" and the church she built where her mother had founded a hostel for pilgrims; in fact this fleeting mention functioned solely to settle Philip's corpse before the family returned home to Rome.[170] In contrast, the text dwelt at length on the changes Eugenia brought to the public sphere of Alexandria, such as large-scale Christian conversions and the legalization of Christianity as the preferred religion of the town.[171] As the key figure in the sacred history of Alexandria (comparable to the female martyrs in the "Deus per angelum" *libellus*), Eugenia's posttrial "re-dressing" involved being wrapped in gold cloth by the joyous crowd and carried triumphantly in procession.[172] For all we know, she then redonned men's clothes. Certainly, once back in Rome, she spent the rest of her life in a monastic community that included both women of all ages and young men, alongside the perpetually silent Protus and Hyacinthus; every Saturday night, they were joined by Pope Cornelius.[173]

This Roman idyll came to an abrupt halt with the launching of an anti-Christian persecution, a section of the narrative that was introduced with a line of brightly rubricated text and a decorated initial.[174] Eugenia had been teaching that the traditional deities were demons and discouraging both sexual intercourse and procreation. A certain Bassilla's embrace of Eugenia's teaching and consequent refusal to marry her fiancé, the prefect Pompeius, resulted in the arrest of both women, as government officials demanded that Bassilla marry and Eugenia sacrifice to the gods.[175] Eugenia, of course, refused, but the bulk of the narrative was long speeches in which the saint painted virginity as a central Christian tenet; she asserted, for instance, that Christ was born of a father who never knew woman and of a mother who never knew man, and was married to a virgin (apparently Eugenia herself) with whom he reproduced without sexual contact.[176] These speeches were central to the *passio Eugeniae* as a reinforcer of the teachings of *Ratio* concerning the preservation of chastity, and the specific reference to the virgin birth tightened the connection with the feast of Christmas, common to Eugenia and Jesus. Furthermore, Eugenia's claim to possess a generative "consciousness fecund through God" demonstrated her missionary ambition,[177] which bore fruit when she unleashed an earthquake in a temple of Diana, pulverizing the entire structure and attracting crowds to witness her contest against imperial executioners.[178] At no point in her ensuing passion was Eugenia's body maltreated in any graphic or sexually redolent way; she was thrown into a dark prison, where she sat calmly glowing like a bright light, and then into the Tiber, where she floated as did St. Peter in the gospels, thus ending her career on an explicit parallel to the Prince of the Apostles.[179] This was a far cry from being reinscribed in an inferior position.

Rather than being a misogynist figure of female inferiority, Eugenia was a syneisactic heroine whose life validated the gender-egalitarian monastic structures of the Anglo-Saxon cultural province in Francia, particularly in relation to intellectual endeavor, while also addressing local concerns about female homoerotic feelings. *Ratio*'s teaching in the *Synonyms* centered, for those in monastic life, on chastity and the battle against libido; these values in particular were illustrated and exemplified in the Karlburg Isidore through the *passio Eugeniae*.

THE KARLBURG FLORILEGIUM (WÜRZBURG UB M.P.TH.F. 13)

A florilegium was a collection of *sententiae* (teachings, opinions) extracted from the works of a variety of authors and organized into chapters devoted to themes such as abstinence, virginity, envy, pride, or wisdom. In this particular example of the genre, the extracts within each chapter were arranged chronologically, beginning with biblical quotations relevant to the theme, proceeding through the Fathers in chronological order, and culminating with the words of the most recent authority, Isidore of Seville. The Bible was the most-cited source, above all the Book of Ecclesiasticus (with 419 citations), followed by Proverbs (with 276 citations), and the letters of Paul (with 164 citations).[180] Beyond the Bible, four sources far outnumbered all others: in uncontested first place came the *Sentences* of Isidore of Seville (with 343 citations), then in roughly equivalent second place came Gregory the Great's *Homilies on the Gospels* (with 138 citations), various letters of Jerome (with 131 citations), and Isidore's *Synonyms* (with 119 citations).[181]

In some cases, the decision to acquire a florilegium was born of pragmatic resignation, such as when (relatively poor) intellectuals recognized that abbreviated versions of, or extracts from, longer texts represented their only affordable (albeit undesirable) option.[182] Yet, the creation of florilegia was never confined to individuals likely to have faced shortages either of books or of cash. In fact, florilegia could function effectively as "coming attractions," enabling collectors to decide which works to acquire, and readers to decide which books in their library to read more carefully, by providing samples from a variety of texts.[183] For instance, Eugippius (d. 533), abbot of a monastery near Naples, made a florilegium of extracts from the works of Augustine with the goal of transmitting the essential aspects of Augustine's teaching in a manageable form.[184] Tellingly, the woman Proba to whom Eugippius dedicated his Augustinian florilegium had in her library all the books excerpted in the collection.[185] Thus, neither the ownership nor the production (as compiler or scribe) of a florilegium should be seen as a stopgap emergency measure.[186]

Furthermore, florilegia must be regarded as serious intellectual texts from another perspective as well. They were frequently intended to advance a theological argument on a subject such as the status of images in Christian worship or "to prove a doctrinal position. . . . Any religious dispute . . . called forth new collections."[187] The first known author to utilize the florilegium format to make a theological argument was Theoderet of Cyrrhus, whose first effort (c. 447) took aim at Monophysitism and whose second compilation marshaled proof texts against all the major heresies of the day.[188] Selection and compilation could be powerful argumentative strategies; for instance, the preferential selection of egalitarian biblical extracts not only argued in favor of egalitarian notions but also effectively (mis)represented the entire Christian tradition as pervasively egalitarian.[189] Furthermore, in an anonymous florilegium format, an argument that might be extremely controversial when articulated through more pointed rhetorical methods approximated the matter-of-fact reflection of a consensus.

In the next section of this chapter, I discuss the lessons taught and points "argued" by the florilegium known as the *Liber* Scintillarum, as well as how those teachings were received, modified, and transmitted by the women of Karlburg who produced the manuscript Würzburg UB M.p.th.f. 13. Unlike many florilegia, this particular collection was not intended primarily as a contribution to a theological controversy. Instead, it contained moral and ethical guidance of great use to members of a monastic community. The anonymous compiler drew "opinions" from a series of older works of moral and spiritual guidance such as the *Synonyms* of Isidore, a special favorite among authors of moral florilegia.[190] She or he then crafted these extracts into a behavioral, ethical, and moral guide that could function as a rule equivalent for men's, women's, or mixed-sex monastic communities. The text was surely acquired at Karlburg above all to serve as a rule equivalent for the house and secondarily as a set of coming attractions to guide the community in its future library acquisitions.

"IT IS THE SPIRIT THAT GIVETH LIFE; THE FLESH PROFITETH NOTHING" (JOHN 6:63)[191]

The overarching, cumulative philosophical thrust of the individual entries in the florilegium known as the *Liber Scintillarum* was the conviction that the physical plane was relatively unimportant, a fundamental principle that resonated strongly with the gender-egalitarian values that characterized the Anglo-Saxon cultural zone on the continent. That women and men were equal in their noncorporeal souls formed part of the fundamental teaching of Austine's *On the Trinity*, an important text in the eighth-century diocese of Würzburg.[192] When one denied significance to the ways in which males and females (seemed to) differ, ways that were inevitably primarily corporeal, and emphasized the ways in which males and females were similar or even identical, ways that were primarily spiritual, one had very little logical choice but to concede (even if grudgingly) the essential equality of the sexes.

The prioritization of spirit over matter could only reinforce gender-hierarchical conceptions if one dichotomized humanity and identified men with (superior) spirit and women with (inferior) matter; however, there is no evidence that such a notion was even known, let alone endorsed, in the Anglo-Saxon cultural zone during the eighth century. Therefore, in the Anglo-Saxon cultural zone on the continent, the prioritizing of spirit over flesh—the celebration of the importance of the spirit and the accompanying denial of importance to the flesh and to fleshly achievements—functioned as an equalizing ideological force between males and females, rather than as a hierarchical justification for the subordination of (the) female(s) to (the) male(s).

The spiritualizing thrust of the Karlburg florilegium was particularly strong in the chapter on virginity, which explicitly taught that bodily virginity, like any other primarily physical or corporeal achievement, was without importance in the absence of spiritual achievements.[193] One of the sayings, attributed by the compiler of the florilegium to the highly authoritative figure of Augustine, has never been identified as "authentically" Augustinian, an example of how the genre (with its lax citation conventions) lent itself to creative remembrance in support of a compiler's intentions.[194] The views of the florilegist here coincided with those of Aldhelm of Malmesbury, Bede, and Theodore of Canterbury, three influential ecclesiastics of seventh- and early eighth-century England. Aldhelm's writings on virginity de-emphasized technically lifelong physical virginity and emphasized instead the practice of chastity at any given moment, independent of prior experiences such as marriage or procreation; all three not only endorsed leaving a spouse to take up a chaste life in a monastic community but also spoke of such a commitment in terms of "*virgines.*"[195] The completely "pure" body was not a goal.

The prioritization of spiritual over physical achievements in the florilegium went so far as to permit martyrs to be overtaken in stature by those who suffered in spirit, for "opinions" of both Jerome and Gregory under the headword "martyrdom" downplayed the importance of spilling blood in favor of mental and spiritual attainments.[196] Chapter 10 on "Abstinence," with seventy-five separate entries, one of the longest in the collection, above all warned against the overvaluation of ascetic practices; not only were eating, drinking, sleeping, and other carnal pleasures treated as goods but also ways to mortify the flesh through rejection of food, drink, sleep, and the like were labeled as useless without outward-looking works of charity such as almsgiving. The antiascetic orientation of the florilegium may have simply been realistic; for instance, moderate alcohol consumption (that is, to make one's heart "joyful" but not to get drunk) may have been all that could be hoped for in a region whose wealth was largely dependent on viticulture.[197] Texts in the Karlburg penitential collection registered a concern with drunkenness while celebrating food, drink, and (re)marriage as God-given goods.[198]

In this regard, the teachings of the florilegium (and the penitential collection) differed markedly from the examples of the martyrs Eugenia and Potitus, whose Karlburg *passiones* rhapsodized over bodily virginity and physical pain. The difference was telling. The hyperbolic, pyrotechnic heroism that readers expected from saints was less useful when it came to the pragmatics of organizing and sustaining a monastic community. Indeed, the ethical stance of the florilegium fell neatly in line with the position of Isidore's *Synonyms*, which (for instance) never mentioned virginity, a bodily achievement whose significance paled before that of ethical behavior. Accordingly, the subject of virginity was relatively unimportant in the florilegium, when measured by the number of entries under the heading, namely, twenty-seven items covering two brief leaves (fols. 11v–12r); this chapter was overshadowed by subject headings of greater ethical significance such as charity (the subject of chapter 1, with 52 entries), the love of God and neighbor (subject of chapter 3, with 67 entries), humility (the subject of chapter 4, with 53 entries), and wisdom (boasting 111 entries). Furthermore, and also in keeping with the message of Isidore's *Ratio*, the florilegium recommended the same spiritual practices highlighted in the *Synonyms*: compunction, prayer, confession, and copious amounts of tears.[199]

One logical ethical conclusion of such sentiments concerning virginity and ascetic practices was the requirement that everyone must be active in the world, or at least the monastic community, and do positive good if they wished to achieve salvation. Chapter 32 ("De doctoribus sive rectoribus") emphasized the importance of teaching as a service to others, of teaching well, of ruling well without cruelty, and of practicing what one preaches rather than falling into hypocrisy. With 110 entries, this chapter was among the very longest in the collection, underlining the sorts of efforts that were most valued by the Karlburg community, which (as previously discussed in this chapter) indeed ran a school.[200] Nothing in the collection implied that this obligation to serve by preaching and teaching did not extend to women, for the scribe of the Karlburg copy, along with those of two of the three other oldest manuscripts, correctly quoted Isidore's *Sentences* on the need for effective preaching to be done "utiliter" (in a useful fashion), rather than "viriliter" (in a manly fashion), an error by one early scribe that Rochais (betraying his own sexism) preferred to the correct reading in his edition of the florilegium.[201] The ethical concerns of the compiler were recognized and reinforced by the ethical emphasis given the codex as it was copied in the Karlburg scriptorium. For instance, the first chapter that was clearly intended to catch the reader's attention through a particularly large and elaborately decorated opening word (the abbreviation "dns" for "dominus") was chapter 14 on "Justice" (fol. 12r).[202]

Virtually every chapter of the florilegium dispensed edifying and gender-neutral ethical advice: not to lose faith, not to lose hope, not to perjure oneself, not to have evil thoughts, not to lie, and so forth. The florilegium lacked any chapter on the subjects "Woman" or "Women." No *sententiae* generalized about the nature of the female, asserted gender-hierarchical notions, or paraded misogynist tropes. The anonymous compiler never pounced on opportunities typically relished by misogynist authors to insert misogynist bromides into certain favorite topics such as Humility, Counsels, Curiosity, Teachers, or Beauty. No opinion recommended greater humility to women. No opinion warned against heeding the foolish advice of women. No authority reviled Eve or Pandora as examples of disastrously curious women. No *sententia* commanded women to hide their beauty so as not to endanger men. Most important, the infamous (albeit probably misunderstood) Pauline dictum in 1 Corinthians 14:33–36 against women teaching, especially in churches, was nowhere to be found.

Both men and women were addressed in all the chapters, one reason that this florilegium (like Isidore's *Synonyms*) became such a widespread and popular text. This included the chapter on Virginity, a virtue sometimes coded as female, despite ample evidence that it mattered intensely to men.[203] Most of the entries in this chapter were gender-neutral, some referred specifically to men (such as "Those men who dedicate their body to continence, should not presume to live with women"),[204] and others to women. Universalizing evenhandedness also characterized chapter 56, "De honore parentum" ("On the Honor of Parents"), which included citations concerning both maternal and paternal authority.[205] The egalitarian orientation of the florilegium message was rendered particularly conspicuous in the Karlburg copy of the text because this section of the compilation called forth not only a real bout of decorative enthusiasm on the part of the scribe-artist Gun(t)za but also some extremely careful copying, both of which reached a high point on folio 44r with chapter 58, "De Acceptione Personarum" ("On the Treatment of Persons"). The contents of the chapter were unanimous in recommending that special consideration not be given to persons, but to their actions, a sentiment consistent not only with gender egalitarianism but also with the broader social egalitarianism of the *passio Eugeniae* discussed earlier in this chapter.[206]

Out of the thousands of individual *sententiae* contained in this florilegium, only a handful could be considered gender-hierarchical. One of these, an excerpt from Jerome's letter to Salvina, appeared in the chapter on Virginity: "A woman's reputation is a tender plant; it is like a fair flower which withers at the slightest blast and fades away at the first breath of wind. Especially is this so when she is of an age to fall into temptation and the authority of a husband is wanting to her."[207] The relatively mild degree of gender hierarchy implicit in this citation was actually moderated by the compiler, who divorced the sentence from its original context (a letter to a wealthy widow with multiple children) and situated it in the context of a discussion of virginity. In the florilegium, concern for the reputation of a woman who lacked a husband's guidance applied to young girls, whose weakness resulted from the impetuousness associated with youth. As such, it was less offensive than Jerome's original letter, an unsolicited missive to an adult, experienced widow. The notion that such a woman would be vulnerable without "the authority of a husband" was unequivocally gender-hierarchical, but that dimension of the message was lost in the florilegium.

This adaptation of Jerome's letter, which disguised his discomfort with autonomous widows and thus purveyed a falsely mild version of his teachings on gender, was but one example of the transformation of an authority and a text through inaccurate or selective incorporation into the florilegium. The compiler of the florilegium and the scribes working in the Karlburg scriptorium did not hesitate to massage even scriptural citations when they threatened to contradict basic gender-egalitarian values. For example, a citation from Ecclesiasticus 19:2, which should have read "Vinum et mulieres apostatare faciunt sapientes" ("Wine and women lead intelligent men astray"), contained—on folio 23v of the Würzburg manuscript—a crucial erroneous substitution of "mueres" for "mulieres." At a minimum, this "error" betrayed a sense of discomfort on the part of the scribe at the moment of copying; at a maximum, it evidenced a deliberate scribal effort to misrepresent some negative aspects of tradition by rendering the citation defective. Similar "mistakes" were made by Dhuoda in the ninth century.[208] As another example, one of the entries in the chapter "De filiis" ("On Children") was a quote from Ecclesiasticus 33:20, which should have read "Filio et mulieri, fratri et amico, non des potestatem super te in vita tua" ("Do not give power over yourself in this life to your son or wife, to your brother or friend"). Yet Gun(t)za wrote on folio 42r: "Filio et mulieri est enim, fratri et amico non des potestatem super te . . ." ("Indeed, give power over yourself in this life to your child and wife, not to your brother and friend").[209]

The most dramatic example of textual adaptation to activate the egalitarian potential of Christian traditions while minimizing their hierarchical aspects concerned the fifty-two selections taken from the *Admonitio* of Pseudo-Basil, one of the florilegist's most frequently cited sources.[210] The compiler's extracts, ripped from their original context in a gynephobic section of the source text, functioned to imply that Basilian authority fully approved of men, even religious men, spending time with women, as long as those men focused on the spiritual or intellectual aspects of their female companions and practiced the sort of discipline of the gaze recommended by Isidore's *Ratio*. For instance, "The wise man does not consider the beauty of the body but of the soul; however the man lacking in understanding gets caught up in carnal things" and "A prudent man averts his eyes from an imprudent woman."[211] The florilegist extracted similar bits of advice from the works of Euagrios Pontikos, whose advice to measure a monk or nun through his or her ability to battle personal fantasies was included in manuscripts meant both for male and female monastic audiences, including the women's house of Schwarzach; the latter's early ninth-century copy of Euagrios's "rule" paired it with the *Synonyms*.[212]

In the full text of the *Admonitio*, the sayings quoted were embedded within a series of essentializing statements labeling "*feminae*" and "*mulieres*" as polluting and categorically warning men in general against any sort of contact with women in general (as opposed to warning them solely about "imprudent" women).[213] The florilegist omitted all those citations, as well as other virulently misogynistic passages such as:

> Therefore, turn your love away from the love of a woman, lest her love exclude you from God's love. . . . Let your heart be pure from all pollution, and do not give your enemy an approach for entering into you. . . . Do not even look with an unashamed eye at the outward appearance of a woman, lest death enter into your soul through those your windows. Do not accustom your ears even to perceiving or hearing her words, lest you conceive evil in your heart. Do not in any way wish to touch the flesh of a woman . . . for whoever touches the flesh of a woman, will not escape without the loss of his soul.[214]

Although Pseudo-Basil consistently exhorted an audience of male readers to take responsibility for their salvation by controlling their own desires and actions, rather than transferring guilt to women as temptresses of men, this advice formed part of a larger misogynistic discourse associating man with a conceptual complex "soul-spirit-mind-heart" that required protection from the conceptual complex "corruption-flesh-woman."

Pseudo-Basil's Woman was inevitably dangerous; in an ideal world, she would be best placed under multiple veils and behind impermeable cloister walls. Pseudo-Basel's views had some fans even in the Anglo-Saxon cultural province in Francia, for the complete text appeared in a late eighth-century manuscript from an unidentified German-insular scriptorium (St. Alban's at Mainz? Fulda?).[215] But this orientation of the (very rare) source text was not taken up into the (wildly popular) florilegium, in which spirit and flesh were far from being battling opposites. Instead, the guiding principle of the florilegium was embodied in a *sententia* from the Gospel of John cited in the chapter devoted to Beauty (*Pulchritudo*): "It is the spirit that giveth life; the flesh profiteth nothing" (John 6:63).[216] Flesh might profit nothing, but it wasn't dangerous.

The notion that women were "unclean" has sometimes been seen as common among medieval Christians.[217] Yet, espousing such a view requires overrating the importance of the (at most) seven copies of the *Admonitio*[218] and underrating the importance of the 361 copies of the florilegium.[219] Rather than vilifying feminine filthiness, our florilegist celebrated female beauty, as with this biblical quote: "As the sun when it riseth to the world in the high places of God, so is the beauty of a good wife for the ornament of her house."[220] The type of beauty meant was, of course, the spiritual kind, which the compiler was able to praise by quoting Pseudo-Basil's *Admonitio*: "That beauty is to be loved, children, which customarily infuses spiritual joy. . . . Christ takes pleasure not in the beauty of the body but in that of the soul, therefore you should also love those things in which God delights."[221]

Related to the mistaken idea that female impurity loomed large in medieval Christian thought is scholarly concern over patriarchal regulatory discourses that imposed impossibly high standards of purity and strict enclosure on religious women.[222] Feminist outrage over the more extreme manifestations and deleterious effects of such ideas should perhaps be tempered by recognition of the existence of hyperstrict regulatory discourses aimed at controlling every move of religious men, such as the declaration by Isidore of Seville that male clerics "should not go about with wandering eyes, nor unbridled or petulant tongue and inflated manner, but they should show modesty and reverence of mind, walking in a simple manner."[223] Indeed, Isidore's rigorous list of "standard" characteristics for men who attained higher ecclesiastical office would have been terrifying to most men: "meekness, patience, sobriety, moderation, abstinence, or rather chastity, so that not only will he abstain from an impure act but also from the error of the eye and the word and the thought."[224] In contrast, the Karlburg florilegium never demanded the impossible of males or females. As a reasoned guide to disciplined, moderate, ethical behavior, it became (like Isidore's *Synonyms*) a standard monastic text, eagerly embraced by generations of nuns and monks. The women of Karlburg were among the first to recognize its potential function as a rule-equivalent.

THE KITZINGEN HOMILIARY: CONSOLATION AND REPENTANCE IN A MUTABLE WORLD

My analysis of the Gun(t)za and Abirhilt manuscripts ends with a discussion of an original homiliary, or collection of sermons, produced (like the "Deus per angelum" *libellus*) by an anonymous compiler active at Kitzingen.[225] By the eighth century, there were innumerable Latin sermons in circulation, many quite brief. It had long been common to compile them into collections, some of which achieved wide circulation. A portion of these homiliaries were devoted to the works of a single author, such as the early ninth-century collection of sermons by Caesarius of Arles (503–543) made for Karlburg by Deacon Reginmaar.[226] Many collections, however, like the homiliary under consideration here, combined works by different authors. The Kitzingen homiliary also combined texts originally aimed at audiences of different genders: a homily by Caesarius addressed to monks, a commentary by Jerome addressed to his female friends, and three Trinitarian sermons addressed to a general audience. Jerome's commentary, originally a word-by-word and line-by-line comment on a string of atomized extracts from the Book of Ecclesiastes (in other words, a classical textual commentary) had already been transformed by an unidentified editor into a (homily-like) series of pearls of wisdom elucidating the famous opening phrase of Ecclesiastes, "*vanitas vanitatum.*"

Monasticism as a lifestyle was not essentially gendered. Both men and women consistently drew inspiration and guidance from the very same texts, whether they were originally composed for male or female audiences.[227] I have emphasized throughout this chapter the gender-neutrality of Isidore's *Synonyms* and of the

Liber Scintillarum as a way to help account for their popularity among the syn-eisactically oriented women of the Anglo-Saxon cultural province in Francia. But that gender-neutrality was likely the source of their larger popularity in the medieval monastic tradition in general. The message of the tiny homiliary was likewise gender-neutral. This slim volume functioned alongside Isidore's *Synonyms* as a crucial guide to the monastic life of discipline and devotion at Kitzingen. In a very few pages, it explained the theological justification for both the penitential practices supported by the *Synonyms* and the humble comportment necessary to maintain a harmonious community. These points were made, in a straightforward manner, through the four sermons at the head of the collection.

The first, pseudo-Augustinian, sermon began with the mystery of the incarnation, hammering home the point that the Son (coequal to the other two persons of the Trinity) took on real flesh from a real Virgin, who was penetrated as by a ray of sunlight. There followed a (genuine) Caesarian sermon on the virtue of true humility as the foundation of all good, on the grounds that Jesus Christ and true humility were one and the same, just as were the devil and pride. An omnipotent God who voluntarily descended into corruptible flesh to live among humans (as elucidated in the first sermon) clearly sought to model humility, just as a devil who was plunged into hell for the sin of pride provided a warning to those tempted to go astray. Calling pride in a monk (and presumably a nun as well) an outright "sacrilegium," Caesarius enjoined his readers to be humble at all times and in all contexts.[228] However, in recognition that a perfectly humble life in full imitation of Christ was not humanly attainable, the compiler of the homiliary moved next to a third (pseudo-Caesarian) sermon on the efficacy of penance. The fourth and final sermon explained the relation of baptism to the resurrection. I focus my discussion here on the third sermon, with its emphasis on the all-important practice of penance.

Before the advent of Christ, ran the argument of the third sermon, the devil reigned in the world and everyone went to hell, because of the sin of Adam who, in paradise, transgressed against divine commandments. To undo the consequences of this prideful act, God sent his son, Jesus, to descend in all humility and be born from a woman as a regular human being. Jesus then conquered the devil through humility by following the law in all subjection, being circumcised and spurned and spit upon and hung on a cross. Having opened the route to heaven for the just, who suffered on earth as he did, Christ graciously offered the potential of salvation to sinners as well: come judgment day, anyone who had done penance, even the most egregious sinner, would avoid hell. God gave humanity the sign that it would always be possible to achieve salvation through repentance by calling out to Adam after the latter sinned, asking "Adam where are you?" ("Adam ubi es?"). Like the last-minute conversion of the Good Thief, dramatized in the Kitzingen crucifixion miniature, the author of this sermon taught that it was never too late to seize the script provided by

Isidore's *Synonyms* and pour forth words of remorse before the Almighty; this was also the view of the Penitential of Theodore, according to which God would award paradise even to a deathbed penitent.[229]

These considerations prepared the reader to face some of the most difficult material in the Bible, namely, the book of Ecclesiastes, through centonized extracts from Jerome's commentary on that text. Reading Ecclesiastes, with its multiple ambiguities and seeming contradictions, was described as a "struggle" from the time of its earliest commentaries.[230] Yet the text proved endlessly fascinating, attracting readers willing to struggle to comprehend the message in its combination of "existential pessimism," "desperate and dramatic hedonism," and "skepticism."[231] This "scrapbook collection of contradictory meditations" boasted as its main paradox the fact that its unrelievedly pessimistic, disappointed narrator Koheleth could be read as a preacher of joy.[232] Crucially, that is how he was understood by Jerome and subsequently by the women of Kitzingen, for "in the abbeys of medieval Europe, the reading of Jerome was inescapable."[233] The cento in the Kitzingen homiliary extracted from Jerome's commentary only a sliver of the scriptural text, the opening statement that "vanity of vanities, vanity of vanities, all is vanity."[234] Yet it also included Jerome's immediate questioning of that pessimistic *cri de coeur*: "If God made all things good, then how can everything be vanity and not only vanity but even vanity of vanities?"[235]

Clearly, all could not be vanity, as Jerome hastened to demonstrate.[236] "Vanity" represented only those temporal things that were to be properly despised as futile, in contrast to the eternal perfection of God, to which all humans were urged to cling.[237] Jerome directed Blasilla in her reading of Ecclesiastes "so as to provoke her to contempt of this world" ("ut eam ad contemptum istius saeculi provocarem");[238] as a corollary, she would be brought to love of other world. Although the sophisticated structure, depth, and erudition of Jerome's commentary were lost in the highly abbreviated version of the text in the Kitzingen homiliary, his fundamental message remained in place: despite the overwrought lament of the narrator Koheleth, all was not absolute vanity, only relative vanity in comparison with God. "For we can say that this world, heaven and earth, sea and all things which are contained within this globe, are good in themselves, but compared to God, they are nothing."[239]

We will return momentarily to the function of the abbreviated Hieronymian commentary in the scheme of the Kitzingen homiliary and in the life of the community, but first we must address the attitude of the text toward women and gender. The relative misogyny of Ecclesiastes was debatable; the misogyny of Jerome's commentary on it was not, for he amplified every potentially antiwoman reverberation in the biblical text.[240] In fact, Jerome turned minor sexist insults into guiding principles of biblical interpretation. For instance, he transformed an isolated passage associating women with matter and men with spirit into an axiom that women "meant" matter in all instances;

therefore, when a biblical figure begat a daughter rather than a son, that was scriptural code signaling the sinfulness or weakness of the man in question, because to produce daughters was to do material works rather than spiritual things.[241] Accordingly, Jerome interpreted a biblical reference to Solomon being captured by a woman as an indication that Solomon had been captured by sin, for woman meant iniquity.[242] Claiming that it was impossible to find a good woman, for "omnes enim me non ad virtutem sed ad luxuriam deduxerunt" ("all have led me not to virtue but to luxury"), Jerome affirmed his own misogyny through the authority of the pagan poet Virgil, who wrote "varium et mutabile semper femina."[243]

Jerome's commentary on Ecclesiastes clearly presented one of those challenging moments for nonsexist Christians seeking to manage the pernicious aspects of their tradition. The centonizer whose work was embraced and transmitted at Kitzingen did an excellent job of suppressing the antiwoman features of Jerome's otherwise useful treatise. Most of his rants vanished completely, but the section containing the Virgilian citation was retained in a radically altered form. The transformation of this passage required a thirty-five-line cut, one of the longest excisions hazarded by the gender-sensitive abbreviator, leaving the following reading:

> Qui eruditus fuerit in scripturis, quanto plus scire coeperit, tanto ei in his cotidie oritur maior obscuritas. Varius et mutabilis est mundus per feminam. Dificile cogitatio alicuius purus inveniri queat. Opera vero, quia per corpus administrentur, alicuius errore permixta sunt.[244]
>
> Whoever is learned concerning scripture, the more he begins to know, the more does greater obscurity arise for him. The world *per feminam* is variable and changeable. It is difficult to find anyone's pure thought. Indeed everyone's works, since they are conducted through the body, are mixed with error.

The narrator here hit on several depressing aspects of life in this vale of tears, all neatly summed up in one of the pithiest of the original *sententiae* added by the centonizer: "Non est iustus qui posit voluntatem dei facere sine lapsu" ("There is no such thing as a just person who can do the will of God without a lapse").[245] The fact that a penitential remedy for those lapses was always available would have saved readers of the homiliary from giving in to utter despair over this "fact," a point to which I shall return. First, however, we must try to understand this (unique and isolated) reference to "woman" in the centonized Jerome.

It would be linguistically possible to translate the middle sentence as "The world is variable and mutable because of (or through) woman" and to read the phrase as an allusion to the "sin of Eve," in other words, as blaming a woman for the postlapsarian situation of humanity. However, to read the passage in this way, we would have to assume that Eve (or woman) was considered particularly culpable for the fall by theologians active in the Anglo-Saxon cultural province in Francia, which was not the case, for all the texts that thematized the fall in local books—four different discussions by Augustine in his gradual Psalm commentaries, the long Marian sermon in the Karlburg passionary's *passio Bartholomei*, and the third (Caesarian) sermon in the Kitzingen homiliary itself—focused exclusively on Adam.[246] Augustine mentioned Eve in only positive ways in the Karlburg copy of his Psalm comments.[247] Finally, the pseudo-Fulgentian sermon at the head of the Kitzingen "Deus per angelum" *libellus* limited the effects of Eve's error to certain ills faced by women and insisted that those disabilities had been removed by Mary.

Within this framework, no one would have understood Woman to be the cause of the variability and changeability of the postlapsarian world or read the reference to "woman" in the cento of Jerome as an allusion to "the sin of Eve." Even a Kitzingen reader who dipped into the full copy of Jerome's commentary on Ecclesiastes available there would have found nothing in his extended misogynist diatribe to associate Virgil's mutable woman with Eve. Therefore, in the context of the cento, the reference to "woman" read as a simple acknowledgment of this depressing, painfully obvious, universally recognized truth: everything (and everyone) that came into the world through woman was mutable and changeable, an undeniable point about the nature of mortal humanity. And for readers of the slim homiliary, acknowledgment of this fact was hardly devastating, because they had already been informed through the sermons that the birth of the (nonmutable) divine savior had created an escape route.

Indeed, even without the sermons, Jerome's own commentary (and its cento in the Kitzingen homiliary) clarified throughout that all was not depressing "vanity" for the Christian believer. The commentary stood in marked contrast to the book of Ecclesiastes itself and to the Old English poem modeled on Ecclesiastes, *The Wanderer* (preserved in the Exeter Book of c. 975). Both of those texts remained mired in despair concerning the transitory nature of existence and the emotional devastation caused by that fact almost to the bitter end, when both made jarring transitions; neither seemed to have a place for God at all, until a sudden tonal change at the end found hope in God.[248] In contrast, Jerome's commentary (like Isidore's *Synonyms*) kept a consolatory divine presence squarely in view throughout the discussion, allowing it to serve as a refutation of the opening cry "vanitas vanitatum." References to the possibility of salvation through Christ abounded, such that no reader could ever imagine that all was lost.[249] Knowing that all had worked out for the best, the reader hardly needed to worry about the variable, changeable nature of the world of mortals, born through women.

Most important, there was always the possibility, and presumably for most people the necessity, of doing penance. The cento of Jerome's commentary (indeed the entire Kitzingen homiliary) culminated with the following call: "While you are in this world, make haste, struggle, do penance while you still have time! Work! God willingly receives penance."[250] This rousing call to penance was combined in the manuscript with a diagram showing a military camp (Plate 7), certainly a depiction of the ruined Roman legionaries' settlement ten kilometers south of Kitzingen at Marktbreit, an abandoned outpost from Mainz.[251] The camp clearly had some significance for the women of the community, for its presence explained certain episodes in the biography of Hadeloga, first abbess of the house.[252] The Kitzingen scribe used the visual image here to illustrate and demonstrate Jerome's contention that all secular things would pass away and thereby encouraged readers to cling instead to eternal God. The incorporation of a diagram into the Kitzingen homiliary as a visual aid to penance was characteristic of the house, which was lucky enough to possess a (unique?) illustrated copy of the *Synonyms*, as well as a full-page crucifixion miniature, the latter also in many ways a spur to penance.

The women of Kitzingen and Karlburg lived monastic lives of discipline and devotion. These lives were structured around the liturgy of the hours, which at least once a day and possibly more than that included a variety of textual readings.[253] Mealtimes and work times were also accompanied by readings.[254] At those key times, they drew on the codices analyzed in this chapter to help structure and guide their lives. From the *Synonyms*, the florilegium, and the homiliary, they learned lessons that were entirely gender-neutral, such as that earthly things were "vanity" but heavenly ones were not. The message could not have been any different in men's monastic communities. In early Carolingian Francia, dedicated monastics, both male and female, did their best to accede to that portion in the kingdom of heaven that no thief or robber or tyrant could take away from them.[255]

PART THREE

CONCLUSIONS

"CONCERNING VIRGINS, I HAVE NO COMMANDMENT OF THE LORD" (1 CORINTHIANS 7:25): CONSECRATED WOMEN AND ALTAR SERVICE IN THE ANGLO-SAXON CULTURAL PROVINCE IN FRANCIA

The introductory sections of this monograph described the Anglo-Saxon cultural province in Francia as a place where men and women took similarly active roles in intellectual life. Subsequent chapters then analyzed the women's books of the region and argued, among other things, that the ideas and imagery in those books supported the participation of women in all aspects of ecclesiastical life, including as performers of liturgy. For instance, the "Deus per angelum" *libellus* showed Cecilia consecrating a church, Agnes wearing a *stola,* and Juliana hearing confession. It is likely that literary imagery such as this reflected the actual participation of consecrated women in the liturgical sphere.

The daily lives of female servants of God were centered on prayer and liturgy.[1] Prohibitions against female participation in the Christian liturgy did not apply to women in general (*feminae*), still less to consecrated women in particular, but rather to laywomen and particularly to married women (the *mulieres* specifically targeted in canon law).[2] No one considered nuns or virgins to be impure beings who had to be kept away from the holy of holies; quite the contrary, such women were considered the epitome of purity and were never specifically devalued in connection with the mass or altar service.[3] Certainly nothing written by the apostle Paul prevented them from approaching the altar, for he wrote, "concerning virgins, I have no commandment of the Lord" (1 Corinthians 7:25).[4]

Accordingly, consecrated women engaged in a wide range of "clerical" activities, often in exchange for donations: they ministered at and around the altar, they offered the chalice to communicants, they brought forward the gifts during mass, they recited from the Gospels and the letters of Paul, they distributed communion, they enacted blessings, they led prayers, they performed solo prayers, they possessed supplies of consecrated hosts for use in exorcisms and healings, they preached, they taught, they baptized children, they engaged in intercessorial prayer, and they chanted the Psalms at public liturgical performances (permitting spectator-donors to verify the discharge of contractual obligations).[5] Everywhere in Latin Europe, abbesses were ordained, were vested in the sacristy, wore miters, carried staffs, heard confessions, administered penance and reconciliation, absolved sins, and excommunicated sinners.[6] On the continent, canonesses played active pastoral roles in the community, effectively as successors of ancient deaconesses.[7] In Anglo-Saxon England, monasteries known as "minsters," including double communities, discharged a variety of parochial, pastoral, and ministerial functions.[8] The inhabitants of one such double house, Whitby, produced a veiled polemic (their biography of Gregory the Great) against priestly hierarchical authority in order to support the pastoral and sacerdotal duties of consecrated women.[9] It has even been suggested that "some bishops allowed women to participate at the altar either as priests or as deacons"[10] and that many early medieval women were formally ordained to perform important liturgical tasks and were generally recognized as clerics.[11] It is surely telling that Pope Zacharias's Roman council of 743 could refer to five distinct categories of clerical women (*presbytera, diacona, nonna, monacha,* and *spiritalis commater*).[12]

All of this justifies exploration of the specific liturgical situation in the Anglo-Saxon cultural province in Francia, where members of women's communities such as Kitzingen and Karlburg may well have officiated in the people's churches run by their houses. Unfortunately, very little relevant evidence survives, for liturgical manuscripts were particularly liable to damage, loss, and destruction; those containing a popular version of the liturgy wore out through overuse, while those containing a superseded version of the liturgy were erased, dismembered, and recycled for their parchment stock.[13] Those with completely up-to-date contents were also susceptible to being scrapped if handwriting styles changed sufficiently to render it difficult for celebrants to decipher them on the fly; thus, even a beautifully laid-out, decorated, rubricated, sectioned, and carefully written sacramentary with oversize letters could become frustratingly inaccessible with the passage of time.[14] Manuscripts lucky enough to weather the Middle Ages then had to face early modern collectors, who were particularly brutal to liturgical books.[15] Still, one important liturgical manuscript survived to illuminate the situation in the Anglo-Saxon cultural province in Francia.

The codex Würzburg, UB M.p.th.q. 32, originally a sacramentary combined with a lectionary, was produced in our region during the second half of the eighth century.[16] The sacramentary was subsequently scraped away and overwritten with the opening sections of the *Discipulus umbrensium* version of the penitential of Theodore (fols. 1–12), leaving the palimpsested undertext illegible.[17] The table of contents for the penitential (fol. 1v) announced a complete text, but the project of transforming the codex was—fortunately—abandoned, and the eighth-century lectionary remained in place (fols. 13r–23v). The readings in the lectionary belonged to no standard schema.[18] I suggest that the liturgical codex was produced by and for the women of Karlburg.

Female liturgists are an astoundingly understudied group, even though they are known to have created some of the most famous liturgical manuscripts in the Latin Christian tradition. Chavasse's study of the Vatican library codex Reginensis Latinus 316, a sacramentary made c. 750 at Chelles, never mentioned that Chelles was a women's house, nor hinted that the gender of the producers had any effect on their work; instead, he treated the codex as a transparent window onto Roman liturgy, transmitted by Franks whose noninterventionist copying skills rivaled those of a digital scanner.[19] Yet, surely the decision of the Chelles nuns to invoke an equal number of male and female saints when composing a prayer asking for help from apostles and martyrs was both deliberate and meaningful.[20]

The only traceable peculiarity of the Würzburg lectionary, part of the votive mass against (or in time of) toothache (fol. 23r), invoked the martyr Quintinus alongside the archangels Orihel and Raguel. Those archangels, along with Tobihel (named as Daniel in the lectionary), were condemned as demons by a Roman synod of 745 and specifically banned as unauthorized names under chapter 16 of the *Admonitio Generalis* (789).[21] The mass must have originated at the women's house of Notre-Dame of Soissons, sixty kilometers from St. Quentin, where those very (generally shunned) archangels were included in the litanies added to the Psalter of Mondsee under Abbess Gisela, Charlemagne's sister.[22] This is one clue connecting the codex with a network of female liturgists, but there is another reason to look to a women's house in the Anglo-Saxon cultural province for the production of the sacramentary-cum-lectionary: the gender-egalitarian nature of the readings prescribed for saints' feasts and other rites.

The lectionary's biblical readings for saints' feasts were common readings for categories of saints, rather than specific readings for particular saints. These gender-egalitarian readings did not participate in the new discourse of the "liturgical *virgo*," a sexist approach of the late eighth century (and after) that explicitly gendered most categories of saint as male while ghettoizing all female saints under the single rubric "virgo."[23] The most dangerous aspect of this discourse for women was the way it removed female saints (even historical figures famous precisely for their martyrdoms) from the martyr category and confined them to the *virgo* category. A *virgo* did not carry the liturgical weight associated with martyrs, illustrated by the notion (in Gregorian sacramentaries) that the chrism made on Holy Thursday was equivalent to the chrism with which the Lord anointed "sacerdotes, reges, prophetas et martyres" (priests, kings, prophets and martyrs).[24] The eighth-century manuscript considered to contain the "ideal" version of the Gregorian Sacramentary (Cambrai, BM 164) labeled saints Agnes and Agatha only as "martyrs," but several early ninth-century copies of the sacramentary added the descriptor "virgo," betraying scribal discomfort with what amounted to a directive to commemorate women using the rite for martyrs.[25]

The lectionary in Würzburg UB M.p.th.q. 32 forced no gendered preconceptions on those who utilized it, for its common readings never implied that the saints of a given category were exclusively, or even more likely to be, male or female.[26] The majority of its readings were sayings of Jesus. Communities and celebrants could determine the application of these sayings to particular saints; that is, they could select which "common" to utilize by choosing from among apostles, confessors, martyrs, or virgins. Nothing prevented a celebrant from associating the following words of Jesus, keyed in the lectionary to the commemoration of martyrs, with Agatha, Agnes, Juliana, Cecilia, or any other female martyr:

> So have no fear of them, for nothing is covered that will not be revealed, or hidden that will not be known. What I tell you in the dark, say in the light, and what you hear whispered, proclaim on the housetops. And do not fear those who kill the body but cannot kill the soul. Rather fear him who can destroy both soul and body in hell. Are not two sparrows sold for a penny? And not one of them will fall to the ground apart from your Father. But even the hairs of your head are all numbered. Fear not, therefore; you are of more value than many sparrows. So everyone who acknowledges me before men, I also will acknowledge before my Father who is in heaven (Matthew 10:26–32).[27]

Furthermore, no celebrant could possibly have felt directed by the Pauline reading associated with virgins to ghettoize every female saint into that group and exclude men from it:

> Now concerning virgins I have no commandment of the Lord: yet I give my judgment, as one that hath obtained mercy of the Lord to be faithful. I suppose therefore that this is good for the present distress, I say, that it is good for a man so to be. Art thou bound unto a wife? seek not to be loosed. Art thou loosed from a wife? seek not a wife (1 Corinthians 7:25–27).[28]

Given the absence of any evidence to the contrary, the eighth-century German-insular lectionary could easily have been produced by female liturgists, very possibly the women of Karlburg. Würzburg UB M.p.th.q. 32, a tiny manuscript, was written on low-quality parchment utilizing an unusually large number of abbreviations to stretch the available writing material to hold the maximum amount of text. Folios 5 and 6 were a number of parchment scraps sewn together to produce a writing surface. Folio 16 required similar care (the sewing up of a major gash down the center of the sheet) to be made usable. A relatively impoverished institution produced this codex in the late eighth century, a time when Karlburg must have been struggling both intellectually and financially: it had been eclipsed in every way by its replacement royal *Eigenkloster* (Kitzingen) and was functioning as an episcopal *Eigenkloster* for a recently founded and not yet wealthy see (Würzburg). Karlburg had even lost its books to Kitzingen yet remained responsible for the governance of the fortress and villa complex surrounding it, as well as the functioning of the people's church there. Fulfillment of those duties would have required a sacramentary-cum-lectionary. The women did their best with few resources until they were closed down by the bishops of Würzburg and the lectionary (along with any other remaining books) was brought to the cathedral; there it was partially erased and overwritten with the penitential.[29]

Saints' feasts were unquestionably celebrated in women's houses; those services may have been open to the lay inhabitants of Karlburg and its vicinity, for the liturgy of the hours, the centerpiece of all monastic life, was often open to the public, including in the case of women's communities.[30] Monastic communities normally possessed multiple churches, interior private ones and exterior public ones (including, as at Karlburg, *Volkskirchen* or people's churches). Indeed, the Karlburg lectionary contained readings for a whole range of rites that could have been performed at the people's church supervised by the community: the consecration of a priest; masses for too much rain, against evil judges, or against bishops who acted evilly; blessings for salt or against toothaches; and exorcisms. The women of Karlburg surely took an active role in those external liturgical performances as well. Certainly, they performed readings, for the Karlburg (Vienna) penitential explained that *famulae Christi* "read the readings in their churches and complete as a ministry whatever pertains to the arrangement of the sacrosanct altar, except what is proper specially to priests and deacons."[31] A further provision noted that a woman could "bring forward the offerings according to the Greeks but not according to the Romans" (a striking concession if "*mulier*" referred to laywomen, as Muschiol suggested),[32] a formulation that effectively left decisions concerning practice up to local communities. It is possible that the Karlburg nuns pushed the edge of the envelope in this sphere and even performed eucharistic services, given recent arguments that women were ordained and recognized as clergy in much of early medieval Europe and that they performed the eucharistic liturgy even when lacking formal ordination.[33] It is unlikely that religious women in the Anglo-Saxon cultural province in Francia were more reticent to act liturgically than were consecrated women elsewhere.

In fact, a local copy of Isidore of Seville's *De ecclesiasticis officiis* indicates that consecrated women in the diocese may have played sacerdotal roles. This practical guide to Christian liturgy, intended to help create a uniform and orderly church in the Visigothic *regnum* after a period of disruptions, achieved not only widespread popularity but also authoritative status in the Carolingian period.[34] Isidore's mixed message—that women were essential to the Christian liturgy in general but barred from specific liturgical activities—was further complicated in practice by the peculiarities of the copy of the work available locally during the eighth century, namely, Würzburg UB M.p.th.q. 18, an eighth-century codex made in England and given to the Würzburg cathedral.[35]

Much of Isidore's treatise was intensely hierarchical. The author's main concern was "church instruments of order and authority," the subordination of women to men in and through marriage being one of these instruments.[36] The second half of the treatise, which "set forth in an orderly fashion the beginnings of those who carry out the ministries of religion in the divine cult," made it absolutely clear that those functions were the exclusive province of men.[37] For instance, Isidore made both the woman Priscilla and the man Aquila of Acts 18:18 male priests and declared that the voices of lectors, "who proclaim the word of God," must be "full of masculine flavor" and free of any feminine tenor.[38] Most pointedly, he explained that the only way for female virgins to distinguish themselves as notable persons in a church setting was to wear a veil, "for it is not permitted for them to speak or teach in the church, and they may not baptize nor offer nor appropriate for themselves a share in any masculine gift or priestly office."[39]

Isidore surely thought he was being crystal clear, but the existence of alternative traditions could cast doubt on even the most clear-cut pronouncements. For instance, while the veil for Isidore did little more than mark a woman as notable for her chastity, some clerics in the Anglo-Saxon cultural province saw a veil as something that permitted its wearer to "dominate" in church and therefore warned against veiling an unworthy woman, such as a priest's concubine.[40] More important, there was even ambiguity in Isidore's own treatise, for his disparaging remarks concerning women and the liturgy came practically at the end of the treatise, whereas he recognized the centrality of women to the divine cult in the opening chapters of part I, which "explained the origins and causes of the offices that are celebrated in common by the church."[41] Isidore began at Sinai, where "Moses was the first to institute choirs. He separated the ranks into men and women, and then, with himself and his sister [Miriam] walking in front, he guided them in choirs to sing a triumphal canticle to God."[42] Both males and females were thus defined as essential to liturgical celebration, not just at the beginning but also through the ages, for in the very next chapter Isidore brought forward the example of Deborah, who was "reported in the Book of Judges to have performed this ministry," to make clear that "not only men, but also women, filled with the divine spirit, had sung the mysteries of God."[43]

Accordingly, mass formulae consistently recognized that those gathered in celebration of the Christian God were both male and female, as in a mass copied at Kitzingen early in the ninth century that, in the space of a few brief lines, referred four times to the worshipers as God's "*famuli*" and "*famulae*."[44] Even average laywomen counted in a liturgical setting; how much more must this have been true of consecrated women? The fact is, consecrated women were fully authorized to sing and chant and psalmodize, and they did so in public, in large numbers, and with enthusiasm.[45] Had this not been the case, it would have been far easier to enforce the sort of gendered segregation around priestly functions that Isidore fantasized about in his *De ecclesiasticis officiis*. Instead, the authorized presence of women in the liturgical thick of things, following the examples of Miriam and Deborah, easily expanded to cover activities other than singing.

Like the author of the penitential noted previously, who conceptualized the symbolism of a virgin's veil in terms of domination, some liturgists drew rather more extensive conclusions from the role of Miriam at Sinai than Isidore might have liked. For instance, the mid-ninth-century Freiburg Pontifical, produced somewhere in the Upper Rhine or in northwest Germany, provided a bipartite ordination rite for an abbess: first she was ordained using the identical (except for gender pronouns and adjectives) rite used for an abbot, on the example of Stephen the protomartyr; then she was ordained "materna in cathedra" on the example of Moses' sister (here named Maria).[46] On the other hand, by the second third of the ninth century, the cathedral clergy at Würzburg settled into a negative view of female liturgical activity, for the scribe of that institution's version of the *De ecclesiasticis officiis* omitted a crucial "non" from his description of Deborah, rendering her a ceremonially active "ignobilis femina" and thus a negative exemplar.[47]

As important as Miriam and Deborah could be, the key exemplary figure for female participation in Christian liturgy was the woman with the alabaster jar, who had by the eighth century been identified as Mary Magdalen. We encountered this figure in the sermons of Augustine and Gregory, as well as in the Kitzingen *libellus*. She also appeared in the first part of Isidore's liturgical handbook, the first time as an example for all Christians of the importance of hearing scripture, for Christ himself acknowledged "that she had 'chosen the better part'" when she "'listened' more intently [than her sister Martha] to 'what he was saying, and sat at the Lord's feet.'"[48] An examination of her second appearance in the treatise reveals how difficult it must have been for misogynist clerics to prevent women from utilizing their authorized ecclesiastical functions to expand into more contentious liturgical territory.

Mary reappeared in Isidore's discussion of the Last Supper, commemorated on the fifth day of the last week of Lent, when Jesus "for the first time handed over to his apostles the mystery of his body and blood."[49] Here the bishop of Seville explained what was to be done in all churches on Holy Thursday: "the altars and the walls and the floors of the church are washed and the vessels that are consecrated to the Lord are purified. And on this day also the Holy Chrism is prepared, because two days before the Passover Mary arranged to perfume the head and feet of the Lord with oil."[50] Isidore acknowledged that the act of a woman lay behind the chrism mass of Holy Thursday, but he discussed this fact in the context of ecclesiastical housekeeping, rather than in the sections of the work dealing with the sacramental activities of male priests and the miracle of the mass, thereby erecting a firewall between Mary and priests. Yet Würzburg UB M.p.th.q. 18 had a "disturbed" textual order, probably as a result of having been copied from an exemplar that had fallen apart and been rebound in the wrong order, with one quire missing completely.[51] In this codex, Mary's unction of Christ became part of Isidore's discussion of the priesthood, which amplified the sacramental charge of her liturgical action. Here, the beginning of I.14 describing (in the words of Ecclesiasticus 50:16) the sacrificial mysteries performed by priests since Old Testament times ("The priest stretched out his hand in offering and he poured out the blood of the grape and he poured out at the foot of the altar a divine odor to the most high prince") was followed immediately by the end of I. 28/29, describing how Mary Magdalen "perfumed the head and the feet of the Lord with oil" ("caput ac pedes domini unguento perfudisse").[52]

The juxtaposition of Mary Magdalen with Hebrew priests in the Würzburg cathedral copy of Isidore's *De ecclesiasticis officiis* glaringly recognized the similarities in their divinely authorized and approved actions. At the very least, it provided food for thought for readers open to extensive female participation in the liturgy; at most, it authorized that participation in the female-run churches of the eighth-century diocese of Würzburg. A tiny but significant error in the Würzburg cathedral copy of Isidore's liturgical guide provides one more glimpse of the situation there. Isidore assigned but a single externally oriented function to communities of consecrated women: to produce clothes for male monks and clerics.[53] But the scribe who, in Anglo-Saxon England, produced this copy of the text was unable to understand the exchange envisioned by Isidore and wrote the nonsensical "ut stes que" where the text called for "vestesque" (or clothes).[54] Anglo-Saxon nuns did more than weave, and so did their counterparts in the Anglo-Saxon cultural province in Francia.

It is not likely that scholars will reach a consensus on the extent of women's historical participation in Christian liturgy anytime soon. The evidence is extraordinarily complex, and the emotional stakes are very high concerning the conclusions drawn from that evidence, which could affect contemporary practice in certain denominations.[55] In the final analysis, a scholar's own lens may be the determining factor in how the ambiguous evidence is interpreted. It takes labor, commitment, and empathy to piece together allusive surviving fragments of evidence and reveal examples of (for instance) late antique ascetic virgins who "eucharisticized."[56] On balance, the cumulative weight of the fragments assembled in this monograph leads me to believe that the consecrated women of the Anglo-Saxon cultural province in Francia played a large variety of active roles, including liturgical ones, in the lay communities over which they ruled.

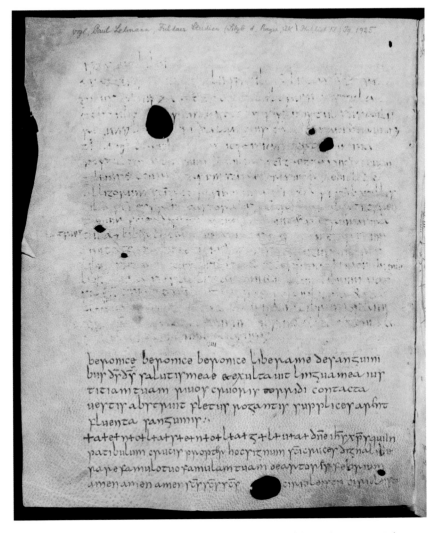

Plate 1: Basel, Öffentliche Universitätsbibliothek F III 15a fol. 17r. (Kitzingen Library Catalogue and related materials.)

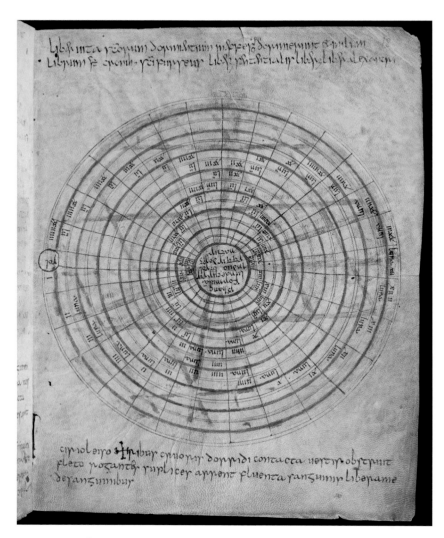

Plate 2: Basel, Öffentliche Universitätsbibliothek F III 15a fol. 17v. (Kitzingen Library Catalogue and related materials.)

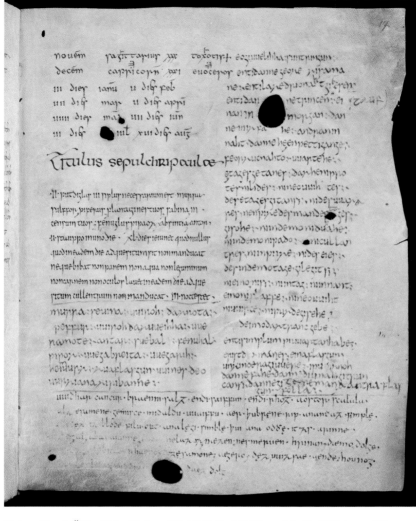

Plate 3: Basel, Öffentliche Universitätsbibliothek F III 15a fol. 18r. (Kitzingen Library Catalogue and related materials.)

Plate 4: Würzburg, Universitätsbibliothek M.p.th.f. 69 fol. 7r. (Kitzingen Crucifixion Miniature [also on cover].)

Plate 5: Würzburg, Universitätsbibliothek M.p.th.q. 28b fol. 43v. (Kitzingen Isidore Lamb of God.)

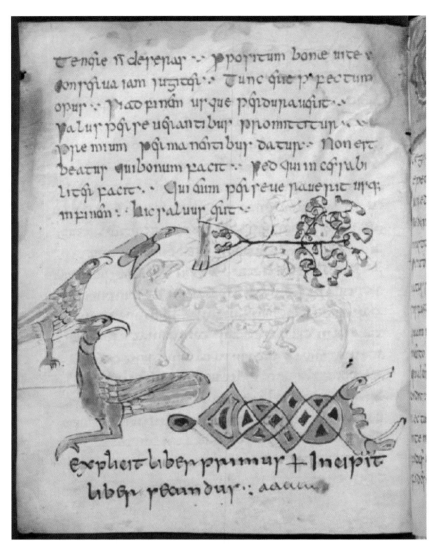

Plate 6: Würzburg, Universitätsbibliothek M.p.th.q. 28b fol. 60v. (Kitzingen Isidore Eagle Illuminations.)

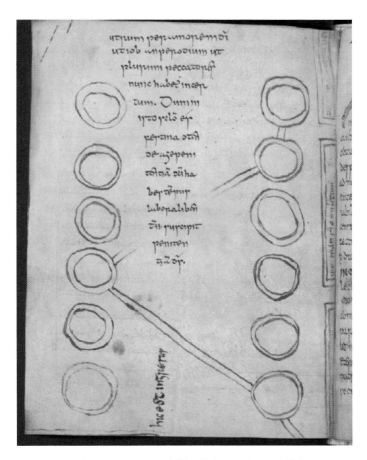

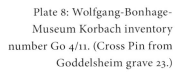

Plate 7: Würzburg, Universitätsbibliothek M.p.th.q. 28b fol. 42v.
(Kitzingen Homiliary Call to Penance.)

Plate 8: Wolfgang-Bonhage-
Museum Korbach inventory
number Go 4/11. (Cross Pin from
Goddelsheim grave 23.)

Plate 10: Volto Santo. (Lucca, Cattedrale di San Martino.)

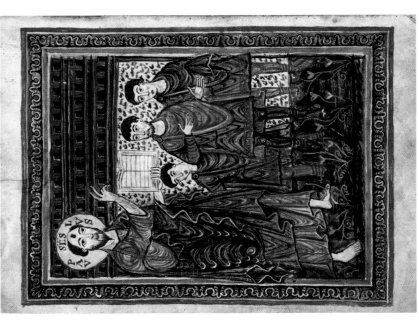

Plate 9: Munich, Bayerische Staatsbibliothek Clm 14345 fol. 7v. (Paul preaching, Altmünster[?] Pauline Epistles.)

CHAPTER NINE

"THROUGH A GLASS DARKLY" (1 CORINTHIANS 13:12): TEXTUAL TRANSMISSION AND HISTORICAL REPRESENTATION AS FEMINIST STRATEGIES IN EARLY MEDIEVAL EUROPE

SPIDERWEBS: RELIGIOUS WOMEN AND TEXTUAL TRANSMISSION

Every early medieval scribe copied only certain texts by earlier authors, ignored others, and edited and situated their "copies" (alongside whatever new writings they produced) in particular ways. Furthermore, many engaged in "unauthorized" practices that modified patristic and biblical traditions, manipulating the writings and reputations of Church Fathers whose views did not match their own. For instance, they adjusted Paul through a series of pseudo-Pauline letters (incorporated into the New Testament), as well as by the widespread *visio Pauli* texts; they conditioned Augustine through dozens of pseudonymous works; and they chopped up the works of virtually every "authority" into tasty morsels and recombined them with decontextualized quotations from other authors in florilegia.

Women as well as men took part in this process, and not in haphazard ways. One of the earliest book-length studies of women's participation in cultural creation, Lewis's 1996 examination of the sister books produced by late medieval Dominican nuns, showed how women worked to render the European tradition more favorable to them by filling their writings with positive images of women.[1] This study of the women's manuscripts from the Anglo-Saxon cultural province in Francia showed how their books reflected and defended both women's integration into intellectual, cultural, political, and religious life (syneisactism) and gender egalitarianism. In closing, we must explore the question of whether some sort of network for the circulation of texts wove together women's communities, facilitating their acquisition of favorable writings. One such spiderweb indeed existed for Chelles and Quedlinburg during the ninth and tenth centuries.[2]

Unfortunately, reconstructing women's transmission networks faces a major obstacle: the small number of surviving manuscripts and early printed books that have been assigned to women's communities.[3] This unjustifiably small number is a legacy of historians' own "indifference or even hostility" to women as creators of culture.[4] Recent feminist scholars have tried to play catch-up. For instance, in 2002 Mary Erler compiled a long list of Englishwomen's books that had not appeared in three previous lists (from 1964, 1987, and 1995) of surviving medieval books from England.[5] Often, however, it is too late, for generations of bureaucrats who considered women by definition historically unimportant destroyed massive amounts of archival evidence for women's religious communities.[6] But we must press on, particularly where it seems likely that searches would prove fruitful.

Remiremont, an institution with extensive elite political and social connections, surely possessed more than the single codex now assigned to it, its famous *Liber memorialis*.[7] How many Remiremont manuscripts were mixed up with books from the nearby men's house of Murbach, whose abbots sometimes served as provosts for the women's community?[8] How many Pfalzel manuscripts found their way into the possession of the archbishops of Trier, who frequented the community both when it was a women's house and, after 1027, when it was given over to men?[9] Surely this prominent women's community possessed more than one book, yet only a late seventh-century copy of Gregory the Great's *Dialogues* has been assigned to their library.[10] And what of St. Irmina/Oeren, in the metropolis of Trier? Implausibly, fragments of an eighth-century homiliary (removed from the binding of their fifteenth-century cartulary) are all that is currently ascribed to that aristocratic women's community.[11] The Nonnberg in Salzburg produced a highly ornamented copy of the Gospels during the second third of the ninth century.[12] How many of the books now associated with the Salzburg cathedral scriptorium were actually made at the Nonnberg? For instance, a copy of the *Liber Scintillarum* ascribed to the cathedral under archbishop Adalram (821–836) was closer to the Nonnberg Gospels than to anything produced under Adalram.[13]

Even the region covered by this study warrants further consideration. Where are the books that belonged to Altmünster in Mainz or to Leoba's retreat in the suburbs of that city? Is one of them the early ninth-century copy of Gregory the Great's *Moralia in Job* by the female scribe Anstrud that passed from a Mainz house of male Carthusians to the Bodleian Library in 1781? Insofar as the charterhouse was founded only in the fourteenth century, its inhabitants must have sourced the older books in their library collection from other communities.[14] What about the library collection of the women's *Reichskloster* Schwarzach, governed by princesses of the Carolingian house? Surely it included more than the collection of monastic rules and other guideline texts, bound together with Isidore's *Synonyms*, that is now Lambach Stiftsbibliothek 31.[15] Finally, how many of the eighth-century manuscripts plundered from Fulda by Hessian troops and brought to Kassel in 1632 hearkened back to the many women's houses taken over by Fulda around 800?[16]

Given our lacunary information on the library collections of women's houses, generalizations about the transmission of texts are bound to be speculative. Nevertheless, we must begin to hypothesize about the intellectual networks that sustained feminist thinkers (including men) during late antiquity and the early Middle Ages. Many late antique religious women on the Italian peninsula lived lives that straddled both halves of the ancient Roman Empire and/or were trained in both Greek and Latin erudition; they must have played crucial roles in the composition of new Latin feminist homilies and *passiones,* and in the Latin translation and adaptation of Greek feminist texts, many of which eventually found their way across the Alps to eighth-century Francia.[17] Early medieval cisalpine women's communities (such as Sant'Agata al Monte in Pavia, San Salvatore in Brescia, and a slew of small Greek houses) surely both continued these composition and translation efforts and superadded the task of assuring textual transmission to the wider Latin world.[18]

Men's communities on both sides of the Alps presumably also played roles. For instance, by the mid–eighth century, San Vincenzo al Volturno controlled a trio of women's Marian houses founded around 665 by Duchess Theodrada of Benevento.[19] Ambrosius Autpertus, monk and then abbot of San Vincenzo, composed notably feminist Marianist works, including a sermon for the feast of the Purification presenting Mary as an instrument of salvation whose importance rivaled that of her Son.[20] His views, whose sources have not been identified, may well have derived from books owned by the Marian communities associated with his house; furthermore, those institutions may have supplied feminist texts that crossed the Alps as a result of the prominent abbot's many connections. Ambrosius dedicated one of his works to Landfrid, founder of the men's community of Benediktbeuern, half of a double house whose women's side was at nearby Kochel.[21] There (at either Benediktbeuern or Kochel), late in the eighth century, someone had borrowed and was copying the Karlburg florilegium codex, while the women's house of Chelles was simultaneously producing for Kochel a copy of Gregory's homilies on the Gospels.[22] What else was exchanged at that moment, when scribes from Bavaria, the Parisian region, and the Anglo-Saxon cultural province in Francia were in touch with one another and with San Vicenzo? Did this constellation bring to Kitzingen the opening Marian homily in the "Deus per Angelum" *libellus,* a sermon composed during the sixth or seventh century on the Italian peninsula by an unidentified feminist known as Pseudo-Fulgentius and transmitted beyond the Alps through the Homiliary of Alan of Farfa, at least two copies of which were owned by Benediktbeuern and Kochel?[23]

The men's house of St. Gallen, "strategically located just north of the Alps," definitely played a role in the transmission of Italian martyr narratives, which appear to have traveled mostly in "small scale 'booklet' style manuscripts."[24] One such booklet, an elaborate novel set in first-century Rome and featuring prominent virgins such as Domitilla, niece of Emperor Domitian, and Petronilla, daughter of St. Peter, was incorporated into a larger passionary produced (apparently) by seven students (scribes in training) at that house near the end of the eighth century.[25] Neither this booklet nor most of the other disconnected (but all Italian) martyr *passiones* in the codex were in any way feminist; to the contrary, the men and boys of St. Gallen commemorated versions of virgins who were consistently in need of instruction and guidance from holy males (such as Nereus and Achilleus).[26] Yet this house had also somehow acquired, and included in their passionary, the oldest known copy of the *conversatio sanctae Justinae* (BHL 2049, pp. 43–58), in which the eloquent speechmaking and behavioral sanctity of that virgin of Nicomedia was responsible for the conversion of a magician, Cyprian, who rose to the rank of bishop and subsequent ordained her as a deaconess ("faciens eam diaconissam," p. 58). Justina's story derived from a long poem by Empress Eudocia, consort of Emperor Theodosius II, who wrote edifying Christian literature during her retirement in Jerusalem from 443 until her death in 460.[27] We shall meet Eudocia again, but for now we are simply left to wonder what individual or institution on the Italian peninsula was responsible for adapting the empress's Greek saint for a Latin audience and putting her on the road to the north.

Another approach to documenting the circulation of feminist ideas and women's books would be to follow the trails of particular authors and texts based on what we already know of (for example) Kitzingen. For instance, given the marked Pelagian leanings of the women of Kitzingen, it was surely no coincidence that copies of his letters (albeit falsely attributed to Jerome) were produced by the nuns of Chelles around 800 and subsequently owned by the canonesses of Quedlinburg.[28] Furthermore, the epitaph of Paula, announced in (but never copied into) the Basel manuscript containing the Kitzingen library catalogue, was included in a collection of grammatical works by Aldhelm and Boniface compiled in northeastern France during the late eighth century by a woman named Eugenia.[29] The unidentified "liber sci Ephraem" on the Basel booklist may also have been a source of feminist imagery, for Ephrem the Syrian (c. 306–373) formed a women's choir to lead his congregation in responses and made women *mallponyoto*, "teachers," in the church, encouraging them to sing out Christian teachings from a raised platform; it was even said that "the whole aim of his teaching was a new world in which men and women would be equal."[30] But the most promising clue on the Kitzingen library catalogue, the "vita sancti malchi monachi," indicated that the eighth-century codex Würzburg UB M.p.th.q. 26 was present (although not necessarily produced) at Kitzingen during the 790s.[31] It contained a *libellus* that I have named "Veri amoris" ("True Love") from its opening words.

"MAKE YOUR VOICE HEARD": THE VERI AMORIS LIBELLUS AND FEMINIST INTELLECTUAL TRADITIONS

The compiler of Würzburg, UB M.p.th.q. 26 combined an abridged version of Apponius's commentary on the Song of Songs (fols. 1–33r), Jerome's *vita Malchi* (fols. 33r–37v), Jerome's letter to Heliodorus (fols. 37v–42r), the *transitus* of John the Evangelist by Pseudo-Melitus (fols. 43–51), and a *vita* of Euphrosyna, a female transvestite saint (fols. 52r–61r). This scribe used holy syneisactic couples (Malchus, John, and Euphrosyna alongside their spiritual companions) to embody the "true love" recommended by Jerome to Heliodorus and celebrated in the voices (of bride and bridegroom) of the Song of Songs: the love of the soul for God.[32]

Although the Song of Songs made no direct mention of God but instead "celebrate[d] the passionate joys and sorrows of unnamed lovers," Christian exegetical tradition spiritualized the text by identifying the royal bridegroom with Christ and the bride with the human soul and/or the church.[33] Commentators such as Apponius and his abbreviator sought to persuade readers that the apparently erotic relations of the Beloved and her Gazelle had nothing to do with *libido* (sexual desire) and everything to do with *caritas* (charity), the "true love" celebrated by Paul in 1 Corinthians 13:11–13 (quoted on the opening page of the *libellus*).[34] Such noncarnal love could be reflected in the relations of human men and women, such as John the Evangelist and Drusiana, whom we already encountered in the Karlburg apostolic passionary.[35] Malchus and Euphrosyna presented additional variations on the theme.

Malchus's constant companion, from youth through decrepit old age, was his *coniunx pudicitiae* (literally "spouse of chastity"), joined to him in soul but not in body. The extremely devout couple reminded Jerome (who claimed to have met them during his adolescence in Syria) of Zachary and Elizabeth, due to their tender loving regard for one another. This particular syneisactic duo had met as captives, both having been sold into slavery by Saracens; when their owners tried to force them to marry, the (unnamed) female captive proposed a chaste marriage to Malchus, who was prepared to die rather than lose his bodily purity. The boy had earlier fled home and family to avoid the marriage his parents had planned for him. The chaste couple lived happily ever after, eventually fleeing their owners to join a double monastic community but meeting daily for long walks in the fresh air.[36]

The *vita Euphrosynae* presented another spiritual pair, a father named Pabnutius and his brilliant, beautiful daughter Euphrosyna, who ran away from home to avoid marriage.[37] Knowing that her father would come looking for her, and suspecting that he would look only in women's communities, Euphrosyna entered a men's house under the name Smaragdus, apparently with the full complicity of the abbot, a spiritual leader to whom Pabnutius frequently turned.[38] When Pabnutius turned to the abbot for consolation on the loss of his beloved daughter, the abbot assigned Smaragdus to the grieving father as his spiritual advisor, a relationship that continued for thirty-eight years without Pabnutius recognizing his wise daughter, whose face had been transformed through tears, prayers, and fasting.[39] Her father remained throughout a prisoner to carnal notions of family, always lamenting the loss of his biological daughter, while his spiritually evolved offspring did her best to teach him contempt for this world, explaining the need to abandon father and mother and brother and sister and to embrace God completely. On her deathbed, she revealed her identity to her father, who died of grief and was buried with his daughter.[40]

The evangelist and his disciple Drusiana, Malchus and his "*coniunx spiritualis*," Euphrosyna/Smaragdus and Pabnutius, and the bride and bridegroom in the Song of Songs were all iterations of the syneisactic ideal of chaste heterosocial love so highly valued by the women of the Anglo-Saxon cultural province in Francia. But there is additional reason to connect the abridgment of Apponius found in this codex with women. Apponius's commentary, probably composed in the early fifth century in Rome, was not particularly popular. The modern critical edition lists only four extant manuscripts, one of the ninth century, one of the eleventh century, one of 1450, and one of 1506. However, the abridged version, known as "Veri amoris" from its opening words (which I have transferred to the *libellus* as a whole), was more widespread. Originating probably in the British Isles or Ireland in the seventh or early eighth century, the abbreviation was brought to the Anglo-Saxon cultural province in Francia during the eighth century; the Würzburg manuscript contained the oldest extant copy of the text and was the source of all later diffusion on the continent.[41] This abridgment reduced the twelve long books of the original to twelve "homilies" by weaving together short extracts from the full text to form a new commentary.[42] In other words, it was—like the version of Jerome's commentary on Ecclesiastes in the Kitzingen homiliary—a cento.

A cento was a patchwork quilt, a Latin loanword from the Greek κέντρον meaning "goad," "prick," "needle" and thus metonymically "a piece of needlework"; it could also be translated as "stitchings" to emphasize the compositional technique of weaving together fragments of older texts to produce a new whole.[43] The terms conventionally utilized to discuss centos thus evoked traditionally female labor spheres; no wonder then that, when a man wrote cento, he described himself "as a good house-wife."[44] The first and most famous centonizer in the Christian tradition was Proba, who, writing in Rome in the last quarter of the fourth century, revealed the hidden Christian message in the works of the Virgil by recombining his words to create a survey of the crucial points in the history of salvation.[45] Proba was attacked by Jerome as a "prating old woman" (*garrula anus*), and her work was considered by many (including Isidore of Seville) to belong among the apocrypha, but her cento remained popular nonetheless.[46] It was copied many times during the eighth and ninth centuries, frequently in combination with Aldhelm's *Aenigmata* (*Riddles*), as in eighth-century manuscripts from Corbie and Lorsch.[47] Her efforts demonstrated that creating a cento effectively created a new text with a new meaning, as did those of Empress Eudocia, "an expert seamstress whose stitchings reveal[ed] a poetic mind."[48] Eudocia's *Homerocentones* transformed quotations from the Iliad and the Odyssey into an epic poem on the creation and fall of man and the life and resurrection of Christ.[49]

Given these examples of women's cento, it is hard to deny the substance of Jerome's anticento critique, namely, its ability to do violence to the centonized author's work.[50] Paraphrasing was a powerful strategy for textual explication and interpretation.[51] Cento could easily be adapted for feminist purposes. Proba, for instance, in reworking the highly regarded Virgil as a Christian prophet, pressed him into service for some sharply feminist points, including the presentation of herself (his mouthpiece) as a prophetic Christian teacher and the development of a typological correspondence in which the serpent's successful temptation of Eve was undone by the serpent's unsuccessful temptation of Christ; her substitution of Eve for Adam in salvation history served "to strengthen Eve's position and to see her as a representative of humanity in general and not as a negative counterpart to Adam."[52]

The very construction of the "Veri Amoris" *libellus* around a centonization of Apponius may point to female involvement. We have encountered the textual stitchings technique before, most prominently in the opening and closing frames of the "Deus per angelum" *libellus*. Centonization was not a strategy exclusive to women, but it was a particularly congenial one, for it enabled women, whose authority as theologians was not a foregone conclusion in late ancient and early medieval Europe, to make original points while superficially deferring to the male authors whose works they abridged. In fact, however, there were also positive reasons to connect women with Apponius, for another eighth-century centonization of his commentary on the Song of Songs, one both different from and less popular than the one in the Würzburg codex, was produced at the double monastery of Bath by a female author-scribe named Burginda.[53]

The attraction of Apponius for women was also a function of the biblical text on which he commented: the Song of Songs. This poetic composition foregrounded a female voice and a (or several) female character(s) and was almost certainly, at least in part, the product of female authorship.[54] As "female literature, as a product of women's culture in ancient Israel . . . where 'contextual liberation theology' might have been born,"[55] the Song of Songs was characterized by "nonsexism, gender equality, and gynocentrism."[56] Yet Apponius further amplified the attractiveness of the Song of Songs for professionally religious women by showing them how to spiritualize the love affair in the biblical text as symbolic of the mutual desire felt between Christ and the human soul. Throughout their courtship, the human soul was personified exclusively in female terms, both in the full text and in the cento: she was *soror* (sister), *amica* (friend), *columba* (dove), *regina* (queen), *concubina* (concubine), *adulescentula* (female adolescent), *sponsa* (wife), *filia* (daughter), and more. Even Christ's soul was sometimes feminized, for instance, as the "queen of queens" (*regina reginarum*).[57]

The love affair ended happily: homily XII left the human soul sitting in the king's garden, in a paradisiacal state similar to that experienced by the wise virgins of the *Visio Pauli*. In the garden of homily XII, Christ asked to hear the voice of his beloved, a female voice. "Let me hear your voice," he said ("fac me audire vocem tuam"), nourishing the dream of religious women everywhere; the scribe of the Würzburg manuscript strengthened this by omitting the "me," so that Christ exhorted his female beloved, "fac audire vocem tuam," or "make your voice heard."[58] Apponius's centonist did her best to make sure that happened, including by engaging in targeted editorial interventions. For instance, she omitted any part of the commentary that was gender hierarchical, such as the commentator's discussion of the virile masculinity of the priesthood and his citation of Paul's notion that God was the head of Christ, Christ the head of man, and man the head of woman (1 Corinthians 11:3).[59]

Although I cannot say where Würzburg UB M.p.th.q. 26 was produced, it seems certain that the compiler of the *libellus* was the beneficiary of a transmission network that enabled her to acquire a series of texts matching her feminist, syneisactic, and gender-egalitarian convictions. The Kitzingen librarian surely exploited a similar network to add the codex to the book collection at her house.

THE CAROLINGIAN REVIVAL AND MASCULINIST INTELLECTUAL TRADITIONS

The dynamics of the textual transmission process became more starkly gendered as a result of the Carolingian reform movement. Charlemagne's "Epistola de litteris colendis," drafted for the king by Alcuin, set an empirewide goal to beef up the education of boys.[60] No one has ever suggested that an improvement in the education of girls resulted from this directive, intentionally or not; indeed, specialists on Carolingian education distinguish quite clearly between the experiences of males and females,[61] and one effect of the new policy must have been to divert resources from women's communities and funnel them toward men's communities. It is not a little ironic that the best and oldest copy of this (circular) letter concerning education in Francia, addressed to Abbot Baugulf of Fulda, survived because it was copied into the Würzburg cathedral's copy of Augustine's *On the Trinity*, produced at Chelles for the newly founded diocese.[62] Thus encouraged, the see of Würzburg and the monastery of Fulda worked together to build up Holzkirchen, a boys' school that soon eclipsed the nearby coeducational school at Karlburg.[63]

The situation was also modified by the Carolingian revival of classical culture, the movement under Charlemagne and Louis the Pious to find long-ignored texts and disseminate them from court and through privileged men's houses. The streams of transmission of dozens of texts (including writings by antifeminist figures such as Tertullian) that would otherwise have been lost ran through the library of the men's house of Lorsch in the Odenwald, built around the principle of systematic collection of classical and patristic texts.[64] Many such "texts came to light because men were looking for them, finding them and transcribing them."[65] Thus, while all newly composed Carolingian-era texts took a positive view of women, marriage, and motherhood and none engaged in overt polemics against women,[66] we should never forget that it was unnecessary to compose fresh antiwoman works; men of the ancient and late ancient Mediterranean (Christian and non-Christian alike) had already composed enough such writings to last any misogynist a lifetime, and it was only necessary to find, disseminate, and canonize those older works.

For instance, the male cathedral clergy of Würzburg developed, during the first half of the ninth century, a striking fondness for Cyprian of Carthage, some of whose writings were passionately antiwoman. Cyprian's most famous misogynistic tract, the *De habitu virginum*, was incorporated into the rule for female religious compiled by Carolingian reformers in 816/817 but was removed from the copy of the compilation produced by the Würzburg cathedral clergy in approximately 820.[67] Clearly there were disagreements among the clerics about the status of religious women, manifested in skirmishes in the scriptorium and guerrilla actions in the library. Perhaps the very same dissident cathedral cleric who cut the leaves out of one manuscript also expressed his skepticism concerning Cyprian's views on another manuscript produced in the cathedral scriptorium during the first third of the ninth century, namely, a virtually complete collection of the writings of Cyprian and Pseudo-Cyprian, combined with a unique list of all the writings attributed to Cyprian at the time.[68] The adoption at Würzburg of the "opera omnia of an authoritative author" approach to collection building necessitated inclusion of the *De habitu virginum* (fols. 48r–55v), but someone wrote a note in the top margin of folio 54v warning readers to approach the text "cautiously." "Hic caute legendum est" read the frame-encased phrase, but the damage was done, and the offensive text canonized along with other works by the venerable bishop. The authority of Cyprian's misogynist views only increased thereafter, as the subsequent Bishops Hunbert (833–842) and Gozbald (842–855) cultivated Cyprian's reputation as a saint. In 835, the cathedral acquired a relic of the martyred bishop of Carthage and dedicated a new proprietary church to him at Ochsenfurt.[69] At this time, the cathedral scriptorium also secured the survival of his ancient passion narrative, which would otherwise have been lost; their copy of the *passio*, marked up for liturgical reading, was clearly used as part of a lively cult to Cyprian.[70]

The systematic collection of works by known authorities was only one side of the methodological coin during the Carolingian movement for reform and renewal. On the other side of the coin was a movement to reject works that could not be ascribed to known authorities, that is, anonymous texts such as the passion narratives of martyrs that formed such an important part of the culture of Karlburg and Kitzingen and frequently contained feminist ideas. The Pseudo-Gelasian Decree, which warned against various martyr narratives and apostolic acts, was originally the idiosyncratic compilation of an unknown figure active on the Italian peninsula during the second quarter of the sixth century; however, during the 790s it rose to the fore in Francia as the standard by which to determine the trustworthiness of texts.[71] Thereafter, anyone interested in ancient martyrs was encouraged to search for information about them only from reliable authors.

One such author was Aldhelm of Malmesbury, whose *Prosa de virginitate* celebrated a number of Roman-era female martyrs. Aldhelm was by no means an antiwoman author; in fact, as a member of the cross-channel syneisactic networks established by the Anglo-Saxon immigrants to Francia, his writings included a significant number of gender-egalitarian images. Yet his take on female martyrs was disturbingly monolithic: all were first and foremost martyrs for virginity.[72] Aldhelm's single-minded construction of these female figures solely as martyrs to bodily purity, rather than as martyrs to bodily purity alongside the political and social considerations that figured so prominently in, for instance, the "Deus per Angelum" *passiones,* was unfortunate, given that anonymous works (such as those in the *libellus*) were being officially devalued just as "authoritative" writings by named authors were being officially promoted. It is striking that Aldhelm's officially approved text struck a chord exclusively with men, the only documented copyists, readers, and commentators of his inspirational tractate.[73] The same was true for the verse version of the work, the *Carmen de virginitate,* witnessed at men's communities such as Lorsch and St. Alban's (Mainz) in the ninth and tenth centuries.[74]

Compared with the small number of women's books I have been able to study here, the masculinist intellectual tradition can seem overwhelming, in part because it has often been able to disguise itself as unmarked by gender, as if it constituted Christian or European or Western tradition *tout court.* Yet an effort to read manuscripts with microscopic intensity and a gendered lens might bring into focus a whole series of feminist strategies to counter that masculinist tradition. Such a level of textual combing, however, can begin only once a larger corpus of women's manuscripts has been identified.

THE CREATION OF FEMINIST CONSCIOUSNESS

Gerda Lerner long ago recognized that both individuals and small groups during the European Middle Ages possessed "feminist consciousness," expressed "resistance to patriarchal ideas," and engaged in "feminist oppositional thought"; she even mentioned Boniface and Leoba by name.[75] In this study, I have provided a detailed accounting of many aspects of "feminist oppositional thought" as it stood in the Anglo-Saxon cultural province in Francia during the eighth century, although I have also been forced to omit (for reasons of space and argumentative elegance) dozens of examples of "resistance to patriarchal ideas" that fell outside the chronological and geographical parameters of the study. For instance, Nuremberg SB Cent. V. App. 96, made by a west Frankish scribe in a German-insular zone in Carolingian minuscule soon after 811, contained a "faulty and problematic" collection of Charlemagne's capitularies: it omitted all of the antiwoman religious/antiabbess legislation of the late eighth and early ninth centuries.[76] Even without piling on additional examples, it seems undisputable that religious women in early Carolingian Francia possessed a "feminist consciousness."

The issue explored in this concluding chapter has been something slightly different: not whether individuals or small groups ever achieved "feminist consciousness" but rather whether those individuals and small groups ever created mechanisms for the sustained transmission of feminist ideas. Lerner also argued that this crucial step was not taken before the eighteenth century and suggested that repeated failures of transmission sentenced each feminist generation to reinventing the wheel ab nihilo.[77] Thus far, I have speculated about the existence of possible networks supporting the circulation of feminist texts; in closing, I hazard the unequivocal assertion that, in at least some areas, a feminist transmission network was firmly in place.

McInerney described the tenth-century author Hrotsvitha as "the first woman to take up the [martyr] stories institutionalized by Ambrose and Prudentius" and continued thus:

> . . . in her retellings the virgin martyr will no longer be an icon of silence for holy women. . . . Hrotsvitha's virgins are characterized not by silence but by a forensic eloquence, which is both passionate and intellectual. . . . If there was . . . an early alternative to the tradition of the patristic writers, embodied in the figure of Thecla and modeling feminine independence and eloquence, it was completely lost. . . . This makes Hrotsvitha's accomplishment even more extraordinary; in her work, founded though it is in the repressive models of the fourth century, the virgin martyr for the first time develops not only subjectivity but attitude."[78]

Yet Hrotsvitha was clearly not the first to narrate the deeds of female martyrs with attitude, for we saw many such figures in the manuscripts from the Anglo-Saxon cultural province in Francia, most of whom were not new creations but rather the result of a prior transmission process. A feminist chain of transmission led from the sixth-century Mediterranean to eighth-century Francia and onward to Hrotsvitha and tenth-century Saxony. The very gendered stereotypes witnessed in the "Deus per angelum" *libellus* (spiritually perceptive women, spiritually blind men) recurred in Hrotsvitha's oeuvre, where "vice, often coupled with paganism, [became] the almost exclusive prerogative of men, and her works abound[ed] in exempla of female virtue."[79]

Despite calls by court-sponsored Carolingian-era reformers for exclusive adherence to reliable narratives by identifiable authors, religious women continued to value and propagate anonymous, unauthorized, feminist martyr imagery. Furthermore, they were frequently supported in their efforts (also despite the existence of masculinist tendencies in "official" circles) by religious men. The monks of Fulda probably played a key role in providing a bridge between the Bonifatian women of Franconian (Frankish) Kitzingen and the canonesses of Hrotsvitha's Saxon Gandersheim through the women's houses in their ambit. One was Karsbach, a house for canonesses in the woods right around Fulda founded after 804 by Gisla, daughter of the Saxon Count Hessi (who had just retired to Fulda), for her daughter Hruodhilt, who appeared in the Fulda necrology of 863 as a *canonica*. Karsbach eventually fell to Fulda entirely.[80] At any point before or after the takeover, Karsbach could have funneled the culture of Kitzingen and Tauberbischofsheim, which was clearly known at Fulda, into Saxon hands. Another path from Kitzingen to Gandersheim would have led through Brunshausen near Gandersheim, which the Saxon Count Liutolf gave to Fulda in approximately 780. This outpost of Fulda, known until the end of the ninth century as the *cella s. Bonifacii*, housed the newly founded women's community of Gandersheim between 852 and 881 while their own buildings were under construction. The founders of Gandersheim, Duke Liutolf and his daughter the first Abbess Hathumot, were descendants of the eighth-century Liutolf and were both born at Brunshausen.[81]

The female martyrs with subjectivity and attitude memorialized by women in sixth-century Italy, eighth-century Francia, and tenth-century Saxony were more than models of female agency. They were also understood to be real women who could claim credit for the historical success of Christianity. Writing about them was a feminist strategy to counter masculinist versions of Christian history, which overlooked women's roles in the Christian past as a way to diminish the potency of their claims for authority in the Christian present. Both the Kitzingen *libellus* and the Karlburg passionary highlighted the centrality of women to the historical process of the establishment of a Christian church, yet another motif favored by Hrotsvitha, most prominently in her play *Gallicanus*, in which the Emperor Constantine's daughter Constantia was the key agent of the Christian conversion of the Roman Empire: "In Gallicanus, Hrotsvit's program [was] to legitimize female presence and authority within the Latin tradition and to rewrite the history of the early church in order to emphasize the contribution of the founding mothers."[82]

This particular historiographical approach to feminist argumentation was relatively common during the eighth through tenth centuries, and indeed beyond. For instance, according to the ninth-to-tenth-century Old English epic *Elene*, thought to have been written by Cynewulf, Constantine's mother (the British-born Empress Helena) was the founding mother of the Anglo-Saxon church.[83] In both *Gallicanus* and *Elene*, "female agency, mastery and leadership" were so prominent that Christianity was "manifested as a feminized religious faith, one also catalyzed through women leaders and educators."[84] Similar profeminist strategies were brought to bear in other histories authored by women both in Carolingian Francia (such as the *Prior Annals of Metz* and the *Liber Historiae Francorum*) and in Ottonian Saxony (such as Hrotsvitha's epics and the *Vita Antiquior Matildae*), which generally foregrounded the political importance of royal and aristocratic women.[85] Sometimes the visual arts were enlisted in the cause of highlighting the historical importance of women, as when an eighth-century artist illustrated an older copy of a chronicle with a new portrait of Empress Helena, shown enthroned and haloed, with a large cross in her left hand and a book in her right hand,[86] or when nuns embroidered altar cloths with images designed to demonstrate "the historical centrality of women to the unfolding of salvation history as well as the potential for contemporary women to continue a tradition of sacramental participation."[87]

Many factors besides gender identity (including idiosyncratic individual or community taste, patronage/matronage, and sheer chance) influenced scriptorial decisions concerning book production. Women's scriptoria sometimes accepted commissions to copy misogynist works, such as when Chelles made a copy of Augustine's *De Genesi ad litteram* for the archbishop of Cologne.[88] Sometimes completely gender-neutral transmission forces were at work, for instance, when the three great Ottonian women's houses of Essen, Gandersheim, and Quedlinburg acquired scientific and classical texts that would have baffled the communities at Karlburg and Kitzingen.[89] These tenth-century Saxon houses were elite establishments where the future officeholders, abbesses, and princesses of the empire were educated; such women exercised leading roles in Ottonian society, both secular and ecclesiastical, that hardly differed from those played by men.[90] The distance of miles and centuries that separated elite Carolingian women from elite Ottonian women witnessed a major evolution in the religious culture of women's communities. Insofar as that evolution included far more progress than decline, we can probably—at least in part—credit the feminist historiographical traditions described here for convincing people that women belonged in positions of power, responsibility, and influence.

Well before Christine de Pizan, intellectual women participated alongside men in the creation of Christian culture and worked to shape that culture so that it would support their own aspirations. They did not write explicit feminist tractates such as would dominate the scene from the fifteenth century onward, but they did argue for the dignity and worth of women (and against patriarchy) in a variety of ways, not least through their sheer participation in the world of books and learning. In our current state of knowledge, we only glimpse—as "through a glass darkly"—a long feminist tradition of anonymous textual production, pseudonymous textual production, pseudonymous centonization, scribal editing, and scriptorial transmission of texts both universalizing and replete with exemplary females. Women and their male allies transmitted the relevant texts and traditions from one religious community to another, so that no woman ever had to throw up her hands in despair, convinced of her own inferiority.

At the beginning of *The Book of the City of Ladies* (1405), the literary character Christine cursed the fact that she was born a woman and claimed that all the books in her fictional library were encouraging her to hate her female self. But the fictional character Christine was soon more than consoled by the glorious history of womankind that the historical writer Christine de Pizan was able to put in the mouths of Reason, Rectitude, and Justice, precisely by drawing on the books full of positive imagery concerning women that filled her actual library.[91] The monumental positive edifice that the historical Christine erected with speed and ease was at least in part a legacy of the efforts of the women and men of the Anglo-Saxon cultural province in Francia.

NOTES

PREFACE
1. Schneir, *Feminism; the essential historical writings*, p. xiv.
2. Schneir, *Feminism; the essential historical writings*, p. xiv.
3. McLaughlin, "Peter Abelard and the dignity of women."
4. Grundmann, *Religiöse Bewegungen im Mittelalter*.
5. McLaughlin, "The Christian Past," pp. 93 and 97 (cited from the 1979 reprint in *Womanspirit Rising*).
6. Fonte, *The Worth of Women*; Ross, *The Birth of Feminism*; Poulain de la Barre, *Three Cartesian Feminist Treatises*; Stuurman, *François Poulain de la Barre and the Invention of Modern Equality*; Cereta, *Collected Letters of a Renaissance Feminist*; Robin, "Humanism and feminism"; Simons, *Cities of Ladies*.
7. Børreson, "Religious Feminism in the Middle Ages"; Griesinger, "Faith and Feminism"; Rubin, "The Languages of Late Medieval Feminism."
8. The "waves" are 1400–1600, 1600–1703, 1700–1800, 1820–1850, 1860–1920 and 1960 onwards (Akkerman and Stuurman, "Introduction," p. 2); King and Rabil, "The Other Voice"; Jansen, *Reading Women's Worlds*, p. 69; Ross, *The Birth of Feminism* p. 1.
9. Lerner, *Creation of Feminist Consciousness*, pp. 12–13; Ruether, "Feminism in World Christianity," pp. 214–217.
10. Klein, "Centralizing feminism," p. 162.
11. Lerner, *Creation of Feminist Consciousness*, pp. 14 and 17.
12. Lerner, *Creation of Feminist Consciousness*, pp. 24–26.
13. Reuther, *Goddesses* p. 306.

1. SYNEISACTISM AND REFORM
1. Nonspecialists may wish to skip the individual manuscript descriptions in Chapter Three (but not the opening discussion of the manuscripts as a group); the information has been concentrated in a single chapter, rather than interspersed throughout the analysis, specifically to permit nonspecialists to easily avoid becoming bogged down in discussions that may be of little interest to them.
2. Humphries, *Communities of the Blessed*, pp. 1 and 4–7.
3. Butzen, *Die Merowinger*.
4. Wittstadt, "Bedeutung."
5. Sims-Williams, *Religion and Literature*.
6. Bischoff, *Latin Paleography*, pp. 93–94.
7. Von Padberg, *Mission und Christianisierung*, pp. 321–31; Classen, "Frauenbriefe," pp. 259–73; Fell, "Some Implications"; Yorke, "The Bonifatian Mission"; I, "Lioba, *dilecta Bonifatii*"; Goetz, *Frauen*, pp. 372–81; Schipperges, *Bonifatius et Socii eius*, passim; Wagner, *Bonifatiusstudien*, passim; Cünnen, *Fiktionale Nonnenwelten*, passim; McNamara, *Sisters in Arms*, pp. 144–47; Urbahn, "'Ich umfasse Dich'"; Orchard, "Old Sources," pp. 29–34; Cünnen, "'Oro pro te sicut pro me'"; Muschiol, "Königshof, Kloster und Mission"; Nolte, "*Peregrinatio–Freundschaft–Verwandtschaft*."

8. McKitterick, "Anglo-Saxon Missionaries in Germany: Personal Connections"; Falck, *Mainz*, pp. 27–28; Green, *Language and History*, p. 343.

9. For the women's letters, see Ferrante, *Epistolae*, at http://epistolae.ccnmtl.colum bia.edu/ (last accessed January 16, 2012). The letters are most often cited from the 1916 *Die Briefe des heiligen Bonifatius und Lullus*, ed. Michael Tangl (= Tangl).

10. Vienna 751 nos. 7, 13, 14, 21, and 28 (Tangl 70, 65, 30, 10, and 35); Schipperges, *Bonifatius ac Socii eius*, pp. 63–64; Orchard, "Old Sources," pp. 20–21.

11. Vienna 751 no. 16 (Tangl 66).

12. Perry, "Radical Doubt," p. 476.

13. Eusebius of Caesarea described how Paul of Samosata was condemned in 267–68 for living with female housemates (*gynaikes syneisaktoi*) (Clark, "John Chrysostom," p. 173). See also Gemmiti, *La Donna in Origine*, pp. 176–82; Cloke, "*This Female Man of God*," pp. 29 and 77–81.

14. Elm and Parisse, eds., *Doppelklöster*.

15. Silvas, *Macrina the Younger*, pp. 18–19; Johnson, "Reviving the Memory of the Apostles," pp. 10–12.

16. Silvas, *Macrina the Younger*, p. 3.

17. Silvas, *Macrina the Younger*, pp. 46–47.

18. Peyroux, "Abbess and Cloister," pp. 50–53; Schulenburg, *Forgetful*, pp. 303–63, especially pp. 323–42; Yorke, "Bonifacian Mission," p. 167.

19. I, "Lioba, *dilecta Bonifatii*."

20. Schipperges, *Bonifatius ac socii eius*, pp. 102–4; I, *L'eloquenza del silenzio*, especially pp. 180–85.

21. Gilchrist, *Gender and Material Culture*, p. 30; Bede, *HE* IV.10, eds. Colgrave and Mynors, pp. 362–65 (for how Abbess Hildilid of Barking had the bodies of all the community's monks and nuns exhumed and placed in a single tomb).

22. Boniface's wish was reported by Raban Maur (*Martyrologium*, ed. McCulloh, p. 99) and Rudolf of Fulda (*Vita Leobae*, ed. Holder-Egger, p. 129). Rudolf called Leoba the "*dilecta*" or "beloved" (p. 124) of Boniface, presumably the equivalent of an *agapeta* (from the Greek term meaning "beloved"), the term used for consecrated Christian virgins who lived, and sometimes slept, albeit without sexual intercourse, with male spiritual companions. The refusal to follow Boniface's wishes was not due to nervousness about opening his grave, for the monks had recently (778) exhumed his body to protect against a Saxon raid (Parsons, "Sites and Monuments," p. 297).

23. Schipperges, *Bonifatius ac socii eius*, pp. 25–27; Wagner, "Die Hedene," pp. 40–41.

24. Fell, "Some Implications," pp. 39–40; Schipperges, *Bonifatius ac socii eius*, p. 53.

25. *Capitula iudiciorum* penitential cc. 9 and 11 (Vienna 2223 fols. 27v and 29v). For the Vienna penitential, see the Appendix to Chapter Three.

26. Wampach, ed., *Urkunden*, vol. 1, nos. 16 and 17.

27. Baltrusch-Schneider, "Klosterleben."

28. *Collectio Vetus Gallica* Chapter xlvii canons 7 and 9, in Würzburg UB MS M.p.th.q. 31 (see below under "*The Carolingian Reform Movement*" for this manuscript).

29. Penitential of Theodore, ch. 15, Vienna 2223 fol. 7v and fols. 8r–8v; see also *Capitula Iudiciorum*, ch. 10, Vienna 2223 fol. 28r.

30. Vienna 2223 *Capitula Iudiciorum*, ch. 9, fol. 27v.

31. Vienna 2223 *Capitula Iudiciorum*, ch. 9, fol. 27v.

32. Vienna 2223 *Capitula Iudiciorum*, ch. 9, fol. 27v.

33. Innes, *State and Society*, pp. 94–96 and 103. Statistics compiled from the charters of Fulda show that women were, in any given year, donors in 35–43 percent of the eighth-century documents, with the percentage of female donors at its height in the years 750–774. During the same period, thirty-five different women acted as witnesses to twenty-nine separate charters given at Mainz, where property transfers were made and recorded according to protocols of public law (Bodarwé, "The Charters of Fulda"). As late as the second quarter of the ninth century, women still appeared in 36.5 percent of charters in the Fulda collection.

34. Rouche, "Des mariages päiens au mariage chrétien"; Vogel, "Les rites."

35. *Liber sacramentorum Gellonensis textus*, ed. Dumas, pp. 411–13 (the "*accio*"); *Liber sacramentorum Gellonensis Introductio, Tabulae et Indices*, eds. Dumas and De-shusses, synoptic tables.

36. Isidore of Seville, *De ecclesiasticis officiis* (*DEO*) II.xx (xviiii), "De coniugatis," ed. Lawson, pp. 89–95, especially 94–95. The epitome of the treatise produced, based on a complete and now-lost exemplar, at and for the Würzburg cathedral during the second third of the ninth century (*LSK*, pp. 123–24; Isidore, *DEO*, ed. Lawson, Appendices A and B, pp. 135*–59*) replaced the hierarchical discussion of marriage with the statement that Eve was initially created as a comfort to Adam, but after the two were ejected from paradise for disobedience, they were commanded to procreate ("Deus enim fecit adam et adiutorium aevam cum procreatione sapientiae dicens crescite et multiplicamini et replete terram, sed facta eadem mulier prius pro solatio quam coniugio fuit, donec a paradiso inoboedientia eiceret"; Würzburg UB M.p.th.o. 4, fol. 32r). An eighth-century copy of the text available in our region (Würzburg, UB M.p.th.q. 18; see Chapter Three) was made on a now-lost English exemplar that was already missing the quire on which would have been found Isidore's subordinationist marital pronouncements, as well as an excoriating diatribe against egalitarian gender conceptions (Lawson, pp. 29*, 129*, and 131*; *DEO* II.19.37–II.23.48, edition pp. 88–99).

37. Beeson, *Isidor-Studien*, p. 99.

38. The scribe of Vienna 2223 fols. 55r–55v omitted every part of Isidore's text that smacked of patriarchy, such as "the term 'mother' (*mater*) is as if the word were 'matter' (*materia*), but the father is the cause" (Isidore, *Etymologies* IX.5.6, ed. Lindsay, trans. Barney et al., p. 206) and "Women stand under the power of their husbands because they are quite often deceived by the fickleness of their minds. . . . Consequently the ancients wanted their unwed women, even those of mature age, to live in guardianship, on account of their fickle minds" (Isidore, *Etymologies* IX.7.30, ed. Lindsay, trans. Barney et al., p. 212).

39. Aldhelm, Letters I, IV, VI, VII, VII, and VIII, in *Prose Works*, trans. Lapidge and Herren, pp. 137, 140, 146–48, 152–53, 155–60, 164–67. See also Aldhelm, *Carmen de Virginitate*, ed. Ehwald, p. 349; Aldhelm, *Prosa de Virginitate*, ed. Gwara, pp. 309*–10* and 316*.

40. Aldhelm, *Prose Works*, trans. Lapidge and Herren, chs. 35 and 36, pp. 96–102.

41. Aldhelm, *Prosa de Virginitate*, ed. Gwara, pp. 296*–303* and note 129; Mettke, *Die althochdeutschen Aldhelmglossen*, pp. 57–65. The booklist of the Würzburg cathedral from approximately 800 included Aldhelm's *De Virginitate* (*LSK*, pp. 142–48, no. 26), perhaps a reference to the eighth-century (fragment of the) prose version (Cambridge, University Library Add. 4219), from an unidentified German-insular scriptorium, whose readings matched those of Würzburg, UB, M.p.th.f. 21, which was produced by

the Würzburg cathedral clergy during the second third of the ninth century (Thurn, *Pergamenthandschriften*, p. 15; Aldhelm, *Carmen de Virginitate*, ed. Ewald, p. 225).

42. Tangl nos. 140, 143, 147, and 148; Orchard, *Poetic Art*, pp. 61–67; Aldhelm, *Prose Works*, trans. Lapidge and Herren, pp. 1–3; Palmer, "The 'Vigorous Rule' of Bishop Lull," pp. 257–58.

43. Heidrich, "Von Plectrude zu Hildegard," pp. 1–6.

44. Nelson, "The Siting of the Council," pp. 154–64; Goetz, *Frauen*, pp. 326–40.

45. Nelson, "The Siting of the Council," pp. 157–62.

46. Mayeski, *Women at the Table*, pp. 66–67; Staab, "Die Königin Fastrada," p. 185.

47. "... ut famulas Dei in monasteriis Germaniae divinis scripturis instrueret" (Raban Maur, *Martyrologium*, ed. McCulloh, p. 99).

48. Boniface wrote to Leoba: "Be it known to you, dear and holy sister, that our brother and fellow priest Torthat has reported to us that in response to his request you are willing to permit a certain maiden to receive instruction for a time, if we would give our consent. Be assured, therefore, that whatever you may see fit to do in this matter for the increase of her merits shall have our consent and approval" (Vienna 751, no. 31 (Tangl 67), trans. Ferrante, http://epistolae.ccnmtl.columbia.edu/letter/376.html).

49. Ranft, *Women and Spiritual Equality*, especially pp. ix–xi.

50. Blamires, *The Case for Women*, pp. 3–4; Schnell, "The Discourse on Marriage," p. 785.

51. McNamara, *Sisters in Arms*, p. 147; Wybourne, "Seafarers and Stay-at-Homes," pp. 246–47; Palmer, "The 'Vigorous Rule' of Bishop Lull," pp. 251–52 and 259.

52. Hochstetler, *A Conflict of Traditions*, pp. 102–4; Lifshitz, "Gender Trouble in Paradise."

53. *Admonitio generalis*, Ch.76 (MGH Capit. I, ed. Boretius, no. 22 pp. 52–62); Collins, *Charlemagne*, pp. 109–11.

54. MGH *Capit* I c. 6, ed. Boretius, pp. 32–37, especially 34.

55. Mordek, *Bibliotheca capitularium*, pp. 72–77, 195–200, 435–38, 698–702.

56. Köbler, *Ergänzungen*, pp. 118–19; Mordek, *Bibliotheca capitularium*, pp. 321–24, 367–68, and 774–79; Machielsen, "Fragments patristiques," p. 488; Kottje, "Hrabanus und das Recht," p. 127.

57. Mordek, "Karolingische Kapitularien" pp. 32–33 and 42–43; Mordek, *Bibliotheca Capitularium*, pp. 949–52; Wolfenbüttel, HAB, Cod. Guelf. 496a Helmst; Weiner, *Initialornamentik*, pp. 15 and 25; Banniard, *Viva voce*, pp. 321–22 and 350; Bullough, "Alcuin before Frankfurt," pp. 578–82.

58. Scheck, *Reform and Resistance*, pp. 59–70.

59. Scheck, *Reform and Resistance*, p. 71.

60. Nelson, "The Siting of the Council," p. 159; Staab, "Die königin Fastrada," p. 186.

61. Falck, *Mainz*, pp. 29–30; Gauthier et al., *Province ecclésiastique de Mayence*, pp. 32 and 36–40; Arens, *Die Inschriften*, pp. 43–45, 343, and 345 (numbers 648 and 650); Ewig, "Älteste Mainzer Patrozinien," p. 159; Krämer, *Handschriftenerbe*, 2.525–26.

62. That expanded version of the letter collection, Vienna 751 fols. 1–78, is available in facsimile (Unterkircher, *Sancti Bonifacii epistolae*).

63. Unterkircher, *Sancti Bonifacii epistolae*, p. 24. The additional series of epistles (plus some extraneous material) begins on fol. 42v. Folios 40r–42r contain five poems (four by Aldhelm) that were probably also not part of the original collection.

64. Vienna 751, no. 101, fols. 64r–65r (Tangl no. 13), a letter written 716–718 by Boniface's student Egburg to her teacher.

65. Munich, BSB, Clm 8112.

66. Vienna 751 no. 34/Tangl 140, Vienna 751 no. 51/Tangl 8, Vienna 751 no. 56/Tangl 143, Vienna 751 no. 63/Tangl 147, Vienna 751 no. 64/Tangl 148, Vienna 751 no. 69/Tangl 98.

67. The de-emphasis on the female members of the Bonifatian circle in Munich 8112 was in part a function of its compiler's relative lack of focus on Boniface. The 1745 binding, with the title "Bonifacii et Gregorii Epistolae" (Letters of Boniface and Gregory), reflected the large number of papal letters added, and their prominence. The first half of the collection (fols. 1–70v) overwhelmingly contained correspondence of officials of the roman see, many not addressed to Boniface: folios 1v–11v contained the letters of Gregory I, folios 12r–16r contained the letters of Gregory II, and folios 16r–61r contained the letters of Zacharias. The isolated letter of Boniface to the pope, embedded in a block of papal letters on folios 17v–21v, implied that—to the compiler of the collection—Boniface was merely the tool of a dynamic papacy. A second letter of Boniface to Zacharias (fols. 47v–49r) consisted largely of a long rubricated salutation lavishing titles of honor on the pope. In the final Roman section of the codex (folios 61r–71r), Boniface's correspondents were primarily members of the Roman clergy, rather than the pope. The second part of the collection (fols. 71r–128v) contained correspondence between Boniface and a variety of secular and religious leaders, including women, north of the Alps.

68. Tangl's edition organized the collection so that the letters involving female authors or recipients appeared, for the most part, further toward the end of the volume than their position in the Vienna manuscript (and the lost eighth-century collection) would have justified. For instance, Boniface's letter to his close friend Bugga, which appeared in the number two spot in the Vienna manuscript (reflecting the lost older collection), became Tangl 94; Lul's equally intimate letter to the "domina abbatissa" Cuneberga, which appeared in the number five spot in the Vienna manuscript, became Tangl 49. And so forth, as Vienna 715 no. 6 became Tangl 46, Vienna 751 no. 13 became Tangl 65, Vienna 751 no. 14 became Tangl 30, Vienna 751 no. 16 became Tangl 66, Vienna 751 no. 20 became Tangl 27, Vienna 751 no. 25 became Tangl 67, Vienna 751 no. 27 became Tangl 41, Vienna 751 no. 28 became Tangl 35, Vienna 751 no. 31 became Tangl 67, Vienna 751 no. 34 became Tangl 140, Vienna 751 no. 37 became Tangl 97, Vienna 751 no. 46 became Tangl 92, Vienna 751 no. 47 became Tangl 128, Vienna 751 no. 56 became Tangl 143, Vienna 751 no. 63 became Tangl 147, Vienna 751 no. 64 became Tangl 148, and Vienna 751 no. 69 became Tangl 98. For the distortion of the evidence concerning women in edited sources, see Röckelein, "Historische Frauenforschung," p. 385.

69. For later, mostly twelfth-century, copies, see Dümmler ed., *Epistolae Bonifatii*, pp. 216–21. One other ninth-century copy is Karlsruhe, Badische Landesbibliothek, Rastatt 22 fols. 2–110 made in Mainz for Fulda (Gugel, *Welche erhaltenen mittelalterlichen Handschriften*, p. 61).

70. McKitterick, *History and Memory*, chapter 11.

71. A copy of the *Collectio Quesnelliana* (created in Gaul or Rome, in approximately 500) was made at Fulda in the early ninth century (now utilized in the binding of several Würzburg manuscripts); see Kéry, *Canonical Collections*, pp. 27–28; Kottje, "Hrabanus und das Recht," p. 127. At least three copies of the first recension of the *Collectio Dionysiana* (compiled around 500 in Rome by Dionysius Exiguus) appear to have been

made in the region around 800: Kassel, Gesamthochschul-Bibliothek, Landesbibliothek und Murhardsche Bibliothek 4° theol. 1, fol. 2–94 (from the Main River valley); Vatican City, BAV, Vatican palatinus latinus 577 fols. 11–69 (from St. Alban's in Mainz or from Fulda), and another copy (written in Anglo-Saxon minuscule) that survives as scraps bound into various manuscripts (Strewe, ed. *Die Canonensammlung des Dionysius Exiguus;* Kéry, *Canonical Collections,* pp. 9–11). The *Concordia Canonum* attributed to Cresconius (produced somewhere in Italy, probably in the Naples area, during the mid to late sixth century, ed. Zechiel-Eckes, *Die Concordia Canonum*) can be found in Oxford, Bodleian Library, Laud misc. 436, from the Würzburg cathedral scriptorium during the first third of the ninth century, and in Wolfenbüttel, HAB, Helmst. 842, a unique reworked version from Fulda during the first half of the ninth century (Kéry, *Canonical Collections,* pp. 33–36; Kottje, "Hrabanus und das Recht," p. 127; Zechiel-Eckes, *Die Concordia Canonum,* pp. 79–85, 147, 332–34, 361, 393–97, and 415). Multiple extracts from the *Collectio Hibernensis,* compiled by an unknown author in Ireland in or before the first half of the eighth century (Wasserschleben, ed., *Die irische Kannonensammlung*), can be found on fols. 1–41 of Würzburg UB M.p.th.q. 31, from an unidentified Anglo-Saxon scriptorium in Germany c. 800 (Kéry, *Canonical Collections,* pp. 73–78; Kottje, "Hrabanus und das Recht," p. 127). The *Collectio Dionysio-Hadriana,* compiled in Rome shortly before 774 on the order of Pope Hadrian, can be found in Würzburg, UB M.p.th.f. 3, produced in an unidentified "mainfrankish" scriptorium at the beginning of the ninth century, in a version that shares both readings and glosses with the *Collectio Wirceburgensis* discussed later (Köbler, *Ergänzungen,* pp. 633–35); (fragmentarily) in Würzburg, UB M.p.th.f. 72, produced at Fulda during the ninth century; and in a series of fragments from a manuscript of c. 800 from the Anglo-Saxon cultural province, now scattered through Würzburg, UB M.p.th.f. 186 and seven other codices (Thurn, *Die Pergamenthandschriften,* p. 84). A ninth-century booklist from Mainz included three copies of the *Dionysio-Hadriana* (Hanselmann, "Der Codex Vat. Pal. 289"; Kéry, *Canonical Collections,* pp. 14–18; Zechiel-Eckes, *Die Concordia canonum,* pp. 146 and 193). Despite "collection" labels, the texts differed both from one another and from published editions (Mordek, *Bibliotheca capitularium,* pp. 961–62).

72. *Collectio Vetus Gallica,* ed. Mordek, in *Kirchenrecht und Reform,* pp. 300–3 and 317–18; Mordek, *Bibliotheca Capitularium,* p. 960; Kéry, *Canonical Collections,* pp. 50–52.

73. *Collectio Vetus Gallica,* ed. Mordek, pp. 454–55.

74. Haines-Eitzen, "'Girls Trained in Beautiful Writing,'" especially pp. 645–46; Haines-Eitzen, *Guardians of Letters,* pp. 104–27, especially pp. 111–12 and 115–16.

75. For the "ad lapidum [*sic*] fluminis" manuscripts, see the Appendix to Chapter Three.

76. Zechiel-Eckes, *Die Concordia canonum,* p. 80; Kéry, *Canonical Collections,* pp. 1–5.

77. The collection was a historical depiction, for each council was introduced by a historical preamble. For instance, the canons of Nicaea on folios 27r–31r were introduced by a discussion of how Silvester, Constantine, and Licinius convened the council to deal with the heresies of Arius (folios 23r–25v), a set of verses on the council (fol. 25v–26r), a copy of the Nicene creed (fol. 26r), and a discussion of the subsequent western condemnation of Arius (fols. 26v–27r).

78. Canons of the Apostles, Canons 6, 7, 18, and 19 (*Collectio Wirceburgensis*, Würzburg, UB M.p.th.f. 146, fols. 18v–19v).

79. Council of Chalcedon, Canon 15 (*Collectio Wirceburgensis*, Würzburg, UB M.p.th.f. 146, fol. 64v).

80. *Collectio Wirceburgensis*, Würzburg, Universitätsbibliothek M.p.th.f. 146, fol. 78v.

81. Council of Laodicea, Canon 11 (*Collectio Wirceburgensis*, Würzburg, Universitätsbibliothek M.p.th.f. 146, fol. 47v). Scholars debate whether references to women as *presbyterae* and the like referred to women as ecclesiastical officeholders or as wives of male officeholders (Muschiol, "Presbytera").

82. Canon 44 of the Council of Laodicea (*Collectio Wirceburgensis*, fol. 49v), which read: "Non oportet mulieres ingredi ad altare" ("It is not fitting for women to accede to the altar"), applied only to married women, not to consecrated women or virgins (Muschiol, *Famula Dei*, pp. 202–22). It is perhaps significant that folio 49v was the only one in the entire manuscript that had serious errors on it, namely, the numbering of the canons was originally incorrect, and had to be corrected to match the table of contents. In addition, the canons of Laodicea (fols 46v–51r) were virtually unglossed (with the exception of some clarification of Greek terminology on fol. 47r) when the rest of the manuscript (through fol. 60v) was very heavily glossed both in Latin and Old High German, a possible indication that this section with its two problematic canons—11 and 44—was valued less than were other sections of the collection.

83. Werminghoff, ed., *Concilia Aevi Karolini*, pp. 245–306, especially pp. 258–73 (the Mainz council).

84. For instance, Canon 12 of the 813 Mainz statutes asserted that monks should "in eorum claustro permaneant, nullusque ex eis foras vadat, nisi per necessitatem ab abbate mittatur in oboedientiam" ("remain permanently in their cloister, and not one of them should wander outside, unless he be sent by the abbot in obedience for some necessity") while Canon 13 provided that professed women should also "in claustris suis permaneant" ("remain permanently in their cloisters"). Canon 19 protected the interior spaces of both men's and women's communities from excessive or unnecessary intrusions by outsiders. See Werminghoff, ed., *Concilia Aevi Karolini*, pp. 264 and 266.

85. Werminghoff, ed., *Concilia Aevi Karolini*, p. 268.

86. Werminghoff, ed., *Concilia Aevi Karolini*, pp. 266–267.

87. Werminghoff, ed., *Concilia Aevi Karolini*, p. 264.

88. "Concordia Episcoporum," ed. Werminghoff, *Concilia Aevi Karolini*, pp. 297–301, especially Canon 8, on the primacy of Chalons (p. 298). Also see the Canons 52–65 of the Council of Chalons (813) concerning female religious (ed. Werminghoff, *Concilia Aevi Karolini*, pp. 284–85), especially Canon 57.

89. Concilium Cabillonense a. 813 Canon 62, ed. Werminghoff, *Concilia Aevi Karolini*, p. 285.

90. MGH Capit I, ed. Boretius, no. 169, pp. 338–42; Schilp, *Norm und Wirklichkeit*, pp. 100–6; Mordek, *Bibliotheca Capitularium* no. 169, especially pp. 952–57 and 1045–58. For the Schwarzach-Aniane connection, see Chapter Two.

91. Würzburg UB M.p.th.q. 25, attribution from Hochholzer, "Zur Herkunft," p. 22, overturning previous attributions to Fulda (Schilp, *Norm und Wirklichkeit*, p. 104; *LSK*, p. 115).

92. Schilp, *Norm und Wirklichkeit*, pp. 126 and 178; Hochstetler, *Conflict of Traditions*, pp. 187–203.

93. Schilp, *Norm und Wirklichkeit*, pp. 89, 97–99, 120, 124, and 178.

94. Würzburg UB M.p.th.q. 25, fols. 2r–13v, 13v–17v, 20r–26v, and 26r–34r.

95. Würzburg UB M.p.th.q. 25, fols. 17v–19v; *Institutio Sanctimonialium*, ed. Werminghoff, *Concilia Aevi Karolini*, pp. 432–33. Only one copy of the *Institutio sanctimonialium* (Munich, BSB, Clm 14431) contains the Cyprian letter.

96. Würzburg UB M.p.th.q. 25, fols. 51v (where it should have been) and 55r–56v (where it is).

97. For instance, concerning penitentials, see Kottje et al., *Penitentialia Minora*, p. ix; Le Bras, "Pénitentiels"; Frantzen, "Significance of the Frankish Penitentials," p. 410.

98. List of houses subjected to Fulda, first third of the ninth century (Fulda, Hessische Landesbibliothek B 1, fol. 31v).

99. Hussong, "Die Reichsabtei Fulda," pp. 89–93; Innes, *State and Society*, pp. 13–17 and 25–26; Weigel, "Straße," p. 36.

100. Lübeck, "Fuldaer Nebenklöster," esp. pp. 1 and 40–44; Wagner, *Bonifatiusstudien*, pp. 65–67.

101. Map of women's religious houses (by Katrinette Bodarwé), in *Krone und Schleier*, p. 160; Martindale, "The Nun Immena," pp. 39–41.

102. The *Capitula ecclesiastica ad Salz data* (MGH Capit. I, ed. Boretius, pp. 119–20, chs. 6–7) appeared in six manuscripts (Mordek, *Bibliotheca capitularium*, pp. 1079–111), and was clearly enforced in the province of Mainz. The oldest copy was written in the Main Valley area during the first third of the ninth century and was thereafter at Mainz (Vatican City, BAV, Vat. Palat. Latinus 289, fol. 1r–1v; Mordek, *Bibliotheca capitularium*, pp. 769–71). The second oldest witness was copied at the end of the ninth or the beginning of the tenth century, perhaps in the (men's) monastery of Werden, and was also in Mainz by the tenth century (Vatican City, BAV, Vat. Palat.lat. 582; Mordek, *Bibliotheca capitularium*, pp. 780–97). A tenth-century compiler, most likely at Mainz, also included most of the capitulary in a collection of which two copies survive (Munich, BSB Clm 3853 and Heiligenkreuz, Stiftsbibliothek 217, both of the tenth century; Mordek, *Bibliotheca capitularium*, pp. 158–72 and 287–305). Women's communities continued to function as educational centers, as required by the *Institutio Sanctimonialium* (Schilp, *Norm und Wirklichkeit*, pp. 73 and 81–83), but the education was supposed to be offered only to committed religious (not lay) women and be carried out in a single-sex environment.

103. Rudolf of Fulda, *Vita Leobae*, ed. Holder-Egger, p. 122; Klöppel, "Die Germania," pp. 174 and 181.

104. Rudolf, *Vita Leobae*, pp. 126 and 129ff.; Mayeski, *Women at the Table*, pp. 61, 72, 74–77, 94, 98, 102–3; Schilp, *Norm und Wirklichkeit*, pp. 51–52.

105. Rudolf, *Vita Leobae*, p. 126.

106. Yorke, "Carriers of the Truth," pp. 56–57.

107. Heene, *Legacy of Paradise*, pp. 200–3, 224–29, and 238.

108. Rudolf of Fulda, *Miracula Sanctorum*, ed. Waitz, p. 339; Hahn, "Fulda," pp. 309–11; Parsons, "Some Churches," pp. 59–61.

109. Raaijmakers, "Een sacraal Landschap," pp. 15–16; Muschiol, "Königshof, Kloster und Mission."

110. Garver, *Women and Aristocratic Culture*, p. 139.

111. Nelson, "Peers."

2. THE ANGLO-SAXON CULTURAL PROVINCE IN FRANCIA

1. Franconia also extended along the Rhine (*Rheinfranken*) and the upper Main (*Ostfranken*) and into some parts of the Odenwald and Hesse.

2. Lindner, *Untersuchungen*, pp. 34–39 and 63; Butzen, *Die Merowinger*, pp. 26–52 and 122–38; Böhme, "Das frühe Mittelalter," pp. 113–14 and 118; Wamser, "Mainfranken," pp. 65–69.

3. Haubrichs, "Sprache," p. 561; Lindner, *Untersuchungen*, pp. 38–42.

4. Banniard, *Viva voce*, pp. 326–28.

5. Dannheimer, "Im Spiegel der Funde," pp. 88–89 and 95–97; Wamser, "Mainfranken," pp. 43–44 and 54–56; Weidemann, "Frühmittelalterliche Burgen," p. 135; Wamers, "Das Untermaingebiet," p. 37.

6. Wickham, *Framing the Early Middle Ages*, pp. 794–805.

7. Falck, *Mainz*, pp. 21 and 48–53; Wamers, *Die frühmittelalterliche Lesefunde*.

8. Wamser, "Zur archäologischen Bedeutung," pp. 324 and 330–31; Innes, *State and Society*, pp. 97–98; Wamers, *Die frühmittelalterliche Lesefunde*; Butzen, *Die Merowinger*, pp. 19–21.

9. Wickham, *Framing the Early Middle Ages*, pp. 805–14.

10. Parsons, "Some Churches"; McKitterick, "Anglo-Saxon Missionaries in Germany: Manuscript Evidence," especially pp. 317–19; Reynolds, "What Do We Mean?" p. 397; Kehl, "Heiligenverehrung," pp. 187–88; Lindner, *Untersuchungen*, pp. 46–51; Butzen, *Die Merowinger*, pp. 60–86 and 99–105; Green, *Language and History*, pp. 284, 302–3 and 346–55.

11. Green, *Language and History*, pp. 325–40.

12. Butzen, *Die Merowinger*, p. 21.

13. Rosenstock, "Siedlungsgeschichte," p. 53; Butzen, *Die Merowinger*, pp. 142–65.

14. Zöller, "Kirchengut," p. 231.

15. Düwel, "Epigraphische Zeugnisse," p. 541.

16. Tangl 50, pp. 84–85; Hartmann, "Rechtskenntnis," p. 14.

17. Lindner, *Untersuchungen* pp. 75–82, 84–90, and map between pp. 80 and 81; Butzen, *Die Merowinger*, pp. 55–60, 72 (where the number of donated churches is thirty-two), and 106–11; Dannheimer, "Im Spiegel der Funde," pp. 98–105; Dinklage, "Hammelburg," p. 40; Wagner, "Die Zehntenschenkung Pippins."

18. *VKB* 1991, pp. 208 and 271; Pescheck, *Archäologiereport Kleinlangheim*; Gerlach, "Pfarrkirche von Kleinlangheim," p. 290.

19. Pescheck, "Frühchristlicher Sakralbau," pp. 10–12; Böhme, "Das frühe Mittelalter," p. 115.

20. *VKB* 1966, p. 164; Klein-Pfeuffer, "Christliche Glaubensvorstellung," pp. 129–30; Falck, *Mainz*, p. 26.

21. Rettner, "Grabhäuser," pp. 105–9. The most venerated individuals were female.

22. For instance, the eighth-century wooden church at Krutzen (*VKB* 1991, p. 237); the church on the villa donated by the woman Ata to Fulda (Stengel, ed., *Urkundenbuch des Klosters Fulda*, vol. 1, no. 71); the Monasterium Rotaha donated to Lorsch in 786 by abbess "Aba deo sacrata filia Theodoni" (Stimming, ed., *Mainzer Urkundenbuch*, vol. 1, pp. 30–31, number 62).

23. Stengel, ed., *Urkundenbuch des Klosters Fulda*, vol. 1, nos. 203, 208, 212, 223, 250, 256, 263, 501, and 509; Dronke, ed., *Codex Diplomaticus*, nos. 189, 210, 214, 217, 224, 272, 344, 398, 409, 458, 480, and 481; Hochstetler, *A Conflict of Traditions*, pp. 173–80. Also

note a funerary inscription of c. 700 for an Abbot Pertram in the massive cemetery at Mainz (Arens, *Die Inschriften der Stadt Mainz*, p. 46).

24. Stengel, ed., *Urkundenbuch des Klosters Fulda*, vol. 1, no. 49; Hochstetler, *A Conflict of Traditions*, p. 70.

25. Ewig, "Die ältesten Mainzer Patrozinien," 156–58; Gauthier et al., *Province ecclesiastique de Mayence*, pp. 33–35 and 41–43; Parsons, "Sites and Monuments," pp. 307–10; Falck, *Mainz*, pp. 18–19.

26. Gauthier et al., *Province ecclesiastique de Mayence*, pp. 23 and 35–36; Falck, *Mainz*, p. 23; Weidemann, "Urkunde," pp. 32–39; Weidemann, "Die hl. Bilhild"; cf. Metzner, "Das Kloster 'Lorsch,'" p. 197.

27. Ewig, "Die ältesten Mainzer Patrozinien," 167–70; Stimming, ed., *Mainzer Urkundenbuch* I. nr. 2b; Wagner, *Bonifatiusstudien*, p. 234; Wagner, "Die Hedene," pp. 30–38. Bilihilt's late eleventh-century biography in Dresden, Sächsische Landesbibliothek A. 128 (from Altmünster), has never been considered reliable, except by Mordek, "Die Hedenen" (pp. 352–55).

28. Falck, *Mainz*, pp. 13–15, 23, and 41; Bodarwé, "Frauenleben," p. 122.

29. Weiner, *Initialornamentik*, pp. 65–68.

30. Gauthier et al., *Province ecclesiastique de Mayence*, p. 35; Rösen, *Klöster in Franken*, p. 81; *VRB* 1991, p. 157.

31. For Amorbach, see note 85.

32. Schiller, *Wanderführer Spessart*, pp. 115–18, 176–222 (especially pp. 188–89); VKB 1991, p. 249.

33. Wamser, "Zur archäologischen Bedeutung," p. 324; Schilp, *Norm und Wirklichkeit*, pp. 76–79.

34. Schiller, *Wanderführer Spessart*, pp. 148–49; Lindner, *Untersuchungen*, pp. 13–14.

35. Weidemann, "Frühmittelalterliche Burgen," pp. 143–44; Emmert, "Gertrudis Tripartita," pp. 9–12; Kübert, *Karlburg*, pp. 53–57; Daul, "Karlburg," p. 83; Rosenstock, "Siedlungsgeschichte," pp. 54–55.

36. Daul, "Karlburg" pp. 46–51; Lenssen, ed., *Gertrud in Franken* p. 34.

37. Kübert, *Karlburg*, p. 52.

38. Rosenstock, "Siedlungsgeschichte," p. 58; Wamser, "Zur archäologischen Bedeutung," pp. 326–28; Munich, Bayerisches Hauptstaatsarchiv Kaiserselekt 69 (reproduced in Lenssen and Wamser, eds., *1250 Jahre Bistum Würzburg*, p. 101).

39. Kübert, *Karlburg*, pp. 20–26; Lindner, *Untersuchungen*, 80–86.

40. Kübert, *Karlburg*, pp. 28–30; Wamser, "Die silberne Pyxis—Landesgeschichtliche Aspekte," p. 146; Wamers, "Die silberne Pyxis—Ikonographie," p. 154; Lenssen and Wamers, eds., *1250 Jahre Bistum Würzburg*, pp. 292–95.

41. Wamser, "Zur archäologischen Bedeutung," p. 331.

42. Wamser, "Zur archäologischen Bedeutung," pp. 321, 328, and 341; Kübert, *Karlburg*, p. 79; Krämer, *Handschriftenerbe*, 1.388; Ettel and Rüdel, "Castellum und villa," pp. 311, 316, and 318; Lifshitz, "Demonstrating Gun(t)za."

43. Gilchrist, *Gender and Material Culture*, pp. 30–31.

44. Wamser, "Zur archäologischen Bedeutung," pp. 319, 329, 332 (especially nos. 9–12), 333 (especially nos. 1–3), 334 (especially nos. 10–11), and 335 (especially nos. 1–3).

45. Kübert, *Karlburg*, pp. 59–64.

46. Kübert, *Karlburg*, p. 30; Wamser, "Zur archäologischen Bedeutung," pp. 323 and 328.

47. Lübeck, "Fuldaer Nebenklöster," pp. 33–37.

48. Wagner, *Bonifatiusstudien*, pp. 92–94; Lindner, *Untersuchungen*, pp. 17–18; Wenisch, *Ochsenfurt*, pp. 8–11 and 28–41.

49. Einfirst (Mattenzell), a rich women's community founded by Count Macco (Matto), was donated to Fulda in 788 by the founder's sons Matto and Megingoz (Lübeck, "Fuldaer Nebenklöster," pp. 13–15; Wagner, *Bonifatiusstudien*, pp. 66–67; Trunk, "Megingozzeshusenscastel," p. 101). It is not certain whether the *monasteriolum* Brachaw north of Bad Kissingen was a men's or women's community; it was donated between 780 and 802 to Fulda by the sisters Reginhilt and Gundhilt (Lübeck, "Fuldaer Nebenklöster," pp. 16–17). There is similar uncertainty concerning the wealthy community of Sala in Saal, which came to Fulda piecemeal through donations by Ellenswind and her son Warmunt (824), the spouses Gundacar and Regingund (806), Sigifrid and his sisters Gunza and Leobniwi (801), and the woman Heijat (796). For Sala, see Lübeck, "Fuldaer Nebenklöster," pp. 18–20.

50. Hochstetler, *A Conflict of Traditions*, pp. 117–67, especially pp. 117–18.

51. Wagner, *Bonifatiusstudien*, pp. 45, 230–31, 234–36; Falck, *Mainz*, pp. 26–27.

52. Wagner, *Bonifatiusstudien*, p. 236.

53. Butzen, *Die Merowinger*, pp. 81–82; Ewig, "Milo et eiusmodi similes."

54. Wagner, *Bonifatiusstudien*, pp. 236 and 238.

55. Wagner, *Bonifatiusstudien*, p. 239, redating Tangl 216 n. 96 to 740–755, rather than 732–754.

56. Tangl 48; Nonn, "Die Nachfolge," pp.62–71; Collins, "Pippin III," pp. 82–83 and 84–85; Airlie, "Towards a Carolingian Aristocracy," p. 113; Becher, "Eine verschleierte Krise," pp. 124–31; Wagner, *Bonifatiusstudien*, pp. 239–40.

57. Rösen, *Klöster in Franken*, pp. 75–76; Zöller, "Kirchengut des hl. Kilian"; Bosl, "Würzburg," p. 27

58. Lindner, *Untersuchungen*, p. 74; Mordek, "Die Hedenen," p. 347; Gerberding, "716," p. 215.

59. Wagner, *Bonifatiusstudien*, p. 242; Schieffer, "Karolingische Töchter," p. 128.

60. Wagner, *Bonifatiusstudien*, p. 242.

61. Wagner, *Bonifatiusstudien*, pp. 246–49; Collins, *Charlemagne*, 32–33; Wolf, "Grifos Erbe," pp. 9–11.

62. Wagner, "Die Äbtissinen," p. 20.

63. Rosenstock, "Die Besiedlung," pp. 50–51.

64. Petzolt, "Abtei Kitzingen," p. 79.

65. Wenisch, *Ochsenfurt*, pp. 70–71. Eventually Ochsenfurt fell under the control of the Würzburg cathedral.

66. Wagner, *Bonifatiusstudien*, p. 92; Petzolt, "Abtei Kitzingen," pp. 77, 79, and 81–82.

67. Wagner, *Bonifatiusstudien*, pp. 47, 54, 70–73, and 82; Wagner, "Die Äbtissinen," pp. 18–20; Schipperges, *Bonifatius ac socii eius*, pp. 148–49. Both Wagner and Schipperges believe that Kitzingen's foundation as a Pippinid *Eigenkloster* predated and was independent of Boniface.

68. Wagner, *Bonifatiusstudien*, pp. 76, 81, and 84–85.

69. Schipperges, *Bonifatius ac socii eius,* pp. 102-4. Frankfurt, Stadt- und UB Praed. 26, a fifteenth-century Bible, is the only codex currently associated with this community (Krämer, *Handschriftenerbe,* 1.1) that survived into the modern era.

70. Haub, "Die ältesten Originalurkunden," p. 125.

71. Innes, *State and Society,* p. 59.

72. Wamser, "Mainfranken," pp. 54-56.

73. Lindner, *Untersuchungen,* p. 16; Butzen, *Die Merowinger,* pp. 79-80.

74. After Leoba's death, the house fell to Hersfeld and was soon after dissolved (Bodarwé, "Frauenleben," p. 141, and number 114 on the list and map in the appendix).

75. The first abbot of Hersfeld was Lul's cousin Baldhard (d. 798), the brother of Berhtgyt and son of Cynehild (Fell, "Some Implications," p. 42). Hersfeld was founded in 736 as a small cell but developed into a monastic community in 760/770 (Butzen, *Die Merowinger,* p. 82).

76. *VKB* 1966, p. 79; *VKB* 1991, p. 113.

77. Hahn, "Fulda," especially pp. 301-4. Fulda was also located four miles from a small men's monastery founded at Lihtolfesbach during the 730s, later taken over by Fulda (Lübeck, "Fuldaer Nebenklöster," pp. 2-10).

78. Hahn, "Fulda," pp. 300-4; Gerlach, "Der Grenzverlauf"; Dinklage, "Hammelburg," pp. 47-48 and 54-56; Stengel, ed., *Urkundenbuch des Klosters Fulda,* vol. 1, nos. 1-31.

79. Lübeck, "Fuldaer Nebenklöster," pp. 19-20 and 28-29.

80. The school at Holzkirchen, run by a *magister,* thrived into the thirteenth century (Lübeck, "Fuldaer Nebenklöster," pp. 21-24 and 29-32; Rösen, *Klöster in Franken,* p. 59; Schneider, *Klöster und Stifte in Mainfranken,* pp. 41-44).

81. Lübeck, "Fuldaer Nebenklöster," pp. 40-44; Wagner, *Bonifatiusstudien,* pp. 65-67; Stengel, ed., *Urkundenbuch des Klosters Fulda,* 1:202. For Einfirst, see note 49.

82. Stengel, ed., *Urkundenbuch des Klosters Fulda,* 1:39. For an alternative (albeit unlikely) interpretation of the donation as for Kitzingen, see Wagner, "Die Äbtissinen," p. 34.

83. Hasdenteufel-Röding, "Studien zur Gründung," pp. 135-36; Hochstetler, *A Conflict of Traditions,* pp. 161-62; Stengel, ed., *Urkundenbuch des Klosters Fulda,* 1:154 (especially p. 129), 1:264, and 1:274 (especially p. 396).

84. Rösen, *Klöster in Franken,* p. 73; Schemmel, "Neustadt," pp. 14-16; Weidemann, "Frühmittelalterliche Burgen," p. 150; Wagner, "Die Äbte," pp. 17-18; Herrmann, "Die Inschrift," p. 70; Wamser, "Erwägungen," pp. 180-83 and pp. 196-201. The tradition that Charlemagne gave the house to Megingaud (Megingoz) after the latter's retirement as second bishop of Würzburg derives from documents generated during a twelfth-century struggle over the autonomy of the house waged between the monks of Neustadt and the bishops of Würzburg, including the twelfth-century *vita Burkhardi* II (discussed at length below) and a forged foundation charter of Charlemagne (Wagner, "Zur Frühzeit," p. 103; Wamser, "Erwägungen," pp. 165-66). They have no reliability for the eighth century.

85. Amorbach, founded c. 734, was unimportant during the eighth century; it was a retreat for male secular clerics and a cell at best, with no signs of a building complex. The oldest manuscript that has ever even been suggested as an Amorbach product, largely on the basis of its Amorbach provenance (Berlin SB-PK theol. Lat. Fol. 480, part of Gregory the Great's Homilies on Ezekiel) dates to the first quarter of the ninth century (Brandis and Becker, *Glanz Alter Buchkunst,* no. 5, p. 23; Fingernagel, *Die Illuminierten Lateinischen Handschriften,* vol. 1, pp. 1-2 and vol. 2, p. 17 Abb. 1-3). Furthermore, the

orientation of Amorbach was not toward the Main Valley but rather toward the southern Odenwald, until—after 800–it was pulled to the north through being yoked to Neustadt and Verden. See Kramer, "Amorbach," p. 33; Störmer, "Amorbach"; Schneider, *Klöster und Stifte,* p. 27; Wamser, "Erwägungen," pp. 166 and 188; Sage, "Die Kirche," p. 209; Rösen, *Klöster in Franken,* pp. 60–61.

86. Vogt, "Zur Frühgeschichte," p. 57.

87. Büll, *Das Monasterium Suuarzaha,* pp. 288–90.

88. Staab, "Die Königin Fastrada," pp. 212–17; Büll, *Das Monasterium Suuarzaha,* pp. 113–31, especially pp. 124–25.

89. Büll, *Das Monasterium Suuarzaha,* p. 25.

90. *Notitia de servitio monasteriorum,* ed. Boretius, MGH Capit. 1, no. 171, pp. 349–352; Mordek, *Bibliotheca Capitularium,* pp. 606–7; Büll, *Das Monasterium Suuarzaha,* pp. 102–8. Schwarzach is the best candidate for the intended possessor of the Würzburg *Institutio sanctimonialium* manuscript (see chapter 1), given that a feature of inclusion on the *Notitia* was the obligation to accept the reforms of Benedict of Aniane (Büll, *Das Monasterium Suuarzaha,* pp. 133–35 and 241). In 844, Theodrada subjected the house to the bishop of Würzburg, but it continued to be ruled by Carolingian imperial princesses, including two daughters of Louis the German, namely, Hildegard (d. 856) and Bertha (Staab, "Die Königin Fastrada," pp. 212–17; Büll, *Das Monasterium Suuarzaha,* pp. 71–76; Semmler, "Monasterium Suuarzaha"; Stoclet, "Gisele, Kisyla, Chelles," pp. 250–51 and 258–64; Rösen, *Klöster in Franken,* pp. 76–78). After the death of Bertha in 877, Schwarzach was transformed into a men's house by Würzburg (Büll, *Das Monasterium Suuarzaha,* pp. 247–86, especially p. 286).

91. The newcomers introduced organized book production, not books. Old High German evidenced a far-reaching exposure to the Latin vocabulary of literacy independent of (and even contrasting with) Old English forms. Tellingly, what Old English speakers did introduce to Old High German was the technical vocabulary necessary for discussing individual letter forms, such as would be required in a scriptorium; for instance, the word for a "letter" (book sign) in Old High German (*buohstab,* as opposed to *rûnstab* for a runic sign) was borrowed from Old English *bōcstæf* (as opposed to *rûnstæf*). For details, see Green, *Language and History,* pp. 256–69.

92. Wolf, "Grifos Erbe," passim and especially pp. 14 and 16; Becher, "Eine verschleierte Krise," especially pp. 131–33.

93. Wagner, *Bonifatiusstudien,* p. 26; Wagner, "Zur Frühzeit," pp. 98–102; Weiner, *Initialornamentik,* p. 40; Ewig, "Beobachtungen zur Entwicklung," p. 226; Ewig, "Saint Chrodegang," pp. 241–42; Wamser, "Erwägungen," p. 165; Herrmann, "Die Inschrift," pp. 69 and 72–75.

94. Wagner, *Bonifatiusstudien,* pp. 9–26 and 61–64; Klüppel, "Die Germania," pp. 165–77. Wagner's argument for the attribution of the biography to Willibald is strengthened by the fact that the oldest copy of the text (in Munich, BSB Clm 1086) was produced in the diocese of Eichstätt during the first half of the ninth century and contained, along with the *vita* of Boniface (fols. 1–44), Hugeburc's biographies of Wynebald of Eichstätt (fols. 44–71) and Willibald of Eichstätt (fols. 71–102); see Bierbrauer, *Die vorkarolingischen und karolingischen Handschriften,* nr. 165.

95. Palmer, "The 'Vigorous Rule' of Bishop Lull," p. 256; Lindner, *Untersuchungen,* p. 53. I would add to Palmer's list Milo of Trier and Reims (Tangl 87; Ewig, "Milo et eiusmodi similes," 194).

96. Willibald, *Vita Bonifatii*, ch. 6, trans. Talbot, p. 127; Duke Hedenus and Duchess Theodrada of Würzburg, with their son Thuring, granted properties (in 704 and 717) in Thuringia and on the Saale River to Willibrord of Echternach (Linder, *Untersuchungen*, pp. 52, 57, 65–66, and 92; Butzen, *Die Merowinger*, pp. 88–89 and 95–96; Sturm, *Kloster Altstadt*, p. 3; Mordek, "Die Hedenen," p. 347; Dinklage, "Hammelburg," pp. 39 and 43–46).

97. All references to Kilian have been collated and analyzed by Dienemann, *Der Kult des heiligen Kilian*, pp. 12–60.

98. Würzburg, UB M.p.th.f. 66, fols. 1r and 208v; Steinmeyer, *Die Kleineren Althochdeutschen Sprachdenkmäler*, no. xxiv, pp. 115–17; Schlosser, *Althochdeutsche Literatur*, pp. 14–15; Weidemann, "Frühmittelalterliche Burgen," p. 136; Dienemann, *Der Kult des heiligen Kilian*, p. 54; Schäferdiek, "Kilian von Würzburg," p. 314; Bostock, *Handbook*, pp. 114–15; Moser, *Würzburg*, pp. 17–21, at p. 21; Zöller, "Kirchengut des hl. Kilian," p. 224.

99. Paris, BN nal 1203 fols. 121v–124v; Lifshitz, *Name of the Saint*, pp. 78–80; Bosl, "Würzburg," p. 26.

100. Schäferdiek, "Kilian von Würzburg," pp. 330–35 and 340; Walter, "Die theologische Streitigkeiten," pp. 15–16; Palmer, "The Frankish Cult of Martyrs"; Mordek, "Die Hedenen," pp. 358–59; Lindner, *Untersuchungen*, pp. 94–95.

101. Schulze, "Das Oratorium und die Grabkirche," pp. 546–47.

102. Collins, *Charlemagne*, p. 92; Lindner, *Untersuchungen*, p. 15; Wamers, "Das Untermaingebiet," pp. 39–44.

103. Levison, ed., *Passio minor Kiliani*. Lindner, who also dated the composition of the text to 788, considered it a political justification for Charles Martel's seizure of territory in the 720s from the Hedeni (*Untersuchungen*, p. 95), a point that would have become moot after the events of the 740s concerning Grifo.

104. Levison, ed., *Passio minor Kiliani*, ch. 14, pp. 727–28. A variant tradition of Kilian's martyrdom appears in the Latin portion of the Martyrology of Tallaght, produced near Dublin c. 830, and in the Martyrology of Raban Maur, written between 842 and 854 (Dienemann, *Der Kult des heiligen Kilian*, pp. 14. 60, 193, and 265; Erichsen, "Kilian, der Märtyrer des Ostens," 212–16; Schäferdiek, "Kilian von Würzburg," pp. 314–15).

105. The *passio maior Kiliani* and the first biography (*vita antiquior*) of Bishop Burkhard, both written in the mid to late tenth century by a single author, reiterated the main outlines of the eighth-century passion narrative (Petersohn, "Zur geographisch-politischen Terminologie," especially pp. 26 and 31–32). However, the *passio maior* of Kilian added an extended foundation narrative for the see of Würzburg, to wit: one day schoolboys at Karlburg and their schoolmaster Atalong received visions telling them to find the body of Kilian (hidden by the evil Geilana); Atalong went to Boniface, who erected a see at Würzburg so that the location chosen by God to harbor the body of a great saint would have a commensurate ecclesiastical dignity (Emmerich, ed., *Passio maior Kiliani*, cc. 20–23). The first biography of Burkhard was effectively an *elevatio et translatio Kiliani*, for the only activity described was Burkhard's elevation, enshrinement, and veneration of the bodies of Kilian and his companions (Wittstadt, "Die älteste Lebensbeschreibung," pp. 14–16). See also Bullin and Ganz, eds. *Dich loben, Dir danken*; Muth, "Kiliandarstellungen"; Mälzer, *Die Würzburger Bischofs-Chronik*; Kummer, *Die Illustration der Würzburger Bischofschronik*; Steidle, "Geilana, Immina" pp. 3–6, 8, 12, and 14–16.

106. Bauer et al., *Die Geschichte Hessens*, pp. 88–91.

107. Lindner, *Untersuchungen*, pp. 102–12.

108. The favorably located right-bank "Stadthügel" was the core of the Merovingian-era settlement, including a royal (Bosl) or ducal (Dinklage) palace and a church that must have been the edifice donated to the new bishop; in contrast, there are no archeological traces of a pre-741 church on the left bank (Bosl, "Würzburg," pp. 32–38; Dinklage, "Hammelburg," p. 38; Wamser, "Die Würzburger Siedlungslandschaft," p. 43; Rosenstock, "Siedlungsgeschichte," pp. 56–58). The rotunda church that crowns the left-bank fortress Marienberg has been associated with the turn of the millennium (Lindner, *Untersuchungen*, pp. 98–101; Roosen-Runge, "Kunstwerke"; Rosenstock, "Siedlungsgeschichte," p. 56); earlier left-bank settlement was concentrated in the fishing village along the riverbank (Rosenstock, "Siedlungsgeschichte," p. 56). Also see Lindner, *Untersuchungen*, pp. 86 and 108–10; Mildenberger, "Ausgrabungen"; Schulze, "Der Dom zu Würzburg"; Schulze, *Der Dom zu Würzburg*.

109. Neither Immina nor a women's monastery in Würzburg appeared in any source prior to the twelfth-century text (Lindner, *Untersuchungen*, p. 67; Hasdenteufel-Röding, "Studien zur Gründung," pp. 123–26).The inspiration for the character was probably Imma, a ninth-century abbess or nun of Karlburg, a recluse at Himmelstadt (a village on the Main River near Karlburg that was also known as Imminestadt), or both, whose remains were venerated at Karlburg until 1236, when the church, fortress, and town were reduced to ruin by the counts of Rieneck, and she was translated to the crypt of the Würzburg cathedral (Grote, *Lexicon*, vol. 1, p. 239; Wagner, "Zur Frühzeit," pp. 106–7; Ettel and Rödel, "Castellum und Villa," p. 316).

110. Bendel and Schmitt, eds. and trans., "Vita sancti Burkhardi," pp. 54–59. The earliest copy is in the fifteenth-century manuscript Oxford, Bodleian Laud misc. 163, from Würzburg (Holder-Egger, ed., *Vitae Burchardi*, pp. 44–45).

111. Bendel and Schmitt, eds. and trans., "Vita sancti Burkhardi," pp. 60–65 and 82–85.

112. Schmale, "Die Glaubwürdigkeit der jüngeren Vita Burchardi."

113. Muth, *St. Burkhard*.

114. Lifshitz, "The Politics of Historiography."

115. Rosenstock, "Zur Genealogie des mainländisch-thüringischen Herzogshauses," p. 31; Mordek, "Die Hedenen," pp. 346–52; Lindner, *Untersuchungen*, pp. 72, 93, and 112–14; Wagner, "Die Äbte von St. Burkhard"; Ettel and Rüdel, "Castellum und villa Karloburg," p. 297; Rösen, *Klöster in Franken*, p. 43; Hasdenteufel-Röding, "Studien zur Gründung," pp. 123–26; Störmer, "Zu Herkunft," p. 16; Werner, *Adelsfamilien*, pp. 99, 106–10, 148–55, and especially p. 168; *LSK* 159–60. See the running notes contradicting the narrative, except during the Immina episode, on the edition by Bendel and Schmitt.

116. Friese, *Studien zur Herrschaftsgeschichte*, pp. 30–36.

117. Wendehorst, "Burchard"; Wendehorst, *Das Bistum Würzburg*. Schipperges expressed skepticism (*Bonifatius ac socii eius*, p. 47).

118. Tangl 49; Fell, "Some Implications," pp. 32–33; Yorke, "Bonifatian Mission," pp. 155–57; McKitterick, "Anglo-Saxon Missionaries in Germany: Personal Connections," pp. 21–24; Schipperges, *Bonifatius ac socii eius*, pp. 109–11.

119. Peyroux, "Abbess and Cloister," p. 219.

120. Böhne, "Bischof Burchard von Würzburg," pp. 50–52; McKitterick, "Frankish Uncial," pp. 383–85, but compare Heyen, *Untersuchungen*; and Werner, *Adelsfamilien*, pp. 326–29.

121. McKitterick, "Anglo-Saxon Missionaries: Manuscript Evidence," pp. 300–10.

122. Oxford, Bodleian Laud miscellaneous 126; Lifshitz, "Demonstrating Gun(t)za," p. 78.

123. Bendel and Schmitt, eds. and trans., "Vita sancti Burkhardi, " pp. 74–75; Hofmann, "Verstreute Blätter," p. 137; *LSK* pp. 72 and 159–60; Weiner, *Initialornamentik*, pp. 40–45.

124. Wagner, "Die Äbte," p. 17. The current structure at St. Burkhard is eleventh century, with no sign of a predecessor building (*VKB* 1991, p. 490).

125. *LSK*, pp. 15 and 22–44.

126. *LSK*, pp. 6–14; Tangl 15; Tangl 105; Yorke, "The Bonifacian Mission," pp. 148–49.

127. *LSK*, pp. 4 and 52. For the "ad lapidum fluminis" manuscripts, see Chapter Three.

3. THE GUN(T)ZA AND ABIRHILT MANUSCRIPTS

1. Würzburg, M.p.th.q. 3 (CLA IX.1431); Schepss, ed., *Priscilliani Quae Supersunt,* pp. viii–xxviii.

2. She wrote her name ("Bilihilt") on the flyleaf (fol. Ar) and a memorial entry ("pro elimosina ettone") for her deceased husband Hetan/Hedan II along the top margin of folio 41r (Lowe, in Morgan Library, Lowe Papers, Box 154 folder 810; Butzen, *Die Merowinger*, p. 80).

3. Cabrera, *Estudio sobre el Priscillianismo*, p. 48; Chadwick, *Priscillian of Avila*; Burrus, *The Making of a Heretic*; and Burrus, "In the Theatre of This Life."

4. Cabrera, *Estudio sobre el Priscillianismo*, pp. 216–218.

5. Schepss, ed., Tractate 1, in *Priscilliani Quae Supersunt*, p. 28, lines 14 ff.

6. D'Alès, *Priscillien et l'Espagne Chrétienne*, p. 87, concerning Schepss, ed., Tractate I, p. 6, lines 5–9.

7. Lopez Caneda, *Prisciliano*, espousing the sexist explanation that women flock to anything novel (p. 181).

8. Chadwick, *Priscillian*, pp. 20–21; Cabrera, *Estudio sobre el Priscillianismo*, pp. 27–28.

9. The two-line title read, "Finit incipit tractatus paschae. lege felix," followed by a Tironian note that might stand for "Amantius," then on the second line "Amantia cum tuis in Christo iesu domino nostro" ("It's finished. Here begins the tractate on Easter. Read, happy, Amantius(?). Amantia, with your [companions/followers] in Jesus Christ our Lord" [Würzburg UB M.p.th.q. 3 fol. 74v]). At some point, the name "Amantia" was incompletely erased. Perhaps these were not personal names but rather references to a chaste couple or syneisactic pair of "beloved ones"?

10. Bischoff, *Latin Paleography*, p. 287.

11. Thurn, *Die Pergamenthandschriften*, p. 86.

12. Cameron, *Christianity and the Rhetoric of Empire*, p. 90; Cabrera, *Estudio sobre el Priscillianismo*, p. 42.

13. Rose, *Ritual Memory*, pp. 46–48.

14. Cabrera, *Estudio sobre el Priscillianismo*, pp. 215 and 218.

15. Schepss, ed., Tractate III, *Priscilliani Quae Supersunt*, pp. 44–56.

16. Banniard, *Viva Voce*, p. 403.

17. Würzburg, Universitätsbibliothek M.p.th.q. 2; *LSK*, p. 243; Jerome, *Commentarius in Ecclesiasten*, ed. Adriaen (with corrections by Thurn, "Zum Text des Hieronymus-Kommentars," pp. 234–44).

18. Würzburg, Universitätsbibliothek M.p.th.q. 2 fol. 1v (accompanied by a little pencil sketch of what looks like a smiling veiled woman); Sims-Williams, "Cuthswith," pp. 5–6, 10–12, 16, 18, and 21; Mälzer and Thurn, *Die bibliothek des Würzburger Domstifts,* pp. 84 and 46–47.

19. Tangl 49; Sims-Williams, "Cuthswith," p. 20; Sims-Williams, *Religion and Literature,* pp. 193 and 239–41; McKitterick, "Anglo-Saxon Missionaries: Personal Connections," pp. 21–22. A possible transporter was Bishop Milred of Worcester (743/745–774/775), who studied Bible and theology under Abbess Hild at Whitby and visited Boniface and Lul in Germany soon before 754 (Sims-Williams, *Religion and Literature,* pp. 193, 230, 237–41, 190–91, 329–31, and 345; Sims-Williams, "Cuthswith," p. 16).

20. Le Moine, "Jerome's Gift to Women Readers," p. 237.

21. Sims-Williams, *Religion and Literature,* p. 196.

22. Jerome, *Commentarius in Ecclesiasten,* ed. Adriaen, p. 249.

23. Christianson, *Ecclesiastes through the Centuries,* p. 6.

24. Arnold, "Kitzingens Anfänge," pp. 16–17.

25. See below note 53 for Paula's epitaph and the discussion of Würzburg, Universitätsbibliothek M.p.th.q. 28b Codex 2 (the Kitzingen Homiliary) for the cento.

26. Fulda, Dommuseum, Bonifatianus 2.

27. Hussey, "The Franco-Saxon *Synonyma,*" pp. 237–38. For the inscription on folio 143v ("ego ragyndrudis ordinavi librum istum"), see Von Padberg and Stork, *Der Ragyndrudis-Codex des Heiligen Bonifatius,* Abb. 22. She was also known as Regentrude and Raegenthryth.

28. Hussey, "The Franco-Saxon *Synonyma,*" pp. 230–31 and 236; Becht-Jördens, "Heiliger und Buch," p. 7.

29. *LSK,* p. 7. The name "gunza" was spelled once with and once without a *t* in Würzburg, UB M.p.th.f. 13 (fols. 8r and 57v). The name had been noticed before; for instance, in 1914, E. A. Lowe reproduced the cryptogram and colophon on folio 57v, and the "gunza" in the bottom margin of folio 8r, then asked, "Is he a scribe?" (New York, Morgan Library, Lowe papers, box 153, folder 809).

30. *LSK,* pp. 6–14. Abirhilt was the last of several scribes on Würzburg, UB M.p.th.f. 45; she signed her name on folio 71v. One of Bischoff's Abirhilt manuscripts appeared on the Würzburg cathedral library catalogue, entered shortly after 800 into a copy of Augustine's *On the Trinity* (Oxford, Bodleian Library, Laud misc. 126 fol. 260r; Lowe, "Eighth-Century List"; *LSK,* plate 14 and pp. 90–148; McKitterick, *Carolingians,* pp. 169–72; Knaus, "Das Bistum Würzburg," p. 953). That codex, Würzburg UB M.p.th.q. 18, a copy of Isidore of Seville's *De ecclesiasticis officiis,* was designated as an "official"; its sole scribe included an anonymous colophon (fol. 64v) describing himself using masculine grammatical forms (Lowe, "Eighth-Century List," p. 8; *LSK,* pp. 102–3 and 142–48; see Chapter One). It is very unlikely that this book was produced at Kitzingen, and it should be removed from the Abirhilt group. The very late biography of the first abbess of Kitzingen, Hadeloga, reported that a house of male canons was attached to the women's monastery at its foundation, but only Heinrich Wagner has ever taken this seriously (Wagner, "Die Äbtissinnen," p. 29), and there is no other hint of adult males resident at Kitzingen who could have produced books there. More important, no color was used in this codex, in stark contrast to all the other women's manuscripts. The decoration style was totally different from that of the Kitzingen Paul (Chapter Four), which used the standard continental (Frankish) fare of fish and bird heads and geometric and

floral/vegetal motifs. Instead, the scribe of Würzburg UB M.p.th.q. 18 (particularly on the title page, fol. 1r) used elongated (both in body and limbs) four-legged beasts and much intertwining (Mälzer and Thurn, *Die Bibliothek des Würzburger Domstifts* abb. 18, p. 99; Weiner, *Initialornamentik*, pp. 279–80). Significantly, Weiner's first list of the "Abirhilt group" omitted the Isidore codex (*Initialornamentik*, p. 18), and he never explained how it fit into the group when he included it on his second list (Weiner, *Initialornamentik*, p. 43). Indeed, the decorative style and the script of the Isidore codex were almost identical to the decoration and script in Würzburg UB M.p.th.f. 62, especially folios 2v and 10v (Thurn, ed., *Comes romanus wirziburgensis*), made in England before the middle of the eighth century and brought to the Main Valley soon afterward (see Chapter Five). Würzburg UB M.p.th.q. 18 copied a lost exemplar of *DEO* from England c. 700, and itself represented the oldest witness of the English transmission of the text (Isidore, *DEO*, ed. Lawson, pp. 129*–131*), and it thus could easily have been made in England and brought to Würzburg for use in the cathedral, as was the *Comes*. Bierbrauer ("Karolingische Buchmalerei," pp. 557–58) associated Munich BSB Clm 6298 (the Homiliary of St. Corbinian) with the Abirhilt group. This also cannot be correct. Munich BSB Clm 6298 was far larger than any of the Abirhilt group manuscripts (and was even larger before it was cut down), was written in columns as was never done in the Abirhilt scriptorium, was written in a much larger script than any in the Abirhilt manuscripts, was written on amazingly thick parchment (particularly fols. 25–38) unlike any in the Abirhilt group, and was made with ink that bled, something that never happened in the Abirhilt group. Furthermore, the ornament on folios 1–24 of Munich BSB Clm 6298 was almost certainly made by the Freising scribe Peregrinus, who made the Florilegium in Munich BSB Clm 6433 under Bishop Arbeo (d. 783; Lehner, *Florilegia*, CCSL 108D, pp. xiii–xiv and xxv–xxvi). Meanwhile, the script of the codex was similar to that in use at Fulda (Lehner, *Florilegia*, p. xxvi; Spilling, "Das Fuldaer Skriptorium," p. 180).

31. Weiner, *Initialornamentik*, pp. 56–57, 82, and 86.

32. For a possible identification of Guntza, see Lifshitz, "Demonstrating Gun(t)za." Abirhilt was perhaps the Abbess Albhilt who governed the women's monastery that "Bleonsuuind ancilla Christi" entered after donating property to Fulda between 780 and 796, possibly Baumerlenbach am Kocher in the diocese of Würzburg (Stengel, ed., *Urkundenbuch des klosters Fulda*, 1, no. 223, p. 321; Dronke, ed., *Codex*, no. 189; Doll, ed., *Traditiones*, n. 13).

33. Knaus, "Das Bistum Würzburg," pp. 952–53; Bischoff, "Die Kölner Nonnenhandschriften," pp. 16–17, 22, 32–34; Ziegler, "Das 'Sacramentarium Gelasianum'"; Wemple, *Women in Frankish Society*, pp. 175–88; McKitterick, "Nuns' Scriptoria"; McKitterick, "Les femmes, les arts et la culture"; McKitterick, "Frauen und Schriftlichkeit"; Schulenburg, *Forgetful*, pp. 96–102; Goetz, *Frauen*, p. 62; Robinson, "A Twelfth-Century *Scriptrix*," pp. 80–90; Lewis, *By Women, for Women, about Women*; Beach, *Women as Scribes*; Beach, "Claustration and Collaboration"; Bodarwé, *Sanctimoniales litteratae*; Classen, *Late-Medieval German Women's Poetry;* Winston-Allen, *Convent Chronicles*; Griffiths, *The Garden of Delights*. Also see Brown, "Female Book-Ownership."

34. Ferrante, *To the Glory of Her Sex*.

35. Bodarwé, *Sanctimoniales litteratae*, pp. 87–98; Haines-Eitzen, "'Girls Trained in Beautiful Writing,'" pp. 630–33. The attempt to discern a peculiarly feminine "Schriftpsychologie" (Bruckner, "Weibliche Schreibtätigkeit"; Bruckner, "Zum Problem der

Frauenschriften") has been discredited (Robinson, "A Twelfth-Century *Scriptrix*," p. 79; Hoffman, "Das Skriptorium von Essen," p. 118).

36. Bénédictins du Bouveret, *Colophons de manuscrits occidentaux* I.2382, II.4442, IV.1265, IV.12885, and II. 5532–34. Only 1 percent (16 of approximately 1,600) of the pre-twelfth-century colophons listed belonged to female scribes (Beach, "Claustration and Collaboration," p. 58). For Burkhard's twelfth-century biography, see Chapter Two. For recent skeptics on the subject of women and book production, see Schilp, *Norm und Wirklichkeit*, pp. 202–3; Weiner, *Initialornamentik*, p. 41; Isidore, *Synonyma*, ed. Elfassi, pp. xlii and xlv.

37. None of the Gun(t)za or Abirhilt group manuscripts appeared on the (apparently comprehensive) Würzburg cathedral library catalogues of c. 800 (see note 30; Knaus, "Das Bistum Würzburg," pp. 977–79) or of c. 1000 (Würzburg, UB M.p.th.f. 40 fols. 1r + 46rv). In 1007, Henry II gave Kitzingen as an *Eigenkloster* to the newly founded bishopric of Bamberg. However, the bishops of Würzburg eventually regained "spiritual" control of the house, and books from the Kitzingen collection began to migrate to the diocesan capital; the process of transferring the collection took place over centuries, including when the house was secularized into a Damenstift (in 1544) and when it was secularized out of existence (in 1803; Walter, *Kitzingen*; Wagner, *Bonifatiusstudien*, p. 92; Petzolt, "Abtei Kitzingen," pp. 77, 79, and 81–82; Krämer, *Handschriftenerbe*, 1.396; Thurn, *Handschriften aus benediktinischen Provenienzen*, p. xviii). Würzburg UB M.p.th.f. 78 and M.p.th.f. 17 bore cathedral ownership marks only from the second half of the thirteenth century, M.p.th.f. 45 only from the fifteenth century, when M.p.th.f. 13, M.p.th.q. 28a, and M.p.th.q. 28b were cut down and rebound in the cathedral (*LSK*, p. 101–3 and 107). Würzburg UB M.p.th.f. 69 bore no such marks of any date; the copy of Paul's letters in the 800 catalogue was probably Würzburg UB M.p.th.f. 12 (*LSK*, p. 102). There is no evidence of early Würzburg ownership of the Priscillian and Jerome codices discussed at the beginning of this chapter (Knaus, "Das Bistum Würzburg," p. 949). Lowe ("An Eighth-Century List," pp. 7–8) suggested that item number 4 ("commentarium") on the 800 list might refer to the Jerome manuscript, on the grounds that the Jerome commentary would have been listed next to works by Bede and Gregory the Great because the codex came via England. Yet Jerome had no "English associations"; surely what was most noteworthy about the manuscript was its ancient Mediterranean provenance.

38. Würzburg UB M.p.th.q. 18 was not on the Basel list, nor could it have been there, even under an erasure, given what we can see and the order of the books. What follows is a full transcription of the Basel Booklist as deciphered by Schrimpf et al., *Mittelalterliche Bücherverzeichnisse*, pp. 9–10. I include it for convenience and for reference purposes but do not endorse every detail of it. For instance, Schrimpf et al. read "cirillae" on line 17 of the catalogue, but it could just as easily be "cicillae."

Key:

? A question mark over a letter or other symbol indicates that a reading is
x: questionable.

(x): A letter or other symbol inside parentheses has been deciphered from traces of ink.

.: A point on the line stands for a single letter or other symbol that has not been deciphered.

– – – –: Dashes stand for groups of letters or (sometimes multiple) words that have not been deciphered.

■: One or more squares stands for a larger or smaller hole in the parchment.

x̄: A line over a letter or symbol reflects an abbreviation symbol in the manuscript.

```
                  ? ??? ?
 1  ist(i) s(unt) nostri libri
    ? ? ?                        _                      ?
 2  au-/ – – – – (ge)lii sci(d)ula s.lucas est me
            ? ?                             ?
 3  d(yc)us a-us / actus apos(t)ulorum (/) pistulae
                                              ?
 4  (p)ost(u)lo■■■rum / apocalipsis / postul scī pauli
                 ■■■
                 ■■■                          ? ??
 5  re(g)um / (li)■■■(b)ri salamonis tr(e)s et■ sapiencia mos. /
 6  thobias / d(an)iel (/) (e)s(ai)as (/) ieremias / cert■■■amina
 7  postuloru(m) o(m)nium .(o)milias scī sup(er) (e)uan
                                                     ? ??
 8  gelium / et commentarium scī gregori su(p)er / ehiel / de
 9  alligorum scī gregori / sino(n)ima scī (e)sid(o)ri scī basillis
                                        _       ? ??
10  (l)iber scī effr(e)m (/) pastoralis scī (g)re(go)ri (li)ber t(r)es sen
11  t(i)arum scī e(si)dori r-arum liber uit(a)s p(a)trum mira
                                                      ? ?      ?
12  cula patrum / liber de cre(at)u(r)ar(um) scī (e)si(do)ri me-(a)rte uir
              _        ??? ??          ? ?
13  ginitate scī – – – liber (s)e(r)mones (sci) (a)ugus(t)ini (t)res
         ???
14  libri / super- (u)ir(g)in(it)at(e) et (u)ita scī ma(l)hi mon(a)hi in u(m̄)
15  libr(i) (/) ui(t)a s(c)I pauli et antoni et in illum librum pas
                                 ??? ???              ?
16  sio scī ciri(aci) omil- -ssio et (s)cī .mli. –sio.et scae
         ? ????
17  ci(ri)llae –ssio – (et) (i)n – – -m librum / sca ui(r)
    ? ? ?? ??                                          ??
18  -s-r –ia –ro- unum (l)ibrum et sca eogenia ci
    ? ?        ???          ?              ??
19  p-s- (s)ci –ori unum (l)ibrum / (et) s.u-s –brum –tam
                                   ?
20  .(ibr).m / - - (s)c. (liber) (l).(brum) um –s .(ibr).(m)
21  liber uita scorum dormientium in effeso qui dormierunt et in ilum
22  librum est cronih / scī furseus liber / sententialis liber / liber alexantri
```

39. Jerome, *Commentarius in Ecclesiasten*, ed. Adriaen, p. 250.

40. Broszinski and Heyne, *Fuldische Handschriften*, no. 19, pp. 58–59; Schrimpf et al., *Mittelalterliche Bücherverzeichnisse*, pp. 3–6; Binz, *Beschreibung*.

41. Gorman, "The Oldest Lists," pp. 55–56.

42. Schrimpf et al., *Mittelalterliche Bücherverzeichnisse*, pp. 12–13 and 94. The Basel codex itself, a copy of Isidore's *De natura rerum*, was not on list. The entry deciphered by Schrimpf et al. (*Mittelalterliche Bücherverzeichnisse*, pp. 5 and 8) as "*Rotarum liber*" (a common title for the *De natura rerum*) is extremely doubtful. Degering combined those two words (of which only *liber* is clear) with the next two words (clearly "vitas patrum") to read "Hieronymi liber vitas patrum" (Schrimpf et al., *Mittelalterliche Bücherverzeichnisse*, p. 199). Because the entry was surrounded by other works of

Isidore, I read, "Isidori liber vitas patrum," that is, Isidore's *De ortu et obitu patrum*, a text definitely owned at Kitzingen (see the discussion below of Würzburg, Universitäts-bibliothek M.p.th.q. 28b Codex 1, the "Deus per angelum" *libellus*).

43. Gorman, "The Oldest Lists," p. 59.

44. Schrimpf et al., *Mittelalterliche Bücherverzeichnisse*, pp. 14–56.

45. Hermann Degering concluded from his examination of the codex: "So a collec-tion of 33 obviously mostly not extensive, in part completely thin little volumes . . . are here named as the collection of the Fulda monastery! Stop! Is that really so certain, as Lehmann and Christ claim, that Fulda was the owner of these 30 volumes? I believe that to throw out the question and to answer it in the negative is one and the same thing. . . . And now one also understands why the list was almost completely erased in Fulda, since it was completely without interest for the Fulda monks." Herrad Spilling also doubted the attribution to Fulda. See Schrimpf et al., *Mittelalterliche Bücherver-zeichnisse*, pp. 4, 197–98, and 200.

46. Schrimpf et al., *Mittelalterliche Bücherverzeichnisse*, p. 5.

47. As Degering also noted (see Schrimpf et al., *Mittelalterliche Bücherverzeichnisse*, pp. 197–98).

48. Schrimpf et al., *Mittelalterliche Bücherverzeichnisse*, pp. 197–98. See the final lines of the booklist on the top margin of Plate 2 (fol. 18r) for insular "s" forms; see the text along the bottom margin of the same folio for insular "g" forms.

49. Arnold, "Kitzingens Anfänge," pp. 19 and 25 (color plate 1).

50. In the ninth century, this Isidoran section was bound with a series of unrelated texts (fols. 24r–32v), while a fragment from the Isidoran section was eventually re-moved to become Copenhagen, Kongelike Bib. Fragm. 19.vii (Gugel, *Welche erhaltenen mittelalterlichen Handschriften*, p. 31).

51. Obrist, "Les Manuscrits du 'De cursu Stellarum' de Gregoire de Tours," pp. 343–44; Obrist, "La representation carolingienne du zodiaque."

52. Di Sciacca, "Isidorian Scholarship," pp. 86–87; Di Sciacca, *Finding the Right Words*, pp. 55–58.

53. De Nie, " 'Consciousness Fecund through God,' " pp. 132–37; Jerome, Letter 108, in *Hieronymus Epistulae*, ed. Hilberg (CSEL 55.1, p. 350). For this epitaph in another women's manuscript, see Chapter Seven.

54. Nedoma, "enti danne geoze zisamane," pp. 175 and 189; Murdoch, "Charms, Prayers and Recipes," p. 59.

55. Baesecke, *Der Vocabularius Sancti Galli*, p. 83.

56. Nedoma, "enti danne geoze zisamane," pp. 169–74; Rauch, " 'Basler Rezept I,' " pp. 526–27; Murdoch, "Charms, Recipes and Prayers," p. 59.

57. Arnold, "Kitzingens Anfänge," p. 20.

58. Diem, *Das Monastische Experiment*, p. 262; Diem, "Rewriting Benedict," pp. 315, n. 10, and 318.

59. Eigil, *Vita Sturmi*, ch. 14, ed. Engelbert, *Die Vita Sturmi,* p. 146; Arnold, "Kitz-ingens Anfänge," pp. 18 and 23; Kehl, "Die Entstehungszeit"; Palmer, *Anglo-Saxons in a Frankish World,* 195–98; Becht-Jördens, "Die Ermordung," p. 98.

60. Eigil made a sufficiently striking impression on some member of the Kitzingen community that she wrote his name ("Eigill") in the top margin of folio 23v of Würz-burg UB M.p.th.f. 13, one of the Karlburg/Gun(t)za group codices that was, by the 790s, at Kitzingen.

61. Nedoma, "enti danne geoze zisamane," pp. 189–90; Arnold, "Kitzingens Anfänge," p. 18.

62. Miller, "The Old High German and Old Saxon Charms," p. 70; Brown, "Female Book-Ownership," p. 57; Schrimpf et al., *Mittelalterliche Bücherverzeichnisse*, Abb 1–2.

63. Miller, "Old High German and Old Saxon Charms," pp. 96–130.

64. Swan, "Remembering Veronica," pp. 22–24, concerning Matthew 9:20–22, Mark 5:25–34, and Luke 8:43–48.

65. For details concerning the remainder of the text, see Barb, "Die Blutsegen," pp. 485–86.

66. London, British Library, Royal 2.A.XX, front cover and fols. 16v and 49rv.

67. For other overlaps, see Barb, "Die Blutsegen," pp. 486–89.

68. Barb, "Die Blutsegen," p. 493.

69. Swan, "Remembering Veronica," pp. 35–36; Brown, "Female Book-Ownership," p. 57.

70. A full-color digitization of the codex can be viewed at http://vb.uni-wuerzburg .de/ub/mpthf69/ueber.html as part of the Virtuelle Bibliothek Würzburg project.

71. Sticht, "Spuren in Wort und Bild," p. 224; Spilling, "Irische Handschriftenüberlieferung," pp. 899–902; Fischer, *Lateinische Bibelhandschriften*, pp. 63 and 173; McGurk, "Oldest Manuscripts," pp. 2–4.

72. Repertoried by *incipit* and *explicit* in Stegmüller, *Initia Biblica*, as follows: folios 7v–8v (Stegmüller 1. 677, for Romans, displaced from their original location), 12v–14r (Stegmüller 1. 684, for I Corinthians), 23v–24r (Stegmüller 1. 700, for II Corinthians), 30v–31v (Stegmüller 1. 707, for Galatians), 35r–35v (Stegmüller 1. 715, through *"carcere,"* for Ephesians), 38v–39r (Stegmüller 1. 728, for Philippians), 41r–41v (an original prologue for I Thessalonians), fol. 43v (a variant of Stegmüller 1. 752, for II Thessalonians), fols. 44v–45r (Stegmüller 1. 736, for Colossians), 47r–47v (a dramatically different variant of Stegmüller 1. 765, for I Timothy), 49v–50r (Stegmüller 1. 772, for II Timothy), 51v–52r (an original prologue for Titus), 53r (Stegmüller 1. 783, for Philemon), and 54r–54v (a variant of Stegmüller 1. 793, for Hebrews). See also Martimort, *Les lectures liturgiques*, pp. 23–25.

73. Würzburg UB M.p. th.f. 69 fol. 7r. The reverse side of the parchment leaf (folio 7v) and the entire next leaf (folios 8r–8v) contain the chapter list for the letters. Without a doubt, folios 7 and 8 were the original folios 1 and 2 of the codex, a point made in an eighteenth-century hand on the bottom of the miniature. At some point, the image was moved to its current position opposite Romans 9. Thurn (*Die Pergamenthandschriften*) stated incorrectly that the text picked up at 9:23 on the top of folio 9r; only the last verse of Romans 9 continued onto that folio.

74. Holcomb, "How Ada Lost Her School"; Budny and Tweddle, "The Early Medieval Textiles at Maaseik"; Budny and Tweddle, "The Maaseik Embroideries"; Garver, "Weaving Words in Silk."

75. Knaus, "Das Bistum Würzburg," pp. 952–53 and 977–79; Thurn, "Libri sancti Kyliani," p. 247.

76. The catalogue also listed "evangelii schedula," "actus apostolorum," "regum," "libri Salomonis tres," "Sapientia," "Tobias," "Daniel," "Isaiah," and "Jeremiah" (Schrimpf et al., *Mittelalterliche Bücherverzeichnisse*, pp. 5–7).

77. Netzer, *Cultural Interplay*, pp. 16 and 149–56.

78. Mälzer, "Das Evangeliar," pp. 66–67; Zimmermann, *Vorkarolingische Miniaturen*, tables 71–72.

79. Wamser, "Zur archäologischen Bedeutung," pp. 329, 332 (nos. 9–12), 333 (nos. 1–3), 334 (nos. 10–11), and 335 (nos. 1–3).

80. Gameson, "The Royal 1.B.vii Gospels," p. 33; Mälzer, "Das Evangeliar," pp. 52 and 64; Thurn, "Die Würzburger Dombibliothek," p. 56; Regul, *Die Antimarcionistischen Evangelienprologe*, no. 12; Fischer, *Lateinische Bibelhandschriften*, pp. 172–73; Zimmermann, *Vorkarolingische Miniaturen*, Text p. 50.

81. Mälzer, "Das Evangeliar," pp. 56–60.

82. Brown, *Augustine of Hippo*, p. 74; Kaczynski, "Authority of the Fathers," p. 21; Bourke, "Augustine," p. 55; Hofer, "Matthew 25," pp. 285–86; Geerlings, "Die Lateinisch-Patristischen Kommentare," p. 5.

83. Schulze, "Das Phänomen der 'Nichtkommentierung,' " pp. 28–30; Schulze, "Das Bild als Kommentar," pp. 335–36; Wittekind, "Die Illustration"; Belghaus, "Inszenierter Dialog"; Hofer, "Matthew 25," p. 285; Geerlings, "Die Lateinisch-Patristischen Kommentare," pp. 3–4; Müller, "Zur Struktur des patristischen Kommentars," pp. 15–16.

84. Gori, "La tradizione manoscritta," pp. 213–28; Augustine, *Enarrationes in psalmos*, ed. Gori, pp. 7–8. The digitized codex is available as part of the Virtuelle Bibliothek Würzburg project (http://vb.uni-wuerzburg.de/ub/lskd/index.html).

85. Gori, "La tradizione manoscritta," pp. 184–86; Augustine, *Enarrationes in psalmos*, ed. Gori, pp. 13–18.

86. Augustine, *Enarrationes in psalmos*, ed. Gori, p. 7.

87. Gori, "La tradizione manoscritta," pp. 194 and 199–200. The copy of Augustine on the Psalms on the Würzburg cathedral catalogue of c. 800 (Lowe, "An Eighth-Century List of Books," number 147) was Würzburg UB M.p.th.f. 64a.

88. Thurn, *Die Pergamenthandschriften*, pp. 31–32.

89. Only the sermons by Gregory included author and title information, the Augustinian ones being both untitled and anonymous, so "Gregory on Ezekiel" was the only way a librarian could have labeled the manuscript. Thurn ("Die Würzburger Dombibliothek," p. 56) believed this small sermon collection went directly from England into the cathedral library during the 740s, but there were no cathedral possession marks on the codex before the fifteenth century (Thurn, *Die Pergamenthandschriften* pp. 31–32).

90. Augustine, Exposition of Psalm 131, trans. Boulding, p. 159, ed. Gori, pp. 295–96; Augustine, Exposition of Psalm 132, trans. Boulding, pp. 176–81, ed. Gori, pp. 321–27.

91. Augustine, Exposition of Psalm 133, trans. Boulding, pp. 187 and 188–89, ed. Gori, p. 339.

92. Augustine, Exposition of Psalm 133, ed. Gori, p. 339, for the excisions in the two Chelles codices Köln Dombibliothek 67 and Berlin SB-PK Philipps 1657; Augustine, *Enarrationes in Psalmos*, ed. Gori, p. 21.

93. This otherwise unattested term was a loanword from the Anglo-Saxon *lǣdend*, also meaning legislator (Köbler, *Ergänzungen*, p. 624; Augustine, Exposition of Psalm 129, ed. Gori, p. 252).

94. Glaser, *Frühe Griffelglosierung*, pp. 66–67, 70–73, 634, and 643; Bergmann, "Die althochdeutsche Glossenüberlieferung," pp. 32–34 and 37–40.

95. Glaser, *Frühe Griffelglosierung*, pp. 55–63; Bergman, "Die althochdeutsche Glossenüberlieferung," pp. 11–29.

96. Glaser, *Frühe Griffelglosierung*, pp. 64, 616–17, and 642; Bergman, "Die althochdeutsche Glossenüberlieferung," pp. 34–35.

97. Chavasse, "Aménagements liturgiques," pp. 75–102; Markus, *Gregory the Great,* p. 16; O'Donnell, "The Holiness of Gregory," pp. 79–80; Bouhot, "Les homélies de saint Grégoire," pp. 225–50.

98. Straw, *Gregory the Great,* p. 6.

99. Ganz, "Roman Manuscripts," pp. 608–13; Thacker, "Memorializing Gregory the Great." According to their library catalogue of c. 800, the women of Kitzingen also possessed three other works by Gregory: his *Homilies on Ezekiel* (probably Würzburg, UB M.p.th.f. 43), his *Dialogues,* and his *Pastoral Care* (Schrimpf et al., *Mittelalterliche Bücherverzeichnisse,* p. 7).

100. *Earliest Life of Gregory the Great,* ed. Colgrave, pp. 116–18.

101. Würzburg, UB M.p.th.f. 47 (Thurn, *Die Pergamenthandschriften;* Weiner, *Initialornamentik,* no. 56 and tables 129–32); Würzburg, UB M.p.th.f. 59 (Thurn, *Die Pergamenthandschriften;* Weiner, *Initialornamentik* no. 57 and table 136); Oxford, Bodleian Library, Laud misc. 275 (Weiner, *Initialornamentik,* no. 37 and tables 143–47; Köbler, *Ergänzugen,* p. 643); Würzburg, UB M.p.th.q. 64 (Krämer, *Handschriftenerbe,* vol. 2, pp. 527–29).

102. Étaix, "Note sur la tradition manuscrite"; Bouhot, "Les homélies de saint Grégoire," pp. 211–12; Gregory I, *Homiliae in Evangelia,* ed. Fiedrowicz, reproducing the eighteenth-century Maurist edition, reprinted also in PL 76:1075–312.

103. Bouhot, "Les homélies de saint Grégoire," pp. 215–25 and 233–34.

104. Homily 36 ended on folio 61r, but much of that folio and all of folio 61v were blank. The sermon series picked up again on the current folio 62r with homily 39. Whoever was responsible for homilies 37 and 38 dropped the ball.

105. Zelzer, *Die alten lateinischen Thomasakten,* pp. xlix–liv. The digitized codex can be accessed on the Virtuelle Bibliothek Würzburg project (http://vb.uni-wuerz burg.de/ub/lskd/index.html).

106. Rose, *Ritual Memory,* pp. 20–21; Lipsius, DAA 1.113–23.

107. Els Rose, project description of "*Dynamics of Apocryphal Traditions in Medieval Religious Culture*" (http://www.e-laborate.nl/en/; last accessed February 6, 2012). See also Zelzer, *Die alten lateinischen Thomasakten,* pp. xxvi and xxxiii; Rose, *Ritual Memory,* pp. 21–22; Lipsius, *DAA* 1.124, 134, and 138–50, especially 149–50.

108. For the contents, see Société des Bollandistes, "BHLms" (http://bhlms.fltr.ucl .ac.be/Nqueryfolio.cfm?numsection=3339&code_bhl=8137a&ville=Montpellier& fonds=FM&cote=055; last accessed February 4, 2012). The Montpellier codex featured what Bischoff considered a "Metz style" of writing, in an early ninth-century form; specialists now consider the codex to belong to the end of the eighth century, when many scriptoria in the Middle Rhine and Moselle regions worked in the "Metz" style (Gribomont, "Une ancienne version," pp. 368–70; personal conversations with Jean-Michel Picard and David Ganz, in Constance, Germany, in May 1998).

109. Thurn, *Die Pergamenthandschriften,* p. 65; CLA IX. 1425.

110. Davies, *Revolt of the Widows;* Macdonald, *The Legend and the Apostle;* Burrus, *Chastity as Autonomy.* This perspective has been challenged (Ng, "*Acts of Paul and Thecla,*" pp. 1–8).

111. Lipsius, *DAA* 1.55, 72–83, 88–89, and 116–17; Johnson, "Reviving the Memory of the Apostles," p. 20.

112. Schepss, "Eine Würzburger lateinische Handschrift," p. 457.

113. Linguistic errors: at the end of John the Evangelist's speech (fol. 2v), "Omnes populos respondisset 'amen' "; Jesus said (fol. 6r) "vade quia ego tecum suum et non te deseram"; two verbs—one singular, one plural—modified "edificia" in a single sentence (fol. 6v); "vindicere" for "vindicare" (fol. 4r), albeit corrected above the line. Order errors: the final passage of the *transitus* described John's metastasis (when his body vanished, leaving manna behind) before the Evangelist even entered his grave, then doubled back to describe his preparations for the big moment (fols. 2v–3r); several lines of a conversation between James and some demons (*Passio Iacobi*, ed. Mombritius, p. 37, line 45) were displaced to a later battle between the apostle and a magus (to Mombritius ed., p. 38, line 6), with an indication (fol. 3v) that it should have been inserted earlier.

114. For instance, "ad ergo" on fol. 6r, then "a tergo" on fol. 13v; "stiatim" on fol. 6r, then "statim" on fol. 13v. For the double opening, see the discussion of the Passion of Thomas below.

115. Other oddities betrayed scriptorial immaturity at Karlburg when the manuscript was being produced. Scribe 1 and scribe 3 (who began a new quire on folio 34r) failed to coordinate the proper breakpoint in the passion narrative of Simon and Jude, resulting in the omission of about two pages (one leaf) worth of material. Scribe 1 inserted folio 33 as a singleton, trying to fill the gap in the narrative, but it was not enough, and no one produced (or at least no one bound in) a second singleton to fill in the lacuna. Another miscalculation, or last-minute change of plan, occurred on folio 20v. There, scribe 2's first intervention in the codex was to erase and rewrite (so as to cram more text into the space) both the ending of the *passio* of Bartholomew and the beginning of the *passio* of Matthew, and then to insert a large, elaborate, decorated initial into the incipit of the Matthew text. The textual manipulations were required to free up more space for the (to scribe 1) unexpectedly large initial that scribe 2 had in mind for this text (the role of scribe 2 being to add decorated initials and make other targeted interventions on the folios copied by scribe 1). Finally, the person responsible for the rubrics was less than completely competent. For instance, the rubric for the *passio* of Bartholomew on fol. 15v set his feast date as iiii Kalends May (April 27), instead of the otherwise ubiquitous August 25 or thereabouts, and the rubric for the *passio* of Matthew on folio 20v was outright nonsensical: "Explicit passio bartheolomeus sancti apostoli feliciter. Sanctus Mattheus apostolus et evangelista. Duo magi et duo."

116. The text is reasonably close to BHL 4320 (PG 5: 1246–50), which the Bollandists ascribed to Pseudo-Melitus (Société des Bollandistes, *BHLms*, online at http://bhlms .fltr.ucl.ac.be/Nquerysaintsectiondate.cfm?code_bhl=4320&requesttimeout=500 [last accessed February 6, 2012]; Thurn, *Die Pergamenthandschriften*; Lipsius, *DAA* Supplement, p. 5) but probably was written by an actual historical Melitus (Lipsius, *DAA* 1.408–11; Schäferdiek, "Die *Passio Johannis*," pp. 374–82).

117. See Chapter Nine.

118. For the prologue, see PG 5, coll. 1239–40.

119. Starowieyski, "La légende de Saint Jacques," p. 195.

120. Van Herwaarden, "The Origins of the Cult of St. James," p. 3.

121. Van Herwaarden, "The Origins of the Cult of St. James," p. 29; Lipsius, DAA 2.2, pp. 201–8.

122. *Passio Iacobi,* ed. Mombritius.

123. Beauxamis, *Abdiae Babyloniae primi episcopi de historia certaminis apostolici libri x*, fols. 45–50; *Passio Iacobi*, ed. Mombritius, p. 664.

124. López Ferreiro, *Historia de la Santa A.M. Iglesia de Santiago*, 1:392–406.

125. Zelzer, ed., *Die alten lateinischen Thomasakten*, pp. 3–42 (BHL 8136).

126. Zelzer, ed., *Die alten lateinischen Thomasakten*, pp. xxiv–xxvi.

127. Henry Chadwick, review of Zelzer; Lipsius, DAA 1.165, 169–70, 254, and 273.

128. Zelzer, ed., *Die alten lateinischen Thomasakten*, pp. xxv–xxxvi.

129. Zelzer, ed., *Die alten lateinischen Thomasakten*, pp. lv–lvi.

130. Orléans, BM MS 341 (late ninth century), Paris, BN MS lat. 17002 (tenth century), and St. Gallen, SB MS 561 (late ninth century); Zelzer, ed., *Die alten lateinischen Thomasakten*, pp. xxxvii–xxxviii and l–li.

131. Zelzer, ed., *Die alten lateinischen Thomasakten*, pp. xxxvii–xxxviii.

132. Würzburg UB M.p.th.f. 78 fol. 6r; Zelzer, ed., *Die alten lateinischen Thomasakten*, pp. xlix, lii, and 34; Schepss, "Eine Würzburger lateinische Handschrift," pp. 452–53.

133. Lipsius, DAA 1.169 and DAA 2.2, pp. 54 and 67–72 (but compare DAA 1.165, where he located the production of the Latin *passio* to late sixth-century Gaul).

134. "Passio Bartholomei," eds. Lipsius and Bonnet, *Acta Apostolorum Apocrypha*, 2.1, pp. 128–50; Van Esbroeck, "La naissance du culte de saint Barthélémy," p. 184.

135. Van Esbroeck, "La naissance du culte de saint Barthélémy," pp. 177 and 192 (but compare Jones, "Ghostly Mentor, Teacher of Mysteries," p. 141).

136. "Passio Bartholomei," eds. Lipsius and Bonnet, *Acta Apostolorum Apocrypha*, 2.1, p. 144; Würzburg UB M.p.th.f. 78 fol. 19v.

137. Würzburg UB M.p.th.f. 78 fol. 16v; "Passio Bartholomei," eds. Lipsius and Bonnet, *Acta Apostolorum Apocrypha*, 2.1, p. 134.

138. Rollason, *Saints and Relics*, pp. 65–70.

139. Jones, "Ghostly Mentor, Teacher of Mysteries," pp. 136–37.

140. Atenolfi, *I Testi Medioevali*, pp. 58–80; Everett, "The Earliest Recension," pp. 883–84.

141. For instance, see the discussion in Chapter Six concerning "Ephigeniam."

142. Atenolfi, *I Testi Medioevali*, p. 13.

143. Weiner, *Initialornamentik*, Plate 54.1, p. 254.

144. Weiner, *Initialornamentik*, Plate 54.2, p. 254.

145. Consider these three changes (all from folio 27r): "venienteo" corrected to "vivente," "coronantem" corrected to "coronandam," and "magistrante" corrected to "ministrante."

146. Because the epilogue has been erroneously taken to refer to a larger group of Latin apostle narratives, it has been treated as separate from the *passio* "proper" (BHL 7550) and given its own BHL number (7551).

147. Rose, *Ritual Memory*, p. 215.

148. Rose, *Ritual Memory*, pp. 215–17.

149. Rose, *Ritual Memory*, pp. 222–23.

150. Rose, *Ritual Memory*, pp. 216 and 224–28.

151. Rose, *Ritual Memory*, pp. 63–64.

152. Rose, *Ritual Memory*, p. 215.

153. Butzen, *Die Merowinger*, p. 82; VKB 1966, p. 79; VKB 1991, p. 113.

154. Lifshitz, *The Name of the Saint*, pp. 50–51.

155. *Passio Simonis et Judae*, ed. Mombritius, *Sanctuarium* 2:534–39.

156. Weiner, *Initialornamentik*, Plate 55 p. 255.

157. Lipsius, *DAA* 2.2, pp. 7 and 50–52.

158. *Passio Philippi* (BHL 6814), ed. Mombritius, *Sanctuarium* 2:385.

159. *LSK*, pp. 6–9 and 107; Robinson, "The 'Booklet.'"

160. A full-color digitization of the codex can be viewed at http://vb.uni-wuerz burg.de/ub/mpthq28b/ueber.html as part of the Virtuelle Bibliothek Würzburg project.

161. Müller, "Zwei Marientexten," transcribed (but did not identify) the text. The most significant error in his transcription was "a ruma" rather than the correct "a ruina primae maledictionis" (fol. 2r).

162. Grégoire, *Les Homéliaires,* pp. 18 and 30. Folios 1r–1v were left blank.

163. Martimort, *Les lectures liturgiques*, p. 85; Hall, "The Early Medieval Sermon," p. 220; Grégoire, *Les Homéliaires*, pp. 7–8, 18–22; Étaix, *Homéliaires Patristiques*, p. 653.

164. Grégoire, *Les Homéliaires* pp. 17, 30, 142–45; Mordek, *Bibliotheca Capitularium*, pp. 883–88.

165. CPMA 908 (Pseudo-Augustine) and CPMA 4828A (Pseudo-Fulgentius), in PL 39:1990–91 (Ps-Augustine sermon 123); PL 65:898–99 (Ps-Fulgentius sermon 36); PLS 2:847 ("sermo antiquus"); and Alvarez Campos, *Corpus*, 6346–48, 6:137–38. CPMA 908, p. 165, located the text to sixth-century Africa.

166. CPMA, 450–3387, pp. 86–562.

167. Le Marié, "L'homéliaire carolingienne."

168. CLA X: 1503; Irblich, *Karl der Grosse*, pp. 66–67; Le Marié, "Un sermon occidentale pseudo-augustinien"; Grégoire, *Les Homéliaires*, pp. 132–33.

169. Isidore, *De ortu et obitu Patrum*, ed. and trans. Chaparro Gómez, ch. 66, pp. 190–93 (BHL 6544), also available in PL 83:129–56 (at 148–49). Müller, "Zwei Marientexten," transcribed (but did not identify) the text.

170. Würzburg UB M.p.th.f. 78 fol. 17r (the Karlburg passionary); Würzburg UB M.p.th.q. 28b fol. 3r (Kitzingen *libellus*); *Passio Bartholomei*, eds. Lipsius and Bonnet, *Acta Apostolorum Apocrypha* 2.1 p. 135.

171. Gagny, ed., *Primasii Commentaria in Epistolas S. Pauli* (with the erroneous attribution to Primasius Hadrumentinus). The selection in the Kitzingen codex diverged slightly from Gagny's edition.

172. De Bruyn, *Pelagius' Commentary*, pp. 10–17.

173. Johnson, "Purging the Poison," pp. 59–77.

174. *Passio Ceciliae* (BHL 1495), ed. Delehaye, *Étude*, pp. 194–220, from Paris BN lat. 10861 and Chartres BM 144. See also Dubois, "Cecile," p. 96; Delehaye, *Étude*, 73–96; McCune, "Four Pseudo-Augustinian Sermons." Her feast fell on November 22. BHL 1495 appeared in 168 of the manuscripts surveyed in the BHLms database (http://bhlms .fltr.ucl.ac.be/Nquerysaintsectiondate.cfm?code_bhl=1495&requesttimeout=500).

175. Arnold, *Caesarius von Arelate*, pp. 459–60 (BHL 1496). The first and last lines of the Kitzingen abbreviation were extremely similar to the first and last lines of the "Franciscan Abbreviation" of Cecilia's *passio*, which appeared in many later medieval lectionaries (Reames,"Recent Discovery," pp. 357 and 361); as a result, copies of this later abbreviation have also, erroneously, been labeled BHL 1496, and the BHLms erroneously identified the *passio* in several fourteenth- and fifteenth-century manuscripts with the text in the Kitzingen *libellus* (http://bhlms.fltr.ucl.ac.be/Nquerysaintsection-date.cfm?code_bhl=1496&requesttimeout=500).

176. Geith, *Priester Arnolts Legende,* pp. 97–98. Her feast fell on February 16.

177. Everett, *Literacy in Lombard Italy.*

178. It is also possible that there was never a single "original" text concerning Juliana, given that her story appeared in an extraordinarily large number of variations and languages (Berschin, "Zur lateinischen und deutschen Juliana-Legende," p. 1006).

179. Geith, *Priester Arnolts Legende,* pp. 35 and 45–46 (although Société des Bollandistes, *BHLms,* and Thurn, *Die Pergamenthandschriften,* p. 103 erroneously identified the text as the full passion narrative known as BHL 4522). Family 1 was best represented by Paris BN lat. 10861. For a corrective to Thurn's description of the *passio Julianae* in Würzburg, UB M.p.th.q. 15 (Thurn, *Pergamenthandschriften*), see Geith, *Priester Arnolts Legende,* pp. 61–62.

180. Josi and Aprile, "Agnese," coll. 383–86. Her feast fell on January 21.

181. Dufourcq, *Étude,* 1:314 and 2:55.

182. D'Arrigo, *Il martirio di sant'Agata,* 1:609 and 612–13.

183. Gordini et al., "Agata." Her feast fell on February 5.

184. Dufourcq, *Étude,* 2:202–6; *Passio Agathae,* ed. Bollandus, *AASS* Feb. I, pp. 615–18; *Passio Agathae,* ed. and trans. D'Arrigo, *Il martirio di Sant'Agata,* 1:359–74.

185. D'Arrigo, *Il martirio di sant'Agata* 1:379–87. Corrections: "immolandis" (fol. 14v) not "Immola diis" (p. 379); "maculavit" (fol. 14v) not "maculant" (p. 381); "tuum" (fol. 14v) not "suum" (p. 381); "curate" (fol. 14v) not "cura te" (p. 381); "volvebant" (fol. 14v) not "volvebatur" (p. 382); "Silvarum" (fol. 14v) not "Silvarii" (p. 382); "teriti motu" (fol. 14v) not "tereamotu" (p. 382); "Tunc" (fol. 14v) not "Denique" (p. 382); "et secretarium" (fol. 14v) not "ad secretarium" (p. 382); "famulam" (fol. 14v) not "famula" (p. 382); "omnis" (fol. 15r) not "omnes" (p. 382); "custodisti me" (fol. 15r) not "custodisti" (p. 383); "tulisti amorem" (fol. 15r) not "tulisti a me amorem" (p. 383); "unculas" (fol. 15r) not "vinculas" (p. 383); "patientium" (fol. 15r) not "patientiam" (p. 383); "postea eum aliquis" (fol. 15r) not "postea aliquis" (p. 384); "iuventus" (fol. 15r) not "inventus" (p. 384); "introibit" (fol. 15r) not "introivit" (p. 384); "deo et e liberationis" (fol. 15v) not "deo et liberationis" (p. 384); "sive" (fol. 15v) not "vel" (p. 385); "defulgantes" (fol. 15v) not "devulgantes" (p. 385); "statim" (fol. 15v) not "factum est" (p. 385); omit "iter" (fol. 15v); "transisset" (fol. 15v) not "transiret" (p. 385); "flumine" (fol. 15v) not "flumen" (p. 386); "hentis" (fol. 15v) not "Hetnas" (p. 386); "licefaciens" (fol. 15v) not "liquefaciens" (p. 386); "inconaverat" (fol. 15v) not "inchovaverat" (p. 387); omit "Christus" fol. 16r; "incendi" (fol. 16r) not "incendii" (p. 387). The assertion that BHL 134 appeared in other codices, in either full (Société des Bollandistes, *BHLms*) or abbreviated (Thurn, *Die Pergamenthandschriften,* p. 95) form, is incorrect.

186. D'Arrigo, *Il martirio di sant'Agata,* 1:381, n. 1 (but compare Löfstedt, "Zum Matthäus-Kommentar").

187. Recent discoveries include commentaries by Pseudo-Remigius of Auxerre (Paredi, "Per le fonti del *Commentum in Matthaeum,*" p. 249), by Pseudo-Gregory I (McNally, "'In nomine Dei summi,'" pp. 128–29), and in the mid-ninth-century "Martinian" style of Carolingian minuscule (Löfstedt, "Fragmente").

188. Passi, "Il commentario inedito," pp. 65–74, 135–36, and 154–56; Löfstadt, "Zum Matthäus-Kommentar"; Löfstadt, ed., *Anonymi in Matthaeum,* p. xv; Gorman, "Frigulus," p. 430; Rittmueller, ed., *Liber Questionum.*

189. Gorman, "Frigulus," pp. 452–53.

190. The "Expositio in Evangelium Matthei" in Munich BSB Clm 6233 (CLA 1252), an eighth-century codex from southern Bavaria; the "Commentarium in Mattheum" in Dresden, Sächsische Landesbibliothek, Staats- und Universitätsbibliothek R. 52 in Anglo-Saxon script of the eighth century; and the commentary on Matthew in Lyons BM 473 from ninth-century Lyons.

191. "Opus Imperfectum," PG 56:611–946; Étaix,"Fragments inédits"; Schlatter, "The Pelagianism of the *Opus Imperfectum*"; Schlatter, "The Author of the *Opus Imperfectum*"; Piédagnel, *Jean Chrysostom*, pp. 98–99, n. 5.

192. Munich BSB Clm 6282, Vienna ÖNB lat. 1007, Prague, Národní Knihovna III E 10 (485), Cologne, Dombibliothek 40, Karlsruhe BLB Augiensis XCIII, and Munich BSB Clm 8110 (Van Banning, ed., *Opus Imperfectum*, pp. xv and xxv–xxvii).

193. Schlatter, "The Author of the *Opus Imperfectum*," p. 367.

194. Biddle, *Tomb of Christ*, pp. 57–58, 68, and 82; Freeman-Grenville, *Basilica of the Holy Sepulchre*, pp. 15 and 45; Ousterhout, "The Temple, the Sepulcher and the Martyrion," pp. 49 and 50.

195. Many available in Wilkinson, *Jerusalem Pilgrims before the Crusades*.

196. Biddle, *Tomb of Christ*, pp. 20–28; Morris, *Sepulchre of Christ*, p. 103; Kötzsche, "Das Heilige Grab," pp. 274–76 and plates 28–33.

197. Freeman-Grenville, *Basilica of the Holy Sepulchre*, pp. 17 and 25; Morris, *Sepulchre of Christ*, p. 63.

198. Kötzsche, "Das Heilige Grab," pp. 274–76.

199. "Haec marmoria rupis januis sex, quinque quoque columnis continetur" (fol. 20r).

200. Kötzsche, "Das heilige Grab," pp. 280–81.

201. See Chapter Four.

202. Pilgrim Vial, Byzantine Collection, Dumbarton Oaks, Washington, D.C., Acc. No. 48.18 (Biddle, *Tomb of Christ*, Figure 18, p. 23; Kötzsche, "Das Heilige Grab," plate 28a–b).

203. Grabar, *Les ampoules*, pp. 11–15; Engemann, "Palästinensische Pilgerampullen," p. 7.

204. Wamers, "Die silberne Pyxis," p. 161; Wamser, "Die silberne Pyxis," p. 146; Bischoff, ed., *Mittelalterliche Schatzverzeichnisse*, no. 56 (although these may refer to or include Thecla vials from Seleucia, rather than Jerusalem vials; see Grabar, *Les Ampoules*, p. 64).

205. Biddle, *Tomb of Christ*, p. 21; Ousterhout, "The Temple, the Sepulcher and the Martyrion," pp. 49 and 50.

206. "Et parietate rotundo simul que quadriformi habitu" (fol. 20r).

207. Morris, *Sepulchre of Christ*, p. 96.

208. Pseudo-Jerome (or pseudo-Augustine), Letter 28: "De exodo in vigilia paschae," ed. Morin, pp. 536–37, lines 9–38; Lambert, *Bibliotheca Hieronymiana Manuscripta*, no. 229, pp. 337–40.

209. Chapters Three, Four, and Five. This was an exegesis of Job 40:19–21.

210. Chapter Five.

211. Bede, *De temporum ratione*, PL 90:575–76.

212. Brown, "Paris, BN lat. 10861," pp. 126, 131–32, and 137.

213. Geith, *Priester Arnolts Legende*, pp. 45–46 and 102–3; Cross, "English Vernacular Saints' Lives," p. 416; D'Arrigo, *Il martirio di Sant'Agata*, 1:469, 471, 601–2, and 649–52.

Both Paris BN lat. 10861 and Würzburg UB M.p.th.q. 28b contained the rare mistake of gendering an obviously female saint as a male in the rubric for her narrative, perhaps reflecting a common exemplar (Paris, BN 10861 fol. 88r: "incipit passio sancti eufemiae"; Würzburg UP M.p.th.q. 28b fol. 12r: "passio sancti agne").

214. Isidore of Seville, *De ortu et obitu patrum*, ed. Chaparro Gómez, pp. 55–74 and 97.

215. Isidore of Seville, *Synonyma*, ed. Elfassi.

216. Elfassi, "Trois Aspects Inattendus," pp. 110–11; Elfassi, "La Langue des *Synonyma*," p. 60; Elfassi, "Les *Synonyma* d'Isidore de Séville: édition critique et histoire du texte," pp. 195 and 515; Elfassi, "Les deux recensions," pp. 154, 173, and 175; Di Sciacca, *Finding the Right Words*, pp. 18–19.

217. A full-color digitization of the codex can be viewed at http://vb.uni-wuerzburg .de/ub/mpthq28a/ueber.html on the Virtuelle Bibliothek Würzburg project.

218. Isidore, *Synonyma*, ed. Elfassi, pp. xxxvii and xlii–xlv; Thurn, "Libri sancti Kyliani," pp. 244–45; Thurn, *Die Pergamenthandschriften*; *LSK*, pp. 28–29; Di Sciacca, *Finding the Right Words*, pp. 51–52, 69, and 72.

219. Elfassi, "Les *Synonyma* d'Isidore de Séville: édition critique et histoire du texte," p. 211; Thurn, "Libri sancti Kyliani" pp. 244 - 245. Elfassi has since suggested a slightly looser connection among the various codices (Isidore, *Synonyma* ed. Elfassi pp. lxxvi–lxxix).

220. Elfassi, "Les *Synonyma* d'Isidore de Séville: édition critique et histoire du texte," pp. 619–20.

221. *Contra* Weiner, *Initialornamentik*, p. 196.

222. Isidore, *Synonyma*, ed. Elfassi, pp. xxviii–xxix, xl, and cviii.

223. Weiner, *Initialornamentik*, pp. 257–58.

224. Because the text skipped from *Synonyms* II.26 (Isidore, *Synonyma*, ed. Elfassi, p. 82) at the very end of one quire (fol. 31v) to *Synonyms* II.82 (Isidore, *Synonyma*, ed. Elfassi, p. 130) at the very beginning of the next quire (fol. 32r), the simple loss of a quire (or "some leaves" as posited by Elfassi, ed. Isidore, *Synonyma*, p. xliii) could account for the lacuna. Nevertheless, the editing seems to have been deliberate (Pilsworth, "Miracles, Missionaries and Manuscripts"; Chapter Seven).

225. *Passio Eugeniae* (BHL 2666), in PL 21: 1105–22 and PL 73:605–20, was unusually faulty (Cross, "*Passio S. Eugeniae*," p. 394). *Passio Potiti* (BHL 6908), in AASS Jan. 1: 754–57 (3rd ed., Jan. II: 36–39), from the eighth-century codex Munich BSB Clm 3514, and in Mottola, *San Potito*, reprinted in Giuffrè, *La passione di San Potito*, pp. 23–41, from the ninth-century codex Vatican City, BAV, Reg. lat. 482. The Karlburg Potitus was sometimes closer to the Vatican copy and sometimes closer to the Munich one. By the ninth century, three only very slightly variant versions of the *passio* (BHL 2666, BHL 2667, and a mixture of the two) were in circulation (Cross, "*Passio S. Eugeniae*," pp. 392–97).

226. New York, Morgan Library, Lowe papers, Box 153, folder 809.

227. The opening of the Eugenia narrative was rubbed away (fols. 37r–38r), and the leaf describing her passion (between fols. 61 and 62) cut out. This certainly happened after the period covered by the present study, for multiple corrections in multiple hands throughout the text demonstrate that it was long valued.

228. Hotchkiss, *Clothes Make the Man*, pp. 131–41.

229. Turin, Bibliotheca Nazionale MS D.V.3; Robinson, "Twelfth-Century Scriptrix," p. 87.

230. BHL 6908, in Munich BSB Clm 3514 (the Codex Velseri; AASS Jan. 1, p. 753; Bierbrauer, *Die vorkarolingischen und karolingischen Handschriften*, 1.16). This text was

longer than the abbreviated Karlburg version, but both could descend from a common exemplar (Mallardo, "S. Potito," pp. 33–36). Although Potitus has been considered legendary, attempts have recently been made to authenticate his martyrdom (Giuffrè, *La passione di San Potito* pp. 11–22, 41, and 45–46).

231. "Missa speciosa quae cotidie debet cantari ad publicam. Missam pro omni populo christiano" (compare Deshusses, *Le sacramentaire Grégorien,* vol. I, nn. 1448, 1449, 1439 and 1450).

232. The full color digitization of the codex can be viewed, as part of the Virtuelle Bibliothek Würzburg project, at http://vb.uni-wuerzburg.de/ub/mpthq28b/index.html. Begin at fol. 43r for codex 3.

233. Sims-Williams, *Religion and Literature,* p. 195. To compare this manuscript with the Kitzingen Isidore on the Virtuelle Bibliothek Würzburg, see Hofmann, *Bayerns Kirche,* p. 35, no. 165.

234. Mälzer and Thurn, *Die Bibliothek des Würzburger Domstifts,* pp. 53 and 101, abb. 20.

235. Defensor, *Liber Scintillarum,* ed. Rochais; Defensor, *Livre,* trans. Rochais, pp. 9–10. A full-color digitization can be viewed at http://vb.uni-wuerzburg.de/ub/mp thf13/index.html as part of the Virtuelle Bibliothek Würzburg project.

236. For what follows, see Defensor, *Liber Scintillarum,* ed. Rochais, pp. vii–xii; and Defensor, *Livre,* trans. Rochais, pp. 16–17 and 21–25.

237. Smith, *Masters of the Sacred Page,* p. 91.

238. Lifshitz, "Demonstrating Gun(t)za," with the correction that Ligugé did already exist around 700 (Heitz, "Fouilles et Datation"; Coquet, "A Ligugé un ensemble exceptionnel").

239. Defensor, *Liber Scintillarum,* ed. Rochais, pp. xii–xiv.

240. Hussey, "Transmarinis litteris," p. 146.

241. Defensor, *Liber Scintillarum,* ed. Rochais, pp. xv–xvii, albeit naming only Benediktbeuern, whose products were very difficult to distinguish from those of Kochel (Bierbrauer, *Vorkarolingischen und karolingischen Handschriften,* 1: 48).

242. Defensor, *Liber Scintillarum,* ed. Rochais, pp. xv–xvii.

243. Defensor, *Liber Scintillarum,* ed. Rochais, pp. xv–xvii.

244. Defensor, *Liber Scintillarum,* ed. Rochais, pp. xv–xvii.

245. Wallach, "Alcuin on Virtues and Vices."

246. Werner, "Iren und Angelsachsen"; Werner, *Adelsfamilien,* pp. 44–46 and 90–94; Anton, "Klosterwesen," pp. 112–24; Lifshitz, "Demonstrating Gun(t)za."

247. Lifshitz, "Demonstrating Gun(t)za"; Raach, *Kloster Mettlach/Saar,* 5–10, 33–35, 83–85. Another "Gunza" donated, with her brother Sigifrid and her sister Leobniuui, people and property on the Saale River to Fulda in 801 (Stengel, ed., *Urkundenbuch des Klosters Fulda,* vol. 1, no. 276). Perhaps this woman was a descendant of the Trier episcopal matriarch. Because of confusion during the production process, the plates that were intended to accompany Lifshitz, "Demonstrating Gun(t)za," were inadvertently omitted. Now that the codex has been made available on the Internet through the project "Virtuelle Bibliothek Würzburg," readers interested in the details of that article can consult the two entries of Gun(t)za's name (fols. 8r and 57v), her highly idiosyncratic abbreviated "dns" alongside a model sketched for her in the margin (fol. 7r), the emphatic marginal cross and accompanying text (fol. 51r), and the feminist alterations to biblical citations (fols. 23v and 42r).

248. Lindner, *Untersuchungen,* pp. 65–67; Wamser, "Zur archäologischen Bedeutung," p. 331.

249. Glaser, *Frühe Griffelglossierung,* pp. 50–51, 74–76, and Appendix (photo of a scratched gloss); Hofmann, "Altenglische," pp. 622–23.

250. A full-color digitization of this codex can be viewed at http://vb.uni-wuerzburg .de/ub/mpthq28b/ueber.html as part of the Virtuelle Bibliothek Würzburg project. Begin at fol. 26r for this portion of the manuscript.

251. Oberleitner et al., eds., *Die Handschriftliche Überlieferung* V/2:544 (sermo app. 245); *PL* 39: 2196–98; Arnold, *Caesarius von Arelate,* p. 462.

252. Caesarius, Sermon 233, in *Sermones,* ed. Morin, CCSL 104, pp. 925–31; *PLS* 4:497–502.

253. PL 67: 1079–81; Étaix, "Sermons ariens inedits, pp. 143 and 146–47.

254. Hauswald, *Pirmins Scarapsus,* pp. cxiv–cxv; Jecker, *Heimat des hl. Pirmins,* pp. 98 and 123.

255. Mai, ed., *Nova Patrum Bibliotheca,* I:174–77; Oberleitner et al., eds., *Die Handschriftliche Überlieferung* V/2 p. 544 (sermo Mai 91).

256. The extracts run through Jerome, *Commentarius in Ecclesiasten,* ed. Adriaen, p. 326 l. 169 (IX.7/8).

257. The cento shared no unique variants with that ancient uncial copy, nor did it agree with its general readings for any significant percentage of time. The Kitzingen cento did share some unique readings with Alcuin's commentary on Ecclesiastes, which frequently quoted Jerome: "imagine umbrae nubis" instead of "imagine, umbra, nube"; "divitibus" instead of "divites"; insertion of "recordatione"; "sapientem" when most witnesses have "mentem" and Würzburg M.p.th.q. 2 has "videntem" (Jerome, *Commentarius in Ecclesiasten,* ed. Adriaen, p. 293, ll. 78–81, p. 295, ll. 145–48, p. 301, ll. 28–32, and p. 301, ll. 42–45, compared with Thurn, "Zum Text des Hieronymus-Kommentars"). The cento copied at Kitzingen was probably made on a version of Jerome that stood in the same stream of transmission as the manuscript utilized by Alcuin, whose commentary can be found in PL 100: 667–722.

258. Berndt, "Skizze zur Auslegungsgeschichte," pp. 20–23, referring to Stegmüller and Reinhardt, eds., *Das Repertorium Biblicum Medii Aevi.*

259. "Quanto magis qui sapientiam fuerit consecutus, tanto magis indignatur subiacere se vitis et procul esse a virtutibus quas requirit" (Würzburg UB M.p.th.q. 28b fol. 38v).

260. Jerome, *Commentarius in Ecclesiasten,* ed. Adriaen p. 273; Würzburg UB M.p.th.q. 28b fol. 39r.

261. Karlsruhe, Badische Landesbibliothek MS. K. 340 (Durlach 36), pp. 109–10; *LSK,* pp. 14, 50–53, and 109–11.

262. Tangl 49 (see Chapter Two).

263. Ettel and Rüdel, "Castellum und villa Karloburg," p. 300, n. 34; Knaus, "Das Bistum Würzburg," p. 952; Krämer, *Handschriftenerbe,* 1:388; Mahadevan, "Überlieferung und Verbreitung," p. 42.

264. Plates of the jewelry produced at Karlburg that inspired the initial decoration in both the Vienna penitentials and the Karlburg florilegium (or vice versa) can be found in Wamser, "Zur archäologischen Bedeutung," pp. 329, 332 (nos. 9–12), 333 (nos. 1–3), 334 (nos. 10–11), and 335 (nos. 1–3).

265. *LSK,* pp. 14 and 51.

266. Köbler, *Ergänzungen,* pp. 636–37; *LSK,* pp. 50, 52, 111, and 140.

267. Würzburg UB M.p.th. f. 146; Köbler, *Ergänzungen,* pp. 637–39; Chapter One.

268. Haggenmüller ("Frühmittelalterliche Bußbücher" pp. 10–11) believed Vienna ÖNB 2223 might have been at Lorsch during the ninth century but considered it more likely that a codex made from Vienna ÖNB 2223 was there. See also Hermann, *Beschreibendes Verzeichnis,* VIII:104–6; *LSK,* p. 53. The other members of the group were Oxford, Bodleian Library, Laud misc. 442, Bede's *Commentary on the Canonical Epistles* (which came to England from the Jesuit College in Würzburg and whose previous possessor was uncertain, since it bore no marks characteristic of the Würzburg cathedral library; *LSK,* p. 51), and Würzburg UB M.p.th. f. 175, an eight-folio fragment of Alcuin's *De virtutibus et vitiis* (Thurn, *Die Pergamenthandschriften,* p. 84; *LSK,* p. 51).

269. Haggenmüller, "Frühmittelalterliche Bußbücher," pp. 10–11; Bouhot, "Les Pénitentiels," pp. 152–155; Meens, "Finding the Appropriate Penance."

270. Meens, "Frequency and Nature," p. 58; Meens, "Finding the Appropriate Penance"; Mahadevan, "Überlieferung und Verbreitung,"p. 48.

271. Wasserschleben, *Die Bussordnungen,* pp. 184–219; Finsterwalder, *Die canones Theodori,* pp. 285–334.

272. Wasserschleben, *Die Bussordnungen,* pp. 220–33; Haggenmüller, *Die Überlieferung,* pp. 148ff. and 194ff.; Haggenmüller, "Frühmittelalterliche Bußbücher," pp. 16–17; Haggenmüller, "Zur Rezeption," p. 158; Kottje et al., eds., *Penitentialia Minora,* p. ix.

273. Bieler, ed., *The Irish Penitentials,* pp. 108–10.

274. Wasserschleben, *Die Bussordnungen,* pp. 505–26; Meens, "Finding the Appropriate Penance"; Mahadevan, "Überlieferung und Verbreitung," pp. 74–75.

275. Mahadevan, "Überlieferung und Verbreitung," pp. 34–37, 42–45, 49, 70, and 74–75.

276. Gregory the Great, *Libellus responsionum,* eds. Ewald and Hartmann, pp. 332–43.

277. Bouhot, "Les Pénitentiels," p. 154.

278. See Chapter One.

279. Fulgentius, *Opera,* ed. Fraipont, *CCSL* 91A pp. 744–60; Fulgentius, *Selected Works,* trans. Eno, pp. 59–107.

280. Fulgentius, *Opera,* ed. Fraipont, *CCSL* 91, pp. 255–73; Fulgentius, *Selected Works,* trans. Eno, pp. 366–83.

281. Gregory of Elvira, ed. Bulhart, *CCSL* 69, pp. 271–72.

282. Bouhot, "Les Pénitentiels."

283. Wasserschleben, *Die Bussordnungen,* pp. 231–47; Haggenmüller, *Die Überlieferung,* pp. 148ff. and 194ff.; Haggenmüller, "Frühmittelalterliche Bußbücher," pp. 16–17; Haggenmüller, "Zur Rezeption," p. 158; Kottje et al., eds., *Penitentialia Minora,* p. ix.

4. "I AM CRUCIFIED IN CHRIST" (GALATIANS 2:20)

1. Description in Chapter Three.

2. Micheli, *L'enluminure,* p. 69.

3. Sticht, "Spuren in Wort und Bild," p. 225; Pulliam, *Word and Image,* pp. 176–78; Zimmermann, *Vorkarolingische Miniaturen,* Text volume, p. 109; Roosen-Runge, "Kunstwerke der Frühzeit," p. 229; Micheli, *L'enluminure,* p. 69; and Weiner, *Initialornamentik,* pp. 19–20.

4. Spilling "Irisiche Handschriftenüberlieferung," pp. 899–902.

5. Haseloff, "Irische Handschriften," especially pp. 93–99; Nees, "Ethnic and Primitive Paradigms"; Mostert, "Celtic, Anglo-Saxon or Insular?"

6. Cutler, "A Byzantine Triptych," p. 10; Hanson, "The Stuttgart Casket," p. 23; Nees, "The Originality of Early Medieval Artists," p. 92; Chazelle, "'Romanness'"; Nees, "On the Image of Christ Crucified," pp. 372–73.

7. Elbern, "Theologische Spekulation"; Sepière, L'Image d'un dieu souffrant; Kornbluth, Engraved Gems; Chazelle, The Crucified God; Harries, The Passion in Art; Hürkey, Das Bild des Gekreuzigten; Grondijs, L'iconographie Byzantine.

8. Saurma-Jeltsch, "Das Bild in der Worttheologie Karls des Grossens," p. 635; Gameson, "The Royal 1.B.vii Gospels," pp. 37 and 43–50.

9. Chapter Three.

10. Monza ampullae 4 and 6–16 and Bobbio ampullae 3–8 (Grabar, Ampoules, plates X, XIV–XXX, and XXXIV–XLI, pp. 21–31 and 34–37).

11. Monza ampullae 1 and 11 (Grabar, Ampoules, plates I–III and XVIII–XXI and pp. 16–17 and 27).

12. Volbach, Early Christian Art, p. 315 and plate 12.

13. Ó Carragáin, Ritual and the Rood, pp. 259–61; Ó Carragáin, "'Traditio evangeliorum.'"

14. Ó Carragáin, "Theological, Liturgical or Devotional?" p. 69.

15. Werckmeister, Irisch-northumbrische Buchmalerei, p. 3.

16. Nees, "On the image of Christ Crucified," pp. 356–60. The Pauline crucifixion artist included only the lance tip and the sponge, both floating near Christ's waist.

17. Eighth-century comparanda include the medallions in the cross painted by a Chelles nun for the Vatican Gelasian Sacramentary and the Echternach Gospels (Sepière, Image d'un Dieu souffrant, p. 69; Werckmeister, Irisch-northumbrische Buchmalerei, pp. 22–36).

18. My arguments here modify substantially those of Lifshitz, "Persistence of Late Antiquity."

19. Brown, "Female Book-Ownership," p. 60.

20. Kessler, "The Book as Icon," pp. 84–85.

21. Vatican City, BAV reg. lat. 316; Paris, BN lat. 12168; Laon, BM 137 (Sepière, Image d'un Dieu souffrant, pp. 68–70 and Plate V; Spilling, "Irische Handschriftenüberlieferung"; Ziegler, "Das 'Sacramentarium Gelasianum'"; Sticht, "Spuren in Wort und Bild," p. 225).

22. Kessler, "The Book as Icon," pp. 84–85.

23. Nees, "On the Image of Christ Crucified," pp. 357–58.

24. Originally Spilling, "Irische Handschriftenüberlieferung," pp. 899–902; most recently, Pulliam (Word and Image, pp. 176–78).

25. Augustine, Ennarationes in Psalmos, eds. Dekkers and Fraipont, CCSL 40:1524.

26. Nees, "On the Image of Christ Crucified," p. 363.

27. Pulliam, Word and Image, pp. 176–77 (although Thurn described the picture as Christ teaching in a boat ["Libri sancti Kyliani," p. 247] and Lowe said it was a saint and nine others in a boat [CLA IX.1424]).

28. Pulliam, Word and Image, pp. 176–77.

29. Veelenturf, Dia Brátha, pp. 121–50, esp. pp. 124–29; Newman, "Die visionären Texte," p. 108.

30. Boenig, *Saint and Hero*, pp. 30–31.

31. Wilson, *Christian Theology*, p. 64.

32. Freeman-Grenville, *The Basilica of the Holy Sepulcher*, p. 20.

33. For instance, Wehrhahn-Stauch, "Christliche Fischsymbolik," pp. 17–18.

34. Chazelle, "An *Exemplum* of Humility," p. 2.

35. Examples from the Index of Christian Art (http://ica.princeton.edu/): Amiens, BM 90; Berlin, SB-PK theol. Lat. Fol. 192; Brussels, BR 138; Cambridge University, Trinity College O.5.8; Cambridge University, Fitzwilliam Museum, McClean 29; Düsseldorf, Universitäts- und Landesbibliothek A.14; Engelberg, SB 78; Florence, Biblioteca Laurenziana Plut XXIII.5; Frankfurt, Stadt und Universitätsbibliothek Bart. 117; Klagenfurt, Priesterseminar s.n.; Leipzig, UB 92; London, British Library Royal 4.E.IX; Milan, Biblioteca Ambrosiana R.70.Supp; Montecassino, Biblioteca Statale del Monumento Nazionale di Montecassino 248; Munich, BSB Clm 18128; Oxford, Bodleian Library, Auctarium D.1.13; Oxford, Bodleian Library, Barlow 26; Oxford, Bodleian Library, Canon. Bibl. Lat. 34; Oxford, Bodleian Library, Laud lat. 3; Oxford, Bodleian Library, Laud lat. 45; Rome, Biblioteca Vallicelliana B.54; St. Gall, SB 64; Sankt Paul im Lavanthal, Stiftsbibliothek (Archiv des Benedictinerstiftes) XXV.1.5; Stuttgart, Württembergische Landesbibliothek II.54; Troyes, BM 626; Valenciennes, BM 84–85. Cambridge University, Trinity College B.5.6–7 combines a portrait of Paul (fol. 3r) with a Trinity (fol. 70r) and an angel (fol. 99r), and Durham, Cathedral Library A. II. 19 contains, in addition to a conventional portrait of Paul (fol. 87v), a depiction of his execution (fol. 250r), a common theme on fourth- and fifth-century sarcophagi (see records 20 R76 ChSbtM S24 020, 20 R76 CySbt S24 010, 20 R76 CyVo S24 002, 20 S22 M2 ChM S24 002, and 20 M36 ChVi S24 010 in the Index of Christian Art). Also see Eleen, *The Illustration of the Pauline Epistles*, pp. 5 and 42.

36. Eleen, *The Illustration of the Pauline Epistles*, pp. 66–71; St. Clair, "A New Moses," p. 23.

37. I arrived at this understanding in February 2007, in the course of many discussions with Jane Rosenthal.

38. Henderson, *From Durrow to Kells*, p. 84.

39. Index of Christian Art, online at http://ica.princeton.edu/. Three additional cross-nimbed figures, not listed in the database, were roughly contemporary with the Pauline crucifixion miniature: the Virgin Mary on fol. 7v of the Book of Kells (produced 750–850), an angel in the apse mosaic of the oratory at Germigny built c. 801 by Theodulf of Orléans, and the (decapitated?) head of a martyr under an altar in an eighth-century manuscript fragment called "of Nájera" in the monastery of Silos (Pulliam, *Word and Image*, pp. 24 and 26–27; Freeman and Meyvaert, "The Meaning of Theodulf's Apse Mosaic," p. 129 and plates 1a, 1b–c, and 2; Fontaine, *Isidore de Séville*, figure 17).

40. Gorman, *Inhabiting the Cruciform God*; Gorman, *Cruciformity: Paul's Narrative Theology of the Cross*; Gorman, *Apostle of the Crucified Lord*.

41. Kessler, "The Book as Icon," pp. 89–90.

42. Despite the stylistic variability, the entire codex was the work of a single scribe-artist (Nees, "On the Image of Christ Crucified," p. 361, n. 50), not the result of a process of accretion over time (in contrast to Budny, "'St. Dunstan's Classbook,'" pp. 127–31).

43. Zimmermann, *Vorkarolingische Miniaturen*, Text Volume, pp. 3–7.

44. Weiner, *Initialornamentik*, pp. 188–91 and 259–73.

45. Weiner, *Initialornamentik*, pp. 188–91 and 259–73; Zimmermann, *Vorkarolingische Miniaturen*, Text Volume, pp. 12–15.

46. Wolfgang-Bonhage-Museum Korbach inventory number Go 4/11, from Goddelsheim (Lichtenfels, Kreis Waldeck-Frankenberg) grave 23; see also Roth and Wamers, *Hessen in Frühmittelalter* catalogue no. 201, p. 285. Other examples include the seventh-century bronze amulet from a woman's burial at Griesheim (Kreis Darmstadt-Dieburg) grave 205, now preserved at the Landesamt für Denkmalpflege Hessen, Abteilung für Vor und Frühgeschichte, Aussenstelle Darmstadt, and the seventh-century bronze cross pendant (to hang from a belt) from a woman's burial at Habitzheim (Otzberg, Kreis Darmstadt-Dieburg) grave 136, now preserved at the Landesamt für Denkmalpflege Hessen, Abteilung für Vor und Frühgeschichte, Aussenstelle Wiesbaden (Roth and Wamers, *Hessen in Frühmittelalter* catalogue nos.183.2, and 196, p. 279).

47. Klein-Pfeuffer, "Christliche Glaubensvorstellung," p. 127.

48. "Paulus, qui ante Saulus, apostolus gentium, advocatus Judaeorum, a Christo de coelo vocatus, in terram prostratus, qui oculatus cecidit, caecatus surrexit, ex persecutore effectus est vas electionis, ex lupo ovis, inter apostolos vocatione novissimus, praedicatione primus . . . atque plus omnibus laborans, multo latius inter caeteros verbi gratiam seminavit, atque doctrinam evangelicam sua praedicatione implevit. Incipiens enim ab Jerosolymis, usque ad Illyricum, et Italiam Hispaniasque processit, ac nomen Christi multarum manifestavit gentium nationibus . . . Raptus sursum in tertium coelum conscendit, demersus deorsum nocte et die in profundo maris fuit . . ." (Isidore, *De ortu et obitu patrum*, PL 83).

49. Eleen, *The Illustration of the Pauline Epistles*, pp. 116–17.

50. Lipsius, *DAA* 1.616 and *DAA* II.1, pp. 176–77.

51. Chazelle, "The Cross," pp. 29–31 and 40–42; Zastrow, "La Croce Cristiana," p. 59.

52. Wehrhahn-Stauch, "Aquila-Resurrectio," pp. 117, 120–21, 124, and 126.

53. Pillinger, *Die Tituli Historiarum*, pp. 12–178, especially p. 115 and Abb. 75.

54. Prudentius, *Works*, trans. Thomson 2:368–69. "Vas electionis: Hic lupus ante rapax vestitur vellere molli / Saulus qui fuerat, fit adempto lumine Paulus / Mox recipit visum, fit apostolus, ac populorum / doctor, et ore potens corvos mutare columbis" (Prudentius, *Carmina*, ed. Bergman, p. 447). Also see Eleen, *The Illustration of the Pauline Epistles*, p. 7

55. The theologian-artist drenched the black crows with blackness, lending them a physical weightiness that is clearer "in the flesh" than in the reproduction.

56. Schrimpf et al., *Mittelalterliche Bücherverzeichnisse*, p. 11. Copies of the *Tituli Historiarum* bore a variety of titles, including "Historiae," or no title at all (Prudentius, *Carmina*, ed. Bergman, p. 434; Bergman, "De codicum Prudentianorum generibus," pp. 6, 36–37 and 57–60; Bergman, *De codicibus Prudentianis*, pp. 8–17, 20–23, 26–27, 30–37, 40–51, 56–57, 61, 69, and 83–89).

57. "Eva columba fuit tunc candida, nigra deinde" (Pillinger, *Die Tituli Historiarum*, p. 20).

58. Alcuin, *De conversione Saxonum*, PL 101:811.

59. Aldhelm, "Carmen de Virginitate," ed. Ehwald, p. 373; Orchard, *Poetic Art*, pp. 6–16 and 171–76.

60. Schrimpf et al., *Mittelalterliche Bücherverzeichnisse*, pp. 5 and 9–10. The oldest extant manuscript of the text was written in the mid–eighth century at the women's

house of Chelles (Gotha, Forschungs- und Landesbibliothek Mbr I. 75 fols. 23–69; Bischoff, "Kölner Nonnenhandschriften," p. 32, n. 60; Chapter One and Chapter Nine).

61. Sepière, *Image d'un Dieu souffrant*, pp. 116–19 and 124–25.

62. Contreni, "Building Mansions in Heaven," p. 683; Hen, "The Structure and Aims," pp. 477–87; Meens, "Frequency and Nature," p. 53.

63. Mordek, *Kirchenrecht*, p. 33.

64. Vienna ÖNB 2223 fols. 54v–55r and 72r; Chapter Three; Bouhot, "Les Pénitentiels," p. 154.

65. Chavasse, *Les Lectionnaires romains*, 2: 11.

66. Van Tongeren, "A Sign of Resurrection," pp. 107–12 and 117.

67. Spilling, "Irische Handschriftenüberlieferung," pp. 899–902.

68. Basel Öffentliche UB F III 15a fol.18r; Schrimpf et al., *Mittelalterliche Bücherverzeichnisse*, p. 9; Diaz y Diaz, ed., *Liber de ordine creaturarum*; Ciccarese, "Le visioni de S. Fursa"; Carossi, *Le voyage de l'âme*, pp. 677–92. The center of Fursey's cult was Lagny-sur-Marne, less than twelve kilometers from the women's house of Chelles, which might have been the source of the text at Kitzingen.

69. Smyth, "Origins of Purgatory," pp. 97 and 108; Sepière, *Image d'un Dieu souffrant*, pp. 116–19 and 124–25.

70. Aldhelm, *Prosa de virginitate*, ed. Ehwald, p. 256; Aldhelm, *The Prose Works*, trans. Lapidge, p. 81; Smyth, "Origins of Purgatory," p. 113; Casiday, "St. Aldhelm on Apocrypha,"pp. 151–52; Tangl 10 and 115; Dinzelbacher, "Die Verbreitung," p. 87.

71. Jiroušková, *Die Visio Pauli*, pp. 3–35.

72. Jiroušková, ed., *Die Visio Pauli*, pp. 918–21 (variants pp. 921–24).

73. Wright, "Some Evidence," pp. 34–37; McNally, "'In nomine Dei summi,'" pp. 121–22. Other copies of this version: Vatican City, BAV, Pal. Lat. 216, an eighth-century manuscript from Reims; St. Gall SB 682, a ninth-century manuscript possibly from the Fulda area; and Leipzig, UB 1608, an early ninth-century codex (Jiroušková, *Die Visio Pauli*, pp. 139–43).

74. Wright, "Some Evidence," p. 37. Compare Dwyer, "An Unstudied Redaction," p. 125.

75. "Et vidi celum apertum et vidi filium dei sedentem ad dexteram patris sui. Et vidi civitatem magnam in celo. . . . Vidi altare dei in medio civitatis et vidi similem filii hominis vestitum podore, erat aspectus eius sicut sol et vestimenta eius sicut nix. Vidi manum eius extendentem super altare dei et laudavit patrem magna voce . . ." (Jiroušková, *Die visio Pauli*, p. 918).

76. Jiroušková, *Die visio Pauli*, pp. 277–83 and 482–94.

77. Anlezark, "The Fall of the Angels," pp. 129–31; Jiroušková, *Die Visio Pauli*, p. 819.

78. "Vidi bestias in medio aque maris quasi pisces in medio maris" (Jiroušková, *Die Visio Pauli*, p. 918).

79. For the homily, see Chapter Three and Chapter Five; for the *libellus*, see Chapter Three and Chapter Six.

80. Gregory I, *Reading the Gospels*, trans. Bhattacharji, p. 84. This was probably also an allusion to Gospel homily 22, also in the Kitzingen copy of his sermons (see Chapter Three), where Gregory explained that the cross penetrated to hell (Gregory I, *Reading the Gospels*, trans. Bhattcharji, p. 43).

81. Gregory I, *Reading the Gospels*, trans. Bhattacharji, pp. 87–88.

82. Gregory I, *Reading the Gospels*, trans. Bhattacharji, p. 61.

83. Wehrhan-Stauch, "Christliche Fischsymbolik," pp. 6–7 and 17–18.

84. Jiroušková, *Die Visio Pauli*, pp. 279 and 919–20. The bishop "non verba recta fecit in vita sua nec misericordiam habuit nec pietatem nec benignitatem nec orationem nec vigilia nec ieiunium in vita sua gerebat," whereas the virgin "ipsaque induit vestimenta salutis et negavit et verba veritatis non referebat in vita sua nec misericordiam nec pietate habebat nec benignitatem nec orationem nec vigilia nec ieiunium in vita sua habuerat" (*Die Visio Pauli,* ed. Jiroušková, p. 919). The bishop was described once as a *senex* but once as "hominem antiquam" (gendered female).

85. Jiroušková, *Die visio Pauli,* pp. 919–21; Dwyer, "An Unstudied Redaction," pp. 123–24.

86. "Vidi quinque libros in manibus earum legentes et audivi vocem earum."

87. ". . . et vocem earum non audivit dominus."

88. The traditional translation of 1 Corinthians 14:34–35 ("Let the women keep silent in the churches; for they are not permitted to speak, but let them subject themselves, just as the Law also says. And if they desire to learn anything, let them ask their own husbands at home; for it is improper for a woman to speak in church") resulted from distorting punctuation strategies utilized by misogynistic editors to turn a sentiment the apostle intended to rebuke into one he approved (Odell-Scott, "Editorial Dilemma"; Odell-Scott, "Let the Women Speak"; Preato, "Did Paul Really Say 'Let the Women Keep Silent'?").

89. "De iustificatione hominis per fidem sine operibus" (Würzburg, UB M.p.th.f. 69 fol. 7v). The dependence of humans on Christ was major theme of Romans 8:24, 8:28, 8:30–31, and 8:34.

90. Eleen, *The Illustration of the Pauline Epistles,* pp. 46 and 50.

91. "De apostolo in corpore suo stigmata domini nostri Jesu Christi portante" (Würzburg, UB M.p.th.f. 69 fol. 34v).

92. ". . . in imitationem Christi multas passiones graviaque corporis sustinuit tormenta" (Isidore, *De ortu et obitu patrum,* PL 83). For use of this text at Kitzingen, see Chapter Six.

93. Kessler, "The Book as Icon," p. 89; St. Clair, "A New Moses," p. 19, figure 1, concerning the Exodus frontispiece on London, British Library Cotton add. 10546 fol. 25v.

94. St. Clair, "A New Moses," pp. 22–23.

95. Desobry, "Le Manuscrit 18," pp. 79–80; Pulliam, "Eloquent Ornament," pp. 24–27 and figure 1; Wright, "Introducing the Medieval Psalter," p. 1, concerning Amiens, BM 18 fol. 1v. The substitution/identification strategy to depict both Christ and David reappeared in the illustration to Psalm 108 (Pulliam, "Eloquent Ornament," pp. 31–34 and figure 8, concerning Amiens, BM 18 fol. 92v).

96. Neuman de Vegvar, "The Echternach Lion," pp. 173–75, concerning Paris, BN lat. 9389.

97. St. Clair, "A New Moses," pp. 21–23; Eleen, *The Illustration of the Pauline Epistles,* pp. 2–3.

98. Bierbrauer, "Karolingische Buchmalerei," pp. 567–69; Helmer, "Clm 14345," in *Katalog.* The codex was long considered to belong to the "Ada School" (Hofmann, *Bayerns Kirche im Mittelalter,* cat. no. 88 and figure 8) before that "school" was dissolved in favor of the notion of a "court school" (Holcomb, "How Ada Lost Her School"). The "Ada school" was associated with the women's monastery of Altmünster in Mainz (see Chapter Two). The codex was owned by a women's house in Regensburg (Obermünster or Niedermünster) by the tenth century.

99. Veelenturf, *Dia Brátha*, pp. 127–30.

100. Würzburg UB M.p.th.f. 69 fol. 41v (reproduced in Weiner, *Initialornamentik*, p. 267).

101. "Ego enim ostendam illi quanta oporteat eum pro nomine meo pati" (Acts 9:16).

102. Hürkey, *Das Bild*.

103. The Volto Santo may date (or copy a lost object) from the eighth century (Ulianich, "Il Cristo crocifisso," pp. 72–74). The Udenheim crucifix in the Gotthard chapel of the Mainz cathedral has been dendrochronologically dated to 610–780 (Beutler, "Der Kruzifixus," with the plates on pp. 1033–35). The Kitzingen artist used techniques similar to those used by the painter of the Echternach Gospels to render draped fabric (Werckmeister, *Irisch-northumbrische Buchmalerei*, plates 14, 16, and 18a). Sepière (*Image d'un Dieu souffrant*, p. 118) saw fish scales in Jesus' clothes.

104. Ulianich, "Il Cristo crocifisso," pp. 70–72 and 75–78.

105. Lumsden, "'Touch No Unclean Thing,'" p. 246.

106. On the (pluriform) "Gallican liturgy," that is, the style of worship current in Francia prior to the Carolingian reforms, see Rose, ed., *Missale Gothicum*, pp. 190–93.

107. "Ad uelandam uirginem," *The Bobbio Missal*, no. 547, p. 167; Ramis, *La Consagracion*, pp. 146–47 and 197. Other versions of the consecration rite, such as the formulae in the Gelasian Sacramentary from Chelles (Ge 793–96 and 800–3) that were repeated in the other eighth-century Gelasian sacramentaries, made similar claims (Ramis, *La Consagracion*, pp. 71–73, 118–19, 126–28, 132, Appendix I, sections 3–10, and Appendix II).

108. See Chapter Three and Chapter Six.

109. Muschiol, *Famula Dei*, p. 294. Chapter 18 of the *Discipulus Umbrensium* version of the Penitential of Theodore (in Vienna ÖNB 2223 and in Würzburg UB M.p.th.q. 32) stated that among the Romans only a bishop could consecrate a *virgo*, whereas among the Greeks a priest could do it. The page containing this text in the Vienna Penitential (fol. 10v), a single sheet inserted into the current manuscript after its original composition and binding, now literally hangs by a thread, a possible indication of some skirmishing among local ecclesiastics. For the codices, see Chapter One and Chapter Three.

110. For instance, in the ninth-century Freiburg Pontifical (Freiburg UB 363 fols. 32r–33v); Constable, "Ceremonies and Symbolism," p. 798; Muschiol, *Famula Dei*, pp. 281, 290, and 293–94.

111. Lifshitz, "Priestly Women, Virginal Men," pp. 96–97.

112. *Liber sacramentorum Gellonensis*, ed. Dumas, pp. 405–10; Ramis, *La Consagracion*, pp. 112–13.

113. *Liber sacramentorum Gellonensis*, ed. Dumas, p. 407; Ramis, *La Consagracion*, p. 82 and Appendix I, section 47.

114. Ramis, *La Consagracion*, p. 86.

115. Ramis, *La Consagracion*, pp. 106–13. This disproves Lynda Coon's contention that male bishops alone managed to capture in their dress the charisma of the Old Testament priests and prophets, leaving female garments to symbolize "submission" (Coon, *Sacred Fictions*, p. 53). For a more evenhanded treatment of male and female clerical dress, see Effros, "Appearance and Ideology"; for the lavish vestments of consecrated women in liturgical settings, see Higley, "Dressing Up the Nuns," pp. 97–101.

116. Paris, BN lat. 12048 fol. 17v; *Liber sacramentorum Gellonensis,* ed. Dumas, figure 11. The saint also wore a pectoral cross, but her exposed ears lacked jewelry, in contrast to the portrait of the laywoman accompanying the oration for a sterile woman wanting to conceive; the latter wore large decorative earrings, a very elaborate headdress, and a biblike piece of fabric bearing an elaborate interlace pattern (Paris, BN lat. 12048, fol. 223; *Liber sacramentorum Gellonensis,* ed. Dumas, p. 415 and figure 108).

117. Jiroušková, *Die visio Pauli,* p. 919 (compare chapters VII and VIII).

118. Origen, *In Numeros homiliae,* ed. Baehrens; Origène, *Homélies sur les Nombres,* trans. Doutreleau; Origen, *Homilies on Numbers,* trans. Scheck; Trigg, *Origen,* pp. 8 and 65–66.

119. Weiner, *Initialornamentik,* p. 48 (albeit while rejecting that any of these books could have been produced by women). The codex could belong to the Kitzingen group. The colophon on fol. 92v, in which the scribe celebrated the end of the hard physical labor of writing with the phrase "sicut naviganti intranti portum, sic et scriptori ultimus versus," could have been written by a woman despite the masculine gender of the nouns, and the book could correspond to any number of entries on the Basel booklist.

120. The tag "omnium inimicorum suorum dominabitur" (Psalm 9:26, or Psalm 10:5 according to the Hebrews), sometimes with the unusual orthography "tominabitur," appeared in Würzburg UB M.p.th.f. 27 on fol. 90v; in Würzburg UB M.p.th.f. 69 on fol. 6v; in Würzburg UB M.p.th.q. 2 on fols. 1r (twice) and 113v; and in Würzburg UB M.p.th.q. 28b Codex 3 on fol. 52r (Sims-Williams,"Cuthswith," p. 3).

121. Trigg, *Origen,* pp. 5, 15, and 43; Gemmiti, *La Donna in Origene,* pp. 95–99; Origen, *Homilies on Numbers,* trans. Scheck, p. xx; Haines-Eitzen, "Girls Trained in Beautiful Writing."

122. Gemmiti, *La Donna in Origene,* p. 147; Origen, *In Numeros homiliae* XXIV.2; *Homilies on Numbers by Origen,* trans. Scheck p. 150.

123. Gemmiti, *La Donna in Origene,* pp. 127 and 154; Origen, *In Numeros homiliae* XXIV.3 ed. p. 231; *Homilies on Numbers by Origen,* trans. Scheck, p. 152.

124. Gemmiti, *La Donna in Origene,* p. 169; Origen, *In Numeros homiliae* XXIV.1–2 ed., p. 229; *Homilies on Numbers by Origen,* trans. Scheck, pp. 149–52. The key portion of the Latin text that utilized the feminine forms and became the basis for the liturgy for consecrating a virgin follows here: "Si ergo 'tollas crucem tuam et sequaris Christum,' si dicas: 'vivo autem, iam non ego, vivit vero Christus in me,' si 'desideret et sitiat anima nostra redire et esse cum Christo,' sicut et Apostolus dicebat . . . tunc 'semet ipsum,' id est animam suam, 'obtulit Deo.' Qui in castitate vivit, corpus suum vovit Deo secundum eum, qui dixit: 'virgo autem cogitat, quomodo sit sancta corpore et spiritu.' Nam et hoc ipsum quod dixit: 'sancta,' ad hoc respicit; sancti enim dicuntur illi, qui se voverunt Deo."

125. Brown, "Homiletic Setting," pp. 71–72.

126. Morin, "Le Plus Ancien *Comes,*" p. 55; Chapter Five, including for the importance of the Gospel reading for this day at Kitzingen.

127. Wenisch, *Ochsenfurt,* pp. 41–49, especially p. 43.

128. Personal observation of Richard W. Unger, February 2013.

129. Smith, "Sacred Journeying," especially pp. 42–44, 51–53, and 55; Hugeburc, *Hoedeporicon.*

130. For instance, Vienna 751 no. 38, fol. 21v (= Tangl 14), where Abbess Eangyth and her daughter Leaburg (aka Bugga) used the metaphor "animarum nostrarum naviculae" to praise Boniface.

131. See note 28.

132. Nauerth and Warns, *Thekla*, plates I–XVI. Another bareheaded, but not negatively charged, female figure was one of the women at Christ's tomb in the top register of the (late fifth- or sixth-century) carved wooden doors of the church of St. Sabina in Rome (Darsy, *Santa Sabina*, pp. 66–73).

133. McGinn, "The Acts of Thecla," pp. 819 and 827, n. 81; Jensen, *Thekla—Die Apostolin*, pp. 113–16.

134. Tangl 38; Ewig, "Milo et eiusmodi similes," p. 189; Orchard, "Old Sources," pp. 35 and 38; Wagner, "Die Äbtissinen des Klosters Kitzingen," pp. 28 and 32–33.

135. Orchard, "Old Sources," p. 22.

136. Willibald, "Vita Bonifatii," trans. Talbot, in Noble and Head, *Soldiers of Christ*, p. 114.

137. Willibald, "Vita Bonifatii," trans. Talbot, in Noble and Head, *Soldiers of Christ*, p. 114.

138. Willibald, "Vita Bonifatii," trans. Talbot, in Noble and Head, *Soldiers of Christ*, pp. 115–16 and 118; also see pp. 123, 129, and 131.

139. Davis, *The Cult of Saint Thecla*, p. vi.

140. Davis, *The Cult of Saint Thecla*, pp. 200–8; Rudolf of Fulda, *Vita Leobae*, ed. Holder-Egger, p. 122.

141. Torjesen, "Reconstruction," p. 291; McGinn, "The Acts of Thecla," pp. 802–3.

142. Burris, "The Syriac *Book of Women*."

143. Burris, "The Syriac *Book of Women*," p. 96.

144. Jensen, "Auf dem Weg zur Heiligen Jungfrau" pp. 45–48; Hayne, "Thecla and the Church Fathers," esp. pp. 210–12 and 215.

145. Schurr, *Iconographie der Heiligen*, pp. 206–16; Johnson, *The Life and Miracles of Thekla*, p. 223.

146. Schurr, *Iconographie der Heiligen*, pp. 209, 211, 214, and 266–67; Davis, *The Cult of Saint Thecla*, pp. 195–200. Some of the Thecla ampullae may have been in the treasury at Milz (see note 9).

147. Rordorf, "Saint Thècle," pp. 77–79.

148. 1 Corinthians 9:5 (see Chapter One).

149. Schüssler Fiorenza, ed., *Searching the Scriptures*, passim; Haines-Eitzen, "Girls Trained for Beautiful Writing"; Haines-Eitzen, *Guardians of Letters*, pp. 111–27, especially pp. 111–12 and 115–16.

150. Boyarin, "Paul," especially pp. 17–20.

151. For the "punctuation" argument concerning 1 Corinthians 14:34–35, see note 88; for the misogynistic interpolation argument, see Haines-Eitzen, "Engendering Palimpsests," p. 184, n. 18.

152. Röckelein, "Gründer, Stifter und Heilige," pp. 72–73. Paul was specially venerated, including through church dedications, at the women's communities of Altmünster (Mainz), Nivelles, Oeren, Paris, Jouarre, Remiremont, and St. Jean of Laon (Ewig, "Älteste Mainzer Patrozinien," p. 168).

153. Hamburger, *Nuns as Artists*, especially p. 102; Hamburger, *The Visual and the Visionary*, p. 190 (see also p. 187).

154. Schulze, "Das Bild als Kommentar," pp. 335–36; Schulze, "Das Phänomen der 'Nichtkommentierung,'" pp. 28–30.

155. Orchard, "Old Sources," p. 22.

5. "WE INTERPRET SPIRITUAL TRUTHS TO PEOPLE POSSESSED OF THE SPIRIT" (1 CORINTHIANS 2:13)

1. Augustine, "Exposition of Psalm 127" (Würzburg, UB M.p.th.f. 17 fol. 33v; trans. Boulding, p. 99; ed. Gori, p. 208).

2. Gregory, "Homily 22" (Würzburg, UB M.p.th.f. 45 fol. 5v; Gregory, *Forty Gospel Homilies,* trans. Hurst, p. 165).

3. Augustine, "Exposition of Psalm 127" (Würzburg, UB M.p.th.f. 17 fol. 33v, trans. Boulding, p. 98, ed. Gori, p. 206).

4. Geerlings, "Die Lateinisch-Patristischen Kommentare," pp. 10–11.

5. Étaix, "Répertoire des manuscrits."

6. Gori, "La tradizione manoscritta," p. 213.

7. Muschiol, *Famula Dei,* p. 198; Peyroux, "Abbess and Cloister," pp. 258–60; McKinnon, "The Book of Psalms," p. 43; Muschiol, "Zeit und Raum," pp. 49–50. Although no surviving psalters have been identified as belonging to the Gun(t)za (or Abirhilt) manuscript group(s), one transcription of the Basel booklist deciphered one of the titles as "Psalmi" (Schrimpf et el., *Mittelalterliche Bücherverzeichnisse,* p. 199).

8. Wright, "Introducing the Medieval Psalter," p. 1; Brown, *Augustine of Hippo,* p. 257; Muschiol, *Famula Dei,* pp. 81, 85, 87–88 and 192–93.

9. Muschiol, *Famula Dei,* pp. 131–32.

10. Wright, "Introducing the Medieval Psalter," p. 2.

11. John, "The Named (and Namable) Scribes," pp. 113 and 115–21.

12. For instance, Clark, "Ideology," especially pp. 165, 168, 170, 172, and 175; Burrus, *"Begotten, Not Made,"* pp. 185 and 190. For a contrary and less well-known view, see Roth, "Mittelalterliche Misogynie."

13. Cloke, *"This Female Man of God,"* pp. 23–24, 212, and 220.

14. Amos, "Early Medieval Sermons," pp. 23 (quote) and 33–34.

15. Kaczynski, "The Authority of the Fathers," pp. 2–3.

16. Kaczynski, "The Authority of the Fathers," pp. 23–24; Otten, "Carolingian Theology," p. 66.

17. Vessey, "Response to Catherine Conybeare."

18. Stark, "Introduction," p. 21.

19. McWilliams, "Augustine's Letters to Women," p. 190.

20. McWilliams, "Augustine's Letters to Women," pp. 197–98; Jerome, *Epistulae,* ed. Hilberg, part 1, nos. 11, 13, 22–34, 37 46, 54, 59, 64, and 65 (twenty nine of seventy letters in the volume).

21. Paris, BN lat. 1 fol. 3v, made at St. Martin of Tours in 846.

22. Le Moine, "Jerome's Gift to Women Readers."

23. Zweierlein, "'Interpretation,'" p. 94; Dorival, "Exégèse Juive et Exégèse Chrétienne," pp. 132–33.

24. Müller, "Zur Struktur des patristischen Kommentars," pp. 17–18.

25. Clancy-Smith, "Exemplary Women," pp. 99–101; Goetz, *Frauen,* pp. 71–103.

26. Von Padberg, *Mission und Christianisierung,* pp. 323 and 331.

27. Tertullian, *De cultu feminarum* 1.1.2, ed. Dekkers, p. 343; Clark, "Ideology," p. 169; Cloke, *"This Female Man of God,"* p. 220; Clark, "Devil's Gateway"; Tertullian, *De exhortatione castitatis,* ed. Friedrich, pp. 1–5; Claesson, *Index Tertullianus.*

28. Hench, ed., *Der Althochdeutsche Isidor,* p. 9; Bede, *In Cantica Habacuc,* ed. Hudson, pp. 381–409; Ward, "'To My Dearest Sister,'" pp. 105–12.

29. Paris, BN lat. 13396 fol. 1v; Hench, ed., *Der Althochdeutsche Isidor*, p. x; Fried, ed., *794*, pp.60–61.

30. Sims-Williams, *Religion and Literature*, pp. 177–210.

31. Quoted in Augustine, "Exposition of Psalm 129," trans. Boulding, p. 129; ed. Gori, p. 251.

32. Brown, *Augustine of Hippo*, p. 446.

33. Brown, *Augustine of Hippo*, pp. 257 and 460–61.

34. Brown, *Augustine of Hippo*, p. 324.

35. Augustine, "Exposition of Psalm 130," ed. Gori, pp. 265–69.

36. Augustine, "Exposition of Psalm 127," ed. Gori, p. 225.

37. The shift in the function of the text from public preaching to learned reading is reflected in small changes, such as the omission of stage directions (Augustine, "Exposition of Psalm 128," ed. Gori, p. 248).

38. Augustine, "Exposition of Psalm 124," trans. Boulding, p. 63; ed. Gori, pp. 156–57.

39. Augustine, "Exposition of Psalm 124," trans. Boulding, pp. 64 and 66; ed. Gori, pp. 157–62.

40. Conybeare, "Spaces between Letters," pp. 66–67.

41. Würzburg, UB M.p.th.f. 17 fols. 14v–19r.

42. Augustine, "Exposition of Psalm 122," trans. Boulding, vol. 6, p. 31; ed. Gori, pp. 109–10.

43. Augustine, "Exposition of Psalm 122" (Würzburg, UB M.p.th.f. 17 fol. 16r; Boulding trans., vol. 6, pp. 33–34; ed. Gori, p. 114).

44. Augustine, "Exposition of Psalm 131," trans. Boulding, pp. 170–71; ed. Gori, pp. 312–14.

45. Augustine, "Exposition of Psalm 132," trans. Boulding, p. 178; ed. Gori, p. 323.

46. Brown, *Augustine of Hippo*, p. 248.

47. Brown, *Augustine of Hippo*, p. 509.

48. Augustine, "Exposition of Psalm 129," trans. Boulding, p. 129; ed. Gori, p. 251.

49. Brown, *Augustine of Hippo*, pp. 154 and 339–75.

50. Cf. Brown, *Augustine of Hippo*, p. 510.

51. Matter, "Christ, God and Woman," p. 170.

52. Stouck, *Medieval Saints*, pp. 39–42.

53. Stouck, *Medieval Saints*, p. 42; Goetz, *Frauen*, p. 59.

54. Coon, *Sacred Fictions*, p. xvii; Clark, "Eusebius on Women."

55. Brown, *Augustine of Hippo*, p. 484.

56. Augustine, "Exposition of Psalm 120" (trans. Boulding, p. 524; WB UB M.p.th.f. 17 fol. 9r; ed. Gori, p. 79).

57. Salisbury, *The Blood of Martyrs*, pp. 178–79.

58. Augustine, "Exposition of Psalm 130," trans. Boulding, p.144; ed. Gori, p. 274. The Karlburg copy of the comment breaks off, mutilated, at chapter 6, line 18 (ed. Gori, p. 270), but this section of the text was definitely originally part of the manuscript (see Chapter Three).

59. Augustine, "Exposition of Psalm 130," trans. Boulding, pp. 146–53, ed. Gori, pp. 274–77 (all of which would have been part of the original codex). The discussion of Stephen in the comment on Psalm 132 (trans. Boulding, pp. 182–83, ed. Gori, pp. 329–32) was omitted from the Karlburg copy.

60. Würzburg, UB M.p.th.f. 17 fol. 19r; Weiner, *Initialornamentik*, initial #1.

61. Augustine, "Exposition of Psalm 123," trans. Boulding, pp. 48 and 54; ed. Gori, pp. 133–37 and 145.

62. Augustine, "Exposition of Psalm 127," trans. Boulding, pp. 102–3; ed. Gori, pp. 212–13.

63. Augustine, "Exposition of Psalm 137," trans. Boulding, p. 255.

64. Brown, *Augustine of Hippo*, p. 497.

65. Brown, *Augustine of Hippo*, p. 397.

66. Cf. Brown, *Augustine of Hippo*, p. 397.

67. Würzburg, UB M.p.th.f. 17 fols. 10r–14v; Augustine, "Exposition of Psalm 121," trans. Boulding, vol. 6, pp. 13–28, especially pp. 18–21.

68. Augustine, "Exposition of Psalm 121," ed. Gori, p. 94; trans. Boulding, p. 20 (as both man and woman).

69. Augustine, "Exposition of Psalm 122," trans. Boulding, p. 39; ed. Gori, p. 123.

70. Augustine, "Exposition of Psalm 122," WB UB M.p.th.f. 17 fol. 17r; trans. Boulding, p. 36; ed. Gori, p. 118.

71. Augustine, "Exposition of Psalm 126," trans. Boulding, pp. 90–91; ed. Gori pp. 196–99; Augustine, "Exposition of Psalm 127," trans. Boulding, pp. 108–9, ed. Gori, pp. 221–22. Augustine made a passing aside, in a citation to 2 Corinthians 11:3, to Eve as having been seduced, with no mention of her as a temptress (Augustine, "Exposition of Psalm 126," trans. Boulding, p. 85; ed. Gori, p. 189).

72. Augustine, "Exposition of Psalm 126," trans. Boulding, pp. 87–89; ed. Gori, pp. 191–95.

73. Würzburg, UB M.p.th.f. 17 fol. 33v; Würzburg, UB M.p.th.f. 64 (Augustine, *Enarrationes in psalmos*, ed. Gori, p. 206).

74. Compare Matthew 26:6–13, Mark 14:3–9, and John 12:2–8.

75. Coon, *Sacred Fictions*, p. 14.

76. Power, *Veiled Desire*, pp. 132–34; Matter, "De cura feminarum," pp. 210–11.

77. Augustine, "Exposition of Psalm 125," trans. Boulding, p. 73; ed. Gori, pp. 170–71; Würzburg UB M.p.th.f. 17 fols. 26v–27r.

78. Augustine, "Exposition of Psalm 125," trans. Boulding, p. 81; ed. Gori, p. 183.

79. Matter, "De cura feminarum," pp. 210–11.

80. Chapter Three; Lifshitz, "Demonstrating Gun(t)za," pp. 76–85.

81. Augustine, *De Trinitate*, ed. Mountain, pp. 333 and 356–80, especially 363–67 and 373–74; Lifshitz, "Demonstrating Gun(t)za," pp. 76–85.

82. Bonner, *Augustine's Doctrine*, p. 498, n. 16; Power, *Veiled Desire*, pp. 131, 136–52, and 167; Matter, "De cura feminarum," pp. 212–13, nn. 4 and 5; Stark, "Augustine on Women," pp. 234 and 241, n. 20.

83. Ruether, "Augustine," pp. 55–56; Stark, "Augustine on Women,"pp. 216, 230, and 234–35.

84. Power, *Veiled Desire*, pp. 151–56.

85. Chapter Four.

86. Augustine, "Exposition of Psalm 129," trans. Boulding, p. 127; ed. Gori, p. 249. The Karlburg copy read: "Quisquis se in profundo intellexerit, clamat, gemit, suspirat, donec de profundo eruatur, et veniet ad eum qui super omnes abyssos sedet . . . donec ad eum veniat anima, donec ad illum liberetur imago ipsius, quod est homo, quae in hoc profundo tamquam assiduis fluctibus exagitata, detrita fiet, et nisi renovetur et

reparetur a deo, qui illam impressit quando formavit hominem – ideoneus esse potuit homo ad casum suum, non est idoneus ad resurrectionem suam – semper in profundo est: nisi liberetur, ut dixi, semper in profundo est" (Würzburg, UB M.p.th.f. 17 fol. 42r).

87. Gregory of Tours, *Libri Historiarum X*, 8.20, ed. Krusch, p. 386.

88. Hartmann, "Rechtskenntnis," pp. 11–13.

89. Augustine, "Exposition of Psalm 125," trans. Boulding, p. 81; ed. Gori, p. 183.

90. Ruether, "Augustine," p. 63.

91. Bowery, "Monica: The Feminine Face of Christ," pp. 76–78; Tinkle, *Gender and Power*, p. 59.

92. Chapter Three.

93. Gregory I, "Homily 23," *Reading the Gospels*, trans. Bhattacharji, p. 56.

94. Chavasse, *Lectionnaires Romains*, 1:49–68.

95. Bouhot, "Les homélies de saint Grégoire," p. 215.

96. Böhne, "Bischof Burchard von Würzburg," pp. 54–56; Clayton, *Cult of the Virgin*, pp. 37–38. The codex opened with a Roman calendar-cum-stational list (fols. 1r–2v). See also Thurn, ed., *Comes*; Morin, "Liturgie et basiliques de Rome," pp. 296–330; Morin, "Le plus ancien *comes*," pp. 46–72 (corrected by Thurn, ed., *Comes*, p. 23); Chavasse, *Lectionnaires Romains*, 2:11–65; Rusch, "A Possible Explanation," pp. 109–11; Martimort, *Les lectures liturgiques*, p. 52; Wegner, *Kirchenjahr und Messfeier*, p. 29; Häussling, "Missarum Sollemnia"; Knaus, "Das Bistum Würzburg," p. 951; Heitz, "Eucharistie," pp. 618–19 and Table XI between pp. 630–32; Thurn, "Libri sancti Kyliani," p. 243; see Chapter Three.

97. Gregory I, *Homiliae in Evangelia*, ed. Fiedrowicz, pp. 23–25. A different set of (so-called Gallican) readings appeared in the marginal notations to the Kilian Gospels (Würzburg, UB M.p.th.q. 1a), produced in what is now northern France around 600 but present in the Würzburg area during the second half of the eighth century (Salmon, "Le système des lectures liturgiques," pp. 38–53). Nevertheless, the system of readings in use in the Anglo-Saxon cultural province was the Roman one (Morin, "Liturgie et basiliques," pp. 328–30).

98. Gregory I, *Reading the Gospels*, trans. Bhattacharji, pp. 11–13 (quotes at 11 and 12); Simón, "Il metodo teologico," pp. 344–45 and 348; Gregory I, *Homiliae in Evangelia*, ed. Fiedrowicz, p.11.

99. Tinkle, *Gender and Power*, pp. 30–31; Clark, *Reading Renunciation*, pp. 70–152.

100. Markus, *Gregory*, p. 45.

101. Simón, "Il metodo teologico," pp. 343–45 and 348 (quote).

102. Markus, *Gregory the Great*, pp. 11–12.

103. Straw, *Gregory the Great*, p. 33.

104. Gregory I, "Homily 26," *Reading the Gospels*, trans. Bhattacharji, pp. 102–3; Gregory I, "Homily 22," *Reading the Gospels*, trans. Bhattacharji, pp. 45–47.

105. Gregory I, "Homily 30," *Forty Gospel Homilies*, trans. Hurst, p. 245; see also Straw, *Gregory the Great*, pp. 124 and 138–40, and Gregory I, "Homily 24," *Reading the Gospels*, trans. Bhattacharji, p. 69.

106. Straw, *Gregory the Great*, p. 104.

107. Gregory I, "Homily 23," *Reading the Gospels*, trans. Bhattacharji, p. 56.

108. "For just as we need to listen to Holy Scripture, to learn the things that were done in the past, so we need equally to consider how to imitate these actions in our own lives" (Gregory I, "Homily 21," *Reading the Gospels*, trans. Bhattacharji, pp. 29–30).

109. Lifshitz, "Gender and Exemplarity."

110. Gregory I, "Homily 23," *Reading the Gospels*, trans. Bhattacharji, p. 54; Bouhot, "Les homélies de saint Grégoire," p. 240.

111. Morin, "Liturgie et basiliques," p. 304; Bouhot, "Les homélies de saint Grégoire," p. 240.

112. "Ecce in resurrectione auctoris nostri ministros eius angelos concives nostros agnovimus (Gregory I, "Homily 21," *Homiliae in Evangelia*, ed. Fiedrowicz, p. 388; *Reading the Gospels*, trans. Bhattacharji, p. 36). For this usage of "to disappear," Biddick, "Bede's Blush," note 11, p. 37.

113. Gregory I, "Homily 21," cc. 4–5, *Homiliae in Evangelia*, ed. Fiedrowicz, pp. 380–83.

114. Gregory I, "Homily 21," *Reading the Gospels*, trans. Bhattacharji, p. 36.

115. Gregory I, "Homily 22," *Reading the Gospels*, trans. Bhattacharji, p. 39.

116. Banniard, *Viva Voce*, pp. 150–72.

117. Gregory, "Homily 22," *Reading the Gospels*, trans. Bhattacharji, pp. 49–50.

118. Gregory, "Homily 29," *Forty Gospel Homilies*, trans. Hurst, pp. 226–35 (on Mark 15:14–20); Bouhot, "Les homélies de saint Grégoire," p. 242.

119. Gregory, "Homily 24" (on John 21:1–14), *Reading the Gospels*, trans. Bhattacharji, especially pp. 63, 66, and 68–69; Bouhot, "Les homélies de saint Grégoire," p. 240.

120. Gregory, "Homily 26," *Reading the Gospels*, trans. Bhattacharji, p. 100; Bouhot, "Les homélies de saint Grégoire," p. 241.

121. It was here, as well as in Gospel Homily 33), that Gregory conflated various biblical women to create an ex-prostitute version of Mary Magdalen (Lifshitz, "Women: *The Da Vinci Code*").

122. Würzburg UB M.p.th.f. 45 fol. 13r; Morin, "Liturgie et basiliques," p. 305; Gregory, "Homily 25," *Homiliae in Evangelia*, ed. Fiedrowicz, p. 442; Bouhot, "Les homélies de saint Grégoire," p. 241.

123. Chapter Four.

124. Köbler, *Ergänzungen*, pp. 625–26.

125. Bergmann, *Die althochdeutsche Glossenüberlieferung*, p.9.

126. Yorke, "The Bonifatian Mission"; Schipperges, *Bonifatius ac Socii Eius*; Jansen, "Maria Magdalena."

127. Gregory I, "Homily 25," *Reading the Gospels*, trans. Bhattacharji, p. 80; "Sed ei magister dicit: 'Noli me tangere.' Non quia post resurrectionem dominus tactum renuit feminarum, cum de duabus ad sepulcrum eius venientibus scriptum sit: 'Accesserunt, et tenuerunt pedes eius.' Sed cur tangi non debeat, ratio quoque additur, cum subinfertur 'Nondum enim ascendi ad Patrem meum.'" (Gregory I, Homily 25, *Homiliae in Evangelia*, ed. Fiedrowicz, p. 456; Würzburg, UB M.p.th.f. 45 fol. 15v).

128. Gregory I, *Libellus Responsionum*, eds. Ewald and Hartmann; Friesen, "Answers and Echoes," pp. 153–57.

129. Thacker, "Memorializing Gregory the Great," p. 81; Friesen, "Answers and Echoes," pp. 157–59.

130. Meens, "Ritual Purity."

131. Meens, "Ritual Purity," p. 34.

132. Gregory, *Libellus Responsionum*, eds. Ewald and Hartmann, pp. 338–40; see Chapter Three.

133. Gregory, *Libellus Responsionum*, eds. Ewald and Hartmann, p. 338 ("valde stultum").

134. Meens, "Ritual Purity," p. 39.

135. Mordek, *Kirchenrecht und Reform*, pp. 79 and 214–29.

136. Meens, "Ritual Purity," p. 42.

137. The *Discipulus Umbrensium* prescribed a three-week fast for noncompliance (Vienna, ÖNB 2223 fol. 8r).

138. *Discipulus Umbrensium*, ch. 26 (Vienna, ÖNB 2223, fol. 14r). The Penitential of Pseudo-Bede in the same manuscript prescribed thirty days for a boy and forty days for a girl (Vienna, ÖNB 2223, fol. 19r).

139. Meens, "Ritual Purity," p. 38.

140. For the contents of Vienna ÖNB 2223, see Chapter Three.

141. Vienna, ÖNB 2223, fol. 41v. Gregory's view that pregnant women could be baptized was consonant with the sixth canon of Neocaesaria, included in another manuscript made at Karlburg around the same time, namely, Würzburg, UB M.p.th.f. 146 fol. 35v (the *Collectio Wirceburgensis*).

142. Thacker, "Memorializing Gregory the Great," p. 81.

143. "Mulieres menstruo tempus non intrent in aecclesiam neque communicant nec sanctimoniales nec laice quod si presumpserint .iii. ebd. peniteat. Beatus vero gregorius papa romanus menstruantem utrumque concessit quod hic prohibetur"(Vienna, ÖNB 2223, fol. 29r).

144. "Non valet" (Vienna, ÖNB 2223, fol. 50r).

145. Nelson, "Peers in the Early Middle Ages," p. 29–32.

146. Gregory I, "Homily 25," *Reading the Gospels,* trans. Bhattacharji, p. 83; "Ecce humani generis culpa ibi absciditur, unde processit. Quia enim in paradiso mulier viro propinavit mortem, a sepulcro mulier viris annunciat vitam: et dicta sui vivificatoris narrat, quae mortiferi serpentis verba narraverat. Ac si humano generi non verbis Dominus, sed rebus dicat: De qua manu vobis illatus est potus mortis, de ipsa suscipite poculum vitae" (Gregory I, Homily 25, *Homiliae in Evangelia*, ed. Fiedrowicz, p. 460).

147. Otfrid's *Evangelienbuch* (863/870) explained John 20:14 to mean that Mary was the antitype of Eve and removed Eve's curse from women (Kochskämper, *"Frau" und "Mann,"* pp. 151–53).

148. Gregory I, *Libellus Responsionum*, eds. Ewald and Hartmann, p. 338.

149. Gregory I, "Homily 25," *Reading the Gospels,* trans. Bhattacharji, p. 72.

150. Gregory I, "Homily 25," *Reading the Gospels,* trans. Bhattacharji, p. 87; "quae sua itinera prava dereliquit.... Tantumque apud eum locum gratiae invenit, ut hunc ipsis quoque apostolis ... ipsa nunciaret" (Gregory I, Homily 25, *Homiliae in Evangelia*, ed. Fiedrowicz, p. 466).

151. Gregory I, "Homily 25," *Reading the Gospels,* trans. Bhattacharji, p. 88; "Ecce omnipotens Deus ubique oculis nostris quos imitari debeamus obicit" (Gregory I, Homily 25, *Homiliae in Evangelia,* ed. Fiedrowicz, p. 468).

152. Gregory I, "Homily 25," *Reading the Gospels,* trans. Bhattacharji, p. 89; "Redite, parvuli filii, ad sinum matris vestrae aeternae Sapientiae; sugite larga ubera pietatis Dei" (Gregory I, Homily 25, *Homiliae in Evangelia,* ed. Fiedrowicz, p. 468).

153. Straw, *Gregory the Great*, pp. 141, 197, 199, 208–9 and 219; Straw, "Purity and Death," p. 22.

154. Gregory I, "Homily 34," *Forty Gospel Homilies,* trans. Hurst, p. 283.

155. See Chapter Six.

156. Gregory I, "Homily 33," *Forty Gospel Homilies,* trans. Hurst, p. 268.

157. Compare Matthew 26:6–13, Mark 14:3–9, and John 12:2–8. The Würzburg *comes* (Würzburg, UB M.p.th.f. 62) pegged the reading to minor weekday masses (Morin, "Liturgie et basiliques de Rome," pp. 300 and 313), but Bouhot calculated that Gregory preached Homily 33 on the fifth Sunday after Pentecost, that is, on Sunday, July 8, 591 (Bouhot, "Les homélies de saint Grégoire," p. 244), which, if correct, would mean that the pope went out of his way to give greater prominence to this sacerdotal female figure.

158. See especially Würzburg, UB M.p.th.f. 45 fols. 42r–45v.

159. Gregory I, "Homily 33," *Forty Gospel Homilies,* trans. Hurst, pp. 270–71.

160. Gregory I, "Homily 33," *Forty Gospel Homilies,* trans. Hurst, p. 272.

161. Gregory I, "Homily 33," *Forty Gospel Homilies,* trans. Hurst, p. 278.

162. Posset, "The 'Palate of the Heart,'" pp. 253–54 and 257–58.

163. Coons, *Sacred Fictions,* pp. 44–50.

164. For Gregory's "sacramental reality," see Straw, *Gregory the Great,* pp. 47–65 and 180–81.

165. *Earliest Life of Gregory the Great,* ed. Colgrave, pp. 104–9; Paul the Deacon, *Vita Gregorii,* PL 75:52–53; John the Deacon, *Vita Gregorii,* PL 75:103.

166. Gregory I, "Homily 32," *Forty Gospel Homilies,* trans. Hurst, p. 265.

167. The *comes* pegged the reading to a minor weekday (Morin, "Liturgie et basiliques de Rome," p. 310), but Bouhot suggested that it was preached on March 22, 593, the sixth Sunday of Lent, the assembly of the faithful for the giving of the creed (Bouhot, "Les homélies de saint Grégoire," pp. 246–49).

168. Gregory I, "Homily 40," *Forty Gospel Homilies,* trans. Hurst, p. 384.

169. Wilkins, "'Submitting the Neck of Your Mind,'" pp. 584–85 and 587–88 (quote).

170. Straw, *Gregory the Great,* p. 54.

171. Straw, *Gregory the Great,* pp. 86–87.

172. Wilkins, "'Submitting the Neck of Your Mind,'" pp. 592–94.

173. Gregory I, "Homily 33," *Forty Gospel Homilies,* trans. Hurst, p. 275.

174. Blamires, *Case for Women,* pp. 145–48.

175. Chapter Three.

176. Munich, BSB Clm 6277; see Bierbrauer, *Vorkarolingische Miniaturen,* 1.50–51 and 2.48–49 (Tafelband).

177. Würzburg UB M.p.th.f. 42 fol. 34r.

178. O'Donnell, "The Holiness of Gregory," pp. 62–64; Meyvaert, "A Letter of Pelagius II," p. 104.

179. "Serpens suggessit, eva velut caro delectata est, adam velut spiritus consensit" (Gregory I, *Libellus Responsionum,* eds. Ewald and Hartmann, p. 343; Vienna ÖNB 2223 fol. 43v).

180. Blamires, *Case for Women,* pp. 185–86; Leyser, "Masculinity in Flux," pp. 105 and 116–18.

181. Chazelle, "Memory, Instruction, Worship," pp. 183 and 202–3.

182. See also Chapter Three concerning Psalm 133.

183. Augustine, "Exposition of Psalm 132," trans. Boulding, p. 179; ed. Gori, p. 325.

184. Astell, "Translating Job as Female," p. 63.

185. Astell, "Translating Job as Female," p. 65.

186. Astell, "Translating Job as Female," p. 69.

187. Conybeare, "Spaces between Letters."

188. Morin, "Pages Inédites," pp. 293–303 and 307.

6. "THE SENSUAL MAN DOES NOT PERCEIVE THOSE THINGS THAT ARE OF THE SPIRIT OF GOD" (1 CORINTHIANS 2:14)

1. Matter, "A Carolingian Schoolbook?" pp. 149–50; Dagenais, *The Ethics of Reading*, p. xviii; Lifshitz, "Gender and Exemplarity."

2. Lifshitz, "Beyond Positivism *and* Genre"; Lifshitz, *Norman Conquest.*

3. Bauer, "Das Bild der Stadt Rom," pp. 193–200, 207–9, and 228.

4. Clemens, *Tempore Romanorum constructa*, p. 87.

5. Mautner, *Das zerbrechliche Leben erzählen*, p. 135.

6. "Animalis homo non percipit quae sunt spiritus Dei" (*Passio Ceciliae* [BHL 1495] ed. Delehaye, *Étude*, p. 209). This quotation was located in a section of the full *passio Ceciliae* that the Kitzingen Anonyma eliminated because it dealt primarily with Valerian and his brother Tiburtius, not Cecilia (*Passio Ceciliae*, ed. Delehaye, *Étude*, pp. 200–14). The Pauline sentiment was nevertheless clearly relevant at Kitzingen, for it was highlighted by a special marginal mark in that community's copy of the Pauline epistles (Würzburg UB M.p.th.f. 69 fol. 16r).

7. "Juliana habens animam rationabilem prudentemque consilium" (Würzburg UB M.p.th.q. 28b fol. 9r).

8. Rebillard, *In Hora Mortis*, pp. 52–53 and 115–18.

9. Heffernan, *Sacred Biography*, pp. 123–84.

10. Vitz, "Gender and Martyrdom"; Wolf, "The Severed Breast."

11. Palmer, *Anglo-Saxons*, p. 278; see also Schneiders, " 'Pagan Past,' " p. 166.

12. Mayeski, *Women at the Table*, p. 11.

13. Chapter Three.

14. Davies, *Revolt of the Widows*; Macdonald, *The Legend and the Apostle*; Burrus, *Chastity as Autonomy* (challenged by Ng, "Acts of Paul and Thecla," pp. 1–8).

15. Lipsius, *DAA* 1:54–56, 61–65, 72–83, 88–89, 116–17, 171, 229, 291, 296–343, 353–59, 457–64, and 515; Bovon, "Editing the Apocryphal Acts," p. 11.

16. Rose, ed., *Missale gothicum*, pp. 266–71; Casiday, "St. Aldhelm," pp. 147–48 and 150; Rose, *Ritual Memory*, p. 3. For a heterodox passage in the *Passio Thomae* (Würzburg UB M.p.th.f. 78 fol. 7v), see Casiday, "St. Aldhelm," pp. 149–50; and Zelzer, ed., *Die alten lateinischen Thomasakten*, p. 10.

17. The Roman Martyrs Project, described at http://www.arts.manchester.ac.uk/cla /projects/romanmartyrsproject/ (last accessed March 23, 2012).

18. Moorhead, "The Byzantines in the West"; Moorhead, "Ostrogothic Italy."

19. De Bruyn, *Pelagius' Commentary*, p. 11; Johnson, *Purging the Poison*, 59–169. See Chapter Three.

20. Von Dobschütz, *Das Decretum Gelasianum*, p. 9; Leyser, "Temptations of Cult."

21. Dufourcq, *Etude*, 1:290, 336, and 359; Dufourcq, *De Manichaeismo apud Latinos.*

22. D'Arrigo, *Il martirio*, pp. 670–71; Dubois, "Cécile," p. 96.

23. Dufourcq, *Etude*, 1:53–54 and 296 (dating the *passio* of Agnes to 514–523); Dufourcq, *Etude*, 2:55 (dating it to the first quarter of the fifth century); Fiorentini and Orioli, *S. Apollinare Nuovo*, pp. 19–21 and pp. 35–37.

24. Matter, "*De cura feminarum*," pp. 207–9; Jenal, "Frühe Formen," pp. 58–59.

25. Nelson, "Perceptions du pouvoir." According to the text of the legend and to the correspondence of Gregory the Great, it was a woman who brought Juliana's relics from Nicomedia to the west, and another woman built her first cult site near Naples; there was also a women's monastery in Naples dedicated to Juliana, founded by a woman named Alexandra (*Passio Julianae*, ed. Bollandus, pp. 868–75; Gregory I, *Registrum Epistolarum*, VII. 84, VII. 85, and IX. 170).

26. For what follows, Jenal, "Il Monachesimo Femminile," pp. 18–19 and 28–31.

27. Brock, "Political Authority."

28. Reynolds, "Social Mentalities," pp. 29 and 33–34.

29. Cf. Granier, "Les échanges culturels."

30. Walter, "Die theologischen Streitigkeiten," p. 26.

31. Würzburg UB M.p.th.f. 78 fols. 10r–10v; Zelzer, ed., *Die alten lateinischen Thomasakten*, p. xiv and 21–22.

32. Chapter Three.

33. Klüppel, "Die Germania," p. 164.

34. Cooper, "Empress and *Theotokos*," p. 49.

35. Clayton, *Cult of the Virgin Mary*, p. 267.

36. ". . . virgo electus a domino et prae ceteris dilectus."

37. Regul, *Die Antimarcionistischen Evangelienprologe*, pp. 11–15, 17–20, 42–44, 71, and 77–94.

38. ". . . custodisti corpus meum ab omni pullutione" (fol. 3r).

39. Hamburger, "Brother, Bride and *alter Christus*," pp. 306–7.

40. Because this portion of the narrative is now currently lost from, but certainly once was part of, the Karlburg passionary (Chapter Three), I take the plot of the episode from Würzburg UB M.p.th.q. 26 fols. 43r–50v (Chapter Three and Chapter Nine); see also Lipsius, *DAA* 1:417–18 and PG 5:1241.

41. Schäferdiek, "Die *Passio Johannis*," pp. 368 and 372.

42. Lipsius, *DAA* 1:496ff.

43. Chapter Three and Chapter Nine.

44. Chapter One.

45. Geisel, *Die Juden im Frankenreich*, pp. 441–97 and 544.

46. Chapter Five.

47. Jesus was "hunc quem iudei crucifixerunt" (fol. 3r) and "quem crucifixerunt iudei" (fol. 5v). This rhetoric recurred in the *passio* of Thomas, where Jesus was "quem iudei occiderunt," "quem iudei crucifixerunt," and "hominen a iudeis occisum" (fols. 14v and 15r).

48. For instance, see his conversion of Filetus through scriptural arguments about the fulfillment of prophesy (fol. 3r).

49. ". . . fantasium fuisse nec verum hominem ex vere virgine natum."

50. Lifshitz, *The Name of the Saint*, pp. 50–51.

51. Rose, *Ritual Memory*, p. 170.

52. Atenolfi, *I Testi Medioevali*, p. 20.

53. Boas, *Primitivism and Related Ideas*, p. 136. See also Kilburn, "The Contrasted 'Other.'"

54. Jolly, "Marked Difference," p. 195.

55. Herrick, *Imagining the Sacred Past*, pp. 61 and 90.

56. Uebel, *Ecstatic Transformation*, pp. 1–4.

57. Zelzer, ed., *Die alten lateinischen Thomasakten*, pp. 4–5.

58. Zelzer, ed., *Die alten lateinischen Thomasakten,* p. 7 (without the variant reading "cantatrix").

59. Zelzer, ed., *Die alten lateinischen Thomasakten,* p. 8.

60. Zelzer, ed., *Die alten lateinischen Thomasakten,* p. 10.

61. Zelzer, ed., *Die alten lateinischen Thomasakten,* p. 11.

62. Zelzer, ed., *Die alten lateinischen Thomasakten,* pp. 12–17.

63. Lipsius, *DAA* 1:271; Zelzer, ed., *Die alten lateinischen Thomasakten,* pp. 34–37.

64. Zelzer, ed., *Die alten lateinischen Thomasakten,* pp. 25–27.

65. Zelzer, ed. *Die alten lateinischen Thomasakten,* p. 28.

66. Zelzer, ed. *Die alten lateinischen Thomasakten,* pp. 29–30.

67. Whitaker's Words, online at: http://lysy2.archives.nd.edu/cgi-bin/WORDS.EXE ?thorum (last accessed March 28, 2012).

68. *Passio Bartholomei,* eds. Lipsius and Bonnet, *Acta Apostolorum Apocrypha,* 2.1, pp. 144–45.

69. The sermon begins on fol. 17 of a current total of 35 leaves, but the first and last folios of the codex have been lost; therefore, the sermon originally began on fol. 18 of a total of 36 leaves.

70. *Passio Bartholomei* eds. Lipsius and Bonnet, *Acta Apostolorum Apocrypha,* 2.1 p. 135. The phrase is in Paris BN lat. 18298, Paris BN lat 17002 and Montpellier H.55.

71. Gössman, "Mariologische Entwicklungen," p. 66–69.

72. *Terra* as *"mater"* (mother) was explicit in the Karlburg passionary and in all manuscripts of the Δ family, but is in the apparatus as a variant reading in *Passio Bartholomei,* eds. Lipsius and Bonnet, *Acta Apostolorum Apocrypha,* 2.1 p. 137.

73. Markschies, "Die neutestamentliche Versuchungsgeschichte," p. 199; Dunning, *Specters of Paul,* pp. 4 and 8–13.

74. "Par enim erat ut qui filium virginis vicerat a filio virginis vinceretur" (*Passio Bartholomei,* eds. Lipsius and Bonnet, *Acta Apostolorum Apocrypha,* 2.1 p. 136).

75. Irenaeus of Lyons was apparently the first theologian to write of a "virgin earth/ virgin birth" typological parallel, but he did so without placing any emphasis on Mary, her agency, or her contribution to the nature of her son; furthermore, his earth was "virgin" because she was as yet untilled and, therefore, unpenetrated (Dunning, *Specters of Paul,* pp. 97–123, especially 110 and 112–14).

76. Markschies, "Die neutestamentliche Versuchungsgeschichte," pp. 199–202.

77. Würzburg UB M.p.th.f. 146 fol. 31r.

78. ". . . cuius initium ante secula a deo patre est sibi initium numquam fuit et omnibus dedit." Although not Paulianist, this formulation could be read as denying the Son coevality and coeternality with the Father; the possibility worried some of the scribes who transmitted the text, for most of the Δ family codices (and Bonnet's edition) said here of Jesus (in line with Nicene Trinitarianism) that he "never had a beginning, was himself always the beginning and gave a beginning to all things" ("nunquam habuit initium, se ipse semper initium fuit et omnibus initium dedit"; *Passio Bartholomei,* eds. Lipsius and Bonnet, *Acta Apostolorum Apocrypha,* 2.1 p. 135).

79. Abramowski, "Histoire de la recherche," pp. 45–46; Dupuy, "La Christologie," pp. 59–60.

80. Vanneufville, "Monophysisme et nestorianisme," pp. 219–20.

81. Abramowski, "Histoire de la recherche," p. 52; Dupuy, "La Christologie," pp. 57–62.

82. Cooper, "Empress and *Theotokos*," p. 44 (challenged by Price, "Marian Piety," p. 38).

83. Chapter Three.

84. Chapter Three.

85. ". . . omnibus notum est judaeos crucifixisse Jesum" (fol. 29r); "qui natus est ex spiritu sancto et ex maria virgine quem tradidit iudas fariseis et illi eum crucifixerunt" (fol. 22v).

86. "qui nullam spernis aetatem non sexsum reprobas, nullam condicionem gratiae tuae ducis indignam, sed in omnium aequalis creator es et redemptor. . . ."

87. Atenolfi, ed., *I Testi Medioevali*, p. 76.

88. "Me, autem, oportet certamen habere cum Hyrtaco."

89. Rose, *Ritual Memory*, pp. 271–73.

90. Hasdenteufel-Röding, "Studien zur Gründung von Frauenklöstern," pp. 112, 113, and 119.

91. Bern, Burgerbibliothek, MS Bongarsiana 611, fol. 86v; Bischoff, "Epitaphienformeln."

92. D'Arrigo, *Il martirio Sant'Agata*, 1:359.

93. Würzburg UB M.p.th.f. 78 fols. 15r–15v; Zelzer, ed., *Die alten lateinischen Thomasakten*, pp. 41–42.

94. Auerbach, *Mimesis*, especially ch. 4.

95. This same contradiction appeared in the copy of the *passio* in Paris BN lat. 10861 (see Chapter Three).

96. Otter, *Inventiones*.

97. The full passion narrative (*Passio Julianae*, ed. Bollandus, p. 878) gave "lxxv" (75).

98. Leupin, *Fiction and Incarnation*, pp. 116–17.

99. Würzburg UB M.p.th.q. 28b fol. 7r; Delehaye, Étude, pp. 207–214.

100. Würzburg UB M.p.th.q. 28b fol. 7v; Delehaye, Étude, p. 214.

101. Heffernan, *Sacred Biography*, p. 5.

102. *Passio Julianae*, ed. Bollandus, p. 877.

103. Olsen, "Cynewulf's Autonomous Women," pp. 225 (quote) and 230.

104. McInerney, *Eloquent Virgins*, p. 2.

105. McInerney, *Eloquent Virgins*, p. 9; Blamires, *Case for Women*, pp. 171–84 and 190–98; Salisbury, *Church Fathers, Independent Virgins*.

106. CLA X: 1502.

107. For instance, in Vienna, ÖNB 1616, fols. 10v–13r.

108. In contrast (for instance) to Vienna, ÖNB 1616 fol. 10v, which began "Sermo sancti Augustini de nativitate domini. Nativitas domini nostri Jesu Christi totum mundum nova adventus sui hodiae luce praefudit. Hodie de caelo deus discendit in hominem ut in coelis homini praepararet ascensum" ("A sermon of St. Augustine on the Birth of the Lord. The birth of our lord Jesus Christ on this day suffused the entire world with the new light of his coming. Today God descended from heaven into a human, in order to prepare in heaven an ascent for humanity").

109. "God brought the Word [Christ] to Mary through an angel," or "God brought word to Mary through an angel."

110. In other manuscripts, the homily began: "And since the devil spoke to Eve through a serpent, and through Eve and her ears brought death to the world, God through an angel brought the Word to Mary" ("Et quoniam diabulus per serpentem Evae locutus, per Evam et eius aures mundo intulit mortem, Deus per angelum ad

Mariam protulit verbum"), cited from Vienna, ÖNB lat. 1616 fols. 10v–11r. See also Alvarez Campos, *Corpus*, nos. 6346–6348, pp. 137–38.

111. Johnson, "*Auctricitas?*"

112. Thraede, "Zwischen Eva und Maria," pp. 132–33.

113. Thraede, "Zwischen Eva und Maria," p. 136.

114. Fulgentius, *Opera*, ed. Fraipont, p. v.

115. Fulgentius, "To Peter on the Faith," trans. Eno, p. 71; Fulgentius, "De Fide ad Petrum," ed. Fraipont, pp. 722–23. For similar sentiments from Justin Martyr, Irenaeus, Ephrem the Syrian, Epiphanius of Salamis, and others, see Gambero, *Mary and the Fathers of the Church*, pp. 46–48, 57–58, 116–17, 124–25, and 128–30.

116. Fulgentius, "Letter to the Widow Galla" and "Letter to Proba," trans. Edo, pp. 301–10 and 313–14.

117. Pseudo-Fulgentius, "Letter to Peter on the Faith," Rules xxii and xxvi, ed. Fraipont, p. 752, in Vienna ÖNB 2223 (see Chapter Three).

118. "Deponite maledictionem praevaricationis et benedictionem restaurationis adsumite, proiecite dolores quos Eva per serpentem accipit, et quos per angelum Maria suscipit honores adsumite" (Würzburg UB M.p.th.q. 28b fol. 2v; Vienna ÖNB 1616 fol. 12v.)

119. *Contra*, for instance, Müller, "Die 'andere Seite.'"

120. "Ideo omnes istos cursus naturae virgo Maria in domino nostro Jesu Christo suscepit, ut omnibus ad se confugientibus feminis subveniret et sic restauraret omne genus feminarum ad se venientium nova Eva" (Würzburg UB M.p.th.q. 28b fols. 2v–3r; Vienna ÖNB 1616 fols. 12v–13r).

121. Grégoire, *Les Homéliaires*, pp. 7 and 71–114; for Alan of Farfa, see Chapter Three.

122. Shapiro, "The Religious Meaning of the Ruthwell Cross"; Farr, "Worthy Women on the Ruthwell Cross," p. 48.

123. Farr, "Worthy Women on the Ruthwell Cross," p. 52.

124. Points such as "salutationem ab angelo et misterium conceptionis agnoscit" (Würzburg UB M.p.th.q. 28b fol. 3r) were drawn from Isidore, *De ortu et obitu patrum*, ed. Chaparro Gómez, chapter 66, pp. 190–93, especially p. 191. The Kitzingen borrowings were unrelated to another late eighth-century anonymous reworking of the text, the *Liber de ortu et obitu patriarcharum*, ed. Carracedo Fraga, c. 41, pp. 44–45.

125. Compare Alvarez Campos, *Corpus Marianum Patristicum*, vol. III, nos. 2773, 2775, 2848, and 2859 and vol. VI, nos. 6429, 6654, 6911, and 7055. The arguments in the Kitzingen *libellus* were closest to, but still went beyond, Bede, *In Lucae Evangelium Expositio*, ed. Hurst, I.i.34, p. 33, and Bede, *Homilia in festivitate annunciationis beatae Mariae* (PL 94:11).

126. "cum a nullo homine nec verbo didicisset nec exemplari ad imitationem invitata, constituit ut virgo specialiter pro amore Dei permaneret."

127. "Specialiter tamen nulla docet historia Mariam gladii animadversione peremptam, quia nec obitus eius uspiam legitur" (Isidore, *De ortu et obitu patrum* c. 66, ed. Chaparro Gómez, p. 193; cited in Würzburg UB M.p.th.q. 28b).

128. I, "La festa della purificazione," pp. 153–64, 175–76, and 209–11.

129. "reperiatur sepulchrum" (Isidore, *De ortu et obitu patrum* c. 66, ed. Chaparro Gómez, p. 193).

130. Schreiner, *Maria*, pp. 468–69.

131. ". . . non de eo quod corpus eius ibi requiescat, sed ad memoriam eius" (Hugeburc, *Hoedeporicon*, p. 98). The text was a double biography of Willibald and his

brother Wynnebald (BHL 8931 and 8996), including the former's travel account (Klüppel, "Die Germania," p. 168).

132. ". . . quia nec obitus eius uspiam legitur, dum non repperiatur sepulchrum"; compare note 129.

133. Brown, *Augustine of Hippo*, p. 342.

134. De Bruyn, *Pelagius' Commentary*, p. 25.

135. De Bruyn, *Pelagius' Commentary*, pp. 26–29.

136. Berlin, SB-PK Nachlass Grimm 139,1 (CLA Supp. 1676).

137. Compare Gagny, ed., *Primasii Commentaria* (in PL 68: 493–96) with De Bruyne, *Pelagius' Commentary*, pp. 133–35.

138. Cf. De Bruyn, *Pelagius' Commentary*, pp. 36 and 49.

139. "Exsaecrantes malum, adherentes bono." Latin versions of the Pauline letter more often have "odientes" (De Bruyne, *Pelagius' Commentary*, p. 186).

140. "Tota puritas debet esse in Christiano, sicut Deus pura lux est" (fol. 3v).

141. Brown, *Augustine of Hippo*, p. 367.

142. Rosenthal and McGurk, "Author, Symbol and Word," p. 188.

143. Carrasco, "The Imagery of the Magdalen," p. 69; see Chapter Five. The passages are Matthew 26:6–13, Mark 14:3–9, Luke 7:36–50, and John 12:1–8.

144. "In spiritu previdit mulier haec quod corpus Domini non potuiset unguere in sepultura gravissima petra clausa." As we saw in connection with the multiple identities and meanings of figures in the crucifixion miniature, the fact that the woman was also the church of gentiles ("Mulier autem id aecclesia gentium est"; fol. 17r) did not erase her human identity.

145. Baby, *The Discipleship of the Women*, pp. 165–208, at p. 207.

146. See Chapter Five for the *imago Dei* and the woman who found the lost coin.

147. The biblical reference was to Joshua 6:17–25. Similar uses of Rahab included James 2:25, Prudentius's *Dittochaeon* (Pillinger, *Die Tituli historiarum*, p. 49), and Bede's *Commentary on the Canonical Epistles* (found, for instance, in the early ninth-century Karlburg codex Oxford Bodleian Laud misc 442 fols. 21r–21v). For the Pseudo-Jerome quote, see Chapter Three.

148. Ó Carragáin, "Crucifixion as Annunciation," p. 504.

149. Ó Carragáin, *Ritual and the Rood*, pp. 83–93.

150. Chapter Three.

151. "Sancta Caecilia virgo carissima absconditum semper evangelium Christi gerebat in pectore suo."

152. "Venit nox in qua suscepit, una cum Valeriano sponso suo, cubili secreta silentia."

153. This was explicit in a passage in the full *passio*, cut by the Kitzingen Anonyma, describing Christians as people who "contempserunt quod videtur esse et non est, et invenerunt illud quod videtur non esse et est" (despise what seems to exist but does not, and have found that which does not seem to exist and does"; Delehaye, *Etude*, p. 208).

154. "One God, one faith, one baptism. One God and father of all, who is above all things and in all of us" (Ephesians 4:5–6).

155. "Caecilia dixit: 'Nescio ubi tu oculos amiseris. Quos deos dicis. Ego et omnes qui sanos oculos habent, saxa vidimus esse et aeramentum'" ("Cecilia said: 'I do not know where you have lost your eyes. You say that these are gods. I and everyone who has healthy eyes, we see that they are stone and bronze'").

156. Mulder-Bakker and Wogan-Browne, "Introduction Part I" p. 2.

157. Underneath the current church of St. Cecilia in Rome sits the baptistery of a fifth- or even third-century church, itself built upon a Roman private house.

158. "Ego sum qui feci Adam et Evam in paradiso praevaricari" ("I am the one who caused Adam and Eve to transgress in paradise").

159. For the "rational soul," see note 7; for the "willing mind," see note 167.

160. "Infantia conputabatur in annis sed erat mentis senectus inmensa" ("She was reckoned to be in infancy according to her years, but the old age of her mind was immeasurable").

161. It falls on fols. 13r–13v of 25 total folios. Since folio 1 is blank, this is the equivalent of folio 12 of 24.

162. "... quod tempus est ut virtus Domini mei Jesu Christi manifestetur, egredemine foras ut solita me Deo in oratione offeram."

163. D'Arrigo, *Il martirio di sant'Agata*, 2:708–14.

164. Schulz, *Der Einfluss Augustins*, pp. 166–72.

165. Agatha's description of herself as acting "viriliter" or "virilely" (fol. 15r) did not imply that a fully liberated woman was one who acted like a man, for the complex of terms *virilitas-virilis-viriliter* had lost any sex-specific connotations already in biblical usage and come to connote energy and strength with no resonance of manliness (Heene, *The Legacy of Paradise*, pp. 248–54).

166. D'Arrigo, *Il martirio di sant'Agata*, 1:372; Mombritius, *Sanctuarium*, c. 94.

167. D'Arrigo, *Il martirio di sant'Agata*, 2:651.

168. This aspect of the narrative evoked paroxysms of theological defensiveness from one of the saint's devotees (D'Arrigo, *Il martirio di sant'Agata* 2:716–718).

169. McInerney, *Eloquent Virgins*, p. 4.

170. Agnes was beautiful, but more beautiful of faith; strikingly, she was not "elegantior castitate" ("more elegant in chastity") in the Kitzingen *libellus*, for that phrase was cut from a description that the Anonyma otherwise retained almost verbatim from the full *passio* (PL 17:735).

171. D'Arrigo, *Il martirio di sant'Agata* 2:695–98.

172. Cross, "English Vernacular Saints' Lives," p. 417.

173. Sorgo, *Martyrium und Pornographie* pp. 255–256.

174. Schulenburg, *Forgetful of Their Sex*, pp. 126–75; Consolino, "Modelli di santità." McInerney's bipolar "virgin martyr" was more nuanced, for she oscillated between a message of female "silence and death" and a message of women's "active speech and liberation" (McInerney, *Eloquent Virgins*, pp. 67–77 and 94–100).

175. The thirteen-year-old Agnes represented the child; Juliana represented the adult woman prepared to marry her fiancé (fol. 9r); Cecilia represented the married woman, in a chaste marriage; Agatha's history "de obitu sanctae agathae" (fol. 14r) only began with her death and burial and focused on her postmortem miracles as protector of Catania (fols. 15r–16r).

176. Riches, "St. George as a Male Virgin Martyr"; Vitz, "Gender and Martyrdom"; Delany, "Hagio, Porn, and Femcrit"; Wogan-Browne, "Saints' Lives and Women's Literary Culture," pp. 6 and 124.

177. This was the implication of the anguished complaint by the demon Jofer when Juliana was torturing him, "O virginitas, quid contra nos armaris?" (*Passio Julianae*, ed. Bollandus, p. 877).

178. Delehaye, *Étude*, p. 199.
179. For instance, Schulenburg, *Forgetful of Their Sex*, p. 127.
180. As opposed to Vienna ÖNB 1616, fol. 11r.
181. For instance, Cazelles, *Lady as Saint*; Miles, *Carnal Knowing*.
182. Bestul, *Texts of the Passion*, pp. 145–64, esp. pp. 159–60.
183. Carrasco, "An Early Illustrated Manuscript of the Passion of St. Agatha," pp. 27–31.
184. *Passio Julianae*, ed. Bollandus, p. 877. On Roman-era judicial torture, see Peters, *Torture*, pp. 22–27 and 35–36.
185. For instance, the full passion narrative of Juliana sentenced her to be burned alive (*Passio Julianae*, ed. Bollandus, p. 878), but the abbreviation just sentenced her to be burned.
186. Easton, "St. Agatha," p. 97.
187. *Passio Julianae*, ed. Bollandus, p. 878.
188. Reames, "Recent Discovery," pp. 343–44. The overwhelming majority of the manuscripts of the full *passio*, and those of the "Franciscan" abbreviation, read "consecrarem" ("I [Cecilia] will consecrate"), but the two early modern editions of the *passio*, and the Golden Legend version, gave "consecrares" ("You [Urban] will consecrate"), a reflection of clerical opposition to sacramental ambitions among the laity.
189. Hofhansl, "Gewänder, Liturgische," p. 163.
190. Schulenburg, *Forgetful of Their Sex*, p. 1.
191. Apostolorum comes, martirum consors, particeps patriarcharum, social angelorum (fol. 10v).
192. "Unus deus, una fides, unum baptizmum (corrected to baptizmam), unus deus et pater omnium, qui supra omnia et in omnibus nobis" (Würzburg UB M.p.th.q. 28b fol. 6v).
193. Aldhelm, *Prose Works*, trans. Lapidge and Herren, ch. 40. It is possible that this text was referenced on the Basel catalogue and available at Kitzingen, perhaps as the current Cambridge University Library Add. 4219; this copy of the treatise, unlike the many known to have been copied and used by men, had no glosses (CLA 2:135; Aldhelm, *Prosa de virginitate,* ed. Gwara, pp. 83*–85*; Lifshitz, "Priestly Women, Virginal Men").
194. Hamburger and Suckale, "Zwischen Diesseits und Jenseits," p. 26; Blamires, *The Case for Women*, p. 9.

7. "AN ETERNAL WEIGHT OF GLORY" (2 CORINTHIANS 4:17)

1. Boretius, ed., *Capitularia regum Francorum* I no. 12, Capitulary of Soissons 744 c. 3, pp. 28–30, and Concilium Germanicum 742 no. 10, pp. 24–26.
2. Schipperges, *Bonifatius ac socii eius*, p. 201.
3. Hochstetler, *Conflict of Traditions*, p. 118; Rudge, "Texts and Contexts," pp. 128–36; César d'Arles, *Oeuvres monastiques*, 1:129–41 and 192.
4. Helvétius, "L'organization des monastères féminins," pp. 153 and 169.
5. Dey, "Bringing Chaos out of Order," pp. 20–24 and 28–29; Diem, "Inventing the Holy Rule," pp. 53–55.
6. Hochstetler, *Conflict of Traditions*, pp. 149 and 159–62.
7. Hochstetler, *Conflict of Traditions*, p. 159; Häussling, *Mönchskonvent und Eucharistiefeier*, pp. 73–84 and 114–73; Semmler, "Le monachisme occidentale."
8. Mériaux, *Gallia irradiata*, pp. 137–42; Jordan, "Gender Concerns," pp. 62–69.
9. Kelly, "The Rule of Patrick."

10. Rudge, "Texts and Contexts," p. 12; Rudge, "Dedicated Women," p. 113.

11. Rudge, "Texts and Contexts," p. 128; Diem, "Inventing the Holy Rule," p. 57.

12. The florilegium was heavily annotated (with as yet undeciphered Latin dry point glosses), demonstrating that it was frequently consulted, as any rule or rule-equivalent might well be (Chapter Three).

13. The statistic for Isidore's use of Jerome is my calculation based on citations in the text as edited and annotated in Isidore, *Synonyma,* ed. Elfassi; for citations to Isidore in the *Liber Scintillarum,* see Elfassi, "Defensor de Ligugé."

14. Munich, BSB CLM 6433; Isidore, *Synonyma,* ed. Elfassi, p. xxxviii; "Freisinger Florilegium," ed. Lehner, *Florilegia.*

15. Karlsruhe, Badische Landesbibliothek, Augiensis CXCVI (Isidore, *Synonyma,* ed. Elfassi, p. xlv).

16. Udine, Biblioteca Arcivescovile e Bartolina 4; Isidore, *Synonyma,* ed. Elfassi, p. lvii.

17. Isidore, *Synonyma,* ed. Elfassi, p. li; Büll, *Das Monasterium Suuarzaha,* pp. 357–60; Elfassi, Les *Synonyma* d'Isidore de Séville: édition critique et histoire du texte," pp. 41, 160, 249; and 637–38; Litschel, ed., *900 Jahre Klosterkirche Lambach,* I.22. It is possible that the two ninth-century texts (recension Φ of the *Synonyms* and the collection of monastic rules) were not fused until a later date.

18. "For this slight momentary affliction is preparing for us an eternal weight of glory beyond all comparison" (2 Corinthians 4:17), cited in Isidore, *Synonyma,* I. 27.

19. Di Sciacca, "Isidorian Scholarship," pp. 77–78, 80, 99–100, and 102; Hussey, "*Transmarinis litteris,*" pp. 148, 150, and 155.

20. Di Sciacca, *Finding the Right Words,* pp. 51–52 and 68–69; Hussey, "*Transmarinis litteris,*" p. 155.

21. *LSK,* p. 96; Di Sciacca, *Finding the Right Words,* pp. 72–76; Hussey, "The Franco-Saxon *Synonyma,*" pp. 237–38; Hussey, "*Transmarinis litteris,*" pp. 141–42, 155–56, and 168; Hussey, "Ascetics and Aesthetics," pp. 38–40 and 53–74; Elfassi, Les *Synonyma* d'Isidore de Séville: édition critique et histoire du texte," pp. 13–123 and 643–834; Elfassi, "Trois aspects inattendus," p. 109.

22. Di Sciacca, *Finding the Right Words,* p. 75.

23. Beeson, *Isidor-Studien,* pp. 52–58; Elfassi, Les *Synonyma* d'Isidore de Séville: édition critique et histoire du texte," pp. 7–9. The "associated" eighth-century manuscript is Munich, BSB Clm. 6433 (see note 14), and the "extraneous" eighth-century manuscripts are Munich, BSB Clm. 14830, Paris, BN lat. 13396, and St. Gallen, SB 194. This statistic excludes two seventh- or very early eighth-century copies: Paris, BN lat. 14086, and St. Gallen SB 226 + Zürich, Zentralbibliothek fragment RP 5–6 (Hussey, "*Transmarinis litteris,*" p. 155).

24. Becht-Jördens, "Heiliger und Buch"; Von Padberg and Stork, *Der Ragyndrudis-Codex,* pp. 27–34; Hussey, "The Franco-Saxon *Synonyma,*" pp. 229 and 237–38; Isidore, *Synonyma,* ed. Elfassi, pp. xxviii–xxix; Chapter Three.

25. Basel, Öffentliche Universitätsbibliothek F.III. 15c (Isidore, *Synonyma,* ed. Elfassi, pp. xxvi–xxvii).

26. Fulda, Hessische Landesbibliothek D1 fols. 133–134v (Elfassi, "Trois aspects inattendus," p. 110, n. 6).

27. Now split between New York, Columbia University Library, Plimpton 129, and New York, Morgan Library, M. 559 (Hussey, "*Transmarinis litteris,*" p. 146; Isidore, *Synonyma,* ed. Elfassi, p. lviii).

28. Isidore, *Synonyma*, ed. Elfassi, pp. xliii–xliv; Di Sciacca, "Isidorian Scholarship," p. 93 and Appendix; Hussey, "The Franco-Saxon *Synonyma*," p. 227; Di Sciacca, *Finding the Right Words*, p. 68.

29. Würzburg, UB M.p.th.q. 28a (Isidore, *Synonyma*, ed. Elfassi, pp. xlii–xliii; Chapter Three).

30. Würzburg, UB M.p.th.q. 28b codex 3 (Isidore, *Synonyma*, ed. Elfassi, pp. xliv–xlv; Chapter Three).

31. Hussey, "Ascetics and Aesthetics," p. 135. The passionate lyricism and beauty of the text are still appreciated in the twenty-first century by those living out monastic vocations, such as Isidore's Castilian translator, Antonio Viñayo González, abbot and prior of San Isidoro de León (Isidoro, *Sinónimos*, trans. Viñayo González, pp. 25–29 and 37–39).

32. Peyroux, "Abbess and Cloister," pp. 111–55.

33. Isidore, *DEO* II.16 (15).17, ed. Lawson, p. 79. For the reception of this text in the Anglo-Saxon cultural zone in Francia, see Chapter Eight.

34. Peyroux, "Abbess and Cloister," pp. 119–23 and 126.

35. In *De ecclesiasticis officiis*, Isidore summed up his chapter concerning the lifestyles of monks and nuns thus: "*Coenobia* of virgins and monks seem to maintain these customs, this life, this institution" (Isidore, *DEO* II.16 (15).17, ed. Lawson, p. 79; Isidore, *DEO*, trans. Knoebel, p. 89).

36. Elfassi, "Les *Synonyma* d'Isidore de Séville," p. 188; Hussey, "Ascetics and Aesthetics," pp. 18–20.

37. Elfassi, "Genèse et Originalité du Style Synonymique," pp. 235–37; Elfassi, "Les *Synonyma* d'Isidore de Séville," pp. 173, 175, 185–86, 188, and 196–97; Elfassi, "Trois Aspects Inattendus," pp. 150–51.

38. Elfassi, "Les *Synonyma* d'Isidore de Séville," p. 172; Elfassi, "Genèse et Originalité du Style Synonymique," pp. 232 and 245.

39. Elfassi, "Les *Synonyma* d'Isidore de Séville," p. 173; Elfassi, "Genèse et Originalité du Style Synonymique," p. 232.

40. "Anima mea in angustiis est, spiritus meus aestuat, cor meum fluctuat. Angustia animi possidet me, angustia animi adfligit me. Circumdatus sum enim malis, circumseptus aerumnis, circumclusus adversis, obsitus miseriis, opertus infelicitate, oppressus angustiis. Non reperio uspiam tanti mali perfugium . . ." (Isidore, *Synonyma*, I. 5, ed. Elfassi, p. 6; cf. PL 83:474–75). All English translations of the text are my own.

41. Elfassi, "Genèse et Originalité du Style Synonymique," pp. 238 and 241.

42. Banniard, *Viva Voce*, pp. 217, 224–34, and 248; Elfassi, "La Langue des *Synonyma* d'Isidore," p. 96.

43. Diem, *Das Monastische Experiment*, p. 62.

44. "Sanctae recordationis Isidorus, archiepiscopus ex Hispania, introducit personam hominis in aerumnis praesentis saeculi sese deflentis . . . cui mirabili concursu ratio obvians, leni hunc moderamine consolatur. . . . Quisquis intenta mente lector nititur pergere, sine dubio repperiet quo pacto caveat vitia, quomodo defleat peccata commissa, qualiterque per lamenta paenitentiae reparatus . . . ut non cum mundi concupiscentiis pereat, sed aeternis praemiis remuneratus vivat cum Christo" (Isidore, *Synonyma*, ed. Elfassi, pp. 3–4; cf. PL 83, pp. 472–73). The Karlburg and Kitzingen copies shared the unique (and clearly erroneous) variant reading "penitentia" rather than "paenitentiae" (Würzburg, UB M.p.th. 28b fol. 43r; Würzburg, UB M.p.th.q. 28a fol. 1r).

45. Isidoro, *Sinónimos*, trans. Viñayo González, pp. 31–32.

46. See Chapter Three and Chapter Five.

47. Instead of "introducit personam hominis. . . . cui mirabili concursu ratio obvians, leni hunc moderamine consolatur," the scribes of both the Ragyndrudis codex (Fulda, Dommuseum Bonifatianus 2) and Würzburg UB M.p.th.q. 28b omitted "hunc" (Isidore, *Synonyma*, ed. Elfassi, p. 3). This same scribe omitted the first sentence ("Isidorus lectori salutem") from Isidore's own Prologue 2, de-emphasizing the masculinity of both the author and the reader (Isidore, *Synonyma*, ed. Elfassi, p. 5).

48. "Moreover two characters are here introduced, a violently weeping human being, and admonishing reason" (Isidore, *Synonyma*, ed. Elfassi, p. 5; cf. PL 83: 474).

49. For example: a fifth-century glyptic on the front cover of a book in the Milan cathedral treasury (Volbach, *Early Christian Art*, p. 330, plate 100) and several sixth-century items from Ravenna, including the Throne of Maximian in the Museo Arcivescovile, sanctuary mosaics in the church of San Vitale, and the sarcophagus of Honorius in the Mausoleum of Galla Placidia (Bovini, *Il cosidetto Mausoleo di Galla Placidia*, figs. 63–64, p. 102).

50. *DACL* I.2: 3202, fig. 1145.

51. *DACL* 2.1, fig. 1690.

52. Klein-Pfeuffer, "Christliche Glaubensvorstellung," pp. 140–41.

53. Sepière, *L'image d'un dieu souffrant*, plate V; Zimmermann, *Vorkarolingische Miniaturen*, Table 144a; Martinet, "Les manuscrits de Sainte-Marie-Saint-Jean de Laon," figure 82; Gaillard, "De *l'Eigenkloster* au monastère royal," pp. 249 and 262.

54. Martinet, "Les manuscrits de Sainte-Marie-Saint-Jean de Laon," pp. 270–71.

55. Ziegler, "Das 'Sacramentarium Gelasianum,'" pp. 64–65 and 85–91.

56. Isidoro, *Sinónimos*, trans. Viñayo González, p. 34.

57. "Nihil mihi te carius, nihil mihi te dulcius. Tu mihi supra vita mea places" or "nothing is dearer to me than you, nothing is sweeter to me than you. You please me beyond even my own life" (Isidore, *Synonyma* II.103, ed. Elfassi, p. 147).

58. "Ubicumque fugero, mala mea me insequuntur; ubicumque me convertero, malorum meorum me umbra comitatur. Velut umbram corporis, sic mala mea fugere non possum. . . . nulli unquam malum feci, nulli calumniatus sum, nulli adversus extiti, nulli molestiam intuli. . . . sine ulla querela apud homines vixi. . . ." (Isidore, *Synonyma* I.6, ed. Elfassi, pp. 6–7; cf. PL 83:475).

59. Di Sciacca, *Finding the Right Words*, p. 18; Von Padberg and Stork, *Der Ragyndrudis Codex*, pp. 74 and 125. The device sometimes appeared in copies of the Λ recension as well, above all, those in the Anglo-Saxon tradition. The PL edition obliterated this aspect of the text (Isidore, *Synonyma*, ed. Elfassi, pp. cxxiv–cxxv and cxxviii).

60. Isidore, *Synonyma*, I.5, ed. Elfassi, p. 6; cf. PL 83:474–75. For the Latin, see note 40.

61. Hussey, "*Transmarinis litteris*," p. 143.

62. Theatrical performances in connection with the liturgies of the saints were common in Italy, Spain, and Gaul during the early Middle Ages (Dunn, *The Gallican Saint's Life*).

63. Isidore, *Synonyma* I.7–21, ed. Elfassi, pp. 7–18; cf. PL 83:475ff.

64. "Cui credam? Cui fidem habeam?" (Würzburg, UB M.p.th.q. 28b fol. 44v), as opposed to "Cui credas? cui fidem habeas?" (Isidore, *Synonyma* I.7, ed. Elfassi, p. 8, cf. PL 83:475).

65. "Omnes in me saeviunt, omnes in exitio meo intendunt, omnes in mortem meam manus suas praeparant" (Isidore, *Synonyma* I.14, ed. Elfassi, p. 13; cf. PL 83:478).

66. The scribe of the Karlburg copy made more use of colored highlighting through this section than elsewhere, for instance in the polychrome "Oportet" in "Oportet nos per multas tribulationes introire in regnum Dei" or "It is fitting that we enter the kingdom of God through many tribulations" (Acts 14:21; quoted in Isidore, *Synonyma* I.27, ed. Elfassi, pp. 22–23; Würzburg M.p.th.q. 28a fol. 8v). Furthermore, although the two recensions (Λ and Φ) diverged substantially from one another in chapter I.26, scribes at Karlburg and Kitzingen somehow managed to include both sets of readings in their copies (folios 8r and 48r respectively), indicating the importance attached to this section of the text.

67. "Non sunt condignae passiones huius temporis ad futuram gloriam" (Romans 8:18); "Quod in praesenti est, momentaneum est et leve tribulationis in nobis; quod aeternum est, supra modum est pondus excellens gloriae" (2 Corinthians 4:17).

68. Isidore, *Synonyma* I.28, ed. Elfassi, p. 24. For the concept of "*probatio*," see Elliott, *Proving Woman*.

69. "Sagittis tuis confoderis, telis tuis vulneraris" (Isidore, *Synonyma* I. 33, ed. Elfassi, p. 28).

70. Isidore, *Synonyma* I.46, ed. Elfassi, p. 38.

71. "Versetur etiam ante oculos tuos imago futuri iudicii" (Isidore, *Synonyma* I.47, ed. Elfassi, p. 38).

72. "Per paenitentiam delicta omnia absterguntur" (Isidore, *Synonyma* I.54, ed. Elfassi, p. 44).

73. "Errorem confiteor, culpam agnosco . . . adtende vocem precantis, audi vocem peccatoris clamantis . . . peccavi, Deus, miserere mei" (Isidore, *Synonyma* I.70–71, ed. Elfassi, p. 56).

74. "Peccata tua Deus a te suspendat" (Isidore, *Synonyma* I.75, ed. Elfassi, p. 61).

75. Compare "Why was I, this wretched one, even born? Why was I thrust into this miserable life?" ("Cur infelix natus sum? Cur in hanc miseram vitam proiectus sum?") with "It would have been better had I not been born, it would have been better had I not been conceived" ("Melius mihi fuerat non esse ortum, melius non fuisse genitum . . .") (Isidore, *Synonyma* I.19 and I.65, ed. Elfassi, pp. 17 and 52).

76. "Qui enim perseveraverit usque in finem, hic salvus erit" (Isidore, *Synonyma* I.78, ed. Elfassi, p. 62).

77. Würzburg UB M.p.th.q. 28b fol. 60v.

78. On the use of two apparently contradictory animals to symbolize Christ in a single image, see Wehrhahn-Stauch, "Christliche Fischsymbolik," p. 4.

79. Isidore, *Synonyma* II.2–7, ed. Elfassi, pp. 63–68.

80. "Cor tuum cotidie discute, cor tuum cotidie examine, privata examinatione occultorum tuorum discute latebras," or "Examine your heart daily, test your heart daily, examine with a private examination the hiding places of your secrets" (Isidore, *Synonyma* II.5, ed. Elfassi, p. 66).

81. McNamer, *Affective Meditation*.

82. Hussey, "Ascetics and Aesthetics," pp. 27–28, 141–44, 181–209, and 214–24, at p. 189. The Book of Cerne is Cambridge, University Library L1.1.10.

83. Isidore, *Synonyma* I.58, ed. Elfassi, pp. 47–48.

84. Isidore, *Synonyma* I.67, ed. Elfassi, pp. 53–54.

85. Pseudo-Bede, Penitential, Chapter 9, ed. Wasserschleben, *Die Bussordnungen*, from Vienna ÖNB 2223, fols. 20v–21r; Chapter Three.

86. Muschiol, *Famula Dei*, pp. 222–37 and 249–63.

87. Diem, "Das Ende des monastischen Experiments," pp. 82–86, 92–95, and 119–21.

88. Mordek, *Kirchenrecht und Reform*, pp. 196–97; Frantzen, "The Significance of the Frankish Penitentials," p. 417.

89. Kerff, "Mittelalterliche Quellen"; compare Haggenmüller, "Frühmittelalterliche Bußbücher."

90. Meens, "Frequency and Nature," pp. 55–61.

91. Pseudo-Bede, Penitential, Chapter 1, ed. Wasserschleben, *Die Bussordnungen*, p. 220; Vienna ÖNB 2223, fol. 17v.

92. Di Sciacca, *Finding the Right Words*, p. 18. On the penitential Psalms (6, 31, 37, 50, 101, 129, and 142), see Driscoll, "The Seven Penitential Psalms."

93. Black, "Psalm Uses in Carolingian Prayerbooks," pp. 1–3, 20–21, 33, and 50–53.

94. Elfassi, "Les *Synonyma* d'Isidore de Séville: édition critique et histoire du texte," pp. 689 and 834.

95. Price, "Informal Penance," pp. 29–33.

96. Price, "Informal Penance," p. 35.

97. Price, "Informal Penance," p. 37.

98. Morrison, "'Know Thyself,'" pp. 378 and 451.

99. Morrison, "'Know Thyself,'" pp. 452–54.

100. Isidore, *Synonyma*, ed.Elfassi, p. 75.

101. Pilsworth, "Miracles, Missionaries and Manuscripts," pp. 67–68, 73, and 75; Chapter Three.

102. For instance, "pacem ama, pacem dilige, pacem cum omnibus retine" or "love peace, value peace, keep peace with everyone" (Isidore, *Synonyma* II.38, ed. Elfassi, p. 92); Di Sciacca, *Finding the Right Words*, pp. 19 and 29–31.

103. For instance, "Cave autem gloriam popularem. Vita admirationem vulgi" or "Beware however of popular glory. Avoid the admiration of the masses" (Isidore, *Synonyma* II.42, ed. Elfassi, p. 95). Additional points included the advice not to carry out wicked commands (II.75, ed. Elfassi, pp. 124–25), to strive to be venerated rather than feared by one's subjects (II.76, ed. Elfassi, p. 126), to render just and fair judgments and observe proper judicial procedure (II. 82–II. 86, ed. Elfassi, pp. 129–34). A sliver of this final section was included in the codex and probably reflected the quire divisions of the exemplar; the decision to halt the copying was likely made in the thick of things, as the scriptorial team gathered what would lie ahead, were they to continue full copying.

104. Isidore, *Synonyma* II.10–II.18, ed. Elfassi, pp. 70–75. The word *libido* appeared sixteen times in these nine chapters.

105. Isidore, *Synonyma* II.19–24, ed. Elfassi, pp. 76–82.The Kitzingen copy currently lacks these and all subsequent chapters.

106. Isidore, *Synonyma* II.25–26, ed. Elfassi, pp. 81–82.

107. "Propter Deum ergo renuntia omnia" (Isidore, *Synonyma* II.94, ed. Elfassi, p. 140, taking the variant reading of the Karlburg copy). Similarly: "Contemne vivens quae post mortem habere non potes" or "despise while alive those things you do not want to have after death" (Isidore, *Synonyma* II.95, ed. Elfassi, p. 141), and a chapter devoted to the theme of humility (II.87, ed. Elfassi, pp. 134–35).

108. Isidore, *Synonyma* II.101–2, ed. Elfassi, pp. 145–47.

109. "Tace usquequo interrogeris, non loquaris nisi interrogatus, non dicas priusquam audias, interrogatio os tuum aperiat. Sint verba tua pauca, tolle verbositatem sermonis

superflui, loquendi modum non excedas, ne inmoderatione linguae incurras periculum" or "Keep silent until you are asked, do not speak unless you are interrogated, do not say anything before you hear something, questioning should open your mouth. Let your words be few, destroy the verbosity of superfluous speech, do not exceed moderation in speaking, do not run the risk of an unmoderated tongue" (Isidore, *Synonyma* II.49, ed. Elfassi, pp. 102–3).

110. It also happens to be missing from the Kitzingen copy in its current state.

111. "Mens enim per oculos capitur" (Isidore, *Synonyma* II. 16, ed. Elfassi, p. 74).

112. Isidore, *Synonyma* II.20–23 and II.87, ed. Elfassi, pp. 77–80 and 134–35.

113. Isidore, *Synonyma* II.88–89 and 91–93, ed. Elfassi, pp. 135–37 and 138–40; *Passio Eugeniae*, Würzburg UB M.p.th.q. 28a, folios 45v and 47r–48v (Eugenia's *ministerium* and her rejection of wealth); *Passio Potiti*, Würzburg UB M.p.th.q. 28a, folios 65v–66r and 69v (Potitus's rejection of money).

114. Ninth-century examples included Chartres BM 106, Munich BSB Clm. 15817, Trier, Stadtbibliothek 137, Valenciennes BM 173, and Würzburg UB M.p.th.f. 33. A 1376 catalogue from the double monastery of Admont listed a now-lost copy of the *Synonyms* combined with *vitae* of Martial, Januarius, and Felicitas (Elfassi, "Les *Synonyma* d'Isidore de Séville: édition critique et histoire du texte," pp. 648–49).

115. Isidore, *Synonyma* I.66 and II.22, ed. Elfassi, pp. 52–53 and 78–79 (both in the Karlburg codex).

116. Isidore, *Synonyma* I.67, ed. Elfassi, pp. 53–54.

117. *Passio Eugeniae*, Würzburg UB M.p.th.q. 28a fol. 62r; PL 73:620; Cross, "*Passio S. Eugeniae*," p. 397.

118. Wittig, "Figural Narrative."

119. "And so Jesus also suffered outside the city gate to make the people holy through his own blood. Let us, then, go to him outside the camp, bearing the disgrace he bore" (Hebrews 13:12–13); Bouhlol, "Rome, cité sainte?" pp. 152–53.

120. Vitz, "Gender and Martyrdom," p. 79.

121. *Passio Potiti*, Würzburg UB M.p.th.q. 28a, fols. 65v–66r and 69v.

122. "In Christi nomine incipit passio sancti Potiti qui sub Antonino imperatore et Gelasio preside passus est" (*Passio Potiti*, Würzburg UB M.p.th.q. 28a, fol. 63r).

123. *Passio Potiti*, Würzburg UB M.p.th.q. 28a, fols. 63r and 66v–70v.

124. *Passio Potiti*, Würzburg UB M.p.th.q. 28a, fols.65r–66r.

125. "Magnum refrigerium" (*Passio Potiti*, Würzburg UB M.p.th.q. 28a, fol. 69r). Additional examples included his expression of desire for torture (fol. 66v), his expression of gratitude for being tortured (fol. 67v), and his request to increase the level of torture (fol. 68r).

126. *Passio Potiti*, Würzburg UB M.p.th.q. 28a, fols. 63v, 68r, and 69r.

127. Rinaldi, "Un Travestimento Agiografico," p. 70.

128. For the popularity of the saint and her cult during the eighth century, particularly in the Anglo-Saxon syneisactic circles, including examples of women who used the name Eugenia, see *Passio Eugeniae*, Würzburg UB M.p.th.q. 28a, fol. 62v; PL 73: 620; Aldhelm, *Prosa de Virginitate*, ed. Ehwald, pp. 297–98; Aldhelm, *Carmen de Virginitate*, ed. Ehwald, p. 431; Costambeys and Leyser, "To Be the Neighbour of St. Stephen," p. 274; Gordini, "Eugenia"; Scheck, *Reform and Resistance*, pp. 62–63; Schreiner, "Kopistinnen," pp. 42–45.

129. Chapter Two.

130. For instance, when Potitus was tortured in the Roman amphitheater, 30,000 spectators cried out, "O quae infantia talis poenis securus potest tolerare" or "Oh, what childhood can safely tolerate such great punishments" (*Passio Potiti*, Würzburg UB M.p.th.q. 28a, fol. 68v; ed. Giuffre, p. 36, with the variant "tantis poenis").

131. Clemens, *Tempore Romanorum constructa*, p. 87.

132. This portion of the narrative was (incompletely) erased at some later date, and still remains somewhat legible (Chapter Three).

133. *Passio Eugeniae*, Würzburg UB M.p.th.q. 28a, fols. 37r *rasa*–38v; PL 73:607.

134. *Passio Eugeniae*, Würzburg UB M.p.th.q.28a, fols. 37v–38r (*partim rasa*), 41r–42v, and 45v; PL 73:607–9 and 611.

135. *Passio Eugeniae*, Würzburg UB M.p.th.q. 28a, fols. 47v–52v; PL 73:612–14.

136. *Passio Eugeniae*, Würzburg UB M.p.th.q. 28a, fols. 56v–62r; PL 73:616–20 (filling in the missing folio between 61 and 62 from PL 73:619–20).

137. *Passio Eugeniae*, Würzburg UB M.p.th.q. 28a, fol. 47r; PL 73:612.

138. *Passio Eugeniae*, Würzburg UB M.p.th.q. 28a, fol. 45v; PL 73:611.

139. *Passio Eugeniae*, Würzburg UB M.p.th.q. 28a, fol. 45v; PL 73:611 gives "mirabilis."

140. "Victricem libidinum omnis pollutionis" (*Passio Eugeniae*, Würzburg UB M.p.th.q. 28a, fol. 53v; PL 73:614–15).

141. Isidore, *Synonyma* II.10–18, ed. Elfassi, pp. 70–75.

142. Quotations from Isidore, *Synonyma* II.8–10, ed. Elfassi, pp. 68–70.

143. Pilsworth, "Miracles, Missionaries and Manuscripts," p. 76; Rudolf of Fulda, *Vita Leobae*, ch. 12.

144. Chapters 2, 9, and 10 of the *Discipulus Umbrensium* version of the penitential by Theodore of Canterbury prescribed penances for frequent sex of a man with a man, frequent sex of a woman with a woman, occasional sex of a man with a boy, the unfulfilled desire of a man for sex with a boy, sex between two brothers, and so on (Vienna 2223, fols. 2r–3r and 5v–6v, also available in Würzburg, UB MS M.p.th.q. 32 fols. 3r–4r). Chapter 10 of the Penitential of Pseudo-Bede tariffed sexual relations both between two laywomen and between two nuns "per machinam," and Chapter 10 of the *Capitula iudiciorum* penitential was almost entirely devoted to male–male same-sex relations (Vienna 2223, fols. 18v and 28r). Furthermore, dozens of ninth-century vernacular enumerations of sins designed for group recitation (in monasteries, public churches, or both) mentioned sodomy and self-gratification; the texts reflected confessional practices going back into the eighth century (Steinmeyer, *Die Kleineren Althochdeutschen Sprachdenkmäler*, pp. 309–64, especially no. xliv. pp. 316–18, the "Würzburg Confession"; Bostock, *Handbook*, pp. 155–57).

145. The Council of Riesbach (799–800) prohibited *sanctaemoniales* from wearing male tunics or trousers and required them to wear women's clothing (Schulenburg, *Forgetful of Their Sex*, p. 163).

146. Würzburg, UB M.p.th.f. 146, fols. 36v–39r; Weiner, *Initialornamentik*, table 140.2; Chapter One.

147. Davis, *The Cult of Saint Thecla*, pp. vi and 141–48 (quotes at p. 143); Hotchkiss, *Clothes Make the Man*, pp. 14 and 134.

148. Dufourcq, *Étude*, 1:300 and 2:112; Hotchkiss, *Clothes Make the Man*, p. 16; Anson, "The Female Transvestite"; Lowerre, "To Rise beyond Their Sex," pp. 55, 63, and 88.

149. Bodarwé, "Ein Spinnennetz," pp. 46–47.

150. Schulenburg, *Forgetful of Their Sex,* pp. 158–59.

151. In a discussion based entirely on Jacobus de Voragine's *Legenda aurea* (c. 1265), Lochrie noted that such texts "raise the possibility that lust is no respecter of gender" (Lochrie, "Between Women," pp. 84 and 86). Bernau noted the homoerotic charge in the Eugenia–Melantia scene but opened up transvestite saints to such a diffuse reading ("the transvestite saint is a figure who arouses desire from all sides") that she ignored the specifically lesbian desire actually dramatized (Bernau, "The Translation of Purity," pp. 26 and 29).

152. Brooten, *Love between Women,* pp. 11, 189, 195, and 213–16.

153. Ivanov and Pichkhadze, "Eupraxia of Olympus" p. 33; Hotchkiss, *Clothes Make the Man,* pp. 131–41.

154. Hotchkiss, *Clothes Make the Man,* pp. 3, 12, 25, and 128.

155. Scheck, *Reform and Resistance,* pp. 73–96.

156. Stofferahn, "Changing Views," pp. 84–85, in reference to Düsseldorf, Universitäts- und Landesbibliothek B3, an early ninth-century manuscript from the "a-b" scriptorium of nuns connected with Corbie, owned by the women's house of Essen by 900 (Bodarwé, "Ein Spinnennetz," pp. 46–47).

157. Roy, "A Virgin Acts Manfully," p. 8.

158. *Passio Eugeniae,* Würzburg UB M.p.th.q. 28a, fols. 52v–53r.

159. Roy, "A Virgin Acts Manfully," p. 11.

160. Roy, "A Virgin Acts Manfully," p. 17.

161. *Passio Eugeniae,* Würzburg UB M.p.th.q. 28a, fol. 53r. The quotation followed the Vulgate text of Matthew 28:2–7, with the modification that the angel told the women, "I will go before you into Galilee" ("praecedam vos in Galileam") rather than "he [Jesus] will go before you into Galilee" ("praecedit vos in Galileam"). The hand of the addition was early Carolingian minuscule; it is therefore uncertain whether the negative text was erased late in the century and immediately replaced with a positive citation, or erased early on and later replaced with a positive citation. The entire process was probably completed while the codex was still at Karlburg, for the Matthew citation in the Karlburg Isidore did not match the Matthew citation in the Kitzingen "Deus per angelum" *libellus* (Würzburg UB M.p.th.q. 28b, fol. 21v); the two scribes thus appear to have used two different Gospel books.

162. *Passio Eugeniae,* Würzburg UB M.p.th.q. 28a, fol. 39r; PL 73:607.

163. *Passio Eugeniae,* Würzburg UB M.p.th.q. 28a, fol. 44r; PL 73:610.

164. *Passio Eugeniae,* Würzburg UB M.p.th.q. 28a, fol. 46v; PL 73:611.

165. "For all of you who were baptized into Christ have clothed yourselves with Christ; there is neither Jew nor Greek, slave nor free, male nor female, for you are all one in Christ Jesus" (Galatians 3:27–28); Chapter Four.

166. After deciding for her slaves that they would convert with and accompany her, Eugenia said, "Let's tonsure my hair so that we won't under any circumstances be separated" (*Passio Eugeniae,* Würzburg UB M.p.th.q. 28a, fol. 39r). This passage was not in the PL version of the text.

167. *Passio Eugeniae,* Würzburg UB M.p.th.q. 28a, fols. 39r–39v; PL 73:607–8 (as "herili habitu").

168. *Passio Eugeniae,* Würzburg UB M.p.th.q. 28a, fols. 42r–42v; PL 73:609.

169. *Passio Eugeniae,* Würzburg UB M.p.th.q. 28a, fols. 45v and 53v; PL 73: 611 and 614.

170. *Passio Eugeniae*, Würzburg UB M.p.th.q. 28a, fol. 56v; PL 73: 616 (with no mention of the church).

171. *Passio Eugeniae*, Würzburg UB M.p.th.q. 28a, fols. 54r–54v; PL 73:615.

172. *Passio Eugeniae*, Würzburg UB M.p.th.q. 28a, fol. 53v; PL 73:615.

173. *Passio Eugeniae*, Würzburg UB M.p.th.q. 28a, fol. 58r; PL 73:617.

174. *Passio Eugeniae*, Würzburg UB M.p.th.q. 28a, fol. 58r.

175. *Passio Eugeniae*, Würzburg UB M.p.th.q. 28a, fols. 60r–61r; PL 73:618–19.

176. *Passio Eugeniae*, Würzburg UB M.p.th.q. 28a, fols. 58r–59v and 61v; PL 73:617–19.

177. De Nie, " 'Consciousness Fecund through God.' "

178. PL 73:620.

179. *Passio Eugeniae*, Würzburg UB M.p.th.q. 28a, fol. 62r (*partim deperdita*); PL 73:620.

180. Defensor, *Liber Scintillarum*, ed. Rochais, pp. 254–55.

181. Defensor, *Liber Scintillarum*, ed. Rochais, pp. 245–54.

182. Hamesse, "A Propos de quelques Techniques," pp. 23–24.

183. Leyser, "Shoring Fragments."

184. Fransen, "D'Eugippius à Bède," pp. 188–89.

185. Leyser, "Shoring Fragments."

186. Leyser, "Shoring Fragments."

187. Uthemann, "Ein Griechisches Florileg"; Cameron, "Social Language." p. 117.

188. Neil, "Towards Defining a Christian Culture," pp. 333–34.

189. Stofferahn, "Changing Views," pp. 79–82 and 85–86.

190. Elfassi, "Trois Aspects Inattendus," pp. 150–51; Elfassi, "Defensor de Ligugé," pp. 243–45. The *Liber Scintillarum* represented the first major use of the *Synonyms*, by a compiler who had access to both recensions of Isidore's text (Elfassi, "Trois Aspects Inattendus," p. 110; Elfassi, "Defensor de Ligugé," pp. 246–47). Elfassi found this puzzling, for he considered it unlikely that anyone could have had access to two different recensions of Isidore's treatise as early as c. 700, the traditional date of composition for the florilegium; however, if I am correct concerning the original composition of the text (see Chapter Three), this aspect of the compilation would be far less puzzling.

191. "Spiritus est qui vivificat; caro non prodest quicquam" (Defensor, *Liber Scintillarum* 53.1, ed. Rochais, p. 176; Würzburg UB M.p.th.f. 13 fol. 40r).

192. See Chapter Two, Chapter Three, and Chapter Five.

193. "Nihil prodest carnem habere virginem, si mente quis nupserit," or "It does no good to have virgin flesh, if someone is married in the mind"; "Nihil prodest virginitas corporis, ubi operatur corruptio mentis," or "Bodily virginity does no good where mental corruption is operative"; "Melius est uxorem ducere quam per libidinis ardorem perire," or "It is better to take a wife than to perish through the ardor of desire"; "Melior est humilis coniugalitas quam superba virginitas," or "Humble conjugality is better than proud virginity" (Defensor, *Liber Scintillarum* 13, ed. Rochais; Würzburg M.p.th.f. 13, fols. 11v–12r).

194. Specifically "Nihil prodest virginitas corporis, ubi operatur corruptio mentis" (Defensor, *Liber Scintillarum* 13.4, ed. Rochais).

195. Hasdenteufel-Röding, "Studien zur Gründung," pp. 57–60.

196. Defensor, *Liber Scintillarum* 73.17 and 73.23, ed. Rochais; Würzburg UB M.p.th.f. 13, fol. 54v; see also Defensor, *Liber Scintillarum* 2.25, ed. Rochais, presumably on the missing first quire of Würzburg UB M.p.th.f. 13.

197. "Vinum enim nobis Dominus ad laeticiam cordis, non ad ebrietatem, donavit," or "For the Lord gave us wine to make our hearts joyful, not for getting drunk" (Defensor, *Liber Scintillarum* 28, ed. Rochais; Würzburg UB M.p.th.f. 13 fol. 23v); Lindner, *Untersuchungen*, pp. 12–15.

198. Penitential of Theodore (*Discipulus Umbrensium* version), chapter 1 (Vienna ÖNB 2223, fol. 2r); Pseudo-Bede, Penitential, ed. Wasserschleben, *Die Bussordnungen*, from Vienna ÖNB 2223, fols. 19v–20r; Fulgentius, *De Fide ad Petrum* Rule 39, ed. Fraipont, in Vienna ÖNB 2223, fol. 72v. For alcohol consumption in women's communities, see Schilp, *Norm und Wirklichkeit*, pp. 76–79.

199. Defensor, *Liber Scintillarum* 6, ed. Rochais.

200. See also Chapter Two.

201. "Tunc enim predicacio utiliter profertur, quando efficaciter adimpletur," or "For that preaching is usefully brought forward, when it is efficaciously fulfilled" (Würzburg UB M.p.th.f. 13, fol. 27v, correctly quoting Isidore, *Sentences* 3.36.2 [PL 83:707], as opposed to "viriliter" in Defensor, *Liber Scintillarum* 32.92, ed. Rochais, p. 132). The other eighth-century manuscripts are St. Gallen SB 124 and Munich BSB Clm 4582.

202. Mälzer and Thurn, *Die Bibliothek*, p. 94 (plate 13).

203. Lifshitz, "Priestly Women, Virginal Men."

204. "Qui corpus suum contenentia dedicant, cum feminis habitare non presumant," and "Melius est uxorem ducere quam per libidinis ardorem perire," or "It is better to take a wife than to perish through the ardor of desire" (Defensor, *Liber Scintillarum* 13.14 and 13.20, ed. Rochais).

205. Defensor, *Liber Scintillarum* 56, ed. Rochais, pp. 181–82; Würzburg, UB M.p.th.f. 13, fols. 41r–41v. Elsewhere the florilegist cited Proverbs 1:8–9: "Hear, my children, the teaching of your father, and do not put away the law of your mother," or "Audi, filii mi, disciplinam patris tui, et ne demittas legem matris tuae" (Würzburg, UB M.p.th.f. 13, fol. 25r, a reading not reflected in Defensor, *Liber Scintillarum* 31.3, ed. Rochais p. 121).

206. For instance, "Non est persona in iudicio consideranda, sed causa," or "The person is not to be considered in a judgment, but the case," and "Causam respicere non personam," or "Look at the case not the person" (Würzburg UB M.p.th.f. 13, fols. 44r–44v; Defensor, *Liber Scintillarum*, ed. Rochais, pp. 190–91; Weiner, *Initialornamentik*, p. 253, plate 53.5).

207. Defensor, *Liber Scintillarum* 13.9, ed. Rochais, quoting Jerome, Letter 79.8.1 to Salvina, in the translation from http://www.ccel.org/ccel/schaff/npnf206.v.LXXIX.html.

208. Dronke, *Women Writers*, p. 36.

209. For more examples, see Lifshitz, "Demonstrating Gun(t)za." The Karlburg scribes were not alone in adjusting the text. For instance, a citation from Jerome that "The man who is strong in grief is no less to be praised than the one who is strong in war" ("Non minus laudandus est vir fortis in luctum quam qui in bellum") was massaged by the scribe of the Zürich copy into the gender-neutral statement "Non minus laudandum est vere fortis in luctum quam in bellum," or "It is not less to be praised to be truly strong in grief than in war" (Defensor, *Liber Scintillarum* 6.9, ed. Rochais, p. 25).

210. Defensor, *Liber Scintillarum*, ed. Rochais, pp. 245–54; Lehmann, ed., *Die Admonitio*; PL 103:683–700.

211. "Sapiens vir non considerat corporis decorem sed animae, insipiens autem in carnalibus se detenet" and "vir prudens ab inprudenti muliere avertit oculos suos" (Defensor, *Liber Scintillarum* 53, ed. Rochais, p. 177; Würzburg UB M.p.th.f. 13, fol. 40r).

212. Defensor, Liber Scintillarum 10.64, 38.43, and 78.48, ed. Rochais, pp. 53, 146, and 226; Diem, *Das Monastische Experiment*, p. 59; Lambach, Stiftsbibliothek 31; Paris, BN lat. 2994A (a women's manuscript); St. Gallen SB 926 and Zürich, Zentralbibliothek Rh. 28 (both labeled as advice for monks).

213. Lehmann, ed., *Die Admonitio*, p. 22.

214. "Reflecte igitur amorem tuum ab amore mulieris, ne te ab amore Dei eius amor excludat. . . . Ab omni pollutione mundum sit cor tuum, et ne des inimico tuo aditum introeundi ad te. . . . Ne inprobo oculo intueris speciem mulierum, ne intret mors in animam tuam per fenestras tuas. Non adcommodes aures tuas ad percipienda verba earum, ne concipias nequitiam in anima tua. Mulieris carnem omnino ne velis tangere . . . qui tangit mulieris carnem, non evadit sine damno animae suae" (Lehmann, ed., *Die Admonitio*, pp. 40–42).

215. Basel, Öffentliche Universitätsbibliothek F.III.15c, fols. 28r–41v.

216. "Spiritus est qui vivificat; caro non prodest quicquam" (Defensor, *Liber Scintillarum* 53.1, ed. Rochais, p. 176; Würzburg UB M.p.th.f. 13, fol. 40r).

217. Angenendt, "'Mit reinen Händen'"; Pomeroy, "Commentary"; De Nie, "Is een vrouw een mens."

218. Diem, *Das monastische Experiment*, p. 114, n. 423, and Appendix, p. 341.

219. Defensor, *Liber Scintillarum*, ed. Rochais, p. vii.

220. "Sicut sol oriens mundo in altissimis Dei, sic mulieris bonae species in ornamentum domus eius" (Würzburg UB M.p. th.f. 13, fol. 19r, correctly quoting Ecclesiasticus 26:21); the edition read: "Sicut sol oriens in altissimis dei, sic mulieres bone species in ornamentis domus eius" (Defensor, *Liber Scintillarum* 21.16, ed. Rochais, p. 96), preferring a corrupt younger manuscript over the correct older Karlburg one.

221. "Pulchritudo diligenda est, filii, quae leticiam spiritalem consuevit infundere. . . . Christus non in corporis sed in animae pulchritudine dilectatur, illa ergo et tu dilige in quibus dilectatur deus" (Defensor, *Liber Scintillarum* 53.3 and 53.5, ed. Rochais, pp. 176–77; Würzburg UB M.p.th.f. 13, fol. 40r).

222. Schulenburg, "Strict Active Enclosure"; Makowski, *Canon Law and Cloistered Women*.

223. "Non vagis oculis, non infreni lingua aut petulanti tumidoque gestu incedant, sed pudorem ac verecundiam mentis simplici habitu incessuque ostendant" (Isidore, *DEO* II.2, ed. Lawson, pp. 53–54; trans. Knoebel, p. 69), just a small part of a long section exacting perfect comportment from men of the cloth (Isidore, *DEO* II.1–II.16, ed. Lawson, pp. 53–79).

224. ". . . mansuetudo, patientia, sobrietas, moderatio, abstinentia, sive pudicitia, ut non solum ab opera se inmundo abstineat sed etiam ab oculi et verbi et cogitationis errore" (Isidore, *DEO* II.5, ed. Lawson, p. 64; trans. Knoebel, p. 77).

225. Würzburg, UB M.p.th.q. 28b codex 2.

226. Karlsruhe, Badische Landesbibliothek 340 (see Chapter 3).

227. For instance, Caesarius's "Vereor" letter to nuns on fighting pride, gluttony, drunkenness, and concupiscence through reading drew almost entirely on texts addressed to monks and priests; it was subsequently rewritten with masculine pronouns but unchanged content (Diem, *Das Monastische Experiment*, p. 168). Caesarius's sermon on the parable of the ten female virgins in Matthew 25:1–23 insisted that the message was intended also for men (Caesarius, Sermon 155, ed. Morin CCSL 104, pp. 632–35).

228. Caesarius, Sermon 233, in *Sermones*, ed. Morin, CCSL 104, p. 930.

229. Penitential of Theodore (*Discipulus Umbrensium* version), chapter 9 (Vienna ÖNB 2223, fol. 6r).

230. Christianson, *Ecclesiastes through the Centuries*, pp. 1–16.

231. Leanza, "I condizionamenti dell'esegesi patristica," p. 38.

232. Christianson, *Ecclesiastes through the Centuries*, pp. 4 and 10.

233. Christiansen, *Ecclesiastes through the Centuries*, p. 104.

234. "Vanitas vanitatum dixit Ecclesiastes, vanitas vanitatum et omnia vanitas" (*Ecclesiastes* 1:2, as quoted in Würzburg UB M.p.th.q. 28b, fol. 38v).

235. "Si cuncta quae fecit Deus valde bona, quomodo omnia vanitas et non solum vanitas verum etiam vanitas vanitatum" (Würzburg UB M.p.th.q. 28b, fol. 38v).

236. Christianson, *Ecclesiastes through the Centuries*, pp. 23 and 26.

237. Christianson, *Ecclesiastes through the Centuries*, pp. 101–2 and 104.

238. Jerome, *Commentarius in Ecclesiasten*, ed. Adriaen, p. 249.

239. "Possumus igitur hunc mundum celum et terram mare et omnia quae in hoc circulo continentur bona quidem per se dicere sed ad deum comparata esse pro nihilo" (Würzburg UB M.p.th.q. 28b, fol. 38v).

240. Christianson, *Ecclesiastes through the Centuries*, pp. 197–201 and 212–13; Le Moine, "Jerome's Gift to Women Readers," pp. 238–39; Laurence, "*Virilis* et *Effeminatus*," pp. 404–5.

241. Jerome, *Commentarius in Ecclesiasten* 2.8, ed. Adriaen, p. 266.

242. Jerome, *Commentarius in Ecclesiasten* 7.26–29, ed. Adriaen, pp. 311–13.

243. Jerome, *Commentarius in Ecclesiasten* 7.26–27, ed. Adriaen, pp. 311–12.

244. Würzburg UB M.p.th.q. 28b, fol. 41v; compare Jerome, *Commentarius in Ecclesiasten*, ed. Adriaen, p. 21, line 4–p. 22, line 12.

245. Würzburg UB M.p.th.q. 28b, fol. 40r.

246. See Chapter Five and Chapter Six. A sermon of Matthew in the Karlburg passionary mentioned, but did not vilify, "Adam's wife" (Chapter Six), while the *passio* of Juliana in the Kitzingen *libellus* as well as Gregory I's *Responsiones* (Chapter Six and Chapter Five) assigned equal blame to Adam and Eve. These were all very brief mentions.

247. Chapter Five.

248. De Lacy, "Thematic and Structural Affinities," pp. 126–29 and 131.

249. For instance, "Si adversus hominem in expugnando robustior extiterit, stabit homo, stabit et christus pro homine suo, pro sodali suo. Non quod solius Christi adversus diabolum virtus infirma sit, sed quod liberum homini servatur arbitrium. Nisi igitur nobiscum Christus domierit et in morte quieverit, calorem aeternam vitae accipere non valemus," or "Should the enemy should be particularly robust in combating a human being, that human being should stand firm, and Christ will also stand firm for his human being, for his companion. It is not that the strength of Christ alone is insufficient to fight the devil, but because it is important to preserve free will for a human being. Thus, unless Christ is at home with us and rests with us, we will not be able to receive the eternal warmth of life" (Würzburg UB M.p.th.q. 28b, fol. 40r; Jerome, *Commentarius in Ecclesiasten*, ed. Adriaen, p. 14, lines 1–4 and 9–10).

250. "Dum in isto seculo es, festina, contende, age penitentiam dum habes tempus. Labora. Libenter suscipit penitentiam Deus" (Würzburg, UB M.p.th.q. 28b, fol. 42v; Jerome, *Commentarius in Ecclesiasten*, ed. Adriaen, p. 26, lines 18–19).

251. Rosenstock, "Die Besiedlung," pp. 48–49.

252. Arnold, "Kitzingens Anfänge," p. 22.

253. Muschiol, *Famula Dei*, pp. 101–2 and 104–7; Muschiol, "Zeit und Raum," p. 41.

254. Muschiol, *Famula Dei*, pp. 176–77.

255. "Hanc solam portionem habemus in regno celorum quam nec fur nec latro nec tyrannus valet auferre et quae nos post mortem sequatur" (Würzburg, UB M.p.th.q. 28b, fol. 40r; Jerome, *Commentarius in Ecclesiasten*, ed. Adriaen, p. 12, ll.32–33).

8. "CONCERNING VIRGINS, I HAVE NO COMMANDMENT OF THE LORD" (1 CORINTHIANS 7:25)

1. Muschiol, *Famula Dei*, pp. 367–70.

2. Muschiol, *Famula Dei*, pp. 202–6.

3. Muschiol, *Famula Dei*, pp. 219–22.

4. For the source of this quotation in one of the liturgical manuscripts from the region, see note 28.

5. Macy, *The Hidden History of Women's Ordination*, pp. 80–86; Muschiol, *Famula Dei*, pp. 182–84, 210–11, and 217.

6. Macy, *The Hidden History of Women's Ordination*, pp. 80–86.

7. Hochstetler, *A Conflict of Traditions*, pp. 76–88.

8. Essays in Blair and Sharpe, eds., *Pastoral Care*; Gilchrist, *Gender and Material Culture*, pp. 25–26.

9. Hollis, *Anglo-Saxon Women and the Church*, p. 12.

10. Macy, *The Hidden History of Women's Ordination*, pp. 14–15 and 77–80.

11. Macy, *The Hidden History of Women's Ordination*, p. 35.

12. Werminghoff, ed., *Concilia Aevi Karolini*, pp. 13–14, including a note about similar legislation in 721.

13. Discussion between Jean-Loup Lemaitre and Reinhard Elze, in *Segni e Riti*, 1:57–58.

14. A sole surviving leaf from one such eighth-century sacramentary in a German-insular hand is now bound as folio 103 into Würzburg UB M.p.th.f. 42, a late ninth-century copy of Gregory the Great's *Regula Pastoralis* (Weiner, *Initialornamentik*, p. 48, catalogue #54 and plate 85; Thurn, *Die Pergamenthandschriften*, pp. 30–31). Other surviving eighth-century sacramentary fragments from the Anglo-Saxon cultural province in Francia include Würzburg M.p.th.f. 176; Wertheim am Main, Fürstlich Löwenstein-Werthheim-Rosenbergisches Archiv, Fragm. 1 (Lit. B. Nr. 1686a); Munich, BSB Clm 29300/4; and St. Petersburg, Historisches Institut der Akademie der Wissenschaften Fragm. 3/625 (Weiner, *Initialornamentik*, pp. 76–77, catalogue #66 and plates 175–78; CLA 9.1372 and **1372; Bierbrauer, *Die vorkarolingischen und karolingischen Handschriften*, 1.110–20).

15. Graham, "Changing the Context."

16. Thurn, Die *Pergamenthandschriften*, p. 106.

17. Finsterwalder, *Die canones Theodori*, pp. 285–334.

18. Wegner, *Kirchenjahr und Messfeier*.

19. Chavasse, *Textes Liturgiques*, p. 7.

20. Chavasse, *Textes Liturgiques*, pp. 34–35, no. 1253.

21. Ewig, "Saint Chrodegang," pp. 48–50.

22. Lifshitz, *The Name of the Saint*, p. 108.

23. Lifshitz, "Gender Trouble in Paradise."

24. Deshusses, *Le sacramentaire Grégorien*, 1:173–74.

25. Deshusses, *Le sacramentaire Grégorien*, 1:121–23 and 125–26.

26. For apostles, the celebrant was to read John 15:12–16, followed by Matthew 10:16–22: "This is my commandment, that you love one another as I have loved you. Greater love has no one than this, that someone lay down his life for his friends. You are my friends if you do what I command you. No longer do I call you servants, for the servant does not know what his master is doing; but I have called you friends, for all that I have heard from my Father I have made known to you. You did not choose me, but I chose you and appointed you that you should go and bear fruit and that your fruit should abide, so that whatever you ask the Father in my name, he may give it to you. . . . Behold, I am sending you out as sheep in the midst of wolves, so be wise as serpents and innocent as doves. Beware of men, for they will deliver you over to courts and flog you in their synagogues, and you will be dragged before governors and kings for my sake, to bear witness before them and the Gentiles. When they deliver you over, do not be anxious how you are to speak or what you are to say, for what you are to say will be given to you in that hour. For it is not you who speak, but the Spirit of your Father speaking through you. Brother will deliver brother over to death, and the father his child, and children will rise against parents and have them put to death, and you will be hated by all for my name's sake. But the one who endures to the end will be saved" (Würzburg UB M.p.th.q. 32, fols. 14v–15r). For confessors, the celebrant was to read Romans 9:22–26, followed by Luke 11: 33–36: "What if God, desiring to show his wrath and to make known his power, has endured with much patience vessels of wrath prepared for destruction, in order to make known the riches of his glory for vessels of mercy, which he has prepared beforehand for glory—even us whom he has called, not from the Jews only but also from the Gentiles? As indeed he says in Hosea, 'Those who were not my people I will call "my people," and her who was not beloved I will call "beloved." ' 'And in the very place where it was said to them, "You are not my people," there they will be called "sons of the living God." ' . . . No one after lighting a lamp puts it in a cellar or under a basket, but on a stand, so that those who enter may see the light. Your eye is the lamp of your body. When your eye is healthy, your whole body is full of light, but when it is bad, your body is full of darkness. Therefore be careful lest the light in you be darkness. If then your whole body is full of light, having no part dark, it will be wholly bright, as when a lamp with its rays gives you light" (Würzburg UB M.p.th.q. 32, fols. 15r–16r).

27. The other reading in the common for martyrs was Revelations 21:4–7: "He will wipe away every tear from their eyes, and death shall be no more, neither shall there be mourning, nor crying, nor pain anymore, for the former things have passed away. And he who was seated on the throne said, 'Behold, I am making all things new.' Also he said, 'Write this down, for these words are trustworthy and true.' And he said to me, 'It is done! I am the Alpha and the Omega, the beginning and the end. To the thirsty I will give from the spring of the water of life without payment. The one who conquers will have this heritage, and I will be his God and he will be my son' " (Würzburg UB M.p.th.q. 32, fols. 16r–16v). The closing reference to a son ("et ille erit mihi filius") would not have been understood as excluding women from the category of martyrs, any more than the reference to a married man in the reading for virgins (to which I turn next) would have been understood as excluding female saints from that category.

28. The other reading in the common for virgins was Matthew 13:44–52: " 'The kingdom of heaven is like treasure hidden in a field, which a man found and covered up. Then in his joy he goes and sells all that he has and buys that field. Again, the kingdom

of heaven is like a merchant in search of fine pearls, who, on finding one pearl of great value, went and sold all that he had and bought it. Again, the kingdom of heaven is like a net that was thrown into the sea and gathered fish of every kind. When it was full, men drew it ashore and sat down and sorted the good into containers but threw away the bad. So it will be at the close of the age. The angels will come out and separate the evil from the righteous and throw them into the fiery furnace. In that place there will be weeping and gnashing of teeth. Have you understood all these things?' They said to him, 'Yes.' And he said to them, 'Therefore every scribe who has been trained for the kingdom of heaven is like a master of a house, who brings out of his treasure what is new and what is old'" (Würzburg UB M.p.th.q. 32, fols. 16v–17v).

29. The codex may be one of the two "lectionari" on the early ninth-century Würzburg library catalogue (*LSK,* pp. 142–148) or one of the three "comiti" (liturgical guides) listed on Würzburg UB M.p.th.f. 57 as stored in the cathedral treasury c. 830–840 (Thurn, "Handschriften der Universitätsbibliothek," p. 210).

30. Muschiol, *Famula Dei,* pp. 114, 123–24, and 133.

31. ". . . in suis ecclesiis lectiones legere et inplere ministerio quae convenient ad conpositionem sacro sancti altaris nisi ea tantum modo que specialiter sacerdotum et diaconorum sunt" (Penitential of Theodore, *Discipulus Umbrensium* version, ch. 22, in Vienna ÖNB, fol. 12v; ; Wasserschleben, *Die Bussordnungen,* p. 209). The ninth-century Würzburg cathedral cleric who intended to palimpsest this entire penitential over an erased older Karlburg sacramentary (in Würzburg UB M.p.th.q. 32) never reached this portion of the text, or the portion cited in note 32.

32. ". . . mulier potest oblationes facere secundum grecos non secundum romanos" (Penitential of Theodore, *Discipulus Umbrensium* version, ch. 22, in Vienna ÖNB, fol. 12v; Wasserschleben, *Die Bussordnungen,* p. 209). See also notes 2 and 3.

33. Macy, "The Ordination of Women," pp. 490–96.

34. Fontaine, *Isidore de Séville,* pp. 199–201.

35. Chapter Three.

36. Isidore, *DEO,* trans. Knoebel, pp. 9 and 97–102.

37. Isidore, *DEO* II, introduction, trans. Knoebel, p. 67.

38. Isidore, *DEO* II.4 and II.11, ed. Lawson, pp. 55 and 71; trans. Knoebel, pp. 70 and 82.

39. Isidore, *DEO* II.18, ed. Lawson, p. 87; trans. Knoebel, p. 95. There were no variants on this section in Würzburg UB M.p.th.q. 18, fols. 56v–57r.

40. *Capitula iudiciorum* penitential c. 10 (Vienna 2223, fols. 6r–6v).

41. Isidore, *DEO* II, introduction, trans. Knoebel, p. 67.

42. "Choros idem Moyses post transitum rubri maris primus instituit, utrorumque sexuum distinctis classibus se ac sorore praeeunte canere deo in choris carmen triumphale perdocuit" (Isidore, DEO I.3(1), ed. Lawson, p. 5; trans. Knoebel, p. 30).

43. "Deinde Debbora, non ignobilis femina, in libro Iudicum hoc ministerio functa repperitur; postea multos non solum viros sed etiam feminas spiritu divino conpletas dei cecinisse mysteria" (Isidore, *DEO* I.4.(2), ed. Lawson, p. 5; trans. Knoebel, p. 30).

44. Würzburg UB M.p.th.q. 28a, fols. 70v–71r.

45. Muschiol, *Famula Dei.*

46. Freiburg UB 363, fols. 30v–32r, quote from fol. 32r.

47. Würzburg UB M.p.th.o. 4, fol. 3r.

48. Isidore, *DEO* I.10, ed. Lawson, p. 9; trans. Knoebel, p. 33. The Gospel episode is Luke 10:39–42.

49. Isidore, *DEO* I.28/29, ed. Lawson, p. 32; trans. Knoebel, p. 51.

50. "Quo die proinde etiam sanctum crisma conficitur quia ante biduum paschae Maria caput ac pedes domini unguento perfudisse perhibetur" (Isidore, *DEO* I. 28/29, ed. Lawson, p. 32; trans. Knoebel, p. 51).

51. Isidore, *DEO*, ed. Lawson, p. 29*. Würzburg UB M.p.th.q. 18 jumped from the middle of I.8/9 to the middle of I.14 (on fol. 5r), leaping directly from prayers to offertories, then continued in proper order until it broke off midway through I.28/29 (on fol. 15r) on the Lord's Supper, and returned to the closing portion of I 8/9, then continued through I.10 on readings (Isidore's first discussion of Mary Magdalen) and beyond in proper order through the previously omitted opening section of I.14, on offertories, which then flowed immediately (on fol. 20rv) into the previously omitted closing section of I.28/29.

52. "Porrexit sacerdos manum suam in libationem et libavit de sanguine uvae et fudit in fundamento altaris odorem divinum excelso principi" (Isidore, *DEO* I.14, ed. Lawson p. 16; trans. Knoebel, p. 39; Würzburg UB M.p.th.q. 18, fols. 20r–20v).

53. "Lanificio etiam corpus exercent atque sustentant vestegue ipsas monachis tradunt, ab hic invicem quod victui opus est resumentes," or "By weaving they also exercise and sustain the body, and they provide this clothing to the monks who are men, bringing back from each of them whatever their means of providing their living is" (Isidore, *DEO* II.16 (15).17, ed Lawson, p. 79; trans. Knoebel, p. 89).

54. Würzburg UB M.p.th.q. 18, fol. 51r (a variant not noted in Lawson's edition).

55. Berger, *Gender Differences,* pp. 32–33 and 160–80.

56. Berger, *Gender Differences,* pp. 88–93.

9. "THROUGH A GLASS DARKLY" (1 CORINTHIANS 13:12)

1. Lewis, *By Women, for Women, about Women,* pp. 54–57.

2. Bodarwé, "Ein Spinnennetz," pp. 31–39 and 43–52.

3. Miglio, "'A mulieribus conscriptos arbitror': donne e scrittura."

4. Hamburger, *Nuns as Artists,* p. 213.

5. Erler, *Women, Reading, and Piety*; Ker, *Medieval Libraries of Great Britain*; Watson, *Medieval Libraries of Great Britain*; Bell, *What Nuns Read*.

6. Bodarwé, "Gender and the Archive," pp. 127–28 and 131.

7. Garver, *Women and Aristocratic Culture,* pp. 79–83.

8. Schilp, *Norm und Wirklichkeit,* p. 157.

9. Heyen, *Untersuchungen,* pp. 7–27 *passim.*

10. Trier, Stadtbibliothek fragment s.n.; CLA Supp. 1808; Krämer, *Handschriftenerbe,* 2:659.

11. Trier, Stadtbibliothek fragment s.n.; CLA Supp. 1807, taken from Trier Stadtbibliothek 2099/686.

12. Munich, BSB Clm 23358; Bierbrauer, *Die vorkarolingischen und karolingischen Handschriften,* Tafelband, pp. 86–87, Textband, p. 78.

13. Munich, BSB Clm 356; Bierbrauer, *Die vorkarolingischen und karolingischen Handschriften,* Tafelband, pp. 85–86.

14. Oxford, Bodleian Laud misc 456; Krämer, *Handschriftenerbe,* 2:532–49.

15. An excellent candidate is Vienna ÖNB 968 (theol. 343); see Hofmann, "Der Lambach-Wiener 'Prosper.'"

16. One candidate is Kassel, Universitäts-Bibliothek 8° theol. 5, produced in Northern France during the eighth century but present in East Francia by the end that century, when Bliidthruut wrote her name on fol. 2r and other words in the dialect of the Fulda region were also added to the codex (CLA 1142).

17. Jenal, "Frühe Formen der weiblichen *vita religiosa*," pp. 50–54, 58–62, and 68–69; Jenal, *Italia ascetica atque monastica*, vol. 1, pp. 15, 23, 82, 84, 89–90, and 112.

18. Andenna, "San Salvatore di Brescia," pp. 209–17; Veronese, "Monasteri femminili in Italia"; Abrahamse, "Byzantine Ascetisicm and Women's Communities," pp. 34–35 and 41–43.

19. Wemple, "Female Monasticism," p. 293.

20. I, *La festa della purificazione*, pp. 198–213, especially p. 204.

21. *Chronicon Benedictoburanum*, ed. Wattenbach, p. 213.

22. Munich BSB Clm. 4582; Chapter Three; Munich BSB Clm 29050; Bischoff, "Kölner Nonnenhandschriften," pp. 21 and 29–30; Stoclet, "Gisèle, Kisyla."

23. Chapter Three.

24. Pilsworth, "Vile Scraps," pp. 177 and 181.

25. St. Gallen, SB 548, pp. 14–43; Scarpatetti, *Die Handschriften der Stiftsbibliothek St. Gallen*.

26. For instance, St. Gallen, SB 548, pp. 15–24.

27. Plant, ed., *Women Writers of Ancient Greece and Rome*, pp. 198–209.

28. Halle, Universitäts- und Landesbibliothek, Qu. Cod. 74; Scheck, "Women's Intellectual Culture."

29. Paris, BN lat. 7560, especially fol. 54; Schreiner, "Kopistinnen," pp. 42–45; Chapter Three.

30. Schrimpf et al., *Mittelalterliche Bücherverzeichnisse*, p. 8; Palmer, "A Single Human Being," pp. 129 and 132.

31. Shrimpf et al., *Mittelalterliche Bücherverzeichnisse* catalogue lines 13–14, manuscript no. 30. The "vita sancti malchi monachi" was paired "in one book" ("in u(m) libri") with at least one other text whose barely legible title Shrimpf gave as "super virginitate," and to which he assigned the catalogue number 29. The entry should probably be understood as referring to the *libellus* as a whole. Gundheri, who placed his colophon in another eighth-century manuscript from the region (Würzburg UB M.p.th.f. 64), may have added the poem on the fall of Rome to Würzburg UB M.p.th.q. 26, fol. 61v (*LSK*, p. 59).

32. For instance, Jerome urged his friend Heliodorus to take up the life of a hermit and break all family ties (Würzburg UB M.p.th.q. 26, fol. 39r; Jerome, *Epistola 14 ad Heliodorum*, ed. Hilberg, CSEL 54:44–52).

33. Astell, *The Song of Songs in the Middle Ages*, p. 1.

34. "When I was a child, I spake as a child, I understood as a child, I thought as a child: but when I became a man, I put away childish things. For now we see through a glass, darkly; but then face to face: now I know in part; but then shall I know even as also I am known. And now abideth faith, hope, charity, these three; but the greatest of these is charity" (quoted in the "Veri Amoris" abridgment of Apponius, Würzburg UB M.p.th.q. 26, fol. 1r). I cite the passage in the King James translation, the source of the Pauline epigram for this chapter.

35. Chapter Three, Chapter Six.

36. *Vita Malchi* (BHL 5190), in Würzburg UB M.p.th.q. 26, fols. 33r–37v; see also *PL* 23:53–60.

37. The published version of the *vita Euphrosynae* (BHL 2723, in *PL* 73:643–53 and *AASS* Feb II: 537–41) varied considerably from the text in the Würzburg manuscript, which I cite here.

38. *Vita Euphrosynae*, Würzburg UB M.p.th.q. 26, fols. 52r–55v.

39. *Vita Euphrosynae*, Würzburg UB M.p.th.q. 26, fols. 56v–59v.

40. *Vita Euphrosynae*, Würzburg UB M.p.th.q. 26, fols. 60r–61r.

41. Apponius, *Apponii in Canticum Canticorum*, eds. de Vregille and Neyrand, pp. xvii–xxv, xxx, and xli–xliii; Apponius, *Commentaire*, trans. de Vregille.

42. Apponius, *Apponii in Canticum Canticorum*, eds. de Vregille and Neyrand, pp. cxix–cxx and 315–90 (edition of "Veri Amoris").

43. Usher, *Homeric Stitchings*, pp. ix and 1.

44. Usher, *Homeric Stitchings*, p. v.

45. Pollmann, "Sex and Salvation," pp. 80 and 87–88; Clark and Hatch, eds. *The Golden Bough*.

46. McGill, *Virgil Recomposed*, p. 155, nn.17 and 19–20; Stevenson, *Women Latin Poets*, p. 69; Jakobi, "Vom Klassizismus zur christlichen Ästhetik," pp. 86–88.

47. Ermini, *Il Centone di Proba*, pp. 62–66; Stevenson, *Women Latin Poets*, p. 69; St. Petersburg, Rossijskaja Nacionalnaja Biblioteka F.xiv.1; Vatican City, BAV pal. lat. 1753; Yaeger, "Did Gower Write *Cento*?" pp. 120–23.

48. Usher, *Homeric Stitchings*, p. 70.

49. Eudocia, *Homerocentones*, ed. Schembra.

50. Usher, *Homeric Stitchings*, p. 11.

51. Hamesse, "A Propos de Quelques Techniques d'Interprétation," pp. 11–13.

52. Pollmann, "Sex and Salvation," pp. 87–92, at p. 89; Leisch-Kiesl, *Eva als Andere*, pp. 152–55; Jakobi, "Vom Klassizismus zur christlichen Ästhetik," pp. 84–86.

53. Boulogne-sur-Mer BM 74 (82), especially fol. 62; CLA 6.738; Sims-Williams, "An Unpublished Seventh- or Eighth-Century Anglo-Latin Letter"; Sims-Williams, *Religion and Literature*, pp. 198–210; John, "The Named and Namable Scribes," pp. 115–21; Apponius, *Apponii in Canticum Canticorum*, eds. de Vregille and Neyrand, pp. 391–463.

54. Brenner, "On Feminist Criticism of the *Song of Songs*," pp. 28 and 32; Goitein, "The *Song of Songs*: A Female Composition," pp. 58–66; Bekkenkamp and Van Dijk, "The Canon of the Old Testament," pp. 67–85; Brenner, "Women Poets and Authors," pp. 86–97; Arbel, " 'My Vineyard, My Very Own, Is for Myself,' " pp. 90–93; Bekkenkamp, "Into Another Scene of Choices," pp. 55–56.

55. Butting, "Go Your Way," p. 143.

56. Exum, "Ten Things Every Feminist Should Know about the Song of Songs," p. 24.

57. "Veri Amoris," Homily IX, lines 51–53, in Apponius, *Apponii in Canticum Canticorum*, eds. de Vregille and Neyrand, p. 365.

58. "Veri Amoris," Homily XII, line 275, in Apponius, *Apponii in Canticum Canticorum*, eds. de Vregille and Neyrand, p. 389.

59. "Veri Amoris," Homily VIII, lines 250ff., in Apponius, *Apponii in Canticum Canticorum*, eds. de Vregille and Neyrand, p. 360, compared with Apponius, *Commentaire sur le Cantique des Cantiques*, Book VIII, chapter 54, trans. de Vregille, SC 421, pp. 306–9; "Veri Amoris," Homily VIII, lines 21–22 (noting only that God is the head of Christ), in Apponius, *Apponii in Canticum Canticorum*, eds. de Vregille and

Neyrand, p. 353, compared with Apponius, *Commentaire sur le Cantique des Cantiques,* Book VIII, lines 81ff., trans. de Vregille, SC 421, p. 246.

60. Contreni, "The Pursuit of Knowledge," pp. 106–9.

61. Contreni, "The Pursuit of Knowledge," pp. 113–14.

62. Oxford, Bodleian Library, Laud misc. 126, folio 1r; Chapter Two and Chapter Three.

63. Chapter Two.

64. Bischoff, *Die Abtei Lorsch,* pp. 71–72, 75–76, and 78.

65. Reynolds, "Introduction," pp. xiv–xvii, at p. xvii.

66. Heene, *Legacy of Paradise,* pp. 16–17, 54, and 261–63.

67. Chapter One.

68. Würzburg UB M.p.th.f. 145, including the so-called *Würzburg Indiculum,* on fols. 43r–v.

69. Wagner, "Zur Frühzeit," p. 108.

70. *Passio Cypriani,* in Würzburg, UB M.p.th.f. 33, fols. 38r–39v, ed. Maier, *Le Dossier du Donatisme,* 1:123–26.

71. Von Dobschütz, *Das Decretum Gelasianum,* 136–39, 351, and 356–57; Berndt, "Das Frankfurter Konzil," p. 540; McKitterick, "Das Konzil im Kontext," 622–27.

72. For instance, Agatha displayed a *castimonia* that stood firm against tortures; Lucia died rather than be married and lose her virginity; Justina suffered horrific, graphic tortures "pro virginitate servanda"; Agnes died to preserve her corporeal integrity; and so forth (Aldhelm, *Prosa de Virginitate,* in Würzburg UB M.p.th.f. 21, fols. 33r–36v; ed. Gwara cc. 41–43 and 45, pp. 589–621 and 631–39).

73. Lifshitz, "Priestly Women, Virginal Men." The main manuscript of the work was Würzburg UB M.p.th.f. 21, produced by and for the cathedral clergy of Würzburg under Bishop Gozbald between 842 and 855 and simultaneously annotated with over a hundred Latin and Old High German glosses in many hands (Aldhelm, *Prosa de Virginitate,* ed. Gwara, pp. 77*–78* and 83*).

74. For Paris, BN lat. 16668 (an eighth-century codex from Lorsch), Vienna ÖNB 969 (a late ninth-century codex from St. Alban's), and Wolfenbüttel HAB Helmst. 365 (400) (a tenth-century codex from St. Alban's); see Krämer, *Handschriftenerbe,* 2.525–26; Irblich, *Karl der Grosse,* pp. 48–49.

75. Lerner, *Creation of Feminist Consciousness,* pp. 14, 17, and 24–26.

76. Mordek, *Bibliotheca Capitularium,* pp. 401–4.

77. Lerner, *Creation of Feminist Consciousness,* pp. 166 and 220.

78. McInerney, *Eloquent Virgins,* p. 88.

79. Wilson, "Introduction," p. 9.

80. Lübeck, "Fuldaer Nebenklöster," pp. 38–40.

81. *VKB* 1966, p. 402.

82. Chance, "Hrotsvit's Latin Drama *Gallicanus,*" p. 205.

83. Chance, "Hrotsvit's Latin Drama *Gallicanus,*" pp. 194–96.

84. Chance, "Hrotsvit's Latin Drama *Gallicanus,*" p. 204.

85. *Annales Mettenses Priores,* ed. von Simson; Hoffman, *Untersuchungen zur karolingischen Annalistik,* pp. 53–61; Bischoff, "Kölner Nonnenhandschriften," p. 31; Haselbach, *Aufstieg und Herrschaft der Karolinger;* McKitterick, "Women and Literacy," p. 24; Hen, "The Annals of Metz"; Nelson, "Gender and Genre"; Nelson, "Gender en Genre"; McKitterick, "*Akkulturation,*" p. 385; Gilsdorf, *Queenship and Sanctity.*

86. In a copy of the Chronicle of Fredegar, in Paris BN lat. 10910, fol. 75r (Zimmermann, *Vorkarolingische Miniaturen* Text, pp. 178–79, Tafel 74b). There was at least one more portrait of an unidentified woman on fol. A of the same manuscript (see the BnF website for cote cliché RC-A-35398).

87. Griffiths, "'Like the Sister of Aaron,'" p. 367.

88. Paris, BN lat. 2706; *CLA* 5.547; Bischoff, "Kölner Nonnenhandschriften," p. 32, n. 60.

89. Compare the books in this study with Bodarwé, *Sanctimoniales litteratae*, pp. 361–480, including demanding works such as Boethius, *In librum Aristotelis de interpretatione* (pp. 417–19); Vitruvius, *On Architecture*; Vegetius, *De re militari* (pp. 441–42); and Flavius Josephus, *Jewish Antiquities* (p. 468).

90. Bodarwé, *Sanctimoniales litteratae*, p. 356.

91. Christine de Pizan, *The Book of the City of Ladies*, trans. Richards.

BIBLIOGRAPHY

WORKS CITED: MANUSCRIPTS

Amiens, Bibliothèque Municipale
18
90

Basel, Öffentliche Universitätsbibliothek
F. III.15a
F. III.15c
F. III.15f

Berlin, Staatsbibliothek-Preussischer Kulturbesitz
Nachlass Grimm 139,1
Theol. lat. fol. 192
Theol. lat. fol. 480
Philipps 1657

Bern, Burgerbibliothek
Bongarsiana 611

Boulogne-sur-Mer, Bibliothèque Municipale
74 (82)

Brussels, Bibliothèque royale de Belgique
138

Cambrai, Bibliothèque Municipale
164

Cambridge University, Fitzwilliam Museum
McClean 29

Cambridge University, Trinity College
B.5.6–7
O.5.8

Cambridge University, University Library
Add. 4219
L1.1.10

Chartres, Bibliothèque Municipale
106
144

Cologne, Dombibliothek
40
67

Copenhagen, Kongelige Bibliotek
Fragm. 19.vii

Dresden, Sächsische Landesbibliothek, Staats- und Universitätsbibliothek
A. 128
R. 52

Durham, Cathedral Library
A. II. 19

Düsseldorf, Universitäts- und Landesbibliothek
A.14
B.3

Engelberg, Stiftsbibliothek
78

Florence, Biblioteca Laurenziana
Plut. XXIII.5

Frankfurt, Stadt- und Universitätsbibliothek
Bart. 117
Praed. 26

Freiburg, Universitätsbibliothek
363

Fulda, Dommuseum
Bonifatianus 2 (on permanent loan from Fulda, Hessische Landesbibliothek)

Fulda, Hessische Landesbibliothek
B 1
D 1

Gotha, Forschungs- und Landesbibliothek
Mbr I. 75

Halle, Universitäts- und Landesbibliothek
Qu. Cod. 74

Heiligenkreuz, Stiftsbibliothek
217

Karlsruhe, Badische Landesbibliothek
Augiensis XCIII
Augiensis CXCVI

Karlsruhe 340 (Durlach 36)
Rastatt 22

Kassel, Universitäts-Bibliothek, Landesbibliothek und Murhardsche Bibliothek der Stadt Kassel
4° theol. 1
8° theol. 5

Klagenfurt, Priesterseminar
S.n.

Lambach an der Traun, Stiftsbibliothek
Cml. 31

Laon, Bibliothèque Municipale
137
423

Leipzig, Universitätsbibliothek
92
1608

London, British Library
Cotton Add. 10546
Royal 2.A.XX
Royal 4.E.IX

Lyons, Bibliothèque Municipale
473

Milan, Biblioteca Ambrosiana
R.70 Supp.

Montecassino, Biblioteca Statale del Monumento Nazionale di Montecassino
248

Montpellier, Bibliothèque Interuniversitaire, Faculté de Médecine
H. 55

Munich, Bayerisches Hauptstaatsarchiv
Kaiserselekt 69

Munich, Bayerische Staatsbibliothek
Clm 356
Clm 1086
Clm 3514
Clm 3853
Clm 4582
Clm 6233

Clm 6277
Clm 6282
Clm 6298
Clm 6433
Clm 8110
Clm 8112
Clm 14345
Clm 14431
Clm 14830
Clm 15817
Clm 18128
Clm 23358
Clm 29050
Clm 29300/4

New York, Columbia University Library
Plimpton 129

New York, Pierpont Morgan Library
E. A. Lowe Papers
M.559

Nuremberg, Stadtbibliothek
Cent. V. App. 96

Orléans, Bibliothèque Municipale
341

Oxford, Bodleian Library
Auctarium D.1.13
Barlow 26
Canon. Bibl. Lat. 34
Laud lat. 3
Laud lat. 45
Laud misc. 126
Laud misc. 163
Laud misc. 275
Laud misc. 436
Laud misc. 442
Laud misc. 456

Paris, Bibliothèque Nationale de France
Lat. 1
Lat. 1622
Lat. 2706
Lat. 2994A
Lat. 7560

Lat. 9389
Lat. 10861
Lat. 10910
Lat. 12168
Lat. 13396
Lat. 12048
Lat. 14086
Lat. 16668
Lat. 17002
Lat. 18298
N.a.l. 1203

Prague, Národní Knihovna
III E 10 (485)

Rome, Biblioteca Vallicelliana
B.54

St. Gallen, Stiftsbibliothek
64
124
150
190
194
226
548
561
682
926

St. Petersburg, Historisches Institut der Akademie der Wissenschaften
Fragm. 3/625

St. Petersburg, Rossijskaja Nacionalnaja Biblioteka
F.xiv.1
Q.v.1.15

Sankt Paul im Lavanthal, Stiftsbibliothek (Archiv des Benedictinerstiftes)
XXV.1.5

Stuttgart, Württembergische Landesbibliothek
II.54

Trier, Stadtbibliothek
137
2099/686
Multiple fragments s.n.

Troyes, Bibliothèque Municipale
626

Turin, Bibliotheca Nazionale
D.V.3

Udine, Biblioteca Arcivescovile e Bartolina
4

Valenciennes, Bibliothèque Municipale
84–85
173

Vatican City, Bibliotheca Apostolica Vaticana
Lat. 5771
Pal. Lat. 216
Pal. Lat. 220
Pal. Lat. 289
Pal. Lat. 577
Pal. Lat. 582
Pal. Lat. 1753
Reg. Lat. 316
Reg. Lat. 482

Vienna, Österreichische Nationalbibliothek
Lat. 1007
Lat. 1556
Lat. 1616
Lat. 2223
751 (theol. 259)
968 (theol. 343)
969

Wertheim am Main, Fürstlich Löwenstein-Werthheim-Rosenbergisches Archiv
Fragm. 1 (Lit. B. Nr. 1686a)

Wolfenbüttel, Herzog August Bibliothek
Guelf. 496a Helmst.
Helmst. 365 (400)
Helmst. 842

Würzburg, Universitätsbibliothek
M.p.th.f. 3
M.p.th.f. 12
M.p.th.f. 13
M.p.th.f. 17

M.p.th.f. 21
M.p.th.f. 27
M.p.th.f. 33
M.p.th.f. 40
M.p.th.f. 42
M.p.th.f. 43
M.p.th.f. 45
M.p.th.f. 47
M.p.th.f. 57
M.p.th.f. 59
M.p.th.f. 62
M.p.th.f. 64
M.p.th.f. 64a
M.p.th.f. 66
M.p.th.f. 68
M.p.th.f. 69
M.p.th.f. 72
M.p.th.f. 78
M.p.th.f. 79
M.p.th.f. 145
M.p.th.f. 146
M.p.th.f. 175
M.p.th.f. 176
M.p.th.f. 186
M.p.th.o. 4
M.p.th.q. 1a
M.p.th.q. 2
M.p.th.q. 3
M.p.th.q. 15
M.p.th.q. 18
M.p.th.q. 25
M.p.th.q. 26
M.p.th.q. 28a
M.p.th.q. 28b
M.p.th.q. 31
M.p.th.q. 32

Zürich, Zentralbibliothek
Rh. 28

WORKS CITED: PRINTED MATERIALS

Abrahamse, Dorothy de F. "Byzantine Asceticism and Women's Monasteries in Early
Medieval Italy." In *Medieval Religious Women 1: Distant Echoes,* edited by John A.
Nichols and Lillian Thomas Shank, 31–49 (Kalamazoo, 1984).

Abramowski, Louise. "Histoire de la recherche sur Nestorius et le Nestorianisme." *Istina* 40 (1995): 44–55.

Affeldt, Werner, ed. *Frauen in Spätantike und Frühmittelalter. Lebensbedingungen— Lebensnormen—Lebensformen* (Sigmaringen, 1990).

Airlie, Stuart. "Towards a Carolingian Aristocracy." In *Der Dynastiewechsel von 751*, edited by Becher and Jarnut, 109–27.

Akkerman, Tjitske, and Siep Stuurman. "Introduction: Feminism in European History." In *Perspectives on Feminist Thought*, edited by Akkerman and Sturrman, 1–33.

Akkerman, Tjitske, and Siep Stuurman, eds. *Perspectives on Feminist Thought in European History: From the Middle Ages to the Present* (New York/London, 1998).

Alcuin of York. *Commentaria super Ecclesiasten*, in PL 100: 667–722.

Alcuin of York. *De conversione Saxonum*, in PL 101: 811–12.

Aldhelm of Malmesbury. *Carmen de virginitate*. Edited by Rudolf Ehwald (MGH AA XV; Berlin, 1919): 327–471.

Aldhelm of Malmesbury. *Prosa de Virginitate*. Edited by Rudolf Ehwald (MGH AA XV; Berlin, 1919): 211–323.

Aldhelm of Malmesbury. *Prosa de Virginitate cum glosa latina atque anglosaxonica (editione rudolfi Ehwald adhibita et aucta)*. Edited by Scottus Gwara (Turnhout, 2001; CCSL 124/124A).

Aldhelm of Malmesbury. *The Prose Works*. Translated by Michael Lapidge and Michael Herren (Ipswich, 1979).

Alvarez Campos, Sergius, ed. *Corpus Marianum Patristicum*, 6 vols. (Burgos, 1970–80).

Amos, Thomas L. "Early Medieval Sermons and the Holy." In *Models of Holiness in Medieval Sermons*, edited by Beverly Mayne Kienzle with Edith Wilks Dolnikowski, Rosemary Drage Hale, Darleen Pryds, and Anne T. Thayer, 23–34 (Louvain-la-Neuve, 1996).

Andenna, Giancarlo. "San Salvatore di Brescia e la Scelta Religiosa delle Donne Aristocratiche tra Eta Longobarda ed Eta Franca (VIII–IX Secolo)." In *Female Vita Religiosa*, edited by Melville and Müller, 209–33.

Angenendt, Arnold. "'Mit reinen Händen.' Das Motiv der kultischen Reinheit in der abendländischen Askese." In *Herrschaft, Kirche, Kultur. Festschrift für Friedrich Prinz zu seinem 65. Geburtstag*, edited by Georg Jenal and Stephanie Haarländer, 297–316 (Stuttgart, 1993).

Anlezark, Daniel. "The Fall of the Angels in *Solomon and Saturn II*." In *Apocryphal Texts and Traditions in Anglo-Saxon England*, edited by Kathryn Powell and Donald Scragg, 121–33 (Woodbridge, 2003).

Annales Mettenses Priores. Edited by Bernhard von Simson. (MGH SRG 10; Hannover, 1905).

Anson, John. "The Female Transvestite in Early Monasticism: The Origin and Development of a Motif." *Viator* 5 (1974): 1–32.

Anton, Hans Hubert. "Klosterwesen und Adel im Raum von Mosel, Saar und Sauer in Merowingischer und Frühkarolingischer Zeit." In *Willibrord, Apostel der Niederlande, Gründer der Abtei Echternach*, edited by Georges Kiesel and Jean Schroeder, 96–124 (Luxemburg, 1989).

Apponius. *Apponii in Canticum Canticorum Expositionem*. Edited by Bernard de Vregille and L. Neyrand (CCSL 19; Turnhout, 1986).

Apponius. *Commentaire sur le Cantique des Cantiques.* Translated by Bernard de Vregille (Sources Chrétiennes 420, 421, and 430; Paris, 1997 and 1998).

Arbel, Daphna V. "'My Vineyard, My Very Own, Is for Myself.'" In *The Song of Songs,* edited by Brenner and Fontaine, 90–101.

Arens, Fritz Victor. *Die Inschriften der Stadt Mainz von frühmittelalterlicher Zeit bis 1650.* (Die Deutschen Inschriften 2; Mainz, 1958).

Arnold, Carl Franklin. *Caesarius von Arelate und die Gallische Kirche seiner Zeit* (Leipzig, 1894).

Arnold, Klaus. "Kitzingens Anfänge. Die erste Erwähnung in der *vita Sturmi* des Eigil von Fulda und die Frühzeit des Klosters Kitzingen." In *"apud Kizinga monasterium,"* edited by Walter, 15–24.

Astell, Ann W. *The Song of Songs in the Middle Ages* (Ithaca, 1990).

Astell, Ann W. "Translating Job as Female." In *Translation Theory and Practice in the Middle Ages,* edited by Jeanette Beer, 59–69 (Kalamazoo, 1997).

Atenolfi, Giuseppi Talamo, ed. *I Testi Medioevali degli atti di S. Matteo l'Evangelista* (Rome, 1958).

Auerbach, Erich. *Mimesis: The Representation of Reality in Western Literature.* Translated by Willard R. Trask (Princeton, 2003).

Augustine. *Enarrationes in Psalmos.* Edited by Eligius Dekkers and Johannes Fraipont, 3 vols. (CCSL 38–40; Turnhout, 1956).

Augustine. *Enarrationes in Psalmos 119–133.* Edited by Franco Gori (CSEL 95 part 3; Vienna, 2001).

Augustine. *Expositions of the Psalms (Enarrationes in Psalmos) 99–120.* Translated by Maria Boulding, OSB (Hyde Park, 2003).

Augustine. *Expositions of the Psalms (Enarrationes in Psalmos) 121–150.* Translated by Maria Boulding, OSB (Hyde Park, 2004).

Augustine. *De Trinitate.* Edited by W. J. Mountain with Fr. Glorie (CCSL 50; Turnhout, 1968).

Augustine. *On the Trinity.* Translated by S. McKenna (Washington, DC, 1963).

Baby, Parambi. *The Discipleship of the Women in the Gospel according to Matthew. An Exegetical Theological Study of Matthew 27:51b–56, 57–61 and 28:1–10* (Rome, 2003).

Baesecke, Georg. *Der Vocabularius Sancti Galli in der Angelsächsischen Mission.* (Halle/Saale, 1933).

Baltrusch-Schneider, Dagmar. "Klosterleben als alternative Lebensform zur Ehe?" In *Weibliche Lebensgestaltung,* edited by Goetz, 45–64.

Banniard, Michel. *Viva Voce. Communication écrite et communication orale du IVe au IXe siècle en Occident latin* (Paris, 1992).

Barb, Alphons Augustinus. "Die Blutsegen von Fulda und London." In *Fachliteratur des Mittelalters. Festschrift für Gerhard Eis,* edited by Gundolf Keil, Rainer Rudolf, Wolfram Schmitte, and Hans J. Vermeer, 485–94 (Stuttgart, 1968).

Bauer, Franz Alto. "Das Bild der Stadt Rom in karolingischer Zeit: Der Anonymus Einsidlensis." *Römische Quartalschrift für christliche Altertumskunde und Kirchengeschichte* 92 (1992): 190–228.

Bauer, Gerd, Heiner Boehncke, and Hans Sarkowicz. *Die Geschichte Hessens. Von der Steinzeit bis zum Neubeginn nach 1945* (Frankfurt, 2002).

Beach, Alison I. *Women as Scribes: Book Production and Monastic Reform in Twelfth-Century Bavaria* (Cambridge, 2004).

Beach, Alison Isdale. "Claustration and Collaboration between the Sexes in the Twelfth-Century Scriptorium." In *Monks and Nuns, Saints and Outcasts,* edited by Sharon Farmer and Barbara Rosenwein, 57–75 (Ithaca, 2000).

Beauxamis, Thomas, ed. *Abdiae Babyloniae primi episcopi de historia certaminis apostolici libri x* (Paris, 1571).

Becher, Matthias. "Ein verschleierte Krise: Die Nachfolge Karl Martells 741 und die Anfänge der karolingischen hofgeschichtsschreibung." In *Von Fakten und Fiktionen. Mittelalterliche Geschichtsdarstellungen und ihre kritische Aufarbeitung,* edited by Johannes Laudage, 95–133 (Cologne, 2003).

Becher, Matthias, and Jörg Jarnut, eds. *Der Dynastiewechsel von 751. Vorgeschichte, Legitimationsstrategien und Erinnerung* (Münster, 2004).

Becht-Jördens, Gereon. "Die Ermordung des Erzbischofs Bonifatius durch die Friesen. Suche und Ausgestaltung eines Martyriums aus kirchenpolitischer Notwendigkeit?" *Archiv für mittelrheinische Kirchengeschichte* 57 (2005): 95–132.

Becht-Jördens, Gereon. "Heiliger und Buch. Überlegungen zur Tradition des Bonifatius-Martyriums anläßlich der Teilfaksimilierung des Ragyndrudis-Codex." *Hessisches Jarhbuch für Landesgeschichte* 46 (1996): 1–30.

Becker, Gustav, ed. *Catalogi bibliothecarum antiqui* (Bonn, 1885; reprint, Hildesheim/New York, 1973).

Bede. *Historia Ecclesiastica Gentis Anglorum.* Edited and translated by Bertram Colgrave and R. A. B. Mynors (Oxford, 1969; reprint with corrections, 1992) = HE.

Bede. *Homilia in festivitate annunciationis beatae Mariae,* in PL 94: 9–14.

Bede. *In Cantica Habacuc Allegorica Expositio.* Edited by J. E. Hudson (CCSL 119B; Turnhout, 1983).

Bede. *In Lucae evangelium expositio.* Edited by D. Hurst (CCSL 120; Turnhout, 1960).

Bede. *De Temporum Ratione,* in PL 90: 520–78.

Bede. *On Tobit and on the Canticle of Habakkuk.* Translated by Seán Connolly (Dublin, 1997).

Beeson, Charles Henry. *Isidor-Studien* (Munich, 1913).

Bekkenkamp, Jonneke. "Into Another Scene of Choices: The Theological Value of the *Song of Songs.*" In *The Song of Songs,* edited by Brenner and Fontaine, 55–89.

Bekkenkamp, Jonneke, and Fokkelien van Dijk. "The Canon of the Old Testament and Women's Cultural Traditions." In *A Feminist Companion to the Song of Songs,* edited by Brenner, 67–85.

Belghaus, Viola. "Inszenierter Dialog: Zur Interaktion von Schrift und Bild in einer mittelalterlichen Handschriftenillustration am Beispiel des Erfurter Codex Aureus (Ms. 249/2869)." In *Der Kommentar,* edited by Geerlings and Schulze, 2:129–62.

Bell, David N. *What Nuns Read: Books and Libraries in Medieval English Nunneries* (Kalamazoo, 1995).

Bendel, Franz-Josef, and Joachim Schmitt, eds. and trans. "Vita sancti Burkhardi Episcopi Wirziburgensis II." *WDGB* 48 (1986): 19–90.

Bénédictins du Bouveret. *Colophons de manuscrits occidentaux des origines au XVIe siècle,* 6 vols. (Fribourg/Suisse, 1965–82).

Berger, Teresa. *Gender Differences and the Making of Liturgical History. Lifting a Veil on Liturgy's Past* (Farnham, 2011).

Bergman, Johannes. *De Codicibus Prudentianis* (Stockholm, 1910).

Bergman, Johannes. "De codicum Prudentianorum generibus et virtute." *Sitzungs-berichte der Kais. Akademie der Wissenschaften in Wien, Philosophisch-Historische Klasse* 157, 5 Abhandlung (Vienna, 1908).

Bergmann, Rolf. *Die althochdeutsche Glossenüberlieferung des 8. Jahrhunderts* (Nachrichten der Akademie der Wissenschaften in Göttingen I. Philologisch-Historische Klasse; Göttingen, 1983, no. 1).

Bernau, Anke. "The Translation of Purity in the Old English *Lives* of St Eugenia and St Euphrosyne." *Bulletin of the John Rylands Library of the University of Manchester* 86 (2004): 11–37.

Berndt, Rainer, ed. *Das Frankfurter Konzil von 794. Kristallisationspunkt karolin-gischer Kultur,* 2 vols. (Mainz, 1997).

Berndt, Rainer. "Das Frankfurter Konzil von 794. Kristallisationspunkt theolo-gischen Denkens in der frühen Karolingerzeit." In *Das Frankfurter Konzil,* edited by Berndt, 1:504–32.

Berndt, Rainer. "Skizze zur Auslegungsgeschichte der Bücher *Proverbia* und *Ecclesiastes* in der abendländischen Kirche." *Sacris Erudiri* 34 (1994): 5–32.

Berschin, Walter. "Zur lateinischen und deutschen Juliana-Legende." *Studi Medievali* 14 (1973): 1003–12.

Bestul, Thomas H. *Texts of the Passion. Latin Devotional Literature and Medieval Society* (Philadelphia, 1996).

Beutler, Christian. *Der Gott am Kreuz. Zur Entstehung der Kreuzigungsdarstellung* (Hamburg, 1986).

Beutler, Christian. "Der Kruzifixus des Bonifatius." In *Das Frankfurter Konzil,* edited by Berndt, 2: 549–53.

Biddick, Kathleen. "Bede's Blush: Postcards from Bali, Bombay, Palo Alto." In *The Past and Future of Medieval Studies,* edited by John Van Engen, 16–44 (Notre Dame, 1994); reprinted in Kathleen Biddick, *The Shock of Medievalism,* 83–103 (Durham, 1998).

Biddle, Martin. *The Tomb of Christ* (Phoenix Mill, 1999).

Bieler, Ludwig, ed. *The Irish Penitentials* (Dublin, 1963).

Bierbrauer, Katharina. "Karolingische Buchmalerei des Maingebietes (Mainz, Würzburg)." In *Das Frankfurter Konzil,* edited by Berndt, 2: 555–70.

Bierbrauer, Katharina. *Die vorkarolingischen und karolingischen Handschriften der Bayerischen Staatsbibliothek,* 2 vols. (Wiesbaden, 1990).

Binz, Gustav. "Beschreibungen der Handschriften F.III.1–15e" (Typescript, Basel Öffentliche Universitätsbibliothek, May 7 1937).

Bischoff, Bernhard. *Die Abtei Lorsch im Spiegel ihrer Handschriften* (2nd ed, Lorsch, 1989).

Bischoff, Bernhard. "Epitaphienformeln für Äbtissinen." *Anecdota Novissima: Quellen und Untersuchungen zur Lateinischen Philologie des Mittelalters* 6 (1984): 150–53.

Bischoff, Bernhard. "Die Kölner Nonnenhandschriften und das Skriptorium von Chelles." In *Karolingische und ottonische Kunst. Werden, Wesen, Wirkung,* edited by Hermann Schnitzler, 395–411 (Wiesbaden, 1957); cited from the expanded version in *Mittelalterliche Studien,* by Bischoff, 1: 16–34 (Stuttgart, 1966).

Bischoff, Bernhard. *Latin Paleography. Antiquity and the Middle Ages.* Translated by Dáibhí O Cróinín and David Ganz (Cambridge, 1990).

Bischoff, Bernhard, ed. *Mittelalterliche Schatzverzeichnisse* (Munich, 1967).

Bischoff, Bernhard, and Josef Hofmann. *Libri sancti Kyliani. Die Würzburger Schreibschule und die Dombibliotheck im VIII u. IX Jahrhundert* (Würzburg, 1952) = LSK.

Black, Jonathan. "Psalm Uses in Carolingian Prayerbooks: Alcuin's *Confessio Peccatorum Pura* and the Seven Penitential Psalms (Use 1)." *Mediaeval Studies* 65 (2003): 1–56.

Blair, John, and Richard Sharpe, eds. *Pastoral Care before the Parish* (Leicester, 1992).

Blamires, Alcuin. *The Case for Women in Medieval Culture* (Oxford, 1997).

Boas, George. *Primitivism and Related Ideas in the Middle Ages* (Baltimore, 1997).

The Bobbio Missal. Edited by André Wilmart and E. A. Lowe (Henry Bradshaw Society vols. LVIII and LXI; London, 1920–24; one-volume reprint, Woodbridge, 1991).

Bodarwé, Katrinette. "The Charters of Fulda as a Source for Women's History." Paper presented at the International Medieval Congress, Leeds, 1996.

Bodarwé, Katrinette. "Frauenleben zwischen Klosterregeln und Luxus? Alltag in frühmittelalterlichen Frauenklöstern." In *Königin, Klosterfrau, Bäuerin. Frauen im Frühmittelalter,* edited by Helga Brandt and Julia K. Koch, 117–43 (Münster, 1996).

Bodarwé, Katrinette. "Gender and the Archive: The Preservation of Charters in Early Medieval Communities of Religious Women." In *Saints, Scholars and Politicians. Gender as a Tool in Medieval Studies. Festschrift in Honour of Anneke Mulder-Bakker on the Occasion of Her Sixty-Fifth Birthday,* edited by Mathilde van Dijk and Renée Nip, 111–32 (Turnhout, 2005).

Bodarwé, Katrinette. *Sanctimoniales Litteratae. Schriftlichkeit und Bildung in den Ottonischen Frauenkommunitäten Gandersheim, Essen und Quedlinburg* (Muenster, 2004).

Bodarwé, Katrinette. "Ein Spinnennetz von Frauenklöstern. Kommunikation und Filiation zwischen sächsischen Frauenklöstern im Frühmittelalter." In *Lesen, Schreiben, Sticken und Erinnern. Beiträge zur Kultur- und Sozialgeschichte mittelalterlicher Frauenklöster,* edited by Gabriela Signori, 27–52 (Bielefeld, 2000).

Boenig, Robert. *Saint and Hero: Andreas and Medieval Doctrine* (Lewisburg, 1991).

Böhme, H. W. "Das frühe Mittelalter am Mittleren Main." In *Führer,* edited by Römisch-Germanisches Zentralmuseum, 95–120 (Mainz, 1975).

Böhne, Winfried. "Bischof Burchard von Würzburg und die von ihm benutzten liturgischen Bücher." *WDGB* 50 (1988): 43–56.

Bonner, Gerald. "Augustine's Doctrine of Man: Image of God and Sinner." *Augustinianum* 24 (1984): 495–514.

Boretius, Alfred, ed. *Capitularia regum Francorum* I (MGH Legum II; Hannover, 1883).

Børreson, Kari Elisabeth. "Religious Feminism in the Middle Ages: Birgitta of Sweden." In *Maistresse of My Wit: Medieval Women, Modern Scholars,* edited by Louise D'Arcens and Juanita Feros Ruys, 295–312 (Turnhout, 2004).

Bosl, Karl. "Würzburg als Pfalzort." *Jahrbuch für Fränkische Landesforschung* 19 (1959): 25–43.

Bostock, J. Knight. *A Handbook on Old High German Literature* (2nd rev. ed., Oxford, 1976 by K. C. King and D. R. McLintock; 1st ed. 1954).

Bouhlol, Pascal. "Rome, cité sainte? La reconquête hagiographique de la topographie urbaine dans le Légendier romain (Ve-Vie siècles)." In *A la recherche des villes saintes. Actes du Colloque franco-néerlandais "Les villes saintes", Collège de France, 10 et 11 mai 2001*, edited by Alain Le Boulluec, 149–75 (Turnhout, 2004).

Bouhot, Jean-Paul. "Les homélies de saint Grégoire le Grand. Histoire des textes et chronologie." *RB* 117 (2007): 211–60.

Bouhot, Jean-Paul. "Les Pénitentiels attribués à Bède le venérable et à Egbert d'York." *Revue d'Histoire des Textes* 16 (1986): 141–69.

Bourke, Vernon J. "Augustine on the Psalms." In *Augustine, Biblical Exegete*, edited by Von Fleteren and Schnaubelt, 55–70.

Bovini, Giuseppe. *Il cosidetto Mausoleo di Galla Placidia in Ravenna* (Vatican City, 1950).

Bovon, François. "Editing the Apocryphal Acts of the Apostles." In *The Apocryphal Acts of the Apostles*, edited by Bovon, Brock, and Matthews, 1–35.

Bovon, François, Ann Graham Brock, and Christopher R. Matthews, eds. *The Apocryphal Acts of the Apostles* (Cambridge, 1999).

Bowery, Anne-Marie. "Monica: The Feminine Face of Christ." In *Feminist Interpretations*, edited by Stark, 69–85.

Boyarin, Daniel. "Paul and the Genealogy of Gender." *Representations* 41 (1993): 1–33.

Brandis, Tilo, and Peter Jörg Becker, eds. *Glanz Alter Buchkunst. Mittelalterliche Handschriften der Staatsbibliothek-Preussischer Kulturbesitz Berlin* (Wiesbaden, 1988).

Brenner, Athalya, ed. *A Feminist Companion to the Song of Songs* (Sheffield, 1993).

Brenner, Athalya. "On Feminist Criticism of the *Song of Songs*." In *A Feminist Companion to the Song of Songs*, edited by Brenner, 28–37.

Brenner, Athalya. "Women Poets and Authors." In *A Feminist Companion to the Song of Songs*, edited by Brenner, 86–97.

Brenner, Athalya, and Carole R. Fontaine, eds. *The Song of Songs. A Feminist Companion to the Bible* (Sheffield, 2000).

Die Briefe des heiligen Bonifatius und Lullus. Edited by Michael Tangl (MGH: Epistolae Selectae, vol. 1, Berlin, 1916; 2nd ed., Berlin, 1955).

Brock, Ann Graham. "Political Authority and Cultural Accommodation: Social Diversity in the *Acts of Paul* and the *Acts of Peter*." In *The Apocryphal Acts of the Apostles*, edited by Bovon, Brock, and Matthews, 145–69.

Brooten, Bernadette J. *Love between Women: Early Christian Responses to Female Homoeroticism* (Chicago, 1996).

Broszinski, Hartmut, and Sivka Heyne. *Fuldische Handschriften aus Hessen mit weiteren Leihgaben aus Basel, Oslo, dem Vatikan und Wolfenbüttel* (Fulda, 1994).

Brown, Michelle P. "Female Book-Ownership and Production in Anglo-Saxon England: The Evidence of Ninth-Century Prayer Books." In *Lexis and Texts in Early English. Studies Presented to Jane Roberts*, edited by Christian J. Kay and Louis M. Sylvester, 45–68. (Amsterdam, 2001).

Brown, Michelle P. "Paris, Bibliothèque Nationale, lat. 10861 and the Scriptorium of Christ Church, Canterbury." *Anglo-Saxon England* 15 (1986): 119–37.

Brown, Peter. *Augustine of Hippo* (Berkeley, 1967; 1999 with a new epilogue).

Brown, Phyllis R., Linda A. McMillin, and Katharina M. Wilson, eds. *Hrotsvit of Gandersheim. Contexts, Identities, Affinities and Performances* (Toronto, 2004).

Brown, Virginia. "Homiletic Setting and a New Witness to Redaction I of the *Visio sancti Pauli*: Funeral Sermons in Beneventan Script (Vat. Borghese 86)." In *Roma, Magistra Mundi: Itineraria Culturae Medievalis. Mélanges offerts au Père L.E. Boyle à l'occasion de son 75e anniversaire,* edited by Jacqueline Hamesse, 73–88 (Louvain-la-Neuve, 1998).

Bruckner, A. "Weibliche Schreibtätigkeit im schweizerischen Spätmittelalter." In *Festschrift für Bernhard Bischoff zu seinem 65. Geburtstag,* edited by Johanne Autenrieth and Franz Brunhoelzl, 441–48 (Stuttgart, 1971).

Bruckner, A. "Zum Problem der Frauenschriften im Mittelalter." In *Aus Mittelalter und Neuzeit: Gerhard Kallen zum 70. Geburtstag,* edited by J. Engel and H. M. Klinkenberg, 171–83 (Bonn, 1957).

Budny, Mildred. "'St. Dunstan's Classbook' and Its Frontispiece: Dunstan's Portrait and Autograph." In *St. Dunstan. His Life, Times and Cult,* edited by Nigel Ramsay, Margaret Sparks, and Tim Tatton-Brown, 103–25 (Woodbridge, 1992).

Budny, Mildred, and Dominic Tweddle. "The Early Medieval Textiles at Maaseik." *Antiquaries Journal* 65 (1985): 353–89.

Budny, Mildred, and Dominic Tweddle. "The Maaseik Embroideries." *Anglo-Saxon England* 13 (1984): 65–97.

Buhl, Wolfgang, ed. *Karolingisches Franken* (Würzburg, 1973).

Büll, Franziskus. *Das Monasterium Suuarzaha. Ein Beitrag zur Geschichte des Frauenklosters Münsterschwarzach von 788(?) bis 877(?)* (Münsterschwarzach, 1992).

Bullin, Wolfgang, and Franz-Ludwig Ganz, eds. *Dich loben, dir danken. 1300 Jahre Mission und Martyrium der Frankenapostel Kilian, Kolonat und Totnan* (Würzburg, 1990).

Bullough, Donald A. "Alcuin before Frankfurt." In *Das Frankfurter Konzil,* edited by Berndt, 2:571–85.

Burris, Catherine. "The Syriac *Book of Women.*" In *The Early Christian Book,* edited by Klingshirn and Safran, 86–98.

Burrus, Virginia. *"Begotten, Not Made." Conceiving Manhood in Late Antiquity* (Stanford, 2000).

Burrus, Virgina. *Chastity as Autonomy: Women in the Stories of the Apocryphal Acts* (Lewiston, 1987).

Burrus, Virgina . "'In the Theater of this Life': the Performance of Orthodoxy in Late Antiquity." *The Limits of Ancient Christianity: Essays on Late Antique Thought and Culture in Honor of R.A. Markus,* edited by William Kingshirn and Mark Vessey, 80–96 (Ann Arbor, 1999).

Burrus, Virgina. *The Making of a Heretic: Gender, Authority and the Priscillianist Controversy* (Berkeley, 1995).

Butting, Klara. "Go Your Way: Women Rewrite the Scriptures (*Song of Songs* 2:8–14)." In *The Song of Songs,* edited by Brenner and Fontaines, 142–51.

Butzen, Reiner. *Die Merowinger östlich des Mittleren Rheins. Studien zur militärischen, politischen, rechtlichen, religiösen, kirchlichen, kulturellen Erfassung durch Königtum und Adel im 6. sowie 7. Jahrhundert* (Würzburg, 1987).

Cabrera, Juliana. *Estudio sobre el Priscillianismo en la Galicia Antigua* (Published Doctoral Thesis, University of Granada, 1983).

Cabrol, Fernand, and Henri Leclerc, with Henri Marrou, eds. *Dictionnaire d'archéologie chrétienne et de liturgie,* 15 vols. (Paris, 1907–53) = DACL.

Caesarius of Arles. *Sermones*. Edited by Germanus Morin (CCSL 103–4; Turnhout, 1953).

Cameron, Averil. *Christianity and the Rhetoric of Empire. The Development of Christian Discourse* (Berkeley, 1991).

Cameron, Averil. "Social Language and Its Private Deployment." In *East and West: Modes of Communication. Proceedings of the First Plenary Conference at Merida*, edited by Evangelos Chrysos and Ian Wood, 111–25 (Leiden, 1999).

Carossi, Claude. *Le voyage de l'âme dans L'Au-delà* (Rome, 1994).

Carrasco, Magdalena. "An Early Illustrated Manuscript of the Passion of St. Agatha (Paris BN lat. 5594)." *Gesta* 24 (1985): 19–32.

Carrasco, Magdalena. "The Imagery of the Magdalen in Christina of Markyate's Psalter (St. Alban's Psalter)." *Gesta* 38 (1999): 67–80.

Casiday, A. M. C. "St. Aldhelm on Apocrypha." *Journal of Theological Studies*, N.S. 55 (2004): 147–57.

Cassidy, Brendan, and Rosemary Muir Wright, eds. *Studies in the Illustration of the Psalter*. (Stamford, 2000).

Cavadini, John C., ed. *Gregory the Great. A Symposium* (Notre Dame/London, 1995).

Cazelles, Brigitte. *The Lady as Saint: A Collection of French Hagiographic Romances of the Thirteenth Century* (Philadelphia, 1991).

Cereta, Laura. *Collected Letters of a Renaissance Feminist*. Translated by Diana Robin (Chicago, 1997).

César d'Arles. *Oeuvres Monastiques I–II: Oeuvres pour les moniales, Oeuvres pour les moines*. Edited and translated by Adalbert de Vogüé and Joël Courreau (Sources Chrétiennes 345 and 398; Paris, 1988 and 1994).

Chadwick, Henry. *Priscillian of Avila. The Occult and the Charismatic in the Early Church* (Oxford, 1976; 2nd ed., 1997).

Chadwick, Henry. "Review of Klaus Zelzer, *Die alten lateinischen Thomasakten*," in *The Classical Review*, N.S., 29 (1979): 156.

Chance, Jane. "Hrotsvit's Latin Drama *Gallicanus* and the Old English Epic *Elene*: Intercultural Founding Narratives of a Feminized Church." In *Hrotsvit of Gandersheim*, edited by Brown et al., 193–210.

Chavasse, Antoine. "Aménagements liturgiques à Rome, au VIIe et au VIIIe siècle." *RB* 99 (1989): 75–102.

Chavasse, Antoine. "L'épistolier romain du codex de Wurtzbourg: son organization." *RB* 91 (1981): 280–331.

Chavasse, Antoine. *Les Lectionnaires Romains de la messe au VIIe et au VIIIe siècle*, 2 vols. (Fribourg, 1993).

Chavasse, Antoine. *Textes liturgiques de l'Eglise de Rome. Le cycle liturgique romain annuel selon le sacramentaire du Vaticanus Reginensis 316* (Paris, 1997).

Chazelle, Celia. "The Cross, the Image and the Passion in Carolingian Thought and Art" (Unpublished PhD Dissertation, Yale University, 1985).

Chazelle, Celia M. *The Crucified God in the Carolingian Era. Theology and Art of Christ's Passion* (Cambridge, 2001).

Chazelle, Celia. "An *Exemplum* of Humility: The Crucifixion Image in the Drogo Sacramentary." In *Reading Medieval Images. The Art Historian and the Object*, edited by Elizabeth Sears and Thelma K. Thomas, 27–35 (Ann Arbor, 2002).

Chazelle, Celia. "Memory, Instruction, Worship: 'Gregory's' Influence on Early Medieval Doctrines of the Artistic Image." In *Gregory the Great*, edited by Cavadini, 181–215.

Chazelle, Celia. "'Romanness' in Early Medieval Culture." In *Paradigms and Methods*, edited by Chazelle and Lifshitz, 81–100.

Chazelle, Celia, and Felice Lifshitz, eds. *Paradigms and Methods in Early Medieval Studies* (New York, 2007).

Christianson, Eric S. *Ecclesiastes through the Centuries* (Oxford, 2007).

Christine de Pizan. *The Book of the City of Ladies.* Translated by Earl Jeffrey Richards (New York, 1982).

Chronicon Benedictoburanum. Edited by Wilhelm Wattenbach, 212–16 (MGH SS 9; Hanover, 1851).

Ciccarese, M. P. "Le visioni de S. Fursa." *Romanobarbarica* 8 (1984–85): 232–303.

Claesson, Gösta. *Index Tertullianus*, 3 vols. (Paris, 1974–75).

Clancy-Smith, Julia. "Exemplary Women and Sacred Journeys: Women and Gender in Judaism, Christianity and Islam from Late Antiquity to the Eve of Modernity." In *Women's History in Global Perspective*, edited by Bonnie Smith, 3 vols, 1: 92–144 (Champaign, 2004).

Clark, Elizabeth. "Devil's Gateway and Brides of Christ." In *Ascetic Piety and Women's Faith. Essays on Late Ancient Christianity*, edited by Elizabeth Clark, 23–60 (Lewiston, 1986).

Clark, Elizabeth. "Eusebius on Women in Early Church History." In *Eusebius, Christianity and Judaism*, edited by H. W. Attridge and G. Hata, 256–69 (Detroit, 1992).

Clark, Elizabeth. "Ideology, History and the Construction of 'Woman' in Late Antiquity." *Journal of Early Christian Studies* 2 (1994): 155–84.

Clark, Elizabeth. "John Chrysostom and the 'Subintroductae.'" *Church History* 46 (1977): 171–85.

Clark, Elizabeth. *Reading Renunciation: Asceticism and Scripture in Early Christianity* (Princeton, 1999).

Clark, Elizabeth A., and Diane F. Hatch, eds. *The Golden Bough, The Oaken Cross. The Vergilian Cento of Faltonia Betitia Proba* (Chico, 1981).

Classen, Albrecht. "Frauenbriefe an Bonifatius. Frühmittelalterliche Literaturdenkmäler aus literarhistorischer Sicht." *Archiv für Kulturgeschichte* 72 (1990): 251–73.

Classen, Albrecht. *Late-Medieval German Women's Poetry: Secular and Religious Songs* (Cambridge, 2004).

Clayton, Mary. *The Cult of the Virgin Mary in Anglo-Saxon England* (Cambridge, 1990).

Clemens, Lucas. *Tempore Romanorum constructa. Zur Nutzung und Wahrnehmung antiker Überreste nördlich der Alpen während des Mittelalters* (Stuttgart, 2003).

Cloke, Gillian. *"This Female Man of God": Women and Spiritual Power in the Patristic Age, AD 350–450* (London/New York, 1995).

Collins, Roger. *Charlemagne* (Toronto, 1998).

Collins, Roger. "Pippin III as Mayor of the Palace: The Evidence." In *Der Dynastiewechsel von 751*, edited by Becher and Jarnut, 75–91.

Consolino, Franca Ela. "Modelli di santità femminile nelle più antiche Passioni romane." *Augustinianum* 24 (1984): 83–113.

Constable, Giles. "The Ceremonies and Symbolism of Entering Religious Life and Taking the Monastic Habit, from the Fourth to the Twelfth Century." In *Segni e Riti*, 771–834.

Contreni, John J. "'Building Mansions in Heaven': The Visio Baronti, Archangel Raphael and a Carolingian King." *Speculum* 78 (2003): 673–706.

Contreni, John J., "The Pursuit of Knowledge in Carolingian Europe." In *The Gentle Voices of Teachers: Aspects of Learning in the Carolingian Renaissance*, edited by Richard E. Sullivan, 106–41 (Columbus, 1995).

Conybeare, Catherine. "Spaces between Letters: Augustine's Correspondence with Women." In *Voices in Dialogue*, edited by Olson and Kerby-Fulton, 57–72.

Coon, Lynda L. *Sacred Fictions. Holy Women and Hagiography in Late Antiquity* (Philadelphia, 1997).

Cooper, Kate. "Empress and *Theotokos*: Gender and Patronage in the Christological Controversy." In *The Church and Mary*, edited by R. N. Swanson, 39–51 (*Studies in Church History* 39; Woodbridge, 2004).

Coquet, Jean. "A Ligugé un ensemble exceptionnel d'art chrétien primitif." *Archeologia* 113 (1977): 23–30.

Costambeys, Marios, and Conrad Leyser. "To Be the Neighbour of St. Stephen: Patronage, Martyr Cult and Roman Monasteries, c. 600–c. 900." In *Religion, Dynasty and Patronage in Early Christian Rome, 300–900*, edited by Kate Cooper and Julia Hillner, 262–87 (Cambridge, 2007).

Cross, J. E. "English Vernacular Saints' Lives before 1000 AD." In *Hagiographies* III, edited by Guy Philippart, 413–27 (Turnhout, 1996).

Cross, J. E. "*Passio S. Eugeniae et Comitum* and the *Old English Martyrology*." *Notes and Queries* n.s. 29 (1982): 392–97.

Cünnen, Janina. *Fiktionale Nonnenwelten: Angelsächsische Frauenbriefe des 8. und 9. Jahrhunderts.* (Heidelberg, 2000).

Cünnen, Janina. "'Oro pro te sicut pro me.' Berthgyths Briefe an Balthard als Beispiele produktiver Akkulturation." In *Übersetzung, Adaptation und Akkulturation im insularen Mittelalter*, edited by Erich Poppe and Hildegard L. C. Tristram, 185–203 (Münster, 1999).

Cutler, Anthony. "A Byzantine Triptych in Medieval Germany and Its Modern Recovery." *Gesta* 37 (1998): 3–12.

Dagenais, John. *The Ethics of Reading in Manuscript Culture. Glossing the "Libro de Buen Amor"* (Princeton, 1994).

D'Alès, Adhémar. *Priscillien et l'Espagne Chrétienne à la fin du IVe siècle* (Paris, 1936).

Damico, Helen, and Alexandra Hennessey Olsen, eds. *New Readings on Women in Old English Literature* (Bloomington, 1990).

Dannheimer, Hermann. "Im Spiegel der Funde. Die Besiedlungsgeschichte nach den archäologischen Quellen." In *Karolingisches Franken*, edited by Buhl, 71–105.

D'Arrigo, Santo. *Il martirio di sant'Agata nel quadro storico del suo tempo*, 2 vols. (Catania, 1988).

Darsy, Felix Marie Dominique. *Santa Sabina* (Rome, 1961).

Daul, Hansjoachim. "Karlburg. Eine Frühfränkische Königsmark" (Unpublished PhD Dissertation, University of Würzburg, 1961).

Davies, Stevan. *Revolt of the Widows: The Social World of the Apocryphal Acts* (Carbondale, 1980).

Davis, Stephen J. *The Cult of Saint Thecla: A Tradition of Women's Piety in Late Antiquity* (Oxford, 2001).

De Bruyn, Theodore. *Pelagius' Commentary on St. Paul's Epistle to the Romans* (Oxford, 1993).

Defensor de Ligugé. *Livre d'Etincelles*. Translated by H. M. Rochais (Sources Chrétiennes 77 and 86; Paris, 1961–62).

Defensor Logiacensis. *Liber Scintillarum*. Edited by Henricus M. Rochais (CCSL 117; Turnhout, 1957).

De Lacy, Paul. "Thematic and Structural Affinities: *The Wanderer* and *Ecclesiastes.*" *Neophilologus* 82 (1998): 125–37.

Delany, Sheila. "Hagio, Porn and Femcrit." Paper presented at the Congress of the Humanities and Social Sciences (Learneds), Montreal, 1995.

Delehaye, Hippolyte. *Étude sur le légendier romain. Les saints de novembre et de décembre* (Subsidia Hagiographica 23; Brussels, 1936).

De Nie, Giselle. "'Consciousness Fecund through God': From Male Fighter to Spiritual Bride-Mother in Late Antique Female Sanctity." In *Sanctity and Motherhood. Essays on Holy Mothers in the Middle Ages,* edited by Anneke B. Mulder-Bakker, 101–61 (New York/London, 1995).

De Nie, Giselle. "Is een vrouw een mens? Voorschrift, vooroordeel en praktijk in zesde-eeuws Gallië." *Jaarboek voor Vrouwengeschiedenis* 10 (1989): 51–74.

Deshusses, Jean. *Le sacramentaire Grégorien. Ses principales formes d'après les plus anciens manuscrits,* 3 vols. (Fribourg-en-Suisse, 1971–82).

Desobry, Jean. "Le Manuscrit 18 de la Bibliothèque Municipale d'Amiens." In *Techniques narratives au Moyen Age,* edited by André Crepin, 73–125 (Amiens, 1974).

Dey, Henrik. "Bringing Chaos out of Order: New Approaches to the Study of Early Western Monasticism." In *Western Monasticism Ante Litteram*, edited by Dey and Fentress, 19–40.

Dey, Hendrik, and Elizabeth Fentress, eds. *Western Monasticism Ante Litteram: The Spaces of Monastic Observance in Late Antiquity and the Early Middle Ages* (Turnhout, 2011).

Diaz y Diaz, Manuel, ed. *Liber de ordine creaturarum. Un anonimo Irlandes del siglo vii* (Santiago de Compostela, 1972).

Diem, Albrecht. "Das Ende des monastischen Experiments. Liebe, Beichte und Schweigen in der *Regula cuiusdam ad virgines.*" In *Female Vita Religiosa,* edited by Melville and Müller, 81–136.

Diem, Albrecht. "Inventing the Holy Rule: Some Observations on the History of Monastic Normative Observance in the Early Medieval West." In *Western Monasticism Ante Litteram,* edited by Dey and Fentress, 53–84.

Diem, Albrecht. *Das Monastische Experiment. Die Rolle der Keuschheit bei der Entstehung des westlichen Klosterwesens* (Münster, 2005).

Diem, Albrecht. "Rewriting Benedict: The *Regula cuiusdam ad virgines* and Inter-textuality as a Tool to Construct a Monastic Identity." *Journal of Medieval Latin* 17 (2006): 313–28.

Dienemann, Joachim. *Der Kult des heiligen Kilian im 8. und 9. Jahrhundert. Beiträge zur geistigen und politischen Entwicklung der Karolingerzeit* (Würzburg, 1955).

Dinklage, Karl. "Hammelburg im Frühmittelalter." *Mainfränkisches Jahrbuch* 11 (1959): 18–63.

Dinzelbacher, Peter. "Die Verbreitung der apokryphen *Visio Sancti Pauli* im mittelalterlichen Europa." *Mittellateinisches Jahrbuch* 27 (1992): 77–90.

Di Sciacca, Claudia. *Finding the Right Words: Isidore's Synonyma in Anglo-Saxon England* (Toronto, 2008).

Di Sciacca, Claudia. "Isidorian Scholarship at the School of Theodore and Hadrian: The Case of the *Synonyma*." In *Quaestio: Selected Proceedings of the Cambridge Colloquium in Anglo-Saxon, Norse and Celtic,* edited by Catherine Jones, 76–106 (Cambridge, 2002).

Doll, L. Anton, ed. *Traditiones Wizenburgenses: Die Urkunden des Klosters Weissenburg, 661–864. Eingeleitet und aus dem Nachlass von Karl Glöckner herausgegeben von Anton Doll* (Darmstadt 1979).

Dorival, Gilles. "Exégèse Juive et Exégèse Chrétienne." In *Der Kommentar,* edited by Geerlings and Schulze, 1: 131–50.

Driscoll, Michael S. "The Seven Penitential Psalms: Their Designation and Usages from the Middle Ages Onwards." *Ecclesia Orans* 17 (2000): 153–202.

Dronke, Ernst F. J., ed. *Codex Diplomaticus Fuldensis* (Kassel, 1850; reprint Aalen, 1962).

Dronke, Peter. *Women Writers of the Middle Ages. A Critical Study of Texts from Perpetua (203) to Marguerite Porete (1310)* (Cambridge, 1984).

Dubois, Jacques. "Cecile." In *Histoire des saints et de la sainteté chrétienne II: La semence des martyrs, 33–313,* edited by André Mandouze, 95–102 (Paris, 1987).

Dufourcq, Albert. *De Manichaeismo apud Latinos quinto sextoque saeculo atque de Latinis Apocryphis Libris* (Paris, 1900).

Dufourcq, Albert, with François Dolbeau. *Étude sur les Gesta Martyrum,* 5 vols. (Paris, 1900–7 and 1988).

Dümmler, Ernestus, ed. *Epistolae Bonifatii* (MGH Epistolae 3, Berlin, 1916).

Dunn, E. Catherine. *The Gallican Saint's Life and the Late Roman Dramatic Tradition* (Washington, D.C., 1989).

Dunning, Benjamin H. *Specters of Paul. Sexual Difference in Early Christian Thought* (Philadelphia, 2011).

Dupuy, Bernard. "La Christologie de Nestorius." *Istina* 40 (1995): 56–64.

Düwel, Klaus. "Epigraphische Zeugnisse für die Macht der Schrift im Östlichen Frankenreich." In *Die Franken. Wegbereiter Europas,* 540–52.

Dwyer, M. E. "An Unstudied Redaction of the *Visio Pauli.*" *Manuscripta* 32 (1988): 121–38.

The Earliest Life of Gregory the Great by an Anonymous Monk of Whitby. Edited by Bertram Colgrave (Lawrence, 1968).

Easton, Martha. "Saint Agatha and the Sanctification of Sexual Violence." *Studies in Iconography* 16 (1994): 83–118.

Edel, Doris, ed. *Cultural Identity and Cultural Integration. Ireland and Europe in the Early Middle Ages* (Dublin, 1995).

Effros, Bonnie. "Appearance and Ideology: Creating Distinctions between Clerics and Laypersons in Early Medieval Gaul." In *Encountering Medieval Textiles and Dress,* edited by Koslin and Snyder, 7–24.

Eigil. "*Vita Sturmi.*" In *Die Vita Sturmi des Eigil von Fulda. Literarkritisch-historische Untersuchung und Edition,* edited by Pius Engelbert (Marburg, 1968), 131–163.

Elbern, Victor. "Theologische Spekulation und die Gestaltungsweise frühmittelalterlicher Kunst." *Frühmittelalterliche Studien* 1 (1967):144–55.

Eleen, Luba. *The Illustration of the Pauline Epistles in French and English Bibles of the Twelfth and Thirteenth Centuries* (Oxford, 1982).

Elfassi, Jacques. "Defensor de Ligugé, Lecteur et transmetteur des *Synonyma* d'Isidore de Séville." In *Munus Quaesitum Meritis. Homenaje a Carmen Codoñer,* edited by Gregorio Hinojo Andrés and José Carlos Fernández Corte, 243–53. (Salamanca, 2007).

Elfassi, Jacques. "Les Deux Recensions des *Synonyma.*" In *L'Édition critique des œuvres d'Isidore de Séville. Les Recensions Multiples,* edited by M. A. Andrés Sanz, J. Elfassi, and J. C. Martin, 153–84 (Paris, 2008).

Elfassi, Jacques. "Genèse et Originalité du Style Synonymique dans les *Synonyma* d'Isidore de Séville." *Revue des études latines* 83 (2006): 226–45.

Elfassi, Jacques. "La Langue des *Synonyma* d'Isidore de Séville." *Bulletin du Cange. Archivum Latinitatis Medii Aevi* 62 (2004): 59–100.

Elfassi, Jacques. "Les *Synonyma* d'Isidore de Séville: édition critique et histoire du texte" (Unpublished PhD Dissertation, École Pratique des Hautes Études, Paris, 2001).

Elfassi, Jacques. "Les *Synonyma* d'Isidore de Séville: un manuel de grammaire ou de morale ? La réception médiévale de l'œuvre." *Revue d'études augustiniennes et patristiques* 52 (2006): 167–98.

Elfassi, Jacques. "Trois Aspects Inattendus de la postérité des *Synonyma* d'Isidore de Séville: Les Prières, les textes hagiographiques et les collections canoniques." *Revue d'Histoire des Textes* n.s. 1 (2006): 109–52.

Elliott, Dyan. *Proving Woman: Female Spirituality and Inquisitional Culture in the Later Middle Ages* (Princeton, 2004).

Elm, K., and M. Parisse, eds. *Doppelklöster und andere Formen der Symbiose männlicher und weiblicher Religiosen im Mittelalter* (Berlin, 1992).

Emmerich, Franz, ed. *Passio maior Kiliani.* In *Der heilige Kilian,* 13–25 (Würzburg, 1896).

Emmert, Jürgen. "Gertrudis Tripartita. Gestalt und Legende der hl. Gertrud von Nivelles." In *Gertrud in Franken,* edited by Lenssen, 9–12.

Engemann, Josef. "Palästinensische Pilgerampullen im F.J. Dölger-Institut in Bonn." *Jahrbuch für Antike und Christentum* 16 (1973): 1–27.

Erichsen, Johannes. "Kilian, der Märtyrer des Ostens—Erhebung und Anfänge des Kultes." In *Kilian. Mönch aus Irland,* 212–37.

Erler, Mary C. *Women, Reading, and Piety in Late Medieval England* (Cambridge, 2002).

Ermini, Filippo. *Il Centone di Proba e la Poesia Centonaria Latina* (Rome, 1909).

Étaix, Raymond. "Fragments inédits de *l'Opus imperfectum in Matthaeum.*" RB 84 (1974): 271–300.

Étaix, Raymond. *Homéliaires Patristiques Latins. Receuil d'études de manuscrits médiévaux* (Paris, 1994).

Étaix, Raymond. "Note sur la tradition manuscrite des *Homélies sur l'Évangile* de saint Grégoire le Grand." In *Grégoire le Grand,* edited by Jacques Fontaine, Robert Gillet, and Stan Pellistrandi, 551–59 (Paris, 1986).

Étaix, Raymond. "Répertoire des manuscrits des homélies sur l'Evangile de saint Grégoire le Grand." *Sacris Erudiri* 36 (1996): 107–45.

Étaix, Raymond. "Sermons ariens inedits." *Recherches Augustiniennes* 26 (1992): 143–79.

Ettel, Peter, and Dieter Rüdel. "Castellum und villa Karloburg. Historische und archäologische Überlieferung." In *1250 Jahre Bistum Würzburg*, edited by Lenssen and Wamers, pp. 297–318.

Eudocia. *Homerocentones*. Edited by Rocco Schembra (Turnhout, 2007).

Everett, Nicholas. "The Earliest Recension of the Life of St. Sirius of Pavia." *Studi medievali* ser 3, 43 (2002): 857–957.

Everett, Nicholas. *Literacy in Lombard Italy, c. 568–774* (Cambridge, 2003).

Ewig, Eugen. "Die ältesten Mainzer Patrozinien und die Frühgeschichte des Bistums Mainz." In *Das erste Jahrtausend,* edited by Victor H. Elbern, 1: 114–27 (Düsseldorf, 1962); reprinted in *SFG* 2: 154–70.

Ewig, Eugen. "Beobachtungen zur Entwicklung der fränkischen Reichskirche unter Chrodegang von Metz." *Frühmittelalterliche Studien* 2 (1968): 67–77; reprinted in *SFG* 2: 220–231.

Ewig, Eugen. "Milo et eiusmodi similes." In *Sankt Bonifatius. Gedenkgabe zum 1200 Todestag,* 412–40 (Fulda, 2nd ed, 1954); reprinted in *SFG* 2: 189–219.

Ewig, Eugen. "Saint Chrodegang et la reforme de l'eglise franque." In *Saint Chrodegang. Communications presentées au colloque tenu à Metz à l'occasion du XIIe centenaire de sa mort,* 25–53 (Metz, 1967); reprinted in *SFG* 2:232–59.

Exum, J. Cheryl. "Ten Things Every Feminist Should Know about the *Song of Songs.*" In *The Song of Songs,* edited by Brenner and Fontaine, 24–35.

Falck, Ludwig. *Mainz im frühen und hohen Mittelalter (Mitte 5. Jahrhundert Bis 1244)* (Düsseldorf, 1972).

Farr, Carol A. "Worthy Women on the Ruthwell Cross. Woman as Sign in Early Anglo-Saxon Monasticism." In *The Insular Tradition,* edited by Karkov et al., 45–61.

Fell, Christine. "Some Implications of the Boniface Correspondance." In *New Readings,* edited by Damico and Olsen, 29–43.

Ferrante, Joan. *Epistolae: Medieval Women's Latin Letters.* Online at http://epistolae. ccnmtl.columbia.edu/.

Ferrante, Joan. *To the Glory of Her Sex: Women's Role in the Composition of Medieval Texts* (Bloomington/Indianapolis, 1997).

Fingernagel, Andreas. *Die Illuminierten Lateinischen Handschriften Deutscher Provenienz der Staatsbibliothek-Preusischer Kulturbesitz Berlin, 8.–12. Jahrhundert,* 2 vols. (Wiesbaden, 1991).

Finsterwalder, P. W. *Die canones Theodori Cantuarensis und ihre Überlieferungsformen* (Weimar, 1929).

Fiorentini, Isotta, and Piero Orioli. *S. Apollinare Nuovo. I Mosaici di Teodorico* (Faenza, 2000).

Fischer, Bonifatius. *Lateinische Bibelhandschriften im frühen Mittelalter* (Freiburg/ Breisgau, 1985).

Fontaine, Jacques. *Isidore de Séville. Genèse et originalité de la culture hispanique au temps des Wisigoths* (Turnhout, 2000).

Fonte, Moderata. *The Worth of Women: Wherein Is Clearly Revealed Their Nobility and Their Superiority to Men.* Translated by Virginia Cox (Chicago, 1997).

Die Franken. Wegbereiter Europas vor 1500 Jahren: König Chlodwig und seine Erben, 2 vols. (Katalog der Austellung Reiss-Museum, Mannheim 1996–97; Mainz, 1997).

Fransen, Paul-Irénée. "D'Eugippius à Bède le Vénérable. A propos de leurs florilèges augustiniens." *RB* 97 (1987): 187–94.

Frantzen, Allen J. "The Significance of the Frankish Penitentials." *Journal of Ecclesiastical History* 30 (1979): 409–21.

Freeman, Ann, and Paul Meyvaert. "The Meaning of Theodulf's Apse Mosaic at Germigny-des-Prés." *Gesta* 40 (2001): 125–39.

Freeman-Grenville, G. S. P. *The Basilica of the Holy Sepulchre of Jesus Christ in Jerusalem* (Jerusalem, 1993).

Fried, Johannes, ed. *794–Karl der Große in Frankfurt am Main. Ein König bei der Arbeit. Ausstellung zum 1200-Jahre Jubiläum der Stadt Frankfurt am Main* (Sigmaringen, 1994).

Friese, Alfred. *Studien zur Herrschaftsgeschichte des Fränkischen Adels der mainländisch-thüringische Raum vom 7. bis 11. Jahrhundert* (Stuttgart, 1979).

Friesen, Bill. "Answers and Echoes: The *Libellus responsionum* and the Hagiography of North-western European Mission." *EME* 14 (2006): 153–72.

Fros, Henry. "Inédits non recensés dans la BHL." *AB* 102 (1984): 163–96 and 355–80.

Führer zu vor- und frühgeschichtlichen Denkmälern 27: Würzburg, Karlstadt, Iphofen, Schweinfurt. Edited by Römisch-Germanisches Zentralmuseum, Mainz (Mainz, 1975).

Fulgentius of Ruspe. *Opera.* Edited by J. Fraipont. (CCSL 91/91A; Turnhout, 1968).

Fulgentius of Ruspe. *Selected Works.* Translated by Robert B. Eno (Washington, D.C., 1997).

Gagny, Jean de, ed. *Primasii Commentaria in Epistolas S. Pauli* (Lyons, 1537; in PL 68: 415–506).

Gaillard, Michèle. "De l'*Eigenkloster* au monastère royal: l'abbaye Saint-Jean de Loan, du milieu du VIIe siècle au milieu du VIIIe siècle à travers les sources hagiographiques." In *L'hagiographie du haut Moyen Âge en Gaule du Nord,* edited by Martin Heinzelmann, 249–62 (Stuttgart, 2001).

Gambero, Luigi. *Mary and the Fathers of the Church. The Blessed Virgin Mary in Patristic Thought.* Translated by Thomas Buffer (San Francisco, 1999).

Gameson, Richard, ed. *The Early Medieval Bible. Its Production, Decoration and Use* (Cambridge, 1994).

Gameson, Richard. "The Royal 1.B.vii Gospels and English Book Production in the Seventh and Eighth Century." In *The Early Medieval Bible,* edited by Gameson, 24–52.

Ganz, David. "Roman Manuscripts in Francia and Anglo-Saxon England." In *Roma tra Oriente e Occidente, Settimane* 49 (2002) 1: 607–49.

Garver, Valerie L. "Weaving Words in Silk: Women and Inscribed Bands in the Carolingian World." *Medieval Clothing and Textiles* 6 (2010): 33–56.

Garver, Valerie L. *Women and Aristocratic Culture in the Carolingian World* (Ithaca, 2009).

Gauthier, Nancy, Brigitte Beaujard, Rollins Guild, and Marie-Pierre Terrien. *Province ecclésiastique de Mayence (Germania Prima), Topographie chrétienne des cités de la Gaule XI* (Paris, 2000).

Geerlings, Wilhelm, "Die Lateinisch-Patristischen Kommentare," in *Der Kommentar,* edited by Geerlings and Schulze, 1:1–14.

Geerlings, Wilhelm, and Christian Schulze, eds. *Der Kommentar in Antike und Mittelalter. Beiträge zu seiner Erforschung,* 2 vols. (Leiden, 2002).

Geisel, Christof. *Die Juden im Frankenreich. Von den Merowingern bis zum Tode Ludwigs des Frommen* (Frankfurt, 1998).

Geith, Karl-Ernst. *Priester Arnolts Legende von der Hl. Juliana. Untersuchungen zur lateinischen Juliana-legende und zum Text des deutschen Gedichtes* (Freiburg/Breisgau, 1965).

Gemmiti, Dante. *La Donna in Origene (con testimonianzi dei primi tre secoli)* (Naples, 1996).

Gerberding, Richard A. "716: A Crucial Year for Charles Martel." In *Karl Martel,* edited by Jarnut, et al., 205–16.

Gerlach, Klaus. "Der Grenzverlauf der Hammelburger Markbeschreibung des Jahres 777." *WDGB* 58 (1996): 9–22.

Gerlach, Stefan. "Pfarrkirche von Kleinlangheim, Landkreis Kitzingen. Nachfolgerin einer grundherrschaftlichen Eigenkirche?" In *1250 Jahre Bistum Würzburg,* edited by Lenssen and Wamser, 289–92.

Gilchrist, Roberta. *Gender and Material Culture. The Archeology of Religious Women* (London/New York, 1994).

Gilsdorf, Sean. *Queenship and Sanctity: The Lives of Mathilda and the Epitaph of Adelheid* (Washington, D.C., 2004).

Giuffrè, Vincenzo. *La Passione di San Potito* (Naples, 2001).

Glaser, Elvira. *Frühe Griffelglossierung aus Friesing. Ein Beitrag zu den Anfängen althochdeutscher Schriftlichkeit* (Göttingen, 1996).

Goetz, Hans-Werner. *Frauen im frühen Mittelalter. Frauenbild und Frauenleben im Frankenreich* (Weimar, 1995).

Goetz, Hans-Werner, ed. *Weibliche Lebensgestaltung im frühen Mittelalter* (Cologne, 1991).

Goitein, S. D. "The *Song of Songs*: A Female Composition." In *A Feminist Companion to the Song of Songs,* edited by Brenner, 58–66.

Gordini, Gian Domenico. "Eugenia." In *Bibliotheca Sanctorum,* edited by Vizzini et al., 5:180–81.

Gordini, Gian Domenico, Renato Aprile, and Aurelio Rigoli. "Agata." In *Bibliotheca Sanctorum,* edited by Vizzini et al., 1:320–35.

Gori, Franco. "La tradizione manoscritta delle *Enarrationes in Psalmos Graduum* di Agostino. Studio Preliminare per l'edizione critica." *Augustinianum* 37 (1997): 183–228.

Gorman, Michael J. *Apostle of the Crucified Lord: A Theological Introduction to Paul and His Letters* (Grand Rapids, 2004).

Gorman, Michael J. *Cruciformity: Paul's Narrative Theology of the Cross* (Grand Rapids, 2001).

Gorman, Michael J. *Inhabiting the Cruciform God: Kenosis, Justification and Theosis in Paul's Narrative Soteriology* (Grand Rapids, 2009).

Gorman, Michael M. "Frigulus: Hiberno-Latin Author or Pseudo-Irish Phantom? Comments on the Edition of the *Liber Questionum in Evangeliis* (CCSL 108F)." *Revue d'Histoire Ecclesiastique* 100 (2005): 425–56.

Gorman, Michael M. "The Oldest Lists of Latin Books." *Scriptorium* 58 (2004): 48–63.

Gössman, Elisabeth. "Mariologische Entwicklungen im Mittelalter. Frauenfreundliche und frauenfeindliche Aspekte." In *Maria*, edited by Gössman and Bauer, 63–85.

Gössman, Elisabeth, and Dieter Bauer, eds. *Maria—für alle Frauen oder über allen Frauen?* (Freiburg, 1989).

Grabar, André, with photographs by Denise Fourmont. *Les Ampoules de sainte terre (Monza-Bobbio)* (Paris, 1958).

Graham, Timothy. "Changing the Context of Medieval Manuscript Art: The Case of Matthew Parker." In *Medieval Art: Recent Perspectives. A Memorial Tribute to C. R. Dodwell*, edited by Gale R. Owen-Crocker and Timothy Graham, 183–205 (Manchester, 1998).

Granier, Thomas. "Les échanges culturels dans l'Italie Méridional du Haut Moyen âge: Naples, Bénévent et le Mont-Cassin aux VIIIe-XIIe siècles." In *Les échanges culturels au Moyen Âge*, edited by Société des Historiens Mediévistes de l'Enseignement Superieur Publique, 89–105 (Paris, 2002).

Green, D. H. *Language and History in the Early Germanic World* (Cambridge, 1998).

Grégoire, Réginald. *Les Homéliaires du Moyen Age. Inventaire et Analyse des Manuscrits* (Rome, 1966).

Gregory I. *Forty Gospel Homilies*. Translated by Dom Hurst, OSB (Kalamazoo, 1990; reprint, Piscataway, 2009).

Gregory I. *Gregor der Grosse, Homiliae in Evangelia/Evangelienhomilien*. Edited and translated by Michael Fiedrowicz, 2 vols. (Freiburg, 1997).

Gregory I. *Libellus Responsionum*. Edited by Paul Ewald and Louis Hartmann, *MGH Epistolae* 2:332–43 (Berlin, 1899).

Gregory I. *Reading the Gospels with Gregory the Great. Homilies on the Gospels 21–26*. Translated by Santha Bhattacharji (Petersham, 2001).

Gregory I. *Registrum Epistolarum*. Edited by Paul Ewald and Louis Hartmann, *MGH Epistolae* 1–2 (Berlin, 1899).

Gregory I. *Grégoire le Grand, Règle Pastorale*. Edited and translated by Bruno Judic (Sources Chrétiennes 381–82; Paris, 1992).

Gregory of Elvira. *Gregorius Illibertanus Faustinus Luciferianus*. Edited by Vinzenz Bulhart (CCSL 69; Turnhout, 1967).

Gregory of Tours. *Libri Historiarum X*. Edited by Bruno Krusch (MGH SRM 1.1; Hanover, 1951).

Gribomont, Jean. "Une ancienne version latine du protévangile de Jacques." *AB* 83 (1965): 365–410.

Griesinger, Emily. "Faith and Feminism in the Middle Ages: The Spirituality of Hildegard of Bingen." In *Medieval Germany: Associations and Delineations*, edited by Nancy van Deusen, 113–36 (Claremont, 2000).

Griffiths, Fiona. *The Garden of Delights. Reform and Renaissance for Women in the Twelfth Century* (Philadelphia, 2006).

Griffiths, Fiona. "'Like the Sister of Aaron': Medieval Religious Women as Makers and Donors of Liturgical Textiles." In *Female Vita Religiosa*, edited by Melville and Müller, 343–74.

Grondijs, L. H. *L'iconographie Byzantine du crucifié mort sur la croix* (2nd ed, Brussels/Utrecht, 1947).

Grote, Otto freiherr, ed. *Lexicon deutscher Stifter, Klöster und Ordenshäuser*, 2 vols (Osterwieck, 1881).

Grundmann, Herbert. *Religiöse Bewegungen im Mittelalter. Untersuchungen über die geschichtlichen Zusammenhänge zwischen der Ketzerei, den Bettelorden und der religiösen Frauenbewegung im 12. und 13. Jahrhundert und über die geschichtlichen Grundlagen der deutschen Mystik.* (Berlin, 1935); English translation as *Religious Movements in the Middle Ages. The Historical Links between Heresy, the Mendicant Orders, and the Women's Religious Movement in the Twelfth and Thirteen Century, with the Historical Foundations of German Mysticism*, translated by Steven Rowan (Notre Dame, 1995).

Gugel, Klaus. *Welche erhaltenen mittelalterlichen Handschriften dürfen der Bibliothek des Klosters Fulda zugerechnet werden?* Vol. I: *Die Handschriften* (Frankfurt, 1995).

Haggenmüller, Reinhold. "Frühmittelalterliche Bußbücher (*Paenitentialia*) und das Kloster Lorsch." *Geschichtsblätter Kreis Bergstraße* 25 (1992): 1–20.

Haggenmüller, Reinhold. "Zur Rezeption der Beda und Egbert zugeschriebenen Bußbücher." In *Aus Archiven und Bibliotheken*, edited by Mordek, 149–59.

Haggenmüller, Reinhold. *Die Überlieferung der Beda und Egbert zugeschriebenen Bußbücher* (Frankfurt, 1991).

Hahn, Hans. "Fulda: Domplatz-Bereich, St. Michael, Petersberg." In *Hessen im Frühmittelalter*, edited by Roth and Wamers, 300–11.

Haines-Eitzen, Kim. "Engendering Palimpsests: Reading the Textual Tradition of the Acts of Paul and Thecla." In *The Early Christian Book*, edited by Klingshirn and Safran, 177–93.

Haines-Eitzen, Kim. *Guardians of Letters. Literacy, Power and the Transmitters of Early Christian Literature* (Oxford, 2000).

Haines-Eitzen, Kim. "'Girls Trained in Beautiful Writing': Female Scribes in Roman Antiquity and Early Christianity." *Journal of Early Christian Studies* 6 (1998): 629–46; reprinted as chapter 2 in Haines-Eitzen, *Guardians of Letters*.

Hall, Thomas N. "The Early Medieval Sermon." In *The Sermon*, edited by Beverly Mayne Kienzle, 203–69 (TSMAO 81–83; Turnhout, 2000).

Hamburger, Jeffrey F. "Brother, Bride and *alter Christus*: The Virginal Body of John the Evangelist in Medieval Art, Theology and Literature." In *Text und Kultur. Mittelalterliche Literatur 1150–1450*, edited by Ursula Peters, 296–327 (Stuttgart, 2001).

Hamburger, Jeffrey F. *Nuns as Artists. The Visual Culture of a Medieval Convent* (Berkeley, 1997).

Hamburger, Jeffrey F. *The Visual and the Visionary. Art and Female Spirituality in Late Medieval Germany* (New York, 1998).

Hamburger, Jeffrey F., and Robert Suckale. "Zwischen Diesseits und Jenseits—Die Kunst der geistlichen Frauen im Mittelalter." In *Krone und Schleier*, 20–39.

Hamesse, Jacqueline. "A propos de quelques techniques d'interprétation et de compilation des textes. Paraphrases, florilèges et compendia." In *Itinéraires de la raison: Etudes de philosophie médiévale offertes à Maria Cândida Pacheco*, edited by José Francisco Meirinhos, 11–34 (Louvain-la-Neuve, 2005).

Hanselmann, J. F. "Der Codex Vat. Pal. 289: Ein Beitrag zum Mainzer Skriptorium in 9. Jahrhundert." *Scriptorium* 41 (1987): 78–87.

Hanson, John. "The Stuttgart Casket and the Permeability of the Byzantine Artistic Tradition." *Gesta* 37 (1998): 13–25.

Harries, Richard. *The Passion in Art* (Aldershot, 2004).

Hartmann, Wilfried. "Rechtskenntnis und Rechtsverständnis bei den Laien des früheren Mittelalters." In *Aus Archiven und Bibliotheken,* edited by Mordek, 1–20.

Hasdenteufel-Röding, Maria. "Studien zur Gründung von Frauenklöstern im frühen Mittelalter. Ein Beitrag zum religiösen Ideal der Frau und seiner monastischen Umsetzung" (Unpublished PhD Dissertation, University of Freiburg, 1988).

Haselbach, Irene. *Aufstieg und Herrschaft der Karolinger in der Darstellung der sogenannten Annales Mettenses priores. Ein Beitrag zur Geschichte der politischen Ideen im Reiche Karls des Großen* (Lübeck, 1970).

Haseloff, Günter. "Irische Handschriften des 7. und frühen 8. Jahrhunderts." In *Kilian. Mönch aus Irland. Aufsätze,* edited by Johannes Erichsen and Evamaria Brockhoff, 93–106 (Munich, 1989).

Haub, Rita. "Die ältesten Originalurkunden im Archiv des Benediktinerinnenklosters St. Walburg in Eichstätt." *Jahrbuch für fränkische Landesforschung* 5 (1996): 123–48.

Haubrichs, Wolfgang. "Sprache und Sprachzeugnisse der merowingischer Franken." In *Die Franken. Wegbereiter Europas,* 559–73.

Häussling, Angelus Albertus. "*Missarum Sollemnia*: Beliebige Einzelfeiern oder Integrierte Liturgie?" In *Segni e Riti,* 2:559–78.

Häussling, Angelus Albertus. *Mönchskonvent und Eucharistiefeier. Eine Studie über die Messe in der abendländischen Klosterliturgie des frühen Mittelalters und zur Geschichte der Meßhäuffigkeit* (Münster, 1973).

Hauswald, Eckhard. *Pirmins Scarapsus. Einleitung und Edition* (Unpublished PhD Dissertation, University of Konstanz, 2006).

Hayne, Léonie. "Thecla and the Church Fathers." *Vigiliae Christianae* 48 (1994): 209–18.

Heene, Katrien. *The Legacy of Paradise. Marriage, Motherhood and Woman in Carolingian Edifying Literature* (Frankfurt, 1997).

Heffernan, Thomas J. *Sacred Biography: Saints and Their Biographers in the Middle Ages* (New York, 1988).

Heidrich, Ingrid. "Von Plectrud zu Hildegard. Beobachtungen zum Besitzrecht adliger Frauen im Frankenreich des 7. und 8. Jahrhunderts und zur politischen Rolle der Frauen der frühen Karolinger." *Rheinische Vierteljahrsblätter* 52 (1988): 1–15.

Heinemeyer, Walter, and Berthold Jaeger, eds. *Fulda in seiner Geschichte. Landschaft, Reichsabtei, Stadt* (Fulda, 1995).

Heitz, Carol. "Eucharistie, Synaxe et Espace liturgique." In *Segni e Riti,* 2:609–30.

Heitz, Carol. "Fouilles et datation de l'ancienne abbatiale Saint-Martin de Ligugé." *Académie des inscriptions et belles-lettres. Comptes-rendus des séances* 4 (1992): 857–67.

Helmer, Friedrich, with Hermann Hauke und Elisabeth Wunderle. *Katalog der lateinischen Handschriften der Bayerischen Staatsbibliothek München: Die*

Handschriften aus St. Emmeram in Regensburg, vol. 3: Clm 14261–14400 (Wiesbaden, 2011).

Helvétius, Anne-Marie. "L'organization des monastères féminins à l'époque mérovingienne." In *Female Vita Religiosa*, edited by Melville and Müller, 151–69.

Hen, Yitzhak. "The Annals of Metz and the Merovingian Past." In *The Uses of the Past in the Early Middle Ages*, edited by Yitzhak Hen and Matthew Innes, 175–90 (Cambridge, 2000).

Hen, Yitzhak. "The Structure and Aims of the *Visio Baronti*." *Journal of Theological Studies* n.s. 47 (1996): 477–97.

Hench, George H., ed. *Der Althochdeutsche Isidor. Facsimile-Ausgabe des Pariser Codex* (Strassburg, 1893).

Henderson, George. *From Durrow to Kells: The Insular Gospel-Books 650–800* (London, 1987).

Henschius, Godefridus. "Commentarius Praevius." *AASS Februarii 2*, edited by Johannes Bollandus and Godefridus Henschius (Antwerp, 1658), 535–37.

Hermann, Julius Hermann. *Beschreibendes Verzeichnis der Illuminierten Handschriften in Österreich VIII : Die Frühmittelalterliche Handschriften des Abendlandes* (Leipzig, 1923).

Herrick, Samantha Kahn. *Imagining the Sacred Past. Hagiography and Power in Early Normandy* (Cambridge, 2007).

Herrmann, Franz Xavier. "Die Inschrift zu Ehren des zweiten Würzburger Bischofs Megingoz, ein Zeugnis des Kulturellen Aufschwungs in der Karolingerzeit." In *1250 Jahre Bistum Würzburg*, edited by Lenssen and Wamers, 69–75.

Heyen, Franz-Josef. *Untersuchungen zur Geschichte des Benedicterinnenklosters Pfalzel bei Trier (700–1016)* (Göttingen, 1966).

Higley, Sarah L. "Dressing Up the Nuns: The *Lingua Ignota* and Hildegard of Bingen's Clothing." *Medieval Clothing and Textiles* 6 (2010): 93–109.

Hochholzer, Elmar. "Zur Herkunft eines Beda-fragments in Angelsächsischer Schrift (WB UB M.p.th.f. 181)." *Mainfrankisches Jahrbuch* 49 (1997): 15–31.

Hochstetler, Donald. *A Conflict of Traditions. Women in Religion in the Early Middle Ages (500–840)* (Lanham, 1992).

Hofer, Andrew. "Matthew 25: 31–46 as an Hermeneutical Rule in Augustine's Ennarationes in Psalmos." *Downside Review* 126 (2008): 285–300.

Hoffman, Hartmut. "Das Skriptorium von Essen in ottonischen und frühsalischen Zeit." In *Kunst im Zeitalter der Kaiserin Theophanu*, edited by Anton Von Euw and Peter Schreiner, 113–54 (Cologne, 1993).

Hoffman, Hartmut. *Untersuchungen zur karolingischen Annalistik* (Bonn, 1958).

Hofhansl, Ernst. "Gewänder, Liturgische." In *Theologische Realenzyklopädie* 13: 159–67 (Berlin, 1984).

Hofmann, Gustav. *Bayerns Kirche Im Mittelalter: Handschriften und Urkunden aus Bayerischem Staatsbesitz* (Munich, 1960).

Hofmann, Josef. "Altenglische und althochdeutsche Glossen aus Würzburg und dem weiteren angelsächsischen Missionsgebiet." *Beiträge zur Geschichte der deutschen Sprache und Literatur* 85 (1963): 27–131; reprinted in and cited from Köbler, *Ergängzungen*, 604–86.

Hofmann, Josef. "Der Lambach-Wiener 'Prosper' (Pomerius) aus Würzburg." *WDGB* 26 (1963): 29–61.

Hofmann, Josef. "Verstreute Blätter eines deutsch-insularen Sakramentars aus Neustadt am Main (Würzburg–Wertheim–Leningrad)." *Mainfränkisches Jahrbuch* 9 (1957): 133–41.

Holcomb, Melanie. "How Ada Lost Her School, and Other Tales of Carolingian Abbesses and the Arts." Paper presented at the International Congress on Medieval Studies, 2005.

Holder-Egger, O., ed. *Vitae Burchardi episcopi Wirziburgensis,* 44–62 (MGH SS 15.1; Hanover, 1887).

Hollis, Stephanie. *Anglo-Saxon Women and the Church: Sharing a Common Fate* (Woodbridge, 1998).

Hotchkiss, Valerie. *Clothes Make the Man. Female Cross Dressing in Medieval Europe* (New York, 1996).

Hugeburc (Huneberc) of Heidenheim. *Vitae Willibaldi et Wynnebaldi,* including the *Hoedeporicon,* edited by O. Holder-Egger, 80–117 (MGH SS 15.1; Hanover, 1887).

Humphries, Mark. *Communities of the Blessed. Social Environment and Religious Change in Northern Italy, AD 200–400* (Oxford, 1999).

Hürkey, Edgar. *Das Bild des Gekreuzigten im Mittelalter. Untersuchungen zu Gruppierung, Entwicklung und Verbreitung anhand der Gewandmotive* (Worms, 1983).

Hussey, Matthew T. "Ascetics and Aesthetics: The Anglo-Saxon Manuscripts of Isidore of Seville's *Synonyma* " (Unpublished PhD Dissertation, University of Wisconsin-Madison, 2005).

Hussey, Matthew T. "The Franco-Saxon *Synonyma* in the Ragyndrudis Codex: Anglo-Saxon Design in a Luxeuil-Scripted Booklet." *Scriptorium* 58 (2004): 227–38.

Hussey, Matthew T. "*Transmarinis litteris:* Southumbria and the Transmission of Isidore's *Synonyma.*" *Journal of English and Germanic Philology* 107 (2008): 141–68.

Hussong, Ulrich. "Die Reichsabtei Fulda im frühen und hohen Mittelalter." In *Fulda in seiner Geschichte,* edited by Heinemeyer and Jaeger, 89–179.

I, Deug-su. "La festa della purificazione in Occidente (secoli IV–VIII)." *Studi medioevali* Series 3, 15 (1974): 143–216.

I, Deug-su. *L'eloquenza del Silenzio nelle fonti mediolatine. Il caso di Leoba, "dilecta" di Bonifacio Vinfrido* (Florence, 2004).

I, Deug-Su. "Lioba, *dilecta Bonifatii.* Eine Liebesgeschichte im 8. Jahrhundert?" *Medieval English Studies* 10 (2002). Online at http://hompi.sogang.ac.kr/anthony/mesak/mes102/IDS.htm (last accessed January 16, 2012).

Index of Christian Art at Princeton University, online at http://ica.princeton.edu/.

Innes, Matthew. *State and Society in the Early Middle Ages. The Middle Rhine Valley, 400–1000* (Cambridge, 2000).

Irblich, Eva. *Karl der Grosse und die Wissenschaft. Ausstellung karolingischer Handschriften der ÖNB zum Europa-Jahr 1993* (Vienna, 1994, 2nd ed).

Isidore of Seville. *De ecclesiasticis officiis.* Edited by C. M. Lawson (CCSL 113; Turnhout, 1989).

Isidore of Seville. *De ecclesiasticis officiis.* Translated by Thomas L. Knoebel (Mahwah, 2008).

Isidore of Seville. *Etymologiae.* Edited by W. M. Lindsay (Oxford, 1911), online at http://penelope.uchicago.edu/Thayer/E/Roman/Texts/Isidore/home.html (last accessed January 17, 2012).

Isidore of Seville. *The Etymologies of Isidore of Seville.* Translated by Stephen A. Barney, W. J. Lewis, J. A. Beach, and Oliver Berghof (Cambridge, 2006).

Isidore of Seville. *De fide catholica contra Iudaeos,* in *PL* 83: 449–538.

Isidore of Seville. *De ortu et obitu Patrum,* in *PL* 83: 129–56.

Isidoro de Sevilla. *De ortu et obitu Patrum. Vida y muerte de los santos.* Edited and translated by César Chaparro Gómez (Paris, 1985).

Isidore of Seville. *Isidori Hispalensis episcopi Synonyma.* Edited by Jacques Elfassi (CCSL 111B; Turnhout, 2010).

Isidore of Seville, *Synonyma,* in *PL* 83: 825–68; reprinted from Faustino Arévalo, ed., *Isidorus Hispalensis Opera Omnia,* 7 vols., 6:472–523 (Rome, 1797–1803).

Isidoro de Sevilla. *Sinónimos.* Translated by Antonio Viñayo González (Leon, 2001).

Ivanov, Sergey A., and Anna Pichkhadze. "Eupraxia of Olympus. An Unknown Transvestite Saint." *AB* 126 (2008): 31–47.

Jacobsen, Werner, Leo Schäfer, and Hans Rudolf Sennhauser with Matthias Exner, Jozef Mertens, and Henk Stöpker. *Vorromanische Kirchenbauten. Katalog der Denkmäler bis zum Ausgang der Ottonen. Nachtragsband* (Munich, 1991) = V K B 1991.

Jakobi, Rainer. "Vom Klassizismus zur christlichen Ästhetik. Die Selbstkonstituierung der christlichen Dichterin Proba." *Hermes* 133 (2005): 77–92.

Jansen, Katherine Ludwig. "Maria Magdalena: *Apostolorum Apostola.*" In *Women Preachers and Prophets,* edited by Kienzle and Walker, 57–96.

Jansen, Sharon L., *Reading Women's Worlds from Christine de Pizan to Doris Lessing. A Guide to Six Centuries of Women Writers Imagining Rooms of Their Own* (New York, 2011).

Jarnut, Jörg, Ulrich Nonn, and Michael Richter, eds. *Karl Martell in Seiner Zeit* (Sigmaringen, 1994).

Jecker, Gall. *Heimat des hl. Pirmins, des Apostels der Alamannen* (Münster, 1927).

Jenal, Georg. "Frühe Formen der weiblichen *vita religiosa* im lateinischen Westen (4. und Anfang 5. Jahrhundert)." In *Female Vita Religiosa,* edited by Melville and Müller, 43–77.

Jenal, Georg. *Italia ascetica atque monastica: Das Asketen- und Monchtum in Italien von den Anfangen bis zur Zeit der Langobarden (ca. 150/250–604)* 2 vols. (Stuttgart, 1995).

Jenal, Georg. "Il Monachesimo femminile in Italia tra Tardo antico e medioevo." In *Il Monachesimo Femminile in Italia dall'alto Medioevo al Secolo XVII a confronto con l'oggi,* edited by Gabriella Zarri, 17–40 (Verona, 1997).

Jensen, Anne. "Auf dem Weg zur Heiligen Jungfrau. Vorformen des Marienkultes in der frühen Kirche." In *Maria,* edited by Gössman and Bauer, 36–62.

Jensen, Anne. *Thekla—Die Apostolin. Ein apokrypher Text neu entdeckt* (Gütersloh, 1999).

Jerome. *Commentarius in Ecclesiasten.* Edited by Marc Adriaen (CCSL 72; Turnhout, 1959).

Jerome. *Epistulae.* Edited by Isidorus Hilberg (CSEL 54–55; Vienna 1910–18).

Jiroušková, Lenka. *Die Visio Pauli. Wege und Wandlungen einer orientalischen Apokryphe im Lateinischen Mittelalter unter Einschluß der alttschechischen und deutschsprachigen Textzeugen* (Leiden, 2006).

John, James J. "The Named (and Namable) Scribes in *Codices Latini Antiquiores.*" In *I Scribi e Colofoni. Le Sottoscrizioni di Copisti dalle origini all'avvento della stampa,* edited by Emma Condello and Giuseppe de Gregorio, 107–21 (Spoleto, 1995).

John the Deacon. *Vita Gregorii Magni.* PL 75: 59–242.

Johnson, David W. "Purging the Poison: The Revision of Pelagius' Pauline Commentaries by Cassiodorus and His Students." (Unpublished PhD Dissertation, Princeton Theological Seminary, 1989).

Johnson, Ian. "*Auctricitas? Holy Women and Their Middle English Texts." In *Prophets Abroad: The Reception of Continental Holy Women in Later Medieval England,* edited by Rosalynn Voaden, 177–97 (Cambridge, 1996).

Johnson, Scott Fitzgerald. *The Life and Miracles of Thekla. A Literary Study* (Cambridge, 2006).

Johnson, Scott Fitzgerald. "Reviving the Memory of the Apostles: Apocryphal Tradition and Travel Literature in Late Antiquity." In *Revival and Resurgence in Christian History,* edited by David Bebbington, 1–26 (*Studies in Church History* 44; London, 2008).

Jolly, Penny Howell. "Marked Difference: Earrings and the 'Other' in Fifteenth-Century Flemish Art." In *Encountering Medieval Textiles and Dress,* edited by Koslin and Snyder, 195–207.

Jones, Graham. "Ghostly Mentor, Teacher of Mysteries: Bartholomew, Guthlac and the Apostle Cult in Early Medieval England." In *Medieval Monastic Education,* edited by George Ferzoco and Carolyn Muessig, 136–52 (London, 2000).

Jordan, Erin L. "Gender Concerns: Monks, Nuns, and Patronage of the Cistercian Order in Thirteenth-Century Flanders and Hainaut." *Speculum* 87 (2012): 62–94.

Josi, Enrico, and Renato Aprile. "Agnese." In *Bibliotheca Sanctorum,* edited by Vizzini et al., 1:382–411.

Kaczynski, Bernice. "The Authority of the Fathers: Patristic Texts in Early Medieval Libraries and Scriptoria." *Journal of Medieval Latin* 16 (2006): 1–27.

Karkov, Catherine E., Robert T. Farrell, and Michael Ryan, eds. *The Insular Tradition* (Albany, 1997).

Kehl, Petra. "Die Entstehungszeit der Vita Sturmi des Eigil." *Archiv für mittelrheinische Kirchengeschichte* 46 (1994): 11–20.

Kehl, Petra. "Heiligenverehrung in der Reichsabtei Fulda." In *Fulda in seiner Geschichte,* edited by Heinemeyer and Jaeger, 181–99.

Kelly, Patricia. "The Rule of Patrick: Textual Affinities." In *Ireland and Europe in the Early Middle Ages: Texts and Transmission,* edited by Próinséas Ní Chatháin and Michael Richter, 284–95 (Dublin, 2002).

Ker, Neil R. *Medieval Libraries of Great Britain: A List of Surviving Books* (2nd ed., London, 1964).

Kerff, Franz. "Mittelalterliche Quellen und mittelalterliche Wirklichkeit. Zu den Konsequenzen einer jüngst erschienem Edition für unser Bild kirchlicher Reformbewegungen." *Rheinische Vierteljahrsblätter* 51 (1987): 275–86.

Kéry, Lotte. *Canonical Collections of the Early Middle Ages (c. 400–1140). A Bibliographical Guide to the Manuscripts and Literature* (Washington, D.C., 1999).

Kessler, Herbert L. "The Book as Icon." In *In the Beginning. Bibles before the Year 1000,* edited by Michelle P. Brown, 77–103 (Washington, D.C., 2006).

Kienzle, Beverly Mayne, and Pamela J. Walker, eds. *Women Preachers and Prophets through Two Millennia of Christianity* (Berkeley, 1998).

Kilburn, Jasmine A. L. "The Contrasted 'Other' in the Old English Apocryphal Acts of Matthew, Simon and Jude." *Neophilologus* 87 (2003): 137–51.

Kilian. Mönch aus Irland. Aller Franken Patron (689–1989). Katalog der Sonderausstellung zur 1300 Feier des Kiliansmartyriums 1989–Festung Marienburg (Munich, 1989).

King, Margaret L., and Alfred Rabil Jr. "The Other Voice in Early Modern Europe: Introduction to the Series." First published in Henricus Cornelius Agrippa, *Declamation on the Nobility and Preeminence of the Female Sex*. Translated by Albert Rabil Jr.(Chicago, 1996); reprinted in all subsequent volumes in the series "The Other Voice in Early Modern Europe," overview at http://www.press.uchicago.edu/ucp/books/series/OVIEME.html.

Klein, Stacy S. "Centralizing Feminism in Anglo-Saxon Literary Studies: *Elene*, Motherhood, and History." In *Readings in Medieval Texts: Interpreting Old and Middle English Literature,* edited by David Johnson and Elaine Treharne, 149–65 (Oxford, 2005).

Klein-Pfeuffer, Margarete. "Christliche Glaubensvorstellung zur Zeit der Mission." In *Kilian. Mönch aus Irland,* 127–43.

Klingshirn, William, and Linda Safran, eds. *The Early Christian Book* (Washington, D.C., 2007).

Klüppel, Th. "Die Germania (750–950)." In *Hagiographies*, edited by Guy Philippart, 2:161–209 (Turnhout, 1996).

Knaus, Hermann. "Das Bistum Würzburg." In *Mittelalterliche Handschriftenkataloge Deutschlands und der Schweiz,* edited by Bernhard Bischoff, 4.2: 948–59 (Munich, 1979).

Köbler, Gerhard. *Ergänzungen, Richtigstellungen, Nachträge, Teileditionen, Nachweise 1993 zu Steinmeyers Edition: Die althochdeutschen Glossen* (Gießen, 1993).

Kochskämper, Birgit. *"Frau" und "Mann" im Althochdeutschen* (Frankfurt, 1999).

Kornbluth, Genevra. *Engraved Gems of the Carolingian Empire* (University Park, 1996).

Koslin, Désirée G., and Janet E. Snyder, eds. *Encountering Medieval Textiles and Dress: Objects, Texts, and Images* (New York, 2002).

Kottje, Raymond. "Hrabanus und das Recht." In *Hrabanus Maurus,* edited by Kottje and Zimmermann, 118–29.

Kottje, Raymond, Ludger Körntgen, and Ulrike Spengler-Reffgen, eds. *Penitentialia Minora Franciae et Italiae saec. VIII–IX* (CCSL 156; Turnhout, 1994).

Kottje, Raymond, and Harald Zimmermann, eds. *Hrabanus Maurus. Lehrer, Abt und Bischof* (Wiesbaden, 1982).

Kötzsche, Lieselotte. "Das Heilige Grab in Jerusalem und seine Nachfolge." In *Akten des XII. Internationalen Kongresses für Christliche Archäologie (Bonn 1991),* edited by Ernst Dassmann, Klaus Thraede, and Josef Engemann, 2 vols., 1:272–90 (*Jahrbuch für Antike und Christentum,* Supplement 20; Munster, 1995).

Krämer, Sigrid. *Handschriftenerbe des deutschen Mittelalters (Mittelalterliche Bibliothekskataloge Deutschlands und der Schweiz, Erganzungsband 1),* 2 vols. (Munich, 1989).

Kramer, Theodore. "Amorbach. Festrede anläßlich der 700-Jahrfeier der Stadt." In *Mainfränkisches Jahrbuch*, 5:31–39 (1953).

Krone und Schleier. Kunst aus Mittelalterlichen Frauenklöstern. Ruhrlandmuseum: Die frühen Klöster und Stifte, 500–1200. Kunst- und Ausstellungshalle der Bundesrepublik Deutschland: Die Zeit der Orden, 1200–1500. Edited by Kunst- und Ausstellungshalle der Bundesrepublik Deutschland, Bonn und dem Ruhrlandmuseum Essen (Munich, 2005).

Kübert, Ernst. *Karlburg—Uralter Fränkische Siedlungsort* (Karlstadt, 1991).

Kummer, Christiane. *Die Illustration der Würzburger Bischofschronik des Lorenz Fries aus dem Jahre 1546* (Würzburg, 1995).

Lambert, Bernard. *Bibliotheca Hieronymiana Manuscripta. La Tradition manuscrite des oeuvres de saint Jérôme*, 4 vols. (Steenbrugis, 1969–72).

Laurence, Patrick. "*Virilis* et *effeminatus* chez saint Jérôme." In *Chartae caritatis. Études de patristique et d'antiquité tardive en hommage à Yves-Marie Duval*, edited by Benoît Gain, Pierre Jay, and Gérard Nauroy, 401–16 (Paris, 2004).

Leanza, Sandro. "I condizionamenti dell'esegesi patristica. Un caso sintomatico: l'interpretazione di Qohelet." *Ricerche Storico Bibliche* 2 (1991): 25–49.

Le Bras, Gabriel. "Pénitentiels." *Dictionnaire de Théologie Catholique* 12/1 coll. 1160–79.

Lehmann, Paul, ed. *Die Admonitio s. Basilii ad Filium Spiritualem* (Sitzungsberichte der Bayerischen Akademie der Wissenschaften, Philosophisch-historische Klasse 1955, Heft 7; Munich, 1955).

Lehner, Albert, ed. *Florilegia* (CCSL 108D; Turnhout, 1987).

Leisch-Kiesl, Monika. *Eva als Andere. Eine exemplarische Untersuchung zu Frühchristentum und Mittelalter* (Cologne, 1992).

Le Marié, Joseph. "L'homéliare carolingienne de Mondsee, témoin de sermons d'un Pseudo-Fulgence." In *Philologia sacra. Biblische und patristische Studien für Hermann J. Frede und Walter Thiele*, edited by Roger Gryson, 568–82 (Freiburg, 1993).

Le Marié, Joseph. "Un sermon occidental pseudo-augustinien témoin du traité sur la Pâque de Méliton de Sardes." *Vetera Christianorum* 17 (1980): 301–11.

Le Moine, Fannie J. "Jerome's Gift to Women Readers." In *Shifting Frontiers in Late Antiquity*, edited by Ralph W. Mathisen and Hagith S. Sivan, 230–41 (Aldershot, 1996).

Lenssen, Jürgen, ed. *Gertrud in Franken: Ausstellung der Diözese Würzburg und der Pfarrei Karlburg 1991 in Marmelsteiner Kabinett* (Würzburg, 1991).

Lenssen, Jürgen, and Ludwig Wamser, eds., *1250 Jahre Bistum Würzburg. Archäologisch-historische Zeugnisse der Frühzeit* (Würzburg, 1992).

Lerner, Gerda. *The Creation of Feminist Consciousness: From the Middle Ages to Eighteen-Seventy* (New York, 1993).

Leupin, Alexandre. *Fiction and Incarnation. Rhetoric, Theology and Literature in the Middle Ages*. Translated by David Laatsch (Minneapolis, 2002).

Levison, Wilhelm, ed. *Passio minor Kiliani, 711–728* (MGH SRM 5; Hanover/Leipzig, 1910).

Lewis, Gertrude Jaron. *By Women, for Women, about Women. The Sister-Books of Fourteenth-Century Germany* (Toronto, 1996).

Leyser, Conrad. "Masculinity in Flux: Nocturnal Emission and the Limits of Celibacy in the Early Middle Ages." In *Masculinity in Medieval Europe,* edited by Dawn Hadley, 103–20 (London, 1999).

Leyser, Conrad. "Shoring Fragments against Ruin? Eugippius and the Sixth-Century Culture of the Florilegium." In *Eugippius und Severin, der Autor, der Text und der Heilige,* edited by Walter Pohl and Maximilian Diesenberger, 65–75 (Vienna, 2001).

Leyser, Conrad. "The Temptations of Cult: Roman Martyr Piety in the Age of Gregory the Great." *EME* 9 (2000): 289–307.

Liber de ortu et obitu patriarcharum. Edited by J. Carracedo Fraga (CCSL 108E; Turnhout, 1996).

Liber sacramentorum Gellonensis Introductio, Tabulae et Indices. Edited by A. Dumas and J. Deshusses (CCSL 159A; Turnhout, 1981).

Liber sacramentorum Gellonensis Textus. Edited by A. Dumas (CCSL 159; Turnhout, 1981).

Lifshitz, Felice. "Beyond Positivism *and* Genre: 'Hagiographical' Texts as Historical Narratives." *Viator* 25 (1994): 95–114.

Lifshitz, Felice. "Demonstrating Gun(t)za: Women, Manuscripts, and the Question of Historical 'Proof.'" In *Vom Nutzen des Schreibens. Soziales Gedächtnis, Herrschaft und Besitz,* edited by Walter Pohl and Paul Herold, 67–96 (Vienna, 2002).

Lifshitz, Felice. "Gender and Exemplarity East of the Middle Rhine: Jesus, Mary and the Saints in Manuscript Context." *EME* 9 (2000): 325–43.

Lifshitz, Felice. "Gender Trouble in Paradise: The Case of the Liturgical *Virgo.*" In *Images of Sanctity: Essays in Honor of Gary Dickson,* edited by Debra Higgs Strickland, 25–39 (Leiden, 2007).

Lifshitz, Felice. *The Name of the Saint. The Martyrology of Pseudo-Jerome and Access to the Sacred in Francia, 627–827* (Notre Dame, 2005).

Lifshitz, Felice. *The Norman Conquest of Pious Neustria. Historiographic Discourse and Saintly Relics, 684–1090* (Toronto, 1995).

Lifshitz, Felice. "The Persistence of Late Antiquity: Christ as Man and Woman in an Eighth-Century Miniature." *Medieval Feminist Forum* 38 (2004): 18–27.

Lifshitz, Felice. "The Politics of Historiography: The Memory of Bishops in Eleventh-Century Rouen." *History and Memory* 10, 2 (1998): 118–37.

Lifshitz, Felice. "Priestly Women, Virginal Men: Litanies and Their Discontents." In *Gender and Christianity in Medieval Europe: New Perspectives,* edited by Lisa Bitel and Felice Lifshitz, 123–43 (Philadelphia, 2008).

Lifshitz, Felice. "Women: *The Da Vinci Code* and the Fabrication of Tradition." In *Why the Middle Ages Matter: Medieval Light on Modern Injustice,* edited by Celia Chazelle, Simon Doubleday, Felice Lifshitz, and Amy G. Remensnyder, 66–76 (New York, 2011).

Lindner, Klaus. *Untersuchungen zur Frühgeschichte des Bistums Würzburg und des Würzburger Raumes* (Göttingen, 1972).

Lipsius, Richard Adalbert. *Die Apokryphen Apostelgeschichten und Apostellegenden. Ein Beitrag zur altchristlichen Literaturgeschichte,* 2 vols. plus supplement (Braunschweig, 1883–90) = Lipsius, *DAA.*

Lipsius, Richard Adalbert, and Maxilian Bonnet, eds. *Acta Apostolorum Apocrypha post Constantinum Tischendorf,* 2 vols. (Leipzig, 1898; reprint, 1959).

Litschel, Helga, ed. *900 Jahre Klosterkirche Lambach. Oberösterreichische Landesausstellung 1989* (Linz, 1989).

Lochrie, Karma. "Between Women." In *The Cambridge Companion to Medieval Women's Writing,* edited by Carolyn Dinshaw and David Wallace, 70–88 (Cambridge, 2003).

Löfstedt, Bengt, ed. *Anonymi in Matthaeum* (CCCM 159; Turnhout, 2003).

Löfstedt, Bengt. "Fragmente eines Matthäus-Kommentars." *Sacris Erudiri* 37 (1997): 141–61.

Löfstedt, Bengt. "Zum Matthhäus-Kommentar in Clm 14311." *Aevum* 75 (2001): 263–66.

Lopez Caneda, Ramon. *Prisciliano. Su Pensiamiento y su Problema historico* (Santiago de Compostela, 1966).

López Ferreiro, Antonio. *Historia de la Santa A.M. Iglesia de Santiago de Compostela,* 2 vols. (Santiago de Compostela, 1898).

Lowe, Elias Avery. *Codices Latini Antiquiores. A Palaeographical Guide to Latin MSS. prior to the 9th Century.* 11 vols. and supplement (Oxford, 1934–71) = CLA.

Lowe, Elias Avery. "An Eighth-Century List of Books." *Speculum* 3 (1928): 3–15.

Löwe, Heinz, ed. *Die Iren und Europa im früheren Mittelalter,* 2 vols. (Stuttgart, 1982).

Lowerre, Sandra. "To Rise beyond Their Sex: Female Cross-Dressing in Caxton's *Vitas Patrum.*" In *Riddles, Knights and Cross-Dressing Saints. Essays on Medieval Language and Literature,* edited by Thomas Honegger, 55–94 (Bern, 2004).

Lübeck, Konrad. "Fuldaer Nebenklöster in Mainfranken." *Mainfränkisches Jahrbuch* 2 (1950): 1–52.

Lumsden, Douglas. "'Touch No Unclean Thing': Apocalyptic Expressions of Ascetic Spirituality in the Early Middle Ages." *Church History* 66 (1997): 240–51.

Macdonald, Dennis R. *The Legend and the Apostle: The Battle for Paul in Story and Canon.* (Philadelphia, 1983).

Machielsen, Johannes. *Clavis Patristica pseudepigraphicorum Medii Aevi* I-II: *Opera Homiletica* (CCSL CPMA I-II; Turnhout, 1990) = CPMA.

Machielsen, Lambert. "Fragments patristiques non-identifiées dans ms. Vat. Pal. 577." *Sacris Erudiri* 12 (1961): 488–539.

Macy, Gary. *The Hidden History of Women's Ordination. Female Clergy in the Medieval West* (Oxford, 2008).

Macy, Gary. "The Ordination of Women in the Early Middle Ages." *Theological Studies* 61 (2000): 481–507.

Mahadevan, Letha. "Überlieferung und Verbreitung des Bußbuchs 'Capitula Iudiciorum.'" *Zeitschrift für Rechtsgeschichte der Savigny-Stiftung: Kanonistiche Abteilung* 72 (1986): 17–75.

Mai, A., ed. *Nova Patrum Bibliotheca* (Rome, 1852).

Maier, Jean-Louis, ed. *Le Dossier du Donatisme,* 2 vols. (Texte und Untersuchungen 134 and 135; Berlin, 1987 and 1989).

Makowski, Elizabeth. *Canon Law and Cloistered Women. Periculoso and its Commentators, 1298–1545* (Washington, D.C., 1997).

Mallardo, Domenico. "S. Potito, un martire dell'Apulia." *Rendiconti della Accademia di Archeologia, Lettere e Belle Arti* 31 (1957): 7–36.

Mälzer, Gottfried. "Das Evangeliar des heiligen Burkhard." In *1250 Jahre Bistum Würzburg,* edited by Lenssen and Wamser, 49–68.

Mälzer, Gottfried. *Die Würzburger Bischofs-Chronik des Lorenz Fries. Textzeugen und frühe Überlieferung* (Würzburg, 1987).

Mälzer, Gottfried, and Hans Thurn. *Die Bibliothek des Wurzburger Domstifts, 742–1803: Eine Austellung der Üniversitätsbibliothek Würzburg* (Würzburg, 1988).

Markschies, Christoph. "Die neutestamentliche Versuchungsgeschichte in der Auslegung der Kirchenväter." *Theologische Zeitschrift* 62 (2006): 193–206.

Markus, Robert A. *Gregory the Great and His World* (Cambridge, 1997).

Martimort, A. G. *Les Lectures liturgiques et leurs livres* (TSMAO 64; Turnhout, 1992).

Martindale, Jane. "The Nun Immena and the Foundation of the Abbey of Beaulieu: A Woman's Prospects in the Carolingian Church." In *Women in the Church,* edited by W. J. Sheils and Diana Wood, 27–42 (*Studies in Church History* 27; Oxford, 1990).

Martinet, Suzanne. "Les manuscrits de Sainte-Marie-Saint-Jean de Laon au VIIIe siècle." In *L'Art du haut Moyen Age dans le Nord-Ouest de la France: Actes du Colloque de St Riquier (22–24 septembre 1987),* edited by Dominique Poulain and Michel Perrin, 263–75 (Greifswald, 1993).

Matter, E. Ann. "A Carolingian Schoolbook? The Manuscript Tradition of Alcuin's *De Fide* and Related Treatises." In *The Whole Book: Cultural Perspectives on the Medieval Miscellany,* edited by Stephen G. Nichols and Siegfried Wenzel, 145–52 (Ann Arbor, 1996).

Matter, E. Ann. "Christ, God and Woman in the Thought of St. Augustine." In *Augustine and His Critics. Essays in Honor of Gerald Bonner,* edited by Robert Dodaro and George Lawless, 164–75 (London/New York, 2000).

Matter, E. Ann. "*De Cura feminarum*: Augustine the Bishop, North African Women, and the Development of a Theology of Female Nature." In *Feminist Interpretations,* edited by Stark, 203–14; reprinted from *Augustinian Studies* 36 (2005): 87–98.

Mautner, Josef. *Das Zerbrechliche Leben Erzählen. Erzählende Literatur und Theologie des Erzählens* (Frankfurt, 1994).

Mayeski, Marie Anne. *Women at the Table. Three Medieval Theologians* (Collegeville, 2004).

McCune, James. "Four Pseudo-Augustinian Sermons *De concupiscentia fugienda* from the Carolingian Sermonary of Würzburg," *Revue d'Études Augustiniennes et Patristiques* 52 (2006): 391–431.

McGill, Scott. *Virgil Recomposed. The Mythological and Secular Centos in Antiquity* (Oxford, 2005).

McGinn, Sheila E. "The Acts of Thecla." In *Searching the Scriptures,* edited by Schüssler Fiorenza and Matthews, 2:800–28.

McGurk, Patrick. "The Oldest Manuscripts of the Latin Bible." In *The Early Medieval Bible,* edited by Gameson, 1–23.

McInerney, Maud Burnett. *Eloquent Virgins from Thecla to Joan of Arc* (New York, 2003).

McKinnon, James W. "The Book of Psalms, Monasticism and the Western Liturgy." In *The Place of the Psalms in the Intellectual Culture of the Middle Ages,* edited by Nancy Van Deusen, 43–58 (Albany, 1999).

McKitterick, Rosamond. "*Akkulturation* and the Writing of History in the Early Middle Ages." In *Akkulturation: Probleme einer germanisch-romanischen Kultursynthese in Spätantike und frühem Mittelalter,* edited by Dieter

Hägermann, Wolfgang Haubrichs, and Jörg Jarnut with Claudia Giefers, 381–95 (Berlin, 2004).

McKitterick, Rosamond. "Anglo-Saxon Missionaries in Germany: Personal Connections and Local Influences." *Vaughn Paper* 36 (Leicester, 1991): 1–40 (reprinted in McKitterick, *The Frankish Kings and Culture*).

McKitterick, Rosamond. "The Anglo-Saxon Missionaries in Germany: Reflections on the Manuscript Evidence." *Transactions of the Cambridge Bibliographical Society* 9 (1989): 291–329 (reprinted in McKitterick, *Books, Scribes and Learning*).

McKitterick, Rosamond. *Books, Scribes and Learning in the Frankish Kingdoms, 6th–9th Centuries* (Aldershot, 1994).

McKitterick, Rosamond. *The Carolingians and the Written Word* (Cambridge, 1989).

McKitterick, Rosamond. "Les femmes, les arts et la culture en Occident dans le haut Moyen Age." In *Femmes et pouvoirs des femmes à Byzance et en Occident (VIe–XIe siècles)*, edited by Stéphane Lebecq, Alain Dierkens, Régine Le Jan, and Jean-Marie Sansterre, 149–62 (Lille, 1999).

McKitterick, Rosamond. *The Frankish Kings and Culture in the Early Middle Ages* (Aldershot, 1995).

McKitterick, Rosamond. "Frankish Uncial: A New Context for the Echternach Scriptorium." In *Willibrord, zijn wereld en zijn werk,* edited by Petronella Bange and Anton Gerard Weiler, 374–88 (Nijmegen, 1990) (reprinted in McKitterick, *Books, Scribes and Learning*).

McKitterick, Rosamond. "Frauen und Schriftlichkeit im frühen Mittelalter." In *Weibliche Lebensgestaltung,* edited by Goetz, 65–118.

McKitterick, Rosamond. *History and Memory in the Carolingian World* (Cambridge, 2004).

McKitterick, Rosamond. "Das Konzil im Kontext der karolingischen Renaissance." In *Das Frankfurter Konzil,* edited by Berndt, 2:635–76.

McKitterick, Rosamond. "Nuns' Scriptoria in England and Francia in the Eighth Century." *Francia* 19 (1992): 1–35.

McKitterick, Rosamond. *Perceptions of the Past in the Early Middle Ages* (Notre Dame, 2005).

McKitterick, Rosamond. "Women and Literacy in the Early Middle Ages." In *Books, Scribes and Learning* by McKitterick, Article XIII 1–43. Original English publication of McKitterick, "Frauen und Schriftlichkeit."

McLaughlin, Eleanor C. "The Christian Past: Does It Hold a Future for Women?" *Anglican Theological Review* 57 (1975): 36–56, reprinted in Carol P. Christ and Judith Plaskow, eds., *Womanspirit Rising: A Feminist Reader in Religion,* 93–106 (New York, 1979; 2nd ed. 1992).

McLaughlin, Eleanor C. "Peter Abelard and the Dignity of Women: Twelfth Century 'Feminism' in Theory and Practice." In *Pierre Abélard–Pierre le Vénérable: Les courants philosophiques, littéraires et artistiques en occident au milieu du XIIe siècle. Abbaye de Cluny 2 au 9 juillet 1972,* edited by Centre Nationale de la Recherche Scientifique, 287–334 (Paris, 1975).

McNally, Robert E. "'In nomine Dei summi': Seven Hiberno-Latin Sermons." *Traditio* 35 (1979): 121–43.

McNamara, Jo Ann. *Sisters in Arms. Catholic Nuns through Two Millennia* (Cambridge, 1996).

McNamer, Sarah. *Affective Meditation and the Invention of Medieval Compassion* (Philadelphia, 2010).

McWilliams, Joann."Augustine's Letters to Women." In *Feminist Interpretations,* edited by Stark, 189–202.

Meens, Rob. "Finding the Appropriate Penance. Two Examples of the Organization of Penitential Manuscripts: Vienna ÖNB lat. 2223 and 2233" (Unpublished typescript, 2000).

Meens, Rob. "The Frequency and Nature of Early Medieval Penance." In *Handling Sins. Confession in the Middle Ages,* edited P. Biller and A. Minnis, 35–61 (Woodbridge, 1998).

Meens, Rob. "Ritual Purity and the Influence of Gregory the Great in the Early Middle Ages." In *Unity and Diversity in the Church,* edited by R. N. Swanson, 31–43 (Oxford, 1996).

Melville, Gert, and Anne Müller, eds. *Female Vita Religiosa between Late Antiquity and the High Middle Ages. Structures, Developments and Spatial Contexts* (Münster, 2011).

Mériaux, Charles. *Gallia irradiata. Saints et sanctuaires dans le nord de la Gaule du haut Moyen Âge* (Stuttgart, 2006).

Mettke, Heinz. *Die althochdeutschen Aldhelmglossen* (Jena, 1957).

Metzner, Ernst Erich. "Das Kloster 'Lorsch' der Königin 'Ute' im römisch-germanischen Kontext." In *Ze Lorse bi dem münster. Das Nibelungenlied (Handschrift C). Literarische Innovation und politische Zeitgeschichte,* edited by Jürgen Breuer, 149–221 (Munich, 2006).

Meyvaert, Paul. "A Letter of Pelagius II Composed by Gregory the Great." In *Gregory the Great,* edited by Cavadini, 94–116.

Micheli, Géneviève L. *L'enluminure du haut Moyen-Age et les influences irlandaises* (Brussels, 1939).

Miglio, Luisa. "'A mulieribus conscriptos arbitror': donne e scrittura." In *I Scribi e Colofoni. Le Sottoscrizioni di Copisti dalle origini all'avvento della stampa,* edited by Emma Condello and Giuseppe de Gregorio, 235–66 (Spoleto, 1995).

Mildenberger, Gerhard. "Ausgrabungen auf dem Marienberg in Würzburg." *Mainfränkisches Jahrbuch* 16 (1964): 294–301.

Miles, Margaret R. *Carnal Knowing: Female Nakedness and Religious Meaning in the Christian West* (Boston, 1989).

Miller, Carol Lynn. "The Old High German and Old Saxon Charms. Text, Commentary and Critical Bibliography" (Unpublished PhD Dissertation, Washington University in St. Louis, 1963).

Mombritius, Boninus. *Sanctuarium siue Vitae sanctorum,* 2nd ed. (Paris, 1910).

Moorhead, John. "The Byzantines in the West in the Sixth Century." In *New Cambridge Medieval History I (c. 500–c. 700),* edited by Paul Fouracre, 118–39 (Cambridge, 2005).

Moorhead, John. "Ostrogothic Italy and the Lombard Invasions." In *New Cambridge Medieval History I (c. 500–c. 700),* edited by Paul Fouracre, 140–61 (Cambridge, 2005).

Mordek, Hubert, ed. *Aus Archiven und Bibliotheken. Festschrift für Raymund Kottje zum 65. Geburtstag* (Frankfurt, 1992).

Mordek, Hubert. *Bibliotheca Capitularium regum Francorum manuscripta. Überliefer-ung und Traditionszusammenhang der fränkischen Herrschererlasse* (Munich, 1995).

Mordek, Hubert. "Die Hedenen als politische Kraft im austrasischen Frankenreich." In *Karl Martell,* edited by Jarnut, Nonn, and Richter, 345–66.

Mordek, Hubert. "Karolingische Kapitularien." In *Überlieferung und Geltung normativer Texte des frühen und hohen Mittelalters,* edited by Hubert Mordek, 25–50 (Sigmaringen, 1986).

Mordek, Hubert. *Kirchenrecht und Reform in Frankenreich. Die Collectio Vetus Gallica. Die Älteste Systematische Kanonensammlung des Fränkischen Gallien* (Berlin, 1975).

Morin, Germain. "Liturgie et basiliques de Rome au milieu du VIIe siècle d'après les listes d'évangiles de Würzburg." *RB* 28 (1911): 296–330.

Morin, Germain. "Pages Inédites de deux Pseudo-Jéromes des environs de l'an 400." *RB* 40 (1928): 289–318.

Morin, Germain. "Le plus ancien *Comes* ou lectionnaire de l'église romaine." *RB* 27 (1910): 41–74.

Morris, Colin. *The Sepulchre of Christ and the Medieval West. From the Beginning to 1600* (Oxford, 2005).

Morrison, Karl F. " 'Know Thyself': Music in the Carolingian Renaissance." In *Committenti e Produzione artistico-letteraria nell'alto medioevo occidentale,* 2 vols. 1:369–479 (*Settimane* 39; Spoleto, 1992).

Moser, Peter. *Würzburg. Geschichte einer Stadt* (Bamberg, 1999).

Mostert, Marco. "Celtic, Anglo-Saxon or Insular? Some Considerations on 'Irish' Manuscript Production and Their Implications for Insular Latin Culture, c. AD 500–800." In *Cultural Identity,* edited by Edel, 92–115.

Mottola, Antonio. *San Potito martire de Ascoli Satriano. Storia e culto* (Foggia, 1992).

Mulder-Bakker, Anneke B., and Jocelyn Wogan-Browne. "Introduction Part I: Household, Women and Lived Christianity." In *Household, Women, and Christianities in Late Antiquity and the Early Middle Ages,* edited by Mulder-Bakker and Wogan-Browne, 1–10 (Turnhout, 2005).

Müller, Daniela. "Die 'andere Seite': Religiöser Aufbruch von Frauen in der irisch-fränkischen Missionierung." *WDGB* 51 (1989): 71–78.

Müller, Hildegund. "Zur Struktur des patristischen Kommentars: Drei Beispiele aus Augustins *Enarrationes in Psalmos.*" In *Der Kommentar,* edited by Geerlings and Schulze, 1:15–31.

Müller, Rudolf. "Zwei Marientexten aus den angelsächsisch geprägten Würzburg des 8. Jahrhunderts." *WDGB* 51 (1989): 485–90.

Murdoch, Brian. "Charms, Recipes and Prayers." In *German Literature of the Early Middle Ages,* edited by Brian Murdoch, 57–72 (Woodbridge, 2004).

Muschiol, Gisela. *Famula Dei. Zur Liturgie im merowingischen Frauenklöstern* (Münster, 1994).

Muschiol, Gisela. "Königshof, Kloster und Mission—die Welt der Lioba und ihre geistlichen Schwestern." In *Bonifatius—Apostel der Deutschen: Mission und Christianisierung vom 8. bis 20. Jahrhundert,* edited by Franz J. Felten, 99–114 (Wiesbaden, 2004).

Muschiol, Gisela. "Presbytera: Female Cleric or Cleric's Wife?"(Conference Paper, International Medieval Congress, Leeds, 1998).

Muschiol, Gisela. "Zeit und Raum—Liturgie und Ritus in mittelalterlichen Frauen-konventen." In *Krone und Schleier*, 40–51.

Muth, Hanswernfried. *St. Burkhard, Würzburg* (2nd ed., Regensburg, 1989).

Muth, Stefan. "Kiliandarstellungen im Bereich Dom/Neumünster." *WDGB* 50 (1988): 687–702.

Nauerth, Claudia, and Rüdiger Warns. *Thekla. Ihre Bilder in der frühchristlichen Kunst* (Wiesbaden, 1981).

Nedoma, Robert. "enti danne geoze zisamane: Die althochdeutsche Fassung des Ersten Basler Rezepts (BR Ib)." *Die Sprache. Zeitschrift für Sprachwissenschaft* 39 (1997): 168–200.

Nees, Lawrence. "Ethnic and Primitive Paradigms in the Study of Early Medieval Art." In *Paradigms and Methods in Early Medieval Studies,* edited by Chazelle and Lifshitz, 41–60.

Nees, Lawrence. "On the Image of Christ Crucified in Early Medieval Art." In *Il Volto Santo in Europa. Culte e imagine del Crocifisso nel Medioevo,* edited by Michele Camillo Ferrari and Andreas Meyer, 347–85 (Lucca, 2005).

Nees, Lawrence. "The Originality of Early Medieval Artists." In *Literacy, Politics and Artistic Innovation in the Early Medieval West,* edited by Celia M. Chazelle, 77–109 (Lanham, 1992).

Neil, Bronwen. "Towards Defining a Christian Culture: The Christian Transforma-tion of Classical Literature." In *The Cambridge History of Christianity, Volume 2: Constantine to c. 600,* edited by Augustine Casiday, 317–42 (Cambridge, 2007).

Nelson, Janet L. "Gender and Genre in Women Historians of the Early Middle Ages." In *L'Historiographie Médiévale,* edited by Jean-Philippe Genet (Paris, 1991); reprinted in Janet L. Nelson, *The Frankish World, 750–900,* 183–97 (London, 1996).

Nelson, Janet L. "Gender en genre bij vrouwelijke geschiedschrijvers in de vroege middeleeuwen." In *In de ban van het verhaal,* edited by Mirjam de Baar et al., 9–25. (*Jaarboek voor Vrouwengeschiedenis* 11; Nijmegen, 1990).

Nelson, Janet. "Peers in the Early Middle Ages." In *Law, Laity and Solidarities: Essays in Honor of Susan Reynolds,* edited by Pauline Stafford, Janet L. Nelson, and Jane Martindale, 27–46 (Manchester, 2001).

Nelson, Janet. "Perceptions du pouvoir chez les historiennes du Haut Moyen Age." *Les Femmes au Moyen Age,* edited by Michel Rouche, 77–85 (Paris, 1990).

Nelson, Janet. "The Siting of the Council at Frankfurt: Some Reflections on Family and Politics." In *Das Frankfurter Konzil,* edited by Berndt, 1:149–65.

Netzer, Nancy. *Cultural Interplay in the Eighth Century. The Trier Gospels and the Making of a Scriptorium at Echternach* (Cambridge, 1994).

Neuman de Vegvar, Carol. "The Echternach Lion: A Leap of Faith." In *The Insular Tradition,* edited by Karkov et al., 167–88.

Newman, Barbara. "Die Visionären Texte und Visuellen Welten religiöser Frauen." In *Krone und Schleier*, 104–17.

Ng, Esther Yue L. "*Acts of Paul and Thecla.* Women's Stories and Precedent?" *Journal of Theological Studies* New Series 55 (2004): 1–29.

Nolte, Cordula. "*Peregrinatio—Freundschaft—Verwandtschaft.* Bonifatius im Austausch mit angelsächsischen Frauen." In *Bonifatius—Leben und Nachwirken. Die Gestaltung des christlichen Europa im Frühmittelalter,* edited by Franz J. Felten, Jörg Jarnut, and Lutz E. von Padberg, 149–60 (Koblenz, 2007).

Nonn, Ulrich. "Die Nachfolge Karl Martells und die Teilung von Vieux-Poitiers." In *Der Dynastiewechsel von 751,* edited by Becher and Jarnut, 61–73.

Oberleitner, Manfred, Franz Römer, Johannes Divjak, Rainer Kurz, and Dorothea Weber, eds. *Die handschriftliche Überlieferung der Werke des heiligen Augustinus,* 7 vols. (Vienna, 1969–97).

Obrist, Barbara. "Les Manuscrits du 'De cursu Stellarum' de Gregoire de Tours et le manuscrit, Laon, Bibliotheque Municipale 422." *Scriptorium* 56 (2002): 335–45.

Obrist, Barbara. "La representation carolingienne du zodiaque. A propos du manuscrit de Bâle, UB F III 16a [sic]." *Cahiers de civilization médiévale* 44 (2001): 3–33.

Ó Carragain, Éamonn. "Crucifixion as Annunciation. The Relation of 'The Dream of the Rood' to the Liturgy Reconsidered." *English Studies* 63 (1982): 487–505.

Ó Carragáin, Éamonn. *Ritual and the Rood. Liturgical Images and the Old English Poems of the Deam of the Rood Tradition* (Toronto, 2005).

Ó Carragáin, Éamonn. "Theological, Liturgical or Devotional? Some Problems in Determining the Context(s) of the Ruthwell and Bewcastle Crosses and of the Ruthwell Crucification Poem." *Old English Newsletter* 16 (1983): 69.

Ó Carragáin, Éamonn. "'Traditio evangeliorum' and 'sustentatio': The Relevance of Liturgical Ceremonies to the Book of Kells." In *The Book of Kells: Proceedings of a Conference at Trinity College Dublin, 6–9 September 1992,* edited by Felicity O'Mahony, 398–436 (Aldershot, 1994).

Odell-Scott, D. W. "Editorial Dilemma: The Interpolation of 1 Cor 14:34–35 in the Western Manuscripts of D, G and 88." *Biblical Theological Bulletin* (July 22, 2000).

Odell-Scott, D. W. "Let the Women Speak in Church: An Egalitarian Interpretation of 1 Cor. 14:33b–36." *Biblical Thinking Bulletin* 13 (1983): 90–93.

O'Donnell, James J. "The Holiness of Gregory." In *Gregory the Great,* edited by Cavadini, 62–81.

Olsen, Alexandra Hennessey. "Cynewulf's Autonomous Women. A Reconsideration of Elene and Juliana." In *New Readings,* edited by Damico and Olsen, 222–32.

Olson, Linda, and Kathryn Kerby-Fulton, eds. *Voices in Dialogue: Reading Women in the Middle Ages* (Notre Dame, 2005).

Orchard, Andy. "Old Sources, New Resources: Finding the Right Formula for Boniface." *Anglo-Saxon England* 30 (2001): 15–38.

Orchard, Andy. *The Poetic Art of Aldhelm* (Cambridge, 1994).

Origen. *Homilies on Numbers by Origen.* Translated by Thomas P. Scheck (Downers Grove, 2009).

Origen. *In Numeros homiliae secundum translationem quam fecit Rufinus.* Edited by W. A.Baehrens (Leipzig, 1921).

Origène. *Homélies sur les Nombres.* Translated by Louis Doutreleau after the edition of André Méhat, notes by Marcel Borret (Sources Chrétiennes 415; Paris, 1996).

Oswald, Friedrich, Leo Schaefer, and Hans Rudolf Sennhauser. *Vorromanische Kirchenbauten. Katalog der Denkmäler bis zum Ausgang der Ottonen* (Munich, 1966) = VKB 1966.

Otfrid. *Evangelienbuch.* Edited by Oskar Erdmann (Tubingen, 1973, 6th ed. improved by Ludwig Wolff).

Otten, Willemien. "Carolingian Theology." In *The Medieval Theologians. An Introduction to Theology in the Medieval Period,* edited by G. R. Evans, 68–82 (Oxford, 2001).

Otter, Monika. *Inventiones. Fiction and Referentiality in Twelfth-Century English Historical Writing* (Chapel Hill, 1996).

Ousterhout, Robert. "The Temple, the Sepulcher and the Martyrion." *Gesta* 29 (1990): 44–53.

Palmer, Andrew. "A Single Human Being Divided in Himself: Ephraim the Syrian, the Man in the Middle." *Hugoye: Journal of Syriac Studies* 1 (1998): 119–63. Online at http://syrcom.cua.edu/Hugoye/Vol1No2/HV1N2Palmer.html (last accessed May 8, 2012).

Palmer, James T. *Anglo-Saxons in a Frankish World, 690–900* (Turnhout, 2010).

Palmer, James T. "The Frankish Cult of Martyrs and the Case of the Two Saints Boniface." RB 114 (2004): 326–48.

Palmer, James T. "The 'Vigorous Rule' of Bishop Lull: Between Bonifatian Mission and Carolingian Church Control." *EME* 13 (2005): 249–76.

Paredi, Paola. "Per le Fonti del *Commentum in Matthaeum* dello Ps.Remigio d'Auxerre (Dal Codice di Ivrea LXXVI/43)." *Aevum* 79 (2005): 249–63.

Parsons, David. "Sites and Monuments of the Anglo-Saxon Mission in Germany." *Archeological Journal* 140 (1983): 280–321.

Parsons, David. "Some Churches of the Anglo-Saxon Missionaries in Southern Germany: A Review of the Evidence." *EME* 8 (1999): 31–67.

Passi, Sara. "Il commentario inedito ai Vangeli attribuito a 'Wigbodus.'" *Studi Medievali*, Ser. 3, 43 (2002): 58–156.

Passio Agathae. Edited by Johannes Bollandus, *AASS Februarii 1* (Antwerp, 1658), 615–18.

Passio Jacobi. Edited by Mombritius, *Sanctuarium*, 2:37–40.

Passio Julianae. Edited by Johannes Bollandus, *AASS Februarii 2 (Antwerp, 1658)*, 868–75.

Passio Philippi. Edited by Mombritius, *Sanctuarium*, 2:385.

Passio Simonis et Judae. Edited by Mombritius, *Sanctuarium*, 2:534–39.

Paul the Deacon. *Vita Gregorii Magni*, PL 75: 42–60.

Perry, R. "Radical Doubt and the Liberation of Women." *Eighteenth-Century Studies* 19 (1985): 472–93.

Pescheck, Christian. *Archäologiereport Kleinlangheim* (Würzburg, 1993).

Pescheck, Christian. "Frühchristlicher Sakralbau in Mainfranken." *Mainfränkisches Jahrbuch* 41 (1989): 1–45.

Peters, Edward. *Torture* (New York, 1985).

Petersohn, Jürgen. "Zur geographisch-politischen Terminologie und Datierung der passio maior sancti Kiliani." *Jahrbuch für fränkische Landesforschung* 52 (1992): 25–34.

Petzolt, Helmut. "Abtei Kitzingen—Gründung und Rechtslage." *Jahrbuch für fränkische Landesforschung* 15 (1955): 69–84.

Peyroux, Catherine Rosanna. "Abbess and Cloister: Double Monasteries in the Early Medieval West" (Unpublished PhD Dissertation, Princeton University, 1991).

Piédagnel, Auguste, ed. and trans. *Jean Chrysostom: Panégyriques de Saint Paul* (Paris, 1982).

Pillinger, Renate. *Die Tituli historiarum, oder, Das sogenannte Dittochaeon des Prudentius: Versuch eines philologisch-archäologischen Kommentars* (Vienna, 1980).

Pilsworth, Clare. "Miracles, Missionaries and Manuscripts in Eighth-Century Southern Germany." In *Signs, Wonders and Miracles. Representations of Divine Power in the Life of the Church,* edited by Kate Cooper and Jeremy Gregory, 67–77 (Studies in Church History 41; Woodbridge, 2005).

Pilsworth, Clare. "Vile Scraps: 'Booklet' Style Manuscripts and the Transmission and Use of the Italian Martyr Narratives in Early Medieval Europe." In *Zwischen Niederschrift und Wiederschrift. Hagiographische und historiographische Texte im Spannungsfeld von Kompendienüberlieferung und Edition,* edited by M. Diesenberger and M. Niederkorn-Bruck, 175–96 (Vienna, 2008).

Plant, Ian Michael, ed. *Women Writers of Ancient Greece and Rome: An Anthology* (Norman, 2004).

Pollmann, Karla. "Sex and Salvation in the Vergilian Cento of the Fourth Century." In *Romane Memento: Vergil in the Fourth Century,* edited by Roger Rees, 79–96 (London, 2004).

Pomeroy, Sarah B. "Commentary on Papers by K.Thraede and A. Demyttenaere." In *Frauen in Spätantike und Frühmittelalter,* edited by Affeldt, 167–70.

Posset, Franz. "The 'Palate of the Heart' in St. Augustine and Medieval Spirituality." In *Augustine, Biblical Exegete,* edited by Von Fleteren and Schnaubelt, 253–78.

Poullain de la Barre, François. *Three Cartesian Feminist Treatises.* Edited and translated by Vivien Bosley and Marcelle Maistre Welch (Chicago, 2002).

Power, Kim. *Veiled Desire. Augustine on Women* (New York, 1996).

Preato, Dennis J. "Did Paul Really Say, 'Let the Women Keep Silent in the Churches'?" (http://www.godswordtowomen.org/Preato2.htm; last accessed February 23, 2012).

Price, Richard. "Informal Penance in Early Medieval Christendom." In *Retribution, Repentance, and Reconciliation,* edited by Kate Cooper and Jeremy Gregory, 29–38. (Studies in Church History 40; Woodbridge, 2004).

Price, Richard. "Marian Piety and the Nestorian Controversy." In *The Church and Mary,* edited by R. N. Swanson, 31–38 (Studies in Church History 39; Woodbridge, 2004).

Prudentius, Aurelii Prudentii Clementis. *Carmina.* Edited by Johannes Bergman (CSEL LXI; Vienna/Leipzig, 1926).

Prudentius. *Works.* Translated by H. J. Thomson, 2 vols. (London/Cambridge, 1949–53).

Pseudo-Jerome. Letter 28: "De exodo in vigilia paschae." Edited by Germain Morin, *S. Hieronymi Presbyteri Opera Pars II: Opera Homiletica,* 536–41 (Maredsous, 1903; revised ed., Turnhout, 1958; CCSL 78).

Pulliam, Heather. "Eloquent Ornament: Exegesis and Entanglement in the Corbie Psalter." In *Studies in the Illustration of the Psalter,* edited by Cassidy and Wright, 24–33.

Pulliam, Heather. *Word and Image in the Book of Kells* (Dublin, 2006).

Raach, Theo. *Kloster Mettlach/Saar und sein Grundbesitz. Untersuchungen zur Frühgeschichte und zur Grundherrschaft der ehemaligen Benediktinerabtei im Mittlalter* (Mainz, 1974).

Raaijmakers, Janneke. "Een sacraal Landschap: Rudolf van Fulda over Hrabanus' Reliekentranslaties." *Millennium. Tijdschrift voor middeleeuwse studies* 14 (2000): 5–21.

Raban Maur. *Rabani Mauri Martyrologium.* Edited by J. M. McCulloh (CCCM, vol. XLIV; Turnhout, 1979).

Ramis, Gabriel. *La Consagracion de la Mujer en las Liturgias Occidentales* (Rome, 1990).

Ranft, Patricia. *Women and Spiritual Equality in Christian Tradition* (New York, 1998).

Rauch, Irmengard. "'Basler Rezept I': Method, Medical Code and the Polysemous Symptom." In *Festschrift für Herbert Kolb,* edited by Klaus Matzel and Hans-Gert Roloff with Barbara Haupt and Hilkert Weddige, 523–27 (Bern, 1989).

Reames, Sherry L. "A Recent Discovery Concerning the Sources of Chaucer's Second Nun's Tale." *Modern Philology* 87 (1990): 337–61.

Rebillard, Eric. *"In Hora Mortis." Évolution de la pastorale chrétienne de la mort aux IVe et Ve siècles dans l'Occident Latin* (Rome, 1994).

Regul, Jergen. *Die Antimarcionistischen Evangelienprologe* (Freiburg, 1962).

Regula cuiusdam ad Virgines, PL 88: 1053–70.

Rettner, Arno. "Grabhäuser—Ausdrucksform christlicher Glaubensvorstellungen?" In *1250 Jahre Bistum Würzburg,* edited by Lenssen and Wamser, 103–10.

Reynolds, Leighton D. "Introduction." In *Texts and Transmission,* edited by Leighton D. Reynolds (Oxford, 1983).

Reynolds, Susan. "Social Mentalities and the Case of Medieval Scepticism." *Transactions of the Royal Historical Society,* 6th Series, 1 (1991): 21–41.

Reynolds, Susan. "What Do We Mean by 'Anglo-Saxon' and 'Anglo-Saxons'?" *Journal of British Studies* 24 (1985): 395–414.

Riches, Samantha J. E. "St. George as a Male Virgin Martyr." In *Gender and Holiness: Men, Women and Saints in Late Medieval Europe,* edited by Samantha E. J. Riches and Sarah Salih, 65–85 (London, 2002).

Rinaldi, Rinaldo. "Un Travestimento Agiografico: la 'Vita S. Potiti' di Leon Battista Alberti." *Studi Umanistici Piceni* 19 (1999): 69–87.

Rittmueller, Jean, ed. *Liber Questionum in Evangeliis* (CCSL 108F; Turnhout, 2003).

Robin, Diana. "Humanism and Feminism in Laura Cereta's Public Letters." In *Women in Italian Renaissance Culture and Society,* 368–84 (Oxford, 2000).

Robinson, Pamela R. "The 'Booklet', a Self-Contained Unit in Composite Manuscripts." In *Litterae Textuales. A Series on Manuscripts and Their Texts,* edited by J. P. Gumbert, M. J. M. De Haan, and A. Gruys, 46–69 (Leiden, 1980).

Robinson, Pamela R. "A Twelfth-Century *Scriptrix* from Nunnaminster." In *Of the Making of Books. Medieval Manuscripts, Their Scribes and Readers. Essays in Honor of M. B. Parkes,* edited by P. R. Robinson and Rivkah Zim, 73–93 (Aldershot, 1997).

Röckelein, Hedwig. "Gründer, Stifter und Heilige—Patrone der Frauenkonvente." In *Krone und Schleier,* 66–77.

Röckelein, Hedwig. "Historische Frauenforschung. Ein Literaturbericht zur Geschichte des Mittelalters." *Historische Zeitschrift* 255 (1992): 377–409.

Rollason, David. *Saints and Relics in Anglo-Saxon England* (Oxford, 1989).

Roosen-Runge, Heinz. "Kunstwerke der Frühzeit. Tradition und Neubeginn." In *Karolingisches Franken,* edited by Buhl, 199–231.

Rordorf, Willy. "Saint Thècle dans la tradition hagiographique occidentale." *Augustinianum* 24 (1984): 73–81.

Rose, Els, ed. *Missale Gothicum e codice Vaticano Reginensi latino 317 editum* (CCSL 159D; Turnhout, 2005).

Rose, Els. *Ritual Memory: The Apocryphal Acts and Liturgical Commemoration in the Early Medieval West (c. 500–1215)* (Leiden, 2009).

Rösen, Hans. *Klöster in Franken. Werke und Gestalten einer europaischen Kulturlandschaft* (Freiburg, 1988).

Rosenstock, Dirk. "Die Besiedlung des Kitzinger Raumes in schriftloser Zeit." In *"apud kizinga monasterium,"* edited by Walter, 29–51.

Rosenstock, Dirk. "Zur Genealogie des mainländisch-thüringischen Herzogshauses der Hedene." In *1250 Jahre Bistum Würzburg*, edited by Lenssen and Wamser, 31–34.

Rosenstock, Dirk. "Siedlungsgeschichte im Frühmittelalter." In *Geschichte der Stadt Würzburg*, edited by Ulrich Wagner, 2 vols., 1:51–61 (Stuttgart, 2001–4).

Rosenthal, Jane, and Patrick McGurk. "Author, Symbol and Word: The Inspired Evangelists in Judith of Flanders' Anglo-Saxon Gospel Books." In *Tributes to Jonathan J. G. Alexander: The Making and Meaning of Illuminated Medieval and Renaissance Manuscripts, Art and Architecture*, edited by Susan L'Engle and Gerald B. Guest, 185–202 (Turnhout, 2006).

Ross, Sarah Gwyneth. *The Birth of Feminism. Woman as Intellect in Renaissance Italy and England* (Cambridge, 2009).

Roth, Detlef. "Mittelalterliche Misogynie–ein Mythos? Die antiken *molestiae nuptiarum* im *Adversus Iovinianum* und ihre Rezeption in der Lateinischen Literatur des 12. Jahrhunderts." *Archiv für Kulturgeschichte* 80 (1998): 39–66.

Roth, Helmut, and Egon Wamers. *Hessen im Frühmittelalter. Archäologie und Kunst* (Ausstellung, Museum für Vor- und Frühgeschichte, Frankfurt, 1984; Sigmaringen, 1984).

Rouche, Michel. "Des mariages päiens au mariage chrétien. Sacré et sacrement." In *Segni e riti*, 835–73.

Roy, Gopa. "A Virgin Acts Manfully: Ælfric's *Life of St. Eugenia* and the Latin Versions." *Leeds Studies in English* n.s. 23 (1992): 1–27.

Rubin, Miri. "The Languages of Late Medieval Feminism." In *Perspectives on Feminist Thought*, edited by Akkerman and Stuurman, 34–49.

Rudge, Lindsay. "Dedicated Women and Dedicated Spaces: Caesarius of Arles and the Foundation of St. John." In *Western Monasticism Ante Litteram*, edited by Dey and Fentress, 99–116.

Rudge, Lindsay. "Texts and Contexts: Women's Dedicated Life from Caesarius to Benedict" (unpublished PhD thesis, University of St. Andrew's, 2006).

Rudolf of Fulda. *Miracula Sanctorum in ecclesias Fuldenses Translatorum*. Edited by Georg Waitz *(MGH SS*, vol. 15.1; Hannover, 1887): 328–41.

Rudolf of Fulda. *Vita Leobae*. Edited by O. Holder-Egger (MGH SS, vol. 15.1; Hannover, 1887): 122–31.

Ruether, Rosemary Radford. "Augustine: Sexuality, Gender, and Women." In *Feminist Interpretations*, edited by Stark, 47–67.

Ruether, Rosemary Radford. "Feminism in World Christianity." In *Feminism and World Religions*, edited by Arvind Sharma and Katherine K. Young, 214–47 (Albany, 1999).

Ruether, Rosemary Radford. *Goddesses and the Divine Feminine: A Western Religious History* (Berkeley, 2005).

Rusch, William G. "A Possible Explanation of the Calendar in the Würzburg Lectionary." *Journal of Theological Studies* NS 21 (1970): 105–11.

Sage, Walter. "Die Kirche auf dem Michelsberg bei Neustadt am Main, Landkreis Main-Spessart." In *1250 Jahre Bistum Würzburg,* edited by Lenssen and Wamser, 209–15.

St. Clair, Archer. "A New Moses: Typological Iconography in the Moutier-Grandval Bible Illustrations of Exodus." *Gesta* 26 (1987): 19–28.

Salisbury, Joyce E. *The Blood of Martyrs. Unintended Consequences of Ancient Violence* (New York, 2004).

Salisbury, Joyce E. *Church Fathers, Independent Virgins* (London, 1991).

Salmon, Pierre. "Le Système des lectures liturgiques contenu dans les notes marginales du manuscrit q. 1a de la Bibliothèque de Wurtzbourg." *RB* 61 (1951): 38–53 and *RB* 62 (1952): 294–96.

Saurma-Jeltsch, Lieselotte. "Das Bild in der Worttheologie Karls des Grossens. Zur Christologie in karolingischen Miniaturen." In *Das Frankfurter Konzil,* edited by Berndt, 2:635–75.

Scarpatetti, Beat Matthias von. *Die Handschriften der Stiftsbibliothek St. Gallen, Bd. 1: Abt. IV: Codices 547–669: Hagiographica, Historica, Geographica, 8.18* (Wiesbaden, 2003).

Schäferdiek, Knut. "Kilian von Würzburg. Gestalt und Gestaltung eines Heiligen." In *Iconologia Sacra. Mythos, Bildkunst und Dichtung in der Religions- und Sozialgeschichte Alteuropas (Festschrift Karl Hauck),* edited by Hagen Keller and Nicolaus Staubach, 312–40 (Berlin, 1994).

Schäferdiek, Knut. "Die *Passio Johannis* des Melito von Laodikeia und die *virtutes Johannis.*" *AB* 103 (1985): 367–82.

Scheck, Helene. *Reform and Resistance. Formations of Female Subjectivity in Early Medieval Ecclesiastical Culture* (Albany, 2008).

Scheck, Helene. "Women's Intellectual Culture—The Case of Quedlinburg." (Paper presented to the Mid-America Medieval Association, University of Missouri–Kansas City, 2007).

Schemmel, Bernhard. "Neustadt am Main und die heilige Gertrud." In *Gertrud in Franken,* edited by Lenssen, 14–16.

Schepss, Georg. "Eine Würzburger lateinische Handschrift zu den apokryphen Apostelgeschichten." *Zeitschrift für Kirchengeschichte* 8 (1886): 449–59.

Schepss, Georg, ed. *Priscilliani Quae Supersunt* (CSEL 18; Leipzig, 1889).

Schieffer, Rudolf. "Karolingische Töchter." In *Herrschaft, Kirche, Kultur. Beiträge zur Geschichte des Mittelalters. Festschrift Friedrich Prinz zu seiner 65. Geburtstag,* edited by Georg Jenal and Stephanie Haarländer, 125–39 (Stuttgart, 1993).

Schiller, Heribert. *Wanderführer Spessart* (6th ed., Stuttgart, 1996).

Schilp, Thomas. *Norm und Wirklichkeit religiöser Frauengemeinschaften im Frühmittelalter* (Göttingen, 1998).

Schipperges, Stefan. *Bonifatius ac Socii Eius. Eine Sozialgeschichtliche Untersuchung des Winfried-Bonifatius und Seines Umfeldes* (Mainz, 1996).

Schlatter, Fredric W. "The Author of the *Opus Imperfectum in Matthaeum.*" *Vigiliae Christianae* 42 (1988): 364–75.

Schlatter, Fredric W. "The Pelagianism of the *Opus Imperfectum in Matthaem.*" *Vigiliae Christianae* 41 (1987): 267–84.

Schlosser, Horst Dieter. *Althochdeutsche Literatur: mit Proben aus dem Altnieder-deutschen: ausgewählte Texte mit Übertragungen und Anmerkungen* (Frankfurt, 1980).

Schmale, Franz-Josef. "Die Glaubwürdigkeit der jüngeren Vita Burchardi. Anmerkungen zur Frühgeschichte von Stadt und Bistum Würzburg." *Jahrbuch für fränkische Landesforschung* 19 (1959): 45–83.

Schneider, Erich. *Klöster und Stifte in Mainfranken* (Würzburg, 1993).

Schneiders, Marc. " 'Pagan Past and Christian Present' in Félire Óengusso." In *Cultural Identity,* edited by Edel, 157–69.

Schneir, Miriam. *Feminism; the Essential Historical Writings. A Reader* (New York, 1972).

Schnell, Rüdiger. "The Discourse on Marriage in the Middle Ages." *Speculum* 73 (1998): 771–86.

Scholz, Bernhard Walter, with Barbara Rogers, trans. *Carolingian Chronicles: The Royal Frankish Annals and Nithard's Histories* (Ann Arbor, 1970).

Schreiner, Klaus. *Maria. Jungfrau, Mutter, Herrscherin* (Munich, 1994).

Schreiner, Peter. "Kopistinnen in Byzanz." *Rivista di Studi Bizantini e Neoellenici* n.s. 36 (1999): 35–45.

Schrimpf, Gangolf, with Josef Leinweber and Thomas Martin, eds. *Mittelalterliche Bücherverzeichnisse des Klosters Fulda und Andere Beiträge zur Geschichte der Bibliothek des Klosters Fulda in Mittelalter* (Frankfurt, 1992).

Schulenburg, Jane Tibbetts. *Forgetful of Their Sex: Female Sanctity and Society ca. 500–1100* (Chicago, 1998).

Schulenburg, Jane Tibbetts. "Strict Active Enclosure and Its Effects on Female Monastic Experience (ca. 500–1200)." In *Distant Echoes,* edited by John A. Nichols, 51–86 (Kalamazoo, 1984).

Schulz, Walther. *Der Einfluss Augustins in der Theologie und Christologie des VIII. und IX. Jahrhunderts* (Halle an der Saale, 1913).

Schulze, Christian. "Das Bild als Kommentar—Zur Problematik von Pflanzendarstellungen in spätantiken und mittelalterlichen Handschriften." In *Der Kommentar,* edited by Geerlings and Schulze, 1: 335–53.

Schulze, Christian. "Das Phänomen der 'Nichtkommentierung' bedeutender Werke." In *Der Kommentar,* edited by Geerlings and Schulze, 2:21–34.

Schulze, Helmut. "Der Dom zu Würzburg." In *1250 Jahre Bistum Würzburg,* edited by Lenssen and Wamser, 76–86.

Schulze, Helmut. *Der Dom zu Würzburg. Sein Werden bis zum späten Mittelalter. Eine Baugeschichte,* 3 vols. (Würzburg, 1991).

Schulze, Helmut. "Das Oratorium und die Grabkirche des Bischofs Megingoz am Platz des späteren neuen 'Allerheiligen-Münsters' in Würzburg." *WDGB* 50 (1988): 545–50.

Schurr, Eva. *Die Ikonographie der Heiligen. Eine Entwicklungsgeschichte ihrer Attribute von der Anfängen bis zur achten Jahrhundert* (Dettelbach, 1997).

Schüssler Fiorenza, Elisabeth, with Shelly Matthews, eds. *Searching the Scriptures,* 2 vols. (New York, 1993).

Segni e Riti nella Chiesa altomedievale Occidentale, 2 vols. (Settimane 33; Spoleto, 1987).

Semmler, Joseph. "Le monachisme occidentale du VIIIe au Xe siècle. Formation et reformation." *RB* 103 (1993): 68–89.

Semmler, Joseph. "Monasterium Suuarzaha. Zu einem neuen Buch." *Zeitschrift für Kirchengeschichte* 107 (1996): 90–99.

Sepière, Marie-Christine. *L'Image d'un dieu souffrant (IXE–Xe siècle). Aux origines du crucifix* (Paris, 1994).

Shapiro, Meyer. "The Religious Meaning of the Ruthwell Cross." In *Late Antique, Early Christian and Medieval Art. Selected Papers,* by Shapiro (New York, 1979).

Silvas, Anna M. *Macrina the Younger, Philosopher of God* (Brepols, 2008).

Simón, Alfredo. "Il metodo teologico di Gregorio Magno. Il processo plurisemantico della analogia metaesegetica." *Benedictina* 53 (2007): 341–63.

Simons, Walter. *Cities of Ladies. Beguine Communities in the Medieval Low Countries, 1200–1565* (Philadelphia, 2002).

Sims-Williams, Patrick. "Cuthswith, Seventh Abbess of Inkberrow, near Worcester, and the Würzburg Manuscript of Jerome on Ecclesiastes." *Anglo-Saxon England* 5 (1976): 1–22.

Sims-Williams, Patrick. *Religion and Literature in Western England, 600–800* (Cambridge, 1990).

Sims-Williams, Patrick. "An Unpublished Seventh- or Eighth-Century Anglo-Latin Letter in Boulogne-sur-Mer ms 74 (82)." *Medium Aevum* 48 (1979): 1–22.

Smith, Julie Ann. "Sacred Journeying. Women's Correspondence and Pilgrimage in the Fourth and Eighth Centuries." In *Pilgrimage Explored,* edited by Jennifer Stopford, 41–56 (York, 1999).

Smith, Lesley. *Masters of the Sacred Page. Manuscripts of Theology in the Latin West to 1274* (Notre Dame, 2001).

Smyth, Marina. "The Origins of Purgatory through the Lens of Seventh-Century Irish Eschatology." *Traditio* 58 (2003): 91–132.

Société des Bollandistes. "BHLms: Index analytique des Catalogues de manuscrits hagiographiques latins publiés par les Bollandistes" (1998). Online at: http://bhlms.fltr.ucl.ac.be/default.htm.

Société des Bollandistes. *Bibliotheca Hagiographica Latina antiquae et mediae aetatis* plus Supplements (Subsidia Hagiographica 6, 12, 70; Brussels, 1898–1901, 1911, and 1986) = BHL.

Sorgo, Gabriele. *Martyrium und Pornographie* (Dusseldorf, 1997).

Spilling, Herrad. "Das Fuldaer Scriptorium zur Zeit des Hrabanus Maurus." In *Hrabanus Maurus,* edited by Kottje and Zimmermann, 165–81.

Spilling, Herrad. "Irische Handschriftenüberlieferung in Fulda, Mainz und Würzburg." In *Die Iren und Europa im frühen Mittelalter,* edited by Löwe, 2:876–902.

Staab, Frank. "Die Königin Fastrada." In *Das Frankfurter Konzil,* edited by Berndt, 1:183–217.

Stark, Judith Chelius. "Augustine on Women: In God's Image, but Less So." In *Feminist Interpretations,* edited by Stark, 215–41.

Stark, Judith Chelius, ed. *Feminist Interpretations of Augustine* (University Park, 2007).

Stark, Judith Chelius. "Introduction." In *Feminist Interpretations,* edited by Stark, 1–45.

Starowieyski, Marek. "La légende de Saint Jacques le Majeur." *Apocrypha: Revue internationale des littératures apocryphes/International Journal of Apocryphal Literatures* 7 (1996): 193–203.

Stegmüller, Friedrich. *Initia Biblica* (Madrid, 1940).

Stegmüller, Friedrich, and Klaus Reinhardt, eds. *Das Repertorium Biblicum Medii Aevi*, 11 vols. (Madrid, 1950–80; online at: http://www.repbib.uni-trier.de/).

Steidle, Hans. "Geilana, Immina und Würzburg." In *Stadt und Frömmigkeit,* edited by Ulrich Knefelkamp, 1–24 (Bamberg, 1995).

Steinmeyer, Elias von. *Die Kleineren Althochdeutschen Sprachdenkmäler* (Berlin, 1916; cited from 3rd ed., Dublin/Zürich, 1971).

Stengel, Edmund, ed. *Urkundenbuch des Klosters Fulda*, 2 vols. (Marburg, 1958).

Stevenson, Jane. *Women Latin Poets: Language, Gender, and Authority from Antiquity to the Eighteenth Century* (Oxford, 2005).

Sticht, Oliver. "Spuren in Wort und Bild—Aspekte der Bibelüberlieferung in Würzburg UB M.p.th.f. 69." *Biblos. Beiträge zur Buch, Bibel und Schrift* 52 (2003): 221–26.

Stimming, Manfred, ed. *Mainzer Urkundenbuch,* 2 vols. (Darmstadt, 1932).

Stoclet, Alain. "Gisèle, Kisyla, Chelles, Benediktbeuren et Kochel. Scriptoria, Bibliothèques et Politique à l'époque carolingienne. Une mise au point." *RB* 102 (1986): 250–70.

Stofferahn, Steven A. "Changing Views of Carolingian Women's Literary Culture: The Evidence from Essen." *EME* 8 (1999): 69–97.

Störmer, Wilhelm. "Amorbach." LTK 1:537.

Störmer, Wilhelm. "Zu Herkunft und Wirkungskreis der merowingerzeitlichen 'mainfränkischen' Herzoge." In *Festschrift für Edouard Hlawitschka,* edited by K. R. Schnith and R. Pauler, 11–21 (Munich, 1993).

Stouck, Mary-Ann. *Medieval Saints. A Reader* (Peterborough, 1999).

Straw, Carole. *Gregory the Great: Perfection in Imperfection* (Berkeley, 1988).

Straw, Carole. "Purity and Death" in *Gregory the Great. A Symposium,* edited by John Cavadini, 16–37 (Notre Dame/London, 1995).

Strewe, A., ed. *Die Canonensammlung des Dionysius Exiguus in der ersten Redaktion* (Leipzig, 1931).

Sturm, Erwin. *Kloster Altstadt bei Hammelburg* (3rd ed., Regensburg, 1988).

Stuurman, Siep. *François Poulain de la Barre and the Invention of Modern Equality* (Cambridge, 2004).

Swan, Mary. "Remembering Veronica in Anglo-Saxon England." In *Writing Gender and Genre in Medieval Literature. Approaches to Old and Middle English Texts,* edited by Elaine Treharne, 19–39 (Cambridge, 2002).

Tertullian. "De cultu feminarum." Edited by Eligius Dekkers, *Tertulliani Opera Omnia,* 342–71 (CCSL 2; Turnhout, 1954).

Tertullian. *De exhortatione castitatis: Ermahnung zur Keuschheit.* Edited by Hans-Veit Friedrich (Stuttgart, 1990).

Thacker, Alan. "Memorializing Gregory the Great: The Origin and Transmission of a Papal Cult in the 7th and Early 8th Centuries." *EME* 7 (1998): 59–84.

Thraede, Klaus. "Zwischen Eva und Maria: das Bild der Frau bei Ambrosius und Augustin auf dem Hintergrund der Zeit." In *Frauen in Spätantike und Frühmittelalter,* edited by Affeldt, 129–39.

Thurn, Hans, ed. *Comes Romanus Wirzeburgensis* (Graz, 1968).

Thurn, Hans. *Handschriften aus benediktinischen Provenienzen: Amorbach, Kitzingen, Münsterschwarzach, Erfurt, Minden, Mondsee* (Die Handschriften der Universitätsbibliothek Würzburg 2.1; Wiesbaden, 1973).

Thurn, Hans. "Handschriften der Universitätsbibliothek Würzburg aus dem Würzburger Domschatz und Heiltum." *Bibliotheksforum Bayern* 10 (1982): 206–11.

Thurn, Hans. "Libri sancti Kyliani—frühe Handschriften der Würzburger Dombibliothek." In *Kilian. Mönch aus Irland*, 238–48.

Thurn, Hans. *Die Pergamenthandschriften der ehemaligen Dombibliothek Würzburg* (Die Handschriften der Universitätsbibliothek Würzburg 3.1; Wiesbaden, 1984).

Thurn, Hans. "Zum Text des Hieronymus-Kommentars zum Kohelet." *Biblische Zeitschrift* N.f. 33 (1989): 234–44.

Thurn, Hans. "Die Würzburger Dombibliothek des frühen Mittelalters." *WDGB* 54 (1992): 55–67.

Tinkle, Theresa. *Gender and Power in Medieval Exegesis* (New York, 2010).

Torjesen, Karen Jo. "Reconstruction of Women's Early Christian History." In *Searching the Scriptures*, edited by Schüssler Fiorenza and Matthews, 1:290–310.

Trigg, Joseph W. *Origen* (London/New York, 1998).

Trunk, P. Leo. "Megingozzeshusenscastel. Eine philologische Anmerkung zur Gründungsurkunde des Klosters Megingaudeshausen." *Mainfränkisches Jahrbuch* 39 (1987): 98–102.

Uebel, Michael. *Ecstatic Transformations. On the Uses of Alterity in the Middle Ages* (New York, 2005).

Ulianich, Boris. "Il Cristo crocifisso rivestito del *colobium* o della tunica (secoli VI–XIII). Note e appunti." In *Ave Crux Gloriosa*, edited by Vittorelli, 59–82.

Unterkircher, Franz, ed. *Sancti Bonifacii epistolae. Codex Vindobonensis 751 der Österreichischen Nationalbibliothek. Faksimile-Ausgabe der Wiener Handschrift der Briefe des heiligen Bonifatius* (Graz, 1971).

Urbahn, Hannah. "'Ich umfasse Dich mit hoechster Liebe.' Der heilige Bonifatius und seine spirituellen Schwestern." In *Meine in Gott geliebte Freundin. Freundschaftsdokumente aus klösterlichen und humanistischen Schreibstuben*, edited by Gabriela Signori, 40–49 (Bielefeld, 1995).

Usher, Mark David. *Homeric Stitchings. The Homeric Centos of the Empress Eudocia* (Lanham, 1998).

Uthemann, Karl-Heinz. "Ein griechisches Florileg zur Verteidigung des Filioque aus dem 7. Jahrhundert? Eine Bemerkung zum Parisinus graecus 1115." *Byzantinische Zeitschrift* 92 (1999): 502–11.

Van Banning, Joop, ed. *Opus Imperfectum in Matthaeum* (CCSL 87B; Turnhout, 1988).

Van Esbroeck, Michel. "La naissance du culte de saint Barthélémy en Arménie." *Revue des études arméniennes* 17 (1983): 171–95.

Van Herwaarden, Jan. "The Origins of the Cult of St. James of Compostela." *Journal of Medieval History* 6 (1980): 1–35 and 133.

Vanneufville, Eric. "Monophysisme et nestorianisme chez Avit de Vienne." In *Clovis, histoire et mémoire. Actes du Colloque International d'Histoire de Reims, du 19 au 25 septembre 1996*, edited by Michel Rouche, 2 vols. 1:217–26 (Paris, 1997).

Van Tongeren, Louis. "A Sign of Resurrection on Good Friday. The Role of the People in the Good Friday Liturgy until c. 1000 A.D. and the Meaning of the Cross." In *Omnes Circumadstantes. Contributions towards a History of the Role of the People in the Liturgy. Presented to Herman Wegman*, edited by Charles Caspers and Marc Schneiders, 101–19 (Kampen, 1990).

Veelenturf, Kees. *Dia Brátha. Eschatological Theophanies and Irish High Crosses* (Amsterdam, 1997).

Veronese, Alessandra. "Monasteri femminili in Italia nell'Alto Medioevo. Confronto con il monasteri maschili per un tentative di analisi 'statistica.'" *Benedictina* 24 (1987): 355–416.

Vessey, Mark. "Response to Catherine Conybeare. Women of Letters?" In *Voices in Dialogue,* edited by Olson and Kerby-Fulton, 73–96.

Vita Euphrosynae, in *PL* 73: 643–53; *AASS* Februarii 2 (Antwerp, 1658), 537–41.

Vita Malchi, in *PL* 23: 53–60.

Vittorelli, Pietro, ed. *Ave Crux Gloriosa. Croci e crocifissi nell'arte dall'VIII al XX secolo* (Monte-Cassino, 2002).

Vitz, Evelyn Birge. "Gender and Martyrdom." *Medievalia et Humanistica* n.s. 26 (1999): 79–99.

Vizzini, Joseph, et al. *Bibliotheca Sanctorum,* 13 vols. (Rome, 1961–70).

Vogel, Cyrille. "Les rites de la célébration du mariage." In *Il matrimonio nelle società altomedioevale,* 397–465 (*Settimane* XXIV (1972); Spoleto, 1977).

Vogt, Gabriel. "Zur Frühgeschichte der Abtei Münsterschwarzach." *Mainfränkisches Jahrbuch* 32 (1980): 49–69.

Volbach, Wolfgang Fritz, with photographs by Max Hirmer. *Early Christian Art* (London, 1962).

Von Dobschütz, Ernst. *Das Decretum Gelasianum de libris recipiendis et non recipiendis* (Leipzig, 1912).

Von Fleteren, Frederick, and Joseph C. Schnaubelt, eds. *Augustine, Biblical Exegete* (New York, 2001).

Von Padberg, Lutz E. *Mission und Christianisierung. Formen und Folgen bei Angelsachsen und Franken in 7. und 8. Jahrhundert* (Stuttgart, 1995).

Von Padberg, Lutz E., and Hans-Walter Stork. *Der Ragyndrudis-Codex des Heiligen Bonifatius* (Paderborn, 1994).

Wagner, Heinrich. "Die Äbte von St. Burkhard zur Würzburg im Mittelalter." *WDGB* 50 (1988): 11–41.

Wagner, Heinrich. "Die Äbtissinen des Klosters Kitzingen." *WDGB* 64 (2002): 9–75.

Wagner, Heinrich. *Bonifatiusstudien* (Würzburg, 2003).

Wagner, Heinrich. "Zur Frühzeit des Bistums Würzburg." *Mainfränkisches Jahrbuch* 33 (1981): 95–121.

Wagner, Heinrich, "Die Hedene, die hl. Bilhildis, und die Erstnennung von Bamberg." *WDGB* 61 (1999): 13–50.

Wagner, Heinrich. "Die Zehntenschenkung Pippins für Würzburg (751/52)." In *1250 Jahre Bistum Würzburg,* edited by Lenssen and Wamser, 35–38.

Wallach, Liutpold. "Alcuin on Virtues and Vices." *Harvard Theological Review* 48 (1955): 175–95.

Walter, Helga, ed. *"apud Kizinga monasterium": 1250 Jahre Kitzingen am Main* (Kitzingen, 1995).

Walter, Helga. *Kitzingen* (Regensburg, 1986).

Walter, Ludwig K. "Die theologischen Streitigkeiten des Frühmittelalters und ihre Widerspiegelung in der Würzburger Kirche des 8. und 9. Jahrhunderts. Ein theologiegeschichtlicher Versuch." *WDGB* 56 (1994): 13–26.

Wamers, Egon. *Die frühmittelalterlichen Lesefunde aus der Löhrstraße in Mainz (Neubau Hilton 2)* (Mainz, 1994).

Wamers, Egon. "Die silberne Pyxis von Pettstadt. Ikonographie und Funktion." In *1250 Jahre Bistum Würzburg*, edited by Lenssen and Wamser, 154–62.

Wamers, Egon. "Das Untermaingebiet im späten 8. Jahrhundert." In *794*, edited by Fried, 37–46.

Wampach, Camillus, ed. *Urkunden und Quellenbuch zur Geschichte der altluxemburgischen Territorien bis zur burgundischen Zeit*, 2 vols. (Luxemburg, 1935).

Wamser, Ludwig. "Archäologische Befunde zur frühmittelalterlichen Topographie und Geschichte Karlburgs." In *Karlburg—Uralter fränkischer Siedlungsort*, edited by Ernst Kübert, 17–39 (Karlstadt, 1991).

Wamser, Ludwig. "Zur archäologischen Bedeutung der Karlburger Befunde." In *1250 Jahre Bistum Würzburg*, edited by Lenssen and Wamser, 319–43.

Wamser, Ludwig. "Erwägungen zur Topographie und Geschichte des Klosters Neustadt am Main und seiner Mark." In *1250 Jahre Bistum Würzburg*, edited by Lenssen and Wamser, 163–203.

Wamser, Ludwig. "Mainfranken—Land und Leute im Spiegel der Archaeologie." In *Kilian. Mönch aus Irland*, 43–88.

Wamser, Ludwig. "Die silberne Pyxis von Pettstadt. Landesgeschichtliche Aspekte." In *1250 Jahre Bistum Würzburg*, edited by Lenssen and Wamser, 141–53.

Wamser, Ludwig. "Die Würzburger Siedlungslandschaft im frühen Mittelalter. Spiegelbild der naturgegebenen engen Verknüpfung von Stadt- und Bistumsgeschichte." In *1250 Jahre Bistum Würzburg*, edited by Lenssen and Wamser, 39–47.

Ward, Benedicta. "'To My Dearest Sister': Bede and the Educated Woman." in *Women, the Book and the Godly. Selected Proceedings of the St. Hilda's Conference 1993*, edited by Lesley Smith and Jane H. M. Taylor, 2 vols., 1:105–12 (Cambridge, 1995).

Wasserschleben, F. W. H. *Die Bussordnungen der abendländischen Kirche nebst einer rechtsgeschichtlichen Einleitung* (Halle, 1851).

Wasserschleben, F. W. H., ed. *Die irische Kannonensammlung* (Leipzig, 1885).

Watson, Andrew G. *Medieval Libraries of Great Britain, a List of Surviving Books, edited by N. R. Ker: Supplement to the Second Edition* (London, 1987).

Wegner, Günter. *Kirchenjahr und Messfeier in der Würzburger Domliturgie des Späten Mittelalters* (Würzburg, 1970).

Wehrhahn-Stauch, Liselotte. "Aquila-Resurrectio." *Zeitschrift des deutschen Vereins für Kunstwissenschaft* 21 (1967): 105–27.

Wehrhahn-Stauch, Liselotte. "Christliche Fischsymbolik von den Anfängen bis zum hohen Mittelalter." *Zeitschrift für Kunstgeschichte* 35 (1972): 1–68.

Weidemann, K. "Frühmittelalterliche Burgen als Zentren der Königs-Herrschaft in den Mainlanden." in *Führer*, 134–65.

Weidemann, Margarete. "Die hl. Bilhild und die Gründung des Altmünsterklosters." In *1300 Jahre Altmünsterkloster in Mainz. Abhandlungen und Ausstellungskatalog*, edited by Ingrid Adam and Horst Reber, 57–63 (Mainz, 1994).

Weidemann, Margarete. "Urkunde und Vita der hl. Bilhildis aus Mainz." *Francia* 21 (1994): 17–84.

Weigel, Helmut. "Straße, Königscentene und Kloster im karolingischen Ostfranken." *Jahrbuch für fränkische Landesforschung* 13 (1953): 7–53.

Weiner, Andreas. *Die Initialornamentik der Deutch-Insular Schulen im Bereich von Fulda, Würzburg und Mainz* (Würzburg, 1992).

Wemple, Suzanne Fonay. "Female Monasticism in Italy and Its Comparison with France and Germany from the Ninth through the Eleventh Century." In *Frauen in Spätantike und Frühmittelalter,* edited by Affeldt, 291–310.

Wemple, Suzanne Fonay. *Women in Frankish Society. Marriage and the Cloister, 500–900* (Philadelphia, 1981).

Wendehorst, Alfred. "Bischofssitz und königliche Stadt—Von der Karolingerzeit bis zum Wormser Konkordat." In *Geschichte der Stadt Würzburg,* edited by Ulrich Wagner, 2 vols, 1:62–73 (Stuttgart, 2001).

Wendehorst, Alfred. *Das Bistum Würzburg I: Die Bischofsreihe bis 1254* (Berlin 1962).

Wendehorst, Alfred. "Burchard." *Lexikon des Mittelalters* 11 (1983): 951.

Wendehorst, Alfred. "Die Iren und die Christianisierung Mainfrankens." In *Die Iren und Europa im früheren Mittelalter,* edited by Löwe, 1:319–29.

Wenisch, Siegfried. *Ochsenfurt. Von der frühmittelalterlichen Gemarkung zur domkapitelschen Stadt* (Würzburg, 1972).

Werckmeister, Otto. *Irisch-northumbrische Buchmalerei des 8. Jahrhunderts und monastische Spiritualität* (Berlin, 1967).

Werminghoff, Albert, ed. *Concilia Aevi Karolini (742–842)* (MGH Leges, Concilia 2.1: 742–817; Hannover/Leipzig, 1906).

Werner, Matthias. *Adelsfamilien im Umkreis der frühen Karolinger. Die Verwandtschaft Irminas von Oeren und Adelas von Pfalzel. Personengeschichtliche Untersuchungen zur frühmittelalterlichen Führungsschicht im Maas-Mosel-Gebiet* (Sigmaringen, 1982).

Werner, Matthias. "Iren und Angelsachsen im Mitteldeutschland. Zur vorbonifatianischen Mission in Hessen und Thüringen." In *Die Iren und Europa im früheren Mittelalter,* edited by Löwe, 239–329.

Wickham, Chris. *Framing the Early Middle Ages. Europe and the Mediterranean, 400–800* (Oxford, 2005).

Wilkins, Walter J. "'Submitting the Neck of Your Mind': Gregory the Great and Women of Power." *Catholic Historical Review* 77 (1991): 583–94; reprinted in Everett Ferguson, ed., *Christianity and Society: The Social World of Early Christianity,* 87–98 (New York, 1999).

Wilkinson, John. *Jerusalem Pilgrims before the Crusades* (Warminster, 1977).

Willibald of Eichstätt. *Vita Bonifatii.* Translated by Talbot. In Thomas F. X. Noble and Thomas Head, eds., *Soldiers of Christ: Saints and Saints' Lives from Late Antiquity and the Early Middle Ages,* 107–40 (University Park, 1994).

Wilson, James H. *Christian Theology and Old English Poetry* (The Hague, 1974).

Wilson, Katharina. "Introduction." In *Hrotsvit of Gandersheim,* edited by Brown et al., 3–10.

Winston-Allen, Anne. *Convent Chronicles. Women Writing about Women and Reform in the Late Middle Ages* (University Park, 2004).

Wittekind, Susanne. "Die Illustration von Augustinustexten im Mittelalter." In *Der Kommentar,* edited by Geerlings and Schulze, 2:101–27.

Wittig, Joseph. "Figural Narrative in Cynewulf's Juliana." *Anglo-Saxon England* 4 (1974): 37–55; reprinted in Robert E. Bjork, ed., *Cynewulf: Basic Readings,* 147–69 (New York, 1996).

Wittstadt, Klaus. "Die älteste Lebensbeschreibung des heiligen Burkard— Lateinischer Text und deutsche Übersetzung." *WDGB* 48 (1986): 7–17.

Wittstadt, Klaus. "Die Bedeutung von Kirche und Glaube für die identität einer historischer Landschaft—aufgezeigt am Beispiel Frankens." In *Landesgeschichte in Deutschland. Bestandsaufnahme. Analyse. Perspektiven,* edited by Werner Buchholz, 335–45 (Paderborn, 1998).

Wittstadt, Klaus, and Wolfgang Weiß. *Das Bistum Würzburg. Leben und Auftrag einer Ortskirche im Wandel der Zeit.* 5 vols. (Strasbourg, 1996).

Wogan-Browne, Jocelyn. *Saints' Lives and Women's Literary Culture, 1150–1300* (New York, 2001).

Wolf, Gunther. "Grifos Erbe, die Einsetzung König Childerics III, und der Kampf um die Macht—zugleich Bemerkungen zur karolingischen 'Hofhistoriographie.'" *Archiv für Diplomatik, Schriftgeschichte, Siegel und Wappenkunde* 38 (1992): 1–16.

Wolf, Kirsten. "The Severed Breast. A Topos in the Legends of Female Virgin Martyr Saints." *Arkiv för nordisk filologi* 112 (1997): 97–112.

Wright, Charles D. "Some Evidence for an Irish Origin of Redaction XI of the *Visio Pauli.*" *Manuscripta* 34 (1990): 34–44.

Wright, Rosemary Muir. "Introducing the Medieval Psalter." In *Studies in the Illustration of the Psalter,* edited by Cassidy and Wright, 1–11.

Wybourne, Catherine. "Seafarers and Stay-at-Homes: Anglo-Saxon Nuns and Mission." *Downside Review* 114 (1996): 246–66.

Yaeger, R. F. "Did Gower Write *Cento*?" In *John Gower: Recent Readings,* edited by R. F. Yaeger, 113–32 (Kalamazoo, 1989).

Yorke, Barbara. "The Bonifatian Mission and Female Religious in Wessex." *EME* 7 (1998): 145–72.

Yorke, Barbara. "Carriers of the Truth: Writing the Biographies of Anglo-Saxon Female Saints." In *Writing Medieval Biography, 750–1250: Essays in Honour of Professor Frank Barlow,* edited by David Bates, Julia Crick, and Sarah Hamilton, 49–60 (Woodbridge, 2006).

Zastrow, Oleg. "La Croce cristiana nell'oreficeria in Lombardia dal VI al XIII secolo." In *Ave Crux Gloriosa,* edited by Vittorelli, 55–67.

Zechiel-Eckes, Klaus. *Die Concordia Canonum des Cresconius. Studien und Edition,* 2 vols. (Frankfurt, 1992).

Zelzer, Klaus, ed. *Die alten lateinischen Thomasakten* (Berlin 1977).

Ziegler, Ulla. "Das 'Sacramentarium Gelasianum' (Vat. Reg. lat. 316) und die Schule von Chelles." *Archiv für Geschichte des Buchwesens* 16 (1976): 2–142.

Zimmermann, Ernst Heinrich. *Vorkarolingische Miniaturen,* 5 vols. (Text and I–IV Plates; Berlin, 1916).

Zöller, Helge. "Kirchengut des hl. Kilian—die Stadt und das Land des Heiligen." In *Kilian. Mönch aus Irland,* 224–37.

Zweierlein, Otto. "'Interpretation' in Antike und Mittelalter." In *Der Kommentar,* edited by Geerlings and Schulze, 1: 79–101.

abbesses: Carolingian reform movement and, 7–9, 11–12; epitaphs of, 128; of Kitzingen, 22, 154; liturgical roles of, 76, 159, 186; monastic rules and, 148

Abelard, Peter, xv

Abirhilt, 32, 41, 58, 223n30, 224n32

Abirhilt manuscripts: "Deus per angelum" *libellus* (Würzburg UB M.p.th.q. 28b codex 1), 49–54; Gregory I's Homilies on the Gospels as (Würzburg UB M.p.th.f. 45), 40–41, 74, 87, 106; Kitzingen homiliary as (Würzburg UB M.p.th.q. 28b codex 3), 58–59, 177–82, 238n257; Kitzingen Isidore as (Würzburg UB M.p.th.q. 28b codex 2), 54–56, 153–58; Kitzingen Paul as (Würzburg UB M.p.th.f. 69), 36–38; overview, 31–37, 223n30. *See also* Gun(t)za and Abirhilt manuscripts

accio nuptialis, 6

Acts of Paul and Thecla, 83, 166

"ad lapidem fluminis" manuscripts, 10, 28, 59–61, 239n268

Ada school, 244n98

Adam: Augustine on, 40, 96–98, 181; in "Deus per angelum" *libellus*, 138, 141; Gregory on, 109; in Kitzingen homiliary, 178, 181, 274n246; in Passions of the Apostles, 124, 125, 181; Proba on, 199; in the Vienna Penitential, 132; in Würzburg UB M.p.th. o.4, 209n36

Admonitio (Pseudo-Basil), 175–76

Admonitio generalis (789), 8, 30, 187

Afra of Augsburg, saint (d.304), 115

Agatha of Catania, saint (d.251): as consecrated virgin, 79, 246n116; "On the Death of Agatha of Catania," 51, 114, 128–30, 134, 136, 138, 139, 141–44, 146, 234n185, 261n165, 261n175; passion of, 51, 114, 128–30, 134, 136, 138, 139, 141–44, 146, 234n185, 261n165, 261n175; Quintianus and, 129, 142, 144

Agnes of Rome, saint (d. c.304): Jesus Christ and, 141–42; passion of, 50–51, 128–30, 134, 136, 138, 139, 141–44, 146, 261n170, 261n175

Alan, abbot of Farfa (d.770), 49, 132, 195

Alcuin of York (c.735–804), 8, 9, 51, 57, 72, 159, 200, 238n257, 239n268

Aldhelm, abbot of Malmesbury (c.639–c.790), 6, 73, 150, 172, 196; *Aenigmata*, 198; *Carmen de virginitate* of, 72, 77, 242n60; *Prosa de virginitate*, 22, 147, 202, 209n41, 262n193, 281nn72–73

altar service: consecrated women and, 185–92; virgins and, 185, 190, 192

Altmünster (St. Mary inside the walls), 5, 18, 29, 31, 76, 194, 216n27, 244n98, 257n152

Ambrosius Autpertus, abbot of San Vincenzo (d.784), 78, 195

Amorbach (Odenwald), 23, 218n85

Ananias of Damascus, 69

Anglo-Saxon cultural province in Francia: book production, 31; Carolingian reform movement in, 7–15; Christianity in, 3, 16–17; consecrated women, altar service and, 185–92; foundation of Würzburg, mythic narratives of expulsion and removal, 25–28; gender relations in, 3–15; historical overview, 3–4; overview, xvi, xvii, 3–4; passions of saints in, 112–16; women and their books in, 29–61. *See also* Main River Valley; *specific topics*

Anglo-Saxon cultural province in Francia, manuscripts. *See* manuscripts

Anglo-Saxons, in Franconia, 16, 18

animal imagery: bird imagery of Kitzingen crucifixion miniature, 70–72, 242n55; *Synonyms* illustration through, 153–58, 266n78

Annianus of Celeda, 51–52

Annunciation, 37; Bartholomew on, 123, 133; in "Deus per angelum" *libellus*, 49, 123, 133–34, 138

"apocalypsis apostoli sancti pauli." See *Vision of St. Paul*

Apocryphal Acts of the Apostles, 30

apostles: Apocryphal Acts of the Apostles, 30, 31. *See also* Passions of the Apostles; saints; *specific apostles*

Apponius, 196–200

Argenteuil, 12, 24

art: gender, spirituality and, 85–86; historical importance of women in visual, 205. *See also* medieval art

artists. *See* theologian-artists; women artists

Astell, Ann, 110–11

Atenolfi, Giuseppi Talamo, 47

Augustine. *See* Augustine, bishop of Hippo

Augustine, bishop of Hippo (354–430), 49; on Adam, 40, 96–98, 181; on biblical characters, 88, 99; on Christian indifference to material conditions, 90–91; on Christian unity, 90–91; Commentary on the Psalms of, 38–40, 68, 87–88, 90–98, 110,

Augustine (cont.)
111, 229n89, 249n37, 249nn58–59; on Eden, 89–90, 95–97, 250n71; on Eve, 89–90, 95–97, 250n71; feminism and, 99; florilegium, 170; gender egalitarianism of, 91–98; gradual Psalms sermons of, 90–96; Gregory I and, 99, 105; on holy women, 88, 90–98; on *imago Dei*, 97; on Job, 110; on martyrs, 93–94; misogyny and, 93–94, 96–98, 110; on Paul, 94, 95; Pelagius and, 135, 136; on saints, 88, 93, 94, 95, 99; on Stephen, 94, 249n59; *On the Trinity* of, 97–98, 152, 154, 171, 200, 223n30; women and, 89, 91, 110–12
Augustine of Canterbury (d.604), 102–3

Bartholomew, apostle: on Annunciation, 123, 133; cult of, 45, 46; passion of, 45–46, 118, 120, 123–25, 231n115
Basel: blood charm, 35–36; recipes, 34–35
Basel booklist, 32–36, 225n37, 225n38, 226n42; visionary literature on, 72–73. *See also* Gun(t)za and Abirhilt manuscripts; Kitzingen library catalogue
Bassilla, noble virgin, 165, 169
Bede (d.735), 48, 54, 90, 134, 172
Benedict of Aniane (747–821), 12
Berhtgyt, *magistra* in Thuringia, 5, 6, 218n75
Berowelf, bishop of Würzburg (d.794), 25, 26
Bible: patriarchy of, 84. *See also specific biblical topics*
biblical books: crucifixion imagery and, 67–68; in Karlburg collection, 38; in Kitzingen library catalogue, 38, 228n76
biblical characters: Augustine on, 88, 99; Gregory I on, 88. *See also specific biblical characters*
biblical commentaries: feminists and, 90; religious women and, 90; women and patristic, 87–90, 111. *See also specific biblical commentaries*
Bilhildis (Bilihilt), 5, 18, 29, 30, 222n2
binary oppositions, and Gregory I, 107–10
bird imagery, of Kitzingen crucifixion miniature, 70–72, 242n55
Bischoff, Bernhard, 28, 31–32, 59
Boniface of Mainz (d.754/755): biography of, 25, 31, 150, 219n94; Leoba and, xvi, xvii, 5, 7, 14, 15, 22, 208n22, 210n48; letters of, 4, 9, 211n67–68; Main River Valley and, 20–25; Paul and, 82–83, 85; Ragyndrudis codex and, 31, 55; women and, 83
Bonifatian syneisactic circle, 3–7, 16–17, 20–23; naval metaphors of, 82, 246n130
Bonifatius ac socii eius, 218n69
Bonnet, Maximilian, 45–46
Book of the City of Ladies, The (Christine de Pizan), 206

book production: Anglo-Saxon cultural province in Francia, 31; gender and, 205; overview, 31; women and, 32, 67. *See also* textual transmission
booklists: overview, 33; Würzburg cathedral, 55, 209n41, 223n30, 225n37, 229n87. *See also* Basel booklist; library catalogues
books. *See* biblical books; manuscripts; women's books; *specific books*
Burginda of Bath, 199
burials: medieval artistic objects and, 70, 242n46; of men and women, 5, 15, 208n22
Burkhard, bishop of Würzburg (d. c.750), 20, 21, 30, 32, 60, 97, 152; overview, 27–28; *vitae Burkhardi* I and II, 24, 26, 27, 218n84, 220n105
Burkhard Gospels, 38

Caesarius, bishop of Arles (460–542), 12, 13, 58, 60, 149, 177, 178, 273n227
canon law collections: Carolingian reform movement and, 9, 211n71, 213n84; overview, 9–13, 211n71; women and, 9–13, 213nn81–82. *See also specific collections*
canonesses, 12, 186, 196, 204
Capitula ecclesiastica ad Salz data, 14, 214n102
Capitula ludiciorum penitential, 60, 61, 103–4, 269n144
Caritius, 122–23
Carolingian reform movement: abbesses and, 7–9, 11–12; in Anglo-Saxon cultural province in Francia, 7–15; canon law collections and, 9–13, 211n71, 213n84; gender relations and, 7–15; masculinist intellectual traditions and, 200–202; men and, 8–9; overview, 7–15; reform councils, 11–12; syneisactism and, 9, 10, 14; textual transmission and, 200–202; women and, 7–15; women's monasteries and, 13–14, 214n102
Cassiodorus (c.485–c.585), 50, 68, 114, 135
Cecilia of Rome, saint: house consecration of, 146, 262n188; passion of, 50, 113, 114, 129, 130, 134, 136, 138–47, 233n175, 255n6, 260n155, 261n157, 261n175, 262n188, 262n193; Valerian and, 139–40, 145–47, 255n6
Cellinga. *See* Zellingen
cenobitic monasticism, 4
centos, 58, 59, 179, 180, 181, 198–99
Charlemagne (742–814) (r.768–814), 8, 25–26, 48; "Epistola de litteris colendis" and, 200; Fulda and, 13, 23; Leoba and, 7, 14; Neustadt am Main and, 23, 218n84; Würzburg and, 25–26
Charles Martel, mayor (c.688–741) (r.718–741), 20, 21
chaste gender relations. *See* syneisactism

Chelles, 12, 193; manuscripts, 28, 40, 67, 68, 78, 97, 98, 154, 187, 195, 196, 200, 205. *See also* Vatican Gelasian Sacramentary

Christ, Carol, xv

Christian imagery: cross-nimbed figures, 69, 241n39; Kitzingen crucifixion miniature and, 65–86, 240n27, 240nn16–17, 241n42; Pauline epistles and, 67–69. *See also* crucifixion imagery

Christian liturgy, altar service and consecrated women, 185–92

Christianity: in Anglo-Saxon cultural province in Francia, 3; feminism and, xv, xvi, xvii, 7, 84; in Franconia, 16–20; indifference to material conditions, 90–91; spirituality and, 140, 260n153; substitution/identification typologies of medieval, 76, 244n95; unity, 90–91; visible church building by female martyrs, 139–47, 204, 261n157; women and, xv, 121. *See also specific Christian topics*

Christine de Pizan (1364–c.1430), xv, xvi, 205, 206

Christmas, abbreviated homily, 49, 130–32, 233n161, 258nn108–10

Chronicle of Fredegar, 205, 282n86

Church Fathers: women and, 88–90. *See also specific patristic topics*

churches: Main River Valley, 16–21, 215n22; Mainz, 18; monastic communities and multiple, 189; visible church building by female martyrs, 139–47, 204, 261n157; Würzburg, 27–28, 221n108

clergy: clerical dress and gender, 78–79, 245n115; Isidore of Seville on purity of male, 177, 273n223; misogyny of male, 201

clothes: clerical dress and gender, 78–79, 245n115; consecrated virgins and, 78–79, 246n116; consecrated women and, 78, 79, 97; crucifixions and, 77, 245n103; Kitzingen crucifixion miniature and, 77, 79, 245n103; nuns and male, 166, 269n145; "putting on Christ like a garment," 78. *See also* transvestism

Collectio Vetus Gallica, 10, 103

Collectio Wirceburgensis (Würzburg UB M.p.th.f. 146), 10–11, 60, 124, 166, 212n77

Comes romanus wirziburgensis, 99, 224n30, 251n96, 254n157, 254n167

commentaries: homilies and, 38–39; overview, 38–39. *See also* biblical commentaries; *specific commentaries*

Commentary on Ecclesiastes (Jerome), 30, 33, 58, 59, 223n19, 225n37; in Kitzingen homiliary, 58, 59, 149, 177, 179, 180–82, 238n257, 274n249; *Synonyms* and, 149, 157, 263n13

commentary on Gospels. *See* Homilies on the Gospels; *specific Gospel commentaries*

Commentary on John 10:1–15, 54, 138–39

Commentary on Matthew 26:1–30, 51–52

Commentary on Paul (Pelagius), 50, 135–36

Commentary on Song of Songs (Apponius), 196–200, 279n34

Commentary on the Gradual Psalms. *See* Commentary on the Psalms

Commentary on the Psalms (Augustine of Hippo), 90, 111, 229n89, 249n37, 249nn58–59; gender in, 92–93, 110; as Gun(t)za manuscript, 38–40, 87; Kitzingen crucifixion miniature and, 68; monastic life and, 87–88; overview, 38–40, 87–88, 91; Song of Ascents in, 94–98; women and, 87

consecrated virgins, 245n107, 245n109, 246n116; overview, 78–80

consecrated women, 9, 11, 14, 27, 113; Anglo-Saxon cultural province in Francia, altar service and, 185–92, 277n31; clothes and, 78, 79, 97; menstruation and, 103, 104

consecration, of Cecilia of Rome's house, 146, 262n188

conversatio sanctae Justinae, 196

Council of Chalons (813), 11, 12, 160, 213n88

Council of Mâcon (585), 98

Creation of Feminist Consciousness, The (Lerner), xvii

Crispina, saint (d.304), 96

crucifix: Udenheim, 77, 245n103; Volto Santo of Lucca, 77, 245n103

crucifixion: clothes and, 77, 245n103; consecrated virgins and, 79, 80; in "Deus per angelum" *libellus*, 134, 136, 137, 138, 146; Kitzingen Paul and, 75–77, 79; of Paul in Kitzingen crucifixion miniature, 76–77, 79–80; Paul on identification with, 77–78

crucifixion imagery, 69; biblical books and, 67–68; functions of, 66; medieval art and, 65–66, 72; overview, 65–66. *See also* Kitzingen crucifixion miniature

Cyneburg, abbess of Inkberrow, 27, 30, 60

Cynehild (Lul's aunt), 5, 218n75

Cynewulf, xvii, 204

Cyprian, bishop of Carthage (d.258), 13, 201

De ecclesiasticis officiis (Isidore of Seville), 189–92, 223n30, 278n51

De habitu virginum (Cyprian), 13, 201

De natura rerum (Isidore of Seville), 34, 35, 226n42, 227n50

De ortu et obitu patrum (Isidore of Seville), 49, 71

De virginitate (Aldhelm of Malmesbury), 72, 242n60

Deborah, biblical figure, 190, 191

Defensor of Ligugé, 57
Degering, Hermann, 34, 226n42, 227n45
demons, 187; Jofer, 141, 145, 146, 261n177
"Deus per angelum" *libellus* (Kitzingen
  Anonyma) (Würzburg UB M.p.th.q. 28b
  codex 1): Annunciation in, 49, 123, 133–34,
  138; crucifixion in, 134, 136, 137, 138, 146;
  Epilogue/Closing (Dominical) Frame,
  51–54, 130, 136–39, 146; Eve in, 131–32, 135,
  141; Female Martyrial Center, 50–51, 113,
  114, 128–30, 134, 136, 138–47, 233n175,
  234n185, 234nn178–79, 255n6, 256n25,
  260n155, 261n157, 261n170, 261n175,
  262n185, 262n188, 262n193; female martyrs
  and, 50–51, 112–14, 129, 130, 134–37,
  139–47; feminism of, 130, 147; gender
  egalitarianism of, 130; overview, 49, 54,
  112–16, 128–47, 130, 235n213; Passions of the
  Apostles and, 112–16, 118, 128; Preface/
  Opening (Marian) Frame, 49–50, 123,
  130–36, 195, 233n161, 258nn108–10;
  Pseudo-Fulgentius and, 49, 131–33;
  theology of womanhood, 128–39; Vienna
  Homiliary compared to, 49, 54, 131–32,
  258n108; Vienna Passionary-Homiliary
  compared to, 130–31; Vienna Penitentials
  compared to, 132; visible church building
  by female martyrs, 139–47, 204, 261n157;
  women and, 118, 128–47
devil, and Jesus Christ, 178
devotion: monastic life, discipline and,
  148–82. *See also* Marian devotion
Dhuoda, 159, 175
Discipulus Umbrensium penitential
  (Theodore of Canterbury), 60, 103, 186, 189,
  245n109, 269n144
Dittochaeon (Tituli Historiarum)
  (Prudentius), 71, 242n56
Dominican nuns, 85, 193
double monasteries, 4–5, 186
Drogo of Austrasia, 21, 25
Drusiana, 117, 256n40

Eadburga, abbess of Thanet or Wimbourne,
  4, 85
Easter: Gospel pericopes, 100–102; Homilies
  on the Gospels and, 87, 100–102; Kitzingen
  crucifixion miniature and, 81
Ecclesiastes. *See* Commentary on Ecclesiastes
Eden: Augustine on, 89–90, 95–97, 250n71;
  Gregory I on, 104–5; in Kitzingen
  homiliary, 180–81, 274n246; in Passions of
  the Apostles, 124, 125
Egeria, 42, 44
Eigil, abbot of Fulda (c.750–822), 35, 36,
  227n60
Elene (Cynewulf), 204

Eliseus, 141
Emhilt, abbess of Milz, 23
Ephigenia, saint, 126–28
Epilogue/Closing (Dominical) Frame (of
  "Deus per angelum" *libellus*), 146; overview,
  51–54, 130, 136–39; Text I: Commentary on
  Matthew 26:1–30, 51–52, 136–37; Text II:
  description of Holy Sepulchre, 52–53, 137;
  Text III: Homily on Matthew 28:1–20,
  53–54, 137–38; Text IV: Sermon on the
  Second Coming, 54, 138–39; Text V:
  Commentary on John 10:1–15, 54, 138–39
"Epistola de litteris colendis," 200
Erler, Mary, 194
Essen, 166, 205, 270n156
Ethiopia, 126–28
Etymologies (Isidore of Seville), 6, 61, 151,
  209n38
Euagrios Pontikos, 175
Eudocia, empress, 196, 198–99
Eugenia of Rome, saint: Bassilla and, 165, 169;
  as Eugenius, 164–66; as female martyr, 164;
  Jesus Christ and, 162–69; Melantia and,
  164–66, 168, 270n151; overview, 164–65;
  passion of, 153, 162–70, 172, 174, 269n132,
  270n161, 270nn165–66; Protus, Hyacinthus
  and, 168–69; *Synonyms* and, 153, 162–70,
  172, 174, 269n132
Eugippius, abbot (d.533), 170
Euphrosyna, saint, 197–98
Euro-American feminism, xv
European feminist history, xvi
Eusebius of Caesarea, 208n13
evangelization: in Passions of the Apostles,
  120; by women, 121
Eve: Augustine on, 40, 95–97, 250n71; in
  "Deus per angelum" *libellus*, 131–32, 135,
  141, 274n246; Gregory I on, 104–5, 109; in
  Kitzingen homiliary, 174, 175, 180–81;
  Otfrid on, 253n147; in Passions of the
  Apostles, 124, 125, 274n246; patristic
  exegesis of, 89–90, 110; Proba on, 199;
  Prudentius on, 72; Virgin Mary and,
  131–32; at Würzburg, 209n36

Fall. *See* Eden
Farr, Carol, 133
Fastrada, queen (765–794) (r.783–794), 7, 8, 24
Fathers of the Church. *See* Church Fathers
feasts, saints, 187, 189
Felicitas, saint (d. 203), 93
Felix of Nola, saint (d.250), 95
female: ritual purity, 103–5, 253n141; saints,
  93, 94, 95, 187–88, 276n26; soul as, 199.
  See also women
female liturgists, 187, 189. *See also* consecrated
  women

Female Martyrial Center (of "Deus per angelum" *libellus*): Jesus Christ and, 139, 141–43, 145, 146, 147; overview, 50–51, 139–47; passion of Agatha of Catania, 51, 114, 128–30, 134, 136, 138, 139, 141–44, 146, 234n185, 261n165, 261n175; Text I: Abbreviated passion of Cecilia of Rome, 50, 113, 114, 129, 130, 134, 136, 138–47, 233n175, 255n6, 260n155, 261n157, 261n175, 262n188, 262n193; Text II: Abbreviated passion of Juliana of Nicomedia, 50, 114, 128–30, 134, 136, 138, 139, 141, 143–45, 146, 234nn178–79, 256n25, 261n175, 261n177, 262n185; Text III: Abbreviated passion of Agnes of Rome, 50–51, 128–30, 134, 136, 138, 139, 141–44, 146, 261n170, 261n175; Text IV: "On the Death of Agatha of Catania," 51, 114, 128–30, 134, 136, 138, 139, 141–44, 146, 234n185, 261n165, 261n175; virgin martyrs in, 143–45, 261n174; Virgin Mary and, 139, 141, 143, 145, 147

female martyrs, 202, 276n27, 281n72; Augustine on, 93–94; "Deus per angelum" *libellus* and, 50–51, 112–14, 129, 130, 134–37, 139–47; Eugenia of Rome as, 164; liturgical sexism against, 187–88; overview, 130; visible church building by, 139–47, 204, 261n157. *See also* virgin martyrs

feminism: in the Anglo-Saxon cultural province in Francia, 3, 7, 9, 10, 15, 31, 83, 84; Augustine and, 98, 99; Christianity and, xv, xvi, xvii, 7, 84; of "Deus per angelum" *libellus*, 130, 134, 138, 147; as Euro-American, xv; Gregory I and, 99, 100, 102, 106, 107, 110; of Kitzingen crucifixion miniature, 80; manuscripts and, 7, 9; medieval, xv–xvii; modern, xv; old, xv; of Origen, 79–80; Passions of the Apostles and, 119, 123–25; patriarchy and, xvii; Paul and, 84; of *Vision of St. Paul*, 73, 75; of women's communities, 83, 84

Feminism: The Essential Historical Writings (Schneir), xv

feminist consciousness, xvii; creation, 202–6

feminist history: European, xvi; feminist strategy of historical representation, 118, 193, 204–6; overview, xv–xvii; Virgin Mary and sacred, 116, 123–25; waves, xvi, 207n8

feminists: biblical commentaries and, 90; hermeneutical strategies of, 84; narratives about saints, 111; patristic texts and, 90; textual transmission as strategy of, 29–31, 42, 89, 90, 92, 93, 111, 193–206; "Veri Amoris" *libellus* and intellectual traditions of, 196–200

florilegium: Augustine, 170; overview, 170–71. *See also* Karlburg florilegium

Francia: overview, 16–17. *See also* Anglo-Saxon cultural province in Francia; Franconia

Franconia: Anglo-Saxons in, 16, 18; Christianity in, 16–20; monastic communities, 17–18, 217n49; overview, 16–17, 215n1

Frauenbewegung, xv. *See also* feminism

Fulda, 13–14, 21, 23, 34–36, 200, 204, 209n33, 218n77; dependent communities, 13–14, 20, 194, 204, 217n49; and Leoba, 5, 14, 15, 34, 83, 165; library catalogue, 33–36, 227n45; manuscripts, 8, 55, 150, 176

Fulgentius, bishop of Ruspe (c.467–532), 49, 51, 61, 72, 132

Fursey, saint (d. 650), 73, 243n68

Gallican Gospel pericopes, 251n97

Gallican liturgy, 78, 245n106

Gallicanus (Hrotsvitha), 204

Gandersheim, 130, 204, 205

garments. *See* clothes

Geith, Karl-Ernst, 50

gender: art, spirituality and, 85–86; book production and, 205; clerical dress and, 78–79, 245n115; in Commentary on the Psalms, 92–93, 110; consecrated virgins and, 78; Gregory I, binary oppositions and, 107–10; *homo* and, 80, 96–98; Kitzingen crucifixion miniature and, 67, 80–82; medieval Europe, women and, 110; patristic gender ideologies, 110–11; spirituality and, 85–86, 171–72

gender egalitarianism: of Augustine, 91–98; of "Deus per angelum" *libellus*, 130; of Karlburg florilegium, 171, 173–77, 272n209, 272nn205–6; of Kitzingen homiliary, 178, 182; of monastic life, 177–78, 273n227; of *Synonyms*, 177–78

gender relations: in Anglo-Saxon cultural province in Francia, 3–15; Carolingian reform movement and, 7–15

gender relations, chaste. *See* syneisactism

Gertrude of Nivelles (626–653), 19

Gisela, abbess of Notre-Dame of Soissons, 187

Gorman, Michael, 51

Gospel pericopes (readings): Easter, 100–102; Gallican, 251n97; Gregory I and, 99–102, 104, 106, 107; Roman, 99, 251n97; in women, 99

Gospels: Burkhard, 38. *See also* Homilies on the Gospels; *specific Gospel commentaries*

gradual Psalms, 88; Augustine's sermons on, 90–96. *See also* Commentary on the Psalms

Gregory I, pope (540–604): Augustine and, 99, 105; on biblical characters, 88; on biblical study, 87; binary oppositions,

Gregory I, pope (cont.)
  gender and, 107–10; on Eden, 104–5; on Eve,
    104–5; on female ritual purity, 103–5,
    253n141; feminism and, 99, 100, 102, 107,
    110; Gospel pericopes and, 99–102, 104, 106,
    107; on holy women, 88, 98–110; Homilies
    on the Gospels of, 40–41, 74, 87–88, 98–107,
    111, 243n80, 251n108; on Job, 110; letters of,
    211n67; on Mary Magdalen, 100–102,
    104–6, 108, 252n121; *Moralia on Job* of, 109,
    110, 194; other works of, 230n99; *Pastoral
    Care* of, 107, 109, 226n38, 230n99;
    Responsiones, 102–3; on saints, 88; sermons
    of, 99–102, 105–7, 254n157, 254n167; on
    women, 110–11
Gregory the Great. *See* Gregory I, pope
Grifo of Thuringia (726–753), 21, 22, 25
Grundmann, Herbert, xv
Gun(t)za and Abirhilt manuscripts, 24;
    Bischoff and, 31–32; overview, 31–37;
    Psalms and, 248n7; *Synonyms* of Isidore of
    Seville as (Würzburg, UB M.p.th.q. 28a
    and 28b), 54–56, 106, 149–70, 266n66.
    See also Abirhilt manuscripts; Gun(t)za
    manuscripts
Gun(t)za manuscripts: Augustine's
    Commentary on the Psalms as (Würzburg
    UB M.p.th.f. 17), 38–40, 87; Karlburg
    florilegium as (Würzburg, UB M.p.th.f. 13),
    56–58, 149, 170–77, 237n247, 273n220;
    overview, 31–37; Passions of the Apostles as
    (Würzburg, UB M.p.th.f. 78), 41–49. *See
    also* Gun(t)za and Abirhilt manuscripts
Gun(t)za of Trier and Karlburg, 31, 57, 58, 174,
    175, 223n29, 237n247
Guthlac of Crowland (673–715), 46

Hadeloga, first abbess of Kitzingen, 22, 182;
    biography of, 223n30
Hamburger, Jeffrey, 85
Hedan I of Würzburg/Thuringia, 220n96
Hedan II of Würzburg/Thuringia, 18, 25, 222n2
Hedeni, 17, 21, 26, 220n103
Hersfeld, 22, 23, 24, 48, 120, 218nn74–75
Hildegard, queen (758–783) (r.771–783), 7,
    25–26
Hildegard of Bingen (1098–1179), xv, 130
Holy Sepulchre, description, 52–53, 137
holy women: Augustine on, 88, 90–98; Gregory
    on, 88, 98–110. *See also* religious women
Holzkirchen, 23, 200, 218n80
homiliary, Kitzingen. *See* Kitzingen
    homiliary
homilies: abbreviated Christmas, 49, 130–32,
    233n161, 258nn108–10; commentaries and,
    38–39; overview, 38–39. *See also specific
    homilies*

Homilies on Numbers (Origen), 78–80,
    246n119
Homilies on the Gospels (Gregory I), 111,
    251n108; as Abirhilt manuscript, 40–41, 74,
    87, 106; Easter and, 87, 100–102; Kitzingen
    crucifixion miniature and, 74; monastic
    life and, 87–88; overview, 40–41, 87–88,
    98–107; underwater imagery of, 74, 243n80;
    women and, 87
Homily on Matthew 28:1–20, 53–54, 137–38
homo, 152, 153; gender and, 80, 96–98; *Homo*
    and, 154–55
Homo (Human Being): *homo* and, 154–55;
    Jesus Christ as, 155, 162; *Ratio* and, 151, 153,
    155, 157–58, 160–61, 163, 165, 265n57, 265n59;
    in *Synonyms*, 151–58, 160–63, 165, 265n57,
    265n59, 266n75
homoeroticism, in passion of Eugenia,
    164–70, 270n151
Hrotsvitha of Gandersheim (935–973), 130,
    203–5
Hugeburc of Heidenheim, 113, 135, 219n94,
    259n131
Human Being. *See* Homo
Hyacinthus, slave, 168–69
Hyrtacus, king in Ethiopia, 126–27

imagery: bird, 70–72, 242n55; *Synonyms*
    illustration through animal, 153–58,
    266n78; underwater, 74, 243n80. *See also*
    Christian imagery; crucifixion imagery
imago Dei (image of God), 80, 97, 138
Immina, abbess of Würzburg, 26–28, 221n109
Institutio sanctimonialium, 10, 12–13, 214n95,
    219n90
intellectual traditions: Carolingian reform
    movement and masculinist, 200–202; "Veri
    Amoris" *libellus* and feminist, 196–200
Isidore of Seville (560–636): *De ecclesiasticis
    officiis* of, 189–92, 223n30, 278n51; *De fide
    catholica contra Judaeos*, 90, 119; *De natura
    rerum* of, 34, 35, 226n42, 227n50; *De ortu
    et obitu partrum*, 49, 54, 71, 133, 227n42,
    259n124; *Etymologies* of, 6, 209n38; as
    inspiration for Kitzingen crucifixion
    miniature, 71; interpolated description of
    Mary by, 49–50, 133–35; on male clerical
    purity, 177, 273n223; on marriage, 6,
    209n36; on religious men and religious
    women, 151, 264n35; *Synonyms* of, 54–56,
    106, 149–71, 173, 177–78, 236n227, 236n230,
    236nn224–25, 263n13, 264n31, 265n57,
    265n59, 265nn47–48, 266n66, 266n75,
    266n78, 266n80, 267n107, 267n109,
    267nn102–5, 268n110, 268n114, 268n119,
    268n125, 269n130, 269n132, 270n161,
    270nn165–66, 271n190

James, brother of John the Evangelist. *See* James the Greater, apostle

James the Greater, apostle, 42–44, 118–20, 231n113

Jerome, saint (347–420), 198–99; Commentary on Ecclesiastes of, 30, 33, 59, 149, 177, 179, 180–82, 223n19, 225n37, 263n13; Karlburg florilegium and letter of, 174–75; letters of, 12–13, 89, 174–75, 197, 279n32; *vita Malchi* of, 196, 197, 279n31; women and, 89

Jesus Christ: Agnes of Rome and, 141–42; devil and, 178; Eugenia of Rome and, 162–69; Female Martyrial Center and, 139, 141–43, 145, 146, 147; as *Homo*, 155, 162; in Kitzingen homiliary, 178, 181, 274n249; Mary Magdalen and, 100–102, 104–6, 108, 252n121; narratives of, 113; Passions of the Apostles and, 117, 119, 121, 124–28, 256n47, 257n78; Paul as messenger of, 77; Potitus and, 162–64; "putting on Christ like a garment," 77–78; as *Ratio*, 155, 158, 162, 165; soul and, 199–200; temptation of, 124; torture of, 145–46; woman with alabaster jar and, 96–97, 105–6. *See also* Christianity; crucifixion; Easter

Jesus Christ, epilogual texts in "Deus per angelum" *libellus*. *See* Epilogue/Closing (Dominical) Frame

Jesus Christ, passion of. *See* Epilogue/Closing (Dominical) Frame

Job, 40, 74, 110, 111

Jofer, 141, 145, 146, 261n177

John the Evangelist, apostle (d.110), 116, 136; assumption of, 117; Commentary on John 10:1–15, 54, 138–39; Drusiana and, 117, 256n40; passion (*transitus*) of, 42, 43, 44, 116, 117, 118, 197, 231n113, 231n116, 256n40; syneisactism and, 117, 197

Jude, saint, 41, 47–48, 116, 118, 119, 125, 231n115

Juliana of Nicomedia, saint (d.304): Eliseus and, 141; Jofer and, 141, 145, 146, 261n177; passion of, 50, 114, 128–30, 134, 136, 138, 139, 141, 143–45, 146, 234nn178–79, 256n25, 261n175, 261n177, 262n185

Justina of Nicomedia, saint (d.304), 196

Karlburg, 21, 22, 24, 28, 32, 36, 53, 66, 200; "ad lapidum fluminis" manuscripts of, 10, 28, 59–61, 239n268; Burkhard Gospels and, 38; monastic life, 87, 88, 91, 148–82; overview, 18–20; sacramentary/lectionary of (Würzburg, UB M.p.th.q. 32), 186–89; Vienna Penitentials of, 60, 61, 72, 103, 104, 132, 166, 172, 238n264. *See also specific topics*

Karlburg florilegium (Würzburg, UB M.p.th.f. 13), 37, 194, 263n12, 272n204;

Admonitio and, 175–76; gender egalitarianism of, 171, 173–77, 272n209, 272nn205–6; as Gun(t)za manuscript, 56–58, 149, 170–77, 237n247, 238n264, 273n220; Jerome letter in, 174–75; men and, 173–76; monastic life and, 149, 170–77; overview, 56–58, 149, 170–77; spirituality of, 171–77, 272n197, 272n201; *Synonyms* and, 171, 173, 271n190; virginity and, 172–74, 272n197; women and, 173–76

Karlburg Isidore (Würzburg, UB M.p.th.q. 28a), 31–32, 37, 54, 55; *Synonyms* illustration through saintly exemplarity in, 162–64, 268n114, 268n119, 268n125, 269n130. *See also* passion of Eugenia; *Synonyms*

Karlburg passionary (Würzburg, UB M.p.th.f. 78). *See* Passions of the Apostles

Karsbach, 204

Kilian, saint and martyr: overview, 25–26; *passio maior Kiliani*, 220n104; *passio minor Kiliani*, 26, 220nn103–4

Kitzingen, 23, 24, 28, 30, 31, 32, 190, 191, 195, 196, 200, 204, 217n67; abbesses of, 22; monastic life, 72–73, 80–81, 148–82; overview, 21–22. *See also specific topics*

Kitzingen Anonyma. *See* "Deus per angelum" *libellus*

Kitzingen crucifixion miniature, 228n73; as author portrait, 69; bird imagery of, 70–72, 242n55; boat trip in, 81–82; Christian imagery and, 65–86, 240n27, 240nn16–17, 241n42; clothes and, 77, 79, 245n103; Commentary on the Psalms and, 68; crucifixion of Paul in, 76–77, 79–80; Easter and, 81; feminism of, 80; gender and, 67, 80–82; Homilies on the Gospels and, 74; Isidore of Seville as inspiration for, 71; Kitzingen community and, 72, 80–81; Kitzingen Paul and, 65–86; Noah's ark and, 81; overview, 36–37, 65–67, 85–86; penance and, 72, 73, 74; religious women's dignity and, 75; underwater imagery of, 74; *Vision of St. Paul* and, 73–75; women and, 84–86

Kitzingen crucifixion miniature artist: Christian imagery inspirations of, 66; as Kitzingen Isidore scribe-illuminator, 56, 153–55; numerical symbolism of, 66–67, 240n17; overview, 65–67; textual inspirations of, 66; as theologian-artist, 66; as woman, 37, 67, 85, 86. *See also* Kitzingen crucifixion miniature

Kitzingen homiliary (Würzburg UB M.p.th.q. 28b codex 3): as Abirhilt manuscript, 58–59, 177–82, 238n257; Adam in, 178, 181, 274n246; Caesarius of Arles and, 177, 178; Commentary on Ecclesiastes in, 177, 179, 180–82, 274n249; consolation and

Kitzingen homiliary (cont.)
repentance in, 177–82; Eden in, 180–81, 274n246; Eve in, 180–81, 274n246; gender egalitarianism of, 178, 182; Jesus Christ in, 178, 181, 274n249; monastic life and, 149, 177–82, 273n227; overview, 58–59, 149, 177–82; penance and, 72, 177–82; sermons in, 177–79, 181; *Synonyms* and, 178
Kitzingen Isidore (Würzburg, UB M.p.th.q. 28b codex 2). See *Synonyms*
Kitzingen library catalogue (in Basel, ÖUB F III 15a), 60, 196; biblical books in, 38, 228n76; overview, 32–36, 225n37, 225n38, 226n42. *See also* Abirhilt manuscripts; Basel booklist; Gun(t)za and Abirhilt manuscripts; *specific Kitzingen texts*
Kitzingen Paul (Würzburg UB M.p.th.f. 69), 223n30; as Abirhilt manuscript, 36–38; crucifixion and, 75–77, 79; Kitzingen crucifixion miniature and, 65–86; overview, 36–38. *See also* Pauline epistles
Kitzingen theologian-artist. *See* Kitzingen crucifixion miniature artist
"know thyself" motif: monastic life and, 158–60; *Synonyms* and, 158–60
Kochel, 57, 109, 195, 237n241

Lamb of God motif, 56, 154, 155, 156, 158, 265n49
Laon Orosius (Laon, BM 137), 154
Leoba of Tauberbischofsheim (710–782): Boniface and, xvi, xvii, 5, 6, 7, 8, 9, 14, 15, 17, 22, 118, 208n22, 210n48; Fulda and, 5, 14, 15, 34, 83, 165; Main River Valley and, 21, 22; overview, 14–15; Schornsheim and, 5, 22, 112, 194; women's monasteries and, 22, 218n74
Lerner, Gerda, xvi, xvii, 202, 203
letters: of Boniface, 4, 9, 211n67–68; of Boniface and Gregory, 211n67; of Jerome, 12–13, 89, 174–75, 197, 279n32; of Lul, 4, 9, 211n68; Mainz collections (Vienna, ÖNB 751 and Munich BSB Clm 8112), 9; overview, 4, 6–7, 9. *See also* women's letters
Lewis, Gertrude Jaron, 193
"Liber de ordine creaturarum" (Pseudo-Isidore), 36, 73
Liber Scintillarum. *See* Karlburg florilegium
library catalogues: Fulda, 33–36, 227n45; overview, 33; Würzburg cathedral, 225n37. *See also* booklists; Kitzingen library catalogue
Ligugé, 57
literature, visionary, 72–73
liturgies: consecrated women, altar service and Christian, 185–92; Gallican, 78, 245n106; manuscripts, 186, 275n14; Roman, 99; sexism against female martyrs, 187–88; theatrical performances in saint, 265n62

liturgists, female, 187, 189. *See also* consecrated women
Louis the Pious (778–840) (r.814–840), 12, 200
Lul, archbishop of Mainz (d.786), 5, 6, 21–23, 25, 27, 30, 48, 60, 120, 218n75, 223n19; letters of, 4, 9, 21, 31, 211n68

Macco (Matto), count, 23, 24, 217n49
Main River Valley: Boniface and friends in, 20–25; churches, 16–21, 215n22; Leoba and, 22; manuscripts, 24–25, 28, 219n91; monasteries, 16–26, 218n74, 218nn84–85; monastic communities, 18, 19, 218n75; wine, 18
Mainz, 16, 17, 112, 164; churches and monasteries of, 18; letter collections, 9
Malchus, saint (d.250), 197
male: Carolingian reform movement and masculinist intellectual traditions, 200–202; saints, 93, 95, 187–88, 276n26. *See also* men
male clergy: Isidore of Seville on purity of, 177, 273n223; misogyny of, 201
male martyrs, 188, 276n27; Augustine on, 94, 107; suffering of, 163
manuscripts, 207n1; centos, 198–99; Chelles, 154, 187; feminism and, 7, 9; liturgical, 186, 275n14; Main River Valley, 24–25, 28, 219n91; regional history and history of ideas, 3–4; University Library of Würzburg, xvi; Würzburg, 28. *See also* book production; booklists; letters; texts; women's manuscripts; *specific manuscripts*
Marian devotion: Passions of the Apostles, syneisactism and, 116–28. *See also* Preface/Opening (Marian) Frame; Virgin Mary
marriage: *accio nuptialis*, 6; Isidore of Seville on, 6, 209n36; during Middle Ages, 5–6, 209n36, 209n38; property and, 5–6; spirituality and, 6; syneisactism and, 4–7
martyr passions. *See* "Deus per angelum" *libellus*; Eugenia of Rome; Potitus; Vienna Passionary-Homiliary
martyrs: Augustine on, 93–94; virgin, 134, 143–46, 203, 261n174, 262n185. *See also* female martyrs; male martyrs; passion narratives, of martyrs; *specific martyrs*
Mary, Virgin. *See* Virgin Mary
Mary Magdalen, 192; Gregory I on, 100–102, 104–6, 108, 252n121; as woman with alabaster jar, 105–6, 108, 191
Matthew, apostle: Commentary on Matthew 26:1–30, 51–52, 136–37; Ethiopian antimagi mission of, 126–28; Homily on Matthew 28:1–20, 53–54, 137–38; passion of, 47, 120, 125–28, 231n115, 232n145

McInerney, Maud Burnett, 203, 261n174
McLaughlin, Eleanor, xv
medieval art: crucifixion imagery and, 65–66, 72; visionary, 73
medieval artistic objects: burials and, 70, 242n46; theology and uses of, 66
medieval book production. *See* book production
medieval Christianity: substitution/ identification typologies of theological, 76, 244n95. *See also* Christianity
medieval Europe: textual transmission as feminist strategy in, 193–206; women and gender in, 110
medieval feminism: overview, xv–xvii; substitute names for 8th century, xvi–xvii. *See also* feminism
medieval scribes, 32, 225n36. *See also specific medieval scribes*
medieval visionary literature, 72–73
Megingoz, bishop of Würzburg (d.783), 25, 26, 218n84
Melantia, 164–66, 168, 270n151
Melitus of Laodikeia, 43, 197, 231n116
men: burials of women and, 5, 15, 208n22; Carolingian reform movement and, 8–9; Karlburg florilegium and, 173–76. *See also* gender; male; marriage; religious men
men's monasteries: Corbie, 56, 76, 198, 270n156; Echternach, 5, 16, 19, 27, 38, 57, 58, 76, 245n103; Franconia, 217n49; Lorsch, 73, 198, 201, 202, 215n22, 239n267; Main River Valley, 8, 18, 23, 218n84; St. Alban's (Mainz), 8, 9, 11, 18, 176, 202; St. Burkhard (Würzburg), 27, 28; St. Gallen, 195; Würzburg, 28. *See also* Fulda
menstruation, and consecrated women, 35, 103, 104
Migdonia, 122–23
Milz, 23, 53, 66, 247n146
Miriam, sister of Moses, 190, 191
misogyny: Augustine and, 93–94, 96–98, 110; of male clergy, 201; patristic, 110; of patristic texts, 89, 96; in texts, 201, 205
modern feminism, xv
Mombritius, Bonino, 43, 48
monasteries: double, 4–5; Main River Valley, 16–26, 218n74, 218n84–85; Mainz, 18; women donors to, 6, 209n33. *See also* men's monasteries; women's monasteries
monastic communities: bishops battles with local, 27; Main River Valley, 18, 19, 218n75; multiple churches of, 189
monastic life: Commentary on the Psalms and, 87–88; discipline and devotion in, 148–82; gender egalitarianism of, 177–78, 273n227; Homilies on the Gospels and,

87–88; Karlburg, 148–82; Karlburg florilegium and, 149, 170–77; Kitzingen, 148–82; Kitzingen homiliary and, 149, 177–82, 273n227; "know thyself" motif and, 158–60; overview, 148–82; penitential confession in, 158–60; *Synonyms* and, 149–70; texts as guidelines for, 148–82; of women, 148–82, 273n227
monasticism, cenobitic, 4
Moralia on Job (Gregory I), 109, 110, 194

naval metaphors: boat trip in Kitzingen crucifixion miniature, 81–82; of Bonifatian syneisactic circle, 82, 246n130
Nelson, Janet, 15
Nestorius, bishop of Constantinople (c.386–450), 125
Neustadt am Main, 23, 29, 218n84
Niedermünster (Regensburg), 128, 244n98
Noah's ark, 81
Nonnberg (Salzburg), 128, 194
Notre Dame de Soissons, 88, 187
numerical symbolism, of Kitzingen crucifixion miniature, 66–67, 240n17

Ó Carragáin, Éamonn, 66
Ochsenfurt, 18, 22, 60, 81, 201, 217n65; overview, 20
Oeren, 19, 28, 57, 194, 247n152
old feminism, xv
Old High German, 34, 90, 213n82, 219n91, 281n73
"On the Death of Agatha of Catania," 51, 114, 128–30, 134, 136, 138, 139, 141–44, 146, 234n185, 261n165, 261n175
On the Trinity (Augustine), 97–98
Opus Imperfectum in Matthaeum (Annianus of Celeda), 51–52
Origen (c.185–254): on consecrated virgins, 80; feminism of, 79–80; *Homilies on Numbers*, 78–80, 246n119; on Mary, 134

Pabnutius, 197–98
paganism, 4, 5, 17, 25, 26, 90, 112, 116, 119, 120, 142, 143, 144, 203
Palmer, James T., 25
passion narratives, of martyrs, 201–2. *See also* "Deus per angelum" *libellus*; Vienna Passionary-Homiliary
passion of Eugenia: homoeroticism in, 164–70, 270n151; *Synonyms* and, 153, 162–70, 172, 174, 269n132, 270n161, 270nn165–66; transvestism in, 164–70, 270n151, 270nn165–66
passion of Jesus Christ. *See* Epilogue/Closing (Dominical) Frame
passion of Virgin Mary, 134

passions of apostles: in Montpellier, Bibliothèque Interuniversitaire, Faculté de Médecine H.55, 42, 44, 45, 124, 230n108; of Paul, 115; of Peter, 115. *See also* Passions of the Apostles; *specific passions of apostles*

passions of saints: of Afra, 115; of Agatha of Catania, 51, 114, 128–30, 134, 136, 138, 139, 141–44, 146, 234n185, 261n165, 261n175; of Agnes of Rome, 50–51, 128–30, 134, 136, 138, 139, 141–44, 146, 261n170, 261n175; in Anglo-Saxon cultural province in Francia, 112–16; of Cecilia of Rome, 50, 113, 114, 129, 130, 134, 136, 138–47, 233n175, 255n6, 260n155, 261n157, 261n175, 262n188, 262n193; of Eugenia, 153, 162–70, 172, 174, 269n132, 270n161, 270nn165–66; of Juliana of Nicomedia, 50, 114, 128–30, 134, 136, 138, 139, 141, 143–45, 146, 234n178–79, 256n25, 261n175, 261n177, 262n185; overview, 112–16; of Potitus, 153, 162–64, 172, 268n125, 269n130; women as writers of, 114. *See also* Passions of the Apostles

Passions of the Apostles (Würzburg, UB M.p.th.f. 78): Adam in, 96, 97, 125; "Deus per angelum" *libellus* and, 112–16, 118, 128; Eden in, 124, 125; evangelization in, 120; Eve in, 124, 125; feminism and, 119; as Gun(t)za manuscript, 41–49; Jesus Christ and, 117, 119, 121, 124–28, 256n47, 257n78; overview, 41–43, 112–28, 231n115; passion of Bartholomew, 45–46, 118, 120, 123–25, 231n115; passion of James the Greater, 43–44, 118–19; passion of John the Evangelist, 43, 117, 118, 231n113, 231n116, 256n40; passion of Matthew, 47, 120, 125–28, 231n115, 232n145; passion of Philip, 48–49, 117–18; passion of Simon and Jude by Pseudo-Abdias, 41, 47–48, 116, 118, 119, 125, 231n115; passion of Thomas, 30, 42–45, 115, 121–22, 128, 231n114; syneisactism, Marian devotion and, 116–28; *Terra* in, 124, 257n72; Virgin Mary in, 123–25; women and, 118, 121–28. *See also specific passions of apostles*

Pastoral Care (Gregory I), 109, 226n38, 230n99

patriarchy: of Bible, 84; feminism as resistance to, xvii

patristic biblical commentary, and women, 87–90, 111

patristic gender ideologies, 110–11

patristic misogyny, 110

patristic texts: feminists and, 90; misogyny of, 89, 96; overview, 88–89; women and, 87–90. *See also* Commentary on the Psalms; Homilies on the Gospels

Paul. *See* Paul of Tarsus, apostle

Paul of Samosata (c.200–275), 124, 208n13

Paul of Tarsus, apostle (5–67): Augustine on, 94, 95; Boniface and, 82–83, 85; Cassiodorus's revision of Pelagius's Commentary on, 50, 135–36; on crucifixion identification, 77–78; feminism and, 84; as Jesus Christ's messenger, 77; Kitzingen crucifixion miniature and crucifixion of, 76–77, 79–80; overview, 69–71; passion of, 115; on syneisactism, 4; Thecla and, 82–84; on virgins, 78; *Vision of St. Paul*, 73–75, 243n73; visions of, 69–71; women and, 75, 83, 244n88, 247n152. *See also* Kitzingen Paul

Paula, Roman matron, 30, 34; epitaph of, 34, 196

Pauline epistles: Christian imagery and, 67–69. *See also* Kitzingen Paul

Pelagius (354–420), 95, 114; Augustine and, 135, 136; Cassiodorus's revision of Commentary on Paul by, 50, 135–36

penance: Kitzingen crucifixion miniature and, 72, 73, 74; Kitzingen homiliary and, 72, 177–82

penitential confession: in monastic life, 158–60; *Synonyms* and, 158–60; women and, 106

penitentials: *Capitula Iudiciorum*, 60, 61, 103–4, 269n144; *Discipulus Umbrensium*, 103, 179, 186, 189, 269n144; of Pseudo-Bede, 159, 269n144; Vienna (Karlburg) Penitentials, 5, 49, 54, 60, 61, 72, 103, 104, 132, 166, 172, 209n38, 239n268, 245n109, 258n108, 269n144

pericopes. *See* Gospel pericopes

Perpetua, saint (d.203), 93, 94

Peter, apostle, 42, 66, 100, 101, 115, 163, 169, 195

Pfalzel, 5, 19, 28, 148, 194

Philip, apostle, 42, 43, 48–49, 117–18, 126

Pippin the Short, king (714–768) (r.752–768), 8, 13, 14, 20, 21, 22, 23

Plaskow, Judith, xv

Plectrude, 6

politics, and women, 6–7

Potitus, saint: Jesus Christ and, 162–64; passion of, 153, 162–64, 172, 268n125, 269n130; suffering of, 163; *Synonyms* and, 153, 162–64, 172, 268n125, 269n130

Preface/Opening (Marian) Frame (of "Deus per angelum" *libellus*), 195; overview, 49–50, 130–36; Text I: abbreviated Christmas homily, 49, 130–32, 233n161, 258nn108–10; Text II: interpolated description of Mary by Isidore of Seville, 49–50, 133–35; Text III: extract from Cassiodorus's revision of Pelagius's Commentary on Paul, 50, 135–36

Priscillian, bishop of Avila (d.385) (r.381–385): syneisactic group of, 29–30; works of, 29–30, 222n2, 222n9
Proba, 170, 198
property, and marriage, 5–6
Prosa de virginitate (Aldhelm of Malmesbury), 202, 281nn72–73
Protus, slave, 168–69
Prudentius, 71, 72, 77, 203, 242n56
Psalms: consecrated women and, 185, 190; Gun(t)za and Abirhilt manuscripts and, 248n7; overview, 76, 88; penitential, 159–60. *See also* gradual Psalms
Pseudo-Abdias, 41, 47–48
Pseudo-Augustine, 178
Pseudo-Basil, 175–76
Pseudo-Bede, 60, 159
Pseudo-Caesarius, 178
Pseudo-Fulgentius: "Deus per angelum" *libellus* and, 49, 54, 131–33, 144, 145, 181, 195; Vienna Penitentials and, 61, 132
Pseudo-Isidore, 36, 73
Pseudo-Jerome, 53, 83, 138
purity: female ritual, 103–5, 253n141; Isidore of Seville on male clergy, 177, 273n223; standards for religious women, 176–77

Quedlinburg, 193, 196, 205
Quintianus, proconsul, 129, 142, 144

Raban Maur, abbot of Fulda (c.780–856), 14, 15, 113, 208n22
Ragyndrudis of Mainz, 31, 223n27
Ratio: Homo and, 151, 153, 155, 157–58, 160–61, 163, 165, 265n57, 265n59; Jesus Christ as, 155, 158, 162, 165; in *Synonyms*, 151, 153, 155, 156–58, 160–65, 169, 173, 175, 265n57, 265n59, 266n80, 267n109
Reginmaar, deacon, 19, 28, 59, 177
Regula cuiusdam ad Virgines, 35, 159
religious men: Isidore of Seville on, 151, 264n35; textual transmission amongst, 195–96, 200–202, 204, 205
religious women: biblical commentaries and, 90; Isidore of Seville on, 151, 264n35; Kitzingen crucifixion miniature and dignity of, 75; medical practice of, 35; purity standards for, 176–77; textual transmission and, 193–96, 203–4; *Vision of St. Paul* and, 74–75. *See also* holy women; women
Remiremont, 88, 194, 247n152
Responsiones (Gregory I), 60, 61, 102–5, 109
Riculf, archbishop of Mainz (d.813), 8, 9
ritual purity, female, 103–5, 253n141
Rochais, Henri, 57
Roman Gospel pericopes, 99, 251n97
Roman liturgy, 99

Rose, Els, 48
Roy, Gopa, 167
Royal Prayerbook (London, British Library, Royal 2.A.XX), 35–36
Rudolf, abbot of Fulda (d.865), 14, 83, 113, 165, 208n22
Ruether, Rosemary Radford, xvi, xvii

Sainte-Marie-Saint-Jean of Laon, 88, 154, 247n152
saints: Augustine on, 88, 93, 94, 95, 99; feasts, 187, 189; female, 93, 94, 95, 187–88, 276n26; feminist narratives about, 111; Gregory I on, 88; history and theology in stories of, 112–47; male, 93, 95, 187–88, 276n26; *Synonyms* illustration through saintly exemplarity in Würzburg M.p.th.q. 28a, 162–64, 268n114, 268n119, 268n125, 269n130; theatrical performances in liturgies of, 265n62; torture of, 145; transvestite, 167; virgins, 188, 276n28. *See also* apostles; *specific saints*
Schneir, Miriam, xv
Schulenburg, Jane Tibbetts, 144, 166
Schwarzach, 12, 18, 24, 149, 154, 175, 194, 219n90
scribes. *See* medieval scribes
Seleucia, shrine of Thecla, 4
self-examination. *See* "know thyself" motif
sententiae (teachings, opinions), 170
Sermon on the Second Coming, 54, 138–39
sermons: by Augustine on gradual Psalms, 90–96; of Gregory I, 99–102, 105–7, 254n157, 254n167; in Kitzingen homiliary, 177–79, 181
Simeon, 134
Simon, saint, 41, 47–48, 116, 118, 119, 125, 231n115
Song of Ascents, 94–98
Song of Songs, 196–200, 279n34
soul: as female, 199; Jesus Christ and, 199–200; *Synonyms* on, 149–53
spirituality: art, gender and, 85–86; Christianity and, 140, 260n153; gender and, 85–86, 171–72; of Karlburg florilegium, 171–77, 272n197, 272n201; marriage and, 6; of *Synonyms*, 149–53; women's, 85
St. Sabina (Rome), 247n132
St. Salvator (Brescia), 12, 195
Stephen, protomartyr, 94, 191, 249n59
Straw, Carol, 107–8, 109
suffering: of male martyrs, 163; of Potitus, 163
symbols, numerical, 66–67, 240n17
syneisactism: Bonifatian syneisactic circle, 82, 246n130; Carolingian reform movement and, 9, 10, 14; group of Priscillian of Avila, 29–30; John the Evangelist and, 117; marriage and, 4–7; overview, 4–5; Passions of the Apostles, Marian devotion and, 116–28; Paul on, 4

Synonyms (Isidore of Seville), 236n227, 236n230, 236nn224–25; appeal of, 150, 264n31; Book I, 156–58; Book II, 157–58, 160–62, 165, 267n107, 267n109, 267nn102–5, 268n110; Commentary on Ecclesiastes and, 149, 263n13; gender egalitarianism of, 177–78; Gun(t)za and Abirhilt manuscripts of, 54–56, 106, 149–70, 266n66; *Homo* in, 151–58, 160–63, 165, 265n57, 265n59, 266n75; illustration through animal imagery at Kitzingen, 153–58, 266n78; illustration through saintly exemplarity at Karlburg, 162–64, 268n114, 268n119, 268n125, 269n130; Karlburg florilegium and, 171, 173, 271n190; Kitzingen homiliary and, 178; "know thyself" motif, penitential confession and, 158–60; monastic life and, 149–70; overview, 54–56, 149–70; passion of Eugenia and, 153, 162–70, 172, 174, 269n132, 270n161, 270nn165–66; passion of Potitus in, 153, 162–64, 172, 268n125, 269n130; prologues of, 152–53, 265nn47–48; *Ratio* in, 151, 153, 155, 156–58, 160–65, 169, 173, 175, 265n57, 265n59, 266n80, 267n109; as spiritual consolation for anguished soul, 149–53; versions, 150, 263n23

"Synopsis of Oppositions in Gregory's World View" (Straw), 108

Tauber Valley, 16, 21; women's monasteries, 22
Tauberbischofsheim, xvi, 5, 8, 14, 21, 22, 23, 34, 60, 204
Terra, 124, 257n72
Tertullian (160–220), 83, 90, 111, 200
texts: inspirations of Kitzingen crucifixion miniature artist, 66; misogyny in, 201, 205; monastic life guidelines from, 148–82. *See also* manuscripts; *specific texts*
textual transmission: Carolingian reform movement and, 200–202; as feminist strategy, 29–31, 193–206; networks amongst women's communities, 193–96; overview, 193; religious men and, 195–96, 200–202, 204, 205; religious women and, 193–96, 203–4; "Veri Amoris" *libellus* and, 196–200. *See also* book production
theatrical performances, in saint liturgies, 265n62
Thecla, saint (apostle), 166, 203; overview, 83–84; Paul and, 82–84, 114; shrine at Seleucia, 4, 42
Thekla, magistra at Kitzingen (d. after 747), 22, 83
Theodore, archbishop of Canterbury (d.690), *Discipulus Umbrensium* penitential of, 60, 103, 186, 189, 245n109, 269n144

theologian-artists: Kitzingen crucifixion miniature artist as, 66; overview, 66; substitution/identification typologies of, 76, 244n95
theology: "Deus per angelum" *libellus* as women's, 128–39; of medieval artistic objects, 66; in stories of saints, 112–47
Thomas, apostle, 101; passion of, 30, 42–45, 115, 121–22, 128, 231n114
Tituli Historiarum. See *Dittochaeon*
torture: of Jesus Christ, 145–46; of saints, 145; of virgin martyrs, 145–46, 262n185
transvestism: nuns in male clothes, 166, 269n145; in passion of Eugenia, 164–70, 270n151, 270nn165–66; saints, 167
Treptia, queen in India, 122, 123

Udenheim crucifix, 77, 245n103
underwater imagery: of Homilies on the Gospels, 74, 243n80; of Kitzingen crucifixion miniature, 74
Urban, 140, 141

Valerian, 139–40, 145–47, 255n6
Vatican Gelasian Sacramentary (Vatican City, Reg. lat. 316), 78, 154, 187, 240n17, 245n107
veils, virgin, 190, 191
"Veri Amoris" *libellus*, 196–200
Veronica (Berenice), St., 35
Vienna Homiliary (Vienna ÖNB 1616), 49, 54, 130–32, 258n108
Vienna Passionary-Homiliary (Vienna ÖNB 1556), 130, 131
Vienna (Karlburg) Penitentials (Vienna ÖNB 2223), 5, 49, 54, 60, 61, 72, 103, 104, 132, 166, 172, 209n38, 239n268, 245n109, 258n108, 269n144; "Deus per angelum" *libellus* compared to, 49, 54, 130–32, 258n108; Pseudo-Fulgentius and, 132
virgin martyrs, 203; Female Martyrial Center and, 143–45, 261n174; torture of, 145–46, 262n185; Virgin Mary as, 134
Virgin Mary, 191; Annunciation, 37, 49, 123, 133–34, 138; Eve and, 131–32; Female Martyrial Center and, 139, 141, 143, 145, 147; feminist sacred history and, 116; interpolated description by Isidore of Seville, 49–50, 133–35; passion of, 134; in Passions of the Apostles, 123–25; as virgin martyr, 134. *See also* Marian devotion
Virgin Mary, prefatory texts in "Deus per angelum" *libellus*. See Preface/Opening (Marian) Frame
virgins, 195, 196; altar service and, 185, 190, 192; consecrated, 78–80, 245n107, 245n109, 246n116; crucifixion and, 79; Karlburg

florilegium and virginity, 172–74, 272n197; Paul on, 78; saints, 188, 276n28; veil of, 190, 191

virgo, 187–88

Visio Pauli. See Vision of St. Paul

Vision of St. Fursey, 73

Vision of St. Paul, 73–75, 243n73

Vision of St. Paul (Visio Pauli), 243n73; feminism of, 73, 75; Kitzingen crucifixion miniature and, 73–75; overview, 73–75; religious women and, 74–75

visionary art, medieval, 73

visionary literature, 72–73

visions, of Paul of Tarsus, 69–71

visual arts, and historical importance of women, 205

vita Burkhardi, 26, 27

vita Malchi (Jerome), 196, 197, 279n31

Volto Santo of Lucca crucifix, 77, 245n103

Walburga, saint (710–777/779), 22

Weiner, Andreas, 223n30

Wenkheim, 23

Whitby, 41, 107, 133, 186, 223n19

Wilkins, Walter, 107

Willibald, bishop of Eichstätt (c.700–c.788) (r.741–788), 21, 22, 25, 82–83, 113, 134, 135, 219n94

wine, Main River Valley, 18

woman with alabaster jar, 96–97, 136, 137; Mary Magdalen as, 105–6, 108, 137, 191

Womanspirit Rising (Christ and Plaskow), xv

women: Augustine and, 89, 91, 110–12; biblical study of, 14, 30, 78 , 87, 89, 90; Boniface and, 83; burials of men and, 5, 15, 208n22; canon law collections and, 9–13, 213nn81–82; Carolingian reform movement and, 7–15; Christianity and, xv, 121; Church Fathers on, 88–90; *Commentary on the Psalms,* 87; "Deus per angelum" *libellus* and, 118, 128–47; donors to monasteries, 6, 209n33; evangelization by, 121; in Gospel pericopes, 99; Gregory I on, 110–11; *Homilies on the Gospels* and, 87; Jerome and, 89; Karlburg florilegium and, 173–76; Kitzingen crucifixion miniature and, 84–86; medieval Europe, gender and, 110; monastic life of, 148–82, 273n227; *Passions of the Apostles* and, 118, 121–28; patristic biblical commentary and, 87–90, 111; patristic texts and, 87–90; Paul and, 75, 83, 244n88, 247n152; penitential confession and, 106; in politics, 6–7; and sacerdotal roles, 8, 79, 133, 137, 146, 186, 187, 189, 254n157; spirituality of, 85; theology and

"Deus per angelum" *libellus,* 128–39. *See also* consecrated women; female; feminism; gender; marriage; religious women; virgins

women artists: Carolingian era, 37, 38. *See also* Kitzingen crucifixion miniature artist

women writers, 41, 52, 78, 111, 116, 130, 132, 136, 145, 204, 205; of Apocryphal Acts of the Apostles, 42, 113, 199; of passions of martyrs, 113, 114; of Passions of the Apostles, 47, 48, 118, 121, 122, 125, 127, 128; of Priscillianist tractates, 29; of *The Vision of St. Paul,* 73, 84, 85. *See also* Burginda; Dhuoda; Hrotsvitha; Kitzingen Anonyma; women's letters; women's manuscripts

women's books: of Anglo-Saxon cultural province in Francia, 29–61; book production, 32, 67. *See also* women's manuscripts

women's letters, 111; overview, 4, 6, 7, 9, 211n68

women's manuscripts, 28; overview, 3–4, 7, 15; problem of survivability of, 193–94, 279n16. *See also* women writers; women's books; women's letters; *specific women's manuscripts*

women's monasteries, xvii, 114; Carolingian reform movement and, 13–14, 214n102; feminism of, 83, 84; Franconia, 17–18, 217n49; Leoba and, 22, 218n74; Main River Valley, 18–26; Tauber Valley, 22; textual transmission networks, 193–96. *See also specific women's monasteries*

Würzburg: bishops, 25; churches, 27–28, 221n108; history, late Merovingian and early Carolingian, 17–28; manuscripts, 28; manuscripts of University Library of, xvi; men's monasteries, 28; mythic narratives of expulsion and removal and foundation of, 25–28. *See also* Augustine; *On the Trinity; specific topics*

Würzburg cathedral, 200, 217n65; library catalogue (in Oxford, Bodleian, Laud misc. 126), 209n41, 223n30, 225n37; scriptorium, 12, 28, 60, 109

Würzburg UB M.p.th.q. 18, 189, 190, 191, 192, 209n36, 223n30

Würzburg UB M.p.th.q. 26 ("Veri amoris" *libellus*), 43, 196–200

Würzburg UB M.p.th.q. 31, 10

Würzburg UB M.p.th.q. 32, 186–89, 276nn26–28, 277n29

Zacharias, pope (679–752), 17, 23, 186, 211n67

Zellingen (Cellinga), 20

Zelzer, Klaus, 44

FORDHAM SERIES IN MEDIEVAL STUDIES

Mary C. Erler and Franklin T. Harkins, series editors

Ronald B. Begley and Joseph W. Koterski, S.J. (eds.), *Medieval Education*

Teodolinda Barolini and H. Wayne Storey (eds.), *Dante for the New Millennium*

Richard F. Gyug (ed.), *Medieval Cultures in Contact*

Seeta Chaganti (ed.), *Medieval Poetics and Social Practice: Responding to the Work of Penn R. Szittya*

Devorah Schoenfeld, *Isaac on Jewish and Christian Altars: Polemic and Exegesis in Rashi and the* Glossa Ordinaria

Martin Chase, S.J. (ed.), *Eddic, Skaldic, and Beyond: Poetic Variety in Medieval Iceland and Norway*

Felice Lifshitz, *Religious Women in Early Carolingian Francia: A Study of Manuscript Transmission and Monastic Culture*